W9-CGK-532

FIFTH EDITION

INTERNATIONAL BUSINESS

Environments and Operations

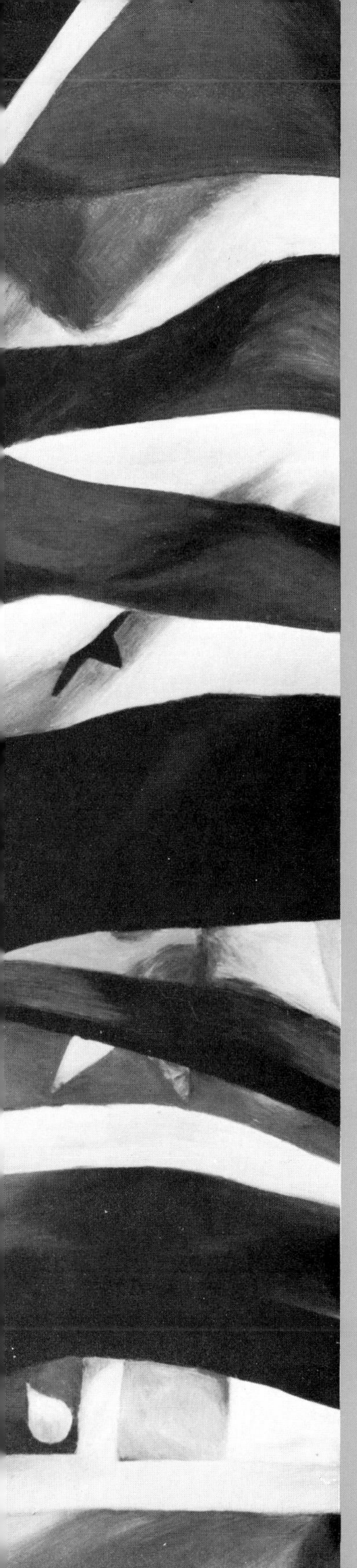

FIFTH EDITION

INTERNATIONAL BUSINESS

Environments and Operations

John D. Daniels
Indiana University

Lee H. Radebaugh
Brigham Young University

ADDISON-WESLEY PUBLISHING COMPANY

Reading, Massachusetts • Menlo Park, California • New York
Don Mills, Ontario • Wokingham, England • Amsterdam • Bonn
Sydney • Singapore • Tokyo • Madrid • San Juan

Sponsoring Editor: *Susan Badger*
Production Supervisor: *Peggy J. Flanagan*
Production Coordinator: *Sarah Hallet*
Text Design: *Vanessa Piñeiro*
Cover Design: *Marshall Henrichs*
Cover Painting: *Jean Seal*
Technical Art Consultant: *Dick Morton*
Illustrators: *Robert C. Forget, George Nichols*
Copy Editor: *Carmen Wheatcroft*
Manufacturing Supervisor: *Roy Logan*

Library of Congress Cataloging-in-Publication Data

Daniels, John D.
International business: environments and operations/by John D. Daniels and Lee H. Radebaugh.—5th ed.
p. cm.
Includes bibliographies and indexes.
ISBN 0–201–15747–0
1. International business enterprises. 2. International economic relations. 3. Investments, Foreign. I. Radebaugh, Lee H. II. Title.
HD2755.5.D35 1988
658. 1'8—dc 19 88–3768
CIP

Reprinted with corrections, June 1989.

CDEFGHIJ-DO-89

PREFACE

Few textbooks survive to a fifth edition. We are gratified that this text is one of the survivors, representing over fifteen years of our collaborative efforts. We believe that our ability to reach a fifth edition is due largely to three factors: (1) continued updating to parallel the rapidly evolving field of international business; (2) the ability to refine methods of presentation that can come only by trial and error over the long life of a book; and (3) the interest and efforts of a large group of academicians who continue to give us critical feedback on content and pedagogy.

To help guide us in preparation of the fifth edition, we sent a large number of questionnaires to people who have taught introductory international business courses in a variety of types of institutions. Based on their familiarity with the fourth edition, we asked what topics should be added, deleted, or emphasized to a different degree. We asked how materials could be presented better. We asked what additional enhancements would best assist in teaching the course. We were gratified that so many professors took the time to give us constructive suggestions.

Although there were too many suggestions to detail them all here, the major ones for the text can be summarized as follows:

- shorten the book,
- simplify the presentation,
- help students identify geographical locations discussed in the text,
- update.

And for the Instructor's Manual:

- add discussion questions,
- update,
- strengthen the multiple-choice test bank.

We have addressed all these points and will discuss them briefly in the following sections.

CONTENT

Since the first edition we have agreed that we would start with a "zero budget," that is, planning anew rather than depending on what we had written before. There has been nothing that could not be altered, no matter how much effort went into the original writing. However, we have started with the same question to guide us: What should be taught in a first course in international business when some of the students will thereafter have little or no direct classroom exposure to the subject and others will use the first course as background for more specialized studies in the area?

We continue to feel strongly that introductory students should be exposed to all the essential elements of international business. But what are these essential elements? From our questionnaire we found a near consensus that our coverage should continue to be as broad as possible. The pervasive feeling is that the field will continue to evolve too rapidly to know for certain what the future essentials will be. It is far better, our respondents reasoned, to risk covering too many things than to risk the omission of emerging issues and approaches that may well turn out to be essentials by the time students enter the work place and need to be informed citizens.

Such broad coverage is both a dilemma and a challenge. The text grew by about three hundred pages between its first and fourth editions, making it increasingly difficult to cover sufficiently in one course. For the fifth edition we have been able to add content but reduce the length by about one hundred pages. This has come about by tightening the style, avoiding some of the repetition from earlier editions, incorporating discussions of future events into existing chapters rather than in a separate chapter, and combining four chapters into two: accounting and tax into one, and management and labor personnel into one. In addition to shortening the overall length, we have moved some material to end-of-chapter appendixes so that instructors may find it easier to omit.

We have maintained essentially the same order of presentation as in the fourth edition. The materials in the basic sections and the order of presentation are as follows: (1) an overview of current international business patterns, with an emphasis on what makes international business different from domestic; (2) the social systems within countries as they affect the conduct of business from one country to another; (3) the major theories explaining international business transactions and the institutions influencing the activities; (4) the financial forms and institutions that measure and facilitate international transactions; (5) the interface between nation-states and the firms attempting to conduct foreign business activities; (6) the alternatives for overall corporate policy and strategy that accommodate global operations; and (7) the concerns and management of international activities that fall largely within functional disciplines.

Our approach is that of the manager rather than that of the social science disciplines from which international business draws its theoretical underpinnings. For example, as we talk about trade policy, we discuss not only the effects of different policies on national objectives but also the courses of action that companies and industries can take in order to influence policy and to react to whatever policy is undertaken.

PRESENTATION

Our objective is still to provide a breadth and depth of coverage greater than that of many of the other introductory texts, while at the same time taking care not to overwhelm students. In order to simplify rather than overwhelm, we have given special attention to the simplification of language and sentence structure so that the materials are easier to understand. Maps have been added throughout, including some in full color, so that students will easily know the location of areas being discussed. The major countries discussed in the cases are highlighted in color on the world map in the middle of the text. Use of this map will help students gain a better frame of reference when discussing the cases. Many new charts and figures have been added to clarify the prose discussions.

One pedagogical technique we have carried over is the use of short cases to introduce and conclude each chapter. This concept has been very well received. Some of the cases are entirely new; others have been updated. All the introductory cases are real and identifiable situations. They are designed to accomplish two objectives: (1) to build the students' interest so that they are motivated to read what is coming in the chapter, and (2) to introduce problems and situations that will be explained further by theories and research findings presented within the chapter that follows. For instance, the first chapter starts with a case dealing with the production and marketing of the three *Star Wars* films, a topic about which almost all students should have some familiarity and interest. Elements of the case are then used as examples within the chapter to illustrate what makes international business different from its domestic counterpart and what types of international business methods were involved.

The closing cases are designed to serve a different purpose from the introductory cases: to present situations for which students must analyze possible actions based on what they have learned from the chapter. In other words, the beginning cases should enhance interest and the recall of essential facts. The concluding cases should enhance the development of critical reasoning skills to apply the essential facts to necessary decision making.

We have also continued the use of extensive updated real-world examples throughout the text to illustrate diverse approaches that individuals, companies, industries, and countries have taken in specific situations. Although these examples help to enliven the presentation, they are not the types of facts that one would ordinarily expect students to remember. Yet most of us have seen examples of students underlining the less critical facts of a chapter while skipping over those things that most instructors would consider to be more important. In order that students do not direct their memory efforts too much to the illustrative data, we are continuing to outline the major points of each section in the margin. These marginal notes have been revised for the sake of emphasis and clarity. New terms are set off in boldface type and are then included in a glossary. Objectives are outlined clearly at the beginning of each chapter, and bulleted lists in each summary recap the chapter's major points.

There is ample use of end notes to aid students and instructors in digging deeper on different subjects, yet we omit names of authors (except those of classics such as David Ricardo) within the chapters themselves so that students are not confused into thinking that these are names that they should remember.

There are three indexes—by company, author, and subject. A simple glance at these and at the end notes will illustrate that the content is up-to-date, worldwide, and easy to access.

Both of us come from diverse functional backgrounds and, furthermore, represent a gamut of opinions on the proper role of business and government in international affairs. In order to develop better coherence among the chapters, we each read, criticized, and contributed to the other's sections. John D. Daniels was charged with Chapters 1, 3, 4, 5, 6, 11, 12, 13, 15, 16, 17, 18, and 21; and Lee H. Radebaugh was charged with Chapters 2, 7, 8, 9, 10, 14, 19, and 20.

ENHANCEMENTS

Earlier in the preface, we discussed several ways in which we improved the fifth edition over the fourth edition. As was mentioned, several of the cases have been replaced, and all of the cases have been updated to reflect new information. We will not identify the replacements and the updatings of the cases at this point. However, there are several other changes in the chapters that instructors and students should find of interest. In order to eliminate some overlap, we removed the discussion of the balance of payments from Chapter 1 and moved that discussion to Chapter 9. In Chapter 2, we changed the section entitled "The Developing Countries" to a new section called "Key Issues in Industrial and Developing Countries" so that we could broaden the discussion to include more areas of the world. Given the increased interest and focus on trade and services, we expanded the discussion on "Services" in Chapter 5 and brought out many issues in the GATT talks in Montevideo.

The discussion of "Foreign Exchange and the International Monetary System" was changed significantly in Chapters 8 and 9. Chapter 8 was simplified a great deal, since some of the technical material that would be more appropriate for an international finance class was considered too detailed for an introductory international business class. Also, the material on compensatory trade and the instruments of foreign exchange was transferred to Chapter 20, which discusses international finance issues. Chapter 9 continues to concentrate on the different factors that determine exchange rates, but there is more of an emphasis on management decisions that are affected by exchange rate changes and how management needs to understand the forces that influence those changes. In Chapter 10, we discuss some of the issues that relate to the 1987 stock market crash as well as the liberalization of capital markets in London, known as the "Big Bang." The discussion on international banking is shortened significantly, and a new section on nonbanking financial services has been added. The focus of the chapter is on the financial institutions that firms can use in accessing cash worldwide.

Chapter 13 reflects some of the possible business effects of reforms such as glasnost on East-West trade. New illustrations are included to show which are the centrally planned economies, how East-West business relations have fluctuated, and what steps must be followed when pursuing business in centrally planned economies.

Chapter 14 concentrates more on the global sourcing and production strategy than did the previous edition, which emphasized logistics and transportation. The import strategy as part of the overall global sourcing strategy is expanded, and the export strategy is retained as one way of penetrating foreign markets. More attention is given to the Japanese trading companies as examples of export/import intermediaries.

Chapter 15 contains up-to-date information on ways companies fight the piracy of their intangible assets. In Chapter 16, we added a discussion on diversification and global versus country-by-country strategies as they affect decisions on where to operate. Chapter 17 was reorganized to bring the structural discussion closer to a discussion on decision-making locations. Sections were added on using subsidiaries effectively and on corporate culture as a control mechanism. In Chapter 18 we strengthened the discussion of the globalization controversy and added a discussion on distributor selection management.

Some of the greatest changes in the book came in Chapters 19, 20, and 21. In Chapter 19, the international accounting and tax chapters were simplified and merged together into one chapter. The management accounting issues were eliminated from this chapter and included in the control chapter. Chapter 20, on international finance, is expanded to include global cash management, financing international trade, foreign exchange risk management, and the international investment decision. The discussion on foreign exchange risk has been simplified. In Chapter 21, we streamlined the two chapters on human resources from the previous edition into one. We also added some information on personnel complexities in cooperative ventures.

INSTRUCTOR'S MANUAL

For the fourth edition, we expanded the instructor's manual significantly. In the fifth edition, we have attempted to improve it further. We have continued to include a minimum of 25 multiple-choice questions per chapter but have improved their quality, based on feedback received from a number of the reviewers and from many of our students. In addition, we have included a number of discussion questions that can be used either in essay exams or in class discussion. Improved software is also being used for the computerized test generator. We hope that you will find the fifth edition instructor's manual to be a significant improvement over the fourth and a big help in developing the course.

ACKNOWLEDGMENTS

We have been fortunate from the start of the first edition to have had colleagues who would take the effort to critique draft materials, react to coverage already in print, advise on suggested changes, and send items to be corrected. Since it is the culmination of efforts over the several editions that has brought us to where we are now, we would like to be able to acknowledge everyone's efforts. However, many more individuals than we can possibly list have helped. We sent a questionnaire to nearly every faculty member who has used the textbook and received a significant number of responses. To those individuals who were kind enough to respond to the questionnaire, we offer our sincere thanks. Several other faculty members were asked to give detailed comments on the drafts of the chapters. Those individuals who were able to help us are as follows: Jean J. Boddewyn, Baruch College; John Garland, University of Kansas; Phillip D. Grub, George Washington University; Rose Knotts, North Texas State University; Paul Marer, Indiana University; Gary Popp, United States International University; William Renforth, Florida International University; Val Ridgway, Colorado State University; Martin E. Rosenfeldt, North Texas State University; Heidi Vernon-Wortzel, Northeastern University.

Several typists and graduate students were extremely helpful to us in the preparation of this edition, and without this anonymous support, we could not have made the necessary changes. Some others were so helpful that we cannot let them remain anonymous. They are Joo Heon Kim and Celia Phillips.

Bloomington, Indiana J. D. D.
Provo, Utah L. H. R.

CONTENTS

PART 1
BACKGROUND

Whether we are managers actively engaged in decision making within an internationally competitive environment or citizens interested in regulating international business to achieve our own objectives, it is useful to know why international business takes place, what advantages accrue to firms operating internationlly, what makes this business different from purely domestic operations, and how these operations relate to a country's overall international economic position.

Chapter 1 sets the stage for a more detailed examination of the above considerations. The chapter begins by defining the field, explaining why the growth has been so great in recent years, and relating the field to both the functional areas of business (for example marketing, finance, and management) and the basic disciplines, such as geography, law, and economics. The chapter continues with an explanation of the multiple forms by which international business may take place. The chapter then examines recent trends in world trade and investment by product and geographic area, along with a brief explanation of the factors that cause changes to take place.

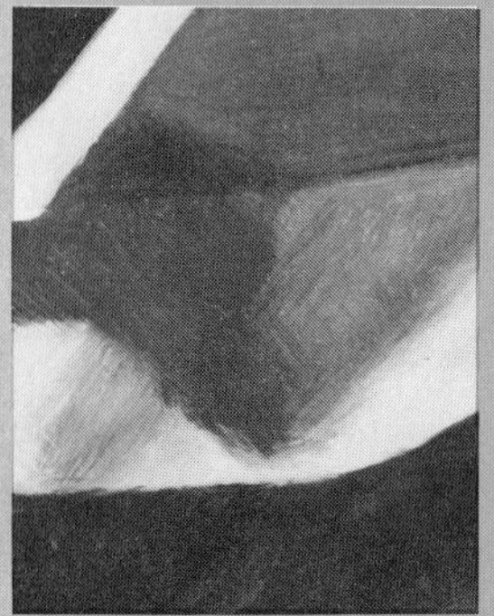

1

CHAPTER INTERNATIONAL BUSINESS: AN OVERVIEW

The world is a chain, one link in another.
Maltese proverb

- To define the field of international business and emphasize the differences between business within the domestic context and business in the international context.
- To illustrate the need to rely on external disciplines (e.g., geography, history, political science, law, economics, and anthropology) because of their impact on how international business is conducted.
- To define and discuss briefly basic terms that relate to international business.
- To introduce the different means—such as exporting, licensing, and investing—a firm can use to accomplish its international objectives.
- To relate the major events causing changes in trade and investment patterns, especially in the post–World War II period.
- To describe the changing composition of world trade in terms of countries and products.
- To examine the patterns of world investment in terms of ownership, location, products, and companies involved.

CASE:

THE STAR WARS TRILOGY[1]

You have probably seen *Star Wars, The Empire Strikes Back,* or *Return of the Jedi.* But you might not know that by 1987 these three films occupied three of the four top spots on the all-time list of revenue earners, making this film sequence the most successful ever produced.

Few films enjoy success when rereleased. Those that have been successful, such as Walt Disney's *Pinocchio,* are generally rereleased only at seven-year intervals. Yet the 1977 film, *Star Wars,* was successfully rereleased five times by 1987. The intergalactic aspect of the trilogy is obvious. Less obvious, though, are the international dimensions, right here on planet earth, that contributed to the films' triumphs.

The deal to produce *Star Wars* was international from the start. George Lucas, the American producer, had written short summaries of two films he wished to make. He took his ideas to every studio in Hollywood; each one turned him down. In desperation, he used his last $2000 to buy a ticket to the Cannes [France] Film Festival, hoping to gain some backing. There he made an agreement with a Hollywood studio for *American Graffiti* and *Star Wars.*

When the time came to film *Star Wars,* cost comparisons were made among technically capable interior facilities. The contract went to a studio outside London. The lower wages of British technicians more than offset the additional costs of transporting personnel from the United States to Great Britain. By the time *The Empire Strikes Back* and *Return of the Jedi* were filmed, the labor cost differentials were no longer significant, but it was convenient to stay on at the English studios, since personnel were working so well together.

Not everything was filmed in England, however. The films' success was due largely to the fact that the extraterrestrial locales appeared authentic. At times the technicians used plates filmed elsewhere to go behind interior scenes shot in England. For instance, in *Star Wars* the Alliance leaders plot the destruction of the Death Star from the secret Rebel base on the planet Yavin. The background for Yavin was in fact the ancient Mayan ruins of Tikal in Guatemala. At other times it was necessary to film on location because of action taking place within rather than in front of scenery. For the scenes in which R2-D2 and C-3PO crash on the desert planet Tatooine, are captured by Jawas, and are sold to a local moisture farmer and his nephew (Luke Skywalker), the filming actually took place on the Sahara Desert in Tunisia. At the beginning of *The Empire Strikes Back* the Rebel force is held up in a hideout on the ice planet Hoth. This was a place above the Arctic Circle in Norway.

In addition to the logistics of filming real actors in different locations, these scenes had to be combined with the miniature effects, which were made at a specially constructed monster factory in California. As shots were completed for *The Empire Strikes Back,* videocassettes had to be transported 6000 miles. Because of transportation and communications advances, global collaboration in filmmaking has become commonplace. These advances enable us to see more realistic-looking scenes than were possible only a few years before *Star Wars.*

The actors were primarily U.S. and U.K. nationals. Carrie Fisher, Harrison Ford, and Mark Hamill, who played Princess Leia Organa, Han Solo, and Luke Skywalker, respectively, were all from the United States. Alec Guinness, who played Ben (Obi-Wan) Kenobi, and Anthony Daniels, who was C-3PO, were both from the United Kingdom. Lord Darth Vader could be characterized as a binational. The actor, David Prowse, is British; however, James Earl Jones, an American, did the voice because of Prowse's strong Devon farmer's accent.

The distribution of the films has been truly international. The expectation of receiving both domestic and foreign income is necessary to justify the risky investment in a high-cost film. About 40 percent of the revenues have come from outside the United States. Some foreign markets have not been penetrated at all, however. For example, most communist countries have prohibited entry. Some other countries, such as Haiti and Mali, have such poor economies that few people can afford to see the films. Even if attendance could be generated, the moviegoers would pay in their local currencies, which are gourdes and francs, respectively. Since the governments are also poor, especially in ownership of other currencies, they would be hard pressed to convert the gourdes and francs to a currency that the producers could use. The film distributors have made separate agreements with each country that shows one of the *Star Wars* trilogy so that revenues will come back to Lucasfilm Ltd. the producer, in U.S. dollars.

Almost everywhere the films have been screened, there has been high public acceptance. This has been due at least partly to good reviews and shrewd marketing, but many films which have these attributes nevertheless fail to become international hits. This difference in success has been ascribed to the films' universal themes. The noted French anthropologist, Claude Levi-Strauss, has observed common threads among the myths, tragedies, and fairy tales in widespread cultures. He attributes this to the fact that the mind classifies by absolute opposition, such as good versus evil. Another explanation may be that there is a bit of child in all of us, all over the world, and George Lucas said, "*Star Wars* is a movie for children." Yet the success has been higher in some countries than in others. In Denmark, for example, revenues have not been stellar because the Danes do not care much for science fiction.

In spite of widespread acceptance it should not be inferred that the films and their promotion have been identical everywhere. The language dubbing of dialogue and/or the placement of subtitles is a costly but standard process necessary to appeal to a mass clientele who do not understand well the original language in films. Subtitles were necessary everywhere, in fact, for the characters speaking languages of foreign planets. These were drawn from combinations of obscure earthly dialects. In *Return of the Jedi,* for example, Jabba the Hutt's language was taken from an Inca-Indian dialect, and the Ewoks' was taken from a combination of five languages that included Mongolian, Tibetan, and Nepali.

Another standard but costly process involves review and approval by censors, without which a film may either be prohibited altogether or restricted to only part of the target audience. The *Star Wars* trilogy was no exception. Although intended for children, censors in a number of countries found scenes too violent for youthful audiences. In Sweden, for example, Lucasfilm had to cut out the sequence of *Return of the Jedi* in which a monster swallows its victims and lets them die slowly and painfully during a thousand-year dinner.

Promotional techniques varied on a country-to-country basis because experienced distributors knew what would most likely attract film patrons. The stars were hustled to Australia to sit for newspaper, radio, and television interviews. In Japan the advertisements were more action oriented than elsewhere. For Spain *The Empire Strikes Back* was entered into the Madrid Film Festival, which gave it national recognition and acceptance.

There has been no need to alter the films technically since 35-millimeter projection has become the worldwide standard for theatrical showings. However, there are no worldwide standards for television. For example, an Italian TV set cannot pick up French programs. Revenues from television transmission are crucial for the success of films, however. So high-quality, expensive conversions must be done for each television transmission system where sales are to be made.

One of the big revenue sources for the *Star Wars* trilogy has been the sale of worldwide rights to such firms as Coca-Cola, Procter & Gamble, and the Atari Division of Warner Communications to produce and sell Star Wars products, ranging from bubble gum and books to wallpaper, piggy banks, and underpants. By the tenth anniversary of the premier of *Star Wars,* the retail sales of these products were more than $2.6 billion. The companies that have been given rights have themselves sometimes depended heavily on foreign operations. For example, more than $400 million in *Star Wars* merchandise has been sold in the United Kingdom. Rather than selling directly abroad themselves, some of the companies have made separate subcontracts with foreign firms to produce and sell particular products in the foreign countries. They have also produced abroad for the U.S. market. Take one company, the Kenner Division of General Mills: Its All Terrain Armored Transport accessories are made in Hong Kong, the *Return of the Jedi* action figures in Taiwan, and the Laser Pistol in Macao. The Chewbacca Bandolier Strap is assembled in Mexico from parts made in the United States.

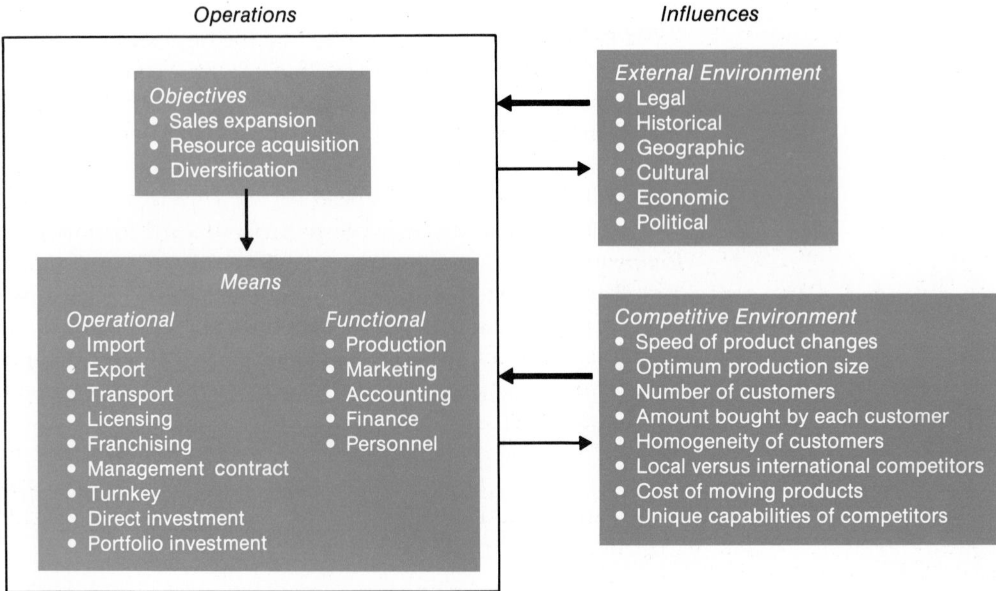

Figure 1.1
International Business: Operations and Influences

INTRODUCTION

The Field of International Business

Private business motives are increased or more stable profits. These are affected by
- Foreign sales
- Foreign resources

Government business may or may not be profit motivated.

International business includes all business transactions that involve two or more countries. Such business relationships may be private or governmental. In the case of private firms the transactions are for profit. Government-sponsored activities in international business may or may not have a profit orientation.

In order to pursue any of these objectives, a company must establish international operational forms, some of which may be quite different from those used domestically. The choice of forms is influenced not only by the objective being pursued, but also by the environments in which the firm must operate. These environmental conditions also affect the means of carrying out business functions such as marketing. At the same time, the company operating internationally will affect, to a lesser degree, the environment in which it is operating. These relationships are illustrated in Fig. 1.1.

Motivation for International Business

There are three major motivations for private firms to pursue international business. These are to expand sales, to acquire resources, and to diversify sources of sales and supplies.

Sales expansion. Sales are limited by the number of people interested in a firm's products and services and by customers' capacity to make purchases. Since the number of people and the degree of their purchasing power is higher for the world as a whole than for a single country, firms may increase their sales potentials by defining markets in international terms.

Ordinarily, higher sales mean higher profits. If, for example, each sales unit has the same mark-up, more volume translates to more profits. Lucasfilm, for example, receives a percentage of the sales made by companies marketing *Star Wars* merchandise; thus Lucasfilm's revenues increase with each additional toy that Parker Kenner sells in the United Kingdom. In fact, profits per unit of sales may increase as sales increase. *Star Wars* cost approximately $10 million to produce; as more people see the film, the average production cost per viewer decreases.

International sales are thus a major motive for firms' expansion into international business. A United Nations study indicated that among the largest industrial firms in the world, about 40 percent of their sales come from outside their home markets.[2]

Resource acquisition. Manufacturers and distributors seek out products and services as well as components and finished goods produced in foreign countries. Sometimes this is to reduce their costs: for example, Lucasfilm used studios in the United Kingdom in the filming of *Star Wars* and Kenner manufactures its Laser Pistol in Hong Kong. The potential effects on profits are obvious. The profit margin may be increased, or cost savings may be passed on to consumers, thereby permitting more people to buy the products. Sometimes foreign procurement is done to gain some unique capability not readily available within one's own country, such as the use of the Arctic snow fields for filming *The Empire Strikes Back.* Such a strategy may allow firms to improve their product qualities or at least differentiate them from their competitors, thus increasing their market shares and profits.

Diversification. Companies usually prefer to avoid wild swings in their sales and profits; so they seek out foreign markets and procurement as a means to this end. Lucasfilm has been able to smooth its yearlong sales somewhat because the summer vacation period (the main season for children's film attendance) varies between the northern and southern hemispheres. It has also been able to make large television contracts during different years for different countries. Many other firms take advantage of the fact that the timing of business cycles differs among countries. Thus while sales decrease in one country that is experiencing a recession, they increase in another that is undergoing recovery. Finally, by depending on supplies of the same product or component from different countries, a company may be able to avoid the full impact of price swings or shortages in any one country that might be brought about, for example, by a strike.

TYPES OF INTERNATIONAL BUSINESS

Companies must choose among different operational forms, as shown in Fig. 1.1, when conducting international business. In making these choices, the companies' own objectives and resources as well as the environments in which the firms operate should be considered. The following discussion introduces the major operating forms, which also correspond closely to the categories in which countries keep records of aggregate international transactions. These transactions are summarized as part of balance of payments accounts, a subject we will discuss in Chapter 9.

Merchandise Exports and Imports

Merchandise exports and imports are usually
- A country's key international economic transaction
- A company's first international business
- Continued even when companies diversify their methods of operating.

Merchandise exports are goods sent out of a country, whereas **merchandise imports** are goods brought in. Since these are tangible goods that visibly leave and enter countries, they are sometimes referred to as visible exports and imports. The terms *exports* or *imports* are used frequently, yet in reality the reference is only to the merchandise exports or imports. In the opening case, the Jedi action figures are merchandise exports for Taiwan when they are sent to the United States and merchandise imports for the United States when they arrive.

Exporting and importing of goods are the major sources of international revenue and expenditure for most countries. Among companies engaged in some form of international business, more are involved in importing and exporting than in any other type of transaction.

Importing and/or exporting is usually, but not always, the first type of foreign operations in which a firm gets involved. This is because at an early stage of international involvement these operations usually take the least commitment and least risk of a firm's resources. For example, firms may be able to export by using excess capacity, thus limiting the need to invest more capital. As will be noted in more detail in Chapter 14, firms may be able to use the services of trade intermediaries who, for a fee, will take on the export-import functions, thus eliminating the need to have trained personnel and a department to carry out foreign sales or purchases.

Exporting or importing are not typically abandoned when firms adopt other international business forms. Although this may sometimes occur, exporting and importing usually continue, either by business with other markets or to complement the new types of business activities.

Service Exports and Imports

Services are earnings other than those from goods.
- Examples are travel, transport, fees, royalties, dividends, interest.

Service exports and imports refer to international earnings other than those from goods sent to another country. Receipt of these earnings is considered a service export, whereas payment is considered a service import. Services are also referred to as invisibles. International business comprises many different types of services.

- They are very important for some countries
- They involve many special international business forms
- They often come after experience with merchandise trade.

Travel, tourism, and transportation. When prints of *Return of the Jedi* were sent from the United States to be shown in Japan, they traveled internationally as did the *Star Wars* actors when they went to Australia to publicize the film. Earnings from transportation and from foreign travel can be an important source of revenue for international airlines, shipping companies, reservations agencies, and hotels. On a national level, such countries as Greece and Norway depend heavily on revenue collected from carrying foreign cargo on their ships. The Bahamas earns much more from foreign tourists than it earns from exporting merchandise.

Performance of activities abroad. **Fees** are payments for the performance of certain activities abroad, such services as banking, insurance, rentals (e.g., the *Star Wars* film), engineering, and management. Engineering services are often handled through **turn-key operations,** contracts for the construction of operating facilities that are transferred to the owner when the facilities are ready to begin operations. Fees for management services are often the result of **management contracts,** arrangements through which one firm provides management personnel to perform general or specialized management functions for another firm.

Use of assets from abroad. **Royalties** are the payment for use of assets from abroad, such as for trademarks, patents, copyrights, or other expertise under contracts known as **licensing agreements.** Royalties are also paid for **franchising,** a way of doing business in which one party (the franchisor) sells an independent party (the franchisee) the use of a trademark that is an essential asset for the franchisee's business. In addition, the franchisor assists on a continuing basis in the operation of the business, such as by providing components, managerial services, or technology.

Firms often move to foreign licensing or franchising after successfully building exports to a market. This move usually involves a greater international commitment than in the early stages of exporting. The greater involvement occurs because the firm commonly has to send technicians to the foreign country to assist the licensee or franchisee in establishing and adapting its production facilities for the new product.

Investments

Key features of direct investment are:

- Control

Direct investments. **Direct investment** takes place when control follows the investment. This can amount to a small percentage of the equity of the company being acquired, perhaps even as little as 10 percent. The ownership

- High commitment of capital, personnel, and technology
- Gain of foreign markets
- Gain of foreign resources
- Higher foreign sales than exporting (often)
- Partial ownership (sometimes)

of a controlling interest in a foreign operation is the highest type of commitment to foreign operations in the given country. Not only does it imply the ownership of an interest abroad, it usually means the transfer of more personnel and technology abroad than when there is no controlling interest in the foreign facility. Because of the high level of commitment, direct investment usually (but not always) comes after a firm has experience in exporting or importing. Direct investment operations may be set up in order to gain access to certain resources or access to a market for the firm's product. Kenner, for example, uses its Mexican direct investment to assemble the Chewbacca Bandolier Strap because this gives access to a resource, cheap labor, for the product's manufacture. Kenner also has direct investments in Europe, which have been made as a means of gaining markets in the countries where the production occurs.

When two or more organizations share in the ownership of a direct investment, the operation is known as a **joint venture.** In a special type of joint venture, a **mixed venture,** a government is in partnership with a private company.

Key components of portfolio investment are

- Noncontrol of foreign operation
- Financial purpose, e.g., loans

Portfolio investments. **Portfolio investment** can be either debt or equity, but the factor that distinguishes portfolio from direct investment is that control does not follow this kind of investment. For U.S. firms as a whole, sales from output produced abroad are many times greater than sales from U.S. production that is sent abroad as merchandise exports.[3] Today most of the world's largest firms have substantial foreign direct investments encompassing every type of business function, such as extraction of raw materials, growing of crops, manufacture of products or components, selling of output, and handling of various services.

Foreign portfolio investments are also important for nearly all firms operating extensively internationally. They are used primarily for financial purposes. Treasurers of companies, for example, routinely move funds from one country to another to get a higher yield on short-term investments. They also borrow funds in different countries.

Multinational Enterprise

Worldwide approach to markets and production is

- Also known as MNC or TNC
- Usually involved in nearly every type of international business practice

The **multinational enterprise,** or MNE, has a worldwide approach to foreign markets and production and an integrated global philosophy encompassing both domestic and overseas operations. Because of the difficulty of ensuring whether a firm has a "worldwide approach," narrower operational definitions emerge. For example, some might say that a firm must have production facilities in some minimum number of countries or be of a certain size in order to qualify as an MNE. The term **multinational corporation,** or MNC, is also quite common in the literature of international business and is often used as a synonym for MNE. We prefer the MNE designation because there are many internationally involved companies such as accounting partnerships that do not use a corporate form.

Another term sometimes used interchangeably with MNE, especially by the United Nations, is **transnational corporation,** or TNC. This term is used also to refer to a company owned and managed by nationals in different countries. To avoid confusion, we shall use TNC only in its latter meaning throughout the text.

Some writers separate MNEs into two categories. The *global company* is one that integrates operations from different countries, such as designing a product or service with a global market segment in mind or making different parts of a product in different countries. The *multidomestic company* is one that allows each country's operations to be independent.

THE EXTERNAL ENVIRONMENT

Drawing on Other Disciplines

Operations in the worldwide environment

- Are affected by social science disciplines
- Cover all functional business fields

Inasmuch as international business operates within the broad context of the world environment, it must draw on the contribution of a number of basic social science disciplines, including geography, history, political science, law, economics, and anthropology. In addition, international business covers the functional business fields such as marketing, management, and finance. These basic disciplines and functional areas play a significant role in the conduct of international business. Consequently, to function effectively in the international environment a manager must have a fundamental grasp of their importance.

A grasp of *geography* is important because it helps managers to determine the location, quantity, and quality of the world's resources and their availability for exploitation. The distribution of these resources gives rise to the production of different products and services in different parts of the world. In our *Star Wars* example, these differences led to the filming of some scenes in Tunisia and others in Norway. Geographical barriers such as high mountains, vast deserts, and inhospitable jungles affect communication and distribution channels for companies in much of the world's economy. Human population distribution around the world and the impact of human activity on the environment exert a strong influence on international business relationships.

An understanding of *history* provides managers with a systematic recording of the evaluation of ideas and institutions. Looking at the past gives international business people a clearer understanding of the functioning of international business activities in the present. History is, after all, the accumulation of human experience that determines how we live today. Technical and institutional developments have expanded the scope of business. For example, the creation of the three *Star Wars* films could not have occurred in the same way at an earlier period. Likewise, certain types of transactions that are not now feasible may be possible in the future whereas others may be carried out in different ways.

Politics has played and will continue to play an important role in shaping worldwide business. *Political Science* sets forth the relationships between business and national political organizations and, in turn, helps to explain behavior patterns of governments and business firms in areas of potentially conflicting interests. Political leadership in each country controls whether and how international business will occur. The prohibition by communist countries of internal distribution of the *Star Wars* films is an example of a political decision that adversely affected international business. The 1988 agreement for McDonald's to start selling bolshoi burgers in the Soviet Union is an example of a more open political policy, *glasnost,* that positively affected international business.

Each country has its own laws on business.

Agreements among countries set international law.

Domestic and international *law* determines largely what the manager of an international company can or cannot do. This includes domestic laws in both the home and host countries that regulate such matters as taxation, employment, and foreign exchange transactions. For example, when *The Empire Strikes Back* was shown in Japan, Japanese law determined how Japanese revenues would be taxed and how revenues could be exchanged from yen to U.S. dollars. U.S. law, in turn, determined how and when the earnings from Japan would be taxed in the United States. International legal agreements between the two countries temper how the earnings are taxed by both nations. Only by understanding the laws for each country where operations may take place and the treaties among nations can companies such as Lucasfilm determine where it might operate profitably abroad.

An appreciation of *economics* gives a manager the tools to determine (1) the impact of an international company on the economy of the host and home countries and (2) the effect of a country's economic policies on the international company. Economic theory also explains why nations exchange goods and services with each other, why capital and people travel from one country to another in the course of business, and why one country's currency has a certain price relative to another's. For example, the decision by Lucasfilm to use British studios was economic. Economics provides a framework for understanding why, where, and when one country can produce goods or services more cheaply than another. The decision not to distribute the films in such places as Haiti was based on a belief that there was insufficient economic wealth to provide a large enough market. The decision to distribute in France was also economic, based not only on France's more prosperous economy, but also on an expectation that the French francs earned from moviegoers would buy enough U.S. dollars to make the showings profitable.

Through the study of *anthropology,* managers may better understand the values, attitudes, and beliefs people have concerning themselves and their environment, thus easing their ability to function in different societies. Recall that Lucasfilm had to cut scenes from *Return of the Jedi* to get permission for children's viewing in Sweden.

Summary comments. The above discussion is intended as an introduction. We shall return to these external environmental situations in greater detail in subsequent chapters. The differences abroad in geography, history, political science, law, economics, and anthropology affect how a company conducts its operations. Yet the amount of adjustment is related to the degree of similarity between the home and foreign countries and is also a function of how many different foreign environments the company is operating.

The Competitive Environment

Each company and each industry has a different competitive environment, which may vary from one country to another. As a result, some firms may be better able to take advantage of foreign opportunities than others. Some firms may also have to deal much more with foreign competition than others within their domestic markets. The most appropriate form of international business opportunity, such as exporting versus licensing, may differ among firms and products, as well as among the countries where the business is undertaken. Some of the most important factors are shown on Figure 1.1 and will be referred to in later chapters. Some trends that are affecting the nature of international competition are briefly explained in the following section.

Time and space shrinkage. A traditional difference between international business and domestic business is that international forms usually encompass greater distances. This increases operating costs and makes control more difficult. But these problems are less prevalent than they used to be. The far-flung production and distribution of the three *Star Wars* films make William Shakespeare's words, "All the world's a stage, and all the men and women merely players," seem prophetic. During Shakespeare's lifetime (1564–1616), most people traveled no more than a few miles from where they were born. The time and cost of moving people or goods from one country to another was so great that sections of the world were quite isolated from each other. Many products that were commonplace in one area were either unknown or rare in another. Since the New World was still being explored (Australia had not even been discovered yet by Europeans), such products as tobacco and potatoes were not introduced into England until after Shakespeare's birth. (One may ponder what the Italian diet must have been before Marco Polo reputedly brought pasta from Asia and the Spaniards introduced tomatoes from South America.) European powers were still fighting to make or break trade monopolies with the Far East so that they could reap the profits from such exotic luxuries as tea. Communications between areas were very slow, although the Dutch did introduce the first airmail service during this period, via pigeon. It was not until four years after Shakespeare's death that the Mayflower sailed from Plymouth, England, to Massachusetts, a trip that took over three months. Another two and a half centuries passed before Jules Verne fantasized that people might encircle the globe in only 80 days.

Business is becoming more global because
- Transport is quicker
- Communications enable control from afar

Technology and geographic expansion. So much that we take for granted today results from the cumulative penetration of technological and geographic frontiers over many decades. Besides the technology to make films, other technology had to be developed in order for the *Star Wars* producers to make and sell the films. Multiple production locations could be used only because videotapes made in the English studio could be transported to California in a day and because actors could travel quickly to locations around the world. Without the transport innovations of the twentieth century, production would have taken so long that the actors might have aged noticeably before the films were completed. Communications developments such as telephone transmission via satellites have not only speeded up interactions, they have allowed people in one country to control operations elsewhere.

Institutional arrangements
- Are made by business and government
- Ease flow of goods
- Reduce risk

Institutional developments. What we now take for granted is also the result of cumulative institutional developments by business and government that let us effectively apply technological innovations. While the ability to distribute films in foreign countries, for example, is due in part to transport advances, it is also related to the evolution of institutional arrangements. Take Lucasfilm's sales to Chile, for example. As soon as the films arrive in Chilean customs, a bank in Santiago would likely collect a distribution fee in pesos from the Chilean distributor and make payment to Lucasfilm in dollars at a bank in the United States. If businesses were still conducted as they were in the era of early caravan traders, Lucasfilm would probably have had to accept Chilean merchandise, such as copper or wine, in payment for the films. The merchandise would have been shipped back to the United States and sold before Lucasfilms could have received a useable income. While such barter transactions still do take place and have been increasing in recent years, they are not the most common means for making international payments. Barter transactions are usually cumbersome, time-consuming, risky, and expensive. The relative ease with which most producers today can get paid for goods and services sold abroad is due to the development of a host of innovations. These include money to replace barter, clearing arrangements to convert one country's currency into another's, insurance to cover damage en route and non-payment by the buyer, and bank credit agreements.

There are numerable other institutional arrangements that have facilitated the conduct of international business. One involves the transport of mail. The first international postal agreement, between France and part of what is now West Germany, was enacted during Shakespeare's life. Today you can send a letter to any place in the world by buying stamps denominated in your own country's currency, regardless of how many countries the letter must pass through en route. Lucasfilm could buy U.S. postage stamps for a letter sent to its Chilean distributors even though the letter might be routed on an Argentine airline that made stops en route in Colombia and Peru. Imagine what it would be like if separate payment and shipment had to be arranged for each country through which a letter passes.

Most large firms operate internationally because
- New products become global quickly
- Firms can produce in different countries
- Domestic firms face international competitors

Development of global competition. Firms today are able to respond to many foreign opportunities more quickly than firms in the past. News about events and innovations in one place is transmitted almost simultaneously elsewhere. One of the results is a more rapid diffusion of new product information and sales in foreign countries, such as Rubik's Cube, which seemed to spread worldwide overnight from its Hungarian origin. Firms can also shift production more quickly from one country to another because of their foreign experience and because goods can be transported efficiently from most places. Coleco, for example, met unexpected demand for its Cabbage Patch Kid dolls but was able to step up output quickly through its production contracts with existing associates in the People's Republic of China and Hong Kong. The dolls were whisked to the U.S. Chirstmas market on chartered jumbo jets.[4] Likewise, companies can separate component and/or product manufacture among countries to take advantage of cost differences. Recall from the opening case that Kenner carried out the more automated part of its Chewbacca Bandolier Strap production in the United States and the more labor-intensive production in Mexico. Some Japanese and South Korean firms are now producing part of their product lines at home and part in the United States, then exporting from each production location.

Because companies can respond to foreign market and production opportunities, competition has become more global. Firms that hitherto operated only domestically and defined their competitors as being domestic are now facing increased competition from foreign firms and from domestic firms that have become international. When they have not recognized and responded to the new global competition, the results have often been catastrophic. A good example is Mesta Machine, one of a handful of U.S. firms that supplied equipment to the U.S. steel industry when the United States dominated steel output worldwide. The firm overlooked technical advances by foreign equipment manufacturers and ignored the rapid growth of foreign markets. Suddenly Mesta found competition from overseas rivals that could offer lower prices, faster delivery, and the technology demanded by the foreign and U.S. steel industry. Mesta responded too late and went bankrupt.[5]

Business Operating Adjustments

A company's specific functional adjustments depend on the environment, the firm's objectives, and its operational form. Recall our *Star Wars* case:

Lucasfilm had to alter its marketing by using different promotion methods for different countries. It undoubtedly had to deal with different labor and accounting regulations for its production in the United Kingdom as well. The choice of business form depends in part on the environment in which the company is operating internationally and in part on the competitive situation facing the firm.

INFLUENCES ON TRADE AND INVESTMENT PATTERNS

Economic Conditions

Economic conditions affect year-to-year trade volume, but trade tends to fluctuate more than economy.

Changes in worldwide affluence since World War II have affected the total value of world trade and investment, the types of products involved, and the proportionate value of international business accounted for by individual countries. Definitive figures on the changes in historic world output are unavailable, but indications are that international trade has remained a fairly constant percentage of gross world product (GWP) over a long period. This does not mean that trade and production will be related in exactly the same way every year. During economic booms, as in much of the 1970s, trade tends to grow more rapidly than production. Conversely, a slow growth rate, such as the period between the two world wars and that of the early 1980s, causes trade to increase more slowly than production. In the late 1980s, both trade and production grew at about the same moderate rate. The reason for this cyclical relationship is that many foreign goods are considered marginal by consumers and government policymakers; thus imports are curtailed as the economy slackens. During the early 1980s, for example, many governments enacted measures to prevent certain imports. Producers may also attempt to export only when they have surpluses and will add capacity to serve foreign markets only if the foreign demand is sustained for a long period.

Rising affluence increases portion of trade in manufactures and lessens portion in agriculture.

Changing world affluence has affected the types of products and their relative importance in world trade. In the mid-nineteenth century, Ernst Engel, a German political economist and statistician, observed that as family incomes increase, the percentage spent on food tends to decrease, whereas the percentage spent on other items tends to remain fairly constant or increase. This is true even though the absolute amount spent on food increases due to substitution of more expensive food items. When the human body has reached the limit of its intake capacity, food purchases are replaced by nonfood items. This trend has decreased the proportion of world trade and investment accounted for by agricultural products and increased the proportion accounted for by the manufacturing sector. In addition to consuming the traditional goods and services, the world mass market now has access to once-rare things such as watches and foreign travel.

Technology

The main effects of technology are

- Changes in products traded
- Changes in trading countries
- Increased trade share of industrial countries

Rapid technological changes in this century have created new products, displaced old ones, and affected the relative positions of countries in world trade and investment. The most obvious examples are new products such as jets, computers, and transistor radios, which make up a large portion of international business. Products that existed in earlier periods have expanded in world trade because of technology in the production process, as with automobiles, or because new uses have been found, as with soybeans and fish meal. Other products have been at least partially displaced by substitutes, such as artificial fibers for cotton, wool, and silk and synthetic rubber and synthetic nitrate for the natural products. Still other products have not grown in demand as rapidly because technology has resulted in methods of conservation. For example, tin cans have become thinner and copper wiring can carry more telephone messages simultaneously; therefore, demand for these metals is not as great as it might be. Since most technical advances have emanated from the most industrialized (richer) countries, firms from these countries control a greater share of the trade and investment in the manufacturing sector, which has been the major growth area. As a result, many of the poorer countries have had a proportionately smaller share of international business.

Wars and Insurrection

Military conflicts

- Change what is produced
- Increase international business risk
- Have a growing global effect on business

Military conflicts disrupt traditional international business patterns as participants divert much of their productive capacity and transportation systems to the war effort. In addition, political animosity and transport difficulties may interfere with trading channels. The composition of trade changes because of a shift from consumer goods to industrial goods that can be used in meeting military objectives. International investment is disrupted since foreign-owned plants are frequently destroyed or expropriated. There is little capital available to move abroad, and even if there were, uncertainties and political regulations would prevent it. Nearly every industrialized country was involved in World War II. Not until 1948, three years after the end of the war, did the volume of world trade return to the 1938 level.

Unlike earlier wars, those in the twentieth century have had far-reaching impact due to increased global interrelationships. A particularly notable example was oil price increases after the Arab/Israeli war of 1973. There has been much concern in the 1980s that the war between Iraq and Iran may have similar results.

Even national disturbances may have widespread international implications. The Chilean disruptions in the early 1970s, for example, had a substantial effect on world copper production and usage. The warring within Lebanon in the 1980s has resulted in a shift in international banking from Beirut to Bahrain and Cyprus.

Political Relationships

Some possible effects of political blocs are
- An increased portion of international business among member countries
- A decreased portion of business with nonmember countries
- Stimulation of international business

Political blocs. The major political schism in recent years has been between the communist and noncommunist countries. (The subject is explored in great depth in Chapter 13.) The result is that very little of total world trade (about 5 percent) is conducted between the two groups. (The total world trade accounted for by the communist countries is about 10 percent.) Direct investment is negligible between the two groups because of restrictions by communist countries on private ownership, particularly from a foreign source.

Since the 1950s several groups of countries have banded together and removed most trade restrictions among themselves. The most notable example is the European Community (EC), which is scheduled to have all trade barriers removed among member countries by 1992. Because of the greater ease of trade among members, a greater percentage of the members' total trade is being conducted within the group. Because of the growth generated within the EC, the members' portion of total world trade has grown. This growth rate, along with the access to larger markets within the community, has also been a major attraction to foreign investors.

Key features of multinational agreements are
- Promotion of consistent and uniform rules
- Exchange of concessions
- Promotion of economic growth

Multinational agreements. In recent years there have been a number of international accords and agreements affecting world business. These have resulted from the realization that countries are increasingly interdependent and that a degree of consistency and uniformity is needed in order to assure a flow of goods and services internationally. Included among the many agreements are the International Monetary Fund (IMF), which has altered currency regulations; the International Air Transportation Association (IATA) and numerous shipping conferences, which set rates and frequencies between international ports; and the International Patent and Trade Mark Conventions, which specify certain property rights for companies operating internationally. In addition to these multilateral activities, countries have signed numerous bilateral tax agreements that prevent international firms from being taxed by both their home and foreign countries on the same earnings. Without these provisions against double taxation, few foreign investments would be economically feasible.

The General Agreement on Tariffs and Trade (GATT), to which most free world and some communist countries are participants, provides a forum for negotiating mutual reductions in trade restrictions. Through tariff conferences, restrictions have been reduced on most items in world trade, and countries have agreed on procedures to simplify the conduct of international trade. Political blocs and multinational agreements are discussed further in Chapter 7.

Another recent development has been the emergence of international agencies, such as the World Bank, the Asian Development Bank, and the

Inter-American Development Bank, which give loans and assistance for government-guaranteed projects. In some cases these have been an alternative to governmental or private capital. In others the funds have been used to finance social and infrastructure development, such as housing and highways, for which alternative funds would not be forthcoming. In these latter cases the agency loans have undoubtedly stimulated trade and direct investment by enabling countries to buy necessary equipment from abroad and by allowing them to build the infrastructure needed for the efficient conduct of business activities. These developments are examined in more detail in Chapter 10.

RECENT WORLD TRADE PATTERNS

Since world trade is unevenly distributed by area and product, it is useful to examine its overall patterns and trends. This examination is helpful for understanding, in a broad sense, where world business opportunities are located.

Divergent Growth Rates

Reasons for industrial countries' growing share of world trade are

- Faster-growing trade in manufactures
- Exceptions made for poor countries with rapid industrialization
- Exceptions made for oil exporters

Economic level of countries. One of the common ways of classifying countries is by their level of economic or industrial development. The high-income countries (Western Europe, the United States, Canada, Australia, New Zealand, and Japan) are usually referred to as either industrial or developed countries. Other noncommunist countries are referred to as developing or lesser developed countries (LDCs). The communist countries are known as centrally planned economies, or CPEs, regardless of whether they have high or low incomes. Precise definitions and further subclassifications of these countries will be covered in Chapter 2.

Figure 1.2 shows that most of the world's exports are among developed countries. Several interrelated factors help to explain the low world trade share by the LDCs. Primarily, LDCs depend heavily on agricultural products and raw materials for their export earnings. Because of the economic and technical factors discussed earlier, earnings from these types of exports have not kept pace with those from manufactured goods. In manufactured production, the developed countries have advantages in world markets because of their technology and their ability to reduce costs through large-scale production or resource capacity to supply their own needs, much less those of other areas.

However, there has been a turnaround in some LDCs' trade positions thanks to three major factors. Foremost has been the ability of oil-exporting countries to raise the price of petroleum exports substantially. During the 1970s the price of oil exports increased more than 1200 percent.[6] Prices fell

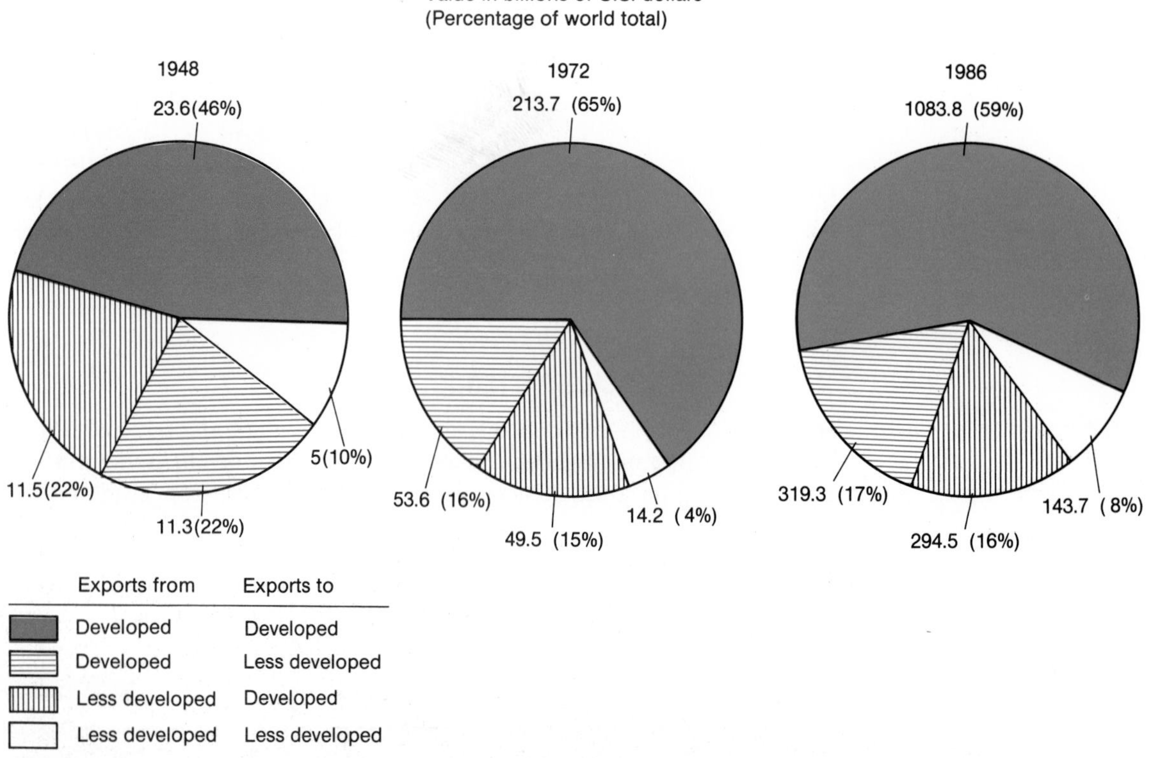

Figure 1.2

Value of Free World Trade Between Developed and Less-Developed Areas, Selected Years

Source: Statistical Yearbook, 1968 (New York: United Nations, 1969), pp. 398–399. *Statistical Yearbook,* 1973 (New York: United Nations, 1974), pp. 402–409, and *Direction of Trade Statistics Yearbook,* 1987 (Washington, D.C. International Monetary Fund, 1987), pp. 8–19, and *Direction of Trade Statistics Annual* 1970–74 (Washington, D.C., International Monetary Fund, n.d.), pp. 8–35.

after 1981, but not nearly as much as they had risen; since then, there has been some fluctuation but no major changes. A second factor has been the rapid industrialization of a number of LDCs, such as Brazil and South Korea, now referred to as newly industrialized countries (NICs). A third factor has been the easier access of LDCs' manufactured products to industrial countries' markets. At the United Nations Conference on Trade and Development (UNCTAD) in 1964 the developing countries began to pressure the industrial nations to give preference to manufactured exports from developing countries. By the end of the 1970s, every industrial country had policies allowing LDC manufacturers easier access than industrial manufacturers. In spite of this turnaround for some LDCs, most LDCs have been able neither to export petroleum nor to industrialize rapidly. For them, there is a downward trend in share of world trade.

Even among the LDCs whose export shares increased, there is some doubt that their successes can continue. In 1988, the United States announced that it would rescind the trade preferences for four countries that had been "too successful"—Hong Kong, Singapore, South Korea, and Taiwan.

Given the position of LDCs, it is not surprising that the ten largest traders are all industrial countries (see Table 1.1). Six of these are members of the EC and conduct a large portion of their trade among themselves, there being far fewer restrictions among EC members than between the EC and other countries.

Since the turn of the century, the portion of U.S. exports

- Has increased in Asia and Canada
- Has decreased in Europe and Latin America

Recent shifts in U.S. trade partners are linked to

- Petroleum trade
- Foreign policy changes
- Asian industrialization

Twentieth-century changes in United States trading partners. The major change in U.S. export markets this century has been the decline in the relative importance of Europe. More than 80 percent of U.S. exports went to Europe before the turn of the century; however, the figure had dropped to about 50 percent by the 1920s and is now only about 30 percent. The biggest gain in exports has been to Asia. Exports to Asia have grown from less than 1 percent at the turn of the century to over 30 percent now, making Asia a larger export market for U.S. products than Europe.[7] Canada is the largest importer of U.S. products.

For U.S. imports, the big losers in proportionate share in this century have been Europe and Latin America. Purchases from Europe, which constituted about half of U.S. imports at the turn of the century, have stayed between 20 and 30 percent per year since the early 1920s. Purchases from Latin America comprised about 30 percent of U.S. imports until 1960; since then the figure has fallen steadily and now accounts for about 15 percent. The major gains in imports over this long-term period have been from Canada and Japan. The growth for Canada has been fairly steady from about 5 percent early in the century to about 20 percent currently. Japan also accounts for approximately 20 percent of U.S. imports, but its growth has been very recent. Japan is the largest exporter to the United States, and Canada is in a close second position. The proportion of imports coming from Asia has grown from a turn-of-the-century figure of about 15 percent of total U.S. imports to about 35 percent now.

Since 1970 the relative importance of U.S. trading partners has shifted considerably, due primarily to three factors: shifts in petroleum trade, foreign policy changes, and greater industrialization of certain Asian countries. Because of increased revenues from oil sales, Mexico, Saudi Arabia, and Venezuela have become more important markets. The People's Republic of China, the Soviet Union, and Egypt have also become more prominent because of foreign policy changes. Increased income from industrialization in Thailand, South Korea, Taiwan, and Malaysia have been responsible for

TABLE 1.1

MAJOR EXPORTING AND IMPORTING COUNTRIES
(in billions of dollars, 1986)

Exports		Imports	
West Germany	243.3	United States	387.1
United States	217.3	West Germany	191.2
Japan	210.8	Japan	127.7
France	124.9	France	127.7
United Kingdom	107.1	United Kingdom	126.3
Italy	97.8	Italy	99.9
Canada	89.9	Canada	85.7
Netherlands	80.6	Netherlands	75.7
Belgium-Luxembourg	68.8	Belgium-Luxembourg	68.6
Switzerland	37.5	Switzerland	41.0

Source: *Direction of Trade Statistics Yearbook, 1987* (Washington D.C., International Monetary Fund, 1987), p. 3.

their taking a larger share of total U.S. exports. The United States brings in a larger portion of its imports from Mexico and Norway because they became new oil suppliers and from Japan, Taiwan, South Korea, and Singapore because of their new industrial product capabilities. The biggest losers in export share to the United States since 1970 have been Canada and West Germany.[8]

Trade by Product Category

Although figures on global trade by product category are always a few years old before they are compiled and published, one can nevertheless discern some trends.

Figure 1.3 shows the growing importance of manufactured goods in world trade up to 1972. Since then the raw materials category has increased substantially at the expense of manufactures because of the increased price of oil. Food exports have continued to decline as a portion of world trade. The U.S. imports and exports show a similar dependence on manufactured products.

As shown in Fig. 1.4, the developed countries account for the majority of world exports in every category except fuels. The centrally planned economies account for a small portion of world trade in all categories. The LDCs have, however, improved their world export share in chemicals, machinery, and other manufacturers during recent years.

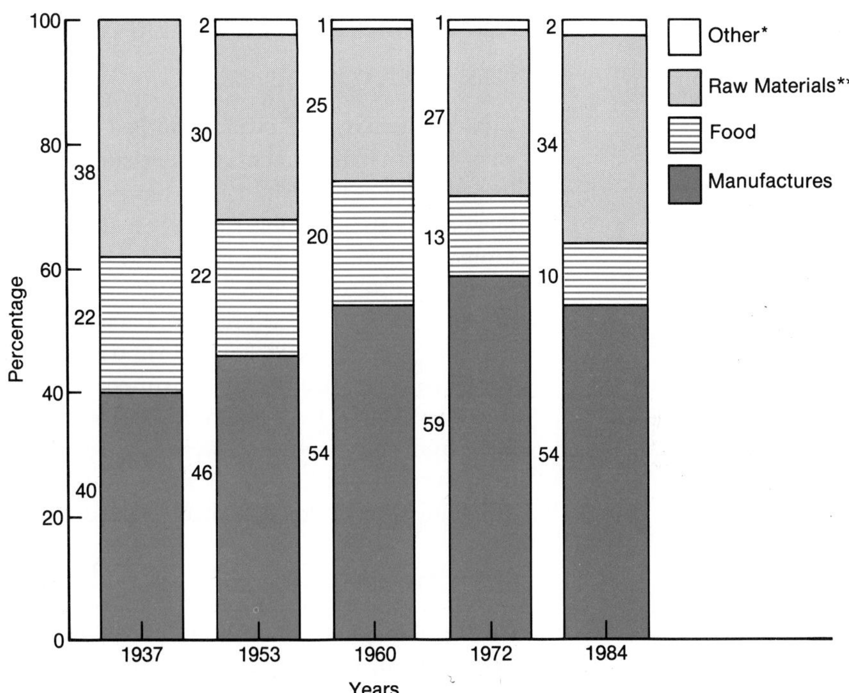

Figure 1.3

World Trade by Major Product Category for Selected Years in Percentage of Total World Trade

Sources: W. S. Woytinski and E. S. Woytinski, *World Commerce and Governments* (New York: Twentieth Century Fund, 1955); *United Nations Statistical Yearbook,* 1973 (New York: United Nations, 1974), p. 56; *International Trade Statistics Yearbook, 1985,* Vol. I (New York: United Nations, 1987), p. 1126.

*Includes such things as live animals and products not classified by reporting countries.

**Includes agricultural raw materials, fuels, minerals, and chemicals.

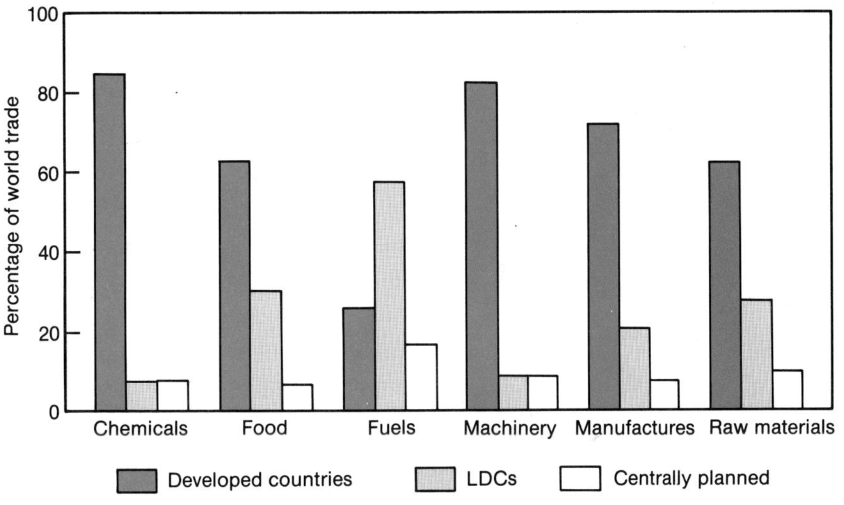

Figure 1.4

World Exports by Type of Country (major product categories, 1984)

Source: International Trade Statistics Yearbook, 1985, Vol. I. (New York: United Nations, 1987), p. 1124.

RECENT DIRECT INVESTMENT PATTERNS

Move to Direct Investment

Until the emergence of international firms, all private foreign investments were portfolio investments rather than direct investments. The push to direct investment began in the 1920s, but even during this period, portfolio movements were about double the direct ones. During the Depression in the 1930s it became obvious that portfolio investors, especially those from the United States who were the main suppliers of foreign capital, had chosen foreign projects poorly. Direct investments fared much better and recovered somewhat in the late 1930s.[9] Since World War II, direct investment by U.S. firms has grown substantially. Direct investment by firms from other industrial countries grew slowly for a number of years after World War II. During this time, firms from those countries were busy rebuilding their domestic markets and they were short of funds to invest on the outside. Since about 1965, their direct investment positions have expanded rapidly.

Direct Investor Description

In direct investment,

- Almost all ownership is by firms from industrial countries
- LDC ownership is starting to grow faster

Country of origin. One way of describing investors is to look at the origin of investment by country. There are no recent estimates of the value of direct investment ownership on a country-by-country basis. The most recent United Nations study did, however, estimate the number of direct investments. Table 1.2 summarizes this information and illustrates that nearly all investment has emanated from a few industrial countries. The United States and United Kingdom comprise together about 60 percent of the world total. The top dozen investing countries account for more than 95 percent.

Although direct investment from industrial countries still accounts for nearly all the world's value (about 98 percent), there has been some recent growth from developing countries. There are now several hundred LDC direct investors that own several thousand foreign investments. Most of this movement has been from the developing countries that have experienced recent industrialization, such as Hong Kong, Singapore, Mexico, Brazil, and Argentina.[10]

At the end of 1986, foreign direct investment in the United States was valued at $209 billion. About 45 percent of this originated from two countries, the United Kingdom and the Netherlands. LDC direct investments make up a substantially higher (10 percent) portion of the direct investment within the United States than the LDC ownership in total world direct investment.[11] Foreign direct investment within the United States has been growing more rapidly in the past few years than the flow of direct investment from the United States to foreign countries. Thus at the end of 1986, the value of direct investment within the United States was about 80 percent of the value of that owned by U.S. interests in foreign countries.

TABLE 1.2

FOREIGN DIRECT INVESTMENT OWNERSHIP BY COUNTRY
(number of affiliates, 1980)

Country	Number	Percent of World Total
United States	33,647	34.3
United Kingdom	24,928	25.4
West Germany	7,392	7.5
France	4,749	4.8
Netherlands	4,370	4.5
Switzerland	4,031	4.1
Sweden	3,369	3.4
Japan	3,029	3.1
Canada	2,991	3.1
Australia	1,885	1.9
Belgium	1,746	1.8
Italy	1,538	1.6
Other	4,289	4.5
Total	97,964	100.0

Source: Figures are compiled from United Nations Centre on Transnational Corporations, *Transnational Corporations in World Development,* Third Survey (New York: United Nations, 1983), pp. 318–326.

Highest growth has been in petroleum and manufacturing because

- There has been faster growth in world consumption
- There are more stringent ownership regulations than in some other sectors.

Economic sector of investment. Between 1929 and 1973 U.S.-owned direct investment shifted toward petroleum and manufacturing (see Fig. 1.5). Although the same type of historical data are not readily available for non-U.S. direct investment, estimates indicate that the U.S.- and non-U.S. investment composition is very similar. Since the early 1970s composition has not changed appreciably. The shift toward the petroleum and manufacturing sectors has been due largely to the faster growth in world consumption of those products. Another factor has been the growing reluctance of many countries to allow foreign ownership of mineral rights, agricultural properties, and transportation and utilities systems.

Highest percentage of investment is

- Petroleum within LDCs
- Manufacturing within industrial countries

The composition of U.S. direct investment abroad varies between developed countries and LDCs. The book value at the end of 1986 showed that manufacturing comprised 45 percent of the investment in developed countries but only 33 percent in LDCs. Petroleum investments were 29 percent in LDCs and only 20 percent in developed countries.[12] This divergence is due partially to circumstance, since oil investments have to be made where the oil is found. Economic conditions are also a major factor, since the developed countries are the main markets for manufactured goods and are large enough to allow for efficient production. The divergence is lessening, since manufacturing investments have been growing more rapidly than petroleum investments in LDCs.

Figure 1.5
Changing Pattern of United States Direct Investment Abroad in Percentages (by value)
Source: Survey of Current Business, various issues.
*Includes transportation,trade, utilities, and other service industries.
**Mining and smelting is included in "other" for 1986.

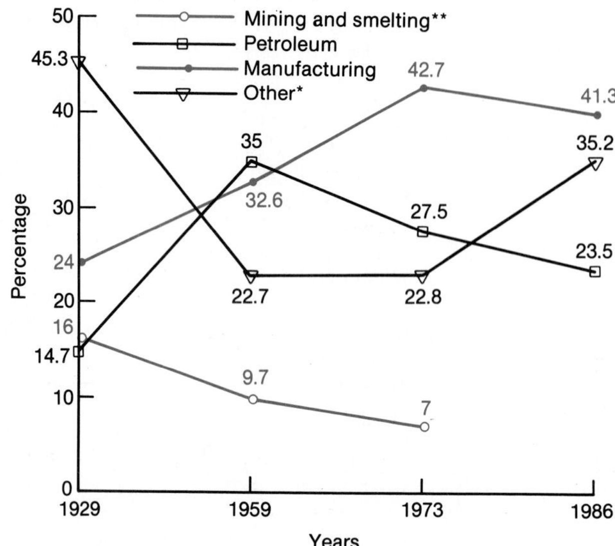

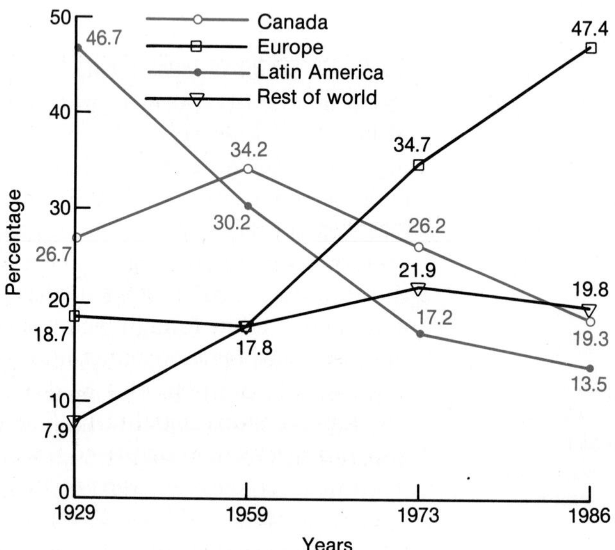

At the end of 1986 the value of foreign direct investment in the United States was distributed in the following sectors: manufacturing, 33%; wholesale trade, 15%; petroleum 14%; and other, 38%.

TABLE 1.3

LOCATION OF FOREIGN DIRECT INVESTMENTS BY AREA
(number of affiliates, 1980)

Country	Number	Percent of World Total
United Kingdom	8239	8.4
Canada	6619	6.7
West Germany	6408	6.5
France	5986	6.1
Australia	5705	5.8
United States	5352	5.5
Netherlands	4084	4.2
Belgium	4014	4.1
South Africa	3873	4.0
Switzerland	2957	3.0
Brazil	2888	2.9
Italy	2535	2.6
Mexico	2355	2.4
Hong Kong	2225	2.3
Spain	2183	2.2
Remainder of Asia	10,164	10.4
Remainder of Europe	9661	9.9
Remainder of Latin America	6359	6.5
Remainder of Africa	4808	4.9
Other	1549	1.6
Total	97,964	100.0

Source: Figures are compiled from United Nations Centre on Transnational Corporations, *Transnational Corporations in World Development,* Third Survey (New York: United Nations, 1983), pp. 318–326.

Investments occur most in industrial countries because they have
- Biggest markets
- Least perceived risk.

LDC-owned investment is largely regional.

Location of investment. Table 1.3 shows that the major recipients of direct investment are industrial countries. Of the top fifteen recipients, only four (South Africa, Brazil, Mexico, and Hong Kong) are generally classified as LDCs. About 54 percent of foreign-owned affiliates are in Europe, and only about 31 percent are in LDCs. This pattern parallels the outward flow of direct investments owned by U.S. enterprises. At the end of 1986, U.S. ownership abroad was about $260 billion, of which a little less than a quarter was located in LDCs. Figure 1.5 shows that Europe has a growing share of U.S.direct investment, whereas Canada and Latin America have declining portions. The portion in Latin America has been declining for a longer period; in the 1920s, nearly half was located there.

There are two primary reasons for the growing interest in developed countries. First, more investments have been market seeking (that is, producing in a country in order to sell the output there), and the developed countries have more income to spend. Second, political turmoil in many LDCs has discouraged investors.

In the case of the direct investment originating from developing countries, most has thus far been to countries within the region where the parent firm is located—for example, Malaysian investments in Thailand. There is some evidence, however, that these investors are now beginning to develop footholds in more distant industrial countries.[13]

Other Forms of International Business

For most companies the two most important forms of foreign business activities are trade and direct investment. These forms also have the biggest impact on regulations governing the private flow of business among countries. That is why we have emphasized the recent patterns of these two types of activities. Other forms, such as licensing, are also important and may even be the most important for individual countries. We shall investigate these other forms from an operational standpoint in later chapters.

SUMMARY

- The cumulative penetration of technologic and geographic frontiers, coupled with institutional development, has resulted in a global competitive environment marked by the use of foreign countries as production bases and sales outlets and by a rapid international diffusion of new products and processes.
- Because of its broad global environment, a number of disciplines (geography, history, political science, law, economics, and anthropology) are useful to help explain the conduct of international business.
- When operating abroad, companies may have to adapt their methods of carrying out business functions. This is because the environment may dictate the appropriate operational method and because the business forms used for foreign operations may differ from domestic ones.
- Among the forms of international business are trade in goods and services, transportation, licensing, franchising, turnkey projects, management contracts, and direct and portfolio investments.
- Multinational enterprises (MNEs) take a worldwide approach to markets and production. They are sometimes referred to as multinational corporations (MNCs) or transnational corporations (TNCs).
- The major factors causing changes in world trade and investment patterns are economic conditions, technology, wars and insurrections, and political relationships.
- Most world trade and direct investment are accounted for by the developed or industrial countries. They are the major importers of all product categories and the major exporters of all except fuels. About 98 percent of direct investment originates from industrial countries, which also receive nearly 70 percent of direct investment.

- A long-term trend has been the increased portion of trade and investment accounted for by the manufacturing sector. During the 1970s, however, the value of raw material exports took a larger share of world trade because of petroleum price increases.

CASE: DISNEYLAND ABROAD[14]

In 1984, Tokyo Disneyland completed its first year of operations. More than 10 million people (9 percent from other Asian countries) visited the park, spending $355 million. This was $155 million more than had been expected, largely because the average expenditure per visitor was $30, rather than the estimated $21 per visitor. During the first year of operations, Tokyo Disneyland had only a $1.3 million deficit instead of an anticipated $14 million one, leaving analysts to expect a profit by year two. This success followed five years of planning and construction since the Walt Disney Corporation entered into an agreement with the Oriental Land Company in Japan.

The Tokyo park is in some ways a paradox. Although such firms as Lenox China and Mister Donut had to adapt to Japanese sizes and tastes, Tokyo Disneyland is a replica of the two parks in the United States. This was required by the management of the Oriental Land Company, who wanted visitors to feel they were getting the real thing. It was also due to the fact that such franchises as McDonald's have enjoyed enormous success in Japan as Japanese youth have embraced American-style culture.

The timing of the Tokyo Disneyland opening coincided with a rise in income and in leisure time among the Japanese, thus contributing to its success. A Disney executive said that a similar rise in income and leisure had contributed to the success experienced when the first park opened near Los Angeles.

That the park itself is nearly identical to the ones in the United States masks the fact that there have been numerous operational adjustments. Probably the most important is in the methods of promotion. Whereas Disney uses its own staff to prepare advertising in the United States, it has relied on outside agencies within Japan to adapt to cultural differences. Even within Japan there are differences. For example, ads outside of Tokyo are more informational whereas those in Tokyo, where the park is well known, rely more on a fun image.

Disney provided no financing for the Tokyo operation. Disney provided master planning, design, manufacturing and training services during construction, and consulting services after completion of the facility. Disney received fees for efforts during construction and receives royalties from admissions and from merchandise and food sales.

The success of Tokyo Disneyland led the company to consider expansion into Europe. In 1985 it announced that it had narrowed its locational choice to two countries, Spain and France. Since the park was estimated to provide about 40,000 permanent jobs and draw large numbers of tourists, the two countries openly courted Disney. Disney, in turn, was likened to Scrooge McDuck, as it openly played off one country against the other to try to get more incentives. Spain offered two different locations, 25 percent of the cost of construction, and claimed it could attract 40 million tourists a year. The French guaranteed 12 million customers a year, the number Disney estimated as the break-even point, and agreed to extend the Paris railway to the park's location (thus linking the park to the rest of Europe) at a cost of about $350 million. Disney finally signed an agreement with the French government in 1986 because of the more central location of Paris and the large number of tourists who visit Paris throughout the year. The park is scheduled to open in 1991.

If Disney had opted for a Spanish location, the park would be much more like the ones in the United States where visitors are outside for almost all amusements. The colder climate in the Paris area will require more indoor shows, focusing on technology and historical themes.

Unlike its Japanese venture, Disney will take a minority ownership in France. In addition, Disney will receive royalties and fees for its unique contributions. The investment for the park is expected to be about $1.2 billion. There will also be satellite investments around the park to include hotels, shopping centers, campgrounds, and other facilities. These will cost another $1.2 billion.

In spite of the economic benefits that the park is expected to bring, many people in France have feared that the park is just one more step toward the replacement of the French culture with that from the United States. In fact, one magazine, *le Nouvel Observateur* showed a giant Mickey Mouse stepping on the rooftops of Parisian buildings. Yet the actor, Yves Montand, summed up the feelings of most young French when he said, "T-shirts, jeans, hamburgers—nobody imposes these things on us. We like them." Walt Disney Productions sought to head off criticism by explaining in the French press that Disney was of French descent, with an original name of D'Isigny rather than Disney.

QUESTIONS

1. What motivated Disney to set up parks abroad, and what might be the pros and cons from the standpoint of the Walt Disney Corporation?
2. Why do you suppose Disney decided to take no ownership in the Japanese operation and only a minority in France?
3. Other than the points mentioned in the case, what other operating adjustments might be necessary to assure success of the foreign operations?

4. Might Disney set up other parks abroad? If so, where? What types of operating forms should Disney consider?

NOTES

1. We wish to acknowledge the cooperation of Robert M. Greber, Chief Executive Officer, and Susan Trembly, Publicity and Advertising Assistant, at Lucasfilm Ltd. for granting interview information. In addition to the interview data, the case relied on data from the following sources: Sid Adilman, " 'Star Wars' Heralds Dawn of Canadian Paycable Amid Ad Blitz for Blockbuster Pix," *Variety,* January 19, 1983, p. 2; Louise Sweeney, "Returns from 'Jedi': Marketing a Megahit," *Christian Science Monitor,* June 30, 1983, pp. 87–8; "$2 Mil. for 'Star Wars' on Aussie TV," *Variety,* March 10, 1982, p. 43; Timothy White, "Slaves to the Empire," *Rolling Stone,* July 24, 1980, pp. 33–37; Jean Vallely, "The Empire Strikes Back," *Rolling Stone,* June 12, 1980, pp. 31–34; Gillian MacKay, "George Lucas Launches the Jedi," *Maclean's,* Vol. 96, May 30, 1983, pp. 42–44; Gerald Clarke, "Great Galloping Galaxies!" *Time,* Vol. 121, May 23, 1983, pp. 62–65; Conrad Phillip Kottak, "Social-Science Fiction," *Psychology Today,* Vol. 106, February 1978, pp. 12–18; "Fun in Space," *Newsweek,* May 30, 1977, pp. 60–61; Aljean Harmetz, "Showing of 'Star Wars' Trilogy Set," *New York Times,* February 28, 1985, p. 20; and *Variety,* June 3, 1987 ("Star Wars," 10th anniversary issue).

2. United Nations Centre on Transnational Corporations, *Transnational Corporations in World Development,* Third Survey (New York: United Nations, 1983), p. 48.

3. The sales from the direct investment were estimated at 108 percent in the U.S. Department of Commerce Benchmark Study. See Ned G. Howenstine, "Gross Product of U.S. Multinational Companies, 1977," *Survey of Current Business,* February 1983, p. 25.

4. Adi Ignatius, "Cabbage Patch Dolls, Believe It or Not, Begin as Bok Choy Way-Ways in China," *Wall Street Journal,* December 8, 1983, p. 34.

5. Thomas F. O'Boyle, "Rise and Fall," *Wall Street Journal,* January 4, 1984, p. 1.

6. *1981 Yearbook of International Trade Statistics,* Vol. 1 (New York: United Nations, 1983), p. 1224.

7. *Survey of Current Business,* December 1984, p. S16.

8. Robert T. Green, "Internationalization and Diversification of U.S. Trade: 1970 to 1981," Department of Marketing Administration Working Paper 83/84-5-1 (Austin: University of Texas, Graduate School of Business, October 1983), pp. 3–7.

9. John H. Dunning, "Capital Movements in the 20th Century," *Lloyds Bank Review,* April 1964, pp. 20–21.

10. Louis T. Wells, Jr., "Guess Who's Creating the World's Newest Multinationals," *Wall Street Journal,* December 12, 1983, p. 26.

11. *Survey of Current Business,* August 1987, p. 90.

12. *Ibid.,* p. 65.

13. Wenlee Ting, "The Emerging Challenge of the NIC Multinationals: Technology, Marketing and Operations," paper presented to the Academy of International Business Annual Meeting, San Francisco, December 1983, pp. 2–3.

14. Data were taken from Michael Dobbs, "Mickey Mouse Storms the Bastille," *Across the Board,* Vol. 23, No. 4, April 1986, pp. 9–11; *Moody's Industrial Manual,* Vol. 2, 1987, p. 5942; "Bonjour, Mickey," *Fortune,* Vol. 113, No. 2, January 20, 1986, p. 8; Peter Lewis, "Disney Advances on Europe," *Maclean's,* Vol. 98, No. 27, July 8, 1985, p. 42; and Terry Trucco, "How Disneyland Beat All the Odds in Japan," *Advertising Age,* Vol. 55, No. 57, September 6, 1984, pp. 14–16.

PART 2

COMPARATIVE ENVIRONMENTAL FRAMEWORKS

The firm operating internationally is affected by and has an immense impact on the environments in which it operates. International business today is conducted among organizations within virtually every conceivable value and institutional framework. Chapter 2 explores first the relationship between a country's economic and political philosophy and its business practices. Next, the adjustments and relations to these economic and political systems by international firms are discussed. Finally, the chapter examines national differences generated by varying levels of economic development. Chapter 3 analyzes the physical and behavioral variations among nations that influence the conduct of business. The chapter concludes with recommendations and caveats for companies coming into contact with alien societies.

2

CHAPTER THE ECONOMIC AND POLITICAL ENVIRONMENTS FACING BUSINESS

Half the world knows not how the other half lives.
—English proverb

- To describe the major political ideologies and how they are practiced.
- To discuss different economic systems in theory and practice.
- To describe the major problems facing different parts of the world.
- To evaluate the role of the foreign firm in different political and economic systems.

CASE:
GULF IN ANGOLA[1]

On November 11, 1975, Angola finally gained its long-sought independence from Portugal. Unfortunately, there was some question as to who should receive the national flag. Before and after independence a bloody civil war engulfed Angola; thousands of people on all sides lost their lives in the struggle. Three major factions had been fighting for control of Angola for a decade. The faction that gained control in late 1975 and early 1976 was the Popular Movement, which had its roots in the leftist opposition to the Portuguese regime. Supported by thousands of Cuban troops and Soviet advisors, the Popular Movement under the leadership of Agostinho Neto was able to expand its sphere of influence from the area surrounding the capitol Luanda to take control of the country.

Two other major factions at the time were UNITA (the National Union for the Total Independence of Angola) and the National Front. UNITA, led by the popular Jonas Savimbi, drew its power base from the Ovimbundu tribe, which claims approximately 40 percent of the country's population. UNITA now operates out of the south of Angola and is especially popular with the West because of Savimbi's anticommunist, moderate, nondoctrinaire form of socialism. The National Front, rooted in the north as part of the ancient Bakongo kingdom, is the third force. It is concerned with separating the northern part of the country from Angola.

Gulf Oil, which was acquired by Chevron, has operated in Angola for more than two decades. In 1975, when the civil war peaked, approximately 7 percent of all Gulf's oil was produced in Angola. However, the war took its toll: Production in 1976 dropped to nearly half the 1975 level. In its 1975 annual report, Gulf stated, "In view of the civil strife in Angola late in December, the Company suspended its operations and temporarily withdrew its personnel from Angola at the request of the U.S. State Department." Gulf also placed royalty payments that were due Angola in a special Treasury bill fund. "Payment was withheld because of conflicting demands from parties contending for political control in Angola. The Company will disburse these funds plus interest earned on them when a government attains control and is generally recognized by the world community."

In April 1976, Gulf moved back into Angola, resumed operations, and paid back taxes and royalties. Pending discussions on a new long-term relationship with the new government, Gulf agreed to continue operating under the same terms that prevailed before operations were suspended in 1975. Finally, in 1978, Gulf signed a new participation agreement with the Angolan national oil company undertaking joint development and exploration projects. In 1978, Gulf drilled its first new well since the 1975–1976 civil war period.

Angola, located on the western coast of sub-Saharan Africa, is wedged in between Zaire and Namibia. Its Marxist government faces some severe problems. A poor transportation infrastructure makes two-way trade difficult for some regions of the country. Farmers are hesitant to engage in more than subsistence agriculture because of a lack of goods to buy. The agricultural sector is inefficient; Angola needs to import 90 percent of its food. France initially provided assistance in developing state grain farms.

Native managers and technicians are also in short supply. When Angola gained independence, it had two airline pilots, one air traffic controller, and forty doctors. The Portuguese managers who had been holding the economy together left, crippling many facilities. Today Brazilians manage hotel facilities; West Germans serve as airline pilots; and workers from Sweden, Italy, and East Germany are training auto mechanics.

Shortly after gaining independence, the Angolan government asked the Portuguese for assistance. The former colonists were considered ideal for several reasons: (1) They speak the language and understand the country; (2) unlike other Europeans, they assimilate easily into the culture and do not establish foreign enclaves; and (3) they are relatively unadvanced in agriculture and business and thus can transfer "appropriate" technology.

West Africa has become one of the world's major oil-producing areas. At one time, Nigeria ranked second behind Saudi Arabia as a supplier of crude oil for the United States. Gulf lists Nigeria and Angola as its two largest foreign suppliers of crude. West Africa is independent of the Arab oil producers, although Nigeria and Gabon are members of OPEC (the Organization of Petroleum Exporting Countries) and Angola at one time aspired to be a member. Its independence from OPEC makes West Africa an attractive source of supply.

Although Gulf has been acquired by Chevron, management remains positive about its future in Angola. In addition, a number of other companies, including Texaco, Cities Service, Boeing, General Electric, Conoco, Arthur D. Little & Co., and General Tire and Rubber have major projects underway in Angola.

However, the large number of Cuban troops in Angola present a problem. Angola's avowedly Marxist government, with its Cuban support, has been very unpopular with U.S. administrations. This situation concerns managers of U.S. companies. As was pointed out by an executive of Cities Service Company, "Time will take care of Angola. The Angolans are more and more development oriented. They aren't interested in politicizing central Africa on behalf of Cuba or the Soviet Union. Our people aren't persona non grata in Angola." A Texaco executive says, "They are pragmatic people. Although they lean toward a Marxist-style government, their Marxist friends can't give them what they need, so they turned to the West."

At one time, Gulf argued for Angola's status quo before a House subcommittee but did not want to lobby too much. Gulf points out that most African nations oppose intervention in Angola because UNITA is supported by South

Africa. Any aid to UNITA could move Angola further from the West and could precipitate an oil cutoff from Nigeria, which historically has supplied a significant percentage of U.S. oil imports. In addition, the Angolan government encourages foreign investment and has enacted a very favorable investment code.

In demonstrating the ability of Gulf to adapt to different political situations, William E. Moffett, Vice-President of Gulf Oil Company, pointed out that Gulf had been operating in Angola with the MPLA government for seven years without significant problems. In fact, Moffett felt that three successive U.S. administrations had accepted the premise that commercial relationships were acceptable, in spite of political differences.

The early 1980s was a period of intense discussion about the role that the United States and its companies should take in Angola, especially as the guerrilla war with Savimbi continued to escalate. In response to an editorial in the *Wall Street Journal* calling for support of Savimbi in order to achieve victory in Angola and criticizing the role of U.S. companies there, Moffett stated,

> *Finally, I would remind you that the presence of Western companies in Angola is not a political or foreign policy contradiction but a sign of real progress and hope. It constitutes a growing recognition by developing countries that wealth cannot be distributed until it is created. There are many ways to achieve "victory"; by helping countries such as Angola to develop their resources and meet their people's aspirations for a better life, we relieve them of the excessive dependence on outside forces that you decry, and provide them a better opportunity to make informed choices about their economic and political future. (*Wall Street Journal, *December 14, 1983, p. 31)*

The Angolan government has worked hard to establish a decent operating environment for foreign investment. In 1985, the Angolan Foreign Minister stated, "We have the principle to protect all foreign enterprises in Angola because we know that the work is for our mutual benefit." The government pays its share in joint venture projects, and it has one of the most favorable investment codes in Africa. However, it also is spending nearly 50 percent of its revenues in the civil war with UNITA. The tremendous cash drain coupled with very inefficient management have created some real problems with the Angolan economy. Foreign investors need to be aware of these problems and decide if the risks are worthwhile.

INTRODUCTION

The three major economies for MNEs are:

- First World: market industrial countries

There are three major world economies in which the multinational enterprise (MNE) may operate successfully. The **First World** is made up of the market industrial countries; the **Second World** consists of the centrally

- Second World: centrally planned economies
- Third World: developing countries.

planned economies; and the **Third World** comprises the developing countries. In each of these three worlds there are different general political and economic frameworks, diverse levels of economic development, and a variety of economic conditions. To each of an infinite number of situations the MNE brings a frame of reference based on its own domestic experience as well as lessons from foreign settings. If the firm is to be successful, management must carefully analyze the interaction of corporate policies with the political and economic environment in order to maximize efficiency. The following economic characteristics must be analyzed and accounted for by management during the preliminary discussions prior to an investment decision as well as during ongoing operations:

Key economic characteristics that must be considered by an MNE.

1. general economic framework: capitalist, socialist, etc.;
2. governmental monetary and fiscal policy;
3. economic stability: cyclical fluctuations, growth, inflation;
4. factor endowment: land, labor, and capital (quality as well as quantity);
5. market size;
6. extent of social overhead capital: power, transportation, communications, etc.;
7. international interaction: balance-of-payments positions, stability of exchange rate, trade patterns.[2]

How important is the economic environment of each country in which the firm operates? As was pointed out in one study, "No industrial enterprise or individual can exist entirely divorced from its environment, and firms both influence and are significantly influenced by the nature of the total environment."[3] The study emphasized that these environmental constraints, which include the economic characteristics listed above, limit the relative efficiency of the firm and thus the society.[4] The purpose of this chapter is to provide managers with background on the political and economic systems that they are likely to encounter and what they need to consider as they make strategic decisions about operations in different countries.

POLITICAL SYSTEMS

The role of the political system is to integrate the society.

The role of the economic system is to allocate scarce resources.

Two major segments of any society that have an enormous impact on the way business is conducted are the political and economic systems. The **political system** is designed to integrate the society into a viable, functioning unit. The **economic system** is concerned with allocating scarce resources among competing users and involves two important matters: the control and coordination of resources and the ownership of property. In contemporary society it is very difficult, if not impossible, to separate political systems from economic systems. Here, however, each type of system will be discussed independently, followed by a synthesis of the two.

Ideology is the systematic body of constructs, theories, and aims that constitute a society.

Pluralistic societies are those with a variety of ideologies.

Ideology can be considered as the systematic and integrated body of constructs, theories, and aims that constitute a society. Most complex societies today are **pluralistic,** meaning that there are different ideologies held by numerous segments rather than one official ideology adhered to by all. These ideologies may be very similar, with only minor differences, or they may have widely divergent points of view. A good example is in Angola, where the three different ethnic (and therefore political) groups formed a coalition government after independence. However, political rivalries broke down the coalition. The resulting government was supported by outside powers and harassed by an ousted member of the former coalition who was aided by other outside interests. The true test of any political system is its capacity to keep divergent ideologies from tearing the society apart.

Political ideologies are many and varied, making it difficult to fit them neatly into a continuum representing degrees of citizen participation in decision making. However, Fig. 2.1 attempts to depict democratic and non-democratic forms of government. The two extremes in a theoretical sense are often considered to be democracy and totalitarianism. From these two theoretical extremes various degrees of participation have emerged and evolved.

Democracy

Democratic systems involve wide participation of citizens in the decision-making process.

In representative democracy, majority rule is achieved through periodic elections.

The ideology of pure **democracy** comes from the ancient Greek concept that citizens should be directly involved in the decision-making process. According to this ideal, all citizens should be equal politically and legally and should enjoy widespread freedoms. In reality, however, complexity increases with the number of citizens, thereby discouraging full participation. As a result, most contemporary societies that espouse democracy have generated various forms of **representative democracy.**

The following features characterize contemporary democratic political systems:

1. freedom of opinion, expression, press, and organization;
2. elections in which voters decide who is to represent them for limited terms of office;
3. an independent and fair court system that has high regard for individual property and rights;
4. a relatively nonpolitical bureaucracy and defense infrastructure;
5. a relative openness of the state.[5]

Totalitarianism

Totalitarianism is the absence of widespread participation in decision making, which is restricted to only a few individuals.

If democracy is at one end of the spectrum, then **totalitarianism** is at the other end. In this case a single party, individual, or group of individuals monopolizes political power and neither recognizes nor permits opposition.

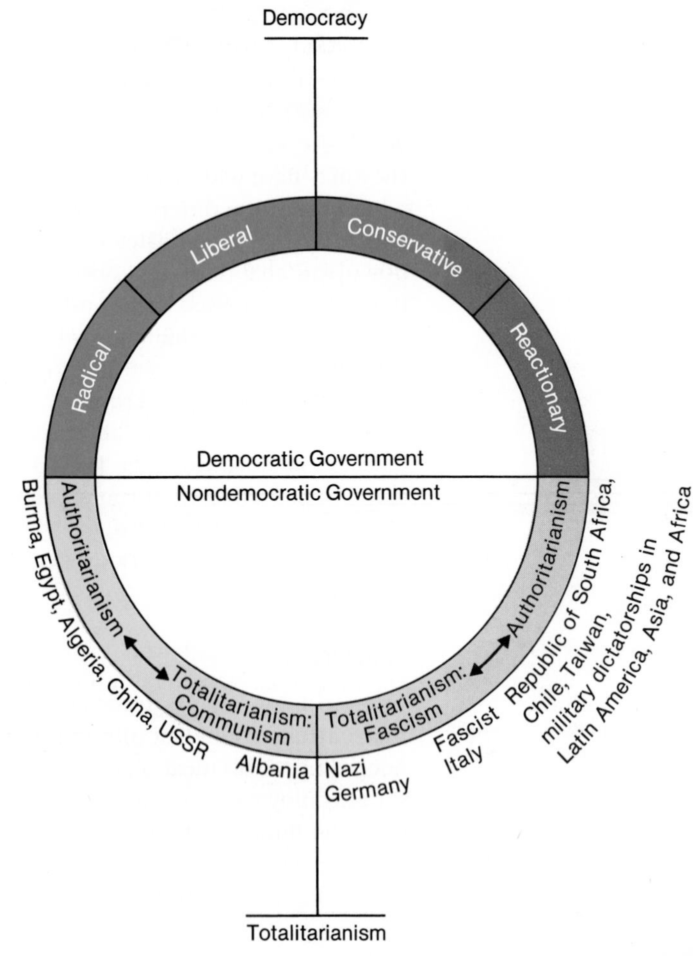

Figure 2.1
The Political Spectrum
Source: Endpaper ("Democracy/Totalitarianism") from *American Democracy in World Perspective* by William Ebenstein, C. Herman Pritchett, Henry A. Turner and Dean Mann, © 1967 by Harper & Row Pub. Co. Reprinted by permission of the publisher.

Communism is a form of totalitarianism initially theorized by Karl Marx.

Theocratic totalitarianism is a form of totalitarianism best exemplified by the Moslem countries in the Middle East.

Secular totalitarianism is a form of totalitarianism rule often enforced through military power and based on worldly rather than religious concepts.

In totalitarianism (i.e., a dictatorship), the opportunity to participate in decisions is restricted to a few individuals.

There are three major forms of totalitarianism in contemporary society. The form most often thought of in the Western context is **communism,** as explained more fully below. However, there are other forms. The sheikdoms of the Middle East as well as Iran thrive on a form of government that could be called **theocratic totalitarianism.** The overthrow of the Shah of Iran supposedly heralded a new era of popular consent for the Ayatollah Khomeini, but his rule has been marked with repression and persecution of nonorthodox factions. **Secular totalitarianism** is found in many Latin American countries, as well as in Egypt and Taiwan. Latin American governments routinely fluctuate between nervous democracy and military dictatorships.

In a theoretical and contemporary sense, **communism** is very complex. Separation of the political and economic systems is virtually impossible. As Karl Marx theorized, the economic system determines the direction taken by a society in political, religious, and philosophical realms. The mechanics and implications of a centrally planned economic system usually espoused in communism will be deferred to another section of the chapter.

According to Marx, two types of revolutions eventually occur in a capitalistic society: political and social. The completion of the political revolution precedes and touches off the social revolution, a long-range phenomenon largely based on economic inequities. Political revolution results in a dictatorship by the proletariat, the working class, which theoretically is to remain for only a short time to smooth the transition during the social revolution. The government would be responsible for organizing society into different groups in order to provide as much input as possible into the decision-making process. Theoretically, as the social revolution approached completion, the dictatorship by the proletariat would disappear, and full communism would take its place.

Contemporary Political Systems

Pure democracy has given way to various forms of representative government in which citizens vote for individuals to represent them and make collective decisions. Voting eligibility may depend on a certain minimum age, as in the United States, or on racial classifications, as in South Africa. South Africa's racial mixture is 73 percent blacks, 15 percent whites, and 12 percent Asians (primarily Indians) and coloreds. The coloreds are a racially mixed category. The racial categories have resulted in a political process involving mainly the whites, even though they are a minority of the population.

Multiple political parties may participate in the process, as in the United States and most other industrial countries, or there may be a single dominant party that controls political power, as in Mexico. Mexico is an interesting case: It is a democracy that has been ruled by one political party, the Institutional Revolutionary Party (PRI), for nearly sixty years. Its members are Mexico's elite, the most educated and experienced in government. The PRI does not have a peculiar ideological thrust other than trying to keep the country together. Another interesting example of changing political situations involves South Korea. For sixteen years, South Korea had been living under a military dictatorship. In 1987, direct elections were held to select a president. The democratic election resulted in a president who had a plurality but not a majority of the votes. In spite of this, a consensus began to build behind the new president as the Korean people were interested in continuing economic growth and progress.[6]

Even casual observation tells that contemporary communism differs from theoretical communism. In reality, the political revolutions have

Figure 2.2
Interrelationships between Control of Economic Activity and Ownership of Factors of Production

Control \ Ownership	Private	Mixed	Collective
Market	A	B	C
Mixed	D	E	F
Command	G	H	I

Control ownership	*Control ownership*	*Control ownership*
A. Market-Private	D. Mixed-Private	G. Command-Private
B. Market-Mixed	E. Mixed-Mixed	H. Command-Mixed
C. Market-Collective	F. Mixed-Collective	I. Command-Collective

resulted in a permanent rather than transitory dictatorship by the proletariat. Also, democratic centralism has given way to totalitarian or autocratic centralism, with no general participation in decision making—especially by those with opposing viewpoints. An important split has developed over the degree and importance of political revolution in achieving social objectives. In addition, the manifestations of communism differ significantly from country to country. Until recently, the Soviet Union had avoided many of the economic changes leading to the introduction of market forces as seen in China. Although it is a communist country, Yugoslavia has been much more regionalized than Cuba or Vietnam, for example. Strong central control has not been as important to Yugoslavia. The Chinese, Vietnamese, and Cuban governments have focused more on agriculture, whereas the Soviet Union and East Germany have developed their industrial infrastructure.

ECONOMIC SYSTEMS

In a market economy, resources are allocated and controlled by consumers, who "vote" through buying goods.

According to a command economy, resources are allocated and controlled by government decision.

In private ownership, individuals own resources.

Economic systems are usually loosely defined as either capitalist, socialist, or mixed. However, it is possible to classify economic systems according to method of resource allocation and control (**market economy** or **command economy**) and to type of property ownership (**private ownership** or **public ownership.**) Expansion of this concept to include mixed ownership and control would result in the taxonomy indicated in Fig. 2.2.

The ownership of factors of production can be viewed as a continuum from complete private ownership at one end to complete public ownership at the other. In reality, no country belongs wholly at one end or the other. For example, the United States is considered to be the prime example of **private enterprise,** yet the government owns some factors of production and actively produces in such sectors of the economy as education, the military, the postal service, and certain utilities. The Soviet Union, which espouses **public ownership** of the means of production, allows small peasant farming on a private basis. Most countries lie somewhere in the mixed category, which is very broad and includes varying degrees of public and private ownership. Likewise, the control of economic activity represents a continuum from market to command economies, with the actual situation lying somewhere in between.

In public ownership, the government owns resources.

Market Economy

In a market economy, two societal units are very important: the **individual** and the **firm.** Individuals own resources and consume products, while firms use resources and produce products. The market mechanism involves an interaction of price, quantity, supply, and demand of resources and products. Labor is supplied by the household if the firm offers an adequate wage. Products are consumed if the price is within a certain range. A firm bases its wages on the quantity of labor available to assume a job. Resources are allocated as a result of the constant interplay between households and firms, as well as the interplay between households and between firms, such as when the input of one firm is the output of another. The key factors that make the market economy work are **consumer sovereignty** and the freedom of the enterprise to operate in the market. As long as both units are free to make decisions, the interplay of supply and demand should ensure proper resource allocation.

The market mechanism involves an interrelationship of price, quantity, supply, and demand.

Consumer sovereignty is the freedom of consumers to influence production through choice.

The market economy has been highly successful in most industrial countries, especially in the United States. A perfect market economy does not exist in the United States owing to three major factors: **large corporations, labor unions,** and the **government.** The large corporation can reduce market pressures somewhat by exerting control over the purchase of resources or the sale of products. Because of the large size of the firm and the relative smallness of each individual shareholder, there is a wide gap between ownership and control of decision making. Decisions may or may not be strictly motivated by the market. The rise in entrepreneurial activities has challenged some of the assumptions of the large firm and injected some dynamism into the economy.

Large corporations, labor unions, and the government limit freedom in a free market.

Labor unions evolved in response to the power exerted by the owners and managers of business over the labor market. Tremendous benefits in terms of salaries, fringe benefits, work conditions, and bargaining power have been won by the unions, but market forces have been disrupted seriously. Many unions control entry into the work force and restrict the freedom of workers to change occupations in response to supply and demand. Wages generally rise rather than fall under the typical union structure, but many firms were able to extract wage concessions from unions during the difficult times of the late 1970s and early 1980s. Although unions are pervasive, they are not homogeneous, as noted in Chapter 21. In the United States, management and unions are confrontational, but in Japan they are supportive of each other. In many European and Latin American countries, unions tend to be much more political than in the United States. In the United Kingdom, unions almost defy description. Government policies continue to shape the U.S. economy. Fiscal and monetary policies have a direct effect on employment, the production and consumption of goods and services (for example, the military), and the growth of the money supply. As will be pointed out in Chapter 5, the government also intervenes in the free flow of goods internationally through protectionist measures.

Centrally Planned Economies

In a centrally planned economy, the government sets goals and decides price and quantity.

In a centrally planned economy, the government tries to harmonize the activities of the different economic sectors. In the extreme form of central command, goals are set for every enterprise in the country and must be followed. The government determines how much is produced, by whom, and for whom. The assumption is that the government is a better judge of how resources should be allocated than is the economy in general and the consumer in particular.

At the heart of a centrally planned economy is its blueprint, generally a five-year plan. Based on this overall plan, specific targets are set each year for each sector of the economy. The governmental plan attempts to harmonize all sectors, since the output of one firm becomes the input of another. A centrally planned economy must rely on the accuracy of government targets instead of on market prices to allocate resources properly. The Soviet Union is a major example of a planned economy, yet market forces are influential to some degree in its labor market, the distribution of consumer goods, part of the production of farm products, and some privately furnished services.

Mixed Economies

Mixed economies are characterized by different mixtures of market and centrally planned economies and public and private ownership of resources.

By definition, no economy is purely market determined or centrally planned. The United States and the Soviet Union represent different ends of the spectrum of mixed economies. In practice, however, mixed economies generally have a higher degree of government intervention than is found in the United States and a greater degree of reliance on market forces than is found in the Soviet Union. Government intervention can be regarded in two ways: actual government ownership of means of production and government influence in economic decision making. Ownership is easy to quantify statistically, but since influence is a matter of policy and custom, it is difficult to measure precisely.

Many industrial countries such as West Germany and Sweden have relatively low levels of government ownership but a strong tradition of social welfare. The United Kingdom also has a strong social welfare system supported by taxes, although the government is involved more heavily in corporate ownership than are Sweden and West Germany.

France's mixed economy uses government-sponsored incentives.

Several industrial economies have a strong mixture of market and command economies. The French economic system, for example, traditionally has depended heavily on private enterprise, but it also relies on strong direction from the government. Special incentives are used on an ad hoc basis to stimulate industrial growth. These incentives include special credit policies, depreciation allowances in certain sectors, favorable treatment of exports, and preference in government orders.

When François Mitterand of the French Socialist Party was elected President of France in 1981 for a seven-year term, the French economy took a strong turn toward central control. President Mitterand's platform included the nationalization of some of the largest companies in France. In keeping with Mitterand's promises, most of the nationalizations took place in large industries that were important for France's strategic future.

The French nationalization effort was weakened temporarily when the Conservatives regained parliamentary control in 1986. The government began to spin off many of its investments to the private sector, a major strategy of the United Kingdom's Prime Minister Margaret Thatcher. However, Mitterand regained control when reelected President in 1988.

Major economic reforms in China include decentralization, incentives, and market mechanisms.

Another country that has been going through rapid change within a centrally planned environment is the People's Republic of China (PRC). Some of the major economic reforms enacted since 1979 are

1. greater decentralization of production and investment decisions to enterprises and farms;
2. stronger incentives with more direct links between material rewards and the work of households and individuals; and
3. greater use of market mechanisms in allocating resources. Credits are available for commercial ventures to market consumer goods and agricultural inputs in rural areas.

These changes have been very visible in the agricultural area. Farmland, draft animals, and implements are assigned to individual households for several (usually five) years. Farmers are free to farm as they wish, but they must sell an agreed-upon amount of their crops to the government and to their village production teams. They can keep the rest for their own use, or they can sell it at the market prices determined by supply and demand. The PRC is not ready to dismantle its statist system totally, but it does allow some flexibility within the system.[7]

Premier Deng Xiaping's pragmatic policies have resulted in a strong move to consumerism in the PRC. A rise in personal income (still less than $300 per year per capita) has caused an increase in consumption, especially of foreign-made goods sold in China. Although 1987 was a difficult year in China politically, the victory of the reformers in the 13th Communist Party Congress in October 1987 ensured that the economic reforms would continue.[8]

Under Gorbachev, the Soviet economy is shifting from total central control.

The economic restructuring initiated in the Soviet Union by General Secretary Mikhail Gorbachev is very interesting. As noted earlier in the chapter, the Soviet Union is a centrally planned economy. "Perestroika" is the Soviet policy of attempting to shift the Soviet Union from an overly centralized command system of management to a more democratic one based on economic reform. The first wave of perestroika came in 1985 when Gorbachev cracked down on drunkenness, absenteeism, waste, and corruption. In May 1986, the government permitted the organization of nonsocialist enterprises. Although only a small portion of the economy is involved in such enterprises, individuals and families can now own businesses independent of the state. In addition, they are allowed to hire workers outside of the family group.

The focus of 1988 and beyond is to reduce the role of the government in strategic planning. On January 1, 1988, a new State Enterprise Law went into effect, resulting in greater management responsibility and control over the financial fate of enterprises. Managers were given increasing control over the use of profits for reinvestment or bonuses for workers.

Gorbachev is also interested in policies that would increase the quality of goods and productivity of resources in the economy. One way to assist in that effort is through joint ventures with Western firms. Formerly, arrangements with Western firms have consisted of contractual arrangements, licensing agreements, and turnkey operations. Under perestroika, foreign investors are allowed to establish joint ventures with Soviet enterprises, resulting in an infusion of capital, technology, and management expertise.[9] A loosening of the Soviet Economy may not result in a complete swing away from the idea of central command, but it should be interesting to watch the impact of market forces on a centrally planned philosophy.

Japan's MITI inspired industrial reorganization.

A final illustration of state intervention is that of Japan. Japan is often called "Japan, Inc.," and for good reason. At the close of World War II, instead of nationalizing key sectors and industries as many countries did, Japan let investment remain in the private sector. Then Japanese policymakers focused more on setting targets and using fiscal incentives to direct investment flows. The Ministry of International Trade and Industry (MITI) was organized to guide industrial development through "strategic planning and authority (both formal and informal) over investment and production priorities."[10]

MITI seemed to be more concerned with developing a vision than with setting up a blueprint for the economy. During the early period of MITI in the 1950s and early 1960s, the key was **protectionism** so that industries could reach economies of scale free of outside competition. However, the 1960s was a period of selective liberalization that involved MITI-inspired industrial reorganizations resulting in industries, such as automobiles and steel, that became formidable world competitors. Structural adjustment to the oil price increases of the 1970s was also inspired and encouraged by MITI as it forced companies to become more energy-efficient. Those companies of highest priority to MITI had to become involved in a program that set out the steps to reduce excess capacity, the timing of such reductions, and restrictions on further expansion. Where necessary, the industries were allowed to establish arrangements to maintain orderly markets under the condition of excess supply and were given government financial support to complete the changes just described.[11]

Two indicators of the role of government in capitalist societies are central government disbursements and revenues as a percentage of gross national product. Figure 2.3 compares data from several countries. Note the wide divergence among countries, with Japan showing the lowest percentages and the Netherlands the highest. As noted earlier, however, Japan's influence in the economy extends beyond actual expenditures.

POLITICAL-ECONOMIC SYNTHESIS

Totalitarian societies are marked by command economy and public ownership.

Except for the discussion on communism, we have made no attempt to link an economic philosophy with a particular political regime, nor a particular political philosophy with any of the economic systems discussed in the previous section. In general, a totalitarian political regime involves public ownership of factors of production and a command economy. Countries that fit into this category would be the East European nonmarket economies such as the USSR, Poland, Yugoslavia, Hungary, Albania, Bulgaria, and East Germany; many African countries, such as Libya, Zambia, Ethiopia, Mozambique, and Angola; Cuba; and China.

However, there are many examples of totalitarian regimes and mixed (primarily capitalistic) economies, especially among the secular totalitarian countries. Some examples of countries in this mix are in the Middle East: Jordan, Saudi Arabia, Bahrain, and Kuwait. Others are in Africa: Cameroon, Gabon, Kenya, and Zaire. The countries in both of these combinations of political-economic systems exhibit total or significant lack of personal individual freedoms.[12]

Many observers think that a democratic form of government is best complemented by private ownership of factors of production and a market economy. This is because the voter is considered to be rational and understands self-interest in the same way that the consumer understands self-interest and prefers to make independent choices. Some countries that fit in this combination of political and economic systems are Japan, the United States, Switzerland, West Germany, Canada, Colombia, Ecuador, Argentina, and South Korea.

However, this view does not apply to democratic socialism. The so-called market socialists feel that since economics and politics are so closely con-

Figure 2.3

Central Government Disbursements and Revenues as a Percentage of GNP of Selected Countries

Source: World Development Report, 1987 (New York: Oxford University Press, 1987).

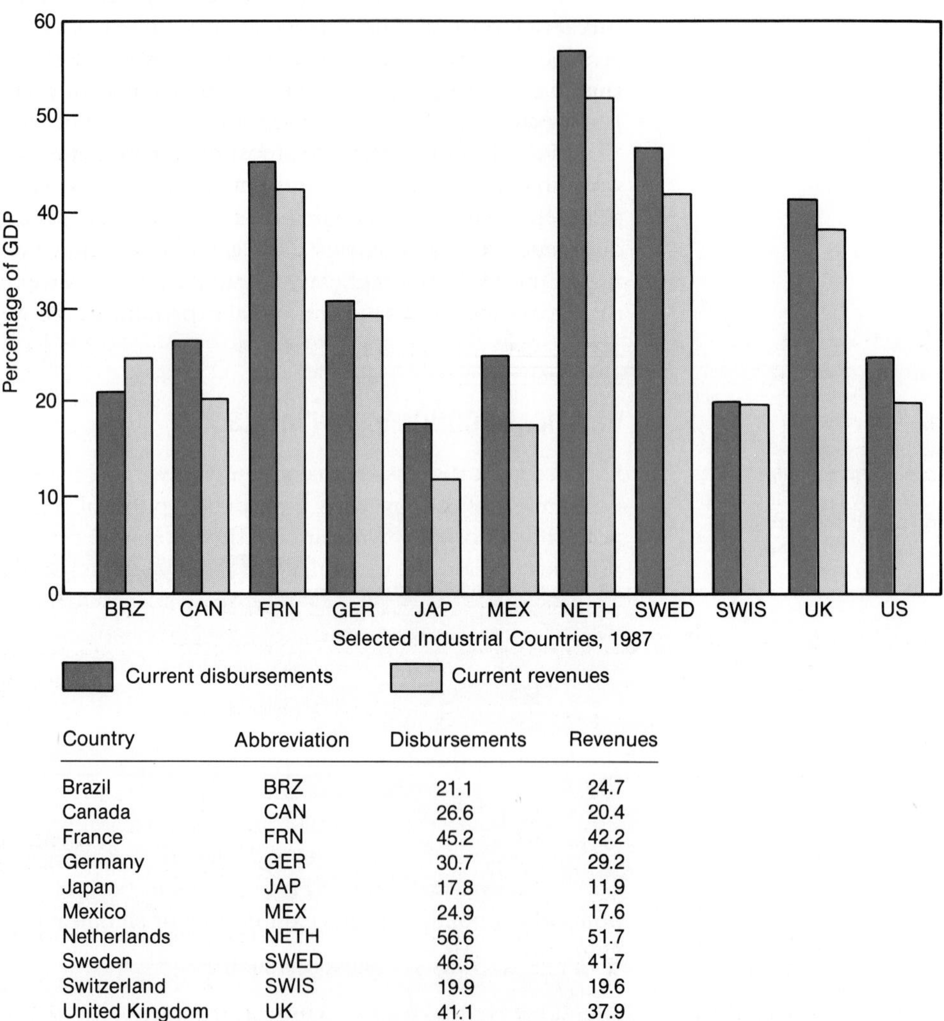

Country	Abbreviation	Disbursements	Revenues
Brazil	BRZ	21.1	24.7
Canada	CAN	26.6	20.4
France	FRN	45.2	42.2
Germany	GER	30.7	29.2
Japan	JAP	17.8	11.9
Mexico	MEX	24.9	17.6
Netherlands	NETH	56.6	51.7
Sweden	SWED	46.5	41.7
Switzerland	SWIS	19.9	19.6
United Kingdom	UK	41.1	37.9
United States	US	24.5	19.8

nected, the voters should rely on their elected government to control the economic system; that is, the part of the economy not owned by the government would be regulated by the government. The rationale for democratic socialism is that in order to have a democratically controlled economy and the economic security necessary for liberty, the economy must be owned or regulated by a welfare-oriented government. Some countries that fit in this combination are Austria, Denmark, France, Greece, Israel, Portugal, Egypt, and Zimbabwe. Countries in the categories just mentioned also tend to allow significant personal freedom for individuals.[13]

Clearly, numerous combinations of political and economic systems are possible. Perhaps the greater the tendency toward political totalitarianism, the greater the reliance on government intervention in ownership and control of the economy. However, most countries that experience relative freedom in political decision making have experimented with different degrees of intervention in the economic system. The extremes are tending to converge to a more even mix of public-private interaction in ownership and control. In the case of the industrial countries, the emphasis seems to be on control rather than on ownership. Three major reasons account for this increased government participation where a quasi–laissez-faire attitude previously existed:

There are three reasons for increased government participation in the economy.

1. the failure of the market mechanism to provide adequately for all sectors of society;
2. the problem of stagnation plaguing many industrial countries during the early 1980s which in some cases has also resulted in deregulation; and
3. increased interdependence of world economies allowing world supply and demand to have a strong impact on national supply and demand.

A movement away from the centrally planned communist model can occur by decentralizing the planning and control process and by allowing certain aspects of the economy to operate on a market rather than a planned basis.

THE ROLE OF THE FOREIGN FIRM

Most foreign firms face the challenge of adjustment. For example, a firm based in the United States is accustomed to the political and economic systems of that country and has devised ways to survive profitably in that particular environment. Upon entering another country for the first time, the firm needs to answer questions such as:

The foreign firm must consider several key issues when entering another country.

1. What is the country's political structure?
2. Under what type of economic system does the country operate?
3. Is the firm's industry in the public or private sector?
4. If it is in the public sector, does the government also allow private competition in that sector?
5. If it is in the private sector, is it moving toward public ownership?

6. Does the government view foreign capital as being in competition or in partnership with public or local private enterprises?
7. In what ways does the government control the nature and extent of private enterprise?
8. How much of a contribution is the private sector expected to make in helping the government formulate overall economic objectives?

The questions appear simple, but owing to the dynamic nature of political and economic events the answers to the questions are complex.

Foreign firms must be aware of their own experiences and how those experiences have helped shape their managerial philosophies and practices. In addition, the firms must determine how the new environment differs from their more familiar domestic environment and decide how managerial philosophy and practice must be changed to adapt to the new political and economic environment. Historically, private enterprise has been very adept at operating in any environment. Its management, marketing, production, and technical skills have been welcomed in a variety of forms in Marxist-Leninist, social democratic, and Third World socialist countries as well as in mixed economy and capitalist countries.

THE CLASSIFICATION OF COUNTRIES

The best classification of countries is provided by the World Bank each year in the *World Development Report.* The different categories are provided in Table 2.1. Note that the specific country groupings include only those countries with a population of 1 million or more.

Twenty-one countries are considered by the World Bank to be industrial market economies, also referred to as industrial economies or industrial countries. As noted in Table 2.1, the industrial countries are basically the twenty-four countries that are members of the Organization for Economic Cooperation and Development (OECD), with the exception of Greece, Portugal, and Turkey. These three latter countries are part of the middle-income developing economies. With the exception of Australia and New Zealand, all of these industrial countries lie in the Northern Hemisphere, giving rise to the "North–South dialogue" so frequently mentioned between industrial and developing countries. Spain is a relatively recent addition to the list of industrial countries. As recently as the 1979 *World Development Report,* Spain was considered a middle-income developing country.

Second World countries have socialist or centrally planned economies.

The Second World countries have been known at different times as socialist countries, centrally planned economies, and East European nonmarket economies. Hungary, Poland, Romania, and China are usually classified as nonmarket economies, but they are included in the middle-income economies as exporters of manufacturers.

TABLE 2.1

WORLD BANK COUNTRY CATEGORIES

I. *Industrial Market Economies**
- Australia
- Austria
- Belgium
- Canada
- Denmark
- Finland
- France
- Federal Republic of Germany
- Iceland
- Ireland
- Italy
- Japan
- Luxembourg
- The Netherlands
- New Zealand
- Norway
- Spain
- Sweden
- Switzerland
- United Kingdom
- United States

II. *Nonmarket Economies*
- Albania
- Angola
- Bulgaria
- Cuba
- Czechoslovakia
- Democratic People's Republic of Korea
- German Democratic Republic
- Mongolia
- Soviet Union

III. *Low-Income Economies*
- 1985 Annual Per Capita GNP of $400 or less

IV. *Middle-Income Economies*
- 1985 Annual Per Capita GNP of $401 or more

A. *High-Income Oil Exporters*
- Bahrain
- Brunei
- Kuwait†
- Libya†
- Qatar†
- Saudi Arabia†
- United Arab Emirates†

B. *Oil Exporters*
- Algeria†
- Cameroon
- Congo
- Ecuador†
- Egypt
- Gabon†
- Indonesia†
- Islamic Republic of Iran†
- Iraq†
- Mexico
- Nigeria†
- Oman
- Peru
- Syria
- Trinidad and Tobago
- Venezuela†

C. *Exporters of Manufactures*
- Brazil
- China
- Hong Kong
- Hungary
- India
- Israel
- Republic of Korea
- Poland
- Portugal
- Romania
- Singapore
- Yugoslavia

D. *Others*

*These twenty-one countries plus Greece, Portugal, and Turkey comprise the Organization for Economic Cooperation and Development (OECD).
†Members of the Organization of Petroleum Exporting Countries (OPEC).
Source: *World Development Report, 1987* (New York: Oxford University Press, 1987).

Developing countries can be
- Low income—per capita GNP of $400 or less
- Middle income—per capita GNP of $401 or more.

Categories of middle-income countries are
- High-income oil exporters
- Oil exporters
- Exporters of manufactures
- Other.

The developing countries are divided into two major categories: low-income economies with per capita GNP of $400 or less and middle-income economies with per capita GNP of $401 or more. The *World Bank Atlas* lists 43 countries as low-income developing countries and 96 countries as middle-income countries, out of a total of 184 countries.

The middle-income countries are subdivided into four other categories. High-income oil exporters are countries whose per capita GNP exceeds approximately $7,500. Most of those countries are also members of the Organization of the Petroleum Exporting Countries (OPEC). Oil exporters are middle-income countries with exports of petroleum and gas accounting for 30 percent of merchandise exports (excluding the high-income oil exporters).

Exporters of manufactures are middle-income developing economies with exports of manufactures accounting for more than 30 percent of exports of goods and services. These countries are sometimes called newly industrializing countries or NICs. The NICs are the newest economic force to reckon with. Their economies are driven by an export philosophy. Many developing countries have pursued a policy of import substitution to solve balance of payments problems, but the NICs—especially the "Four Tigers" of South Korea, Taiwan, Hong Kong, and Singapore—have pursued a successful program of export promotion. The "Four Tigers" have been able to capitalize on low wage and production costs, coupled with relatively stable currency values vis-à-vis the U.S. dollar to capture an increasingly large percentage of the U.S. import market. The last category would be all other middle-income developing countries not included elsewhere.

With only a few exceptions, the low-income countries are found in Asia, Africa, and Latin America. Middle-income countries are much more widespread geographically, but a majority of Latin America's population is in middle-income countries. African nations tend to be more concentrated in the lower–middle-income countries, and Latin American nations tend to be more concentrated in the upper–middle-income countries.

Although these are the major groups of countries identified by the World Bank for a variety of reasons, there are also other groups. Many of them will be discussed in Chapter 7 on Regional Economic Integration. However, there are also some other interesting groups. The first is the Group of 7, whose members are major industrial countries: Canada, France, Germany, Italy, Japan, the United Kingdom, and the United States. This group is usually synonymous with meetings of Finance Ministers and Central Bank Governors. In addition, the heads of state of the Group of 7 meet annually to discuss world affairs. An expansion of this group is the Group of 10, the Group of 7 countries plus Belgium, the Netherlands, Sweden, and Switzerland. (Even though this group was expanded to 11 in 1983 with the addition of Switzerland, it is still referred to as G-10.) The developing countries have banded together in the Group of 77, which expanded to 127 members in mid-1986. The Group of 77 functions as a caucus for the developing countries on economic and political matters before various UN bodies. A subset of this group, the Group of 24, was established in 1972 to work specifically with international monetary questions.[14]

Key Indicators

Table 2.2 provides comparative indicators for the different country groupings. As the groupings move from low-income to industrial market countries, the distribution of gross domestic product (GDP) shifts in emphasis from agriculture to industry to services.

The geographical distribution of wealth is even more dramatically illustrated in Fig. 2.4. The world's wealth is primarily in the industrial countries. The high-income oil exporters are quite wealthy, but the income distribution

TABLE 2.2
BASIC INDICATORS (1985)

	Population (millions)	Life Expectancy at Birth	Distribution of Gross Domestic Product (percent)		
			Agriculture	Industry	Services
Industrial market	737.3	76	3	36	61
Low-income	2439.4	60	32	33	35
Middle-income	1242.1	62	14	34	52
High-income oil exporters	18.4	63	2	58	39
Oil exporters	523.3	58	17	36	47
Exporters of manufactures	2098.3	64	21	35	44

Source: *World Development Report, 1987,* published for the World Bank (New York: Oxford University Press, 1987), pp. 202–203, 206–207.

is not as even as it is in the industrial countries. Surprisingly, the exporters of manufactures have a low level of per capita GNP. However, the data is distorted by the presence of China and India, which have per capita GNPs of $310 and $270, respectively. The rest of the countries among exporters of manufac tures tend to be classified as upper–middle-income, a category which has a per capita GNP of $1,850.

KEY ISSUES IN INDUSTRIAL AND DEVELOPING COUNTRIES

Drucker identifies three key areas of change in the world economy.

A number of significant changes have occurred in the world economy in recent years. Drucker points out three key areas in which the world economy has changed, resulting in changes within countries as well as between countries.[15]

The first key issue is that the primary-products economy has separated from the industrial economy. In the mid-1970s, analysts predicted that within a decade, there would be severe shortages in raw materials, which would lead to a rise in prices and a shift in wealth from industrial to developing countries (where a large share of the world's raw materials is found). Since 1977, however, raw materials prices have dropped significantly. This has occurred as a result of increased production of existing raw materials, new sources of raw materials, and the shift in global production to products that are not raw-material intensive. As a result, developing countries cannot generate significant cash flow from their raw materials to pay off debt and acquire capital goods to assist in infrastructure development.

The second key trend is that production has separated from employment in most of the industrial countries. Manufacturing production has risen steadily in the industrial countries and remained a constant 23 to 24 percent of GNP. However, manufacturing employment has fallen as firms have improved productivity and production has shifted to high-tech, knowledge-

Figure 2.4
Per Capita GNP by Major Country Category
Source: World Development Report, 1987 (New York: Oxford University Press, 1987), pp. 202–203.

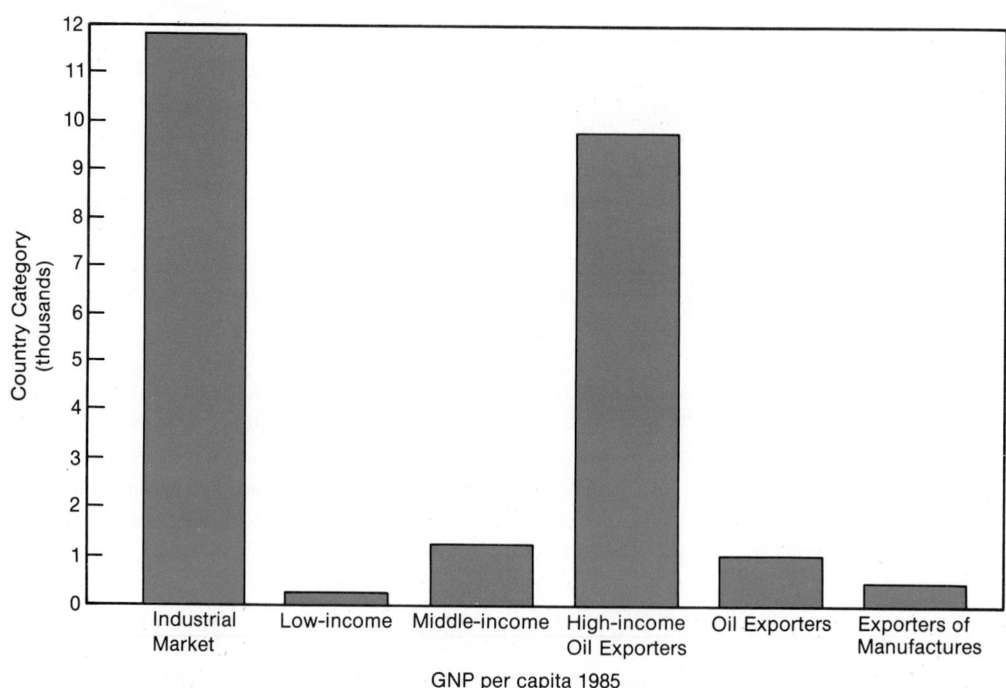

Country Category	GNP per Capita, 1985
Industrial Market	$11,810
Developing Country:	
Low-income	270
Middle-income	1,290
High-income oil exporters	9,800
Oil exporters	1,060
Exporters of manufactures	520

intensive products. Employment in the non-manufacturing sector of the industrial economy, such as information processing and other high-tech services, has increased.

The final major trend identified by Drucker is that capital movements have become more important than goods movements in driving the world economy. Worldwide trade in goods and services is approximately $2.5 to $3.0 trillion per year, compared with the turnover in cash in eurocurrency markets of approximately $75 trillion per year.[16] (A eurocurrency is any currency banked outside of its home country and thus free from government controls.) This means that the flow of capital is highly unstable, reacting to inflation, interest rates, and confidence in a country's political and economic system instead of on the flow of goods and services. As a result it is very difficult to predict what will happen to the world economy.

As noted at the beginning of the chapter, a variety of cultural, legal, political, and economic issues influence the management of the MNE at home and abroad. These issues vary considerably depending on the country where the firm is operating. Obviously, the environment in a developing country such as China is very different from that of an industrial country such as West Germany.

Even though there is a wide disparity among the developing countries, there are many shared problems and characteristics. Some of the most common problems mentioned are inflation, external debt, weakening currencies, shortage of skilled workers, political instability, war and insurrection, mass poverty (primarily in Africa), rapid population growth, weakening commodity prices, and reliance on imported oil.

Five key economic issues are
- Economic growth
- Inflation
- Trade strategy
- Payments imbalances
- Country debt.

Issues such as trade policy, the investment climate, the importance of regional economic integration in promoting trade and investment, foreign exchange, the impact of the MNE on host societies, and doing business in and with non-market central command economies are discussed at great length in other chapters. We cannot discuss in this chapter every problem of concern to industrial and developing countries. In this section of the chapter, however, we will discuss five issues (in addition to the three dimensions in the changed world economy described above) that could influence management decisions in industrial and developing countries: economic growth, inflation, trade strategy, payments imbalances, and country debt. We will close with some comments on the dialogue between industrial and developing countries known as the North-South Dialogue.

Economic Growth

Developing countries have exhibited strong growth but are riskier.

The MNE would prefer to have every country in the world politically stable, with low rates of inflation and high rates of real growth. Even if the firm does not expand market share in each market, it would be able to increase revenues at the same pace as the general economy. Developing countries provide large market potential and exhibit strong economic growth overall, although they tend to be riskier than the industrial countries. Figure 2.5 illustrates real growth in GDP between industrial and developing countries from 1973–1986. Although growth in developing countries has been slightly better than it has been in the industrial countries, the two have essentially kept pace with each other. Economic growth is monitored very closely by MNE management. A review of the annual report of any MNE will show comments about the impact of economic growth abroad on the financial performance of the firm, especially on the specific industry and products of the firm.

Recently, strong growth has occurred in low-income countries and exporters of manufactures.

There has been weak growth in industrial countries.

As noted in the data accompanying Fig. 2.5, growth in recent years has been especially strong in two categories: low-income countries and exporters of manufactures. The growth in the first category is largely a result of the low-income countries' low base. The growth in the second category is significant, since exporters of manufactures are moving closer to the industrial category. Slowing growth in the industrial countries is a troublesome sign. These countries tend to ignite growth for the rest of the world. As noted in Chapter 1, the developing countries rely on the industrial countries as a market for products. A significant recession in the industrial countries would spell disaster for the developing countries as well.

Movement to privatization is increasing in industrial and developing countries.

An interesting trend in the 1980s has been the increasing privatization of business. The moves to absorb industry in the public sector in the 1960s and 1970s has not been very successful in the industrial or developing countries. As mentioned earlier in the chapter, a number of British state-owned com-

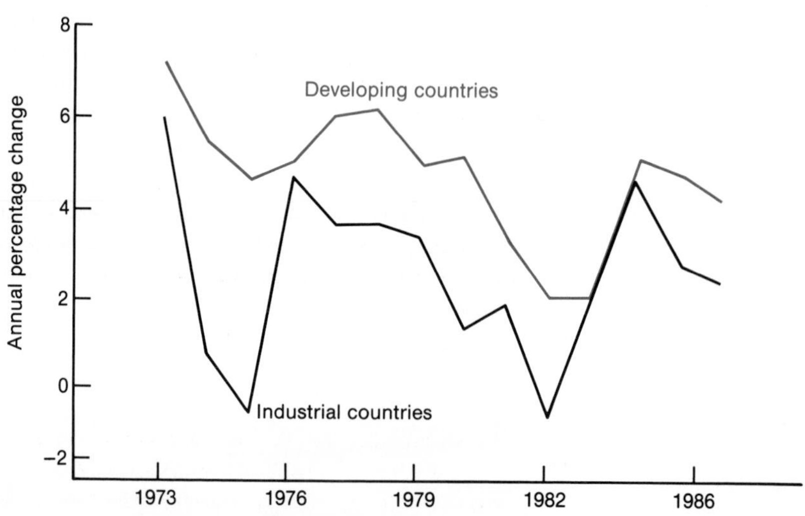

Country group	1973–1980 average	1981	1982	1983	1984	1985	1986
Developing countries	5.4	3.4	2.1	2.1	5.1	4.8	4.2
Low-income countries	4.6	4.8	5.6	7.7	8.9	9.1	6.5
Middle-income countries	5.7	2.8	0.8	0.0	3.6	2.8	3.2
Oil exporters	6.0	4.1	0.4	−1.9	2.3	2.2	−1.1
Exporters of manufactures	6.0	3.3	4.2	4.9	7.8	7.8	7.0
High-income oil exporters	7.9	1.4	−0.5	−6.9	1.2	−3.8	8.2
Industrial market economies	2.8	1.9	−0.5	2.2	4.6	2.8	2.5

Figure 2.5
Real GDP Growth, 1973–1986
Source: World Development Report, 1987 (New York: Oxford University Press, 1987), pp. 15–16.

panies were sold to individual shareholders as Prime Minister Thatcher continued her conservative revolution in the United Kingdom. A center-right coalition in France, headed by Jacques Chirac, defeated the socialists in 1986 and began to sell off many of the companies taken over by the government when François Mitterand was first elected president. Similar trends have emerged in developing countries, principally in Africa, which have found that state socialism does not generate enough economic growth.

Inflation

Inflation moderated in the 1980–1985 period but is still significant for some developing countries, especially Argentina, Brazil, and Israel.

Inflation is an important aspect of the economic environment (see Chapter 9) because of its influence on interest rates, exchange rates, the cost of living, and general confidence in a country's political and economic system. For example, fear of inflation in Japan and West Germany accounts for the unwillingness of those countries to inflate their economies in order to achieve more rapid economic growth. However, the magnitude of inflation in many developing countries is incomprehensible to most people in the industrial world. During the period of 1980–1985, inflation increased in Argentina by 342.8 percent, in Brazil by 147.7 percent, in Bolivia by 569.1 percent, and in Israel by 196.3 percent.[17] Argentina suffered inflation in 1984 of between 600 and 700 percent a year. Brazil's inflation during that same period was over 200 percent a year. In 1988, inflation was expected to reach 400 percent in Brazil.

What are the major reasons for inflation? Briefly, there is too much money chasing too few goods. In other words, the demand for products exceeds the supply. Sometimes the money supply expands too rapidly, putting a lot of money in people's hands when there are not enough goods for them to buy. This pushes up prices on available goods. Thus government monetary policy is critical. Fiscal policy can also be important: The government can expand its service programs, for example, by putting more purchasing power in people's hands without expanding the production of goods.

As a result, two major ways to control inflation are to control the money supply and control government spending. If the money supply is controlled, the economy will not be able to expand very rapidly. As the economy slows down, pressure on prices also begins to drop. The problem with this strategy is that slow economic growth can result in unemployment, an explosive situation in many developing countries.

In highly inflationary environments, it is difficult for firms to plan for the future and run profitable operations. Prices change almost daily in order to maintain a sufficient cash flow to replace inventory and keep the firm operating. Accurately forecasting inflation is challenging, so firms end up underpricing or overpricing products, which results in a shortage of cash flow in the first situation or a price that is too high to maintain market share in the second situation.

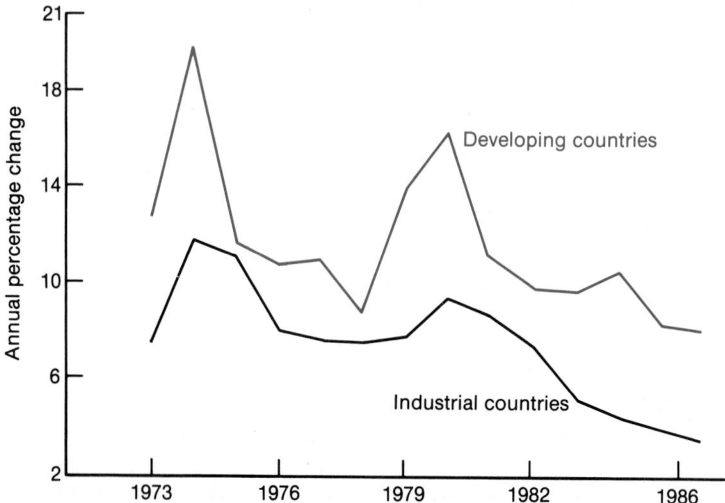

Figure 2.6
Inflation, 1973–1986

Note: Inflation is calculated as the change in the GDP deflator. For developing countries, the data points indicate median values; for industrial countries, average values.

Source: World Development Report, 1987 (New York: Oxford University Press, 1987), p. 16.

Inflation of the magnitude of a Bolivia, Argentina, or Brazil also creates problems for firms that deal in international markets. If the exchange rate depreciates at the same pace as inflation, then the prices that foreigners pay for exports of the inflationary country will not really change. But if the exchange rate does not change as much as inflation is forcing companies to raise their prices, the local companies will soon find that they cannot compete in world markets.

Inflation weakens the value of a currency and destabilizes a country politically.

Inflation causes political destabilization. If the government tries to control inflation by controlling wages, the real income of the populace declines and frustration sets in. If the government decides to do nothing, the country runs the risk of having the economy deteriorate to the point that real incomes fall anyway. To institute fiscal rigor when the government is in a fragile position in the first place is very difficult. In spite of the problems created by inflation, inflationary countries can still offer strong profits for traders and investors. Brazil has been able to fuel its economic growth largely through inflation and soften the impact of inflation through special fiscal policies. Its large market and relatively strong per capita income have created good opportunities, in spite of the uncertainty and instability.

As shown in Fig. 2.6, inflation has dropped steadily since 1980, especially in the industrial countries where it fell from 9.3 percent to 3.4 percent at the end of 1986. Prices have dropped in the developing countries also, mainly as a result of the fall in oil prices and commodities prices. A real key to stable economic growth is control over inflation. The fastest growth in inflation during the 1980–1985 period was in the countries considered to be high debtors. As mentioned above, Brazil was a key highly inflationary country in 1987 and 1988, with Mexico not far behind.

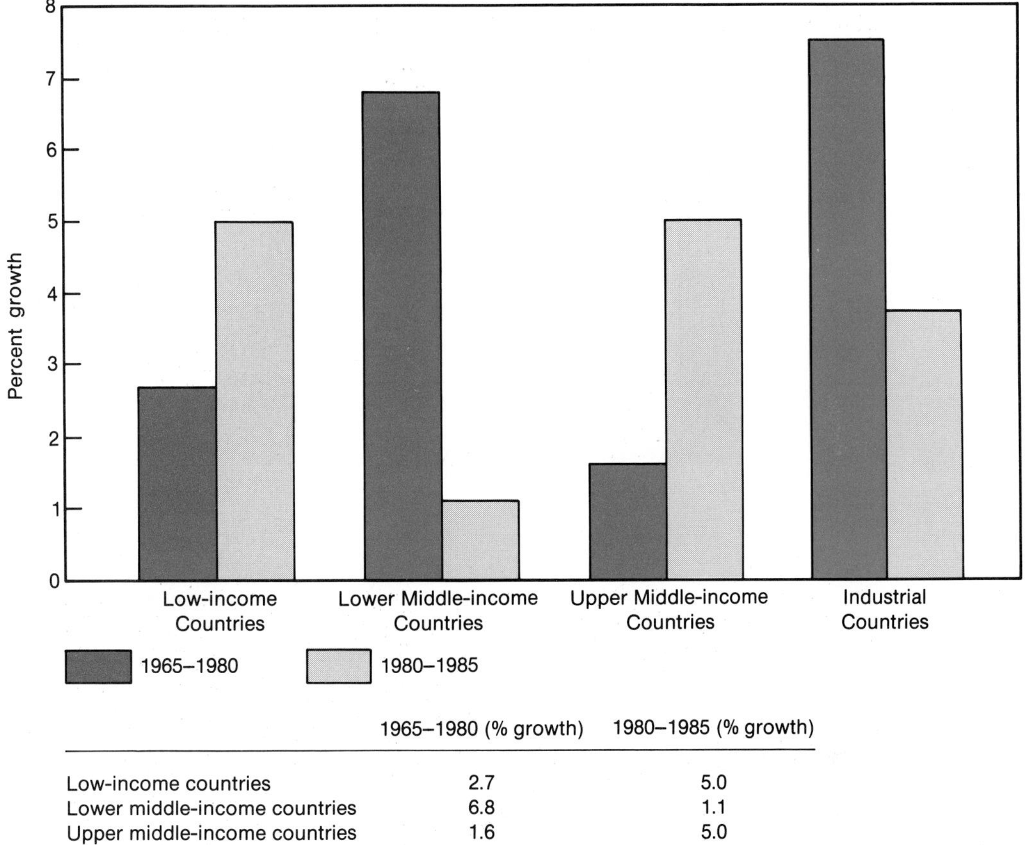

	1965–1980 (% growth)	1980–1985 (% growth)
Low-income countries	2.7	5.0
Lower middle-income countries	6.8	1.1
Upper middle-income countries	1.6	5.0
Industrial countries	7.5	3.7

Figure 2.7

Average Annual Growth Rate in Exports

Trade Strategy

In Chapter 1, we discussed trade patterns among the different regions of the world and in different product groups. Note the growth in exports and imports in different country categories since 1965 shown in Figs. 2.7 and 2.8. The developing countries showed an increase in growth rate in the 1980–1985 period over the 1965–1980 period. Exports from industrial countries declined during that period. It is particularly disturbing to note that exports from lower–middle-income countries did not grow as rapidly in 1980–1985 as they did in 1965–1980 in the lower–middle-income countries.

Different countries have very different trade strategies. Investments by MNEs in industrial countries typically are established to service local markets, which also tend to be relatively free to exports and imports. Developing

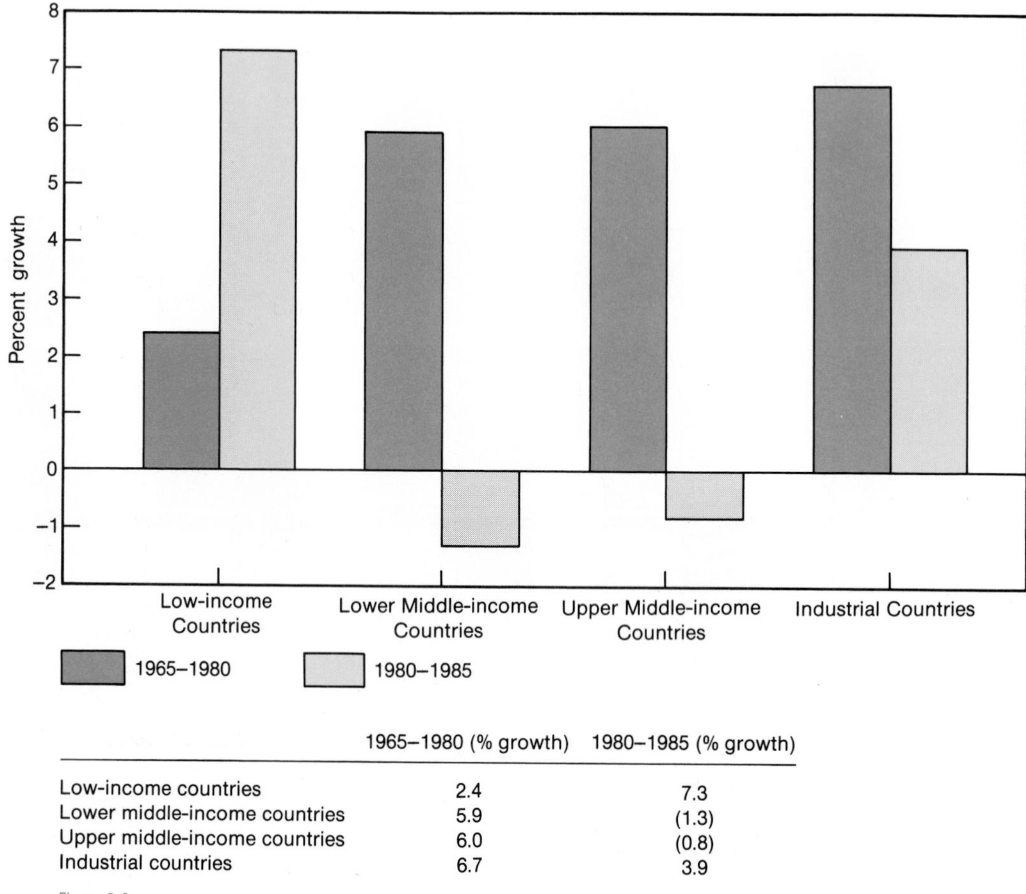

	1965–1980 (% growth)	1980–1985 (% growth)
Low-income countries	2.4	7.3
Lower middle-income countries	5.9	(1.3)
Upper middle-income countries	6.0	(0.8)
Industrial countries	6.7	3.9

Figure 2.8

Average Annual Growth Rate in Imports

countries, however, often have adopted specific strategies to encourage exports or impede imports. Figure 2.9 on p. 61 summarizes these strategies. MNE management must understand the country's attitude toward trade, since it may have an impact on the type of investment undertaken. The criteria for the four categories are defined by the World Bank as follows:

The four major trade strategies adopted by developing countries are

- Strongly outward-oriented
- Moderately outward-oriented
- Moderately inward-oriented
- Strongly inward-oriented.

1. Strongly outward-oriented countries. Trade controls are either nonexistent or very low in the sense that any disincentives to export resulting from import barriers are more or less counterbalanced by export incentives (such as Hong Kong, Korea, and Singapore).
2. Moderately outward-oriented countries. The overall incentive structure is biased toward production for domestic rather than export markets. But the average rate of effective protection for the home markets is relatively low (such as Brazil, Chile, and Israel).

Period	Strongly outward oriented	Moderately outward oriented	Moderately inward oriented	Strongly inward oriented
1963–1973	Hong Kong, Korea, Republic of Singapore	Brazil Cameroon Colombia Costa Rica Côte d'Ivoire Guatemala Indonesia Israel Malaysia Thailand	Bolivia El Salvador Honduras Kenya Madagascar Mexico Nicaragua Nigeria Philippines Senegal Tunisia Yugoslavia	Argentina Bangladesh Burundi Chile Dominican Republic Ethiopia Ghana India Pakistan Peru Sri Lanka Sudan Tanzania Turkey Uruguay Zambia
1973–1985	Hong Kong, Korea, Republic of Singapore	Brazil Chile Israel Malaysia Thailand Tunisia Turkey Uruguay	Cameroon Colombia Costa Rica Côte d'Ivoire El Salvador Guatemala Honduras Indonesia Kenya Mexico Nicaragua Pakistan Philippines Senegal Sri Lanka Yugoslavia	Argentina Bangladesh Bolivia Burundi Dominican Republic Ethiopia Ghana India Madagascar Nigeria Peru Sudan Tanzania Zambia

Figure 2.9

Classification of forty-one developing economies by trade orientation, 1963–1973 and 1973–1985

Source: World Development Report, 1987 (New York: Oxford University Press, 1937), p. 83.

3. Moderately inward-oriented countries. The overall incentive structure distinctly favors production for the domestic market. The average rate of effective protection for home markets is relatively high (such as Mexico and the Philippines).

4. Strongly inward-oriented countries. The overall incentive structure strongly favors production for the domestic market. The average rate of effective protection for home markets is high (such as Argentina and India).[18]

TABLE 2.3

CURRENT ACCOUNT BALANCE, 1980–1986 (billions of dollars)

Country group	1980	1981	1982	1983	1984	1985	1986
Developing countries	−69.1	−106.7	−103.0	−57.2	−32.1	−37.4	−35.5
Low-income countries	−17.0	−13.9	−8.9	−6.7	−8.1	−25.9	−22.0
Middle-income countries	−52.1	−92.8	−94.1	−50.5	−24.0	−11.5	−13.5
Oil exporters	1.4	−22.7	−30.0	−7.8	1.4	−2.2	−19.0
Exporters of manufactures	−33.9	−27.5	−23.3	−8.4	1.7	−8.8	6.0
High-income oil exporters	88.5	74.0	26.0	1.2	1.5	12.1	−9.4
Industrial countries	−38.2	2.4	1.4	−2.9	−35.1	−24.7	21.6
United States	8.4	12.8	−1.4	−38.2	−95.8	−104.4	−126.7
Other industrial countries	−46.6	−10.4	2.8	35.3	60.7	79.7	148.3
Total[a]	−18.8	−30.3	−75.6	−58.9	−65.7	−50.0	−23.3

Note: Net official transfers are excluded. Data for developing countries are based on a sample of ninety countries.
a. Reflects errors, omissions, and asymmetries in reported balance of payments statistics on current account, plus balance of listed groups with countries not included. Negative numbers reflect a deficit, positive numbers a surplus.
Source: *World Development Report, 1987* (New York: Oxford University Press, 1987), p. 17.

Explanations for why firms trade and why governments intervene in trade are discussed in Chapters 4 and 5. There are some interesting facts on macroeconomic performance of countries grouped by their trade orientation. Countries that are strongly outward oriented tend to have a higher average percentage growth in real GDP, a higher average percentage growth in per capita GNP, a larger percentage of gross domestic savings relative to GDP, and a larger percentage growth in manufactured exports than do countries in other categories. They also tend to exhibit lower rates of inflation.[19]

Payments Imbalances

Table 2.3 highlights the current account balances, exports minus imports of goods, services, and unilateral transfers, of different country categories from 1980–1986. The picture in the developing countries has improved steadily since 1981, especially among the exporters of manufactures.

The industrial countries as a group also performed well over the 1980s, with the notable exception of the United States. The U.S. deficit on current account of $126.7 billion was offset by the surplus in the other industrial countries of $148.3 billion. The huge deficit in the United States has been a constant source of contention between the United States and the rest of the world. Since a country's balance of payments must always be stable, the United States has been able to offset its current account deficit with an inflow of capital from abroad. Foreign governments and individuals have been willing to invest in the United States due to relatively high real interest rates, political stability, a strong local economy, and general confidence in the political and economic system of the United States. In addition, U.S. firms in the early 1980s began to invest more in the United States than abroad, thereby reducing the outflow of foreign direct investment. As a result, the United States has been buying foreign products and selling the strength and stability of the U.S. economy. Some feel that this heavy reliance on foreign capital has made the United States the world's largest debtor. However, the money has flowed in as a result of economic opportunity in a significantly different way from that of Mexico, Brazil, and Argentina.

Some would argue that a surplus is evidence of a mercantilist government policy. Surplus countries tend to be fairly satisfied with their situation. However, pressure has been placed in recent years on large surplus countries such as Taiwan and Japan to open their markets and stimulate consumption in order to reduce the surplus. Deficit countries have been under pressure to increase exports and correct fundamental economic imbalances in order to slow down imports and bring the trade deficit up to a more even balance.

Country Debt

One of the consequences of the rapid increase in the cost of oil during the 1970s was the equally rapid increase in debt as developing countries sought assistance from private or government institutions in other countries to finance oil imports and other products necessary for development. Debt in the developing countries increased from $86.6 billion in 1971 to $753.4 billion in 1986.[20] Of the 1986 total, it was estimated that 63.5 percent was owed to private institutions and the rest to official government agencies.

Figure 2.10 identifies the major developing country debtors. Note the tremendous size of the debt in countries such as Mexico and Brazil. Table 2.4 provides some data about the developing countries as a whole. The **debt service ratio** is the ratio of interest payments plus principal amortization (the payment of the original loan balance) to exports. The debt service ratio has been increasing over the past six years, which means that countries are not able to use as much of their export earnings as they would like for economic development. An increasing share of it is going to service their debt.

The overall data hides the critical problem faced by some large debtors in servicing their debt. Brazil and Mexico, the two largest debtors in the world, have debt service ratios of 34.8 percent and 48.2 percent, respectively. Clearly, it is important to have a diversified economy so that manufacturing exports can be used to help service that debt.

As noted earlier, debt of developing countries increased dramatically during the 1970s and 1980s. The first crisis was felt by the international banking community in Poland in the 1970s. At that time it appeared that Poland would have to default (or not pay its obligations), and many experts were unsure of the impact on the international financial community. The next crisis came in August 1982 when Mexico, with nearly four times the debt of

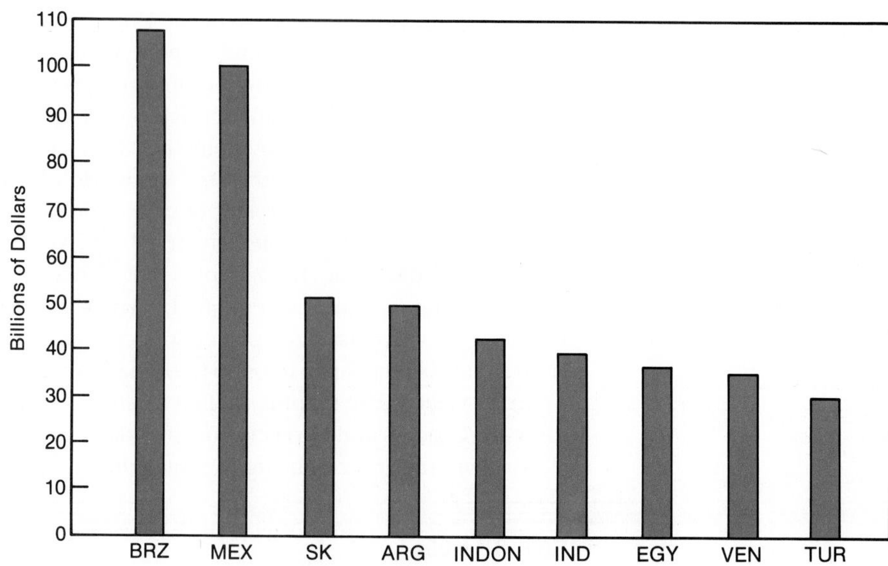

Country	Abbreviation	Current Debt (in billions)
Brazil	BRZ	$108.0
Mexico	MEX	100.3
South Korea	SK	51.6
Argentina	ARG	49.8
Indonesia	INDON	42.7
India	IND	39.7
Egypt	EGY	36.8
Venezuela	VEN	35.3
Turkey	TUR	30.3

Figure 2.10

Third World Debtors (in billions of dollars)

Source: Morgan Guaranty Trust Co., "Brazil Will Press for Concessions Won by Mexico," published in *Wall Street Journal,* Jan. 9, 1987, p. 24.

Poland, could not fulfill its debt service obligations. As a result, it was forced to reschedule principal and interest payments. When a country reschedules debt, it changes the interest rate of the loan and/or the timing of the payments of principal and interest.

Debt rescheduling involves:

- restructuring of payments
- extension of long-term loans
- maintenance or extension of short-term credit.

Most of the large debtors, especially Brazil and Argentina, were in the same position and had to go through reschedulings at the same time. Interestingly, fourteen countries rescheduled $8 billion of debt in 1981, ten countries rescheduled $4 billion in 1982, but it was estimated that twenty-four countries restructured debt worth $71.1 billion in 1986. Of that total, $43.7 billion involved the Mexican debt. Debt rescheduling typically involves some combination of the following: (1) restructuring of principal

TABLE 2.4

DEBT INDICATORS FOR DEVELOPING COUNTRIES, 1980–1986 (percent, unless otherwise noted)

Indicator	1980	1981	1982	1983	1984	1985	1986
Ratio of debt to GNP	20.6	22.4	26.3	31.4	33.0	35.8	35.4
Ratio of debt to exports	90.0	98.0	117.6	134.8	121.2	143.7	144.5
Debt service ratio	16.0	17.5	20.6	19.4	19.5	21.4	22.3
Ratio of debt service to GNP	3.7	4.0	4.6	4.5	4.9	5.3	5.5
Ratio of interest service to exports	6.9	8.3	10.4	10.1	10.3	10.8	10.7
Total debt outstanding and disbursed (billions of dollars)	428.6	490.8	551.1	631.5	673.2	727.7	753.4
Private debt as a percentage of total debt	63.1	64.5	65.0	65.8	65.7	63.9	63.5

Note: Data are based on a sample of ninety developing countries. Data for 1986 are estimates.

Source: *World Development Report, 1987* (New York: Oxford University Press, 1987), p. 18.

payments falling due during an agreed consolidation period, (2) the related extension of new long-term loans, and (3) understandings to maintain or extend short-term credit lines.[21]

In 1987, the crisis, especially among the Latin American debtors, reached critical proportions. Brazil declared a moratorium on interest and principal payments to commercial creditors, basically a suspension of payments, arguing that it could not afford the $5 billion in annual interest payments, an amount that was 12 percent of its federal budget.[22] As a result of the high degree of uncertainty in Latin American loans, many banks set aside reserves that equaled an average of 25 percent of their Latin loans in case the loans would not be repaid. At that time, many experts were predicting that the reserves would have to go even higher. Banks establish reserves by reducing earnings and increasing the reserve account. This allows them to reduce earnings a little each year, especially in profitable years, rather than wait for a major default and reduce earnings all at once. The problem is that the reduction in earnings also reduces the lending ability and financial strength of the banks.

Latin countries also were trying to create novel ways to reduce the debt pressure by, for example, converting debt into equity. A debt-equity swap is based on a foreign lender's exchanging its dollar debt in a developing country for real assets in that country, such as equity in a local business. The equity investment would be made in the local currency. The exchange rate is set by the government for the dollar/local currency swap, and it is often at a discount from the official exchange rate. Thus the dollar debt would yield less local currency for the swap transaction than if the transaction were allowed to take place in the official market. This implies that the debt has actually lost value due to the credit problems of the debtor nation, so the swap exchange rate reflects that value. In 1988, the Mexican government unsuccessfully attempted to convert some of its debt into equity. It also converted some of its debt into bonds at a significant discount (similar to the rationale described above in the debt/equity swaps) but backed by U.S. government securities.

The International Monetary Fund has played a crucial role in helping the debtor nations restructure their economies. In country after country the IMF has recommended strong economic restrictions as a precondition for receiving loans from the IMF. These loans are almost a necessity for the international commercial banks to reschedule their loans. Restrictions have involved a combination of export expansion, import substitution, and a drastic reduction in public spending. In Mexico, for example, the government deficit was running at an estimated 17.6 percent of GDP in 1982, and the IMF gave the government a target of 5.5 to 6.5 percent, a substantial reduction in government spending.[23] By 1985, the Mexican deficit was 7.7 percent.

In many developing countries, these radical requirements have touched off heated debate and have sorely tested the political stability of the governments in power. Once the IMF sets targets, it monitors those targets periodically as a precondition to releasing funds. The private international banks often use the results of this monitoring to determine their policies.

MNE management is concerned about the high debt situation because of the difficulty caused in operating in that type of environment. Imports are often curtailed, and hard currency is difficult to come by. In addition, a variety of macroeconomic measures might be instituted to control debt, including slowing down economic growth, which would have a negative impact on sales opportunities for firms.

NORTH–SOUTH DIALOGUE

In 1964 in Geneva, the first session of the **United Nations Conference on Trade and Development (UNCTAD)** was held, leading to what is now called the North–South dialogue. (The North reflects the industrialized and the South the developing countries.) At this time, a new international economic order was identified,

> *based on equity, sovereign equality, interdependence, common interest, and cooperation among all States, irrespective of their economic and social systems, which shall correct inequalities and redress existing injustices, make it possible to eliminate the widening gap between the developed and the developing countries, and ensure steadily accelerating economic and social development and peace and justice for present and future generations.*[24]

None of the pronouncements emanating from the session were particularly new, but the collective resolve of the developing countries (i.e., the South) appeared to be stronger than ever.

The North–South dialogue focused on:
- Stabilization of earnings and prices
- Reduction of trade barriers
- Increased aid
- Debt moratorium
- Private investment.

Since 1974, various meetings focused on specific problems have been held in order to continue the North–South dialogue. In particular, the developing countries have expressed major concern in the following areas: stabilization of export earnings and commodity prices; reduction of trade barriers in the developed countries; increased aid; debt moratorium; and additional private investment. The basic concern is how to transfer wealth from the developed to the developing countries. Even though each side has moderated its position, a wide gap continues to exist between what the developing countries want and what the developed countries want and are willing to give.

UNCTAD V, held in Manila in 1979, may have started a new era of cooperation and understanding in the dialogue. The four main areas of emphasis in the conference were: (1) trade and financial-flow aspects of the relationships between developed and developing countries; (2) emphasis on growing interdependence between different parts of the world economy; (3) efforts to bring socialist countries into the dialogue on economic issues; and (4) emphasis on trade liberalization and concern about expanding protectionism.[25] Unlike the conflict-ridden earlier sessions of UNCTAD, the mood seemed to be one of greater cooperation.

The UNCTAD VI meetings held in Yugoslavia in 1983 focused on the problems of debt and protectionism. At that meeting, the Group of 77 identified the following points as the key focus for the discussions:

The UNCTAD VI meeting held in 1983 focused on four major points.

1. automatic debt relief;
2. an increase in world liquidity through the IMF;
3. greater aid and private bank lending to developing nations;
4. freer access for developing country exports to the markets of the rich.[26]

The meeting was not as fruitful as the Group of 77 had hoped, however. Industrialized countries acknowledged that protectionism hurts the developing countries and agreed to open access to their markets more as the recovery took hold. But they also encouraged the richer developing countries to do the same for their poorer neighbors. This suggestion met with some resistance from the developing countries, which felt that they needed barriers to allow their own infant industries to develop. The industrial countries also opposed discussions of increasing liquidity because they viewed the World Bank and the International Monetary Fund (IMF) as better suited to deal with those issues. UNCTAD originally was organized to deal with commodity issues, whereas the World Bank and IMF were geared toward financial issues. In addition, the industrial countries have greater control over the World Bank and the IMF than they do over UNCTAD. The industrial North in effect seemed to feel that the developing South would see a lot of their problems disappear as the impact of the recovery "trickled down" to the developing countries.

UNCTAD VII (1987) focused on universal growth.

UNCTAD VII, held in Geneva in 1987, decided to focus more on promoting development, growth, and international trade. Three objectives in particular were established by the managing director of UNCTAD: (1) Establish in each country growth-oriented structural adjustment programs; (2) acquire financing appropriate to the situation of overindebtedness; and

(3) put into place a universal growth-oriented adjustment effort.[27] A major accomplishment at the meeting was a final agreement on the establishment of a common fund for commodities. Rather than serve as a buffer fund for commodities (which will be discussed in more detail in Chapter 7), the fund will be used to help develop new markets for commodities of commodity-dependent countries or by helping the countries diversify. This is significantly different from what was originally envisioned in 1977.

EXTERNAL INFLUENCES ON DEVELOPMENT

Multilateral Institutions

IMF provides financial support to developing countries and assists in restructuring the economy.

World Bank provides infrastructure development for developing countries.

The road to development is complex, making it difficult for the developing countries to meet the challenges alone. The International Monetary Fund (IMF) and World Bank are instrumental in the development process. IMF provides financial support for countries suffering severe balance of payments problems, which includes most of the developing countries. As noted earlier in the section on debt, this financial assistance, although multilateral, comes with strings attached. Countries are often forced to make substantial and politically unpopular concessions for IMF support. At times, countries have felt too much loss of sovereignty involved in IMF financing.

The World Bank also provides financing, especially in infrastructure development such as roads, communications, and power, in low-income developing countries. In a World Bank study, three problems were identified with respect to the economies of developing countries: (1) overvalued currencies and trade restrictions that have discouraged local production; (2) government pricing and tax policies that have kept the cost of imported fertilizer and equipment high and the price of agricultural products low; and (3) overreliance on government.[28] The World Bank intends to take a more active role in helping countries alter their basic economic policies in return for aid, which would bring their policy more in line with that of the IMF.

The Multinational Enterprise

Third World MNEs are primarily from resource-rich, labor-rich, and rapidly industrializing countries.

The 1970s brought a flurry of books and articles on the impact of the MNE in developing countries. MNEs were accused of a variety of problems, including the destruction of the nation-state. Several factors challenge this perception: (1) a shift in bargaining power toward the nation-state; (2) a dispersion in multinationals to include home countries other than the United States, thus eliminating the United States as the sole source of economic influence; (3) the development of multinationals by developing countries themselves; (4) the emergence of more multinationals including a larger number of smaller, more flexible enterprises; and (5) greater flexibility on the part of multinationals in adapting to local situations.[29] One of these points deserves elaboration: Third World multinationals, usually coming from the rapidly developing middle-income countries, have increased dramatically in recent years. These

MNEs come primarily from three different types of developing countries: resource-rich (such as OPEC members); labor-rich and rapidly industrializing (such as Hong Kong, Taiwan, and South Korea); and market-rich, rapidly industrializing (such as Brazil, Mexico, and the Philippines).[30] Governments in these countries tend to be committed to international business activities. MNEs from the developing countries also tend to be more readily accepted in sister countries since they are "part of the group" and are not perceived to be as threatening as MNEs from the industrialized countries.

The strength of these MNEs comes from their special experience with manufacturing for small home markets. Since they bring the skills that the host countries have not experienced and that the traditional western MNEs have forgotten, they are more competitive in other developing countries where markets are small and labor costs are low.[31] The impact of industrial-country MNEs on developing countries is complex. Chapter 11 examines the major issues in greater depth.

A humorous description of the MNE appeared in the London *Economist:*

> *It fiddles its accounts. It avoids or evades its taxes. It rigs its intra-company transfer prices. It is run by foreigners, from decision centres thousands of miles away. It imports foreign labour practices. It doesn't import foreign labour practices. It overpays. It underpays. It competes unfairly with local firms. It is in cahoots with local firms. It exports jobs from rich countries. It is an instrument of rich countries' imperialism. The technologies it brings to the third world are too old-fashioned. No, they are too modern. It meddles. It bribes. Nobody can control it. It wrecks balances of payments. It overturns economic policies. It plays off governments against each other to get the biggest investment incentives. Won't it please come and invest? Let it bloody well go home.*[32]

Many developing countries are finding that they need to provide a better climate for foreign investment in order to have access to the capital and technology of the industrial country MNEs as a key part of their industrial strategy. For years, Mexico would not allow majority ownership for most new investment. However, the debt problems of the early 1980s caused them to change their legislation in order to attract more capital. They found that incurring debt was not the best route, and as a result, in 1984 began to improve the investment climate and restore the confidence of foreign investors in the hopes of attracting more capital.[33]

MNEs have a great deal to offer developing countries in terms of capital, technology, managerial expertise, and access to world markets. As the oil companies have learned, however, they need to be increasingly flexible about the way profits are to be earned. Licensing agreements, production agreements, management contracts, and joint ventures are sometimes taking the place of wholly owned direct investments. As host countries improve their basic operating environments to attract investment and the MNEs adjust their operating strategies to these environments, development will increase and profits will be earned.

SUMMARY

- There are three major world economies: The First World is made up of the market industrial economies, the Second World consists of the centrally planned economies, and the Third World is comprised of the developing countries.
- The role of the political system is to integrate the society; the role of the economic system is to allocate scarce resources.
- Most complex societies are pluralistic; in other words, they encompass a variety of ideologies.
- Democracy involves wide participation in the decision-making process, whereas totalitarianism involves only a relative few in the process. Totalitarian regimes can be communistic, theocratic, or secular.
- Most democracies have multiple political parties, whereas some, such as Mexico, have a dominant political party.
- All economic systems have to decide who is to own and control resources. A market system allows individuals to allocate and control resources; a command economy allows the government to allocate and control resources. A command economy is compatible with a totalitarian political system; a market economy is compatible with a democracy.
- A multinational enterprise (MNE) that enters a country needs to determine the nature of the political and economic system and how it can fit into that system.
- Developing countries are divided into low-income (per capita GNP of $400 or less) and middle-income (per capita GNP of $401 or more). Middle-income developing countries are divided into high-income oil exporters, other oil exporters, exporters of manufactures, and other countries not included in one of the above categories.
- As countries move from low-income to industrial market economies, the distribution of Gross Domestic Product (GDP) shifts in emphasis from agriculture to industry to services.
- Drucker identifies three major changes in the world economy: the primary-products economy has separated from the industrial economy, production has separated from employment, and capital movements have become more important than goods movements in driving the world economy.
- Some of the greatest problems facing the developing countries are inflation, external debt, weakening currencies, shortage of skilled workers, political instability, war and insurrection, mass poverty, rapid population growth, weakening commodity prices, and reliance on imported oil. Developing countries have exhibited strong growth, but they are riskier places of investment than the industrial countries.

- Inflation today is not as bad as it was during the 1970s, but it is still a problem in some countries, such as Argentina, Brazil, and Israel.
- The trade strategy of countries ranges from strongly outward-oriented (such as Hong Kong and Korea) to strongly inward-oriented (such as Argentina and India).
- Many of the large debtor nations have had to restructure their loans due to an inability to meet principal and interest payments.
- The UNCTAD meetings are focusing on growth and solving the problem of indebtedness. The International Monetary Fund (IMF) is concerned with stabilizing exchange rates and helping countries resolve their indebtedness problems. The World Bank is concerned with providing capital for development of the Third World.

CASE:
BATA, LTD.[34]

In 1986, management of Bata, Ltd. had a critical decision to make concerning its investment in South Africa. It had operated in South Africa for 55 years but now had to weigh its commitment to an operation employing 3200 mostly black employees and generating about one percent of its worldwide revenues of more than $1 billion. A rapidly deteriorating economic and political environment forced management to make a decision about whether or not to sell its operations.

As difficult as this situation appeared to be, it is not the first time that Bata management had to deal with a difficult political environment. As war swept across Europe in 1939, Tom Bata was faced with a difficult situation. His father, of the ninth generation of a family of shoemakers in Czechoslovakia, had built a worldwide shoe network in 28 countries, using machinery and the mass production technology of the 1920s. But now Tom was left with the responsibility of expanding that empire during a period of great uncertainty worldwide. Because of the invasion of the Nazis and the uncertain future that occupation held, Bata took 100 Czech families and emigrated to Canada in order to preserve his father's business.

Since that time, Bata's decision has been ratified through strong growth worldwide. Bata, Ltd. is a family-owned business whose production facilities produce hundreds of millions of shoes annually, generating over $1 billion in revenues through sales in 6000 Bata-owned retail outlets and 125 independent retailers in 115 nations. Its 85,000 employees work in over ninety factories and five engineering facilities, as well as the retail operations mentioned earlier. Bata's influence is so pervasive that it makes and sells one out of every three shoes manufactured and sold in the noncommunist world. In fact, the word for shoe in many parts of Africa is "bata."

Bata, Ltd. operates as a decentralized operation that is free to adjust to the local environment, within parameters. Tom Bata travels extensively to check on quality control and to ensure good relations with the governments of the countries where Bata, Ltd. operates.

Although Bata, Ltd. has factories in more than 90 countries and operations of one form or another in over 100, it does not own all of those facilities. Where possible, it owns 100 percent of the operations. In some countries, however, the government requires less than majority ownership. In India, for example, 60 percent of the stock of the local Bata operations trades on the Indian stock exchange, and in Japan, Bata, Ltd. owns only 9.9 percent of the operations. In some cases, Bata, Ltd. provides licensing, consulting, and technical assistance to companies in which it has no equity interest.

Bata, Ltd.'s strategy for servicing world markets is interesting. Some MNEs try to lower costs by achieving economies of scale in production, which means that they produce as much as possible in the most optimal-sized factory and then service markets worldwide from that single production facility. Bata, Ltd. tries to service its different national markets by producing in a given market nearly everything it sells in that market. Part of the reason for this strategy is that Bata, Ltd. can achieve economies of scale very quickly because it has a fairly large volume in the countries where it produces.

This may seem difficult to believe, especially since Bata, Ltd. has production facilities in some African nations where it is the sole industry. However, Bata, Ltd. feels that it can achieve economies of scale very easily because it is a labor-intensive operation. Bata, Ltd. also tries to get all of its raw materials locally. This is not possible in some cases, especially in some of the poorer developing countries. However, it tries to have as much value-added as possible in those countries.

Another of Bata, Ltd.'s policies is that it prefers not to export production; rather, it chooses local production to service the local market. Obviously, that rule is not fixed, since the company produces in only 90 countries but has distribution in over 100. Sometimes Bata, Ltd. becomes entangled with local governments when it imports some raw materials but does not export. Then it has to adjust to the local laws and requirements for operation.

Bata, Ltd. avoids excessive reliance on exports partly because of the risk. For example, if an importing country were to restrict trade, Bata could possibly lose market opportunity and market share. In addition, Mr. Bata noted the benefit to the developing country of not exposing itself to possible protectionism:

> *We know very well what kind of a social shock it is when a plant closes in Canada. Yet in Canada we have unemployment insurance and all kinds of welfare operations, and there are many alternative jobs that people can*

> *usually go to. In most of the developing countries, on the other hand, it's a question of life and death for these people. They have uprooted themselves from an agricultural society. They've come to a town to work in an industry. They've brought their relatives with them because working in industry, their earnings are so much higher. Thus a large group of their relatives have become dependent on them and have changed their lifestyle and standard of living. For these people it is a terrible thing to lose a job. And so we are very sensitive to that particular problem.*

Bata, Ltd. operates in a variety of different types of economies. It has extensive operations in both the industrial democratic countries and the developing countries. It has been soundly criticized (as have been most MNEs) for operating in South Africa and thus tacitly supporting the white minority political regime, and it has also been censured for operating in other totalitarian regimes such as Chile. Bata counters by pointing out that the company has been operating in Chile for over forty years, during which a variety of political regimes have been in power.

Although Bata's local operations have not been nationalized very many times, the company has had some fascinating experiences. In Uganda, Bata's local operations were nationalized by Milton Obote, denationalized by Idi Amin, renationalized by Amin, and finally denationalized by Amin. During that time the factory continued to operate as if nothing had happened. Mr. Bata's explanation for finally being left alone is that, "Shoes had to be produced and sold, materials had to be bought and wages paid. Life went on. In most cases, the governments concluded it really wasn't in their interest to run businesses, so they cancelled the nationalization arrangements."

Despite Bata, Ltd.'s ability to operate in any type of political situation, Mr. Bata prefers a democratic environment. He feels that while both democratic and totalitarian regimes are bureaucratic, a democracy holds the potential to discuss and change procedures whereas under totalitarianism it is sometimes wise to remain silent.

Bata, Ltd. has a multifaceted impact on a country. The basic strategy of the company is to provide footwear at affordable prices for the largest possible segment of the population. The product, footwear, is a necessity rather than a luxury. The production facilities are labor-intensive, so jobs are created, which increases consumers' purchasing power. Although top management may come from outside of the country, local management is trained to assume responsibility as quickly as possible. Because the company tries to get most of its raw materials locally, suppliers are usually developed. Since Bata, Ltd. likes to diversify its purchases, it usually develops more than one supplier for a given product, which leads to competition and efficiencies.

Typically Bata, Ltd. brings in its own capital resources at the start-up of a new operation, but it is also skillful in utilizing international capital markets. More than once Bata, Ltd. used the resources of the International Finance Corporation (IFC), a division of the World Bank that provides development financing for private enterprise projects in developing countries. One of Bata's most recent attempts at IFC financing was to expand a tannery in Bangladesh. The importance of getting IFC support is that Bata, Ltd. would be much more likely to attract other debt and equity capital once it had received IFC approval. All of the five previous Bata projects supported by the IFC had been successful, and the loans had been paid back.

The South African dilemma presented unique challenges for Bata management, however. South Africa, whose population ranks just below those of Nigeria, Egypt, and Ethiopia, has long been considered a good place to invest because of its large market size. South Africa's per capita GNP is the largest in Africa, however. The country's main attraction has been the incredibly high rate of return that companies can earn, owing largely to low labor costs and mineral wealth. The relatively large market still allows firms to achieve economies of scale in production while exploiting the low labor costs.

But the situation has deteriorated rapidly in recent years. The system of apartheid, which has resulted in a political, social, and economic separation of blacks, coloreds, and whites, has characterized South Africa for decades, and change has been slow. However, government opposition has begun to unite around the concept of one man, one vote. Black nationalists will settle only for total voting rights, whereas the white government refuses that concept at all costs. Rioting has left many dead and has heightened the uncertainty of South Africa's political future. The African National Congress (ANC), the outlawed political party that is the black majority's largest representative body, opposes capitalism and would nationalize all industry, whether domestic or foreign-owned.

South Africa's 0.8 percent growth during 1980–1985 was significantly below that of the average of 1.7 percent for upper–middle-income developing countries. In addition to a relatively stagnant economy and political strife, pressure has come from foreign firms and governments. A number of U.S. firms including Apple Computer, Coca Cola, Ford, International Harvester, General Motors, IBM, Honeywell, and Warner Communications, have sold or significantly reduced their investments in South Africa. In 1984, only seven U.S. companies had pulled out of South Africa. In 1985, forty pulled out; in 1986 fifty left; and by mid-1987, thirty-three firms had already withdrawn. U.S. investment in South Africa had dropped in half between 1982 and 1986. Even the U.S. consulate in Johannesburg had lost faith in the future of South Africa, noting that South Africa was on its way to becoming "just another African country: chronic debtor, import-starved... a repressive regime unable to manage its own domestic constituency in any positive way."

The Canadian attitude toward South Africa was also poor. Canada's government issued very conservative voluntary guidelines on new investments in South Africa. As a result, Bata management was forced to examine its investment and decide if it was worth the uncertainty of the environment, both at home and in South Africa.

QUESTIONS

1. Why do you think that a developing country might allow Bata, Ltd. to operate locally?
2. Do you agree with Bata's assessment of the riskiness of exporting? How do you think the developing countries might react to that assessment?
3. Explain why Bata, Ltd.'s operations might be less susceptible to serious political influence than some other types of companies.
4. Discuss the pros and cons of Bata, Ltd.'s remaining in South Africa.

NOTES

1. Data for the case were taken from *Annual Reports* (Gulf, 1975–1983); Chevron *Annual Report* (1986); *The Wall Street Journal,* March 27, 1981, p. 1; *The Wall Street Journal,* November 8, 1979, p. 20; *New York Times,* February 2, 1981, p. D1; *New York Times,*June 27, 1981, p. 1; *Economist,* May 22, 1976, p. 93; *Economist,* July 21, 1976, pp. 52–53; *Business Week,* August 10, 1981, pp. 52–63; "U.S. Interests, Public and Private, in Angola," *The Wall Street Journal,* December 14, 1983, p. 31; "Gulf Oil's Role in Southern Africa," *The Wall Street Journal,* January 26, 1984, p. 33; Barry Shlachter, "Portuguese Come Back to Angola," *Deseret News,* September 9–10, 1982, p. 14A; Sam Levy, "Ex-Colonies Ponder a Return of Portuguese Settlers," *The Wall Street Journal,* September 24, 1986, p. 29; Steve Mufson, "Marxist Angola Is Accommodating Host to Oil Firms, Other Western Enterprises," *The Wall Street Journal,* November 13, 1985, p. 34; "Angola's Resilient Rebel," *U.S. News & World Report,* February 10, 1986, p. 11; "Angola: Trapped in the Cross Fire," *U.S. News & World Report,* February 16, 1987, pp. 30–31; Lee Lescaze, "Angola's Inept, Indifferent Marxist Elite Run a Nation Where 'Nothing Gets Done,' " *The Wall Street Journal,* February 19, 1987, p. 30.

2. Adapted from Richard N. Farmer and Barry M. Richman, *Comparative Management and Economic Progress* (Homewood, Ill.: Richard D. Irwin, 1965), p. 30.

3. Farmer and Richman, p. 25.

4. Farmer and Richman. For similar ideas, see Hans Schollhammer, "Strategies in Comparative Management Theorizing," in *Comparative Management: Teaching, Training and Research,* Jean Boddewyn, ed. (New York: Graduate School of Business Administration, New York University, 1970), p. 22; Richard W. Wright, "Organizational Ambiente: Management and Environment in Chile," *Academy of Management Journal,* March 1971; and Bernard D. Estafen, "System Transfer Characteristics: An Experimental Model for Comparative Management Research," *Management International Review,* no. 2–3 (1970).

5. Robert Wesson, *Modern Government—Democracy and Authoritarianism,* 2nd ed. (Englewood Cliffs, N.J.: Prentice-Hall, Inc., 1985), pp. 41–42.

6. Laxmi Nakarmi, "Korea Votes for Economic Stability," *Business Week,* December 28, 1987, p. 69.

7. *World Development Report, 1984* (Washington, D.C.: World Bank, 1984), p. 54.

8. Maria Shao, "Laying the Foundation for the Great Mall of China," *Business Week,* January 25, 1988, pp. 68–69.

9. Peter Galuszka, Bill Javetski, John Pearson, and Rose Brady, "Reforming the Soviet Economy," *Business Week,* December 7, 1987, pp. 76–80, 84, 88.

10. *World Development Report,* 1984, p. 67.

11. *Ibid.*

12. "Freedom House Comparative Survey of Freedom for 1987," *Freedom at Issue,* January-February, 1987, p. 33. This survey has an interesting matrix that plots political systems on one axis and economic systems on the other. Examples of countries are included in each cell in the matrix.

13. *Freedom at Issue, op. cit.*

14. Michael P. Blackwell, "From G-5 to G-77: International Forums for Discussion of Economic Issues," *Finance and Development,* December 1986, pp. 40–41.

15. Peter F. Drucker, "The Changed World Economy," *Foreign Affairs,* Vol. 64, No. 4, Spring 1986, pp. 768–791.

16. Drucker, *op. cit.,* p. 782.

17. *World Development Report,* 1987 (New York: Oxford University Press, 1987), pp. 202–203.

18. *World Development Report,* 1987, pp. 82–83.

19. *World Development Report,* 1987, p. 84.

20. "The Banker's Guide to LDC Debt," *Banker,* March 1981, pp. 90–91; *International Letter,* No. 518 (Chicago: Federal Reserve Bank of Chicago, January 27, 1984), p. 2; *World Development Report,* 1987.

21. *World Development Report,* 1987, p. 20.

22. Jeffrey Ryser, Stephen Baker, and Elizabeth Weiner, "The Debtors' Revolt Is Spreading in Latin America," *Business Week,* December 28, 1987, pp. 88–89.

23. "Will Mexico Make It?," *Business Week,* October 1, 1984, pp. 74–77.

24. From "The Declaration on the Establishment of a New International Economic Order," reprinted in Paul Rogers, ed., *Future Resources and World Development* (New York: Plenum Press, 1976), p. 135.

25. Mahmud al Burney, "A Recognition of Interdependence: UNCTAD V," *Finance & Development,* September 1979, p. 18.

26. Paul Lewis, "Aid and Trade Are in the Air at North–South Talks," *New York Times,* June 12, 1983, p. 8F.

27. "Conditions in Global Economy Prompt Renewed Focus on Growth," *IMF Survey,* July 27, 1987, p. 233.

28. Art Pine, "World Bank Drafts Long-Term Aid Plan That Pressures Poor Countries to Change," *Wall Street Journal,* August 21, 1981, p. 4.

29. Paul Streeten, "Multinational Revisited," *Finance & Development,* June 1979, pp. 39–42.

30. David A. Heenan and Warren J. Keegan, "The Rise of Third World Multinationals," *Harvard Business Review,* January–February 1979, pp. 102–103.

31. Louis T. Wells, Jr., "Guess Who's Creating the World's Newest Multinationals," *Wall Street Journal,* December 12, 1983, p. 22.

32. "Controlling the Multinationals," *Economist,* January 24, 1976, p. 68.

33. "Why Only a Few Companies Are Betting on Mexico's Future," *Business Week,* October 1, 1984, p. 78.

34. The material for the case was taken from the following sources: Dean Walker, "Shoemaker to the World," *Executive,* January 1981, pp. 63–69; Gary Vineberg, "Bata Favors Free Trade but Tempers Asia Stance," *Footwear News,* Vol. 39, No. 24, June 13, 1983, pp. 2ff.; Ira Breskin and Gary Vineberg, "Parent Bata Looks after Farflung Footwear Family," *Footwear News,* Vol. 39, No. 23, June 6, 1983, pp. 1ff.; Ira Breskin, "Globe-Trotting Bata, Ltd.: A World Bank Customer," *Footwear News,* Vol. 38, No. 38, October 4, 1982, p. 23; "After Sullivan," *The Economist,* June 13, 1987, p. 71; Elizabeth Weiner and Steve Mufson, "All Roads Lead out of South Africa," *Business Week,* November 3, 1986, pp. 24–25; Jonathan Kapstein, John Hoerr, and Elizabeth Weiner, "Leaving South Africa," *Business Week,* September 23, 1985, pp. 104–112.

3

CHAPTER

THE HUMAN AND CULTURAL ENVIRONMENTS FACING BUSINESS

"To change customs is a difficult thing."
—Lebanese proverb

- To demonstrate how human-cultural environments are examined and to show some of their principal limitations.
- To highlight human physical characteristics peculiar to different countries and to show the effects of these characteristics on efficiency of business practices worldwide.
- To examine major customs that differentiate business practices from country to country.
- To present guidelines for multinational firms that want to expand into foreign operations.

CASE:
PARRIS-ROGERS INTERNATIONAL[1]

When Prime Minister Margaret Thatcher made an official visit to Saudi Arabia, the first ever by a British head of government, she deferred to Islamic custom on appropriate attire for women. She wore a long-sleeved, ankle-length dress throughout the day. During her talks with King Khalid, she wore a net veil over her face. This deference was a symbolic gesture to show her sensitivity to the Saudi culture, which helped to gain acceptance of her proposals to Saudi officials.

A year before Mrs. Thatcher's visit, Parris-Rogers International (PRI), a British publishing house, sold its floundering Bahraini operations, which had been set up to edit the first telephone and business directories for five Arab states on or near the Arabian peninsula, plus the seven autonomous divisions making up the United Arab Emirates. (See the map on Fig. 3.1.) Like many foreign firms, PRI was drawn to the Middle East in the 1970s because of the burgeoning business brought on by the rising oil prices. Whereas Prime Minister Thatcher had protocol officers to advise her when she visited Saudi Arabia, PRI had no such guidance. The resultant lack of understanding and failure to adapt to a different culture contributed directly to PRI's failure.

Most of the oil-rich states have had an acute shortage of local personnel to work on their development projects. Consequently, foreign workers have comprised a large portion of their work forces, for example, 60 percent of Saudi Arabia's in 1985. When PRI could not find sufficient qualified people locally, it filled four key positions through advertisements in London newspapers. Angela Clarke, an Englishwoman, was hired as editor and researcher, and three young Englishmen were hired as salesmen. The four left immediately for Bahrain. None of them had visited the Middle East before; all expected that they could carry out business in their accustomed way.

The salesmen, hired on a commission basis, expected that by moving aggressively they could make the same number of calls as would be normal in Great Britain. They were used to working about eight hours a day, to having the undivided attention of potential clients, and to restricting most conversation to the specifics of the business transaction.

What the salesmen sometimes found instead was less time to sell because of the Moslem requirement to pray five times per day and because of a further reduction of the work day during the holy month of Ramadan. Appointments often began after the scheduled time. When the salesmen finally got in to see Arab businessmen, they were often invited to go to a café, where the Arabs would divert the conversation to idle chitchat. Whether in a café or in the office, the drinking of coffee or tea seemed to have precedence over the business matter. It seemed further to the salesmen that the Arab

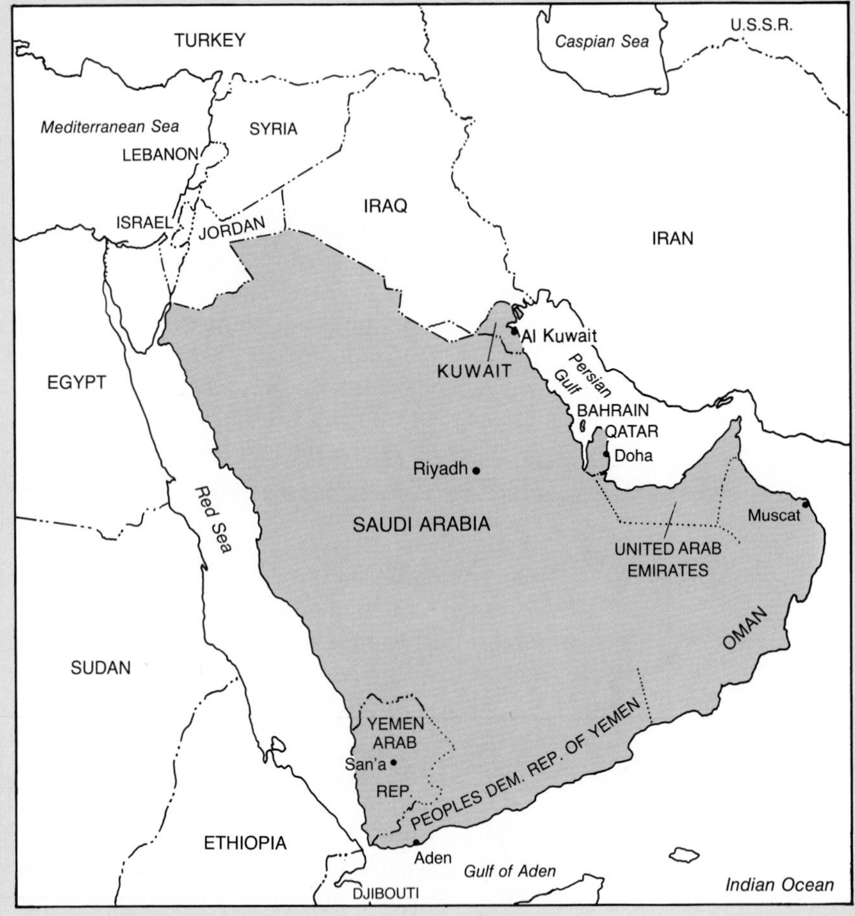

Figure 3.1

PRI's Business Contract in the Middle East

Note: PRI's contract included Bahrain, Kuwait, Oman, Qatar, Saudi Arabia, and the United Arab Emirates (Abu Dhabi, Ajman, Dubai, Fuzaira, Ras al-Khaimah, Sharjah, and Umm al-Qaiwain).

businessmen placed little importance on the appointments, since they frequently diverted their attention to friends who joined them at the café or in the office.

Angela Clarke was paid a salary instead of a commission, so PRI bore all of the expense resulting from her work's being thwarted in unexpected ways. PRI had based its government contract prices to prepare telephone directories on its English experience. The preparation turned out to be more time-consuming and costly. In the traditional Middle Eastern city there were no street names or building numbers. Ms. Clarke had to do a census of Bahraini establishments, identifying each with such prepositions as "below," "above," or "in front of" some meaningful landmark, before getting to the expected directory work.

Other problems occurred because of Angela Clarke's status as a single woman. She was in charge of the research in all thirteen states and was to have hired freelance assistants in most of them. Yet because she was a single woman, her entry to Saudi Arabia was denied by Saudi authorities. Her visa for Oman took six weeks each time to process. These experiences were particularly frustrating for Ms. Clarke because both Saudi Arabia and Oman sometimes eased the entry of single women when their business was of high local priority. In the states that she could enter, she sometimes was required to stay only in hotels that government officials had approved for foreign women. Even there, she was prohibited from eating in the dining room unless accompanied by the hotel manager. Her advertisements to hire assistants were met by personal harassment and obscene telephone calls.

PRI's salesmen never adjusted in the new environment. Instead of pushing PRI to alter its commission scheme, they tried to change the way that Arab businessmen were dealing with them. For example, after a few months the salesmen refused to join their potential clients for refreshments. They became visibly irritated at "irrelevant" conversations, delays, and interruptions from outsiders. The Arab businessmen responded negatively. In fact, PRI received so many complaints from Arab businessmen that the salesmen had to be replaced. But by then, irrevocable harm had been done to PRI's sales.

Angela Clarke fared better, thanks to her compromises to Arab customs. She began wearing a wedding ring and registering at hotels as a married woman. When traveling, she ate meals in her room, conducted meetings in conference rooms, and had all incoming calls screened by the hotel operators. To avoid arrest by decency patrols, she wore long-sleeved blouses and below-the-knee length skirts in blue or beige. When PRI left the area, Angela Clarke stayed on to work for a Japanese bank in Bahrain. Still, in spite of her compromises, her inability to enter Saudi Arabia had forced PRI to send a salesman there in her place who was not trained to do the research.

The rapid growth and intrusion of foreigners into the region has created adjustment problems for foreigners and for the local societies as well. On one hand, foreign workers provide needed skills for the increasingly complex economy; on the other hand, Middle-Easterners fear that their presence will erode deep-seated values and traditions. In many cases, foreigners are expected to conform; in others, they are allowed to pursue their own customs in isolation from the local populace. For example, most Western television programming is immoral according to traditional Islamic standards. In some places, foreigners may acquire unscramblers to view Western television fare, but local people may not.

The Saudi government also had second thoughts about some of the culture's double standards. At one time, for example, male and female hotel guests were allowed to swim in the same pools in Saudi Arabia. This permission was rescinded, however: Saudis frequent the hotels and thus could be corrupted by viewing "decadent" behavior. Another example of a reevaluation of standards involved the availability of certain foods. When Angela Clarke and the salesmen first arrived in Bahrain, there were prohibitions on the sale of pork products, including imported canned foods. This prohibition was later modified, but grocers had to stock pork products in separate rooms in which only non-Muslims could work or shop.

These dual and changing standards for foreigners and citizens make adapting difficult for foreigners. This situation has been further complicated because the Middle East is going through such substantial, but uneven, economic and social transformation. This was well described as follows:

> *Changes that in other countries have been spread out over several generations are being accomplished in [a] few short years. Diesel trucks and jet airplanes are replacing camel caravans, but the camel has not yet been discarded. Modern architecture and broad, tree-lined avenues are replacing mudbrick houses on twisting streets, but mudbrick buildings are still evident. Nomads (Bedouins) are beginning to drive from place to place; but it is common to see a pickup truck or a Mercedes parked beside a traditional tent.*[2]

As contact increases between Arabs and Westerners, there will be increased cultural borrowing and meshing of certain aspects of traditional behavior. This meshing is apt to come slowly. A noted anthropologist summarized the Americans' misconception of change by the Saudis:

> *We tend to think of them as underdeveloped Americans—Americans with sheets on. We look at them as undereducated and rather poor at anything technological. All we have to do is to make believers out of them, get them the proper education, teach them English, and they will turn into Americans.*

In fact, when Saudi students who have spent time abroad return home they revert to traditional behavior. Likewise, foreigners, after completing an assignment in Saudi Arabia, return to their traditional behaviors. These behaviors indicate how deeply rooted both Saudi and Western traditions are.

INTRODUCTION

A business employs, sells to, buys from, is regulated by, and is owned by people. Therefore an international company must consider differences in groups of people or societies in order to predict and control its relationships and operations. The PRI case illustrates how human differences give rise to different business practices in varying parts of the world. When doing business abroad, a company should determine if the usual business practices in a foreign country differ from its home country experience or from what its management ideally would like to see exist. If customs differ, international management must then decide what, if any, adjustments are necessary to operate efficiently in the foreign country.

Some differences, such as acceptable attire, are discerned easily whereas others may be more difficult to perceive. For example, people in all cultures respond in given ways to situations, and as such, they take many things for granted. They expect that people from other cultures will respond the same way as those in their own culture, and they anticipate that duties and privileges will be similar to those of people in similar stations or positions in their own societies. All of these expectations may be disproven in another culture. In the PRI case, for example, the British salesmen budgeted time and considered that drinking coffee and chatting about nonbusiness activities in a café were "doing nothing," especially if "there was work to be done." The Arab businessmen, on the other hand, had no compulsion to finish at a given time, viewed time in a café as "doing something," and considered "small talk" a necessary prerequisite for evaluating whether the potential business partners could interact satisfactorily. Because of their belief that you "shouldn't mix business and pleasure," the Englishmen became nervous when friends of the Arab businessmen intruded. Yet the Arabs felt that "people are more important than business" and that there was nothing private about business transactions.

No one can learn all the differences in cultural norms between one's own country and the foreign place of business. Managers can, however, pinpoint those cultural areas that have been noted to cause the greatest operational problems. By understanding cultural differences, they can also note subtle differences.

Even when a company successfully identifies the differences in the foreign country where it intends to do business, must it alter its customary or preferred practices to be successful there? This is not an easy question. Although the PRI case illustrates the folly of not adjusting, international companies nevertheless have been very successful sometimes at introducing many new products, technologies, and operating procedures to foreign countries. Sometimes these introductions did not run counter to deep-seated attitudes, and in some cases the local society is willing to accept behaviors from foreigners that it would not accept from its own citizens. For example, an American female executive said, "I do business comfortably in Japan. I don't find myself subjected to the same kind of sexism that, they tell me, is prevalent in other areas of Japanese life. I am treated as an American businessperson.... Most people overseas are well aware of the differences between Americans and themselves."[3]

The Nation-State as Proxy of Society

The nation-state is a useful proxy of society because
- boundaries are cause and effect of national differences in norms
- laws fall primarily along national lines.

There is no universally satisfactory definition of a society; however, a **nation-state** is a workable shorthand approximation for use in international business since basic similarity among people is both a cause and effect of national boundaries. Furthermore, the laws governing business operations apply primarily along national lines. This does not imply that everyone in a country is alike; nor does it suggest that each country is unique in all respects. There are,

Limitations of country-by country analysis occur because
- not everyone in a country is alike
- variations within some countries are great
- commonalities link groups from different countries.

however, certain physical, demographic, and behavioral norms that may alter methods of conducting business from one country to another.

In using the nation-state as a point of reference, it should be understood that there is much greater variation within some countries than within others. Geographic and economic barriers may make it difficult for people in some countries to move from one region to another, thus limiting their interactions. In addition, government control may be so decentralized that the laws and government programs enhance regional separation. Even if there are no substantial geographic barriers, linguistic, religious, and ethnic differences within a country usually retard a fusing of the population into a homogeneous state. India, for example, is much more diverse than Denmark for all the reasons just given.

Of course, nationality is not the only way of grouping people. Everyone belongs to various other groups—for example, those based on profession, age, religion, and place of residence. There are many commonalities that might in some ways link groups from different countries more closely together than groups within a country. For instance, people in urban areas differ in certain attitudes from people in rural areas and managers have different work-related attitudes than production workers regardless of the country examined.[4] Therefore if we compare countries, we must be careful to examine relevant groups. If, for example, a firm is interested in predicting how a group of British scientists and a group of French scientists might work together, it would be more appropriate to see if there are differences in the two groups' approaches to solving problems rather than whether British and French problem-solving approaches in general are different. The common occupational bond might make scientists in the two countries more similar to each other than to nonscientists within either of the countries.

TYPES OF VARIABLES

There are too many human variables and different types of business functions for an exhaustive cause–effect discussion in one chapter. Depending on how we classify physical and behavioral variables and the business activities that they might influence, we can easily arrive at hundreds, or even thousands, of direct relationships.[5] This chapter concentrates on just a few of the variables that have been noted to influence business practices substantially. While we can describe a few of the effects that these may have on the process of management within this and subsequent chapters, we must let the reader anticipate the full range of possible adjustments. The latter part of the chapter highlights alternative approaches for determining and dealing with differences that exist in foreign countries as well as the changes in international firms themselves as they come in contact with new human environments.

PHYSICAL ATTRIBUTES

Variation

Differences in dominant characteristics can influence conduct of business.

Each country comprises people whose physical attributes vary widely; nevertheless, there are usually dominant characteristics. The variations are due largely to genetics and become less noticeable as people migrate and intermarry. Even in the absence of mixing with other groups, gene frequency (and thus, physical characteristics) may change over a period of time because of natural selection as humans adapt to the changing physical environment. There is also some evidence that the cultural environment, including social norms and responses, may affect physical attributes.[6]

International businesspeople must grasp the sometimes-subtle differences that may influence the conduct of business. For example, the susceptibility in a given population to certain diseases may affect the market for pharmaceutical products. But neither the market for automobiles nor the accounting practices of pharmaceutical firms would be affected by this tendency.

Appearance

Businesspeople must consider societies' self-stereotypes.

Appearance is among the most noticeable of human variations. While most such differences are apparent readily, there are a host of subtle variations that may be overlooked by nondiscriminating outsiders. For example, Asians complain that Western films and advertisements frequently depict Orientals' national backgrounds incorrectly. For example, they may identify a Chinese person as a Japanese or a Korean as a Thai.

Individuals' size would seem to be an obvious difference. However, one U.S. company unsuccessfully attempted to sell men's slacks in Japan based on U.S. tailoring patterns. Before the company discovered the sizing error, a competitor, who cut clothing to fit the slimmer Japanese customer, had preempted the market. In another case, a U.S. firm had good initial sales for its brassieres in West Germany but then witnessed a rapidly declining demand. Initially the decline was attributed wrongly to higher labor costs, which had to be passed on to consumers. Additional research revealed that there were size variations between German and U.S. women. This difference was complicated by varied buying behavior on the part of the German women, who were not prone to try on merchandise in the store or to return it because of discomfort. Instead, they simply did not make repeat purchases. As a result, there was an initial lack of the necessary feedback.

Physical differences must be taken into consideration in such business functions as product changes, machinery height, and selection of advertising message. Also, idealized traits have an impact. People often have culture-wide wishful stereotypes. For example, U.S. advertisements typically depict individuals who are younger and thinner than the majority of the people toward whom the product is aimed. In West Germany, the tall Nordic type is the ideal, though most Germans are actually no taller than the average Pole or French person.[7]

BEHAVIORAL ATTRIBUTES

Businesspeople agree that cultural differences exist, but disagree on what they are.

In every society there are specific learned norms based on attitudes, values, and beliefs. These norms constitute societal **culture.** Visitors remark on differences; experts write about them; and people managing affairs across countries find that results cannot be fully explained by economic models.[8] Great controversy exists, however, as to what these differences are because of an acknowledged problem of measuring variances.[9] Culture cannot be isolated easily from such factors as economic and political conditions and institutions. An opinion survey, for example, may reflect a short-term response to temporary economic conditions rather than the basic values and beliefs that will have longer-term effects on how business can be managed. Different cultures may share values, but may order them differently if it becomes necessary to trade off the achievement of one for another. This is illustrated by a question posed to groups of Asian and U.S. businessmen: "If you were on a sinking ship with your wife, your child, and your mother who could not swim, which one would you save if you could rescue only one?" In the United States, about 60 percent chose the child and about 40 percent the wife, with none choosing the mother. All of the Asians chose the mother.[10] Although this example is outside the business realm, it illustrates that different nationalities may prioritize among organizational objectives differently. Businesspeople must be very tentative about proclaiming existing differences and appropriate reactions.

Despite these problems, considerable research conducted in recent years indicates that some aspects of culture are significantly different across national borders and have a substantial impact on how business is conducted normally in different countries. There also has been an upsurge in studies comparing business operations in industrial countries, whereas most interest historically was in primitive areas where little international business occurs. One of the common means of research has been the reliance on trained experts, usually cultural anthropologists, to relay their observations of a national character. This method was used extensively during World War II, for example, to predict how the enemy would react to different situations. Another method is to compare carefully paired samples of organizational practices from two or more countries. The following discussion highlights some of the major findings of such research.

Group Affiliations

Affiliations can be:
- Ascribed
- A reflection of resources and position
- Acquired

All countries' populations are commonly subdivided into groups, and individuals belong to more than one group. Affiliations determined by birth are known as **ascribed group memberships;** these include differentiations based on sex, family, age, caste, and ethnic, racial, or national origin. Among **acquired group memberships** (those not determined by birth) are religion, political affiliation, and professional and other associations. The type of membership often reflects individuals' place in the social stratification system as well. Every society has stratification, such as valuing people in managerial and technical positions over production workers.

Performance capability is viewed most highly in some societies.

Egalitarian societies place less importance on group membership.

Competence versus group affiliation. In some societies, peoples' acceptance for jobs and promotions is based primarily on performance capabilities. This is the norm in the United States, for example. This does not mean, of course, that there is no discrimination against people in the United States because of their sex, race, or religion. However, the belief that competence should prevail is valued sufficiently highly that legislative and judicial actions in recent years have aimed at instituting that value. This value is far from universal. In many cultures, competence is of secondary importance, and the belief that it is right to place some other criterion ahead of competence is held just as strongly as competence is in the United States. Whatever factor is given primary importance—such as the relative weight given to seniority, sex, or some other factor—will largely affect who is eligible to fill certain positions and how their compensation will be determined primarily.[11]

The more egalitarian, or open, a society is, the less difference ascribed group membership will make in access to rewards. Sometimes membership rigidity actually extends to legal proscriptions. For example, in South Africa, blacks, whites, and coloreds enjoy eligibility for certain jobs. Frequently, memberships simply prevent large groups of people from getting the preparation that would equally qualify them. In countries with poor government education systems, elite groups send their children to private schools while other children receive inferior public education.

Country-by-country attitudes vary toward
- male versus female roles
- importance of youth vs. older age
- family versus nonfamily ties.

Importance of different group memberships. Although there are almost unlimited ways of defining group memberships, three types of international contrasts (sex, age, and family) should indicate both how widespread these differences are and how important they are to business considerations.

Sex-based Groups

There are strong country-specific differences in attitudes toward males and females. Recall the case at the beginning of this chapter and the fact that the female editor for PRI could not get permission to enter Saudi Arabia. Saudi Arabia is the most extreme example of behavioral rigidity related to sex. There, separation is maintained at a greater level even than in most other Islamic countries. Schools are separate as is most social life: Only about 10 percent of women work outside the home; those who do remain separate from men. To get to work, women are prohibited legally from driving cars and are socially restricted from riding in a taxi without a male relative. Most of the jobs for women are in professions with little or no male contact, such as teaching or giving medical treatment to other women. When women do work in integrated organizations, the Saudis feel it necessary to put partitions between them and male employees.

In Saudi Arabia, the sheltering of women is also reflected in education statistics. The ratio of males to females in elementary school is 1.5 to 1; in universities it is over 2 to 1.[12] Even between countries in which women constitute a large portion of the working population there are vast differences in the types of jobs considered "male" or "female." In thirty-seven African countries less than 5 percent of the manufacturing employees are women, yet in Mali, the figure is over 70 percent. In El Salvador over 25 percent of managerial positions are filled by women, compared to less than 10 percent in Peru and Venezuela.[13]

Expected male and female behaviors may carry over to other aspects of the work situation as well. For example, Molex, a U.S. manufacturer of connectors which has a manufacturing facility in Japan invited its Japanese workers and their spouses to a company dinner one evening. Neither wives nor female employees appeared. To comply with Japanese standards, the company now has a "family day" which is acceptable for female attendance.[14]

Age-based Groups

Age involves some curious variations. Many cultures assume that age and wisdom are correlated, with a resultant seniority-based system of advancement. Until the 1980s in the United States, retirement at age 60 or 65 was mandatory in most companies, and relative youthfulness has even been an advantage. This quest for youthfulness does not, however, carry over to the U.S. political realm, where there are relatively high minimum age requirements for many posts with no mandatory retirement age.

Family-based Groups

In some societies, especially Mediterranean and Latin American countries, the family constitutes the most important group membership. An individual is accepted largely on the basis of the social status or respectability of his or her family rather than on individual achievement. Because family ties are so strong, there also may be a compulsion to cooperate closely within the family unit but to be distrustful of links involving others. Within Greek businesses, for example, workers in family restaurants cooperate and mobilize their efforts to attain success much better than workers in large organizations where people are from many different families.[15]

Barriers to employment on the basis of age or sex are undergoing substantial changes in many parts of the world. Thus statistical and attitudinal studies even a few years old are unreliable. One of these changes has involved the growing number of women and men in the United States in occupations previously dominated by the other sex. Between 1975 and 1985, for example, the portion of male secretaries, telephone operators, and nurses rose substantially as did the portion of female architects, bartenders, and bus drivers.[16] During the same period in Saudi Arabia the percent of female enrollment in universities more than doubled.

Local attitudes may force hiring by local norms or opinions.

Some effects on international business hiring practices. Even if individuals have the qualifications for a certain position and there are no legal barriers for hiring them, social obstacles may still have an impact. Other workers, customers, local shareholders, or governmental officials may oppose certain groups, creating an added risk of failure.

Class structures may be so rigid within one type of group that they are difficult to overcome in other contexts. One U.S. firm set up a plant in Taiwan without realizing the strength of the class structure, which is built largely on the military hierarchy. The U.S. managers hired the person they thought would be the most qualified individual to head the organization. In practice, however, he consistently deferred to a subordinate who had outranked him during their military experience. In many African countries the tribal relationship is still very important. To attract workers in some rural areas, it may be necessary to get permission from tribal chiefs by compensating them.

Importance of Work

Most people work for more than basic necessities in industrial countries.

There are different motives for work in different places.

People work for a number of reasons. Most people in industrial societies could satisfy their basic needs for food, clothing, and shelter by working fewer hours than they do. What, then, motivates them to work more? Reasons for working and the relative importance of work among human activities may be explained largely by the interrelationship of the cultural and economic environment of the country in which one lives. The differences in motivation help to explain management styles, product demand, and levels of economic development.

Attitudes may change as economic gains change.

Protestant ethic. Max Weber, a German sociologist, observed near the turn of the century that the predominantly Protestant countries were the most economically developed. This **protestant ethic,** he reasoned, was an outgrowth of the Reformation, a time when work was viewed as a means of salvation. Adhering to this belief, people preferred to transform productivity gains into additional output rather than into additional leisure.[17] Although few societies today hold to this strict basic concept of work for work's sake, leisure is valued more highly in some societies than in others. In the United States, for example, where incomes probably allow for considerably more leisure than most people take, there is still much disdain for, on the one hand, the millionaire playboy who contributes nothing to society and, on the other, for the person who lives on welfare. People who are forced to give up work, such as retirees, complain strongly of their inability to do anything "useful." This view may be contrasted with those that predominate in some other societies, such as rural India, where the living of a simple life with minimum material achievements is still considered a desirable end in itself.

In industrial countries today personal economic achievement is thought commendable. The same holds true for some rapidly developing Asian countries. In contrast, it has been argued that many economies are characterized by limited economic needs that are an outgrowth of the culture. If incomes start to rise, workers tend to reduce their efforts so that personal income remains unchanged.[18] A number of observers have argued that this may be a very short-lived phenomenon and that expectations rise slowly on the basis of past economic achievement. Most of us believe we would be happy with just "a little bit more"—until we have that "little bit more," which then turns out to be not quite enough.

People are more eager to work if

- rewards for success are positive
- there is some uncertainty of success.

Belief in success and reward. One factor that influences the attitude toward working is the perceived likelihood of success and rewards. The concepts of success and reward are closely related. Generally people have little enthusiasm for efforts that seem too easy or too hard—in other words, where the probability of success or failure seems almost certain. For instance, few of us are eager to run a foot race against either a snail or a race horse because the outcome in either case is too certain. Our highest enthusiasm is when the uncertainty is high, probably by racing another human of about our same ability. The reward for successfully completing an effort, such as winning our imaginary foot races, may be high or low as well. People will usually work harder at any task, such as winning one of the foot races, when the reward from success is high compared with the reward from failure.

The same tasks performed in different countries will have different probabilities of success and different rewards associated with both success and failure. In cultures where the likelihood of success from working is low *and* where the perceived rewards of success are also low, there is a tendency to view work as a necessary evil. This may exist in harsh climates, in very poor areas, or among subcultures who experience discrimination. At the other extreme, there is also little enthusiasm for the work itself. This has been noted in Scandinavia, for example, where rewards tend to be high and are similar, regardless of how hard one works because the Scandinavian tax structure and public policies redistribute income from high earners to low earners. The greatest enthusiasm for work exists where high uncertainty of success is combined with some probability for a very positive reward for success.[19]

Work ethic is related to economic achievement.

Work as a habit. Another factor in the trade-off between work and leisure is that the pursuit of leisure activities may itself have to be learned. After a long period of sustained work, people may have problems in deciding what to do with free time. This view helps to explain the continued drive for greater achievement in some societies that already have considerable material goods. One study, in attempting to determine why some parts of Latin America developed a higher economic level and desire for material achievement than others, attributed differences to the fact that some Spanish settlers worked themselves rather than using slave or near-slave labor. In such areas as Antioquia in Colombia, the Spanish settlers thus developed a work ethic and became the industrial leaders of the country.[20] So, when comparing the importance of work from one country to another, the effects of habit cannot be overlooked. An international firm may thus find it easier in some societies than in others to motivate its work force with shorter work weeks or longer vacation periods.

High-need achievers want
- personal responsibility,
- calculated risks,
- performance feedback.

Lower-need achievers prefer smooth social relationships.

High-need achievement. The **high-need achiever** is a person who will work very hard to achieve material or career success as opposed to a person who is more concerned with developing smooth social relationships or spiritual achievements.[21] Three attributes distinguish the high-need achiever:

1. liking situations that involve personal responsibility for finding solutions to problems;
2. setting moderate achievement goals for taking calculated risks; and
3. wanting concrete feedback on performance.

The average manager's interest in material or career success varies substantially from one country to another,[22] which explains situations in which the local manager reacts differently than the international firm may expect or wish. For instance, a purchasing manager with a high affiliation need may be much more concerned with developing an amiable and continuing relationship with suppliers than in reducing costs and speeding delivery. Or in some countries the local managers may place such organizational goals as employee and social welfare ahead of the foreign firm's priorities for growth and efficiency.

Need hierarchy. The **hierarchy of needs** is one well-known motivation theory.[23] (See Fig. 3.2.) According to this scheme, people try to fulfill lower-order needs sufficiently before moving on to higher ones. A person will work

Figure 3.2
Need Hierarchy Comparisons

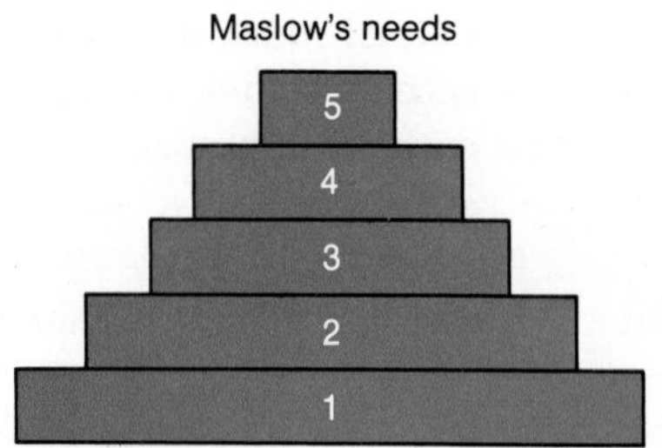

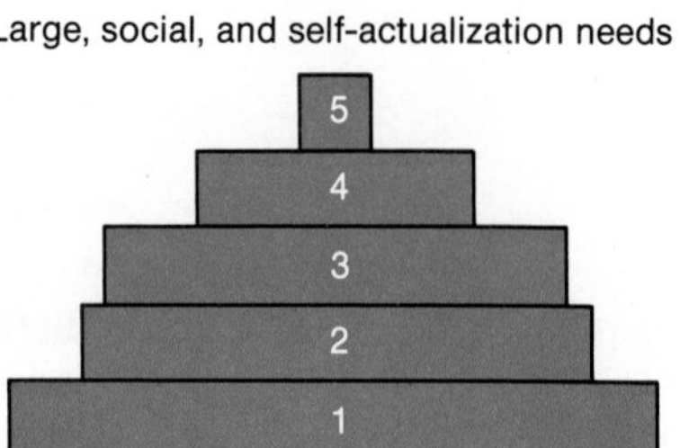

to satisfy a need, but once it is fulfilled it is no longer a motivator. This fulfillment is not an all-or-nothing situation. However, because lower-order needs are more important, they must be more nearly fulfilled before triggering a higher-order need to be an effective motivator. For instance, the physiological needs may have to be 85 percent satisfied before triggering a safety need. The safety need may have to be only 70 percent satisfied before triggering the social need, and so on. The relative fulfillment requirements are shown by the horizontal bars in part A of Fig. 3.2.

The importance of needs differs among countries.

This theory is helpful for differentiating the reward preferences employees have in different countries. In very poor countries, most workers may be so deprived that a firm can motivate them by concentrating solely on the provision of enough food and shelter. Elsewhere, other needs will have to be gratified to motivate workers. Observers have noted that people from different countries attach different importance to various needs and even place some of the higher-order needs in different orders. One of the most extensive studies involved data from 116,000 questionnaires from employees within the same U.S. multinational firm in fifty countries. Among the findings was that the employees in the Netherlands and the Scandinavian countries placed more importance on social needs and less on self-actualization than did the employees in the United States. In other words, in Scandinavia and the Netherlands group-centered motivation methods may have a more positive impact on employees than individual job-enrichment methods, which are important in the United States.[24]

Importance of Occupation

The perception of "best" jobs varies somewhat by country.

In every society, certain occupations carry a perception of greater economic, social, or prestige reward than others. This view will determine to a great extent the numbers and qualifications of people who will seek employment in a given occupation as individuals compete for high-reward jobs. Although overall patterns are universal (for example professionals ranked ahead of street cleaners) there are some national differences. For instance, physicians tend to be ranked higher than university professors in the United States, probably because of the importance in the United States of financial rewards.

The rank is reversed in Japan, probably because of the importance the Japanese attach to education and their emphasis on clean occupations.[25] The reluctance of educated people to dirty their hands or associate directly with operative workers has sometimes made it difficult to get lower-level managers in Latin America. To generalize, in Latin American culture there is a class of leisure, a class of people who work with their minds, and a third class of people who work with their hands.[26] The importance of business as a profession is also predictive of the degree of difficulty that an international firm may have in hiring qualified managers. In many countries, people with the desired educational qualifications prefer to work in governmental posts rather than in business. Therefore, the international firm in such a situation may have to undertake more training programs because it must hire relatively uneducated people.

Another international difference involves the desire to work for an organization versus being one's own boss. More Belgians and French people than most people of other nationalities prefer, if possible, to go into business for themselves. Going by the number of retail establishments in these countries compared on a per capita basis with the number in most other countries, we may conclude that this is true. Psychological studies also show that French and Belgian workers place a greater importance on personal independence from the organizations employing them than workers in many other countries.[27]

Jobs with low prestige usually go to people whose skills are in low demand. In the United States, for example, such occupations as babysitting, delivering newspapers, and carrying groceries traditionally have been done largely by teenagers, who grow out of the jobs through additional age and training. In most less-developed countries, these are not transient occupations; rather, they are filled by adults who have very little opportunity of moving on to higher-reward positions. (In the United States, as well, there has been a recent concern that menial jobs are becoming less transient.)

Self-Reliance

There are national variations in the preference for autocratic versus participatory leadership and self-determination versus fatalism.

Superior–subordinate relationships. There are national differences in the preferences for autocratic versus consultative managerial styles. Austria, Israel, New Zealand, and the Scandinavian countries are among those having a strong preference for superiors to consult with subordinates before making decisions. Some countries with the highest preference for autocratic leadership are Malaysia, Mexico, Panama, Guatemala, and Venezuela. There is a significant correlation between countries' preferences for autocratic leadership and the incidence of autocratic political leadership.[28] Clearly, organizations may find it easier to initiate worker participation methods in some countries than in others.

Trust. Although trust is difficult to measure, various studies indicate that national groups differ in the degree to which individuals have trust in others.[29] The greater the trust, the greater the ability and eagerness of people to establish rapport with others. Where trust is high, both managers and subordinates have more desire for participative than authoritative decision making; they actually tend to function this way. Certainly one of the factors leading to acceptance of new products, as in the United States, is the trust in the manufacturer and the legal system that individuals will not be cheated. There may be similar acceptance in dealing with a new firm. Some nationalities have high levels of trust and get right to the point in a business discussion. Conversely, people of some other nationalities may spend more time in preliminary discussion before getting down to business. This difference, although partially due to cultural formalities, is also affected by the need of some groups to seek more cues as to whether they can trust others in a business relationship. In some parts of the world nearly all transactions among individuals are carried out by cash rather than check as an assurance of payment. In this type of environment, it is difficult to raise funds through the sale of company shares, since people prefer to place their funds in visible assets they can control themselves.

Degree of fatalism. If people believe strongly in self-determination they may be willing to work hard to achieve goals and to blame and reward themselves and others for performance. A belief in fatalism, on the other hand, may be a barrier to the acceptance of a basic cause–effect relationship. Religious differences play a part: Conservative Christian, Buddhist, Hindu, and Moslem societies tend to view occurrences as "the will of God." In such an atmosphere it is difficult to persuade personnel to plan ahead. Even getting workers to cooperate in accident or damage prevention—by checking tire pressure, for example—may be hard. Studies show that there are national differences even among managers in fairly developed societies.[30]

Individual versus group. In many Western countries, people look up to personal achievement. In fact, people compete openly with each other within a company's work place in order to gain a greater share of compensation or prestige rewards. Based on this background, at a meeting of his professional staff in Asia, a U.S. design engineer singled out an individual to credit him for his performance on a project. Rather than motivating the employee or others to perform well, the design engineer's comment created embarrassment for people at the meeting. In Japan, collective effort is valued and the Japanese are reluctant to single out individuals.[31]

We have already discussed the varying degree of importance in different societies of the family unit as a group. There are also differences in what is normally conceived to constitute a family. In some countries, for example, the nuclear family dwelling containing a husband, wife, and minor children is customary; however, this is not the pattern for most people in the world. Instead, the same household may contain a vertically extended family (several generations) and/or a horizontally extended one (aunts, uncles, and cousins). This difference has a number of effects on business. Material rewards from an individual's work may be less effective in such societies, since these rewards attract and are divided among more people. Geographic mobility is reduced, since more people in a family would have to find new jobs. Purchasing decisions may be more complicated because of the interrelated roles of family members. Even if the extended family does not live together, mobility may be reduced because people prefer to remain near relatives. Security and social needs also may be met more extensively at home rather than in the work place.

Communications

All languages are complex and reflective of environment.

Common language within countries is a unifying force.

Language. Linguists have determined that even very primitive societies have complex languages that reflect the environment in which people live. Because of varying environments, it is often difficult to translate directly from one language to another. For example, people living in the temperate zone of the Northern Hemisphere are accustomed to referring to summer as roughly the months of June, July, and August, whereas people in tropical zones may use the term *summer* to denote their dry season, which varies substantially in time of year from one country to another. Some things simply do not translate. For instance, in Spanish there is no word to refer to everyone who works in a business organization. Instead there is one word, *empleados,* which refers to white-collar workers, and another word, *obreros,* which refers to laborers. This differentiation reflects the substantial class difference attributed to each group. Another interesting difference in phrasing between English and Spanish, which undoubtedly reflects attitudes, is that a clock "runs" in English but "walks" in Spanish.

Languages such as English and Spanish have such widespread acceptance that there is generally not a high compulsion for native speakers to learn other languages. Commerce and other cross-border associations can be conducted easily with other nations that have the same official language. When a second language is studied, the choice is usually based on the utility in dealing with other countries. English and French traditionally have been common choices because of the commercial links developed during colonial periods. In countries that do not share a common language with other countries (e.g., Finland and Greece) there is a much greater need to study a second or multiple languages in order to function internationally. But English, especially American English, is being added to languages worldwide. Some 20,000 English words have entered the Japanese language; the Russian word for tight denim pants is *dzhinsi* (pronounced "jeansy"); and the arbiter of the

French language added over 600 English words to its standard usage in 1986.[32]

Even within the same language there may be substantial differences. The terms *corn, maize,* and *graduate studies* in the United Kingdom correspond to *wheat, corn,* and *undergraduate studies,* respectively, in American English. Although the wrong choice of words is usually just a source of brief embarrassment, a poor translation may be tragic. Bad translations have been blamed for structure collapses at construction sites in the Middle East.[33] In contracts, correspondence, negotiations, advertisements, and social gatherings, words must be chosen carefully.

Language itself may reflect the internal cohesion of a country as well as its relative ability to deal with other countries. In some countries, such as Japan and Portugal, almost everyone has the same native language. However, in about half the countries of the world, there are multiple language groups which may be very difficult to unify. In some cases, the official language of the country may actually be spoken by only a minority of the inhabitants. This is true in India and Zaire, where, nevertheless, most power has accrued to people who number among those few who speak the official language.[34]

Silent language includes such things as color, distance, time, and status cues.

Silent language. Not all communication occurs in the form of a formal language. We all give and receive messages by a host of cues other than formal language: These other cues form a **silent language.**[35] For example, a particular color conjures up meanings based on experience within our own culture. In most Western countries, black historically has been associated with death, yet white in parts of the Far East and purple in Latin America have the same connotation. To be successful, the color of products and their advertisements must relate to the consumers' frame of reference.

Distances between people during conversation is a learned process that differs by society. For example, in the United States the customary distance for a business discussion is five to eight feet; for personal business it is eighteen inches to three feet.[36] When the distance is closer or greater than is customary, a person tends to feel very uneasy. A U.S. manager conducting business discussions in Latin America may constantly be moving backward to avoid the closer conversational distance to which the Latin American official is accustomed. At the conclusion of the session, both parties may have an unexplainable distrust of the other.

Punctuality is another confusing area. For a business appointment in the United States, participants usually arrive early. For a dinner at someone's home, guests arrive on time or a few minutes late; for a cocktail party, they may arrive a bit later. In a foreign country, the accepted punctuality may differ drastically. A U.S. businessperson in Latin America, for example, may consider it discourteous that the Latin American manager does not keep to the appointed time. Latin Americans may find it equally discourteous if the U.S. businessperson arrives for dinner at the invited time.

Cues concerning a person's relative position may be particularly difficult to grasp. A U.S. businessperson, who tends to place a greater reliance on objects as prestige cues, may underestimate the importance of a foreign counterpart who has no large private office with a wood desk and carpeting. A foreigner may react similarly if U.S. counterparts open their own garage doors and mix their own drinks.

Cues are perceived selectively and differ among societies.

Perception and processing. We perceive cues selectively. We may identify by any of our senses (sight, smell, feel, sound, taste) and by various ways within each of these. For example, visually we can sense color, depth, and shape. Among societies, there are differences in the cues used to perceive things. This is partly physiological—for example, genetic differences in eye pigmentation enable some groups to differentiate colors more finely. Another reason for differences is related to culture—for example, relative richness of vocabulary can cause people to notice subtle differences in color.[37] Vocabulary differences reflect cultural differences: For example, there are more than 6000 different words in Arabic for camels, their body parts, and the equipment associated with camels.[38]

Regardless of social differences, once people perceive cues, they process them. Information processing is universal in that all societies categorize, plan, and quantify. In terms of categorization, we bring objects together according to their major shared function. Something to sit upon is thus called a chair in English whether it is large or small, made of wood or plastic, upholstered or not. All societies have future and conditional tenses; thus all societies plan. All societies have numbering systems as well. But the specific ways societies go about grouping things, dealing with the future, and counting differ substantially.[39]

Idealists settle principles first and prefer mass action.

Pragmatists
- settle small issues first
- want specific measurable achievements.

Evaluation of information. Although there are vast differences within countries, there are nevertheless national norms in the degree to which people try to settle principles before they try to settle small issues or vice versa: **idealism** versus **pragmatism.** From a business standpoint, differences manifest themselves in a number of ways. The idealist sees the pragmatist as too interested in trivial details, whereas the pragmatist sees the idealist as too theoretical. Labor, in a more pragmatist society, tends to ask for very specific things, such as a pay increase of one dollar per hour. In a more idealistic society, labor tends to make vague demands, depending on mass action to demonstrate its principles.[40]

Morals and Etiquette

There is no universally accepted moral behavior.

The way we normally act in our native culture may be subject to different degrees of acceptance and interpretation in another society. Practices that are accepted in one locale may even be considered immoral in another. The depiction of a man and woman in close contact for an advertisement in a Western country must be changed in many Asian countries to fit a moral context in which even holding hands in public is taboo. U.S. motion picture exports illustrate different moral conceptions based on different attitudes toward punishment for crimes, body exposure, sexual explicitness, and violence.

Gift giving represents an etiquette dilemma. If a Western businessperson in the Far East fails to bring small but thoughtful gifts to the Far Eastern counterpart, that official may not only consider it a breach of etiquette, but may also feel that the foreign businessperson places little interest or emphasis on the meeting. At the same time, if they are not invited into private homes, some foreign managers, unaware that such invitations are not customary, may develop the same wrong opinion of Far Eastern associates.

In many places it is customary to give payments to governmental officials in order to obtain their services or to obtain governmental contracts. While these payments are not part of coded regulations and may even be condemned officially, they are well embedded in local common-law practices. In Mexico, for example, it is common for companies to give tips once a month to the postman. Otherwise, the mail simply gets lost.[41] The going rate of payment is rather easily ascertained and is usually graduated on the basis of ability to pay. It is a fairly efficient means of taxation in countries that pay civil servants poorly and do not have means of effectively collecting income taxes. Still, many of these tips or bribes are frequently viewed by home country constituents as so immoral that home country laws are enforced against practices in foreign operations. (This subject is discussed in greater detail in Chapter 11.)

Unfortunately, there are so many behavioral rules that businesspeople cannot expect to memorize all of them for every country where business relations might occur. Even the form of address to use is something that varies widely, such as whether to use the given or the surname, which of several surnames to use, and whether a wife takes the husband's name.[42] Fortunately, though, there are fairly up-to-date guide books which have been compiled geographically based on the experience of many successful international managers.[43]

RECONCILIATION OF INTERNATIONAL DIFFERENCES

Are Cultures Converging?

There are three scenarios of cross-cultural contact:
- smaller cultures are absorbed by national and global ones
- subcultures transcend national boundaries

Contact across cultures worldwide is more widespread than ever before. Several factors, including advances in transportation and communications along with rising personal incomes allow people to enjoy greater freedom to travel. Global competition has grown also, so that many of the same international companies compete against each other in many different parts of the world. These factors have led to a leveling of cultures. More similar products

- organizations are more similar worldwide but people in organizations are holding on to cultures.

are demanded and more similar methods are used to produce them globally. International companies also act to bring in new products that may then influence changes in culture, such as the playing of street hockey in Singapore after Toys 'R' Us introduced equipment there.[44] Many small cultural groups are being absorbed into more dominant national ones, and in recent years, many regional languages have become extinct.

On the other hand, there is evidence of emerging subcultures within countries because of the influx of people who retain traditional ways rather than assimilate completely. There is also evidence that some groups accept new ideas, products, and technologies more readily than others. All of these factors might lead to future problems in defining culture along national lines. The distinct subcultures within a country may have less in common with each other than with subcultures in other countries.

There is a third possibility that cultures will converge in some, but not all, respects. Clearly, organizations are becoming more similar internationally in what they produce and in what technologies they use. However, people within the same organizations are continuing to hold onto their national differences as strongly as ever.[45] In other words, some tangibles are becoming more universal; but the way people cooperate, attempt to solve problems, and are motivated are not becoming more universal.

Cultural Awareness

Problem areas in cultural awareness are:

- things learned subconsciously
- stereotypes
- societal subgroups.

Regardless of which of the above three scenarios might emerge, there is nearly a consensus that at least some cultural differences will persist, thereby complicating international business. Where these differences exist, businesspeople must decide whether and to what extent they should adapt home country practices to the foreign environment. But before making that decision, managers must be aware of what the differences are. This is not an easy task. There is much disagreement about the differences and no foolproof method of building better cultural awareness.

In any situation, some people are more prone to say the right thing at the right time while others unintentionally offend. Most people are more aware of differences in things that they have learned consciously, such as table manners, than in things that they have learned subconsciously, such as methods of approaching problem solving. Still, there is general agreement that awareness and sensitivity can be improved. In this chapter we have presented a framework of human cultural factors that have been especially noted to cause business adjustments on a country-to-country basis. By paying special attention to these factors, businesspeople can start building awareness.

Reading about and discussing other countries and researching how people from other countries regard the home culture can be very instructive. The opinions presented must be measured carefully. Very often they represent unwarranted stereotypes, an accurate assessment but only of a subsegment of the particular country, or a situation that has since undergone change. By getting varied viewpoints, businesspeople can judge assessments of different cultures better. They can also observe the behavior of those people who are well accepted or those with whom one would like to be associated in a given society in order to emulate their behavior.

Fitting Needs to the Company Position

Not all companies need the same degree of foreign cultural awareness. Nor must a particular company have a consistent degree of awareness during the course of its operations. Refer to Fig. 3.3 for an illustration of relative needs. The further a firm moves from domestic operations on any one of the four axes shown, the more effort needs to be placed on building awareness of cultural differences. Ordinarily, there is no need for a company to tackle multiple functional adjustments in multiple dissimilar countries simultataneously.

Axis A in Fig. 3.3 may be related to the international business objectives introduced in Chapter 1. Near the center are foreign operations aimed toward achieving a limited functional objective. For example, in a purely market-seeking operation, such as exporting from the home country, the company must be aware of cultural factors that may influence the marketing program. Consider advertising, which may be affected by the real and wishful physical norms of the target market, the roles of group membership in terms of status and buying decisions, and the perception of different words and images. A company undertaking a purely resource-seeking international activity can ignore the effects of cultural variables on advertising, but must consider factors that may influence supply, such as methods of managing a foreign labor force. With multi-functional activities, such as producing and selling a product in a foreign country, the added functions warrant concern with a wider array of cultural relationships. At the far extreme are operations that are integrated across various countries. In these situations, a firm must consider the cultural differences between its home country and a foreign country and the distinctions among the various foreign countries involved.

Axis B shows that the more countries in which a firm is doing business, the more cultural nuances it must consider. Think of the adjustments a manager from corporate headquarters who visits the company's foreign distributors would undergo. The more countries visited, the more cumbersome the trip would be and the more predeparture training time would be needed.

The relationship between the similarity between countries and the relative need for cultural adjustment is shown on the C Axis. For example, a U.S. firm starting business in Australia will find greater similarity to its cultural experience than if it were starting a new business in Japan.

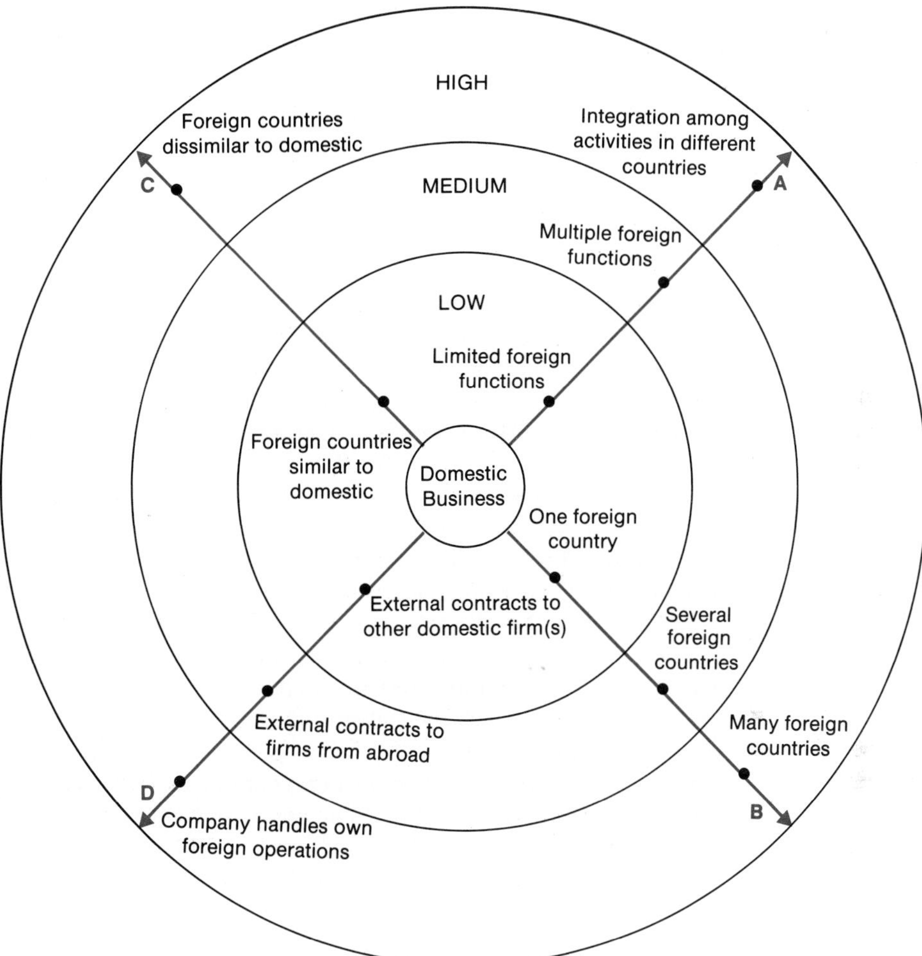

Figure 3.3
Cultural Awareness Needs Related to Foreign Operations

A company may handle foreign operations on its own or it may contract another firm to handle them, as shown on the D Axis in Fig. 3.3. The risk of making operating mistakes because of misunderstanding may be effectively reduced if operations are turned over to another firm. If the firm contracts with another domestic firm experienced in the foreign country, it can avoid direct dealings with the foreign environment. If the business is contracted to a foreign firm, then the company must understand the cultural nuances that may influence the relationship between the two companies, such as the means of negotiating an agreement or the ordering of objectives for the operation. As a company gains experience in the foreign country, its managers normally learn to operate efficiently there and may then consider internalizing activities that it had previously contracted to another firm.

Since companies usually increase foreign operations over a period of time, they may expand their knowledge of cultural factors in tandem with their expansions of foreign operations.

Dangers of Polycentrism

Polycentrists are overwhelmed by national differences and risk not introducing workable changes.

Polycentrism is a geographic decentralization so that "our man in Rio" conducts business in what he says is "the Brazilian way."[46] At an extreme, the term characterizes an individual or organization being "overwhelmed by the differences, real and imaginary, great and small, between its many operating environments."[47] Since most discussions on foreign business focus on uniquenesses abroad and the attendant problems that international firms have encountered, it is understandable that many managers develop this attitude. If, in reviewing domestic business practices, managers concentrated on the numerous failed actions due to misjudged markets, resistance to change, and misunderstood communications, they might become overly cautious in their own operating environments as well. In reality, it is uncertain whether companies' practices abroad are more prone to failure than those at home.

If a company's views are too polycentric, the company may shy away from certain areas or from transferring intact home country practices or resources that, in fact, may work well abroad. For example, American Express assembled its worldwide personnel managers for an exchange of views. The complaints from the overseas managers centered on certain corporate directives that "do not fit our country." The impression generated was that foreign operations were so unique that each overseas office should develop its own procedures independently. Further talks revealed, however, that the complaints focused on a particular personnel evaluation form. To delegate the proposed control would risk not introducing some of the other standard forms and procedures that had worked successfully abroad. Furthermore, it would risk duplication of efforts, which may have been more costly than the problems of trying to administer the ill-suited evaluation directives. The additional discussions also generated comments for the first time from the personnel managers in U.S. domestic offices who had received the same corporate instructions. They concluded that they had as many problems with the personnel form as had their foreign counterparts: The problem, originally attributed to environmental differences, was in fact universal.

If an international firm is to compete effectively with local firms, it must usually perform some functions in a distinct way. Polycentrism may lead to such extensive delegation or to such extensive imitation of proven host country practices that innovative superiority is lost. Furthermore, control may be diminished as operations for each country move separately in order to foster local rather than worldwide objectives.

Dangers of Ethnocentrism

Ethnocentrists overlook national differences;
- ignore important variables
- think change easily introduced
- believe home country objectives should prevail.

Ethnocentrism is the belief that one's own group is superior. The term is used in international business to describe the firm or individual so imbued with the belief that what worked at home should work abroad that environmental differences are ignored. Ethnocentrism may fall into three categories. One type involves the oversight of important variables because a manager has become so accustomed to certain cause–effect relationships in the home country that differences abroad are ignored. To combat this type of ethnocentrism, the manager can refer to checklists of human variables in order to assure that the major factors are at least considered. A second type of ethnocentrism involves recognizing differences but assuming that the introduction of changes is both necessary and easily achieved. The problems accompanying this type of attitude will be discussed in the next section. A third type is manifested by the firm that, although recognizing both the environmental differences and the problems of change, operates abroad in order to achieve home-country rather than foreign or worldwide objectives. This type of operation may result in adverse long-term competitive viability because (1) the company does not perform as well as competitors, and (2) it develops opposition to its practices from host governments.

Change Agent or Changed Agent?

International firms often follow hybrid of home and foreign norms.

Between the extremes of polycentrism and ethnocentrism are hybrid business practices that are not exactly like the international company's home operations and not exactly like those of the typical host country firm. These are the most common means of reconciling differences. When the host-country environment is substantially different, the international firm must decide whether to get people in the host country to accept something new (in which case the firm will be acting as a change agent) or to have the firm itself make changes.

Managers must consider their own versus foreign value system.

Value system. It is much easier for someone to adapt to things that do not challenge that person's value system than to things that do. Whether someone eats a salad before or after the main course is usually a matter of some flexibility. Such things as different degrees of exposing one's body or the paying of bribes to government officials may, however, present needs for moral adjustment. In many cases, though, the foreigner or foreign firm may not be expected to adhere to the national norm. For example, many practices that Western culture considers "wrong" are either customary elsewhere or have been abolished very recently and could even be reinstated. These include chattel slavery, polygamy, concubinage, child marriage, and the burning of widows.[48] Although foreigners are not expected to participate in these practices, the exposure may be so traumatic to them that the foreigners cannot perform their duties efficiently.

The person who moves to a foreign country frequently encounters **culture shock,**"a generalized trauma one experiences in a new and different culture because of having to learn and cope with a vast array of new cultural cues and expectations, while discovering that your old ones probably do not fit or work."[49] Culture shock usually occurs near the beginning of a foreign assignment. If someone gets an extreme case of culture shock, his or her usefulness in a foreign assignment may be greatly impaired; fortunately, most people's culture shock begins to ebb after a month or two. Some patterns and implications for foreign transfers are discussed in Chapter 21.

The Society for Applied Anthropology, whose members advise agencies on instituting change in different cultures, has adopted a code of ethics to protect foreign cultures with which they come into contact. Among the considerations is whether or not a project of planned change will actually benefit the target population. This respect of other cultures is itself a Western cultural phenomenon that goes back at least as far as St. Ambrose's fourth century advice of "When in Rome, do as the Romans do." Elsewhere there has been no such compulsion to adjust. Because of differences in value systems in terms of what is a benefit, implementing this code is challenging.

The cost of making change may exceed benefits gained.

Cost-benefit of change. A firm must consider its sometimes opposite objectives of cost minimization and sales maximization along with its resources. We have noted, for example, that international firms tend to introduce the same or only slightly altered products into foreign markets instead of designing what would be best suited for maximum acceptance in those markets. This may make sense, even though it is costly to convince people to buy "the next best thing" and even though sales are not maximized. The cost of designing and producing a new product may make the product too expensive and the firm may lack the resources to make large-scale product changes.

Resistance to change may be lower if the number of changes is not too great.

Resistance to too much change. When Sears, Roebuck decided to open its first retail store in Spain, a major problem occurred with suppliers. Sears tried to deal with these suppliers in much the same way as it operates with U.S. suppliers. Among the many changes that Sears tried to introduce at the start were payments by check, firm delivery dates, standard sizes, no manufacturer's labels, and larger orders. Suppliers balked or did things their old way, claiming forgetfulness.[50] Acceptance by suppliers may have been easier had Sears made fewer demands on them at one time, and the company could have phased in its other policies over a period of time.

The more the change upsets the things important in the value system, the more resistance the firm will experience.

Importance of change. A Spanish textile factory opened in a community of Guatemala and tried to install training methods, work hours, and a host of other production "improvements" commonplace in more developed areas.

Not only did people refuse to work, but soldiers had to protect the factory from the community. The management retracted and gave in on those things that were most important to the potential workers. These included a four-hour period between shifts so that male workers could attend to agricultural duties and female workers could do household chores and nurse their infants. The laborers were willing to work Saturday afternoons in order to compensate for production lost during shift breaks.[51] The important lesson of this is that the more a change disrupts basic values, the more the people affected will resist the change. When changes do not interfere with deep-seated customs, then accommodation is much more likely. By giving in on matters that were most important to the workers, the foreign firm was able to gain an effective and committed work force.

People are more willing to implement change when they are involved in the decision.

Participation. One way to avoid undue problems if changes are to be introduced is to promote participation. By discussing the possibility of change, the firm may ascertain how strong resistance might be, stimulate the recognition of a need for improvement, and slacken fears of adverse consequences among individuals who otherwise might feel they have no say in their own destinies. Managers sometimes think of delegation or participation as characteristic of highly developed countries where people have the backgrounds to make substantial contributions. Experience with economic development programs, however, indicates that participation in even the most backward communities of the world may be extremely important. Two of the most successful development programs on record are the Vicos project in Peru and the Etawah project in India.[52] Unlike some other development programs, these projects relied heavily on participation in planning and enactment by the people of the communities.

People are more apt to support change when they see personal or reference group rewards.

Reward sharing. Sometimes a proposed change may have no foreseeable benefit for the people whose support is needed to assure its success. Production workers, have little incentive to shift to new work practices unless they see some benefits for themselves. A U.S. firm manufacturing electrical appliances in Mexico moved workers easily from radio to black-and-white television production. When the firm introduced color televisions, however, product defects inexplicably increased. The company learned that the workers were eager to turn out high-quality black-and-white sets because they or their friends might be consumers. The expensive color sets, though, were so far beyond their reach that the workers had no incentive to be careful in production. The firm therefore developed a bonus system for quality;[53] rewards may be in monetary compensation or prestige.

Managers should convince those who can influence others.

Opinion leaders. By discovering the local channels of influence, an international firm may locate opinion leaders to help speed up the acceptance of change. In Ghana, government health workers frequently ask permission and seek the help of village witch doctors before inoculating people or spraying huts to fight malaria. This achieves the desired result without destroying important social structures. Opinion leaders may emerge in different places, such as among youth in a rapidly changing society. An interesting use of this concept in Mexico involved sending low-level workers rather than supervisors to the parent plant in the United States. These workers returned as heroes among their peers and were emulated when they demonstrated new work habits.[54]

Firms should time change when there is likely to be least resistance.

Timing. Many good ideas never get applied effectively because they are ill-timed. Change brings uncertainty and insecurity: A labor-saving production method creates resistance because people fear losing their jobs. Fewer impediments will occur if the labor-saving methods are introduced when there is a labor shortage rather than a surplus, regardless of what management says will happen to employment. Attitudes and needs may change slowly or rapidly, so keeping abreast of these changes helps in determining timing. Volkswagen introduced small cars in the United States when substantial numbers of consumers were ready for small cars. The Henry J. and Crosley, two other small cars, were introduced to the U.S. market a few years earlier, too soon to be successful.

International firms
- change some things abroad
- change themselves when encountering foreign environments
- learn things abroad which they can apply at home.

Learning abroad. The discussion thus far has centered on the interaction between the international firm and the host society. The firm not only affects the relationship but may also be affected by it. It may change things abroad or alter its own activities to fit the foreign environment; it may also learn things that will be useful in its own home country or other operations.

The national practices most likely to be scrutinized for possible use in other countries are those from the countries that are doing best economically.[55] For example, there was a great focus on the British cultural character in the nineteenth century, when Britain was the economic leader. Then, at the turn of the century, attention was diverted to Germany and the United States. There has been a recent shift in attention toward Japan and South Korea as business theorists and practitioners have debated whether some of their successful business practices can be adopted successfully elsewhere. Whether a company is importing or exporting practices, one must consider the same factors when questioning whether and how change can be introduced.

SUMMARY

- National norms for physical and behavioral characteristics require international firms to evaluate their business practices.

- A given country may contain very distinct societies. Companies must also realize that people from some groups share more with people from certain foreign countries. People may also have more in common with similar groups in foreign countries than with people from different groups in their own countries.
- There are notable group differences in physical variations. Businesspeople must consider the effects that these variances may have on their practices as well as wishful stereotypes.
- Societal culture includes norms of behavior based on attitudes, values, and beliefs. Businesspeople agree that there are national differences but disagree as to what these differences are.
- Group affiliations based on sex, family, age, caste, religion, political preference, associations, and ethnic, racial, or national origin often reflect a person's degree of access to economic resources, prestige, social relations, and power. Among the effects of affiliations on business is the determination of who may be qualified and available for given jobs.
- Most people work far more than is necessary for the satisfaction of basic food, clothing, and shelter needs. The relative importance of work may be explained largely by the interrelationship of the cultural and economic environment. Among the explanations for a drive to work are the Protestant ethic; the degree to which people believe that work will bring success; a work ethic based on habit; achievement motivation; and fulfillment of higher-order needs.
- Occupations carry different perceptions of economic, social, and prestige rewards in different countries. People gravitate to jobs for which they perceive high rewards. The many international differences result in varied attitudes toward working for an organization (particularly business) versus self-employment.
- Self-reliance depends on trust of others and attitude toward nature and fate, whether a person believes an autocratic or participative relationship is preferable, and on cooperative group membership, especially the family.
- We communicate through formal language, through silent language based on culturally determined cues, and through prevailing morals and etiquette. We even evaluate much information on the basis of our own cultural backgrounds. Subtle distinctions can result in much misunderstanding in cross-national dealings.
- Controversy exists over whether and how national cultures are converging as they come into greater contact with each other.
- In encountering a foreign environment there are dangers of excessive polycentrism or of ethnocentrism.

- In deciding whether to encourage a foreign populace to adjust to an international firm's accustomed practices or whether to develop new practices to fit a given population, the company should proceed with caution. Among the considerations are the cost and benefit to the firm of each alternative; the importance of the change to both parties; the possibility of participation in decision making; the way rewards of change may be allocated; the identity of opinion leaders, and the right timing.
- There has usually been more interest in diffusing business practices from those countries that are showing the most economic success. Cultural factors may determine whether or not they will work in another society.

CASE: JOHN HIGGINS*

In 1962, Leonard Prescott, vice-president and general manager of Weaver-Yamazaki Pharmaceutical of Japan, believed that his executive assistant, John Higgins, was losing his effectiveness in representing the U.S. parent company because of his extraordinary identification with the Japanese culture.

Weaver Pharmaceutical, with extensive international operations, was one of the largest U.S. drug firms. Its competitive position depended heavily on research and development (R&D). Sales activity in Japan had begun in the early 1930s through distributorship by Yamazaki Pharmaceutical, a major producer of drugs and chemicals in Japan. World War II disrupted sales, but Weaver resumed export sales to Japan in 1948 and captured a substantial market share. To prepare for increasingly keen competition from Japanese producers in the foreseeable future, Weaver decided to undertake local production of some of its product lines. In 1953 the company began preliminary negotiations with Yamazaki, which culminated in the establishment of a jointly owned and operated manufacturing subsidiary in 1954.

Through the combined effort of both parents, the subsidiary soon began to manufacture sufficiently broad lines of products to fill the general demands of the Japanese market. Importation from the United States was limited to highly specialized items. The company conducted substantial research and development on its own, coordinated through a joint committee of both parents to avoid unnecessary duplication of efforts. The subsidiary had turned out many new products, some of which were marketed suc-

*Reprinted from *Stanford Business Cases 1963* with the permission of the publishers, Stanford University Graduate School of Business, 1963 by the Board of Trustees of the Leland Stanford Junior University. This is a condensed version of the original by M. Y. Yoshino.

cessfully in the United States and elsewhere. Weaver management considered the Japanese operations to be one of the most successful of its international ventures. It felt that the company's future prospects were promising, especially since steady improvement was occurring in Japan's standard of living.

The subsidiary was headed by Shozo Suzuki, who as executive vice-president of Yamazaki and also president of several other subsidiaries, limited his participation in Weaver-Yamazaki to determination of basic policies. Daily operations were managed by Prescott, who was assisted by Higgins and several Japanese directors. Though several other Americans were assigned to the venture, they were concerned with R&D and held no overall management responsibilities.

The Weaver Company had a policy of moving American personnel from one foreign post to another with occasional tours in the international division of the home office. Each assignment generally lasted for three to five years. Since there was a limited number of expatriates, the personnel policy was flexible enough to allow an employee to stay in a country for an indefinite period of time if he or she desired. A few Americans had stayed in one foreign post for over ten years.

In 1960, Prescott replaced the former general manager, who had been in Japan since 1954. Prescott was experienced at international work, having spent most of his twenty-five-year career with the company in its international work. He had served in India, the Philippines, and Mexico and had spent several years in the home office international division. He was delighted with the challenge to expand the Japanese operations. After two years there, Prescott was pleased with the progress the company had made and felt a sense of accomplishment in developing a smoothly functioning organization.

He became concerned, however, with the notable changes in Higgins's attitude and thinking. Prescott felt that Higgins had absorbed and internalized the Japanese culture to such a point that he had lost the U.S. point of view. He had "gone native," resulting in a substantial loss of his administrative effectiveness.

Higgins was born in a small Midwestern town; after high school in 1950, he entered his state university. Midway through college, he was drafted. Since he had shown an interest in languages in college, he was given an opportunity to attend the Army Language School for intensive training in Japanese. After fifteen months he was assigned as an interpreter and translator in Tokyo. While in Japan, he took further courses in Japanese language, literature, and history. He made many Japanese friends, fell in love with Japan, and vowed to return there. In 1957, Higgins returned to college. Since he wanted to use the language as a means rather than an end in itself, he finished his college work in management rather than in Japanese. He graduated with honors in 1958 and joined Weaver. After a year in the company training program he was assigned to Japan.

Higgins was pleased to return to Japan, not only because of his love for Japan, but also for the opportunity to improve the "ugly American" image abroad. Because of his language ability and interest in Japan, he was able to intermingle with broad segments of the Japanese population. He noted that Americans had a tendency to impose their value systems, ideals, and thinking patterns upon the Japanese, believing that anything American was universally right and applicable. He felt indignant about American attitudes on numerous occasions and was determined to remedy it.

Under both Prescott and his predecessor, Higgins's responsibilities included troubleshooting with major Japanese customers, attending trade meetings, negotiating with government officials, conducting marketing research projects, and helping with day-to-day administration. Both bosses sought his advice on many difficult and complex administrative problems and found him capable.

Prescott mentally listed a few examples to describe what he meant by Higgins's "complete emotional involvement" with Japanese culture. In 1961, Higgins married a Japanese woman who had studied in the United States and graduated from a prestigious Japanese university. At that time, Higgins asked for and received permission to extend his stay in Japan for an indefinite period. This seemed to Prescott to mark a turning point in Higgins's behavior.

Higgins moved to a strictly Japanese neighborhood, relaxed in a kimono at home, used the public bath, and was invited to weddings, neighborhood parties, and even Buddhist funerals. Although Weaver had a policy of granting two months' home leave every two years with paid transportation for the employee and his family, Higgins declined his trips, preferring to visit remote parts of Japan with his wife.

At work, Higgins had also taken on many characteristics of a typical Japanese executive. He spent a great deal of time listening to the personal problems of his subordinates, maintained close social ties with many of the men in the organization, and had even arranged marriages for some of the young employees. Consequently, many employees sought Higgins's attention to register their complaints and demands with management. These included requests for more liberal fringe benefits in the form of recreational activities and acquisition of rest houses at resort areas. Many employees also complained to Higgins about the personnel policy that Prescott had installed. This involved a move away from promotion based on seniority to one based on superiors' evaluation of subordinates. The employees asked Higgins to intercede on their behalf. He did so and insisted that their demands were justified.

Although Prescott felt it helpful to learn the feelings of middle managers from Higgins, he disliked having to deal with Higgins as an adversary rather than an ally. Prescott became hesitant to ask Higgins's opinion because he invariably raised objections to changes that were contrary to the Japanese norm. Prescott believed that there were dynamic changes taking place in traditional Japanese customs and culture, and he was confident that many of Higgins's points were not tied to existing cultural patterns as rigidly as

Higgins seemed to think. The opinion was bolstered by the fact that many of the Japanese subordinates were more willing to try out new ideas than Higgins was. Prescott further thought that there was no point in a progressive American company's merely copying the local customs. He felt that the company's real contribution to Japanese society was in bringing in new ideas and innovations.

Recent incidents had raised some doubts in Prescott's mind as to the soundness of Higgins's judgment, which Prescott had never before questioned. For example, there was a case involving the dismissal of a manager who in Prescott's opinion lacked initiative, leadership, and general competency. After two years of continued prodding by his superiors, including Prescott himself, the manager still showed little interest in self-improvement. Both Higgins and the personnel manager objected vigorously to the dismissal because the company had never done this before. They also argued that the man involved was loyal and honest and that the company was partially at fault for having kept him on for the last ten years without spotting the incompetency. A few weeks after the dismissal, Prescott learned accidentally that Higgins had interceded on behalf of the fired employee and had gotten Yamazaki Pharmaceutical to take him on. When confronted, Higgins simply said that he had done what was expected of a superior in any Japanese company.

Prescott believed these incidents suggested a serious problem. Higgins had been an effective and efficient manager whose knowledge of the language and the people had proved invaluable. On numerous occasions, his American friends envied Prescott for having a man of Higgins's qualifications as an assistant. Prescott also knew that Higgins had received several outstanding offers to go with other companies in Japan. Prescott felt that Higgins would be far more effective if he could take a more emotionally detached attitude toward Japan. In Prescott's view, the best international executive was one who retained a belief in the fundamentals of the U.S. point of view while also understanding foreign attitudes. This understanding, of course, should be thorough or even instinctive, but it also should be objective, characterized neither by disdain nor by strong emotional attachment.

QUESTIONS

1. How would you contrast Higgins's and Prescott's attitudes toward the implementation of U.S. personnel policies in the Japanese operations?
2. What are the major reasons for these differences in attitude?
3. If you were the Weaver corporate management person responsible for the Japanese operations and the conflict between Higgins and Prescott had come to your attention, what would you do? Be sure to first identify some alternatives and then make your recommendations.

NOTES

1. Most data were taken from an interview with Angela Clarke, a protagonist in the case. Additional background information came from Kenneth Friedman, "Learning the Arabs' Silent Language: Interview with Edward T. Hall," [the noted anthropologist quoted in the case] *Bridge,* Spring 1980, pp. 5–6 ff.; Samira Harfoush, "Non-Traditional Training for Women in the Arab World," *Bridge,* Winter 1980, pp. 6–7 ff.; "British Premier Visits Saudi Arabia," *New York Times,* April 20, 1981, p. A2; Karen Elliott House, "Modern Arabia," *Wall Street Journal,* June 4, 1981, p. 1 ff.; David Ignatius, "A Saudi Job Offers Hordes of Foreigners a Chance to Prosper," *Wall Street Journal,* March 20, 1981, p. 1.; and The Economist Intelligence Unit, *Country Profile: Saudi Arabia, 1986–87* (London: Economist Intelligence Unit, 1986), p. 11.

2. Eve Lee, "Saudis as We, Americans as They," *Bridge,* Winter 1980, pp. 6–7ff.

3. Lorna V. Williams, "Women in International Business," *American Way,* February 18, 1986, p. 51.

4. Marshall H. Segall, *Cross-Cultural Psychology: Human Behavior in Global Perspective* (Monterey, Calif.: Brooks/Cole Publishing Company, 1979), p. 143; and Luis R. Gomez-Mejia, "Effect of Occupation on Task Related, Contextual, and Job Involvement Orientation: A Cross-Cultural Perspective," *Academy of Management Journal,* Vol. 27, No. 4, 1984, pp. 706–720.

5. Richard N. Farmer and Barry M. Richman, *Comparative Management and Economic Progress,* rev. ed. (Bloomington, Ind.: Cedarwood Publishing, 1970), pp. 20–21, for example, list fifteen behavioral variables relating to each of thirty-six business functions. George P. Murdock listed seventy-two cultural variables in "The Common Denominator of Culture," in *The Science of Man in the World Crises,* Ralph Linton, ed. (New York: Columbia University Press, 1945), pp. 123–142.

6. S. Gunders and J. W. M. Whiting, "Mother–Infant Separation and Physical Growth," *Ethnology,* 7, No. 2, April 1968, pp. 196–206, and Thomas K. Landauer and J. W. M. Whiting, "Infantile Stimulation and Adult Stature of Human Males," *American Anthropologist,* Vol. 66, 1964, p. 1008.

7. James F. Downs and Herman K. Blebtreu, *Human Variation: An Introduction to Physical Anthropology* (Beverly Hills, Calif.: Glencoe Press, 1969), p. 197.

8. Ian Jamieson, *Capitalism and Culture: A Comparative Analysis of British and American Manufacturing Organizations* (Farnborough, England: Gower Press, 1980), Chapter 1.

9. Nancy J. Adler and Jill de Villafranca, "Epistemological Foundations of a Symposium Process: A Framework for Understanding Culturally Diverse Organizations," *International Studies of Management and Organization,* Winter 1982–1983, pp. 7–22.

10. James A. McCaffrey and Craig R. Hafner, "When Two Cultures Collide: Doing Business Overseas," *Training and Development Journal,* Vol. 39, No. 10, October 1985, p. 26.

11. Harry C. Triandis, "Dimensions of Cultural Variation as Parameters of Organizational Theories," *International Studies of Management and Organization,* Winter 1982–1983, pp. 143–144.

12. *1987 Statistical Yearbook* (Nancy, France: UNESCO, 1987), 3-96, 3-267.

13. "Women in a Changing World," *Women at Work* (Geneva, Switzerland: International Labour Office, 1985, no. 1), pp. 19, 40.

14. Kenneth Dreyfack, "You Don't Have to Be a Giant to Score Big Overseas," *Business Week,* April 13, 1987, p. 63.

15. Triandis, *op. cit.,* p. 146.

16. Carol Hymowitz, "More Men Infiltrating Professions Historically Dominated by Women," *Wall Street Journal,* February 25, 1981, p. 31; "The Job Market Opens up for the 68-Cent Woman," *New York Times,* July 26, 1987, p. E6.

17. Max Weber, "The Protestant Ethic and the Spirit of Capitalism," and Kember Fullerton, "Calvinism and Capitalism," both in *Culture and Management,* Ross A. Webber, ed. (Homewood, Ill.: Richard D. Irwin, 1969), pp. 91–112.

18. J. H. Boeke, *Economics and Economic Policy of Dual Societies* (New York: Institute of Pacific Relations, 1953), pp. 39–41.

19. Triandis, *op. cit.,* pp. 159–160.

20. Everett E. Hagen, *The Theory of Social Change: How Economic Growth Begins* (Homewood, Ill.: Richard D. Irwin, 1962), p. 378.

21. David C. McClelland, *The Achieving Society* (Princeton, N.J.: D. Van Nostrand Company, 1961); David C. McClelland, "Business Drives and National Achievement," *Harvard Business Review,* July–August 1962, pp. 92–112; M. L. Maehr and J. G. Nicholls, "Culture and Achievement Motivations: A Second Look," *Studies in Cross Cultural Psychology,* in Neil Warren, ed. (London: Academic Press, 1980), Vol. 2, Chapter 6.

22. George W. England and Raymond Lee, "Organizational Goals and Expected Behavior among American, Japanese and Korean Managers—A Comparative Study," *Academy of Management Journal,* December 1971, pp. 425–438, examined eight organizational goals for three countries; McClelland, *op. cit.,* compared managers in the United States, northern Italy, southern Italy, Turkey, and Poland.

23. Abraham Maslow, *Motivation and Personality* (New York: Harper & Brothers, 1954).

24. Geert Hofstede, "National Cultures in Four Dimensions," *International Studies of Management and Organization,* Spring–Summer 1983, p. 68; for an earlier comparison among countries, see Mason Haire, Edwin Ghiselli, and Lyman Porter, *Managerial Thinking* (New York: John Wiley & Sons, 1966), pp. 90–103.

25. Donald Treiman, *Occupational Prestige in Comparative Perspective* (New York: Academic Press, 1977), especially appendix C.

26. Robert R. Rehder, *Latin American Management Development and Performance* (Reading, Mass.: Addison-Wesley, 1968), p. 16.

27. Hofstede, *op. cit.,* pp. 54–55.

28. Hofstede, *op. cit.,* pp. 50–57.

29. See, for example, Geza Peter Lauter, "Sociological–Cultural and Legal Factors Impeding Decentralization of Authority in Developing Countries," *Academy of Management Journal,* September 1969, Vol. 12, No. 3, pp. 367–378; Richard B. Peterson, "Chief Executives' Attitudes: A Cross-Cultural Analysis," *Industrial Relations,* May 1971, Vol. 10, No. 2, pp. 194–210; G. Katona, B. Strumpel, and E. Zahn, "The

Sociocultural Environment," in *International Marketing Strategy,* H. B. Thorelli, ed. (Middlesex, England: Penguin Books, 1973).

30. L. L. Cummings, D. L. Harnett, and D. J. Stevens, "Risk, Fate, Conciliation and Trust: An International Study of Attitudinal Differences among Executives," *Academy of Management Journal,* September 1971, p. 294, found differences among the United States, Greece, Spain, Central Europe, and Scandinavia.

31. McCaffrey and Hafner, *op. cit.,* p. 26.

32. Vivian Ducat, "American Spoken Here—and Everywhere," *Travel & Leisure,* Vol. 16, No. 10, October 1986, pp. 168–169.

33. Christian Hill, "Language for Profit," *Wall Street Journal,* January 13, 1977, p. 34.

34. Vern Terpstra and Kenneth David, *The Cultural Environment of International Business,* 2d ed. (Cincinnati: South-Western Publishing Company, 1985), p. 23.

35. This term was first used by Edward T. Hall, "The Silent Language in Overseas Business," *Harvard Business Review,* May–June 1960, and included five variables (time, space, things, friendship, and agreements).

36. *Ibid.*

37. For a survey of major research contributions, see Harry C. Triandis, "Reflections on Trends in Cross-Cultural Research," *Journal of Cross-Cultural Psychology,* March 1980, pp. 46–48.

38. Benjamin Lee Whorf, *Language, Thought and Reality* (New York: John Wiley & Sons, 1956), p. 13.

39. Segall, *op. cit.,* pp. 96–99.

40. E. Glenn, *Man and Mankind: Conflict and Communication between Cultures* (Norwood, N.J.: Ablex, 1981).

41. William Stockton, "Bribes Are Called a Way of Life in Mexico," *New York Times,* October 25, 1986, p. 3.

42. Peter Gosling, "Culture and Commerce: What's in a Name?" *Southeast Asia Business,* No. 6, Summer 1985, pp. 30–38.

43. Two recent examples are Roger E. Axtell, *Do's and Taboos around the World,* (Janeville, Wis.: Parker Pen Company, 1986); and Neil Chesanow, *The World-Class Executive* (Toronto: Bantam Books, 1985).

44. Mark Maremont, Dori Jones Yang, and Amy Dunkin, "Toys 'R' Us Goes Overseas—and Finds that Toys 'R' Them Too," *Business Week,* No. 2982, January 26, 1987, p. 71.

45. J. D. Child, "Culture, Contingency and Capitalism in the Cross-National Study of Organizations," in *Research in Organizational Behavior,* L. L. Cummings and B. M. Staw, eds. (Greenwich, Conn.: JAI Publishers, 1981), Vol. III, pp. 303–356; Andre Laurent, "The Cross-Cultural Puzzle of International Human Resource Management," *Human Resource Management,* Vol. 25, No. 1, pp. 91–102.

46. David P. Rutenberg, *Multinational Management* (Boston: Little, Brown and Company, 1982), p. 19.

47. Hans B. Thorelli, "The Multi-National Corporation as a Change Agent," *The Southern Journal of Business,* July 1966, p. 5.

48. Bernard Lewis, " 'Western Culture Must Go', " *Wall Street Journal,* May 2, 1988, p. 18.

49. Philip R. Harris and Robert T. Moran, *Managing Cultural Differences* (Houston: Gulf Publishing Company, 1979), p. 88, quoting Kalervo Oberg.

50. "Problems of Opening a Retail Store in Spain," *Wall Street Journal,* March 27, 1967, p. 1.

51. Manning Nash, "The Interplay of Culture and Management in a Guatemalan Textile Plant," *Culture and Management,* Ross A. Weber, ed., pp. 317–324.

52. Conrad M. Arensberg and Arthur H. Niehoff, *Introducing Social Change: A Manual for Americans Overseas* (Chicago: Aldine, 1964), pp. 123–125.

53. John D. Daniels, "U.S. Subsidiary Adjustments to the Mexican Labor Force," *Journal of International Business Studies,* Spring 1971, p. 19.

54. *Ibid.*

55. Ian Jamieson, "The Concept of Culture and Its Relevance for an Analysis of Business Enterprise in Different Societies," *International Study of Management and Organization,* Winter 1982, pp. 71–72.

3

PART

THEORIES AND INSTITUTIONS: TRADE AND INVESTMENT

Why do trade and investment take place? What are the governmental institutions that enhance or retard trade and factor mobility? What would happen if there were no institutions? These are the major questions considered in this part.

Chapter 4 considers the question of why foreign trade takes place. The theory of international trade is developed, and the advantages of specialization resulting from trade are discussed. Chapter 5 presents the arguments against a free flow of trade among countries and the mechanisms by which nations regulate both the inward and outward flow of goods across their borders.

Chapter 6 is concerned with still another essential aspect of the field of international business: the reasons behind direct foreign investment. In this context the close relationship between trade and investment is also examined. Chapter 7 deals with the major agreements—both bilateral and multilateral—by which nations have joined together to effect a unified or cooperative policy.

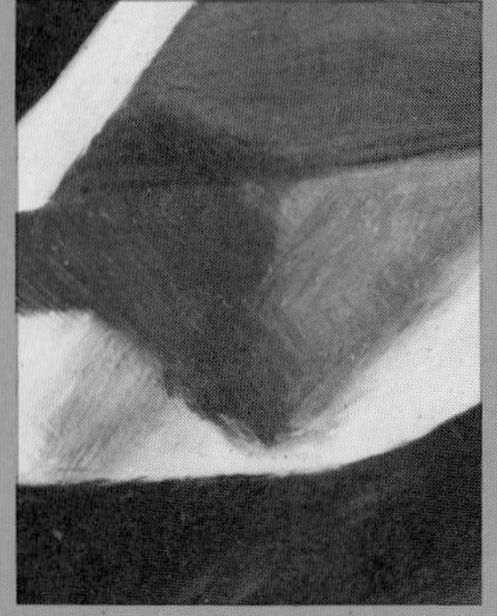

4

CHAPTER

INTERNATIONAL TRADE THEORY

"A market is not held for the sake of one person."
—African (Fulani) proverb

- To explain what trade patterns would exist if trade could move freely.
- To discuss how global efficiency can be increased through free trade.
- To point out the underlying assumptions of trade theories.
- To introduce prescriptions for targeting trade patterns.
- To explore how business decisions determine what trade takes place.

CASE:
SRI LANKAN TRADE[1]

Sri Lanka, which means resplendent land, is an island country of more than sixteen million people off the southeast coast of India. Lying just above the equator, it is 270 miles long and 140 miles across at its widest points. (See map in Fig. 4.1.) It has a hot tropical climate with two monsoon periods; yet the central mountain region is cool enough to experience frost. Known as Ceylon from the early sixteenth century until 1972, Sri Lanka is in many ways typical of most developing countries. It has a low per capita income (about $380 per year), a high dependence on a few primary products for earning foreign exchange, insufficient foreign exchange earnings to purchase all of the desired consumer and industrial imports, and a high unemployment rate. In many other ways, though, Sri Lanka is atypical of developing nations. By various measurements comparing the quality of life among countries, Sri Lanka ranks fairly high. Its 86 percent literacy rate is one of the highest in Asia, and its standards of nutrition, health care, and income distribution are among the best in the Third World. Its life expectancy of 70 years is one of the highest in the developing world, and its recent population growth rate of 1.4 percent per year is one of the lowest.

Although Sri Lanka did not become independent until 1948, it has a long recorded history of international trade. By the middle of the third century B.C., special quarters of its capital were set apart for "Ionian merchants." King Solomon sent his galleys to Sri Lanka to purchase gems, elephants, and peacocks to woo the Queen of Sheba. Sinbad and Marco Polo sailed there. Sri Lanka sent ambassadors to Claudius Caesar in the Roman Empire and later established trade links with China. One by one the European powers came to dominate the island in order to acquire products unavailable in their own countries. The Portuguese, for example, sought such products as cinnamon, cloves, and cardamon, and the English developed the island's economy on tea, rubber, and coconuts, replacing rice as the major agricultural crop.

Since its independence, Sri Lanka has looked to international trade policy as a means of helping to solve such problems as (1) foreign exchange shortage, (2) overdependence on one product and one market, and (3) insufficient growth of output and employment.

Foreign exchange is needed for buying imports. Advances in international communications and transportation have contributed to rising Sri Lankan expectations, which in turn, have translated into preferences for foreign products or for foreign machinery to produce them. These desires have grown more rapidly than foreign exchange earnings have.

Sri Lanka also has been concerned about its overdependence on a single export product and market. Until 1975, more than half of Sri Lanka's export

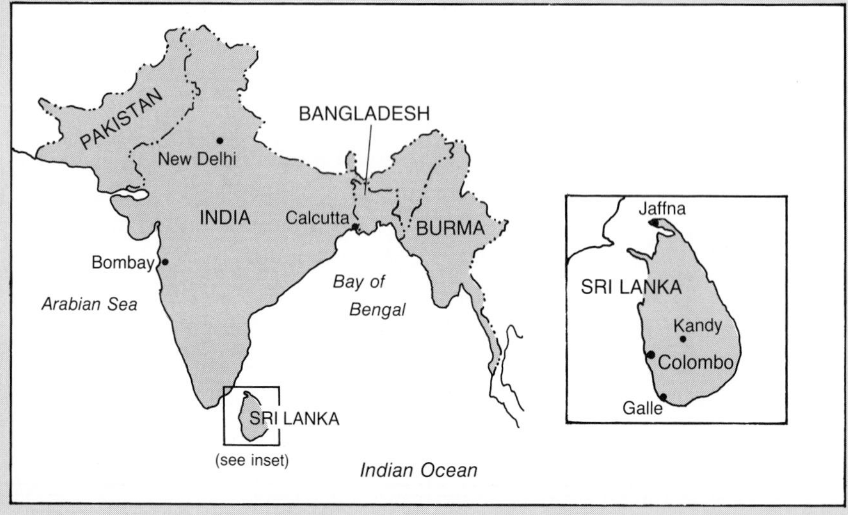

Figure 4.1
Map of Sri Lanka

earnings were from tea. This made Sri Lanka vulnerable in two ways. First, the world demand for tea has not grown as rapidly as that for many other products, particularly manufactured ones. Therefore, tea has not offered as viable a means of increasing economic growth, employment, or foreign exchange earnings as some other products. Second, tea prices can fluctuate substantially from one year to another because of bumper crops or natural disasters in any tea-exporting country. For example, the wholesale price of tea has changed by as much as 90 percent from one year to the next. This makes planning for long-term business or government projects very difficult. Because Sri Lanka is a former British colony, many Sri Lankans also have been concerned that the country cannot be politically and economically independent as long as trade is so centered on the British market. At the time of independence, for example, one-third of Sri Lankan exports went to the United Kingdom. Sri Lanka is thus potentially vulnerable to British political demands and economic downturns.

Because of these varied but interrelated problems, Sri Lanka has attempted since independence to earn more foreign exchange by exporting more of its traditional commodities. In addition, Sri Lanka has sought to diversify its production. From independence in 1948 until a change of government in 1977, the emphasis was on the restriction of imports in order to encourage local production, which would thus save foreign exchange. Since then the focus has been on the development of new industries that can export a part of their production and thus earn more foreign exchange. Whether the diversification has been for import substitution or export development, the intended outcome has been to create growth and jobs by using unemployed people and other unemployed resources. By moving to new products, the country expects to be less dependent on the tea market and on sales of that product into the traditional British market.

The decision to develop exports of nontraditional products raises the questions of what those products should be and how to get firms to produce them for foreign markets. In 1977 the newly elected government in Sri Lanka was determined that any assistance should be given to those industries that would give Sri Lanka the best potential advantage of competing in world markets. The government took numerous steps to ease restrictions on imports in order to judge where competitive advantages lay. Authorities reasoned that the industries that could survive import competition were the most likely to become competitive in export markets.

Governmental authorities were not satisfied to sit back and wait for imports to determine the whole future industrial thrust. They reasoned that some entirely new industries might have to be assisted. Additionally, there was a desire to make some short-term export gains in order to develop credibility for the export development program. The export development division of the Ministry of Industries was instrumental in creating a methodology to identify appropriate products for development and promotion.

An obvious way of selecting product groups was to identify nontraditional products that were already being exported in small amount, since this ability to export indicated potential growth. The export development division also sought to find other products for which Sri Lanka might have a potential advantage in competing abroad. They first identified products that would have a high need for semiskilled and skilled labor for three reasons: (1) labor costs in Sri Lanka were low; (2) the labor force was fairly well educated; and (3) there was a good deal of unemployment and underemployment. The division narrowed that group of products to include only those for which Sri Lanka had indigenous raw materials for production and packaging. This was deemed to be an important competitive indicator because it would be costly to import materials that would then have to be processed before being reexported. Finally, the division examined market conditions where Sri Lanka was most apt to be able to sell. This examination was based on an analysis of demand in two types of markets: (1) those where Sri Lanka had special market concessions and therefore would experience minimal trade barriers and (2) those that were geographically close to Sri Lanka and could be served with minimum transport costs.

Seventeen products emerged and were ranked by export potential and expected benefits for the country. The leading items were:

- processed tea (packaged teabags, and instant tea)
- ready-made garments (shirts, pajamas, and dresses)
- chemical derivates of coconut oil
- edible fats
- bicycle tires and tubes
- other rubber products such as automobile tires and tubes.

Other items included canvas footwear, passionfruit juice, canned pineapple, ceramicware, seafood (lobsters and shrimp), handicraft items, and gems.

This identification of the most likely competitive industries encouraged some businesspeople to consider investments in new areas. Additionally, the government established industrial development zones. Companies that produced in and exported their production from the zones could qualify for up to a ten-year tax holiday plus another fifteen years of tax concessions, depending on the size of the investment and the number of employees. They could also bring in goods and components without paying import taxes on them at the time of import. The import tax was deferred until the ensuing products were sold domestically. If the items were reexported, there was no import tax.

The first manufacturers to take advantage of the incentives were textile and footwear producers who had special access to the U.S. and European markets. Since then the products have become more diverse. During 1986 such operations as the production of PVC film, carpets, and data-entry were approved.

Sri Lanka continues to have a shortage of foreign exchange. As imports have entered Sri Lanka more easily and as incomes have risen, consumers have demanded even more foreign products. As a result, Sri Lanka has restricted large consumer items but has allowed smaller items, such as watches, to enter freely because of a belief that they would otherwise be smuggled in.

However, the move to establish new export industries is accomplishing many of its objectives. Manufacturing has grown as a portion of total exports and tea has fallen. There has also been a dispersion of Sri Lankan export markets, with such countries as the United States, Saudi Arabia, West Germany, and India gaining in importance. Whereas one-third of exports once went to Britain, no single country now accounts for as much as 15 percent of Sri Lankan sales.

INTRODUCTION

Universal trade questions focus on

- What products?
- With whom?
- How much?

In the introductory case, Sri Lankan authorities, like authorities in all countries, wrestled with the problems of what, how much, and with whom the country should import and export. Once they made decisions, officials enacted trade policies to achieve the desired end results. These policies, in turn, affected business: They influenced what products companies might be able to sell in Sri Lanka from both Sri Lankan and foreign sources. The trade policies also affected what companies could produce in Sri Lanka for sale in either the domestic or the foreign market. Although Sri Lankan officials set policies to conform to the country's unique conditions and objectives, they relied on a body of trade theory shared by officials around the world.

Some theories explain trade patterns in absence of government interference.

Some theories explain what government actions should strive for in trade.

Whereas some theories precede events (e.g., Einstein's theory of relativity was a necessary antecedent to the atomic experiments that followed several decades later), international trade took place long before any trade theories evolved. Sri Lankan trade, for example, predated recorded trade theories by more than 1500 years.

Two types of trade theories have emerged since the sixteenth century. The first type of theory deals with the natural order of trade: That is, it examines and explains what trade patterns would exist if trade were allowed to move freely among countries. These theories pose questions of how much, which products, and with whom a country will trade in the absence of restrictions among nations. Not all of these particular theories consider all of these questions; their focuses are shown in Table 4.1 under the heading "Description of Natural Trade." Note that two of these theories are also prescriptive: That is, they posit that a system of unrestricted trade should prevail. They are marked "No" for the question, "Should government control trade?" Some other theories of the first type are merely descriptive: That is, they explain what does or will happen but do not judge the result. The second type of theory prescribes governmental interference with the free movement of goods and services among countries in order to alter the amount, composition, and direction of trade. These theories are marked "Yes" under the question, "Should government control trade?" in Table 4.1.

Since no single theory explains all natural trade patterns and since all prescriptions are relevant to some of the actions taken by governmental policymakers, this chapter examines a variety of approaches. However, the subject of governmental interference in trade is so broad that an entire chapter is devoted to discussion of many of the specific arguments and methods (see Chapter 5). Both the descriptive and prescriptive approaches have considerable impact on international business. They provide insights about favorable market locales as well as potentially successful products. The theories also increase understanding on what kinds of government trade policies might be enacted and predict how they might affect competitiveness.

MERCANTILISM

According to mercantilism, countries should export more than they import.

Why has Sri Lanka been so dependent on primary, rather than manufactured, products? Perhaps the answer lies in an economic philosophy promoted by a number of writers during the period from 1500 to 1800.[2] This economic philosophy, **mercantilism,** was based on the premise that a country's wealth relied on its holdings of treasure, usually in the form of gold. Trade was an integral part of this economic philosophy; consequently, mercantilism was the first trade theory.

According to mercantilism, governments should export more than they import, and if successful, they would receive the value of their trade sur-

TABLE 4.1

EMPHASIS OF MAJOR THEORIES

Theory	Description of natural trade			Prescription of trade relationships			
	How much is traded?	What products are traded?	With whom does trade take place?	Should government control trade?	How much should be traded?	What products should be traded?	With whom should trade take place?
Mercantilism	—	—	—	Yes	X	X	X
Neomercantilism	—	—	—	Yes	X	—	—
Absolute advantage	—	X	—	No	—	X	—
Country size	X	X	—	—	—	—	—
Comparative advantage	—	X	—	No	—	X	—
Factor proportions	—	X	X	—	—	—	—
Product life cycle (PLC)	—	X	X	—	—	—	—
Country similarity	—	X	X	—	—	—	—
Dependence	—	—	—	Yes	—	X	X

pluses in the form of gold from the country or countries that ran deficits. During this period, nation-states were emerging, and gold served to consolidate the power of central governments. The gold was invested in armies and national institutions that would solidify people's primary allegiances to the new nation rather than to such traditional units as city-states, religions, and guilds.

But how could countries export more than they imported? Trade was conducted largely by governmental monopolies. Restrictions were placed on most imports and subsidies on many exports. Colonies, such as Sri Lanka under British rule, supported this trade objective first by supplying many commodities that the colonizing country might otherwise have had to buy from a nonassociated country. Second, the colonial powers sought to run trade surpluses with their own colonies as a further means of obtaining revenue. They did this not only by monopolizing the colonial trade but also by preventing the colonies from manufacturing. This way the colonies had to export the less-valued raw materials and import the more-valued manufactured products.

Since acceptance of the mercantilist philosophy faded in about 1800, few actual prohibitions were set by colonial powers on the development of industrial capabilities within their colonies; but there were few encouragements, either. Institutional and legal arrangements continued to tie the trade of colonies to their industrialized mother countries. Sri Lanka, like the many other countries that have attained independence since World War II, began with a production structure and a trade pattern that closely resembled those of colonies during the heyday of mercantilist economic thought. Efforts to alter this pattern are discussed later in this chapter in the section on independence, interdependence, and dependence.

Carry-over of Terminology

A favorable balance does not necessarily indicate a beneficial situation.

Some of the terminology of the mercantilist era has endured. The term **favorable balance of trade,** for example, is still used to indicate that a country is exporting more than it is importing. An **unfavorable balance of trade** is indicative of a trading deficit. Many of these terms are misnomers: For example, the word *favorable* implies benefit whereas *unfavorable* suggests disadvantage. In fact, it is *not* necessarily beneficial to run a trade surplus; nor is it necessarily disadvantageous to run a trade deficit. If a country is running a trade surplus, or favorable balance of trade, for the time being it is receiving goods and services from abroad of less value than it is sending out.[3] In the mercantilist period the difference was made up by a transfer of gold, but today the difference usually is made up by granting credit to the deficit country. If that credit is not repaid in full, the so-called favorable trade balance actually may turn out to be disadvantageous for the country with the trade surplus.

Neomercantilism

In neomercantilism, a country attempts to run export surplus to achieve some political or social objective.

In recent years the term **neomercantilism** has been used to describe countries that apparently try to run favorable balances of trade in an attempt to achieve some social or political objective. For instance, a country may try to achieve full employment by sending its surplus production abroad because there is inadequate demand at home. Or a country might attempt to maintain political influence in an area by sending the area more merchandise than it receives from that area.

ABSOLUTE ADVANTAGE

According to Adam Smith, a country's wealth depends on its available goods and services rather than gold.

So far we have ignored the question of why countries need to trade at all. Why can't Sri Lanka (or any other country) be content with the goods and services produced within its territorial confines? Under mercantilist policy, many countries tried to become as self-sufficient as they possibly could by producing things locally.

In his 1776 book *The Wealth of Nations* Adam Smith questioned the mercantilists' assumption that a country's wealth depends on its holdings of treasure.[4] He said instead that the real wealth of a country consists of the goods and services available to its citizens. Smith developed the theory of **absolute advantage,** which holds that different countries can produce different goods more efficiently than others. On the basis of this theory he questioned why the citizens of a country should have to buy domestically made goods that they could purchase more cheaply from abroad.

Smith reasoned that if trade were unrestricted, each country would specialize in those products for which it had a competitive advantage. Resources would shift to the efficient industries because countries could not compete in the inefficient ones. Through specialization, countries could increase their efficiency: (1) because labor could become more skilled by repeating the same tasks; (2) labor would not lose time in switching from the production of one kind of product to another; and (3) long production runs would provide incentives for the development of more effective working methods. A country then could use the excess of its specialized production to buy more imports than it could have otherwise produced. But in what products should a country specialize? Although Smith felt the marketplace would make the determination, he thought that a country's advantage would be either natural or acquired.

Natural Advantage

Natural advantage refers to climate and natural resources.

A country may have a **natural advantage** in the production of a product because of climatic conditions or because of access to certain natural resources. The climate may dictate, for example, what agricultural products can be produced more efficiently. Sri Lanka's efficiency in the production of tea, rubber, and coconuts, for example, is due largely to advantageous climatic conditions.

Sri Lanka imports wheat and dairy products. If Sri Lanka were to increase its production of wheat and dairy products, for which its climate is less suited, it would have to use land now devoted to the cultivation of tea, rubber, or coconuts, thus decreasing the output of those products. At the same time, the United States could produce tea (perhaps in hothouses), but at the cost of diverting resources away from products such as wheat for which its climate is naturally suited. Both countries can trade tea for wheat and vice versa more cheaply than they could become self-sufficient in the production of both. Moreover, the more diverse the climates of two countries, the more likely they will have natural trade advantages with each other.

Most countries must import ores, metals, or supplies of fuel from other countries whose natural resources are plentiful. No one country is large enough or sufficiently rich in physical resources to be independent of the rest of the world except for short periods. Sri Lanka, for example, exports natural graphite but must import its supply of natural nitrates. Another natural resource is soil, which, when coupled with topography, is an important determinant of the type of product to be produced most efficiently in different areas.

The variation in natural advantages in different places also helps to explain where certain manufactured or processed products might be best produced, particularly if transportation costs can be reduced by processing an agricultural commodity or natural resource prior to exporting. Recall that Sri Lankan authorities sought to identify industries that could use its primary commodities such as tea. The instant tea processing would likely save bulk and transportation costs on tea exports. To make canned liquid tea could add weight, however, thus lessening the internationally competitive edge.

Acquired Advantage

Acquired advantage refers to technology and skill development.

Most of the world's trade today consists of manufactured goods rather than agricultural goods and natural resources. The production location of these goods today is due largely to an **acquired advantage,** commonly referred to as product or process technology. An advantage in product technology refers to an ability to produce a different or differentiated product. Denmark, for example, exports silver tableware, not because there are rich Danish silver mines but because Danish companies have developed distinctive products. An advantage in process technology refers to an ability to produce a homogeneous product more efficiently. Japan, for example, has exported steel in spite of having to import iron and coal, the two primary ingredients necessary for steel production. A primary reason for Japan's success is its steel mills, which encompass new, labor-saving and raw-material-saving processes.

Resource Efficiency Example

The idea of absolute advantage in international or domestic trade can be explained by picturing two countries (or regions within one country) and two commodities. In this example, we assume the countries are Sri Lanka and the United States and the commodities are tea and wheat. Since we are not yet considering the concepts of money and exchange rates, we shall treat the cost of production in terms of the resources needed to produce either tea or wheat. This is a realistic treatment in that real income depends on the output of goods associated with the resources used to produce them.

We start with the assumption that Sri Lanka and the United States each have the same amount of resources (land, labor, and capital), which can be used to produce either tea or wheat. Let us say that 100 units of resources are available in each country (shown in Fig. 4.2). In the case of Sri Lanka we assume that it takes four resources to produce one ton of tea and ten resources per ton of wheat. In the United States it takes twenty resources per ton of tea and five resources per ton of wheat. Sri Lanka is thus more efficient (that is, takes fewer resources to produce) in the production of tea than the

Figure 4.2
Production Possibilities with Absolute Advantage

ASSUMPTIONS

Sri Lanka
1. 100 resources available
2. 10 resources to produce a ton of wheat
3. 4 resources to produce a ton of tea
4. Uses half of resources per product when there is no foreign trade

United States
1. 100 resources available
2. 5 resources to produce a ton of wheat
3. 20 resources to produce a ton of tea
4. Uses half of resources per product when there is no foreign trade

PRODUCTION	Tea	Wheat
Without Trade:		
Sri Lanka (Point A)	12.5	5
U.S. (Point B)	2.5	10
Total	15.0	15
With Trade:		
Sri Lanka (Point C)	25.0	0
U.S. (Point D)	0	20
Total	25.0	20

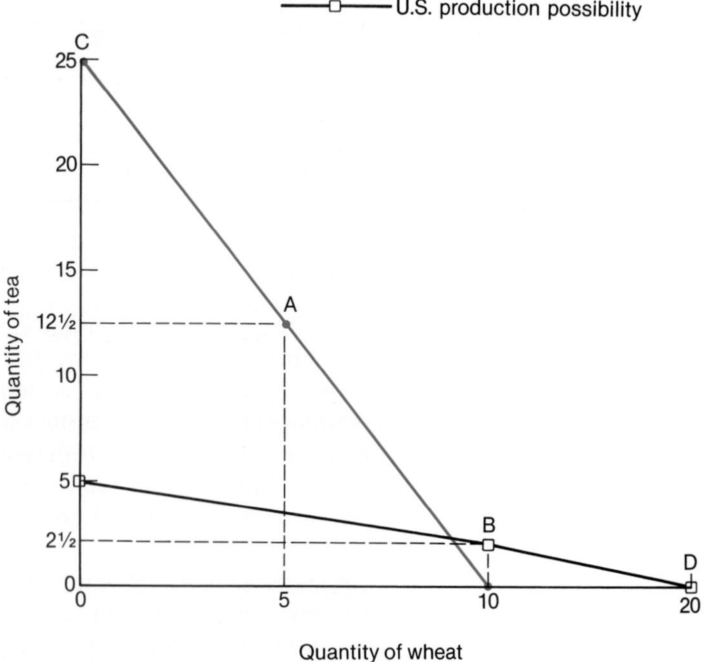

United States, and the United States is more efficient than Sri Lanka in the production of wheat.

Consider a situation in which the two countries have no foreign trade. If Sri Lanka and the United States were each to devote half of their resources for the production of tea and half to the production of wheat, Sri Lanka would be able to produce 12.5 tons of tea and 5 tons of wheat (point A in Fig. 4.2), whereas the United States could produce 2.5 tons of tea and 10 tons of wheat (point B in Fig. 4.2). Since each country has only 100 resources, neither country can increase the production of wheat without decreasing the production of tea or vice versa. Without trade the combined production of the two countries would then be 15 tons of tea (12.5 plus 2.5) and 15 tons of wheat (5 plus 10). If each of the two countries were to specialize in the commodity for which it had an absolute advantage, Sri Lanka could then produce 25 tons of tea and the United States 20 tons of wheat (points C and D in Fig. 4.2). We can see then that by specialization the production of both products can be increased (from 15 to 25 tons of tea and from 15 to 20 tons of wheat). By trading, the two countries can have more tea and more wheat than would be available to them without trade.

Theory of Country Size

Bigger countries have several differences from smaller countries. They:

- Tend to trade smaller portion of output or consumption
- Have more varied resources
- Have higher transport costs for foreign trade
- Can handle large-scale production

The theory of absolute advantage does not deal with country-by-country differences in specialization; however, some recent research based on country size helps to explain how much and what type of products will be traded.

Resource variety. The **theory of country size** holds that because countries with large land areas are more apt to have varied climates and natural resources, they are generally more nearly self-sufficient than smaller countries. Most of the very large countries such as Brazil, China, India, the United States, and the Soviet Union import much less of their consumption and export much less of their production than small countries such as Iraq, the Netherlands, and Iceland.[5] Although this relationship holds generally true, there are exceptions. Albania, for example, is a small country for which trade is a small percentage of national income because of its stringent restrictions on trade.

Transport costs. Although the theory of absolute advantage ignored transport costs, these costs do affect large and small countries differently. Normally, the further the distance, the higher are the transport costs, and the average distances for trade are greater for large countries than for small countries. Assume, for example, that the normal maximum distance for transporting a given product is 100 miles and that beyond that distance, prices increase too substantially. Most of the production and consumers in the United States are more than 100 miles from the Canadian or Mexican borders. In the Netherlands, however, almost the entire production and market are within 100 miles of its border. Transportation costs thus make it more likely that small countries such as the Netherlands will trade.

Scale economy. In addition to the comparison of countries' size by land area, countries also may be compared on the basis of their economic size. Countries with large economies and high per capita incomes are more likely to produce goods that use technologies requiring long production runs because these countries develop industries to serve their large domestic markets.[6] These same industries tend to be competitive in export markets as well.

COMPARATIVE ADVANTAGE

The Logic

Trade gains will occur even though the country may have absolute advantage on all products because it must give up less efficient output to produce more efficient.

What happens when one country can produce all products at an absolute advantage? In 1817, David Ricardo examined this question and expanded on Adam Smith's treatise on absolute advantage. He developed the theory of **comparative advantage.** This theory holds that there may still be gains from trade if a country specializes in those products that it can produce more efficiently than other products without regard to whether or not the country has an absolute advantage vis-à-vis other countries.[7] While this may seem incongruous initially, a simple analogy should explain the logic of this theory. Imagine that the best physician in a particular town also happens to be the best medical secretary. Would it make economic sense for the physician to handle all the administrative duties of the office? Definitely not. The physician can earn more money by devoting all professional energies to working as a physician, even though that means having to employ a less skillful medical secretary to manage the office. In the same manner a country will gain if it concentrates its resources on the production of the commodities that it can produce most efficiently. It will then buy, from countries less well endowed in terms of resources or skills, those commodities that it has relinquished. Like the physician, the country will concentrate its efforts on the production of those commodities for which comparative efficiency is greatest.

A Demonstration

In the following example we assume that the United States is more efficient in the production of both tea and wheat than Sri Lanka. The United States thus has an absolute advantage in the production of both products. In this example it takes Sri Lanka ten resources to produce either a ton of tea or a ton of wheat, whereas it takes the United States only five resources to produce a ton of tea and four resources for a ton of wheat. (See Fig. 4.3.) As in the earlier example

ASSUMPTIONS

Sri Lanka
1. 100 resources available
2. 10 resources per ton of wheat
3. 10 resources per ton of tea
4. Uses half of resources per product when no foreign trade

United States
1. 100 resources available
2. 4 resources per ton of wheat
3. 5 resources per ton of tea
4. Uses half of resources per product when no foreign trade

PRODUCTION	*Tea*	*Wheat*
Without trade:		
Sri Lanka (Point A)	5	5
U.S. (Point B)	10	12½
Total	15	17½
With trade (increasing tea production)		
Sri Lanka (Point C)	10	0
U.S. (Point D)	6	17½
Total	16	17½
With Trade (increasing wheat production)		
Sri Lanka (Point C)	10	0
U.S. (Point E)	5	18¾
Total	15	18¾

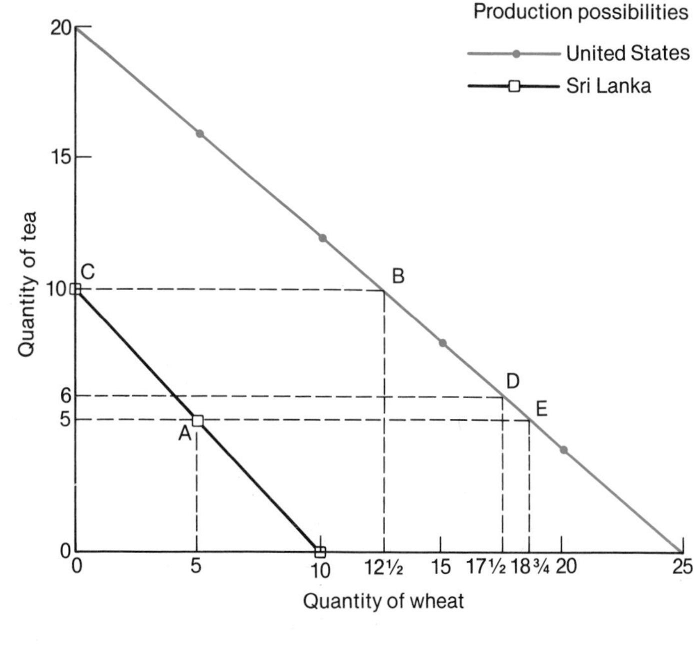

Figure 4.3
Production Possibilities with Comparative Advantage

of absolute advantage, we once again assume that each country has a total of 100 resources available. If each country uses half of its resources in the production of each product, Sri Lanka can produce 5 tons of tea and 5 of wheat (point A on Fig. 4.3). The United States can produce 10 tons of tea and 12.5 tons of wheat (point B on Fig. 4.3). Without trade, neither country can increase its production of tea without sacrificing some production of wheat or vice versa.

Although the United States has an absolute advantage in the production of both tea and wheat, the United States has a comparative advantage only in the production of wheat. This is because its advantage in wheat is comparatively greater than its advantage in tea. By using the same number of resources the United States can produce 2.5 times as much wheat as Sri Lanka but only twice as much tea. Although Sri Lanka has an absolute disadvantage in the production of both products, Sri Lanka has a comparative advantage (or less of a comparative disadvantage) in the production of tea. This is because Sri Lanka is half as efficient in tea and only 40 percent as efficient in wheat production.

Without trade, the combined production would be 15 tons of tea (5 in Sri Lanka plus 10 in the United States) and 17.5 of wheat (5 in Sri Lanka plus 12.5 in the United States). By opening up trade the production of tea, wheat, or a combination of the two can be increased. If we increase the production of tea without changing the amount of wheat that could have been produced before trade, the United States could now produce all 17.5 tons of wheat by using seventy resources (17.5 tons times 4 per ton). The remaining thirty U.S. resources could be used for the production of 6 tons of tea (thirty resources divided by five per ton). These are shown as point D in Fig. 4.3. Sri Lanka would use all of its resources in the production of 10 tons of tea (point C in Fig. 4.3). The combined wheat production has stayed at 17.5 tons but, the tea production has increased from 15 to 16 tons.

If we increase the production of wheat while leaving tea production the same as it was before trade took place between the two countries, Sri Lanka could use all its resources on the production on tea, yielding 10 tons (point C on Fig. 4.3). The United States could produce the remaining 5 tons of tea by using twenty-five units of resources. The remaining seventy-five units of U.S. resources could now produce 18.75 tons of wheat (seventy-five divided by four). These are shown as point E in Fig. 4.3. Without sacrificing the tea available before trade, wheat production has increased from 17.5 to 18.75 tons.

If the United States were to produce somewhere between points D and E in Fig. 4.3, both tea and wheat production would increase over what was possible before trade took place. Whether the production targets are for an increase of tea, wheat, or a combination of the two, both countries can gain by having Sri Lanka trade some of its tea production to the United States for some of the United States' wheat output.

Some Assumptions

Full employment is not a valid assumption.

Full employment. The earlier analogy of the physician/medical secretary assumed that the individual could stay busy full time practicing medicine. If we relax this assumption, then the advantages of specialization are less pervasive. The physician might, if unable to stay busy full time with medical duties, do secretarial work without having to forego the physician's higher income. Both the theories of absolute and comparative advantage likewise assume that resources are fully employed. Since they have many unemployed resources, some countries have sought to restrict imports in order to employ idle resources although they are then not employed efficiently.

Countries' goals may not be limited to efficiency.

Efficiency objective. A second assumption of the physician/medical secretary analogy is that the individual who can do both medicine and office work is interested primarily in profit maximization or maximum efficiency. There are a number of reasons why the individual might not choose to work full-time at medical tasks. Administrative work might simply be very relaxing and self-fulfilling. The physician might fear that the hired secretary will be unreliable. The physician may wish to maintain secretarial skills in case that administration, rather than medicine, commands higher wages in the future. Countries also often pursue other objectives than output efficiency: They may fear too much specialization because of the vulnerability brought about by changes in technology and price fluctuations.

Two countries, two commodities. For the sake of simplicity, Ricardo's and our example assumed a very simple world of only two countries and two commodities. Although this is unrealistic, it does not limit the theory. Economists have applied the same reasoning to demonstrate the efficiency advantages with multiproduct and multicountry situations.

Transport costs. Neither the theory of absolute nor that of comparative advantage considered the cost of moving products from one country to another, but this is not a serious limitation. Although specialization might save the number of resources necessary for producing goods, resources are also needed to move the goods internationally. If it costs more resources to transport the goods than are saved through specialization, then the advantages of trade are negated.

Resources are not as mobile or immobile as the theories state.

Mobility. The absolute and comparative advantage theories assume that resources can move freely from the production of one good to another domestically but are not free to move internationally. Neither of these assumptions is completely valid. The misplaced clothing worker in New England, for example, may not move easily into an aerospace job in California. Rather, this worker will have difficulty working in such a different industry and might have trouble moving to a new area. Contrary to the theories, there is some mobility of resources internationally, although not as much as there is domestically. In recent years, for example, a significant number of Sri Lankan workers have been employed in the Middle East. The questions of domestic and international mobility will be discussed in the next two chapters.

FACTOR PROPORTIONS THEORY

According to the factor proportions theory, factors in relative abundance are cheaper than factors in relative scarcity.

In their theories of absolute and comparative advantage, Smith and Ricardo showed how output could be increased by having countries specialize in the products for which they have an advantage. But their theories did not help to identify which types of products would most likely give a country an advantage. They assumed that the free market would lead producers to move to the goods that they could make more efficiently as they were unable to compete in other areas. About a century and a quarter later two Swedish economists, Eli Heckscher and Bertil Ohlin, developed the **factor proportions theory,** which reasoned that differences in countries' endowments of labor relative to their endowments of land or capital would explain differences in factor costs. They proposed that if labor were abundant in relation to land and capital, for example, labor costs would be low and land and capital costs high. If labor were scarce, then the price of labor would be high in relation to the price of land and capital. These factor costs would lead countries to excel in the production and export of products using their abundant and cheaper factors of productions.[8]

Land–Labor Relationship

On the basis of the factor proportions theory Sri Lankan authorities reasoned that they were likely to have a competitive advantage for products using large numbers of semiskilled workers. This was a production factor that they had in abundance.

The factor proportions theory seems logical on the basis of a casual observation of worldwide production and exports. Where there are many people relative to the amount of land—for example, Hong Kong and the Netherlands—it would seem, and it is so, that land prices are very high. Neither Hong Kong nor the Netherlands, regardless of their climate and soil conditions, would seem likely to excel in the production of goods requiring large amounts of land, such as sheep or wheat. These products are left to countries such as Australia and Canada where there is abundant land relative to the number of people. Casual observation of manufacturing in relation to the labor–land proportions also seems to substantiate the theory. In Hong Kong, for example, the most successful industries are those for which technology permits the use of a minimum amount of land relative to the number of people employed; there, clothing production can be achieved in multistoried factories where there is a small distance among workers on any level. Hong Kong does not compete in the production of automobiles, which requires much more space per worker.

Labor–Capital Relationship

Production factors are not homogeneous, especially labor.

When labor is abundant in relation to capital, cheap labor rates and export competitiveness in products requiring large amounts of labor relative to capital would be expected. The opposite would be anticipated when labor is scarce. India, Iran, and Tunisia, for instance, excel in the production of handmade carpets that differ in appearance as well as production method from the machine-made carpets produced in the United Kingdom and the United States using cheap capital.

U.S. imports have high intensity of less-skilled labor.

U.S. exports are labor-intensive compared with U.S. imports.

Studies examining the labor-to-capital relationship have shown that export competitiveness is sometimes surprising, however. For example, Wassily Leontief found that among overall industries in the United States, those that were more successful at exporting had a higher labor intensity than those that faced the most import competition.[9] Because of the presumption that the United States has abundant capital relative to labor this surprising finding is known as the **Leontief paradox.** Several possible explanations have been proposed for this finding.

One of the most plausible has been that the Heckscher-Ohlin theory assumes erroneously that production factors are homogeneous. Labor skills are, in fact, very different within and among countries, since different people have different training and education. Training and education require capital expenditures that do not show up in traditional capital measurements, which include only plant and equipment values. By modifying the Heckscher-Ohlin theory to account for different labor groups and the capital invested to train these groups, the factor proportions theory seems to hold. If we look at labor, not as a homogeneous commodity, but rather by categories of labor, we find that the industrial countries actually have a more abundant supply of highly educated labor (to which a high capital expenditure has been made) than of other types. Industrial country exports embody a higher proportion of professionals such as scientists and engineers; thus they are using their abundant production factors. LDC exports, on the other hand, have a high intensity of less-skilled labor.[10]

Different Production Methods

The factor proportions analysis becomes more complicated when the same product might be produced by different methods, such as with either high inputs of labor or high inputs of capital. Canada produces wheat in a capital-intensive (lots of machinery per worker) method because of its abundance of low-cost capital relative to labor. In India, on the other hand, the same wheat is produced by using many fewer machines because there is abundant and cheap labor. Where there is more than one way of producing the same output, it is the relative input cost in relation to output that determines what country can produce the same product more cheaply. The fact that products can be produced in different ways is another possible explanation of the Leontief paradox in that the U.S. industries facing the most competition because of cheap foreign labor are the ones that have responded most by substituting machines for labor.

THE PRODUCT LIFE CYCLE

According to the PLC theory, the production location for many products goes from one country to another in the products' life cycles.

Another theory attempts to explain world trade and investment patterns in manufactured products on the basis of stages in a product's life.[11] Only that part of the theory dealing with trade aspects will be covered in this chapter. Chapter 6 will emphasize the investment aspects of the theory. Briefly, the theory of **product life cycle (PLC)** states that certain kinds of products go through a cycle consisting of four stages (introduction, growth, maturity, and decline) and that the location of production will shift internationally depending on the stage of the cycle. These four stages are a continuum rather than fully differentiated from each other. Nevertheless, we shall describe each stage in terms of its major characteristics.

Stage 1: Introduction

The introduction stage is marked by:

- Innovation in response to observed need
- Exportation by the innovative country
- New product.

Innovation, production, and sales in same country. New products are usually developed because there is a need and market for them. Since there is generally more observation of nearby market conditions, the development is more apt to be in response to domestic than foreign needs. In other words, a U.S. firm is most apt to develop a new product because of observed needs in the U.S. market, a French firm because of perceived French needs, and so on. Once a research and development group has created a new product, that product could theoretically be manufactured anywhere in the world, even though its sales are intended primarily for the market where consumer needs were first observed. In practice, however, the early production generally occurs in a domestic location as well because the company wishes to use its excess capacity and because it is useful to locate near the intended consumers in order to get quick market feedback.

Industrial countries, especially the United States. Since the early manufacturing and sales of new products occur primarily in countries that make product innovations, it is useful to know where new products are developed. Indications are that during the last few decades nearly all of the world's technology emanates from the developed countries and that over half originated in the United States.

A number of reasons account for the dominant position of industrial countries, especially the United States. These include the high incomes, which allow for risking expenditures on research that may or may not yield gainful results, and the availability of scientists and engineers. In the United States there is a particular awe of science dramatized by such adjectives as "wonder," "miracle," and "magic" when referring to new products, and a contingent of consumers who generally believe that "new" is better than "old."

The recent supremacy of the United States does not imply that all product innovations originate in the United States. In fact, there is evidence that the U.S. share of new products has been declining and that Japan may now be the world's leading innovator.[12] For the purpose of explaining the PLC theory, however, we shall assume that the new products have originated in the United States.

Exports and labor. Although most sales are for the domestic market during the introduction stage of a product cycle, a small part of the production may be sold to customers in foreign markets who have heard about the new product and actively seek it. These foreign customers are most likely to be in other industrial countries because of similarities in income levels which create similar market segments.

At this stage the production process is apt to be quite labor-intensive in comparison to the way the product will be produced at a later stage. Because the product is not yet standardized, it is necessary to produce it by a process that permits rapid changes in product characteristics as dictated by feedback from the market. This implies high labor input as opposed to automated production, which is more capital-intensive. A second factor influencing the early labor intensity is that process technology (the capital machinery necessary to produce a product on a large scale) usually comes later than the development of product technology. It is only when sales begin to develop very rapidly (Stage 2) that there is an incentive to build machinery capable of producing the product on a large scale. At the introductory stage, sales growth may be too uncertain to warrant the high development costs of the new process machines.

The fact that the United States excels in the development of new products that are generally made in labor-intensive ways helps us to understand the Leontief Paradox, which showed that the United States generally exports labor-intensive products. Since U.S. labor rates are known to be among the highest in the world, how can the United States compete? One view is that it is due to the monopoly position of original producers, which allows producers to pass on costs to consumers who are unwilling to wait for possible price reductions later on. There is much evidence of this behavior based on eventual price decreases of products such as calculators and videocassette recorders. Another line of thought is that although U.S. labor is paid a high hourly wage, its education and skill level make it adept and efficient when production is not yet standardized. When production becomes highly automated, it becomes less competitive because unskilled labor may be quickly trained to perform highly repetitive tasks efficiently. Interestingly the United States enjoys its best manufacturing export advantage in those industries in which production workers are most highly paid, such as aerospace. The least competitive are the industries with lower wage rates, such as clothing.[13]

Stage 2: Growth

Growth is characterized by:
- Increases in exports by innovating country
- More competition
- Increased capital intensity
- Some foreign production

If sales begin to grow after a product is introduced, there is an incentive for competitors to break the monopoly position. They can often do this by making slight product changes, which overcome proprietorship created through patents. At the same time, demand is liable to be growing substantially in foreign markets, particularly in other industrial countries. In fact, demand may grow sufficiently to justify the capital expenditure to produce in some foreign markets in order to overcome transport charges and tariffs.

The output at this stage is likely to stay almost entirely in the foreign country with the new manufacturing unit. Let us say, for example, that U.S. production had a monopoly that has been broken by Japanese output. The Japanese output will be sold mainly in Japan because: (1) there is growth in the Japanese market; (2) unique product variations are being introduced for Japanese consumers; and (3) Japanese costs may still be high owing to production start-up problems.

Because sales are growing fast in many markets, there are greater incentives at this level for the development of process technology. However, technology may not yet be well developed because of the number of product variations introduced by different competitors who are trying to take a leadership position by gaining market share. The production process may therefore still be characterized as labor-intensive during this stage but becoming less so. The original producing country will increase its exports in this stage but face the loss of certain key export markets for which local production has commenced.

Stage 3: Maturity

Maturity includes:
- Decline in exports from innovating country
- More product standardization
- More capital intensity
- Increased competitiveness of price factor
- Production starts in LDCs

In Stage 3, maturity, worldwide demand begins to level off although it may be growing in some countries and declining in others. In the mature stage of production there is often a shakeout of producers so that product models become highly standardized, making cost a more important competitive weapon. Longer production runs become possible for foreign plants, which in turn reduces per unit cost. The lower per unit cost enables sales to increase more in LDCs.

Since markets and technologies are widespread, the innovating country no longer has a production advantage. In fact, there are incentives to begin moving plants to LDCs where unskilled but inexpensive labor can be used effectively on standardized (capital-intensive) work processes.

Stage 4: Decline

Decline is characterized by:
- Production concentrated in LDCs

As a product moves to a declining stage, those factors occurring during the mature stage continue to evolve. The markets in industrial countries decline more rapidly than in LDCs as affluent customers spend disposable income on

- Innovating country is net importer

ever-newer products. By this time, market and cost factors have dictated that almost all production is situated in LDCs.

Verification and Limitations of PLC Theory

There have been a number of attempts to verify the PLC theory. Studies have found behavior to be consistent with the predictions of the PLC model for certain consumer durables, synthetic materials, and electronics.[14]

The PLC model seems to hold for many industries but there are many other types of products for which this behavior would not be expected.[15] One such product type would be that for which, because of very rapid innovations, the life cycle is too short to have time to achieve cost reductions by moving production from one country to another. For many electronic products today, for example, product obsolescence occurs so rapidly that there is little international diffusion of production. Another is a luxury-type product for which cost is of little concern to the consumer. A third type of product is one for which international transportation costs are so high that there is little opportunity for export sales regardless of the stage within the product life cycle. A fourth type of product is one in which a firm can use a differentiation strategy, such as advertising, in order to maintain consumer demand without competing on the basis of price.[16]

Regardless of the type of product, there has been an increased tendency by MNEs to introduce new products at home and abroad almost simultaneously. In so doing, they eliminate the leads and lags that are assumed to exist as a product is diffused from one country to another. Furthermore, companies are increasingly producing abroad simply to take advantage of production economies rather than in response to growing foreign markets. For example, Singer produces certain sewing machine models in Brazil to sell in export markets, not to supply sewing machines to Brazil.

DETERMINATION OF TRADING PARTNERS

A number of factors help to explain why a country trades more with one partner than with another.[17] The most important of these are described in this section.

Country Differences

Most trade theories emphasize differences among countries:
- Climate
- Factor endowments
- Innovative capabilities

Thus far in this chapter, the theories to explain why trade takes place have concentrated on differences among countries. On the basis of these theories we would expect that the greater the dissimilarity among countries, the greater potential there would be for trade. For example, big differences in climatic conditions would create different capabilities of producing agricultural products. Differences in labor or capital intensities would lead countries to be able to produce different types of products efficiently. Differences in innovative abilities would affect how a product's production will move from one country to another during its life cycle. These theories tend to explain most of the trade among dissimilar countries, such as trade between an industrial country and an LDC.

Country Similarity Theory

Most trade today occurs among seemingly similar countries.

When we observe actual trade patterns, we see that most of the world's trade occurs among countries that have similar characteristics. Most trade occurs among industrialized countries that have highly educated populations and are located in temperate areas of the world. On this basis, overall trade patterns seem to be at variance with the traditional theories that emphasize country-by-country differences.

The fact that so much trade takes place among industrial countries is due to the growing importance of acquired (product technology) advantage as opposed to natural advantage in world trade. The **country similarity theory** holds that, having developed a new product in response to observed market conditions in the home market, a producer will then turn to markets that are perceived to be the most similar to those at home. In other words, consumers in industrial countries will have a high propensity to buy high-quality and luxury products, whereas consumers in lower income countries will buy few of these products.[18]

Although the markets within the industrial countries might have similar demand characteristics, there are differences in how these countries specialize in order to gain acquired advantages. For example, the British have for some time excelled in biochemistry and applied engineering, the Germans in synthetics chemistry, and the French in pharmacology. It is also known that substantial country-to-country differences exist in how they apportion their R&D expenditures, thus giving rise to the development of different technical and product capabilities in different industrial countries.[19]

Pairs of Trading Relationships

Although the theories of country differences and similarities help to explain broad world trade patterns, such as between industrial countries and LDCs, they do little to help us understand specific pairs of trading relationships. Why, for example, will a particular industrial country buy more from one LDC than another? Why will it buy from one industrial country versus another? Although there is no single answer to these questions that will explain all product flows, the distance between two countries explains more of these world-trade relationships than any other factor. This is especially true for products for which the transport cost is high relative to the production cost.

Cultural similarity, as indicated by language and religion, also helps to explain much of the direction of trade. Apparently importers and exporters find it easier to do business in a country that they perceive as being similar. Likewise, much of the trade between specific industrial countries and LDCs is explained by historic colonial relationships. Importers and exporters find it easier to continue business ties than to develop new distributorship arrangements in countries where they are less experienced.

INDEPENDENCE, INTERDEPENDENCE, AND DEPENDENCE

No country is completely dependent or independent, though some are nearer one extreme or other.

The concept of independence, interdependence, and dependence must be viewed along a continuum. Imagine independence at one extreme and dependence on the other, with interdependence somewhere in the middle. There are no countries located at either extreme of this continuum; however, some tend to be nearer one extreme than the other.

Independence

Too much independence means doing without certain things.

In a situation of **independence,** a country would not rely at all on others. Since all countries trade, no country is completely independent economically from other countries. Therefore it is hard to imagine how life would be without the accessibility of goods and services produced in a foreign country. The most recent observation of a society's possible economic independence occurred when hunters reported on the Tasaday tribe on the island of Mindanao in the southern Philippines. Although some scientists have called the Tasadays a hoax, many others believe that the Tasadays may have been the last group on earth to live in virtual isolation. From the end of World War II to the death of dictator Enver Hoxha in 1985, Albania is the closest recent experience of a country in near-isolation.[20] Because they lacked goods, services, and technologies from other societies, Tasadays and Albanians enjoyed certain advantages. They did not have to worry, for example, that another society might cut off their supply of essential foods or tools. At the same time, both the Tasadays and Albanians did without a variety and quantity of products.

Governmental policy has focused on achieving the advantages of independence without paying too high a price in terms of consumer deprivation. China and India, for example, have pursued much more economic independence than have Brazil and Mexico, with different results in different periods.[21] Earlier in this chapter we showed that large countries typically depend much less on foreign trade than do small countries. Even consumers in large countries could suffer through policies to promote more independence. The degree of suffering would depend on the type of product. The elimination of coffee or tea imports into the United States would probably involve less of a hardship, for example, than the cessation of foreign purchases of certain essential metals, such as manganese, cobalt, and chromium. In between are products that could be produced domestically, but at a much higher price. No country today seeks complete independence; however, most try to forge their trade patterns so that they are minimally vulnerable to foreign supply and demand problems.

Interdependence

Interdependence is mutual dependence.

One of the ways of limiting vulnerability to problems of foreign events is through **interdependence**, or the development of mutually needed trade. France and West Germany, for example, have highly interdependent economies. Each of the two countries depends about equally on the other as a trading partner. Therefore, France is not too vulnerable to the possibility that West Germany would cut off supplies or markets because France could retaliate effectively.

Dependence

Too much dependence means vulnerability to events in other countries.

In recent years, many developing countries have decried their **dependence** on the sale of one primary commodity and/or one country as a customer and supplier. Because LDC economies are small, they tend to be much more dependent on a given industrial country than the industrial country is dependent on the LDC. Mexico, for example, depends on the United States for over 60 percent of its imports, whereas the United States depends on Mexico for less than 5 percent of its imports. Mexico can thus be much more

Figure 4.4
Dependence on Leading Commodity for Export Earnings

Source: 1986 Yearbook of International Trade Statistics, Vol. I (New York: U.N. Department of International Economic and Social Affairs, 1988). The figures by the pie slices refer to the number and percentage of countries. For example, three industrial countries (15 percent of all industrial countries) depend on their leading two digit SITC commodity for 25 to 50 percent of their exports.

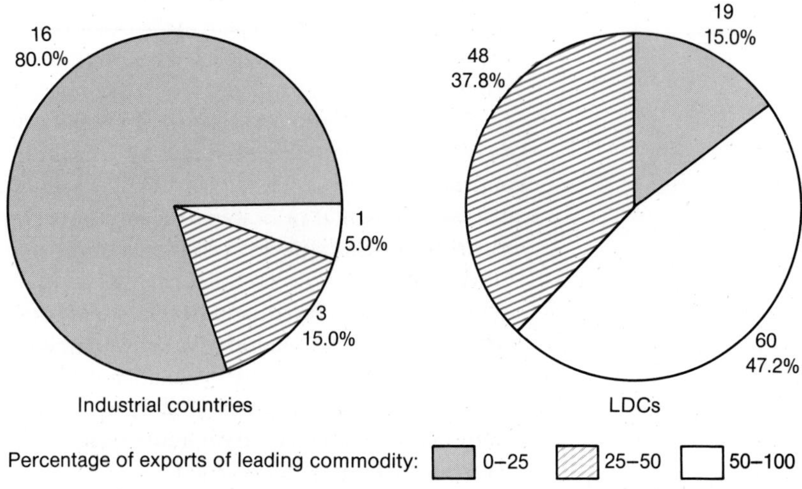

TABLE 4.2

SELECTED LDC DEPENDENCE ON ONE COMMODITY FOR EXPORT EARNINGS

Country	Commodity	Percent of export earnings
Burma	Rice	55.2
Colombia	Coffee	52.4
Cuba	Sugar	74.1
Ghana	Cacao	47.7
Iraq	Petroleum	98.1*
Jamaica	Inorganic chemicals	61.8
Kiribati	Crude fertilizers	84.6
Macao	Clothing	61.7
Mali	Cotton	51.2
Mauritania	Iron ore	48.1
Niger	Uranium and thorium ores	79.3
Sierra Leone	Semiprecious stones and crude metals	70.4
Somalia	Live animals	83.7

*From the *1983 Yearbook of International Trade Statistics,* Vol. I.

Source: *1984 Yearbook of International Trade Statistics,* Vol. I (New York: U.N. Department of International Economic and Social Affairs, 1986).

adversely affected by U.S. policies than the United States can be affected by Mexican policies. The dependence by an LDC on an industrial country also has led to a widespread belief that this will retard the LDC's development.[22] This fear of dependency has led many LDCs to try to change their production and trade patterns, as reflected in the opening case on Sri Lanka.

Figure 4.4 shows that there is only one industrialized county (Iceland) out of twenty whose leading export accounts for as much as 50 percent of total export earnings. Among the developing countries, however, 60 percent are dependent on one commodity for at least 50 percent of their export earnings. A selected list of high-commodity dependencies by LDCs is given in Table 4.2.

The developing countries are also somewhat more dependent on one trading partner than are industrial countries. (See Fig. 4.5). The trading partner on whom the developing country typically depends is almost always an industrial country. Some examples are shown in Table 4.3. Only one industrial country (Canada) conducts over half its trade with one partner, the United States.

Although theorists and policymakers wishing to lower dependency have proposed a number of different approaches, they all propose that LDCs intervene in the foreign trade markets. As was shown in the introductory case, Sri Lanka has attempted to diversify its exports by developing non-traditional products for which policymakers feel that Sri Lanka can ultimately be competitive in world markets.

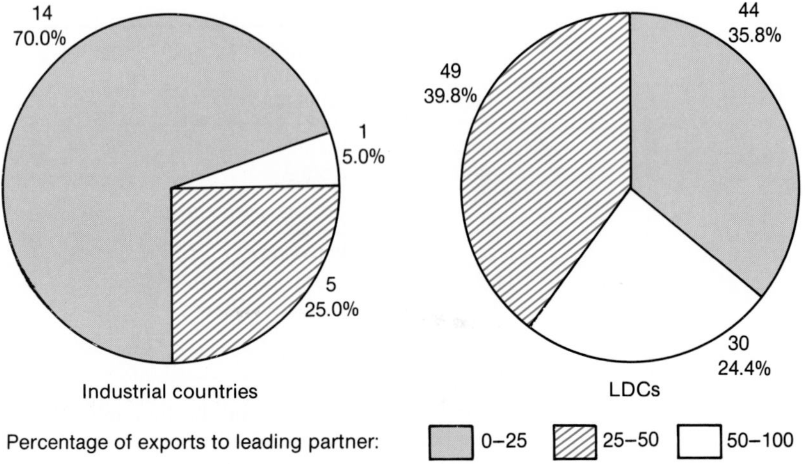

Figure 4.5
Dependence on Major Export Partner

Source: 1986 Yearbook of International Trade Statistics, Vol. I (New York: U.N. Department of International Economic and Social Affairs, 1988). The figures by the pie slices refer to the number and percentage of countries. For example, five industrial countries (25 percent of all industrial countries) depend on one trading partner for 25 to 50 percent of their exports.

TABLE 4.3

SELECTED LDC DEPENDENCE ON ONE TRADING PARTNER

LDC	Export market	Percent of LDC's exports
Afghanistan	U.S.S.R.	59.4
Brunei	Japan	67.7
Central African Republic	France	44.1
Mauritius	U.K.	50.5
Mexico	U.S.	58.1
Somalia	Saudi Arabia	84.1

Source: *1984 Yearbook of International Trade Statistics,* Vol. I (New York: U.N. Department of International Economic and Social Affairs, 1986).

SOME DIFFERENCES AMONG DEVELOPING COUNTRIES

In foregoing discussions we emphasized that most LDCs depend on the export of primary products. The manufactured goods they export are usually mature products requiring high inputs of unskilled or semi-skilled labor. While these distinctions are true overall, they nevertheless obscure some differences among groups of developing countries. For those countries that do export manufactured goods, the type of good and country can be put primarily into one of three categories. The first is the group of countries made up of Hong Kong, Singapore, Taiwan, South Korea, Israel, Portugal, and Greece. These countries all lack natural resources and have concentrated on exporting mature labor-intensive products. They have all placed a heavy emphasis on marketing, design, and information about foreign markets as a means of being competitive. A second group of countries made up of

Yugoslavia, Argentina, Brazil, Mexico, and Turkey have natural resources which they can use for further processing into manufactured goods. They also have large enough domestic markets to develop scale economies. These countries have had success in exporting capital goods, chemicals, and other intermediaries. The third group of countries made up of India, Pakistan, Egypt, and Indonesia (large poor nations) have developed exports of standardized intermediate goods such as textiles, plywood, and cement that are not typical labor-intensive commodities.[23]

WHY COMPANIES TRADE

Most theories are made on the basis of countries but trade decisions are usually made by companies.

Incentives to export include:

- use for excess capacity
- reduced production costs per unit
- increased mark-up
- spread of sales risk

Incentives to import include:

- cheaper supplies
- additions to product line
- reduction of risk of nonsupply

Most trade theories take an approach from a country standpoint. In other words, they approach trade with a question such as, "Why should Sri Lanka trade?" Regardless of the advantages that countries may gain by trading, trade ordinarily will not reach fruition unless businesses within the country perceive that there are opportunities for exporting and importing. Since companies have a limited number of resources, they must decide whether to exploit those resources domestically or internationally. Only if they see that the international opportunities might be greater than the domestic ones will they divert those resources to the foreign sector. To understand why trade takes place, it is therefore useful to understand the trade advantages accruing to individual businesses.

Export Opportunities

Use excess capacity. Companies frequently have immediate or long-term output capabilities for which there is inadequate domestic demand. This may be in the form of known reserves of natural resources or product-specific capabilities that cannot easily be diverted to the production of other goods for which there might be an adequate domestic demand.

As shown earlier in this chapter, small countries tend to trade more than large countries. This is partially due to their need to use excess capacity when process technology is relatively fixed to produce efficiently only on a large scale. Take automobile production, for example: Volvo has a much greater need to export from the small Swedish market than does General Motors from the large U.S. market.

Cost reduction. Studies have shown that a company can generally reduce its costs by 20–30 percent each time its output is doubled, a phenomenon known as the **experience curve.**[24] For instance, if we assume a 20 percent cost reduction and an initial cost of $100 per unit, the second unit produced will cost $80, the fourth $64, and so on. The reduction may come about because of one of several factors: covering fixed costs over a larger output; becoming more efficient because of the experience of having produced more units; and making quantity purchases of materials and transportation. Therefore it is obvious that the market leader may garner cost advantages over competitors. One way a company can increase output is by defining its market in global rather than domestic terms.

More profitability. A producer might be able to sell the same product at a greater profit abroad than at home. This may come about because of a different foreign than domestic competitive environment. One such reason is that the product may be in a different stage of its life cycle abroad. Thus a mature stage at home may force domestic price cutting, whereas a growth stage abroad may make price reductions unnecessary there. Greater profitability may come about because of different government actions at home or abroad (for example, differences in the taxation of earnings or differences in regulations on prices).

Risk spreading. By spreading sales in more than one country market, a producer might be able to minimize fluctuations in demand. This may come about because of differences on a country-to-country basis in the timing of business cycles and because the life cycle of products might be in different stages in different countries. Another factor in the spreading of risks through exportation is that a producer might be able to develop more customers, thereby reducing its vulnerability to losing a single or a few customers.

Import Opportunities

The impetus for getting involved in trade may come either by the exporter or by the importer. In either case, there must be both a seller and a buyer. Impetus may come from an importer because a firm is seeking out cheaper supplies, components, or products to be used in its home market or in a foreign country where it has production facilities. Or a firm may be actively seeking new products that have been innovated abroad in order to complement its existing lines. This will give the company more to sell; it might also enable the importer to use excess capacity in its own distribution sales force.

An importer, like an exporter, might be able to spread its operating risks. By developing alternative suppliers, the firm is less vulnerable to the dictates or problems of any single supplier. In the 1960s, for example, many large steel customers in the United States, such as the automobile industry, diversified their steel purchases to include European and Japanese suppliers. This reduced the risk of supply shortages for the U.S. automobile industry in case of a strike among steelworkers in the United States. At the same time, though, it contributed to the problems of the steel industry within the United States.

Trade Impediments

Trade impediments include:
- Lack of knowledge about opportunities
- Lack of information on trade mechanics
- Fears about risks
- Trade restrictions

Although there are often advantages for firms in commencing importation or exportation, many factors can impede firms' entry into trading relations. These in turn affect the full materialization of trade among countries. First of all there may be imperfect knowledge of markets in foreign countries so that a producer does not take advantage of the avenues open to it. Or a producer might be aware of potential demand in foreign countries but nevertheless not know the mechanics of exporting and distributing in foreign markets. The process of exporting, after all, involves a whole new set of terminology and institutions. A company might also perceive that exporting or importing is too risky. A potential exporter may fear, for example, that payment will not be forthcoming, that payment will be in a currency that cannot easily be used, or that the competitive environment abroad is too unknown or disorderly. A potential importer may fear that supplies are too uncertain given the greater distance between countries and the problems of strikes and unrest abroad.

Governmental policies might either enhance or retard the movement of trade. Policies to improve imperfect knowledge about the foreign environment might positively increase trade. Direct restrictions on the importation or exportation of goods are detriments. It is safe to say, though, that all governments in the world have policies that both enhance and retard trade. In the Sri Lankan case at the beginning of the chapter, the Sri Lankan government sought to remove some marketing imperfections by helping to identify industries of likely international competitiveness. At the same time, however, Sri Lanka set direct import restrictions on a number of products.

SUMMARY

- Trade theory is useful because it helps to explain what might be produced competitively in a given locale, where a company might go to produce a given product efficiently, and whether governmental practices will interfere with the free flow of trade among countries.
- Some trade theories deal with the question of what will happen to international trade in the absence of governmental interference; others prescribe how government should interfere with trade flows in order to achieve certain national objectives.
- Mercantilist theory proposed that a country should try to have a favorable balance of trade (export more than it imports) in order to receive an influx of gold. Neomercantilist theory also seeks a favorable balance of trade, but its purpose is to achieve some social or political objective.
- Adam Smith developed the theory of absolute advantage, which holds that consumers will be better off if they can buy foreign-made products that are priced more cheaply than domestic ones.

- According to the absolute advantage theory, a country may produce goods more efficiently because of a natural advantage (e.g., raw materials, climate) or because of an acquired advantage (e.g., technology or skills).
- The theory of country size holds that because countries with large land areas are more apt to have varied climates and natural resources, they are generally more nearly self-sufficient than smaller countries. A second reason for their greater self-sufficiency is that their population centers are more likely to be located at a greater distance from other countries, thus raising the transport costs of foreign trade.
- The comparative advantage theory holds that total output can be increased through foreign trade even though one country may have an absolute advantage in the production of all products.
- Some of the assumptions of the absolute and comparative trade theories that have been questioned by policymakers are that full employment exists, that output efficiency is the major objective, that there are no transport costs among countries, that resources move freely within countries, and that resources are immobile internationally.
- The factor proportions theory holds that the relative factor endowments in a country of land, labor, and capital will determine the relative costs of these factors. These costs, in turn, will determine what goods a country can produce most efficiently.
- The product life cycle (PLC) theory states that many manufactured products will first be produced in the countries whose research has developed the new product. This is almost always an industrialized country, with the United States accounting for the largest share in recent years. Over the life of the product, however, the production will tend to become more capital intensive and be shifted to foreign locations.
- According to the country similarity theory of trade, most trade today takes place in manufactured goods among industrial countries because there are more similar market segments among these countries.
- LDCs have increasingly been concerned that they are too vulnerable to events in other countries because of their high dependence on one export product and/or one trading partner. As they try to be more independent of the external environment, however, they face the risk that their own consumers may have to pay higher prices or do without some goods.
- Although most trade theories deal with country-to-country benefits and costs, it is usually at the firm level that trading decisions are made. Companies may perceive trading advantages because of using excess capacity, lowering production costs, and spreading risks. They may not commence foreign trading activities, however, because of not knowing about opportunities or how to take advantage of them.

CASE: THE CASHEW[25]

The cashew tree is best known today for its nuts, which account for about 20 percent of the value of nuts produced worldwide—about equal to almonds or hazelnuts.

The fruit of the tree (known as the cashew apple), however, drew earlier attention. The Tupi Indians of Brazil first harvested the cashew apple in the wild. They later introduced it to early Portuguese traders, who in turn propagated the plant in other tropical countries. But attempts to grow the tree on plantations proved unsuccessful because the cashew was vulnerable to insects in the close quarters of plantations. Instead, some of the abandoned plantation trees propagated new trees in the wild where they thrived in the forests of India, East Africa, Indonesia, and Southeast Asia.

Several factors inhibited early use of the cashew nut. First, cashew fruit matures before the nut, so the fruit is spoiled by the time the nut can be harvested usefully. Second, the processing of cashew nuts is tedious and long. In the 1920s, though, a processing industry developed in India. The nuts became more valuable than the fruit because of growing popularity among Indian consumers. India maintained a virtual monopoly on cashew processing until the mid-1970s. This monopoly was due to a combination of three factors: First, India was the largest producer of wild cashews; second, early demand occurred in India, meaning that any other country would have to incur added transport charges in order to reach the Indian market; third, and most importantly, the Indian workers were particularly adept at the process technology.

Cashew nut processing was performed in a very labor-intensive manner, requiring manual dexterity and low labor rates. The nut is contained beneath layers of shell and thin skin. To remove the shell, the nut must be placed in an open fire for a few minutes and then tapped (while still hot) with a wooden hammer. If the nut is broken in the tapping, its value decreases considerably. Once the shell is removed, the nut is placed in an oven for up to ten hours, after which the skin is removed by hand while the nut is still warm. Removal is done without fingernails or any sharp objects that can mark or break the surface. The nuts are then sorted and graded into twenty-four different categories by the size of the pieces. The highest-quality grade typically sells for about four times the price of the lowest grade, which is sold almost entirely to the confectionery industry.

Through the years several factors began to threaten India's prominence as a cashew producer. First there was a shortage of Indian-grown raw nuts as demand grew in the United States and the United Kingdom. Since the nuts were grown in the wild and unsuited to plantation growth, India turned to East Africa (e.g., Mozambique, Tanzania, and Kenya) for supplies. Those countries were experiencing high unemployment and were at first eager to sell the raw nuts.

By the 1950s, India was no longer the world's major consumer. Consequently, the East African countries began to realize that they might be able to bypass India by processing the raw nuts themselves. Cashew-processing methods were well known, so there was no technological obstacle. Another barrier blocked early competition from East Africa, however. The Indian workers had worked on homemade handicrafts when they were very young, and, as a result, by the time they were employed in cashew processing, could perform delicate hand operations efficiently. Without this childhood training, the East Africans were at a disadvantage. This was because workers broke too many nuts and were too slow to make output profitable.

Although the African failure granted a reprieve to the Indian industry, it put them on notice that they were vulnerable to supply cutoffs. The Indian Council for Agricultural Research, the International Society for Horticultural Sciences, and the Indian Society for Plantation Crops expanded efforts to increase India's raw nut production. Concomitantly, three different companies developed mechanical equipment to replace hand processing. The Sturtevant Tropical Products Institute developed a method now used by a London equipment manufacturer, Fletcher and Stewart, which cracks the shells with a steel plate. Oltremare Industria of Italy and Widmer and Ernst of Switzerland both developed shell-cutting machines. Equipment was sold to East African countries and to Brazil in the 1970s. These countries decreased their raw nut exports to India in order to maintain supplies for their own processing.

Two factors have kept India's hand-processing industry afloat. First, the new machinery breaks many nuts, so that Indian processors still have little competition in the sale of higher-grade cashew nuts. At any time, however, newer machinery might solve the breakage problem, again threatening the approximately 200 Indian processors and their 300,000 employees. Furthermore, there is increased competition for the lower-grade output. The second factor responsible for the enduring Indian industry is that their processors have been able to obtain more raw nuts as Indian raw nut production has increased. Pesticide technology now makes cashew tree plantations feasible, thus increasing the number of trees per acre. Furthermore, Indian experimentation in hybridization, vegetative propagation, and grafting and budding techniques promises to increase the output per tree to five times what it was in the wild.

During the 1980s, Indian processors felt vulnerable to two more threats. One was political; the other technological. First, since India could no longer compete as well in its traditional North American and European markets for lower-grade nuts, a larger portion of those nuts was sold in the Soviet Union, which had become India's largest cashew nut customer in terms of tonnage.

The Soviet Union bought the nuts at a price above world market levels, and its buying habits were believed to have a political motive. By buying large quantities at a high price, the Soviet Union might have considerable political influence in India, especially in the Kerala area where the processing industry is centered. At any time these sales might decline drastically for political reasons.

Second, there was the potential for an excess cashew nut supply, which can result from plantation techniques and improved technology in India and elsewhere. To find outlets for a possible nut glut, the All-India Coordinated Spices and Cashew Nut Improvement Project has centered on finding new markets for products from the cashew tree. The cashew apple, for example, is available in far greater tonnage than the cashew nut. It has been discarded in the past because processors could get either fruit or nut but not both, and the nuts have been considered more valuable. Experimentation is going on to harvest both the fruit and the nut. The fruit is also being studied for commercial use in candy, jams, chutney, juice, carbonated beverages, syrup, wine, and vinegar. A second area of research is in the use of cashew nut shell liquid, which was once discarded as a waste product and is now used extensively in industrial production of friction dusts for formulation in brake linings and clutch facings. It has also been used in the formulation of particle board and in tanning processes. Thus far, however, the extraction of cashew nut shell liquid has been too costly to make it fully competitive with some other types of oils.

QUESTIONS

1. What trade theories help to explain where cashew tree products have been produced historically?
2. Might India lose its competitive advantage in future cashew nut production? Why or why not?
3. If you were an Indian cashew processor, what alternatives might you consider to maintain future competitiveness?

NOTES

1. Data for this case were taken from *1983 Commodity Yearbook* (Jersey City, N.J.: Commodity Research Bureau, Inc. 1983), p. 340; "The Business Outlook: Sri Lanka," *Business Asia,* February 6, 1981, p. 48; "Sri Lanka Investment: Inside or Outside the Free Trade Zone?" *Business Asia,* April 24, 1981, pp. 134–135; P. Murugasu, "Selecting Products for Export Development," *International Trade Forum,* October–December 1979, pp. 4–7; International Monetary Fund, *Direction of Trade Statistics Yearbook 1982* (Washington, D.C.: IMF, 1982), p. 345; "United States Congress Speaks on Sri Lanka," bulletin issued by the Embassy of the Democratic Socialist Republic of Sri Lanka, Washington, April 1979; Lucien Rajakarunanayake, "Sri Lanka: Patterns of Serendipity," (Washington, D.C.: Embassy of Sri Lanka, May 1975); Colin de Silva, "Sri Lanka, the 'Resplendent Isle,' " *New York Times,* February 14, 1984, Sec. xx, p. 9; *World Development Report, 1987* (Washington, D.C.: The World Bank, 1987), p. 11.

2. The mercantilist period is not associated with any single writer. A good coverage of the philosophy of the era may be found in Eli Heckscher, *Mercantilism* (London: George Allen & Unwin, 1935).

3. For a discussion of the problems in running a trade surplus, see Maria Shao, William J. Holstein, and Steven J. Dryden, "Taiwan's Wealth Crisis," *Business Week,* No. 2993, April 13, 1987, pp. 46–47.

4. The book has been reprinted by various publishers. For the specific references of this chapter the edition used was Adam Smith, *The Wealth of Nations* (New York: The Modern Library, n.d.).

5. Stephen P. Magee, *International Trade* (Reading, Mass.: Addison-Wesley Publishing Company, 1980), pp. 10–12.

6. G. C. Hufbauer, "The Impact of National Characteristics and Technology on the Commodity Composition of Trade in Manufactured Goods," in *The Technology Factor in International Trade,* Raymond Vernon, ed. (New York: Columbia University Press, 1970), pp. 145–231.

7. David Ricardo, *On the Principles of Political Economy and Taxation,* originally published in London in 1817 has since been reprinted by a number of different publishers.

8. Bertil Ohlin, *Interregional and International Trade* (Cambridge, Mass.: Harvard University Press, 1933).

9. W. W. Leontief, "Domestic Production and Foreign Trade: The American Capital Position Re-examined," *Economia Internationale,* February 1954, pp. 3–32.

10. See, for example, Anne O. Krueger, "Trade Policies in Developing Countries," in *Handbook of International Economics,* Vol. 3, Ronald W. Jones and Peter Kenen, eds. (Amsterdam: North-Holland, 1984), pp. 519–569; and Bela Balassa, *The Newly Industrialized Countries in the World Economy* (New York: Pergamon Press, 1981), chap. 7.

11. Raymond Vernon, "International Investment and International Trade in the Product Life Cycle," *Quarterly Journal of Economics,* May 1966, pp. 190–207; Paul Krugman, "A Model of Innovation, Technology Transfer, and the World Distribution of Income," *Journal of Political Economy,* Vol. 87, April 1979, pp. 253–266; David Dollar, "Technological Innovation, Capital Mobility, and the Product Cycle in North–South Trade," *American Economic Review,* Vol. 76, No. 1, pp. 177–190.

12. See, for example, Paul Streeten, "Technology Gaps between Rich and Poor Countries," *Scottish Journal of Political Economy,* November 1972, Vol. XIX, No. 3, pp. 213–230; and Theresa Tellez, "Science, Technology and the Matter of Choice," *Science and Public Affairs,* October 1973, p. 55, for LDC estimates. Estimates of the U.S. portion are from National Science Foundation studies reported in Victor K. McElheny, "U.S. Science Lead Is Found Eroding," *New York Times,* March 14, 1976, p. 1. For more recent country-by-country comparisons of R&D expenditures, see Barnaby J. Feder, "Europe's Technology Revival," *New York Times,* May 21, 1984, p. D1 +; and William J. Broad, "Novel Technique Shows Japanese Outpace Americans in Innovation," *New York Times,* March 7, 1988, p. 1 +.

13. Daniel J. B. Mitchell, "Recent Changes in the Labor Content of U.S. International Trade," *International Labor Relations Review,* April 1975, pp. 355–375.

14. For good summaries of the studies to test the theory as well as recent tests, see James M. Lutz and Robert T. Green, "The Product Life Cycle and the Export Position of the United States," *Journal of International Business Studies,* Winter 1983, pp. 77–93; and Alicia Mullor-Sebastian, "The Product Life Cycle Theory: Empirical Evidence," *Journal of International Business Studies,* Winter 1983, pp. 95–105.

15. Ian H. Giddy, "The Demise of the Product Life Cycle in International Business Theory," *Columbia Journal of World Business,* Spring 1978, pp. 90–97.

16. This has been argued as a factor enabling industrial countries to charge high prices to LDCs while purchasing LDC manufactured products at the lowest possible prices. See Frances Stewart, "Recent Theories of International Trade: Some Implications for the South," in Henry Kierzowski, ed., *Monopolistic Competition and International Trade* (Oxford: Oxford University Press, 1984).

17. For a good overview of studies on this subject as well as an empirical analysis, see Rajendra K. Srivastava and Robert T. Green, "Determinants of Bilateral Trade Flows," *Journal of Business,* Vol. 59, No. 4, October 1986, pp. 623–639.

18. Stefan B. Linder, *An Essay on Trade Transformation* (New York: Wiley Publishing, 1961).

19. Michael J. Thomas, "The Location of Research and Development in the International Corporation," *Management International Review,* No. 1, 1975, p. 39.

20. Kenneth MacLeish, "Stone Age Cavemen of Mindanao," *National Geographic,* August 1972, pp. 219–249; Seth Mydans, "In Mindanao: Ancient Tribe or a Hoax from the 1970's," *New York Times,* December 7, 1987, p. 6; Robin Knight, "Albania Peeks out, Never Forgetting 'Life Is Earnest,' " *U.S. News & World Report,* Vol. 102, No. 18, May 11, 1987, p. 36.

21. Bela Balassa, "The Cambridge Group and the Developing Countries," *The World Economy,* Vol. 8, No. 4, September–October 1985, pp. 201–218.

22. For a very good survey of the literature (pro and con) on this point, see José Antonio Ocampo, "New Developments in Trade Theory and LDCs," *Journal of Developing Economics,* Vol. 22, No. 1, 1986, pp. 129–170.

23. Hollis Chenery and Donald Keesing, "The Changing Composition of Developing Country Exports," in Sven Grassman and Erik Lundberg, eds., *The World Economic Order: Past and Prospects* (London: Macmillan, 1981), pp. 82–116.

24. See, for example, Boston Consulting Group, *Perspective in Experience* (Boston: Boston Consulting Group, 1970); and Robert D. Buzzell, Bradley T. Buzzell, Gale Sultaw, and Ralph G. M. Sultaw, "Market Share: A Key to Profitability," *Harvard Business Review,* Vol. 58, No. 1, 1975.

25. Data for this case were taken from "L'Anacarde ou Noix de Cajou," *Marches Tropicaux,* June 13, 1980, pp. 1403–1405; R. J. Wilson, *The Market for Cashew Nut Kernals and Cashew Nutshell Liquid* (London: Tropical Products Institute, 1975); J. H. P. Tyman, "Cultivation, Processing and Utilization of the Cashew," *Chemistry and Industry,* January 19, 1980, pp. 59–62; Jean-Pierre Jeannet, "Indian Cashew Processors, Ltd.," ICH Case 9-378-832 (Boston: Harvard Business School, 1977); Jean-Pierre Jeannet, "Note on the World Cashew Nut Industry," ICH Case 9-378-834 (Boston: Harvard Business School, 1977).

5

CHAPTER

GOVERNMENTAL INFLUENCE ON TRADE

A little help does a great deal.
—French proverb

- To evaluate the rationale for governmental policies to enhance and/or restrict trade.
- To examine the effects of groups and trade-offs among groups on trade policies.
- To compare the protectionist arguments used in developed versus developing countries.
- To study the potential and actual effects of governmental intervention on the free flow of trade.
- To give an overview of the major means by which trade is restricted.
- To show that governmental trade policies create business uncertainties.

CASE: AUTOMOBILE IMPORTS[1]

The beginning of 1989 marked seven years since Japan began its "voluntary" limitation of automobile exports to the United States. Had Japan not voluntarily limited the exports through negotiations with the United States, the United States would certainly have imposed even more restrictive sanctions. Different groups have disagreed on whether the Japanese automobile imports should have been limited, whether the agreements have served the objectives for which they were intended, and whether new controls should be placed on the importation of vehicles. A U.S. Special Trade Representative vowed to end import restrictions. The president of the United Auto Workers (UAW) union responded that more imports would "punish the workers for the greed of their bosses." How did this situation develop?

Between 1979 and 1980, just prior to the first voluntary limitations, the foreign share of the new car market in the U.S. increased from 17 percent to 25.3 percent. Clearly, the U.S. automobile firms and their workers were in trouble. A beleaguered American Motors sold out to Renault, a French automaker, in an attempt to maintain operations. Chrysler was forced to sell most of its foreign subsidiaries, primarily to Peugeot, to raise working capital and then announced the largest losses ever registered by a company. Chrysler's loss record was eclipsed within a week by Ford. General Motors' working capital was drastically reduced. By the end of 1980, 193,000 out of 750,000 members of the UAW were unemployed.

There was considerable disagreement on the exact cause of the automobile import problem and on how to alter the competitive situation. Managers of the U.S. automobile firms and officials of the UAW spoke out in favor of restricting imports. This was a milestone because the automobile industry and its union had long been supporters of free trade, having publicly opposed import restrictions on such products as steel in the past.

Although imports were rising at the same time that sales by U.S. firms were decreasing, factors other than imports were contributing to the problems of the U.S. automobile industry. U.S. consumers historically have preferred the large cars with rear-wheel drive that Detroit produced. Although there was a jump in small-car sales after the 1973 oil embargo, Americans largely maintained their demand for larger cars. The U.S. auto firms thus felt that they could prolong the life of present facilities rather than writing them off quickly and going through the very costly process of building new plants or converting old ones before their useful lives ran out. The rapid increase in gasoline prices during 1979 and 1980 was unexpected and led to a rapid switch in demand among those decreasing numbers of consumers demanding cars at all. A general recession and unprecedented high interest rates reduced car sales drastically.

The U.S. automakers were not holding their own in sales of small cars that they had been producing for several years. Japanese producers, the primary exporters to the United States, were evidently just as surprised as Detroit about the sudden shift in demand. The Japanese lacked capacity to fill U.S. orders quickly, yet many buyers were willing to wait six months for delivery of a Honda rather than purchase a U.S.-manufactured model. Reasons for the American preference for the Japanese automobiles were debatable. One argument claimed that price differences created by labor cost differences were the cause. Those who accepted the cost differential argument largely favored the taxing of imports in order to raise their prices. Yet on the basis of canvassing 10,000 U.S. households, the Motor and Equipment Manufacturers Association found that imports strongly outranked U.S. small cars in perceived fuel economy, engineering, and durability. People who accepted these results felt that imports should not be limited.

The arguments for protecting or aiding the U.S. auto industry were based on two premises: (1) that the costs of unemployment are higher than the increased costs to consumers of limiting imports and (2) that U.S. production could become fully competitive with imports if it were helped with its temporary problems. The first premise is based on such factors as personal hardships for persons displaced in the labor market; lost purchasing power, which adversely affects demand in other industries; and the high taxes needed to support unemployment insurance and food stamps. A *New York Times* poll showed that 71 percent of Americans felt that it was more important to protect jobs than to get cheaper foreign products. The second premise is based on such factors as the historical competitive capability of the U.S. producers, the possibility of scale economies of U.S. production, and the much higher productivity possible with new plants. Furthermore, U.S. production costs would not have to drop as low as those in Japan, since it costs the Japanese about $500 per unit to ship vehicles to the United States.

Opponents of protection thought that the present problems were due to errors in management decisions. Thus, they said, the firms should not be rewarded by having consumers or taxpayers pay for seeing the companies through the crisis. Any assistance, even short-term, they felt, would result in at least one of the following: higher taxes because of subsidies to companies; higher prices for foreign cars (which are preferred by many consumers); or the necessity of buying domestic cars (which are perceived as inferior). Another antiprotection group felt that government assistance in limiting imports would result in foreign retaliation against U.S. industries that were more competitive with foreign production. Japan, for example, might curtail purchases of U.S.-made aircraft.

The UAW was clearly more interested in maintaining jobs than in protecting the U.S. auto firms. UAW representatives were instrumental in helping to convince Volkswagen and Honda to set up U.S. assembly operations. The UAW wanted much more, though; it pushed for having 75 percent of Volkswagen and Honda parts made in the United States. This push for local content ran counter to some of the policies being pursued by the U.S. auto firms that were trying to produce "global" cars in order to gain maximum economies of scale and buying specific parts that could be produced more cheaply in certain countries, such as die-cast aluminum parts in Italy. The Ford Escort, for example, which was assembled in the United States, Britain, and West Germany, contained parts from many countries. The UAW sought public support through newspaper and radio advertisements and managed to get several states to buy U.S.-made vehicles, as the union urged (unless the purchases were "inconsistent with the public interest"). Opponents of protection, mainly consumers, were generally unorganized; thus there was no major promotion effort to counter the UAW. The result was a negotiation with Japan in 1981 to limit its automobile exports to the U.S.

The U.S. auto industry recovered and by 1984 was announcing record profits. The turnaround was due partially to recovery from the recession, which lifted auto sales. But the restrictions also played a part: General Motors (GM), Ford, and Chrysler were able to invest heavily in more automated plants and to trim inventory costs.

Another factor in the industry's recovery was an increased U.S. demand for more expensive (and more profitable) cars. Some people claimed that this was a natural phenomenon of the market, since gasoline prices went down again. Others alleged that it was an outgrowth of the import restrictions, which gave U.S. consumers little choice except to buy more expensive cars. Because Japanese producers were not able to increase U.S. profits by selling more cars, they did so instead by selling more luxurious models and raising prices. During the three years of the original export restraints, the average Japanese import increased by $2600; and a Wharton Econometrics study attributed $1000 of this to import restraints. In the meantime, U.S.-made cars' prices increased by 40 percent. These price increases made both U.S. and Japanese producers more profitable. GM, Ford, and Chrysler have all given yearly bonuses of over a million dollars to their chairmen because of their firms' record earnings.

Although the Japanese have continued a restraint on sales, they have increased their allocation from 1.68 million units in 1982 to 2.3 million in 1988. The effect on U.S. employment has been minimal as producers have turned to more automated means of production. The high profits increased the bargaining power of U.S. automobile production workers so that they increased their earnings relative to other production workers. This has stimulated even further automation.

In the meantime the UAW has been concerned that the automobile import restraints largely affect only Japan and only assembled vehicles. Ford announced that it would spend $500 million to produce 130,000 Mazda cars per year in Mexico for sale in the United States. (Ford owns 25 percent of Toyo Kogyo, which makes Mazdas.) The House of Representatives voted to require that cars sold in the United States have up to 90 percent U.S. content, but the bill did not pass the Senate.

INTRODUCTION

All countries seek to influence trade. Each has:

- Economic, social, and political objectives
- Conflicts among objectives
- Pressure groups

The preceding case shows why and how automobile imports were limited into the United States. This is not atypical: No country in the world permits unregulated flow of goods and services across its borders. Restrictions commonly are placed on imports and occasionally on exports. Direct or indirect subsidies frequently are given to industries to enable them to compete with foreign production either at home or abroad. In general, governmental influence is exerted in an attempt to satisfy economic, social, or political objectives. The objective of increasing automobile workers' employment is such an example. Often there are conflicts among objectives (e.g., increased employment versus lower consumer prices of automobiles) as well as considerable disagreement as to the potential effects of trade policies (e.g., employment increases for auto workers versus possible decreases for aircraft workers).

Not surprising, any proposal for changes in trade regulations results in heated debates among individuals and interest groups who believe they will be affected. However, these interest groups that are most directly affected are apt to speak most loudly. People whose livelihood depends on U.S. automobile production (workers, owners, suppliers, and local politicians) perceive losses from import competition to be very great. Workers see themselves as having to take new jobs in new industries, perhaps in new locales. There may be prolonged periods of unemployment, reduced incomes, and insecure work and social surroundings. These people are liable to become a very strong pressure group. Workers in an industry that is indirectly affected by retaliation, such as aircraft, do not perceive the same threat and are less vocal. The same thing is true for consumers, even though they must pay the higher prices of both foreign and domestically made cars. Although their aggregate costs are great, these costs are so diffused throughout society that consumers are not likely to join together to protest import limitations very strongly.

THE RATIONALE FOR GOVERNMENTAL INTERVENTION

Unemployment

Unemployed can form effective pressure group for import restrictions.

Pressure groups are a real entity that challenge governmental policymakers and businesspeople. There is probably no more effective a pressure group than the unemployed because no other group has as much time and incentive to write letters to congressional representatives or to picket.

Import restrictions to create domestic employment:

- May lead to retaliation by other countries

One of the problems of restricting imports to create jobs is that other countries might retaliate. The most often-cited example was when the United States raised import restrictions to their highest level in history in 1930. In a matter of months, other countries countered with their own

- Are met by less retaliation if done by small countries
- May decrease export jobs owing to price increases for components
- May decrease export jobs owing to lower incomes abroad

limitations. The United States lost rather than gained jobs as its exports diminished.[2] In recent years, new import restrictions by a major country have almost always brought quick retaliation. When automobile imports from Japan were restricted, for example, Japanese pressure groups forced import restrictions on American orange juice.

Two factors may mitigate the problems of retaliation. First, there may be less tendency to retaliate against a small country that places barriers on imports. Thus a small country may be able to increase employment more easily by imposing trade barriers. Second, if redistribution because of retaliation decreases employment in a capital-intensive industry but increases it in a labor-intensive industry, employment objectives may be attained.

Even if there is no retaliation, the net number of jobs gained for the economy as a whole through producing domestically is bound to be less than the number of people who would be employed in the newly protected industry. That is because many people would otherwise be employed in handling the imports. In the case of the United States, for example, it is estimated that 194,000 jobs are related directly to the imported car industry. These include such workers as employees of importers, dealers, and distributors of foreign cars and workers in U.S. plants that make foreign-car parts.[3]

Imports may also help create jobs in export industries. Take Caterpillar Tractor, one of the largest exporters in the United States. It buys crankshafts from West Germany and Japan to cut costs enough to be competitive in foreign markets.[4] Imports stimulate exports less directly by increasing foreign income and foreign exchange earnings, which are then spent on new imports by the foreign country.

Costs of import restrictions:
- Possibly include higher prices
- Possibly include higher taxes
- Should be compared with costs of unemployment

If import restrictions do result in a net increase in domestic employment, there will still be costs to some people in the domestic society through higher prices or higher taxes. The first three years of voluntary export restraint is estimated to have cost $160,000 per job saved.[5] If protection seems permanent, the domestic industry may lag behind in technical and product development as well.

These costs of higher prices or higher taxes must be compared with the costs of unemployment if workers are displaced through free trade. It may be necessary to find some means by which individuals are compensated for their losses and by which they move to new employment. These tasks are challenging: First, it is hard to put a price tag on anxieties created by having to be idle, change jobs, or move; second, it is difficult for working people to understand that they may be better off financially by having part of their taxes go to help support people whose positions were lost because of imports; finally, it may be equally difficult to convince people to accept handouts in lieu of their old jobs.

Many countries give assistance to workers who are affected adversely by imports. Some observers argue that too little is done in the way of retraining and relocation. Assistance is received in the form of supplements to unemployment benefits, and workers spend the funds for living expenses in the hope that they will be recalled to old jobs.

Infant Industry Argument

The infant industry argument says that production becomes more competitive over time because of:

- Gaining economies of scale
- Efficiency of workers

One of the oldest arguments for protection from imports was presented as early as 1792 by Alexander Hamilton. The logic of the **infant industry argument** for protection is that initial output costs for an industry in a given country may be too high to be competitive in world markets, but that over a period of time the costs will decrease sufficiently so that efficient production will be achieved. Two reasons account for the lowering of costs over a period of time. First is the concept of **economies of scale.** Because of high fixed costs, a company may have to reach a certain level of output and sales to reduce total unit costs to the level of competition, assumed in this case to be foreign competition. The second is the **learning curve concept.** This is based on the premise that initial production may be costly because of the inexperience of workers and managers, but that as they gain experience, their output will grow so that unit costs of production decrease. Proponents of the infant industry argument hold that the domestic infant industry should be guaranteed a large share of the domestic market so that adulthood ultimately is reached.

While it is reasonable to expect costs to decrease over a period of time, they may not go down sufficiently. Therefore, there are some problems in using trade protection as a means of gaining international competitiveness for a domestic industry. The first is the challenging identification of industries that have a high probability of reaching adulthood. Examples of industries, such as automobile production in Brazil and Japan, that grew to be competitive because of government protection are available. In many other cases, however (e.g., automobile production in Argentina and Australia) the industries are still in an infantile state even after many years of operation. If infant industry protection is given to an industry that does not reduce costs sufficiently, chances are the owners, workers, and suppliers will constitute a formidable pressure group that effectively may prevent the import of a cheaper competitive product.

Even if policymakers can ascertain which industries may effectively reach adulthood, it does not necessarily follow that governmental assistance should be given. There are, of course, many examples of entrepreneurs who endure early losses in order to gain future benefits, and policymakers may argue that assistance should be given only if entry barriers to new firms are very high. Some segment of the economy must absorb the higher cost of local production during infancy. Most likely the consumer will pay higher prices;

however, a government may subsidize the industry so that consumer prices are not increased, in which case the taxpayer absorbs the burden. For the infant industry argument to be fully viable, future benefits should exceed early costs.

The automobile import case at the beginning of this chapter raises interesting questions about the infant industry argument. We have all heard of second childhoods, but is the automobile industry in the United States in its second infancy? Can this U.S. industry overcome some of its present disadvantages? Or does the automobile industry, like people, go around only once? In other words, has the absolute or comparative advantage shifted to other countries, thus precluding U.S. ability to compete effectively in the future? If efficiency can be reached, who should incur the short-term costs: investors, taxpayers, or consumers?

Industrialization Objectives

Countries seek protection to promote industrial production because:

- There is faster demand growth than agriculture
- It brings in investment funds
- It diversifies economy
- It brings more price increases than primary products

In recent years many countries have sought to increase their level of industrialization for several reasons:

1. This will increase output more than an emphasis on agriculture;
2. Inflows of foreign investment in the industrial area will promote growth;
3. Diversification away from traditional agricultural products or raw materials is necessary to stabilize trade fluctuation; and
4. The prices of manufactured goods tend to rise more rapidly than the prices of primary products.

Industrial countries are generally better off economically than nonindustrial countries. Since the Industrial Revolution in England, a number of countries have developed an industrial base while largely preventing competition from foreign-based production. This, for example, was the experience of the United States, Japan, and the Soviet Union. As in the infant industry argument, the premise here is that cheaper products from abroad would prevent the establishment of domestic industry if free market conditions were allowed to prevail. The **industrialization argument** differs from the infant industry argument in that proponents argue that objectives will be achieved even though domestic prices do not become competitive on the world market.

Marginal agricultural returns. In many developing countries there are frequently surpluses of population engaged in agriculture. This is particularly true in economies such as India or Egypt, which have little additional arable land available. In other words, large numbers of people may be able to leave the agricultural sector without greatly affecting the country's agricultural output. If these surplus workers can be employed in the manufacturing sector, their output is likely to contribute a net gain to the economy because so little agricultural production is sacrificed in the process. If the cost of the domestically produced manufactured product is higher than an imported one, sales of the imported product must be restricted to ensure survival of the domestic industry. This will result in either higher prices or taxes; nevertheless, real output should rise in the economy.

In a country's shift from agriculture to industry:

- Output increases if marginal productivity of agricultural workers is very low
- Demands on social and political services in cities may increase
- Development possibilities in agricultural sector may be overlooked

Shifting people out of agriculture is not without risks. One danger is that individuals' expectations may be raised and left unfulfilled, thus leading to excessive demands on social and political services. Indeed, one of the major problems facing poor countries today is the massive urban migration of people who cannot be absorbed easily. There is no work for them either (1) because the industrialization process has proceeded too slowly or (2) because the migrants lack the rudimentary skills and work habits necessary for employment in manufacturing.[6] A second risk is that agriculture may in fact be a better means of effecting additional output than industry. Not all poor countries are utilizing their lands fully; nor is industrial development the only means of economic growth. Such countries as the United States, Canada, and Argentina grew rapidly during the nineteenth century, in large part through agricultural exports, and they continue to profit from such exports. Australia, New Zealand, and Denmark maintain high incomes along with substantial agricultural specialization. A third problem in shifting people from agriculture is that if protection is to be given to manufacturing enterprises, policymakers must decide on which type so that the additional consumer prices and taxes are minimized. A fourth issue is that too much of a rural-to-urban shift may reduce agricultural output in developing countries, thus further endangering their self-sufficiency. Interestingly, most of the world's agricultural production and exports come from the so-called industrial countries.

If import restrictions keep out foreign manufacturers, foreign firms may invest to produce in restricted area.

Promoting investment inflows. In Chapter 6 we will show that import restrictions are a major impetus for direct investment movements, particularly those regulating the purchase of foreign-produced manufactured products. The influx of foreign firms may hasten the move from agriculture to industry as well as contribute to growth by adding to the stock of capital and technology per worker employed. It may also add to employment, which is an especially attractive benefit from the standpoint of most policymakers.

Diversification. Export prices of most primary products undergo great fluctuations.[7] Whether due to such uncontrollable factors as weather affecting supply or business cycles abroad affecting demand, price variations can wreak havoc on economies that are dependent on the export of primary products. This is particularly true when an economy depends very heavily on one commodity for employment of its population and for its export earnings. Recall from Chapter 4 that a large number of developing countries depend heavily on just one primary commodity. Many developing countries can afford foreign luxuries one year but are unable to afford replacement parts for essential equipment the next.

A greater dependence on manufacturing is no guarantee of stable export earnings. The gross national product of most less-developed countries (LDCs) is small; consequently, a change may simply shift dependence to one or two manufactured products from one or two agricultural ones. The basic risk of having all economic eggs in one basket has not been removed.

Terms of trade for LDCs may deteriorate because:
- Demand for primary products grows more slowly
- Production cost savings in primary products will be passed on to consumers

Terms of trade. The **terms of trade** refer to the quantity of imports that a given quantity of a country's exports can buy. The prices of raw materials and agricultural commodities have not risen as fast as the prices of finished products. As a result, over a period of time it will take more primary products to buy the same amount of manufactured goods. Further, the demand for primary products does not rise as rapidly, so LDCs have become increasingly poorer in relation to developed countries. This supposedly warrants protection of emerging manufacturing enterprises that replace traditional products.[8] The declining terms of trade for LDCs have been explained in part by lagging demand for agricultural products and by changes in technology that have saved on raw-material utilization. A further explanation sometimes offered is that, because of competitive conditions, savings due to technical changes that lower production costs of primary products are largely passed on to consumers, whereas cost savings in manufactured products go to higher profits and wages.[9]

Controversy over whether industrialization should emphasize
- products to sell domestically or
- products to export

Import substitution versus export promotion. By placing restrictions on imports a country may produce goods for local consumption that it formerly imported. This is known as **import substitution.** In recent years many countries have questioned whether import substitution is the most appropriate way to develop new industries through protection. Realizing that if the protected industries do not become efficient, these countries see that consumers may have to pay high prices or taxes for an indefinite period of time to support these industries. They have also noted that since capital equipment and other supplies usually must be imported, foreign exchange savings are minimal. Furthermore, they have witnessed the rapid growth of countries such as Taiwan and South Korea, which have had a favorable balance of payments by promoting export industries, a process known as **export-led development.** For these reasons, some countries are aiming their industrialization efforts on industries for which export markets should logically exist, such as the processing of raw materials that they are now exporting. This move affects international companies' strategies: They are required increasingly to export from the countries where they are producing whereas formerly they could sell all their outputs in each country where they produced.

In reality, it is not so easy to distinguish between the two types of industrialization, nor is it always possible to develop exports. Industrialization may initially result in import substitution, yet export development of the same products may be feasible at a later date. The fact that a country concentrates its industrialization activities on products for which it would seem to have a comparative cost advantage does not guarantee that exports can be generated. There are a variety of trade barriers, to be discussed later in this chapter, that are particularly problematic to the development of manufacturing exports from nonindustrialized countries.

Relationships with Other Countries

Balance of payments adjustments. In Chapter 9 we will examine in detail the fact that in order to correct balance-of-payments problems a country may change the value of its currency relative to others, adjust the rate of domestic price change, or influence individual accounts in the balance of payments. Since the trade account is a major component within the balance of payments for most countries, there are numerous attempts by governments to modify what would have been an import or export movement in a free market situation.

Trade restrictions may have an uneven effect on industries but a country can choose to restrict the least essential imports.

Trade influence differs from the other two means of adjustment primarily because of greater selectivity. This may be either an advantage or a disadvantage compared to the other adjustment mechanisms. If a country is running a deficit, for example, either a devaluation or a domestic deflation can make domestically produced goods and services less expensive than foreign ones. This has widespread effect on both imports and exports as well as on such service accounts as tourism. Because of the breadth of industries affected, fairly small changes relative to other countries' prices may substantially affect payments balances. Furthermore, this minimizes the burden of adjustment on any single industry. Direct trade influence may, however, allow a country to choose the types of products or services to be affected. For example, the importation of luxury items may be curtailed, whereas no change may be made in rules or prices governing imports of needed foodstuffs.

Export restrictions may:

- Keep world prices up in monopoly situation
- Involve high cost to prevent smuggling
- Lead to substitution

Price-control objectives. A few countries hold monopoly or near-monopoly control of certain resources. To maintain control and pursuant high prices, strict export regulations are enforced. Australia, for example, has for over fifty years prohibited the export of Merino rams, considered the top-quality wool producers in the world. Unfortunately, this type of policy encourages smuggling and requires high costs to prevent smuggling. Brazil lost its world monopoly and practically its total world market position in natural rubber after a contrabandist brought rubber plants into Malaysia. South Africa and Colombia pay high prices to prevent diamonds and emeralds, respectively, from flooding world markets. A second problem is that if prices are kept too high, substitutes may be developed. For example, high prices of Chilean natural nitrate led to the development of a synthetic, and high sugar prices in the mid-1970s led to the development of a corn derivative substitute.

Export restrictions may:

- Keep domestic prices down by increasing domestic supply
- Give producers less incentive to increase output
- Shift foreign production and sales

A country may also limit exports of a product in short supply so that domestic consumers may buy the good at a lower price than if foreign purchasers were allowed to bid the price up. In recent years, Argentina has done this with wheat and the United States with hides and soybeans. The primary danger in these policies is that the lower prices at home will not entice producers to expand domestic output, whereas foreign output is expanded. This may lead to long-term market loss.

Import restrictions may:

- Prevent dumping, be used to put domestic producers out of business
- Get other countries to bargain away restrictions
- Get foreign producers to lower their prices

There is a fear that producers from one country will price products so artificially low in a given market that they drive other producers out of business, resulting in a costly dislocation for displaced workers and industries from other countries. If entry barriers are high for new firms, the surviving producers may even be able to extract monopoly profits or withhold supplies to help other industries in their own countries. There have been allegations that Hitachi, the only producer of a key chip, delayed deliveries to Cray Research, the leading U.S. supercomputer producer, to give Japanese computer makers an advantage.[10] The ability to price artificially low abroad may result from high domestic prices due to a monopoly position at home or the result of home government subsidy or sponsorship policies. The underpricing of exports (usually below cost or below the home country price) is often referred to as **dumping.** Home country consumers or taxpayers seldom realize that they are in effect subsidizing foreign sales. A group of Japanese did boycott purchases of Japanese color television sets after it was disclosed that the sets were being sold in the United States at prices far below those in Japan.[11]

Another pricing concept is the use of trade restrictions as a means of forcing other countries to bargain away restrictions of their own. In 1971, for example, the United States placed a 10 percent surcharge on all dutiable imports. The surcharge was quickly negotiated away as some other countries, particularly Japan, reduced barriers to the importation of U.S. products. The danger in this mechanism is that each country may escalate restrictions rather than bargain them away.

A final price argument for governmental influence on trade is the **optimum tariff theory,** which holds that a foreign producer will lower its prices if a tax is placed on its products. If this occurs, benefits shift to the importing country. For example, assume that an exporter has costs of $500 per unit and is selling to a foreign market for $700 per unit. With the imposition of a 10 percent tax on the imported price, the exporter may choose to lower the export price to $636.36 per unit which, with a 10 percent tax of $63.64 would keep the price at $700 for the importer. The exporter may feel that a price higher than $700 would result in lost sales; thus a profit of $136.36 per unit instead of the previous $200 per unit is still better than no profit at all. An amount of $63.64 per unit has thus shifted to the importing country. While in actual practice examples of products whose prices did not rise correspondingly to increased costs of taxes may appear, the behavior is very difficult to predict in advance.

Fairness. All countries regulate how their companies can produce. These standards reflect the accepted social and environmental values of their citizens, such as requirements for worker safety or the disposal of wastes. Since these vary from one country to another, the costs incurred by producers also vary. It is argued, therefore, that cost differences do not necessarily reflect efficiency differences; rather, they reflect differences in social and environmental values. Some industries affected by import competition, for example the U.S. television and steel industries, reason that their own governments should protect them because foreign producers do not have to adhere to the same stringent requirements that raise production costs.[12]

In protecting essential industries, countries must:

- Agree on essential businesses
- Consider costs and alternatives
- Consider political consequences

Political objectives. Much governmental influence on trade cannot be explained through economic rationales. One of the major considerations is the protection of essential domestic industries during peacetime so that in wartime the country is not dependent on foreign sources of supply. This argument for protection has much appeal in rallying support for barriers to the importation of foreign-produced goods. However, in time of a real crisis or military emergency, almost any product could be considered essential. Because of the high cost of protecting an inefficient industry or domestic substitute, the **essential industry argument** should not be (but frequently is) accepted without a careful evaluation of costs, real needs, and alternatives. Once an industry is afforded protection, it is difficult to terminate it. On the basis of the strategic argument the United States government subsidizes domestic production of silicon so that domestic chipmakers will not have to depend entirely on foreign suppliers.[13]

Defense arguments are also used to prevent exports of strategic goods to potential enemies. The United States, for example, restricts the export of certain goods to communist countries. This policy may be valid if a country assumes that it needs products from the potential enemy less than the potential enemy needs its products. Even if this assumption is made, it is possible that the so-called enemy country may simply find sources of supply from other countries or develop a capability of its own. Closely akin to this is the restriction of exports on raw materials that could be sold competitively, because of fear that essential supplies will become depleted.

Trade controls on other than strategic goods also may be used as a foreign policy weapon to try to prevent another country from easily meeting its economic and political objectives. A good example was the cessation of trade between the United States and Cuba, a situation that is discussed in the case at the end of Chapter 13.

There are many other examples of governments' influencing trade for political reasons: Aid, credits, and purchases frequently are tied into a political alliance or even to votes within international bodies. Most major powers buy at higher than world prices from certain LDCs in order to maintain their influence on those countries. The United States did this with sugar; France, with citrus products. In country-to-country negotiations, government officials may even trade off some of the economic advantages of their own nations' firms in order to gain political advantages.

FORMS OF TRADE CONTROL

The previous discussion centered on the end objectives sought by governmental influence on trade. Attaining any of the objectives depends in great part on groups at home who pressure for actions they believe will have the most positive (or least negative) influence on them. Since the actions taken on foreign trade by one country will have repercussions abroad, retaliation from foreign governments looms as another potential obstacle to the achievement of the desired objectives. The choice of alternative instruments to achieve the trade goal is therefore important, since domestic and foreign groups may respond differently to them. One of the ways the types of influence may be classified is to distinguish between (1) those that influence quantity movements by directly influencing prices and (2) those that affect quantity movements directly. Another common distinction is between tariff barriers and nontariff barriers. Tariffs influence prices, and nontariff barriers may affect either price or quantity directly.

Tariffs

Tariffs may:

- Be on goods entering, leaving, or passing through country
- Be for protection or revenue
- Be per unit or per value

The most common type of trade control is the **tariff** or **duty,** a governmental tax levied on goods shipped internationally. If collected by the exporting country, it is known as an **export tariff;** if collected by a country through which the goods have passed, it is a **transit tariff.** By far the most common is the **import tariff.**

Import duties serve primarily as a means of raising the price of imported products so that competitively produced domestic goods will gain a relative price advantage. A duty may be classified as protective in nature even though there is no domestic production in direct competition. For example, if a country wishes to reduce the foreign expenditures of its citizens because of balance-of-payments problems, authorities may choose to raise the price of some foreign products, even though there is no close domestic substitute, in order to curtail consumption temporarily.

Tariffs also serve as a means of governmental revenue. Although of little importance to the large industrial countries, the import duty is a major source of revenue elsewhere because governmental authorities may have more control over ascertaining the amount and nature of goods passing across their frontiers and collecting a tax on them than they do over determining and collecting individual and corporate income taxes. Revenue tariffs are most commonly collected on imports; however, many raw material-exporting nations use export duties extensively, such as New Caledonia's tariff on nickel. When the United States threatened to place an import tariff for protectionist reasons on compressors originating in Singapore, Singapore countered with an export tariff that afforded the protection while giving the tax revenue to Singapore rather than to the United States.[14] Transit duties were historically a major revenue source for countries but have nearly been abolished through governmental treaties.

A tariff may be assessed on the basis of a tax per unit, in which case the duty is known as a **specific duty.** It may also be assessed as a percentage of the value of the item, in which case it is known as an **ad valorem duty.** It is not uncommon for both a specific duty and an ad valorem duty to be charged on the same product, in which case it is known as a **compound duty.** A specific duty is easier to assess because it is not necessary for customs officials to determine a value on which to calculate a percentage. During normal periods of price rises, the specific duty will, unless changed, become a smaller percentage of the value and therefore less restrictive to imported goods.

One of the major tariff controversies concerns the relationship between industrial countries' treatment of manufactured exports from developing countries that are seeking to diversify by selling nontraditional manufactured products. Raw materials frequently can enter developed markets free of duty; however, once processed, those same materials usually have a tariff assigned to them. Since an ad valorem tariff is based on the total value of the product, nonindustrial countries have argued that the **effective tariff** on the manufactured portion is higher than would be indicated by the published tariff rate. For example, a country may charge no duty on coffee beans but assess a 10 percent ad valorem tariff on instant coffee. If $5 for a jar of instant coffee covers $2.50 in coffee beans and $2.50 in processing costs, the $0.50 duty is effectively 20 percent on the manufactured portion, since the beans could have entered free of duty. This has made it more difficult for developing countries to find markets for their manufactured products. In addition, many of the products that developing countries are best able to produce are the ones that in industrial countries are produced by employees who are ill equipped to move easily to new employment. The result is the formation of pressure groups to keep out these products. It has been estimated that the tariffs in industrial countries on items of most export interest to LDCs are about twice as high as those on manufactured imports as a whole.[15]

Nontariff Barriers: Direct Price Influences

Governmental subsidies may help their firms be competitive.

- Those to overcome market imperfections are least controversial.
- There is little agreement on "unfair" subsidies.
- There is a recent increase in export credit assistance.

Subsidies. Although countries sometimes resort to direct payments to producers for losses they incur by selling abroad, governments most commonly give other types of assistance to their firms to make it cheaper or more profitable for them to sell overseas. For example, most countries provide an array of services for their companies that are potential exporters including: providing information; sponsoring trade expositions; and establishing contacts for businesses overseas.[16] These types of service subsidies are frequently more justifiable from an economic standpoint than tariffs, since arguably they are designed largely to overcome market imperfections rather than create them. Furthermore, there are certainly economies to be gained by disseminating information widely. Other countries are not likely to complain about such types of assistance. On the other hand, some observers may contend that users should be the only ones to share the costs. At any rate, export assistance is apt to result in less opposition at home than the imposition of import restrictions.

Other types of subsidies are more controversial, and producers frequently assert that they face unfair competition from subsidized exports. What exactly constitutes a subsidized export? On this point there is little agreement. Does Canada subsidize exports of fish because it gives grants to fishermen to buy trawlers? Did Britain subsidize steel when the government-owned steel company had severe losses? Did the United States prevent some automobile imports because the state of Pennsylvania made many concessions to convince Volkswagen to locate its plant there?[17] Recent questions also have been raised about various governments' support of research and development (e.g., the U.S. government funds 55 percent of U.S. R&D, much of which results in exported military and consumer products)[18] and tax programs that directly or indirectly affect export profitability. (Some of these tax programs will be discussed in Chapter 19.)

Some other types of government assistance to exporting warrant mention, including foreign aid and loans. These forms are nearly always "tied"—that is, the recipient must spend the funds in the donor countries, making some products competitive abroad that would otherwise be uncompetitive. Most industrial countries also provide repayment insurances for their exporters, thus reducing the risk of nonpayment for overseas sales. In the 1980s, industrial countries progressively lowered their export credit rates, which were already below market rates, in an effort to stimulate their own exports. One of the schemes used has been the combining of aid with loans so that the rate on paper does not look as low to competitor nations as it really is.[19]

An undervalued exchange rate will make a country's goods more competitive.

Exchange rate manipulations. Exchange rate determination will be discussed in full in Chapter 9. For now, however, it is enough to know that if a country can keep its currency value so that it buys less of foreign currency than it might in a free market determination, its products will have a relative cost advantage.

It is hard for customs to determine if invoice price is honest, therefore:

- Customs may arbitrarily increase duty
- Valuation procedures have been developed.

Customs valuation. In order to determine the value of an imported product for affixing an ad valorem duty, customs officials used to have fairly wide discretion. Even though the invoice value of a shipment might be $100, customs officials might use the domestic wholesale or retail price or even an estimation of what it would cost if the product were produced domestically. This meant that they might charge a 10 percent duty on a value much higher than the $100. The discretion was permitted to prevent exporters and importers from declaring an arbitrarily low price on invoices in order to avoid paying as high a tariff as they would otherwise. In practice, however, the discretionary powers were sometimes used as an arbitrary means of preventing the importation of foreign-made products by assessing the value too high.

Most industrial countries have now agreed on a sequence of techniques for assessing values. They must first use the invoice price. If there is none or if the authenticity is doubtful, they must then assess on the basis of the value of identical goods and then on the basis of similar goods coming in at about the same time. If these techniques cannot be used, customs officials may compute a value based on final sales value or on reasonable cost.[20] The difficulty of arriving at a fair price is illustrated by complaints that imports of Polish golf carts were injuring U.S. domestic producers. Although tariff restrictions were based first on a higher assessment than the invoice value, there was disagreement because of the different methods of determining costs in Poland and in the United States and the fact that none of the carts was sold in Poland. It took five years to remove the excess valuation.[21]

Another customs valuation problem can be traced to the fact that so many different products are traded. It is easy (by accident or on purpose) to classify a product so that it will pay a higher duty. With over 13,000 categories of products a customs agent must use discretion to determine if silicon chips should be considered as "integrated circuits for computers" or as "a form of chemical silicon." In a 1988 case the U.S. Customs Service had to determine whether Japanese-made sport utility vehicles were cars or trucks. They assessed the 25 percent truck duty instead of the 2.5 percent duty for cars. Surprisingly, Japanese exporters were pleased with this ruling; if the vehicles were categorized as cars, the voluntary export limitation program would not have allowed their entry.[22]

Other direct price influences. Countries frequently use other means to affect prices, including special fees, for example, for consular and customs clearance and documentation; the requirement that customs deposits be placed in advance of shipment; and the establishment of minimum prices at which goods can be sold after they have customs clearance.

Nontariff Barriers: Quantity Controls

A quota:

- May set total amount to be traded
- May allocate amount by country

Quotas. The most common type of import or export restriction from a quantity basis is the **quota.** From the standpoint of imports, a quota most frequently limits the quantitative amount of a product allowed to be imported in a given year. The amount frequently reflects a guarantee that domestic producers will have access to a certain percentage of the domestic market in a given year. For many years, the sugar import quota of the United States was set so that U.S. producers would have about half the home market. In this case the quotas were allocated further by country on the basis of political considerations rather than price. Consumer prices of imported sugar equaled the price of more expensive domestically produced sugar, since the lowering of the consumer price on imports could not increase the quantity of imports sold. This restriction of supply usually will increase consumer prices because there is little incentive to use price as a means of increasing sales. In the case of import tariffs the gains from price increases to consumers are received in the form of government revenue in the importing country. In the case of quotas, however, the gains are most likely to accrue to producers or exporters in the producing country as added profits.[23] Windfall gains could accrue to middlemen in the importing country if they bought at a lower open market price and then sold at the higher protected domestic price.

Import quotas do not necessarily protect domestic producers. Japan, for example, maintains quotas on many agricultural products not produced in Japan. Imports are allocated as a means of bargaining for sales of Japanese exports as well as to avoid excess dependence on any one country for essential food needs, which could be cut off in case of adverse climatic or political conditions.

Export quotas may be established to assure that domestic consumers will have a sufficient supply at a low price, to prevent depletion of natural resources, or to attempt to raise an export price by restricting supply in foreign markets. The various **commodity agreements** in recent years have allocated exports by producing countries and restricted their output so that prices will be raised to importing countries.

A specific type of quota that prohibits all trade is known as an **embargo.** As in the case of quotas, embargoes may be placed on either imports or exports, on whole categories of products regardless of destination, on specific products to specific countries, or on all products to given countries. Although embargoes are used generally for political purposes, the effects may be economic.

According to "buy local" practices

- Governmental purchases give preference to domestically made goods
- Government sometimes legislates preference for domestically made goods

"Buy local" legislation. If governmental purchases are a large portion of total expenditures within a country, the determination of where governmental agencies will make their purchases is of added importance in international competitiveness. Most national governments give preference to their own producers in the purchase of goods, sometimes in the form of content restriction (that is, a certain percentage of the product for governmental purchase must be of local origin) and sometimes through price mechanisms. For example, a governmental agency may be able to buy a foreign-made product only if the price of the foreign product is some predetermined margin below that of a domestic competitor. Sometimes the preference for local products is even more subtle: For example, the Nippon Telegraph and Telephone Public Corp. (NTT), a Japanese quasi-government telecommunications monopoly in the world's second largest telecommunications market, purchases only a very small portion of its equipment from foreign sources. Foreign firms claim that they have had superior technology and prices, but in practice they have been excluded from the market.[24]

There is an abundant legislation worldwide that simply prescribes a minimum percentage of domestic value that must be encompassed in a given product for it to be sold legally within the country. The office of the U.S. Trade Representative says that of the fifty countries it monitors, forty have such performance requirements.[25] In the introductory case on automobile imports, the local content proposed for cars sold in the United States would be, if implemented, such a type of legislated protection. Among those implemented already in other countries are Mexico's requirement that 50 percent of automobile components be made there and Brazil's requirement that companies purchase domestically made computers.

Other types of trade barriers include:

- Arbitrary standards
- Licensing arrangements
- Administrative delays
- Reciprocal requirements
- Service restrictions

Standards. Countries commonly have set classifications, labeling, and testing standards in a manner that allows the sale of domestic products but inhibits the sale of foreign-made products. These are sometimes ostensibly for the purpose of protecting the safety or health of the domestic populace. However, imports often have been tested under more onerous conditions (e.g., imported cars in Japan) than have domestic products.[26]

Specific permission requirements. Many countries require that potential importers or exporters secure permission from governmental authorities before conducting trade transactions, a procedure known as a **licensing arrangement.** To gain a license, a company may even have to send samples abroad in advance. The use of licenses not only may restrict imports or exports directly by denial of permission, but also may result in further deterrence of trade because of the cost, time, and uncertainty involved in the process. Similar to a licensing arrangement is a **foreign exchange control.** For instance, in order to import a given product an importer in an exchange control country must apply to governmental authorities to secure foreign exchange to pay for the product. Once again, the failure to grant the exchange coupled with the time and expense of completing forms and awaiting replies constitute an obstacle to the conduct of foreign trade. Specific permission requirements also may be placed on exports. In an effort to prevent potential military technology from falling into the hands of communist countries the United States places specific export permission requirements on certain products and to certain destinations. These will be discussed further in Chapter 13.

Administrative delays. Closely akin to specific permission requirements have been intentional administrative delays on entry, which raise uncertainty and the cost of carrying inventory. For example, France required that all imported videotape recorders arrive through a small customs entry point that was both remote and inadequately staffed. The resultant delays effectively kept Japanese recorders out of the market until there was a negotiated "voluntary export quota" whereby Japan limited its penetration of the French market.[27] Peruvian customs officials routinely take months to clear merchandise and then charge customs storage fees that amount to a high portion of the import's value.

Reciprocal requirements. In recent years there has been an upsurge in requirements that exporters effectively take merchandise in lieu of money: For example, Colombia paid for buses from Spain's ENESA with coffee, and China purchased railroad engineering services from Italy's Tecnotrade with coal.[28] Since these transactions often require exporters to find markets for goods outside their lines of expertise, many firms avoid this type business. These barter transactions, often referred to as **countertrade** or **offsets,** will be discussed in greater detail in Chapter 20.

Restrictions on services. Trade restrictions usually are associated with governmental interference with the international movement of goods. In addition to earnings from the sale of goods abroad, many countries depend substantially on revenue from the foreign sale of such services as transportation, insurance, consulting, and banking. These services account for about 30 percent of the value of all international trade.[29] There have been reports of widespread discrimination by countries favoring their own firms. Among the complaints have been that Japanese airlines get cargo cleared more quickly in Tokyo than do foreign carriers; that Argentina requires automobile imports to be insured en route with Argentine firms; that West Germany requires models for advertisements in West German magazines to be hired through a West German agency (even if the advertisement is made abroad); that Spain restricts the dubbing of foreign films, forcing people to read subtitles; and that West Germany prohibits its insurance brokers from helping German clients to arrange insurance abroad.[30]

The Role of GATT

GATT is the major trade liberalization organization:

- Sets rules for negotiations
- Monitors enforcement

The most important trade liberalization activity in the post-World War II period has been through the General Agreement on Tariffs and Trade (GATT). GATT has given the world a basic set of rules under which trade negotiations take place and a mechanism for monitoring the implementation of these rules.

Most favored nation clause. To belong to GATT nations adhere to the **most favored nation (MFN)** clause. MFN means that if a country, such as the United States, gives a tariff reduction to another country—for example, from 20 percent to 10 percent on wool sweaters from Australia—the United States would grant the same concession to all other countries of the world. The MFN applies to quotas and licenses as well. Although MFN initially was intended to be unconditional, countries have always made exceptions to it.[31]

The most important exceptions are as follows:

1. Manufactured products from developing countries have been given preferential treatment in comparision to those originating from industrial countries;
2. Concessions granted to other members of a trading alliance, such as the European Community (EC), have not been extended to other countries;
3. Nations that arbitrarily discriminate against products from a given country are not necessarily given MFN treatment by the country whose products are discriminated against;
4. Nonsignatory countries are not always treated in the same way as those that grant concessions;
5. Countries sometimes stipulate exceptions based on their existing laws at the time of signing a GATT agreement; and
6. Exceptions are made in times of war or international tensions.

The first exception provides that most industrial countries grant tariff preferences to developing countries under the Generalized System of Preferences (GSP). Under the second exception the United States and Israel agreed in 1985 to remove all tariffs on each other's products without giving the same benefits to other countries. Under the third exception the United States does not grant MFN treatment to a number of communist countries. The fourth exception allows that only countries signing the Government Procurement Code are granted automatic permission to bid on public works contracts open to foreign bids. Under the fifth exception Switzerland excludes agricultural trade. Finally, under the last exception the United Kingdom suspended MFN treatment to Argentina during the two countries' war in the South Atlantic.

GATT-sponsored rounds. GATT's most important activity has been the sponsoring of "rounds," which have led to a number of multilateral reductions in tariffs and nontariff barriers for its membership. The process of granting reductions is across the board: In other words, countries may agree to lower tariff rates by 50 percent over some specified period of time. Given the thousands of products traded, it would be nearly impossible to negotiate each product separately and even more difficult to negotiate each product separately with each country separately. Nevertheless, each country brings to the negotiations certain products that it considers exceptions to its own across-the-board reductions. That a series of negotiations have resulted in vast tariff reductions indicates not only that countries are committed to work jointly toward freer trade, but that tariffs are the easiest trade barrier to tackle.

The most recently concluded conference, the Tokyo Round in 1979, resulted in an overall reduction in tariffs by about 33 percent. For example, tariffs between the United States and the EC were reduced by 35 percent each way, and U.S. imports into Japan by 40 percent. In spite of these tariff reductions the primary thrust of the negotiations involved grappling with the increasingly important and complex nontariff barriers, especially in five specific areas: industrial standards, government procurement, subsidies and countervailing duties, licensing, and customs valuation. In each of these five areas, conference members agreed on a code of conduct for GATT nations.[32] (The Montevideo Round began in 1986, has shifted discussions to Geneva, and is expected to continue in negotiations until 1990.)

The Agreement on Industrial Standards provides for treating imports on the same basis as domestically produced goods. Similarly, the Agreement on Government Procurement calls for treating bids by foreign firms on a nondiscriminatory basis for most large contracts.

The Agreement or Code of Conduct on Subsidies and Countervailing Duties recognizes domestic subsidies as appropriate policy tools whose implementation, however, should avoid any adverse impact on other countries. Export subsidies are prohibited, the only exception being agricultural products. This agreement also spells out procedures regarding the possibility of using countervailing duties against a second country if the first country believes its domestic firms are being harmed by the second country's subsidy. The question of agricultural subsidies is one of the major controversies within the Montevideo Round.

The Licensing Code commits members to simplify their licensing procedures significantly and to treat both foreign and domestic firms in a nondiscriminatory manner.

The Customs Valuation Code calls for either c.i.f. or f.o.b. valuation (invoice value with or without transportation and insurance included) and specifically bans certain types of valuation methods, such as basing valuation on the selling price of a product in the importing country. The specific procedures were discussed earlier in the chapter in the section on customs valuation.

GATT as monitor. There is general agreement that tariff-reduction agreements are difficult to enforce. There are simply too many subtle means that countries use to circumvent the intent of the Tokyo negotiations. Furthermore, there is one important area on which participants were unable to agree in the Tokyo Round: the use of temporary safeguards against severe domestic disruptions caused by expanding imports. GATT still allows safeguard measures that can reverse the injurious effects of increases in imports that, in turn, result from trade liberalization moves. In such a situation the injured nation may cancel a previously negotiated action that liberalized trade as long as the country feels that this move is necessary to prevent further injury, particularly in the form of increased unemployment in the affected industry.

In practice very few safeguards have been imposed under the new GATT rules. However, there have been a number of "voluntary" limitations on exports, such as the example of Japanese limits on auto exports to the United States in the opening case. The voluntary restraint can circumvent the GATT agreement because neither the importing country nor the exporting country complains to the GATT Council in Geneva (the organization's ruling body), and GATT can do nothing without a complaint.

What can GATT do if there are complaints? First, investigations take place to determine if the allegations are valid. If the complaints are valid, then countries may pressure the offending party to change its policies. At the extreme, other GATT members could rescind MFN treatment to the violating country; however, such an extreme measure has not become necessary. The mutual commitment to cooperate has been sufficient to gain widespread compliance with GATT directives. In 1988, for example, the United States eliminated custom-user fees after the GATT Council investigated complaints from Canada and the EC; and Japan lifted quotas on eight processed food products which had raised complaints in the United States.

MESHING PROTECTION AND INTERNATIONAL STRATEGY

When facing import competition, firms can

- Try to get protection
- Make domestic output competitive
- Move abroad

Governmental actions concerning trade usually are examined in terms of their effects on such broad objectives as balance of payments, income distribution, employment, and tax receipts or on such narrow objectives as decreasing steel imports versus increasing citrus exports as a trade-balancing measure. The very fact that changes in governmental actions may alter substantially the competitiveness of facilities in given countries creates uncertainties about which businesses must make decisions.[33] These decisions affect companies that are facing import competition as well as those whose exports are facing protectionist sentiment.

Foreign Competition and U.S. Auto Makers

Take the case at the beginning of this chapter about automobile manufacturers in the United States during recent years. Foreign competition was taking a larger proportion of the U.S. market. Consequently, a U.S. company wishing to maintain sales in the domestic market had a number of options including: (1) pushing for import restrictions or other forms of government assistance; (2) effecting internal adjustments, such as cost efficiencies, product innovations, or improved marketing; (3) moving production to a lower-cost country and exporting to the United States; and (4) concentrating on market niches where there is less import competition. Clearly, there are substantial costs, as well as considerable uncertainty as to outcome, associated with any one of these options.

The U.S. automobile industry was successful at lobbying for the first option. The U.S. firms also pursued the second option by instituting various cost-saving measures. Ford estimated its cost level in 1984 to be $4 billion a year less than in 1979.[34] Cost breakthroughs are not always feasible; if they do occur, the innovations may be short-lived as foreign competitors respond with like improvements. The effect of the movement of production abroad (option 3), such as Ford's plan to source in Mexico, could be negated if the United States afterward prohibited importation from the foreign plant. The likelihood of import restrictions in such a situation would be inversely related to the number of producers following this option. In other words, if Ford, Chrysler, and GM all went to foreign sourcing, there would likely be no strong coalition to push for import controls on the foreign production, except from labor. The Big Three auto firms have also followed the fourth option. Each has made arrangements for Japanese companies to supply small cars for them so that they can concentrate more of their production efforts on the larger cars, for which there is little foreign competition. A company should attempt to assess costs and probabilities of each alternative before embarking on a program.

The potential protection of the U.S. auto industry also created problems for firms that were planning to export to the U.S. market. They could lobby against the protection, try to devise process or product technologies that would overcome the restrictive measures, or locate their production in the United States. As was the case for domestic producers, each of these options involved costs and risks. As was the situation with U.S. auto firms, Japanese auto firms followed each of their alternatives to some extent. They lobbied with the Japanese government to take steps to counter U.S. actions. They developed allies, such as associations of foreign car importers, to lobby on their behalf in the United States. They continued efforts to reduce costs in case tariffs might be imposed. They developed capabilities for adding more luxury items so that profits might not diminish if quotas were imposed. They also negotiated arrangements to produce outside Japan such as in Mexico and the United States in case sanctions would be taken only against Japanese output.

Approaches to the International Environment

From the preceding discussion it is clear not only that firms may take different approaches to counter changes in the international competitive environment, but also that their attitudes toward protectionism are influenced by the investments that they have made already to develop their international strategies.[35] Companies that depend primarily on trade (whether market seekers or resource acquirers) and those that have integrated their production among different countries are most apt to lose with increased protectionism. Companies with single or multi-domestic production facilities (such as production in the United States to serve the U.S. market and production in Mexico to serve the Mexican market) are most apt to gain through protectionist measures.

SUMMARY

- Despite the potential resource benefit of free trade, no country permits an unregulated flow of goods and services.
- Given the possibility of retaliation and the fact that imports as well as exports create jobs, it is difficult to determine the effect on employment of protecting an industry.
- Policymakers have not yet solved the problem of redistribution of income through changes in trade policy.
- The infant industry argument for protection holds that without governmental prevention of import competition, certain industries would be unable to pass from high-cost to low-cost production.
- Because industrial countries generally are more economically advanced than nonindustrial ones, governmental interference is often argued to be beneficial if it promotes industrialization.
- Direct influence on trade is used as a more selective means of solving balance-of-payments disequilibrium than resorting to either changes in currency values or to internal price adjustments.
- Trade controls are used to control prices of goods traded internationally. This includes protection of monopoly positions, prevention of foreign monopoly prices, greater assurance that domestic consumers get low prices, and getting foreign producers to lower their profit margins.
- Much of the interference in the free flow of goods and services internationally is motivated by political rather than economic concerns including: maintenance of domestic supplies of essential goods and prevention of potential enemies from gaining goods that would help them achieve their objectives.
- Many nonindustrial countries are seeking export markets within the industrialized world for their manufactured products but argue that the effective tariffs on their products are too high.
- Trade controls that directly influence price and secondarily influence quantities include tariffs, subsidies, multiple exchange rates, arbitrary customs valuations, and special fees.

- Trade controls that directly affect quantity and secondarily affect price include quotas, "buy local" regulations, licensing, foreign exchange controls, arbitrary standards, administrative delays, and requirements to take goods in exchange.
- The development of an international strategy will greatly determine whether firms will benefit best from protectionism or from some other form of countering international competition.

CASE: STEEL IMPORTS[36]

At the end of World War II the U.S. steel industry was the most powerful in the world, and it seemed that no one would challenge its supremacy. By 1950, U.S. raw steel production accounted for 47 percent of the world's supply. However, this share fell to about 10 percent by the early 1980s, where it has since stabilized. Not only has the U.S. world share of production fallen, the United States has become a net importer of steel. Steel companies in the United States have argued that import figures understate the inroads of foreign competition because so much additional steel enters in finished products such as automobiles and pipes. Steel jobs in the United States fell by more than 200,000 between 1981 and 1987.

Worldwide, several factors are important for understanding the evolving competitive situation. One involves additional capacity created in countries that are relatively new to steel production. Many developing countries consider domestic mills essential for their industrialization objectives, and the need for steel output is viewed for security and prestige purposes. These countries have been able to increase capacity because the technology, except for certain specialty steels, has become widespread and easily attainable. Because of the high priority placed on steel, many countries have been willing to forego other development projects in order to build mills or have received financial assistance from outside for construction. Turkey, for example, received both U.S. and Soviet long-term, low-interest government loans to finance its steel output. Since the early 1970s the largest capacity increase has been among Third World countries; they have a substantial, growing excess capacity. The excess in the United States, Europe, and Japan has been over 50 percent in the 1980s. Steelmakers in all three regions have been planning and effecting capacity cuts.

Given the high fixed costs of steel production, a second factor affecting steel competition is that much of the world's production is government owned. Some observers argue that these firms will continue operating regardless of whether they cover their short-term costs. Because of employment pressures in countries such as France, it has been politically very difficult to cut back production more rapidly in the state facilities. Export markets have been used as an instrument of maintaining more output. The state-owned companies in such countries as Spain and Argentina have been reporting record losses but continue exporting at low prices. In addition to direct ownership, it has been argued that governmental assistance through tax incentives, reorganization schemes, provision for long-term, low-interest loans, and waiving of environmental requirements have placed U.S. steel producers at a disadvantage vis-à-vis some foreign producers.

A number of other factors have contributed to the ability of foreign steel producers to compete effectively in the United States. One such consideration is technology: Although U.S. firms claim that their newest plants are as advanced as any, the average age of plants in some countries is much lower than that of U.S. plants, so these plants are more productive on average. In addition, Japanese workers receive less compensation than U.S. workers and when on strike, they typically continue working and signify their demands by wearing armbands. American firms once guaranteed their workers pay increases that exceeded increases in productivity in order to gain a "no strike" clause in labor contracts. By 1987, American steelworkers made more than U.S. production workers in any other manufacturing sector (e.g., 135 percent more than apparel workers). Yet the 1987 labor contract between USX, the largest U.S. steel producer, called for wage cuts.

Another factor concerns production location. Most U.S. mills were built many years ago in the corridor of states bordering the Great Lakes. These locations minimized transportation costs for raw materials and for finished steel to be shipped to industrial users in this same corridor. If a firm wants to use cheaper iron from Brazil and to sell to the expanding industrial and population base in the South and West, these locations may no longer be optimal. Japan, the largest steel exporter to the United States, situates its production largely at deep-water ports. The Japanese industry now has an estimated cost advantage on purchases of raw materials even though they are imported. Despite these advantages, Japan is increasingly importing steel from Taiwan and South Korea, both countries with lower labor rates and newer plants, on the average, than Japan's. South Korea's Pohang Iron & Steel is now considered the world's most efficient steelmaker. In addition to its efficiency advantage, the average South Korean steelworker earns only one-third the salary of a Japanese steelworker.

Regardless of the source of competition, there is a general agreement that there must be major new investment and restructuring of the U.S. steel industry if it is to align its costs with those of imported steel. The steel industry in the United States has argued the difficulty of making this investment because of poor earnings records of recent years. This has been contested by critics who pointed to U.S. Steel's (now USX) acquisition of

Marathon Oil when it apparently lacked funds for technological improvements. Critics also have blamed industry managers for spending funds for years at hopelessly obsolete (now being retired) plants rather than targeting outlays to viable facilities.

Four competitive responses appear to offer some hope for the future of the steel industry in the United States. The first has been a move to so-called minimills, which have specialized products, the latest technology, and proximity to markets. These plants are competitive, and their combined capacity and sales are growing. The second has been a move by foreign steel firms, such as Nippon Kokan of Japan, to buy into the U.S. industry, thus infusing funds and technology while eliminating a foreign competitor. The third has been a move by U.S. producers to buy semifinished steel from abroad, thus cutting costs at an important level of production. For instance, Korea's Pohang has a joint venture in the United States with USX, to which hot-rolled coils are shipped from Korea. The fourth has been a move to merge firms in the industry in order to gain administrative scale economies, to complement production, and to phase out less competitive plants while maintaining a full product line. An example of this was the Republic Steel–LTV merger plan.

In spite of these moves, the steel industry in the United States has pushed for stringent protection. In 1984 the U.S. imposed a flat ceiling of 1.7 million tons a year on imports of semifinished steel. Twenty-nine steel-making countries participated in voluntary quotas to fill this overall quota. By late 1987 many steel customers in the United States complained that the quotas, when coupled with steel capacity cuts, meant higher prices, delayed deliveries, and inability to get steel of the needed specifications. Some, such as Handy & Harman's Indiana Tube Corp., were even considering the movement of their production abroad to overcome the supply problem.

QUESTIONS

1. Should the United States seek to maintain a steel industry even if it could not become cost effective with foreign steel?
2. Should foreign producers be allowed to export steel to the United States at a price below their cost?
3. Can the United States again become cost efficient in the production of steel vis-à-vis foreign competition?
4. What types of governmental assistance might the United States give to the steel industry to help it compete more effectively with foreign steel? What are the advantages and disadvantages of each option?
5. If the steel industry in the United States does not receive assistance, what other options does it have?
6. Contrast the differences and similarities of the U.S. steel situation with those of the automobile case at the beginning of the chapter.

NOTES

1. The data for the case were taken from "U.S. Trade Agency Facing Crucial Decision on Detroit's Plea for Auto Import Curbs," *Wall Street Journal,* November 7, 1980, p. 29; "Car Wars," *Wall Street Journal,* February 15, 1980, p. 1; "Japan Asks Its Car Firms to Limit Exports to U.S. and Start American Production," *Wall Street Journal,* February 13, 1980, p. 2; "U.S. Autos Losing a Big Segment of the Market—Forever?" *Business Week,* March 24, 1980, pp. 78–85; "Made in U.S.A.—with Foreign Parts," *New York Times,* November 9, 1980, sec. 3, p. 1ff.; "7 of 10 Americans Agree," *New York Times,* November 6, 1980, p. A23; "Pressure Mounts to Restrict Auto Imports by Japan," *Wall Street Journal,* November 19, 1980, p. 2; Clyde H. Farnsworth, "House, 219–199, Votes to Require U.S. Made Parts in Imported Cars," *New York Times,* November 4, 1983, p. A1; Amal Nag, "The Politics of Auto-Import Quotas," *Wall Street Journal,* October 17, 1983, p. 30; Art Pine, "U.S. Bid to Limit '84 Car Imports Spurned by Japan, Which Seeks 1.9 Million Units," *Wall Street Journal,* October 26, 1983, p. 2; Donald Woutat, "GM and Ford Bonuses Raise Questions about Import Curbs, Union's Restraint," *Wall Street Journal,* April 16, 1984, p. 10; Leslie Wayne, "The Irony and Impact of Auto Quotas," *New York Times,* April 8, 1984, p. F1 +; "Brock Vows to End Import Quotas on Japanese Cars," *Wall Street Journal,* May 3, 1984, p. 29; Morgan O. Reynolds, "Unions and Jobs: The U.S. Auto Industry," *Journal of Labor Research,* Vol. 7, No. 2, Spring 1986, pp. 103–126; Robert D. Hershey, Jr., "Unemployment Rate Dips to 5.9% Behind Growth in Manufacturing," *New York Times,* August 1, 1987, p. 1; Rachel Dardis and Jia-Yeong Lin, "Automobile Quotas Revisited: The Costs of Continued Protection," *The Journal of Consumer Affairs,* Vol. 19, No. 2, Winter 1985, pp. 277–292; Susan Chira, "Japan Confirms It Will Continue U.S. Quota of 2.3 Million Cars," *New York Times,* January 30, 1988.

2. James J. Kilpatrick, "How Not to Create Jobs," *Nation's Business,* March 1983, Vol. 77, No. 1, p. 5.

3. John Andrew, John Helyar, and Bill Johnson, "Silver Lining," *Wall Street Journal,* February 29, 1984, p. 1.

4. *Ibid,* p. 19

5. Robert W. Crandell, "Import Quotas and the Automobile Industry: The Costs of Protectionism," *Brookings Review,* Summer 1984, pp. 8–16.

6. For an interesting account of the absorption problem, see Warren J. Bilkey, "Perceived Shortages of Unskilled Labor in Labor Surplus Economies: Costa Rica, El Salvador, Dominican Republic, and Mexico," *Journal of International Business Studies,* Fall 1972, pp. 1–16.

7. United Nations, Instability in Export Markets in Underdeveloped Countries (New York: United Nations, 1952), pp. 4–6, showed average annual fluctuations of 14 percent during the first half of this century.

8. Peter F. Drucker, "The Changed World Economy," *Foreign Affairs,* Vol. 64, No. 4, Spring 1986 discusses recent occurrences. Lloyd G. Reynolds, "Economic Development in Historical Perspective," *American Economic Review,* May 1980, p. 92, surveys an earlier period.

9. Supportive of the premises are Raul Prebisch, *The Economic Development of Latin America and Its Principal Problems* (New York: United Nations Department of

Economic Affairs, 1950); Charles P. Kindleberger, *The Terms of Trade: A European Case Study* (New York: John Wiley & Sons, 1956), and W. Arthur Lewis, *Aspects of Tropical Trade, 1883–1965* (Stockholm: Almquist and Wiksells, 1969). Nonsupportive are M. June Flanders, "Prebisch on Protectionism: An Evaluation," *Economic Journal,* June 1964; Theodore Morgan, "The Long-Run Terms of Trade between Agriculture and Manufacturing," *Economic Development and Cultural Change,* October 1959; and Gottfried Haberler, "Terms of Trade and Economic Development," in *Economic Development of Latin America,* H. Ellis, ed. (New York: St. Martin's Press, 1961).

10. John Diebold, "Beyond Subsidies and Trade Quotas," *New York Times,* November 2, 1986, p. F3.

11. "A Boycott Tunes Down Japan's TV Makers," *Business Week,* No. 2166, March 6, 1971, p. 41.

12. John M. Culbertson, "The Folly of Free Trade," *Harvard Business Review,* No. 5, September–October 1986, pp. 122–128.

13. Hazel Bradford and Evert Clark, "When the Pentagon Wants Something America Doesn't Have," *Business Week,* No. 2970, October 27, 1986, p. 46.

14. "Singapore Places Duty on Company's Exports to U.S. for First Time," *Wall Street Journal,* December 12, 1983, p. 35.

15. N. Hutton, "The Salience of Linkage in International Economic Negotiations," *Journal of Common Market Studies,* Nos. 1 and 2, 1975, p. 147.

16. F. H. Rolf Seringhaus, "The Impact of Government Export Marketing Assistance," *International Marketing Review,* Vol. 3, No. 2, Summer 1986 offers a detailed discussion of the effects.

17. Robert B. Reich, "Beyond Free Trade," *Foreign Affairs,* Vol. 61, No. 4, Spring 1983, p. 786.

18. For these and many other examples, see "One Man's Subsidy Is Another Man's Poison," *Economist,* March 11, 1978, pp. 77–78.

19. "U.S. Fails to Get Pact Limiting Direct Aid in Trade Financing," *Wall Street Journal,* April 16, 1984, p. 32.

20. "Tokyo Round: (3) New Customs Valuation Rules," *World Business Weekly,* March 10, 1980, p. 14.

21. "Trade Unit Ruling Sets End to Penalty Duty on Poland's Golf Carts," *Wall Street Journal,* May 21, 1980, p. 10.

22. Clyde H. Farnsworth, "If He Says It's Broccoli, It's Broccoli," *New York Times,* May 25, 1984, p. A18; Melinda Grenier Guiles, "Japanese Sport Utility Vehicles Remain in Truck Category, Bypassing Car Quota," *Wall Street Journal,* March 28, 1988, p. 2.

23. Joan Berger, "Tariffs Aren't Great, but Quotas Are Worse," *Business Week,* No. 2989, March 16, 1987, p. 64.

24. Michael Berger, "Phone Market: Japan Keeps Hanging up on the U.S.," *Business Week,* March 11, 1985, p. 67.

25. Kenneth N. Gilpin, " 'Local Content' Laws Posing New Obstacles for World's Exporters," *International Herald Tribune,* June 27, 1983, p. 17+.

26. See, for example, Jimmey S. Hillman, "Nontariff Barriers: Major Problems in Agricultural Trade," *American Journal of Agricultural Economics,* August 1978, pp.

491–501; "Wrapping Up the MTN Package," *Business America,* April 23, 1979, pp. 5–6; "Japan: Barriers that Slow Ford Escort Sales," *Business Week,* December 1, 1980, p. 60.

27. "Japan to Curb VCR Exports," *New York Times,* November 21, 1983, p. D5.

28. "New Restrictions on World Trade," *Business Week,* July 19, 1982, p. 119.

29. John Templeman, Bill Javetski, Jeffrey Reyser, and Barbara Buell, "The New Trade Talks Look Jinxed," *Business Week,* No. 2965, September 22, 1986, p. 47.

30. Laura Wallace, "Rising Barriers," *Wall Street Journal,* October 5, 1981, p. 1; Nina Darnton, "Spain Restricting the Dubbing of Foreign Movies," *New York Times,* June 4, 1984, p. C11; Chris Best, "Free Trade in the International Insurance Industry," *Risk Management,* August 1986, p. 12; J. J. Boddewyn and Iris Mohr, "International Advertisers Face Government Hurdles," *Marketing News,* May 8, 1987, p. 20.

31. Gary C. Hufbauer, "Should Unconditional MFN Be Revised, Retired, or Recast?" in *Issues in World Trade Policy,* R. H. Snape, ed. (New York: St. Martin's Press, 1986), pp. 32–55; Frieder Roessler, "The Scope, Limits and Function of the GATT Legal System," *The World Economy,* Vol. 8, No. 4, September 1985, pp. 287–298.

32. Ann V. Morrison, "Tokyo Round Agreements Set Rules for Nontariff Measures," *Business America,* Vol. 9, No. 14, July 7, 1986, pp. 11–13.

33. For a good discussion of alternatives when faced with import competition, see Ingo Walter and Kent A. Jones, "The Battle over Protectionism: How Industry Adjusts to Competitive Shocks," *Journal of Business Strategy,* Vol. 2, No. 2, Fall 1981, pp. 37–46.

34. "Ford Posts Record Net in Quarter," *New York Times,* April 27, 1984, p. D1.

35. For a discussion of MNE changes in their lobbying effort for protectionism see Giles Merrill, "Coping with the 'New Protectionism': How Companies Are Learning to Love It," *International Management,* Vol. 41, No. 9, pp. 20–26.

36. Data for this case were taken from "Why the Trigger Price Omits Specialty Steel," *Business Week,* October 20, 1980, pp. 44–45; "South Korea Goal: Join List of Top Steelmakers," *New York Times,* February 4, 1979, special section, p. 32; "Import Protection for Steel Faulted," *New York Times,* February 14, 1980, p. A7; "Basic Problems," *Wall Street Journal,* September 30, 1983, p. 1+; Steven Greenhouse, "National in Japanese Steel Deal," *New York Times,* April 25, 1984, p. D20+; Thomas F. O'Boyle and J. Ernest Beazley, "U.S. Steel Bid Stirs Debate inside Firm," *Wall Street Journal,* February 3, 1984, p. 25; Steven Greenhouse, "Many E.E.C. Roles in Steel Dispute," *New York Times,* January 16, 1984, p. D8; Thomas F. O'Boyle, "Forging a Link," *Wall Street Journal,* December 20, 1983, p. 1; "The Rebirth of Steel," February 16, 1984, p. 34; Donald F. Barnett and Louis Schorsch, *Steel: Upheaval in a Basic Industry* (Cambridge, Mass.: Ballinger, 1984); and "Its a No-Win Situation for Both Sides at USX," *Business Week,* No. 2981, January 19, 1987, p. 55; J. Ernest Beazley, "Big Steel's Push to Extend Import Quotas Draws Debate," *Wall Street Journal,* December 30, 1987, p. 2.

6

CHAPTER WHY DIRECT FOREIGN INVESTMENT TAKES PLACE

Who moves picks up, who stands still dries up.
—Italian proverb

- To explain why controlled or direct investments are viewed differently by investors and governments than noncontrolled or portfolio investments.
- To demonstrate how foreign direct investment may be acquired.
- To evaluate the relationship and possible substitution between foreign trade and international factor mobility, especially direct investment.
- To classify the major types of direct investment motivation.
- To show why trade is often not feasible as a means for a firm to service foreign markets, thus necessitating foreign investment.
- To illustrate the circumstances that lead companies to seek foreign supplies through their direct foreign investments.
- To show how and why government actions influence the movement of direct investment.
- To introduce the advantages that direct investors have vis-à-vis domestic firms.

CASE: BRIDGESTONE TIRE COMPANY[1]

The Bridgestone Tire Company is the largest tire producer in Japan, with 50 percent of that market. During the 1970s its sales grew sixfold. Between 1978 and 1987 it grew from the fifth to the third largest tire company in the world. Although most of the company's sales efforts have been geared toward the Japanese market, foreign sales have been increasing. Part of these foreign sales have been indirect because Bridgestone is a major supplier to Japanese automobile firms. Since they are part of the original equipment on exported Japanese automobiles, Bridgestone tires arrive in foreign markets where the company makes little or no export effort. Direct exports are also important. Bridgestone's top management believes that it is essential to grow outside of Japan, assuming that by 1990 or 1995 there will be only four or five major tire companies in the world. Management also believes that it will be difficult to sustain growth in Japan because it is hard to exceed 50 percent of the market.

In 1987 Bridgestone announced it would expand its truck and bus tire plant in Tennessee in order to produce about two million passenger tires a year by 1990. This was seven years after the company's president stated that the firm's first priority would be the establishment of a manufacturing investment in the United States. Probably the major factor influencing this priority was the firm's high direct and indirect export sales to the United States. These sales have given Bridgestone a solid indication that it could compete against firms with established U.S. sales and manufacturing facilities. By 1987 one out of every ten new cars sold in the United States carried Bridgestone tires. Some dealers carried Bridgestone tires as replacements as well; however, Bridgestone had only 2 percent of this larger market. Bridgestone has become more confident about its ability to manage and control an automobile tire manufacturing investment in the highly competitive U.S. market. Part of this confidence is due to Bridgestone's success with foreign manufacturing facilities in four developing countries, its success in Australia after buying out Uniroyal there, and its success with U.S. truck tire manufacture after buying a Firestone facility in 1982.

Then in 1988, Bridgestone surprised analysts by buying Firestone's tire operations for $2.6 billion. This gave them five North American plants supplying about 40 percent of the tires for North American vehicles built by Ford and 21 percent of those built by General Motors as well as plants in Portugal, Spain, France, Italy, Argentina, Brazil, and Venezuela. Although Bridgestone remained the world's third largest tire company, the acquisition put them very close to the two largest firms, Goodyear and Michelin.

But why should Bridgestone manufacture automobile tires in the United States? Why not continue exporting, since sales have grown by this means? Several factors have current or potential negative impact on Bridgestone's export activities to the United States. The first of these is government-imposed restrictions. Although imports of replacement tires comprised a very small part of the U.S. market, these imports could be restricted if sales of U.S. tires go down. More probable could be action taken against imports of Japanese automobiles, thus jeopardizing the sale of original equipment tires. The possibility of import restrictions already had led four major Japanese automakers to begin some U.S. production, and all opted for U.S.-made tires once their plants were operating. Toyota, by the way, bought 40 percent of Bridgestone's original equipment tires. Finally, because of Japan's huge trade surplus with the United States, the United States could conceivably place overall restrictions on the import of Japanese products.

Exports might also be imperiled if Japanese costs went up in relation to American costs. Because of high transportation costs for tires, which are bulky relative to their value, it is usually difficult to ship tires over a large distance except as part of original vehicle equipment. Bridgestone's overseas shipping expenses ranged between $3 and $12 per tire, depending on size. U.S. producers even depended on multiple U.S. plant locations in order to minimize transport costs. It was generally conceded that a one-plant firm in the United States could not maintain sales on both the east and west coasts. Bridgestone's ability to overcome the high transport costs was due largely to the low value of the yen relative to the U.S. dollar. Since most of Bridgestone's costs were in yen, a fall in the yen resulted in a cheaper price in terms of U.S. dollars. When the yen strengthens, Bridgestone's dollar costs go up. By mid-1986 the strong yen put the competitive sales price below Bridgestone's break-even point. The yen strengthened even more in 1987 and 1988, making it even more difficult to serve the U.S. market by exporting to it.

INTRODUCTION

Foreign sales are increasingly being made from controlled foreign production facilities; this is termed **direct foreign investment.** No one explanation or theory encompasses all the reasons for this increase.[2]

The preceding case illustrates the multiplicity of factors influencing the decision of one firm to produce in a foreign country. Before deciding to invest in the United States, Bridgestone faced a sequence of decisions. One of the first was whether or not to serve foreign markets. Bridgestone was content with the Japanese market as long as it could expand rapidly within that market. However, once the company reached a large and fairly stable share of a maturing market, the choices were either product diversification or geographic diversification if growth was to be sustained. Either type of diversification would involve new risks because of operating in new arenas. Bridgestone chose to diversify geographically because its managers believed its competitive advantage was more specific to the production of tires than to knowledge of the Japanese market. (For example, Bridgestone spends more on R&D than Goodyear, the world's largest tire manufacturer. The high level and concentration of R&D expenditures has led Bridgestone to make notable breakthroughs in both product and process technologies.)[3] Bridgestone first entered foreign markets through exporting and was successful. However, management felt that it could not sustain an export market to the United States because of the high transport cost of tires, the possibility of U.S. government import restrictions or preferences by final or industrial consumers for a U.S.-made product, and an uncertain cost structure created by the changing yen-dollar relationship. Bridgestone still might have chosen to license its technologies and/or its name to producers already in the U.S. market, which would have generated revenues without the risk of operating in an alien environment. By this time, though, the perceived risk of operating in the United States was minimal because of Bridgestone's growing foreign experience and its probable ability to sell output to Japanese automakers with whom the company had experience. There were also competitive reasons for Bridgestone's not licensing. The company felt that it must be located in growth markets if it were to survive the expected shakeout in the industry. The transfer of technology to other tire producers eventually might undermine Bridgestone's ability to compete in other markets.

Neither the motives nor the methods for acquiring direct investment as illustrated in the case are conclusive. This chapter will further examine these various motives and methods.

The growth of direct foreign investment has resulted in a heightened interest in four other questions:

1. What effect does the investment have on national economic, political, and social objectives?
2. Should a firm choose to operate abroad by some form other than direct investment, such as licensing?
3. What is, or should be, a firm's pattern of investment in terms of where to operate abroad?
4. What are the hidden costs and problems of operating in foreign environments?

These questions will be discussed from an introductory standpoint in this chapter. Then they will be explored more thoroughly in subsequent chapters: question 1 in Chapter 11; question 2 in Chapter 15; question 3 in Chapter 16; and question 4 in Chapters 18–22.

THE MEANING OF DIRECT FOREIGN INVESTMENT

The Concept of Control

In Chapter 1 we said that for direct investment to take place, control must follow the investment. The amount of ownership share necessary for control

Direct investment usually implies 10 or 25 percent ownership.

is certainly not clear-cut. If stock ownership is widely dispersed, then a small percentage of the holdings may be enough to gain weight in managerial decision making. On the other hand, even a 100 percent share does not guarantee control. If a government dictates whom a firm hires, what the firm must sell at a specified price, and how earnings will be distributed, then we could say that control has passed to the government. These are all decisions that governments frequently have imposed on foreign or domestic investors operating within their confines. But it is not necessarily only governments that may wrest control from whoever holds the voting shares. If some resource needed for the firm to operate is not regulated by the firm's owners, then whoever does control the resource may exert substantial influence. Because of the difficulty of identifying direct investments, governmental offices have had to establish arbitrary definitions, usually indicating ownership of either 10 or 25 percent of the voting stock in a foreign enterprise as minimum for an investment to be considered direct.

The Concern over Control

In foreign investment, decisions of national importance may be made abroad.

Governmental concern. Why is there concern over whether an investment is controlled from abroad? Many critics worry that the national interest will not be best served if a multinational firm makes decisions from afar on the basis of its own global or national objectives. For example, General Motors (GM) owns a 100 percent interest in Vauxhall Motors in the United Kingdom. The control of Vauxhall by GM in this direct investment means that GM's corporate management in the United States must be concerned directly with and make decisions about personnel staffing, the export prices, and the retention versus payout of profits in Vauxhall. The British public also is concerned in this case because decisions that directly affect the British economy are being (or at least can be) made in the United States. The British government, on the other hand, owns slightly less than 1 percent of GM. Since this is not enough for control, the British government does not have to expend time and effort in making management decisions for GM. Nor is the U.S. populace concerned that vital GM decisions will be made in Britain. This should not imply that noncontrolled investments are unimportant. They may affect substantially a country's balance of payments (see Chapter 9), and they may play an important part in a firm's financial management and strategy (see Chapter 21).

When investors control an organization, they:

- Are more willing to transfer technology and other competitive assets
- Usually use cheaper and faster means of transferring assets.

Investor concern. Control is also very important to many investors who are reluctant to transfer certain vital resources to another domestic or foreign organization that can make all its operating decisions independently. Valuable patents, trademarks, and management know-how then could be used to undermine the competitive position of the original holders, who transferred these resources.[4] In the introductory case, for example, Bridgestone was hesitant to transfer either product technology, such as its SuperFiller radials, or process technology, such as its mold changeover methods, to other companies. Bridgestone's management is well aware of how acquired technology can be used to catch a leader. Between the end of World War II and 1979, much of Bridgestone's technology came from Goodyear, which held a noncontrolling interest in Bridgestone. Another reason for control is to make decisions that serve global as opposed to country level objectives. Operating costs may also decrease when there is control. This is because (1) the parent and subsidiary are likely to have a common corporate culture, (2) a company can use its own managers, who understand its objectives, (3) protracted negotiations with another company are avoided, and (4) possible problems of enforcing an agreement are evaded.[5] This self-handling is often referred to as **internalization.** This desire for control does not imply that the control of foreign operations is always preferable. There are many circumstances in which assets are transferred to noncontrolled entities; which is one of the subjects of Chapter 15.

Methods of Acquisition

Direct investments usually, but not always, involve some capital movement.

Direct investment traditionally has been considered an international capital movement that crosses borders when the anticipated return (accounting for the risk factor and the cost of transfer) is higher overseas than at home. Although most direct investments involve some type of international capital movement, an investor may transfer many other types of assets. Such organizations as Western Hotels have transferred very little capital to other countries. Instead, Western has transferred managers, hotel cost controls, and reservations capabilities in exchange for equity in foreign hotels. An example of a direct investment made completely by transferring nonfinancial resources instead of capital was the Plessey (British) acquisition of Airborne Accessories Corporation of New Jersey. Plessey had two assets that were vital to Airborne Accessories: technology and established sales capabilities outside the United States. Plessey offered the owners notes in exchange for the ownership. Although the interest and principal on these notes was to be paid strictly out of the earnings of the acquired company, the owners reasoned that this interest was a higher return than they could get by continuing to own and manage Airborne themselves.[6]

Aside from committing nonfinancial resources, there are two other means of acquiring assets that do not involve international capital movements in a normal sense. First, if a business earns funds in a foreign country, these may be used to establish an investment. For example, if a firm exports merchandise but holds payment for those goods abroad, the settlement could be used to acquire an investment. In this case the company merely has exchanged goods for equity. Although this is not a method used extensively for initial investment, the use of retained earnings is a major means of expanding abroad. Initially a firm may transfer assets abroad in order to establish a sales or production facility. If the earnings from the facility are used to increase the value of the foreign holdings, direct investment has increased without a new international capital movement. The second means is by trading equity between firms in different countries. For example, Naarden in the Netherlands acquired a share of Flavorex in the United States by giving the Flavorex owners stock in the Naarden Company.

In several of the preceding examples a firm in one country acquired an interest in an ongoing business operation in another country. Alternatively the investors could have established an entirely new company abroad. In either case the investors' ownership of voting shares might have been less than 100 percent: If it were less, the remainder could be (1) widely rather than narrowly held and (2) owned by private rather than by governmental sources. The rationale and implications of these various alternatives will be elaborated on in Chapter 15.

THE RELATIONSHIP OF TRADE AND FACTOR MOBILITY

Both finished goods and production factors are partially mobile internationally.

Whether capital or some other asset is transferred abroad initially to acquire a direct investment, the asset is a type of production factor. Eventually, the direct investment usually involves the movement of various types of production factors as investors infuse capital, technology, personnel, raw materials, or components into their operating facilities abroad. Therefore it is useful to examine the relationship of trade theory to the movement of production factors.

The Trade and Factor Mobility Theory

Chapter 4 explained that trade often occurs because of differences in factor endowments among countries. A country such as Canada, with abundant arable land relative to its small but educated labor force, may cultivate wheat in a highly mechanized manner. This wheat may be exchanged for handmade sweaters from Hong Kong, which require abundant semiskilled labor and little land.

Historical treatises on trade assumed that the factors of production were nearly immobile internationally and that trade could move freely. In actuality there are many natural and imposed barriers that make both finished goods and production factors partially mobile internationally. Factor movement is an alternative to trade that may or may not be a more efficient allocation of resources. If the factors of production were not free to move internationally as assumed by early economic theorists, then trade would ordinarily be the most efficient way of compensating for differences in factor endowments. If neither trade nor the production factors could move internationally, a country would often have to forego consuming certain goods. Alternatively, countries could produce them differently, which would usually result in decreased worldwide output and higher prices. We can only speculate on the astronomical cost of coffee if it were produced, say, in hothouses in Arctic regions. In some cases, however, the inability to utilize foreign production factors may stimulate efficient methods of substitution, such as the development of new materials as alternatives for traditional ones or of machines to do hand work. The development of synthetic rubber and rayon undoubtedly was accelerated because wartime conditions made it impractical to move silk and natural rubber, as well as silkworms and rubber plants.

Substitution

In substitution, there is pressure for most abundant factors to move to area of scarcity.

Whenever the factor proportions vary widely among countries, there are pressures for the most abundant factors to move to countries of greater scarcity so that they can command a better return. Thus in countries with an abundance of labor relative to land and capital, there is a tendency for laborers in that country to be unemployed or poorly paid; if permitted, these workers will gravitate to countries with relatively full employment and higher wages. Likewise, capital will tend to move away from countries where it is abundant to those where it is scarce. Mexico is thus a net recipient of capital from the United States, and the United States is a net recipient of labor from Mexico.

If finished goods and production factors were both completely free to move internationally, then the comparative costs of transferring goods and factors would determine the location of production. A hypothetical example should illustrate the substitutability of trade and factor movements under different scenarios.

Assume: (1) that the United States and Mexico have equally productive land available at the same cost for the growing of tomatoes; (2) that the cost of transporting tomatoes from the United States to Mexico or from Mexico to the United States is \$0.75 per bushel; and (3) that workers from either country pick an average of two bushels per hour during a thirty-day picking season. The only differences in price between the two countries are due to labor and capital cost variations. The labor rate in the United States is assumed to be \$20.00 per day or \$1.25 per bushel; in Mexico it is assumed to be \$4.00 per day or \$0.25 per bushel. The cost of capital needed to buy seeds, fertilizers, and equipment costs the equivalent of \$0.50 per bushel in Mexico and \$0.30 per bushel in the United States.

If neither tomatoes nor production factors can move between the two countries, then the cost of tomatoes produced in Mexico for the Mexican market would be \$0.75 per bushel (\$0.25 of labor plus \$0.50 of capital), whereas those produced in the United States for the U.S. market would be \$1.55 per bushel (\$1.25 of labor plus \$0.30 of capital). If trade restrictions on tomatoes were eliminated between the two countries, the United States would import from Mexico because the Mexican cost of \$0.75 per bushel plus $0.75 of transportation cost to move them to the United States would be less than the $1.55 cost of growing them in the United States.

Consider another scenario in which neither country allows the importation of tomatoes but in which both countries allow certain movements of labor and capital. An investigation shows that Mexican workers can enter the United States on temporary work permits for an incremental travel and living expense of $14.40 per day per worker or $0.90 per bushel. At the same time, U.S. capital can be enticed to invest in Mexican tomato production provided that it receives a payment equivalent to $0.40 per bushel, less than the Mexican going rate but more than it would earn in the United States. In this situation, Mexican production costs per bushel would be $0.65 ($0.25 of Mexican labor plus $0.40 of American capital). U.S. production costs would be $1.45 ($0.25 of Mexican labor plus $0.90 of travel and incremental costs plus $0.30 of American capital). Note that each country could reduce its production costs (Mexico from $0.75 to $0.65 and the United States from $1.55 to $1.45) by bringing in abundant production factors from abroad.

With free trade and the free movement of production factors, Mexico would produce for both markets by importing capital from the United States. According to the above assumptions, that would be a cheaper alternative than sending labor to the United States. In reality, neither production factors nor the finished goods that they produce are completely free to move internationally. Some slight changes in imposing or freeing restrictions can greatly alter how and where goods may be produced most cheaply. In the case of the United States in recent years there has been more legal freedom for capital to flow out than for labor to flow in. There has been a resultant increase in U.S.-controlled direct investment to produce goods that are then imported back into the United States.

Complementarity of Trade and Direct Investment

Factor mobility via direct investment often stimulates trade movements due to:

- Components
- Complementary products
- Equipment to subsidiaries

In spite of the increase in direct investments to produce goods for re-import, an interesting occurrence is that firms usually export substantially to their foreign facilities. Many of these exports would not occur if overseas investments did not exist. In these cases, factor movements stimulate rather than substitute for trade. One reason for this phenomenon is that domestic operating units may ship materials and components to their foreign facilities for use in a finished product. For example, the Mexican government requires that all automobiles sold in Mexico be assembled there. Chrysler therefore has an investment in Mexico to which parts are shipped from the United States. (Yet the amount of parts from the United States has decreased as Mexico has required more local purchases.) The foreign subsidiaries or affiliates also may buy capital equipment or supplies from home country firms because of the confidence in performance and delivery or because of desires for maximum worldwide uniformity. A foreign facility may produce part of the product line while serving as sales agent for exports of its parent's other products. Bridgestone, for instance, continued to export its automobile tires from Japan while using the sales force from its U.S. truck tire manufacturing operations to handle the imports.

DIRECT INVESTMENT MOTIVATION

Business or government motivations
- expand markets
- acquire supplies or resources

Government motivation may additionally be to gain political advantage

The reasons that firms engage in direct investment ownership are no different than those outlined in Chapter 4 for their pursuit of international trade. These are:

1. to expand markets by selling abroad,
2. to acquire foreign resources (e.g., raw materials, production efficiency, knowledge).

When government is involved in direct investment an additional motive may be to attain some political advantage. These three objectives in turn may be pursued by any one of three forms of foreign involvement. One of these, the sale of services (e.g., licensing or management contracts) often is avoided either for fear of the loss of control of key competitive assets or because of greater economies from self-ownership of production. The following discussion will concentrate on the remaining two forms: trade and direct investment. We will emphasize why direct investment is chosen in view of the fact that most firms consider it riskier to operate a facility abroad than at home.

MARKET EXPANSION INVESTMENTS

Transportation

Transportation increases cost too much for some products.

Early trade theorists usually assumed away the cost of transporting goods from one place to another. More recent location theorists have considered total landed cost (cost of production plus shipping) to be more relevant. When transportation is added to production costs, some products become impractical to ship over a great distance. In the opening case, we showed that one of the factors influencing Bridgestone's decision to invest in the United States was the high cost of transporting tires relative to the production price of tires. Numerous other products that are impractical to ship great distances without a very large escalation in the price quickly come to mind: A few of these products and their investing companies are newspapers (Thompson Newspapers, Canadian); margarine (Unilever, British-Dutch); dynamite (Nobel, Swedish); and soft drinks (Pepsico, U.S.). For these firms, it is necessary to produce abroad if they are to sell abroad.

Excess domestic capacity

- Usually means exporting rather than direct investment.
- May be competitive through variable cost pricing.

Lack of domestic capacity. As long as a company has excess capacity at its home country plant, it may be able to compete effectively in limited export markets in spite of the high transport costs. This could be because the fixed operating expenses are covered through domestic sales; thus foreign prices can be set on the basis of variable rather than full cost. Such a pricing strategy may erode as foreign sales become more important or as output nears full plant capacity utilization. This helps to explain why firms, even those with products for which transport charges are a high portion of total landed costs, typically export before producing abroad. The other major factor is that companies want to get a better indication that they can sell a sufficient amount in the foreign country before committing resources for foreign production.

This reluctance to expand total capacity while there is still substantial excess capacity is not unlike a domestic expansion decision. Internationally as well as domestically, growth is incremental. To understand this process, it is useful to draw a parallel of how growth may take place domestically. The simplest example is the firm that makes only one product. Most likely, this firm will begin operations near the city where its founders are already residing and will begin selling in only the local or regional area. Eventually, sales may be expanded to a larger geographic market. As capacity is reached, the firm may build a second plant in another part of the country to serve that region and save on transportation costs. Warehouses and sales offices may be located in various cities in order to assure closer contact with customers. Purchasing offices may be located close to suppliers in order to improve the probability of delivery at low prices. In fact, the company may even acquire some of its customers or suppliers in order to reduce inventories and gain economies in distribution. Certain functions may be further decentralized geographically, such as the location of financial offices near a financial center. As the product line evolves and expands, operations continue to disperse. In the pursuit of foreign business it is not surprising that firms find it necessary to acquire assets abroad.

In large-scale process technology, large-scale production and export usually reduce unit landed costs since fixed costs are covered.

In small-scale process technology, country-by-country production usually reduces unit landed costs since transportation is minimized.

Scale economies. Transportation costs must be examined in relation to the type of technology used to produce a good. The manufacture of some products necessitates plant and equipment that use a high fixed capital input. In such a situation, especially if the product is highly standardized or undifferentiated from competitors, the cost per unit is apt to drop significantly as output increases. Products such as ball bearings, alumina, and semiconductor wafers fall into this category. Such products are exported substantially because the cost savings from scale economies overcome the added transport expenses to get goods to foreign markets. Products that are more differentiated and labor-intensive, such as pharmaceuticals and certain prepared foods, are not as sensitive to scale economies. For these types of products, transportation costs may dictate smaller plants to serve national rather than international markets.[7] David's Cookies, for example, first entered the Japanese market with ingredients mixed in the United States. However, there was little cost reduction by mixing bigger batches of batter; consequently, David's switched to Japanese ingredient preparation to overcome the transport cost incurred when exporting.[8]

Trade Restrictions

If imports are highly restricted:

- Companies often produce locally to serve market.
- Firms are more prone to produce locally if market potential is high in relation to scale economies.

Chapter 5 showed that for various reasons there are numerous ways in which a government can make it impractical for a firm to reach its market potential through exportation alone. The firm may find it *must* produce in a foreign country if it is to sell there. For example, Mexico announced that within five years, locally produced microcomputers would have to comprise 70 percent of the market. Although many producers questioned whether the same prices and quality could be maintained as when they exported, they nevertheless were reluctant to abandon a growing market.[9] Such governmental pronouncements are not unusual. They undoubtedly favor large companies that can afford to commit large amounts of resources abroad and make foreign competitiveness more difficult for the smaller firms, which can afford only to export as a means of serving foreign markets.

How prevalent are trade restrictions as an enticement for making direct investments? There are substantial numbers of anecdotal examples of firms' decisions to locate within protected markets, yet studies of aggregate direct investment movements present disagreements on the importance of trade barriers.[10] A possible explanation for the fact that some studies have not found import barriers to be an important enticement is that the studies have had to rely on actual tariff barriers as the measurement of restrictions. This reliance overlooks the importance of nontariff constraints, indirect entry barriers, and potential trade restrictions. In the opening case, Bridgestone reacted to these latter impediments to trade rather than to the actual existence of tariffs on tires. Almost certainly import barriers are a major enticement to direct investment, but they must be viewed alongside other factors, such as the market size of the country imposing barriers.

Import trade restrictions, for example, have been highly influential in enticing automobile producers to locate in Mexico. Similar restrictions by Central American countries have been ineffective because of their small markets. However, Central American import barriers on products requiring lower amounts of capital investment and therefore smaller markets (e.g., pharmaceuticals) have been highly effective at enticing direct investment.

Consumer-Imposed Restrictions

Government-imposed legal measures are not the only trade barriers to otherwise competitive goods: Consumer desires also may dictate limitations.

Consumers sometimes prefer domestically made products due to:

- Nationalism
- A belief that their own products are better
- A fear that foreign-made goods may not be delivered on time
- A compatibility between these products and local preferences.

For example, consumers may have a preference for buying domestically made goods even though these are more expensive. They may also demand that merchandise be altered so substantially that foreign production becomes feasible. The question of preference for domestically made products may be due to nationalistic feelings, to a belief that foreign-made goods are inferior, or to a fear that service and spare parts will not be obtainable easily for imported wares.

Nationalism. The impact of nationalistic feelings on investment movements is not assessed easily; however, some evidence does exist. There have been active campaigns at times in many countries to persuade people to buy locally produced goods. In the United States, for instance, attempts have been made in recent years to boycott Polish hams, Japanese Christmas ornaments, and French wines. In the mid-1980s many U.S. manufacturers promoted "made in the USA" to appeal to consumers in areas that had been hit with import competition.[11] Fearful that adverse public opinion might lead to curbs on television imports, some firms announced the establishment of production plants in the United States.[12]

Product image. The link between product image and direct investment is clearer than the one between nationalism and direct investment just discussed. The image may stem from the merchandise itself or from beliefs concerning after-sales servicing. In tests using commodities that were identical except for the label of country origin, consumers were found to view wares differently on the basis of product source.[13] Although there are examples of eventual image changes, such as the general improvement in the image of Japanese products concomitant with the image decline for U.S. products, it may be slow and costly for a company to overcome image problems created by manufacturing in a country having a lower-image status for a particular product. Consequently, there may be advantages in producing in a country with an already-existing high image. For example, a Canadian electronics producer found U.S. consumers reluctant to purchase its products because of a belief that Canadian electronics were inferior to U.S. electronics. When part of the output was shifted to the United States and "made in U.S.A." was put on the label, this problem disappeared.[14]

Delivery risk. There is considerable consumer fear that parts for foreign-made goods may be difficult to obtain from abroad. Industrial consumers often prefer to pay a higher price to a producer located nearby in order to minimize the risk of nondelivery due to distances and strikes. For instance, Hoechst Chemical of West Germany located one of its dye factories in North Carolina because that region's textile industry feared delivery problems from the cheaper German imports.

Product change. Often a company must alter a product to suit local tastes or requirements, which may compel the use of local raw materials and market testing. Test marketing and altering a product at a great distance from the production is most difficult and expensive. Coca-Cola, for example, sells some drinks (made from local fruits) abroad that are not available in the United States. It is assuredly much cheaper to make these drinks overseas.

The necessity of product alteration has two other effects on company production. Initially, it means an additional investment; as long as an investment is needed to serve the foreign market anyway, management might consider locating facilities abroad. Next, product alteration may mean that certain economies from large-scale production will be lost, which may cause the least-cost location to shift from one country to another. The more the product has to be altered for the foreign market, the more likely that the production will be shifted abroad. Two of the factors influencing the decision of Volkswagen to set up U.S. production facilities, for example, were the ever-increasing safety requirements set by the U.S. government and the desire for new options by U.S. consumers, which were different from those needed to sell in other parts of the world. But these changes were not sufficient to garner a large share of the U.S. market; and Volkswagen announced the closing of its U.S. assembly operations in 1987.[15]

Following Customers

Companies can keep customers by producing abroad when customers produce abroad.

There are many examples of companies that sell abroad indirectly: That is, they sell products, components, or services domestically that become embodied in a product or service that their domestic customer then exports. Bridgestone, for example, sold tires to Toyota and Honda, which in turn exported fully assembled cars (including the tires) to foreign markets. In these situations the indirect exporters commonly follow their customers when those customers make direct investments. Bridgestone's consideration for making automobile tires in the United States was based partially on a desire to continue selling to Honda and Toyota once those companies initiated U.S. production. Bridgestone's truck tire investment was in turn instrumental in Yasuda Fire & Marine Insurance Co.'s decision to establish a U.S. investment in order to provide workman's compensation insurance to Bridgestone's U.S. operations.[16]

Following Competitors

In oligopoly industries, competitors tend to make direct investments in a given country at similar times.

Within oligopoly industries (those with few sellers), several investors often establish facilities in a given country within a fairly short time period.[17] Much of this concentration may be explained by internal or external changes, which would affect most oligopolists within an industry at approximately the same time. In many industries, for example, capacity expansion cycles are similar for most firms. Thus the firms would consider logically a foreign investment at approximately the same time as their domestic capacity point is approached. Externally, they might all be faced with changes in import restrictions or market conditions that indicate a move to direct investment in order to serve consumers in a given country. In spite of the prevalence of these motivators, much of the movement by oligopolists seems better explained by defensive motives.

Much of the research done in game theory shows that people often make decisions based on the "least damaging alternative." The question for many firms is, "Do I lose less by moving abroad or by staying at home?" Let us say that some foreign market may be served effectively only by an investment in the market, but the market is large enough to support only one producer. One way of facing this problem would be for competitors to set up one joint operation and divide profit among them; however, antitrust laws might discourage or prevent this. If only one firm decides to establish facilities, it will have an advantage over its competitors by garnering a larger market, spreading its R&D costs, and making a profit that can be reinvested in other areas of prone to follow quickly rather than let the firm gain advantages. Thus the decision is based not so much on the benefits to be gained, but rather on the greater losses sustained by not entering the field. In most oligopoly industries (e.g., automobiles, tires, petroleum), this pattern emerges and helps to explain the large number of producers relative to the size of the market in some countries.

Closely related to this is the decision to invest in a foreign competitor's home market to prevent that competitor from using high profits therein to invest and compete in other parts of the world. This type of aggressive strategy will be discussed more fully in Chapter 16.

Changes in Comparative Costs

The least costly production location changes due to inflation and wage rates.

A company may export successfully because its home country has a cost advantage. The home country cost advantage depends on the price of the individual factors of production, the size of operations, transportation of finished goods, and the productivity of the combined production factors. None of these conditions affecting cost is static; consequently, the least-cost location may change over time. Another factor affecting Volkswagen's decision to locate in the United States was the fact that during the 1970s, German wage rates (measured in dollars) grew much faster than those in the United States, owing largely to a rise in the value of the mark relative to the dollar. Volkswagen estimated a 10 percent cost savings by producing in the United States rather than in West Germany for that market. But Volkswagen closed its U.S. operations after eleven years in order to source from even lower-wage facilities in Mexico and Brazil.[18]

The concept of shifts in comparative costs of production is closely related to that of resource-seeking investments. A firm may establish a direct investment to serve a foreign market but eventually import into the home country from the country to which it was once exporting. Some of these concepts will be discussed in the following section on supply-oriented investments.

SUPPLY-ORIENTED INVESTMENTS

There is a cartoon showing Santa Claus speaking to his elves; the caption reads, "I'm sorry to report that after the first, I'll be moving operations to Taiwan."[19] This cartoon is consistent with the popular image of direct investments motivated by cheap foreign labor used to make imported products. While this does take place, the explanation overlooks some of the costs of producing abroad. For example, Lionel Trains moved from the United States to Mexico but had so many problems with training and communications that the company moved back after a few years. Furthermore, there are cost advantages from direct investment that are not fully encompassed in the popular image.

Vertical Integration

In vertical integration, raw materials, production, and marketing often occur in different countries.

Most vertical integration is supply-oriented.

Vertical integration involves gaining control of different stages as a product moves from its earliest production to its final distribution. As products and their marketing become more complicated, there is a greater need to combine resources located in more than one country. If one country has iron, a second has coal, a third has the technology and capital for making steel and steel products, and a fourth the demand for the steel products, there is a great interdependence among the four and a strong need to establish tight relationships in order to ensure the continuance of the production and marketing flow. One way of adding assurance to this flow is by gaining a voice in the management of one of the foreign operations by investing in it. Most of the world's direct investment in petroleum may be explained through this interdependence concept. Since much of the petroleum supply is located in countries different from those with a heavy petroleum demand, the oil industry has become integrated vertically on an international basis.

Certain economies also may be gained through vertical integration. The greater assurance of supply and/or markets may allow a firm to carry smaller inventories and spend less on promotion. It also may permit considerably greater flexibility in shifting funds, taxes, and profits from one country to another through artificial intercompany transfer prices, as will be discussed more fully in Chapter 20.

Advantages of vertical integration may accrue to a firm by either market-oriented or supply-oriented investments in other countries. There are examples of both. Of the two, however, there have been more examples in recent years among manufacturers to gain raw materials in other countries than vice versa. This is because of the growing dependence on raw materials in LDCs and the lack of resources by LDC firms to invest substantially abroad. This movement of capital and technology to LDCs is consistent with a theory that holds that factor mobility is most efficient when the more mobile factors, such as capital, move so as to be combined with the less mobile ones, such as natural resources. Without the capital movement the natural resources otherwise might not be exploited efficiently.[20]

Rationalized Production

In rationalized production, different components or portions of product line are made in different parts of the world. Advantages are:

- Factor cost differences
- Long production runs

Challenges are:

- Satisfying governments that local production takes place
- Higher risk of work stoppage
- Record keeping.

Companies increasingly produce different components or different portions of their product line in different parts of the world—**rationalized production**—to take advantage of varying costs of labor, capital, and raw materials. One such example are the more than 1300 plants in Mexico, known as *maquiladores,* which are integrated with operations in the United States. Semifinished goods can be exported to Mexico duty free, as long as they will be reexported from Mexico. Once the labor-intensive portion of the production is accomplished in Mexico, such as the sewing of car seats for General Motors or the building of television cabinets for Panasonic, duties in the United States are charged only on the amount of value added in Mexico.[21]

Many companies shrug off the possibility of rationalized production of parts because of the risks of work stopping in many countries due to a strike or a change in import regulations in just one country. An alternative to parts rationalization is the production of a complete product in a given country but only part of the product range within that country.[22] A U.S. subsidiary in France, for example, may produce only product A, another subsidiary in Brazil only product B, and the home plant in the United States only product C. Each plant sells worldwide so that each can gain scale economies and take advantage of differences in input costs that may affect total production cost differences. Each may get concessions to import because of demonstrating that jobs and incomes are developed locally.

Access to Production Factors

A company's presence in a country may improve knowledge flow and access to other resources.

The concept of seeking abroad some input not easily or cheaply available in the home country closely resembles vertical integration. Many foreign firms have offices in New York in order to gain better access to the U.S. capital market or at least to know what is happening within that market that can affect other worldwide capital occurrences. The search for knowledge may take other forms as well. It may be a U.S. pharmaceutical firm in Peru conducting research not allowed in the United States. It may be C.F.P. (French), which bought a share in Leonard Petroleum to learn U.S. marketing in order to compete better with other U.S. oil firms outside the United States. It may be McGraw-Hill, which has an office in Europe to uncover European technical developments.

Foreign acquisitions may give firms faster and cheaper access to certain resources. Because of the technical lead of the United States in semiconductors, such firms as Siemens and Robert A. Bosch from West Germany have found it more expeditious to acquire U.S. firms with advanced capabilities than to develop them independently.[23] The ability to gain access to technology has been a very important factor in the decision to invest by foreign firms in the United States.[24]

The Product Life Cycle Theory

The product life cycle theory shows that:

- New products are produced mainly in industrial countries
- Mature products are more likely to be produced in LDCs

One explanation for changes in the location of production is called the **product life cycle (PLC) theory.**[25] (Recall the explanation of the theory in relation to trade and production location in Chapter 4.) This theory shows, because of market and cost reasons, how production of many products moves from one country to another as a product moves through its life cycle. The production occurs during the introductory stage of the life cycle in only one (usually industrial) country. As production moves next to other industrial countries as well during the product's growth stage, the original producer may decide to invest in the foreign facilities to earn profits there. At the mature stage when production shifts largely to developing countries, the same firm may decide to control those operations as well.

Governmental Investment Incentives

Governmental incentives may shift the least-cost location of production.

In addition to putting restrictions on imports, countries frequently encourage direct investment inflows by offering tax concessions or a wide variety of other subsidies. Such incentives are offered by the central governments of every industrial country except the United States and Japan[26] as well as by the LDCs. Among the direct assistance are tax holidays, accelerated depreciation, low-interest loans, loan guarantees, subsidized energy or transport, and the construction of rail spurs and roads to serve the plant facility.[27] These incentives affect the comparative cost of production among countries, enticing companies to invest there to serve national or international markets.

POLITICAL MOTIVES

Governments take ownership in or give incentives to direct investors to:

- Gain supplies of strategic resources
- Develop spheres of influence

In Chapter 4 we showed that trade sometimes has been undertaken historically for political motives. During the mercantilist period, for example, European powers sought colonies in order to control their foreign trade and extend the sphere of influence of the mother countries. Since colonialism is no longer an acceptable practice, it is argued that many of the old colonial aims may be achieved by having companies control vital sectors in the economies of LDCs.[28] For instance, if a U.S. firm controls the production of a vital raw material in an LDC, it can effectively prevent unfriendly countries from gaining access to the production. It may also be able to hold down prices to the home country, prevent local processing, and dictate its own operating terms. Observers have pointed out, for example, that Great Britain, France, Italy, and Japan established national oil companies with governmental participation (B.P. C.F.P., E.N.I., and J.P.D.C., respectively) in order to lessen the reliance on U.S. multinational petroleum firms, which might give preference to the United States in the allocation of supplies.[29] In the process of gaining control of resources, much political control is transferred to the industrial nations.

Governmental encouragement of MNE expansion to other developed countries may be aimed toward gaining greater control over vital resources. Japan, for example, is highly dependent on foreign sources for certain foodstuffs, lumber, and raw materials. For example, Japanese governmental agencies have assisted national companies to undertake foreign investments in these sectors in order to protect supplies in Japan.[30]

The control of resources is not necessarily the political aim for encouraging direct investors. During the early 1980s, for example, the U.S. government instituted various incentives designed to increase the profitability of U.S. investment in Caribbean countries unfriendly to Cuba's Castro regime. The reasoning was that the incentives would lure more investment to the area, causing the economies of the friendly nations to strengthen. This would in turn make it difficult for unfriendly leftist governments to gain control. (This situation is treated in the case at the end of Chapter 12.)

Where there is governmental ownership and control of companies, not all of these governmental enterprises have become multinational. There are simply too many objectives for government ownership other than control over foreign economies. Even if the government enterprise has foreign facilities, it does not necessarily mean that political motives just described prompted the investment.[31] For example, the firm may be acting in terms of any of the economic motives discussed earlier in the chapter.

MULTIPLE MOTIVES

A combination of factors, rather than one, usually explain a direct investment.

Although previous discussions within this chapter have categorized investments by separate motives, in reality most decisions to invest abroad, such as the Bridgestone Case at the beginning of the chapter, are based on multiple motives. Another such combination of influences may be illustrated by Brazilian automobile investments.

As the automobile became a mature product, there were considerable opportunities for saving labor costs by moving operations to a country having cheap labor, such as Brazil. One problem, however, is that economies of large-scale operations are needed to reduce the total cost of the vehicles. As long as car imports were permitted by Brazil, the U.S. and European producers could serve the Brazilian market more cheaply by exporting than by manufacturing a low volume in Brazil for that market. To move *all* operations to Brazil would be too costly and would so disrupt domestic operations that some type of home government sanctions would be inevitable. However, in the next stage, Brazil required local production as a requisite for serving the Brazilian consumer. Consequently, Ford, General Motors, Chrysler, Volkswagen, Daimler Benz, Saab-Scandia, Alfa Romeo, and Fiat established facilities, and production began in 1957. The car companies built plants because the Brazilian market was deemed too important to lose and too important for competitors to have to themselves. Now output is high, and Brazil is a major exporter, even sending components back to home countries.[32]

Political motives for investment are seldom isolated from economic motives. To encourage companies to invest abroad, governments must consider the objectives of the potential investors. U.S. policymakers, for example, reasoned that many U.S. firms might find it advantageous to tap cheap labor sources in the Caribbean. Consequently, legislation was enacted to allow certain Caribbean output to enter the United States virtually free of restrictions. Investors, acting purely on economic motives, helped to achieve governmental objectives.

ADVANTAGES OF DIRECT INVESTORS

Most successful domestic firms, especially ones with unique advantages, invest abroad.

Direct investment makes firms more successful domestically.

Are companies big because they are multinational or are they multinational because they are big? Such a "chicken-and-egg" type question has hounded direct investment theorists: On one hand, there is evidence that the very successful domestic firms are most likely to commit resources to direct investments; on the other hand, ownership of foreign direct investment appears to make firms more successful domestically.

Monopoly Advantages Prior to Direct Investment

One explanation for direct investment is that investors perceive a monopoly advantage over similar companies in the countries to which they go. The advantage is due to the ownership of some resource that is unavailable at the same price or terms to the local firm. The resource may be in the form of access to markets, patents, product differentiation, management skills, or the like. Because of the greater cost usually incurred by transferring resources abroad and the perceived greater risk of operating in a different environment, the firm will not move unless it expects a higher return than at home and a higher return than the local firm abroad.[33]

Certain monopoly advantages may accrue to large groups of firms and explain their relative ability and willingness to move abroad. One such observation has been made in reference to the cost and access to capital.

When the capital component is an integral part of a new investment, the company that can borrow in a country with a low interest rate has an advantage over the company that cannot. Prior to World War I, Great Britain was the largest source for direct investment because of the strength of sterling and the resulting lower interest rates on borrowing sterling funds. From World War II until the mid-1980s the strength of the U.S. dollar gave an advantage to U.S. firms. More recently this advantage has shifted to Japanese firms.[34]

Related to this is the relative power of different currencies in terms of the plant and equipment they will purchase. During the two and half decades immediately following World War II, the U.S. dollar was very strong, and it was perhaps overvalued in later years. As a result, by converting dollars to other currencies, U.S. firms could purchase a greater output capacity in foreign countries than they could after the dollar began to slide downward in 1971. The reverse was true for firms from such countries as West Germany and Japan, which invested more heavily in the United States during the late 1970s and mid-1980s when the yen and mark increased their purchasing power.[35]

Currency values do not, however, provide a strong explanation of direct investment patterns. There was a two-way investment flow between the United States and West Germany and the United States and Japan when the dollar was weak as well as when the dollar was strong. Then in the first half of the 1980s, U.S. companies were not increasing investment abroad significantly, whereas foreign companies were investing heavily in the United States in spite of the strong dollar. The major reasons were high real interest rates in the United States and a relatively strong U.S. economy. In the late 1980s, when the dollar was weak again, there were record flows of direct investment both to and from the United States.[36] The currency strength situation therefore only partially explains direct investment flows and must be viewed along with other multiple motives for direct investment.

Advantages after Direct Investment

Firms with foreign investments
- Tend to be more profitable
- Tend to have more stable sales and earnings.

In order to support large-scale expenditures (such as expenditures for R&D) that are necessary to maintain a domestic competitive viability, companies frequently must sell on a global basis.[37] To do this, they often must establish direct investments abroad. The advantage accruing to MNEs rather than to purely domestic firms by spreading out some of the costs of product differentiation, R&D, and advertising is apparent in a comparison of the domestic profitability of the two types of firms. Among groups of similar size that spent comparable amounts on advertising and employed comparable numbers of scientists and engineers, the MNEs in every case earned more on their domestic investments than did the purely domestic firms.[38]

Economies in different countries are in different stages of the business cycle at different times. Companies that operate in these different economies are known to be able to reduce fluctuations in year-to-year sales and earnings more than firms operating only in a domestic environment,[39] thereby effectively reducing their operating risks.

SUMMARY

- Direct investment is the control of a company in one country by an organization from another country. Because control is difficult to define, arbitrary minimum ownership of the voting stock is used to explain direct investment.
- Governments have concern about who controls enterprises within their confines for fear that decisions will be made contrary to the national interest.
- Firms often prefer to control foreign production facilities because (1) the transfer of certain assets to a noncontrolled entity might otherwise undermine the competitive position and (2) there are economies of buying and selling with a controlled entity.
- Although a direct investment usually is acquired by transferring capital from one country to another, capital is not usually the only contribution made by the investor or the only means of gaining equity. The investing firm may supply technology, personnel, and markets in exchange for an interest in a foreign country.
- The factors of production and finished goods are only partially mobile internationally. Moving either is one means of compensating for differences in factor endowments among countries. The cost and feasibility of transferring international production factors versus finished goods will determine which alternative results in cheaper costs.
- Although a direct investment may be a substitute for trade, it also may stimulate trade through sales of components, equipment, and complementary products. Foreign direct investment may be undertaken to expand foreign markets or to gain access to supplies of resources or finished products. In addition, governments may encourage direct investments for political purposes.
- The price of some products increases too substantially if they are transported internationally; therefore foreign production is necessary to tap foreign markets.
- Companies usually try to hold out on establishing foreign production as long as they have excess domestic capacity.
- The degree to which scale economies lower production costs influences whether production is centralized in one or a few countries or dispersed among many countries.

- Since most direct investments are intended for selling the output in the country where the investments are located, governmental restrictions that prevent the effective importation of goods are probably a most compelling force causing firms to establish their direct investments.
- Consumers may feel compelled to buy domestically made products even though these products are more expensive. They also may demand that products be altered to fit their needs. Both of these consumer demands may dictate the need to establish foreign operations to serve foreign markets.
- Direct investment sometimes has chain effects: When one company makes an investment, some of its suppliers follow with investments of their own, followed by investments by their suppliers, and so on.
- In oligopoly industries, companies from the same industry often invest at about the same time in a foreign country. This occurs sometimes because they are responding to similar market conditions and sometimes because they wish to negate competitor's advantages in the markets.
- Vertical integration is needed to control the flow of goods across borders from basic production to final consumption in an increasingly interdependent and complex world distribution system. It may result in lower operating costs and enable firms to transfer funds among countries.
- Rationalized production involves the production of different components or different products in different countries to take advantage of different factor costs.
- The least-cost location of production may change over time, especially in relation to stages of the life cycle of a product. In general, advanced countries have a cost advantage in the production of new products, and LDCs have an advantage in mature products. The least-cost production location may change because of governmental incentives that effectively subsidize production.
- Governments may encourage their firms to invest abroad in order to gain advantages over other countries.
- Most investments are made because of interrelated multiple motives.
- Monopolistic advantages help to explain why firms are willing to take what they perceive to be higher risks of operating abroad. Certain countries and currencies have had these advantages; thus this helps to explain the dominance of firms from certain countries at a given time.
- Foreign investment may enable firms to spread certain fixed costs vis-à-vis domestic firms. It also may enable firms to gain access to needed resources, to prevent competitors from gaining control of needed resources, and to smooth sales and earnings on a year-to-year basis.

CASE: ELECTROLUX ACQUISITIONS[40]

Electrolux, the world's largest manufacturer of electrical household appliances, once pioneered the marketing of vacuum cleaners. However, not all products bearing the Electrolux name have always been controlled by the Swedish firm. For example, Electrolux vacuum cleaners were sold and manufactured independently in the United States from the 1960s until 1987. The Swedish firm also manufactures Eureka vacuum cleaners.

Electrolux pursued its early international expansion largely to gain economies of scale through additional sales. The Swedish market was too small to absorb fixed costs as much as the home markets for competitive firms from larger countries. When additional sales were not possible by exporting, Electrolux still was able to gain certain scale economies through the establishment of foreign production. Research and development expenditures and certain administrative costs thus could be spread out over the additional sales made possible by foreign operations. Additionally, Electrolux concentrated on standardized production to achieve further scale economies and rationalization of parts.

Until the late 1960s, Electrolux concentrated primarily on vacuum cleaners and the building of its own facilities in order to effect expansion. Throughout the 1970s, though, the firm expanded largely by acquiring existing firms whose product lines differed from those of Electrolux. The compelling force was to add appliance lines to complement those developed internally. Its profits have enabled Electrolux to go on an acquisitions binge. Electrolux acquired two Swedish firms that made home appliances and washing machines. Electrolux management felt that it could use its existing foreign sales networks to increase the sales of those firms. In 1973, Electrolux acquired another Swedish firm, Facit, which already had extensive foreign sales and facilities. Electrolux acquired vacuum cleaner producers in the United States and in France; to gain captive sales for vacuum cleaners, the company bought commercial cleaning service firms in Sweden and in the United States. Also Electrolux bought a French kitchen equipment producer, Arthur Martin, along with a Swiss home appliance firm, Therma, and a U.S. cooking equipment manufacturer, Tappan.

Except for the Facit purchase, these acquisitions all involved firms with complementary lines that would enable the new parent to gain certain scale economies. However, not all of the acquired firms' products were related, and Electrolux sought to sell off unrelated businesses. In 1978, for example, Electrolux bought a diverse Swedish firm, Husqvarna, because of its kitchen equipment lines. Electrolux was able to sell Husqvarna's motorcycle line but could not get a good price for the chain saw facility. Reconciled to being in the chain saw business, Electrolux then acquired chain saw manufacturers in Canada and Norway, thus becoming one of the world's largest chain saw producers. The firm made approximately fifty acquisitions in the 1970s.

In 1980, Electrolux announced a takeover distinguished from those of the 1970s. It offered $175 million, the biggest Electrolux acquisition to date, for Granges, Sweden's leading metal producer and fabricator. Granges was itself a multinational firm (1979 sales of $1.2 billion) with about 50 percent of its sales outside of Sweden. The managing directors of the two firms indicated that the major advantage of the takeover would be the integration of Granges' aluminum, copper, plastics, and other materials into Electrolux's appliance production. Many analysts felt that the timing of Electrolux's bid was based on indications that Beijerinvest, a large Swedish conglomerate, wished to acquire a nonferrous metals mining company.

After the Granges takeover, Electrolux resumed its acquisition of appliance firms. It bought Italy's Zanussi to become Europe's top appliance maker with 23 percent of that market. In 1986 it acquired White Consolidated Industries, the U.S. manufacturer of such appliance brands as Frigidaire, White-Westinghouse, Kelvinator, and Gibson.

Electrolux was becoming a global appliance producer even though this traditionally has been an industry in which companies have sold little outside their home countries. Varying sizes of kitchens from one country to another complicated international standardization of models. But Electrolux was betting that life-styles in the industrialized nations would be increasingly similar; thus the company could take advantage of economies of scale in technical breakthroughs and designs.

Meanwhile, other producers were growing through consolidation as well. For instance, Maytag acquired such brands as Magic Chef, Admiral, and Norge. Table 6.1 shows the major global competitors in appliances.

TABLE 6.1

ESTIMATED WORLDWIDE APPLIANCE SALES BY MAJOR FIRMS (1987)

Firm	Headquarters Country	Millions of U.S. Dollars
Electrolux	Sweden	$5,100
General Electric	United States	4,350
Matsushita Electric	Japan	4,180
Whirlpool	United States	3,959
Bosch-Siemens	West Germany	2,200
Philips	Netherlands	2,000
Maytag	United States	1,580

Source: Sales figures are taken from data from Goldman Sachs as quoted in *Business Week*, November 2, 1987, p. 94

In 1988 Anders Scharp, president of Electrolux, said that industry consolidation would not allow for much more growth through acquisition of household appliance firms. Further Electrolux acquisitions would concentrate on outdoor products and commercial appliances.

QUESTIONS

1. How do Electrolux's reasons for direct investment differ from those of Bridgestone at the beginning of the chapter?
2. How has Electrolux's strategy changed over time? How have these changes affected its direct investment activities?
3. What are the main advantages and possible problems of expanding internationally primarily through acquisitions as opposed to a company's building its own facilities?
4. Should Electrolux have taken over Granges?
5. What will be the future global competitive situation in household appliances and how does that fit with the Electrolux strategy?

NOTES

1. Data for the case were taken from Urban C. Lehner, "Bridgestone Looks Overseas for Growth," *Wall Street Journal,* June 17, 1981, p. 1; Edward Noga, "Bridgestone," *Automotive News,* April 20, 1981, p. E10; Edward Noga, "Bridgestone Tries U.S. Market," *Advertising Age,* April 6, 1981, p. 85; David Pauly, "Bridgestone Tire: Made in Japan," *Newsweek,* August 11, 1980, pp. 62–64; Mike Tharp, "Bridgestone, Japan's Tire Giant, Now Seeking International Role," *New York Times,* November 21, 1980, p. D4; "Japan: Why a Tiremaker Wants a U.S. Base," *Business Week,* January 14, 1980, p. 40; Bernard Krisher, "A Different Kind of Tiremaker Rolls into Nashville," *Fortune,* Vol. 105, No. 6, March 22, 1982, pp. 136–145; Zachary Schiller and James B. Treece, "Bridgestone May Try an End Run around the Yen," *Business Week,* No. 2983, February 2, 1987, p. 31; Roger Schreffler, "Bridgestone's New Rolling Thunderbolt, *Automotive Industries,* Vol. 165, No. 12, December 1985, p. 55; Gregory Stricharchuk, "Foreign Tire Firms Want More of the Robust U.S. Market," *Wall Street Journal,* November 11, 1987, p. 26; Jonathan P. Hicks, "A Global Fight in the Tire Industry," *New York Times,* March 10, 1988, p. 29; Gregory Stricharchuk, "Japanese Firm Defends Price for Firestone," *Wall Street Journal,* March 21, 1988, p. 2.

2. Some recent surveys of the considerable number of explanations may be found in Jean J. Boddewyn, "Foreign and Domestic Divestment and Investment Decisions," *Journal of International Business Studies,* Vol. XIV, No. 3, Winter 1983, pp. 23–35; A. L. Calvet, "A Synthesis of Foreign Direct Investment Theories and Theories of the Multinational Firm," *Journal of International Business Studies,* Spring–Summer 1981, pp. 43–60; John H. Dunning, "Toward an Eclectic Theory of International Production," *Journal of International Business Studies,* Spring–Summer 1980, pp. 9–31; Robert Grosse, "The Theory of Foreign Direct Investment," *Essays in Interna-*

tional Business, No. 3, December 1981, pp. 1–51; M. Z. Rahman, "Maximisation of Global Interests: Ultimate Motivation for Foreign Investments by Transnational Corporations," *Management International Review,* Vol. 23, No. 4, 1983, pp. 4–13; and Alan M. Rugman, "New Theories of the Multinational Enterprise: An Assessment of Internalization Theory," *Bulletin of Economic Research,* Vol. 38, No. 2, 1986, pp. 101–118.

3. Krisher, *op. cit.,* p. 141. Schreffler, *loc. cit.*

4. This desire to hold a monopoly control over certain information or other proprietary assets has been noted by such writers as M. Casson, "The Theory of Foreign Direct Investment," Discussion Paper Number 50, (Reading, Engl.: University of Reading International Investment and Business Studies, November 1980); Stephen Magee, "Information and the MNC: An Appropriability Theory of Direct Foreign Investment," in *The New International Economic Order,* Jagdish N. Bhagwati, ed. (Cambridge, Mass.: The MIT Press, 1977), pp. 317–340; Alan M. Rugman, *Inside the Multinationals: The Economics of Internal Markets* (New York: Columbia University Press, 1981).

5. David J. Teece, "Transactions Cost Economics and the Multinational Enterprise," *Berkeley Business School International Business Working Paper Series,* No. IB–3, 1985.

6. "Plessey Co. Acquires Airborne Accessories for $8.9 Million Notes," *Wall Street Journal,* February 21, 1968, p. 6.

7. Yves Doz, "Managing Manufacturing Rationalization within Multinational Companies," *Columbia Journal of World Business,* Fall 1978.

8. Clyde Haberman, "Made in Japan: U.S. Cookie," *New York Times,* February 17, 1984, p. B6.

9. Lawrence Rout, "Mexico Limits U.S. Makers of Computers," *Wall Street Journal,* February 1, 1982, p. 31.

10. Studies that found import barriers to be an important enticement include Sanjaya Lall and N. S. Siddharthan, "The Monoplistic Advantages of Multinationals: Lessons from Foreign Investment in the U.S." *The Economic Journal,* Vol. 92, No. 367, September 1982, pp. 668–683; T. Horst, "Firm and Industry Determinants of the Decision to Invest Abroad," *Review of Economics and Statistics,* August 1972, pp. 256–266; John H. Dunning, *American Investment in British Manufacturing Industry* (London: Allen and Unwin, 1958); and D. Orr, "The Determinants of Entry: A Study of the Canadian Manufacturing Industries," *Review of Economics and Statistics,* Vol. 57, 1975, pp. 58–66. Those not finding import barriers to be important include R. E. Caves, M. E. Porter, A. M. Spence, and J. T. Scott, *Competition in the Open Economy: A Model Applied to Canada* (Cambridge, Mass.: Harvard University Press, 1980); and B. Balassa, "Effects of Commercial Policy on International Trade, the Location of Production and Factor Movements," in *The International Allocation of Economic Activity,* Bertil Ohlin, ed. (New York: Holmes & Meier, 1977).

11. Kenneth Dreyfack, "Draping Old Glory around Just about Everything," *Business Week,* No. 2970, October 27, 1986, pp. 66–67.

12. "Toshiba Plans to Build Color-TV Plant in U.S.," *Wall Street Journal,* April 5, 1977, p. 43, and "Mitsubishi U.S. Unit to Assemble TV Sets in Irvine, California, Plant," *Wall Street Journal,* April 14, 1977, p. 7, shows two examples of responses to nationalistic advertisements by Zenith.

13. Philippe Cattin, Alain Jolibert, and Coleen Lohnes, "A Cross-Cultural Study of 'Made in' Concepts," *Journal of International Business Studies,* Vol. XIII, No. 3, Winter 1982, pp. 131–141; Robert D. Schooler, "Bias Phenomena Attendant to the Marketing of Foreign Goods in the U.S.," *Journal of International Business Studies,* Spring 1971, pp. 71–80; A. Nagashima, "A Comparison of Japanese and U.S. Attitudes toward Foreign Products," *Journal of Marketing,* January 1970, pp. 68–74.

14. John D. Daniels, "Recent Foreign Direct Manufacturing Investment in the United States," *Journal of International Business Studies,* Summer 1970, p. 128.

15. "Why VW Must Build Autos in the U.S.," *Business Week,* February 16, 1976, p. 46; and John Templeman, "What Ended VW's American Dream," *Business Week,* October 7, 1987, p. 63.

16. Steven P. Galante, "Japanese Have Another Trade Barrier: Limiting Business to Compatriot Firms," *Wall Street Journal,* April 12, 1984, p. 36.

17. Edward B. Flowers, "Oligopolistic Reactions in European and Canadian Direct Investment in the United States," *Journal of International Business Studies,* Fall–Winter 1976, pp. 43–55; Frederick Knickerbocker, *Oligopolistic Reaction and Multinational Enterprise* (Cambridge, Mass.: Harvard University, Graduate School of Business, Division of Research, 1973). For opposing findings, see Lall and Siddharthan, *loc. cit.*

18. "Why VW Must Build Autos in the U.S." *op. cit.,* p. 48; and John Holuska, "Volkswagen Will Shut U.S. Plant; Competition and Slow Sales Cited," *New York Times,* November 21, 1987, p. 1.

19. "Salt and Pepper," *Wall Street Journal,* December 15, 1983, p. 31.

20. K. Kojima, *Direct Foreign Investment: A Japanese Model of Multinational Business Operations* (London: Croom Helm, 1978).

21. Brian O'Reilly, "Business Makes a Run for the Border," *Fortune,* Vol. 114, No. 4, August 18, 1986, pp. 70–76; and Dudley Althaus, "Manufacturing in Mexico," *Dallas Times Herald,* September 21–27, 1987, p. 1+.

22. Doz, *loc. cit.*

23. "Global Report," *Wall Street Journal,* January 16, 1978, p. 6.

24. Riad A. Ajami and David A. Ricks, *Motives of Non-American Firms Investing in the United States,* College of Administrative Science, Working Paper Series (Columbus: Ohio State University, 1980).

25. Raymond Vernon, "International Investment and International Trade in the Product Cycle," *Quarterly Journal of Economics,* May 1966, pp. 191–207.

26. "National Policies toward Foreign Direct Investors," *FRBNY Quarterly Review,* Winter 1979–1980, p. 28.

27. Robert Weigand, "International Investments: Weighing the Incentives," *Harvard Business Review,* Vol. 61, No. 4, July–August 1983, pp. 146–152.

28. Among the many treatises on this subject is Carlos F. Diaz Alejandro, "International Markets for Exhaustible Resources, Less Developed Countries and Transnational Corporations," in *Economic Issues of Multinational Firms,* Robert G. Hawkins, ed. (New York: JAI Press, 1977).

29. M. Y. Yoshino, *Japan's Multinational Enterprises* (Cambridge, Mass.: Harvard University Press, 1976), pp. 53–57.

30. Terutomio Ozawa, "Japan's Resource Dependency and Overseas Investment," *Journal of World Trade Law,* January–February 1977, pp. 52–73.

31. For a good discussion of differences in European government-owned enterprises, see Renato Mazzolini, *Government Controlled Enterprises* (New York: John Wiley & Sons, 1979).

32. Lewis H. Diugid, "Brazil to Supply Pinto Power," *Washington Post,* October 1, 1972, p. H7; "The Brazilian Motor Vehicle Industry," *Notes on International Business Research,* No. 10 (Cambridge, Mass.: M.I.T. Press, August 1975).

33. Stephen H. Hymer, *A Study of Direct Foreign Investment* (Cambridge, Mass.: M.I.T. Press, 1976); and Alan M. Rugman, "Internationalization as a General Theory of Foreign Direct Investment: A Re-Appraisal of the Literature," *Weltwirtschaftliches Archiv,* Band 116, Heft 2, 1980, pp. 365–379.

34. Robert Z. Aliber, "A Theory of Direct Foreign Investment," in *The International Corporation,* Charles P. Kindleberger, ed. (Cambridge, Mass.: M.I.T. Press, 1970), pp. 28–33; Robert Johnson, "Distant Deals," *Wall Street Journal,* February 24, 1988, p. 1.

35. William Glasgall, "Foreign Investors Are Keeping the Pot Boiling," *Business Week,* No. 2974, November 24, 1986, p. 84.

36. Louis Uchitelle, "Overseas Spending by U.S. Companies Sets Record Pace," *New York Times,* May 20, 1988, p. 1+.

37. N. H. Prater, "Foreign Participation in the U.S. Market," *Industrial Development,* Vol. 152, No. 3, May/June 1983, pp. 20–22.

38. Thomas Horst, "American Multinationals and the U.S. Economy," *American Economic Review,* May 1976, p. 153.

39. Joseph C. Miller and Bernard Pras, "The Effects of Multinational and Export Diversification on the Profit Stability of U.S. Corporations," *Southern Economic Journal,* Vol. 46, No. 3, 1980, pp. 792–802; Alan M. Rugman, "Foreign Operations and the Stability of U.S. Corporate Earnings: Risk Reduction by International Diversification" (Vancouver, Simon Fraser University, 1974); A. Servern, "Investor Evaluation of Foreign and Domestic Risk," *Journal of Finance,* May 1974, pp. 545–550.

40. Background data on Electrolux may be found in "Why Electrolux Wants a Materials Supplier," *Business Week,* February 18, 1980, pp. 78–79; "Company Briefs," *Wall Street Journal,* October 19, 1979, p. 5; Alan L. Otten, "Electrolux, a Big Success in Appliances, Is Helped by Decentralized Operations," *Wall Street Journal,* June 4, 1980, p. 16; "Electrolux to Proceed with Granges Offer, Providing Sweden Acts," *Wall Street Journal,* June 18, 1980, p. 29; "Electrolux Suspends Its Purchases of Stock in TI Group of Britain," *Wall Street Journal,* February 21, 1984, p. 38; Sharon Tully, "Electrolux Wants a Clean Sweep," *Fortune,* Vol. 114, No. 4, August 18, 1986, pp. 60–62; "On a Verge of a World War in White Goods," *Business Week,* November 2, 1987, pp. 91–94; "Electrolux Shifts the Focus of Its Acquisition Program," *Wall Street Journal,* March 22, 1988, p. 27.

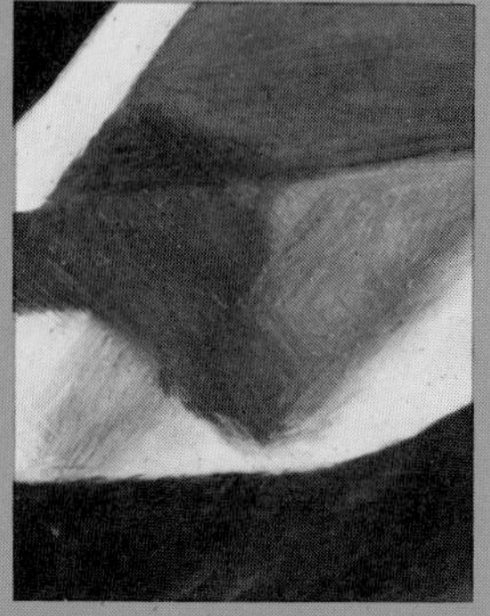

CHAPTER 7

CROSS-NATIONAL COOPERATION AND AGREEMENTS

Marrying is easy, but housekeeping is hard.
—German proverb

- To define different forms of regional economic integration.
- To describe the static and dynamic benefits of regional economic integration.
- To trace the development of the European Community (EC) as an illustration of regional economic integration.
- To describe the rationale for, and current trends in, commodity agreements.
- To discuss other bilateral and multilateral treaties affecting international business.

CASE:

INCIDENT: FORD IN EUROPE—THE EARLY YEARS[1]

When the European Economic Community (EEC) was first organized in 1957, U.S. multinational enterprises (MNEs) had to change their method of servicing European markets. The large size of the U.S. market allowed these firms to achieve economies of scale so that they could export to the EEC. After the EEC was established and tariff barriers were erected to protect domestic industries, foreign firms were forced to invest in EEC countries or lose their markets. They were accustomed to large-scale organizations and had the financial and managerial resources to handle the expansion.

One such example is the Ford Motor Company. Ford first began operating in Europe through its British subsidiary in 1913 and its German subsidiary in 1926. During the next several decades, however, Ford's European operations were separate operating subsidiaries reporting to Ford but not coordinating their policies in any meaningful way. This occurred for two reasons: Individual countries had: (1) different preferences and (2) unique tariff and nontariff barriers to trade. In its 1960 *Annual Report,* Ford management noted that:

> *The historical patterns of trade and commerce among nations are undergoing significant changes. Trade groupings, such as the European Economic Community and the European Free Trade Association, are being established. Similar groupings are being considered in Latin America and by some of the African countries. Further changes in trade patterns have been brought about in a number of countries by government regulations that make it advantageous to manufacture locally.*
>
> *The Company and its subsidiaries are responding to these trends, which bear promise of increasing competition for world automobile markets, by exploring opportunities to strengthen and to expand their international operations.*

As a result of the changing environment, Ford executives realized that they could begin considering Europe as one common market rather than a collection of individual markets. Shortly after the establishment of the EEC, Ford changed its management structure to include the European operations under one umbrella organization in order to exploit the economies of scale that were beginning to develop in the EEC. The two large manufacturing centers in Great Britain and West Germany were to remain central to the new strategy, but they were no longer considered separate, independent operating companies. Ford decided it was best to obliterate national boundaries, which was challenging because of nationalistic tendencies on the part of country management. As was noted by the West German managing director,

> *The pooling of the two companies cut the engineering bill in half for each company, provided economies of scale, with double the volume in terms of*

purchase—commonization of purchase, common components—and provided the financial resources for a good product program at a really good price that we could still make money on.

Ford initially began developing and selling European cars rather than engineering separate cars in each market, a strategy that resulted in the Escort, Capri, and Fiesta models among others. Not only did Ford design and assemble similar automobiles throughout Europe, but it also designed common components to be used in Ford cars. To show the importance of market size in developing this plan, one Ford executive commented: "Neither the British nor German company could have come up with the Capri separately, tooled it separately. Only with the whole volume of Europe in prospect did the Capri become a viable product development program."

As Ford continued its European expansion, it explored the possibility of having its European unit merge with Fiat in order to allow Ford's strength in Northern Europe to combine with Fiat's strength in Southern Europe. However, both sides were so strong and so convinced of the need for control that the proposed merger never occurred. Ford needed control to guarantee that the timing of its global strategy, which was developed in the United States, could be maintained. Fiat, on the other hand, was controlled by the Agnelli family in Italy, and loss of control to a foreign company, especially one from a country not a member of the EEC, would have been explosive politically. In addition, Fiat's management could not accept a subordinate role to Ford's management. Clearly, mergers are never easy, but cross-border mergers can often introduce unique problems.

In the late 1980s, a relatively cohesive Europe continued to be an important force in Ford's strategy. Donald E. Petersen, Chairman of Ford, was determined to globalize the company. Part of his strategy involved centralizing the development of a specific car or component wherever in the world Ford has the greatest expertise. Ford of Europe's comparative advantage with respect to the rest of the company is in the small car market. The European company is responsible for developing a common suspension and undercarriage for compact cars that will be built and sold in the United States as well as in Europe. The growing sophistication of Ford in Europe has resulted largely from the harmonization and growth of the European Community.

INTRODUCTION

During the Depression of the 1930s, the world plunged into a period of isolation, trade protection, and economic chaos. Then in the mid- to late-1940s, a spirit of intergovernmental cooperation emerged from the wreckage of World War II. The spirit of cooperation was designed to promote economic growth and stability. This chapter discusses some of the important forms of such cooperation, such as regional economic integration and commodity agreements. The establishment of these agreements is an important source of influence on MNEs, as Ford learned in the opening case. The agreements define the size of the market and the rules under which the firm must operate. Firms in the initial stage of expansion abroad need to be aware of the regional groups that encompass target countries. As firms proceed along the scale of multinationalism, they find that their organizational structure and operating strategies must conform to and take advantage of regional integration. As noted in the opening case, Ford altered its European organization soon after the formation of the EEC. This chapter explains how these regional groups impact structure and strategy.

European Evolution to Integration

The OEEC (forerunner of the OECD) is the organization of European countries assisted by the Marshall Plan.

World War II left a wake of economic as well as human destruction throughout Europe. To facilitate utilization of aid from the Marshall Plan, a U.S. plan to provide aid to Europe after World War II, the sixteen-nation **Organization for European Economic Cooperation (OEEC)** was established in 1948 with the encouragement of the United States. Its purposes were to improve currency stability, combine economic strength, and improve trade relations. However, the OEEC did not appear strong enough to provide the necessary economic growth, so further efforts at cooperation were initiated.

The EC or EEC allows the economic integration of European countries leading to a free flow of resources, a harmonization of policies, and a common external tariff.

One major school of thought adhered to the idea that a common market should be developed, which would: (1) result in the elimination of all restrictions to the free flow of goods, capital, and persons; (2) allow for the harmonization of economic policies; and (3) create a common external tariff. The result was the creation of the **European Economic Community (EEC)** through the Treaty of Rome in March 1957. It involved West Germany, Belgium, the Netherlands, Luxembourg, France, and Italy. As noted in Fig. 7.1, the membership of the EEC has since been broadened to include the United Kingdom, Ireland, Denmark, Greece, Spain, and Portugal. It now embraces the title **European Community (EC),** which implies a broader form of cooperation.

European Free Trade Association

EFTA is an example of a free trade area.

The second major school of thought rejected the notion of total integration and favored instead a free trade area, which would allow for the elimination of all restrictions on the free flow of industrial goods among member nations and would permit each country to retain its own external tariff structure. This approach would provide the benefits of free trade among members but would allow each country to pursue its own economic objectives with outside countries. This was especially true for Great Britain, which had developed favorable trade relationships with Commonwealth countries. From the British point of view, a common external tariff would result in too much cooperation and restriction of individual sovereignty.

Figure 7.1
Europe: the EEC and EFTA

Commonwealth countries is a voluntary association of forty-eight independent nations, including the United Kingdom and most of its former colonies.

Following the second line of thought, the Stockholm Convention of May 1960 resulted in the creation of the **European Free Trade Association (EFTA)** which involved seven of the OEEC countries that were not partners in the EEC: Austria, Denmark, Norway, Portugal, Sweden, Switzerland, and the United Kingdom. The composition of the EFTA has changed since to include Austria, Finland, Iceland, Norway, Sweden, and Switzerland, as illustrated in Fig. 7.1. These countries were concerned about a unified European effort in economic integration and reaffirmed their interest in working toward a broader solution. However, there were still many problems that led to their creating the EFTA:

1. the lack of desire to harmonize social and economic policies, as would be required by the EEC;

2. the special arrangements between the United Kingdom and the Commonwealth nations;
3. the political neutrality of Austria, Sweden, and Switzerland.

REGIONAL ECONOMIC INTEGRATION

Economic integration abolishes economic discrimination between national economies.

During the 1950s and 1960s regional economic integration gained significant momentum. **Economic integration** can be defined

> *as a process and as a state of affairs. Regarded as a process, it encompasses measures designed to abolish discrimination between economic units belonging to different national states; viewed as a state of affairs, it can be represented by the absence of various forms of discrimination between national economies.*[2]

If we assume that discrimination actually affects economic activity between the countries in question, integration can be seen as valuable.

Major efforts of economic integration include: EC, EFTA, LAIA, and COMECON.

Geographic proximity is an important reason for economic integration.

When we consider some of the major efforts of economic integration, such as the European Community (EC), the European Free Trade Association (EFTA), the **Latin American Integration Association (LAIA),** and the **Council for Mutual Economic Assistance (COMECON,** an association of communist countries), the concept of geographic proximity looms as important. The major reasons for this are:

> *(a) the distances to be traversed are shorter in the case of neighboring countries; (b) tastes are more likely to be similar, and distribution channels can be more easily established in adjacent economies; and (c) neighboring countries may have a common history, awareness of common interests, etc., and hence be more willing to coordinate policies.*[3]

Also important are the notions of ideological and historical proximity. For instance, Cuba and Mongolia are both members of COMECON because of their similar political philosophies.

There are five major forms of economic integration:

Major forms of economic integration include:
- Free trade area: no internal tariffs
- Customs unions: common external tariffs
- Common market: factor mobility
- Economic union: harmonization of economic policies
- Complete economic integration.

1. *Free trade area* (FTA). Tariffs are abolished among the members of the **free trade area (FTA),** but each member maintains its own external tariff against the non-FTA countries. Two examples of this form of economic integration are EFTA and the Latin American Free Trade Association (LAFTA), which was abolished in 1980 and replaced with the **Latin American Integration Association (LAIA),** a looser form of free trade association.
2. *Customs union.* In the case of a **customs union,** a common external tariff is combined with the abolishment of all internal tariffs. This was the first stage of the EC and is also descriptive of the Andean Group, the

Central American Common Market (CACM), and the **Caribbean Community and Common Market (CARICOM),** the other major groups in Latin America.

3. *Common market.* In a **common market**, all of the characteristics of a customs union are combined with the abolishment of restrictions on factor mobility. This is the state that the EC is currently enjoying.
4. *Economic union.* In an **economic union,** common market characteristics are combined with some degree of harmonization of national economic policies. This is the theoretical direction in which the EC is moving.
5. *Complete economic integration.* The **complete economic integration** stage of the economic union "presupposes the unification of monetary, fiscal, social, and counter-cyclical policies and requires the setting up of a supra-national authority whose decisions are binding for the member states."[4] Some would say that the institution of the European Parliament was a step in the direction of political unification of Europe, a condition nearly essential for economic integration. However, this process of unification is still in its infancy.

Economic Effects of Integration

Economic integration reduces discrimination among participating nations.

As noted in Chapter 5, the imposition of tariff and nontariff barriers disrupts the free flow of goods and therefore resource allocation. However, the institution of a customs union reduces discrimination among participating nations even though it often increases, or at least maintains, discrimination with nonparticipating nations. Thus the formation of the EC resulted in a reduction of tariffs and the increased mobility of goods among EC member nations, although outsiders, such as the United States, still had to leap a large tariff barrier to do business in the EC.

The impact of a customs union can be static or dynamic. When trade barriers are reduced, consumers tend to purchase goods with the best quality at the cheapest price. The static effect of economic integration implies that resources shift from the least efficient to the most efficient producers of goods that consumers demand. Companies that are protected in their domestic markets face real problems when the barriers are eliminated as they attempt to compete with more efficient producers.

Integration has dynamic effects: As markets grow, firms achieve economies of scale of production.

Dynamic effects account for changes in total consumption and for changes in internal and external efficiencies as a result of growth in market size. The reduction of barriers automatically increases total demand. As resources shift to the more efficient producers, firms are able to expand output to take advantage of the larger market. This dynamic change in market size allows firms to produce goods at a cheaper price, since the fixed costs of the business can be spread out over more and more units of production.

Efficiency increases due to competition.

An important dynamic effect is an increase in efficiency due to increased competition. The EC has encouraged the merger of smaller member firms into more efficient economic units that can compete with U.S. and Japanese multinationals. In addition, the EC is trying to get firms to cooperate more in a variety of ways, such as through joint research and development (R&D) and joint production efforts. Very few cross-border mergers and efforts actually have worked. A major drawback is the lack of a unified company law in Europe. Each country has a different approach to taxation and labor legislation, among other things, so it is often to a company's advantage to set up separate subsidiaries in each country where it does business. Airbus, a pan-European aircraft manufacturer, is competing successfully against the U.S. giants. Although it is a consortium of Aerospatiale of France, British Aerospace PLC, Messerschmitt-Boelkow-Blohm G.m.b.H. of West Germany, and Construcciones Aeronauticas S.A. of Spain, it is based in France under French law.[5]

In 1987–1988, a series of mergers took place in the software industry in Europe. Many of the initial mergers were national in scope, especially among French software developers, whereas much of the rest of Europe belonged to small entrepreneurial ventures. However, large and complex programs require large-scale development costs, so many cross-border mergers began. In 1988, CAP Group PLC of Britain and SemaMetra S.A. of France agreed to merge, resulting in a new firm called Semacap PLC, which would be the second largest computer software developer in Europe.[6]

Nationalism is a major barrier to integration.

However, nationalism has prevented many cross-border mergers. National pride precludes significant progress. As noted in the opening case, the Ford/Fiat venture fell apart largely due to nationalism, as well as different objectives. It will be interesting to track the success of cross-European mergers over the next decade.

Benefits from Reducing Barriers—Some Examples

Table 7.1 lists several of the more important groups involved in one form of economic integration or another. All of the groups have achieved at least free trade area status, and some (such as the EC) are dabbling in various forms of factor mobility and harmonization of economic policies.

The large, relatively homogeneous U.S. market is a strong rival to other forms of economic integration.

The sizes of the different groups are notable. Integration is aimed at providing a large market in which companies can grow and achieve economies of scale. The regional groups are struggling just to achieve the same market size that the United States has as a single country. In addition, the United States operates with a common language, common currency, and a generally common set of laws. Thus it is easier for the United States to achieve the economies of a large market than it is for a group like the LAIA, which contains eleven countries, or the EC, which has twelve countries.

The EC and COMECON have a high percentage of intrazonal trade. African and Latin American groups have a low percentage.

Trade liberalization. Although trade liberalization has been one of the major goals of any form of economic integration, it has met with varying success. The EC has been one of the most successful of all, with 57 percent of its exports going to its member countries. EFTA, on the other hand, exports 13.6 percent of its products to other member countries of the EFTA; interestingly, it exports 52.9 percent of its products to EC member countries. Intraregional exports as a percentage of total exports are less than 10 percent in Latin America, and most Latin American countries trade more with the United States than they do with each other. COMECON trade is approximately 60 percent.[7]

TABLE 7.1

COMPARATIVE DATA ON MAJOR TRADE GROUPS, THE UNITED STATES, AND JAPAN

	1985 Population[a] (in Millions)	1985 GNP[b] (in Billions of U.S. Dollars)	Per Capita GNP[b] (in U.S. Dollars)	Percent of World Exports (1985)[c]
COMECON (Council of Mutual Economic Assistance)	462.7	1,699.6	3,720.0	8.9
LAIA (Latin American Integration Association	343.8	600.2	1,745.6	5.3
EC (European Community)	322.0	2,561.5	7,955.9	30.7
ASEAN (Association of South East Asian Nations)	287.0	213.5	743.8	4.3
United States	239.3	3,993.9	16,690.0	13.4
ECOWAS (Economic Community of West African States)	173.3	98.2	600.6	1.1
Japan	120.8	1,365.0	11,300.0	11.1
Andean Pact	80.1	123.5	1,541.5	1.4
EFTA (European Free Trade Association	31.8	391.9	12,307.7	7.6

[a] Data for Ivory Coast Population is from *Europa Yearbook, 1987.*
[b] Data for Ivory Coast GNP is from *Europa Yearbook, 1987.* Data shown for COMECON is for 1984; data for 1985 is unavailable.
[c] Data shown for COMECON is for 1982; data for 1985 is unavailable. Data for Brunei, Cape Verde, Gambia, Guinea-Bissau, Ivory Coast for 1985 is unavailable and not included in export percentage.
The countries included in the above groups are as follows:
COMECON: Bulgaria, Czechoslovakia, Cuba, East Germany, Hungary, Mongolia, Poland, Romania, Vietnam, and Soviet Union.
LAIA: Argentina, Bolivia, Brazil, Chile, Colombia, Ecuador, Mexico, Paraguay, Peru, Uruguay, and Venezuela.
EC: Belgium, Denmark, France, Greece, Ireland, Italy, Luxembourg, Netherlands, Portugal, Spain, United Kingdom, and West Germany.
ASEAN: Indonesia, Malaysia, Philippines, Singapore, and Thailand.
ECOWAS: Benin, Burkina, Cape Verde, Gambia, Ghana, Guinea, Guinea-Bissau, Ivory Coast, Liberia, Mali, Mauritania, Niger, Nigeria, Senegal, Sierra Leone, and Togo.
Andean Pact: Bolivia, Colombia, Ecuador, Peru, and Venezuela.
EFTA: Austria, Finland, Iceland, Norway, Portugal, Sweden, and Switzerland.
SOURCE: *World Development Report, 1987* (Washington, D.C.: The World Bank, 1987).

The various African forms of regional integration provide for free trade status, but very little intrazonal trade goes on. Their experience is very similar to that of Latin America except that their primary markets lie in Europe rather than the United States. This is so because the EC has given preferential status to a number of developing countries in Africa, the Caribbean, and the Far East. They also have strong ties from former colonial status. Similar status has been accorded to EFTA and other non-EC countries in Europe. Another part of the explanation lies in the size of the market. As shown in Table 7.1, ECOWAS has a market size of 172.7 million people and an average per capita GNP of only $618.2 per year, whereas ECOWAS countries can export to the EC, with a population of 321.9 million people and a per capita GNP of $11,060 per year. Since most ECOWAS countries export raw materials rather than finished goods, their intrazonal capacity is quite small. In contrast, the EC countries need raw materials.

European Community. Complexity always breeds bureaucracy. The simpler forms of integration, such as a free trade area and customs union, usually can be managed by a coordinating committee larger than it needs to be but adequate for the job. However, the more complex forms of integration, such as in the EC, have developed a very extensive bureaucracy to protect the goals and rules of the group of countries.

Major institutions of the EC include: the Commission, the Council of Ministers, the Parliament, and the Court of Justice.

The key to the EC's success is the balance between common and national interests monitored and refereed through four major institutions: the Commission; the Council of Ministers; the Parliament; and the Court of Justice. The Commission, headquartered in Brussels, Belgium, comprises a President, six Vice-Presidents, and ten other members whose allegiance is to the EC rather than to an individual government, although the members are appointed by the various governments. The Commission is the EC watchdog: It is supposed to draw up policies, implement them when approved by the Council of Ministers, and ensure that treaties and laws are adhered to by member nations.

The Council of Ministers, also headquartered in Brussels, is composed of one representative from each of the member governments. It is entrusted with making the major policy decisions for the EC.

Headquartered in Luxembourg, the Parliament is basically an advisory body elected directly in each member country. Its representatives tend to adhere to particular political and economic views rather than the wishes of the individual governments. Representatives of different countries with similar political leanings can form coalitions to increase their power base. Figure 7.2 illustrates how the composition of the Parliament changed between the first group elected in 1979 and the new group comprised of those elected in 1984 and those added in 1986 with the admission of Spain and Portugal. In the first few years of operation, the Parliament exhibited little political power, although it must approve the budget of the EC. Individual EC member governments are reluctant to surrender too much national sovereignty to the

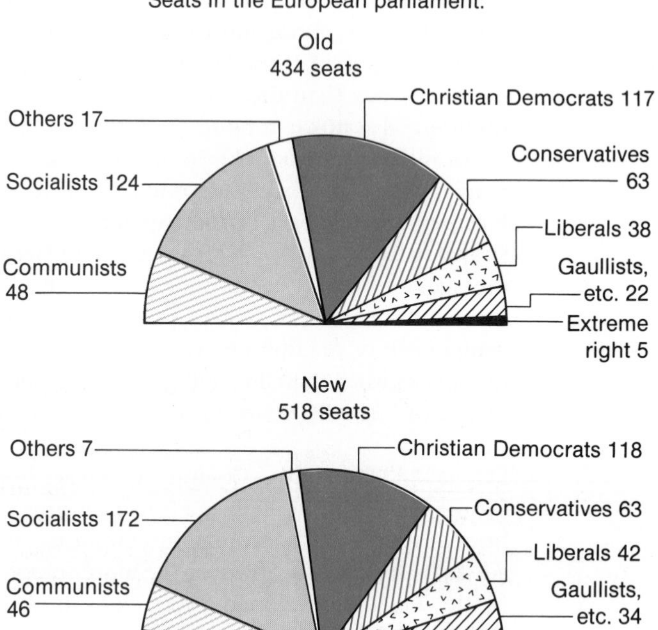

Figure 7.2
Europe from Left to Right: Composition of the European Parliament, 1979 and 1987.
Source: The Economist, June 23, 1984, p. 32, and *Europa Yearbook, 1987,* p. 142.

Europarliament. The Parliament serves primarily to advise on legislative proposals made by the Commission to the Council. The advent of Spain and Portugal resulted in a slight loss of power by the conservative side of Parliament. However, that probably will not have a significant impact on Parliament's agenda. Despite the EC's desire to have the Parliament be a working group with committees, member governments have been reluctant to surrender much power. In some respects, Parliament's inability to function effectively is a good example of the difficulty that the EC has had in completely unifying.[8]

The Court of Justice, also headquartered in Luxembourg, is composed of one member from each country in the EC. It serves as a supreme appeals court for EC law. The Commission or member countries can bring other members to the Court for failing to meet treaty obligations. For example, the Commission brought suit against Spain in 1987 for failing to ease certification requirements on the import of computers, peripheral equipment, and other hi-tech products because it considered these nontariff barriers in violation of membership in the EC.[9] Likewise, member countries, firms, or institutions can bring the Commission or Council to the Court for failure to act properly under the treaty.

Obviously, not every regional economic group is so organized. In most cases there is a commission responsible for formulating and implementing policy and a series of committees responsible for making recommendations to the commission. But the EC is a more ambitious undertaking than most; and it is growing. Growth brings various problems, which tend to keep the bureaucracy increasing. The EC has grown from the original six countries to an enlarged group of nine (with the additions of Denmark, the United Kingdom, and the Republic of Ireland in 1973), to ten (with the addition of Greece in 1981), and most recently to twelve (Spain and Portugal in 1986).

Harmonization of Policies in Europe

The reduction of internal trade barriers by free trade areas and the adoption of a common external tariff by customs unions have been the major benefits of economic integration. After working for over thirty years to reduce trade barriers, the EC has finally decided to eliminate all barriers by 1992, thus totally integrating the European market for goods and services. This is expected to have an important impact on trade and investment in Europe for members of the EC as well as for outside trading partners.

In addition to trade-liberalization policies, there are other dimensions to economic integration in the EC. Some of the major policies are the common agricultural policy, the free flow of labor, and the free flow of capital.

Common agricultural policy. One of the most famous of the EC's common policies involves the **common agricultural policy (CAP).** The farm policy features four main points:

1. Free trade of agricultural products. This policy is still slightly hampered by nontariff barriers.
2. Price supports to guarantee high prices to farmers. This policy especially concerned the United Kingdom before its entry into the Common Market. There was fear that higher continental farm prices would have a damaging inflationary effect. The policy is also a major source of concern in relationships between the United States and the EC.
3. A series of variable levies or duties on farm imports. This would ensure that competitive foreign products would not be sold at less than prevailing continental prices.
4. Agricultural modernization projects. These would be undertaken to try to make farming in the EC more efficient.

The agricultural policy has been challenging for the EC since it consumes 60 percent of its budget. Policies have caused major problems, such as the butter surpluses of 1986–1987 that resulted in butter's being used for animal feed and industrial lubricants. The governments that do not benefit as much from farm supports, such as Italy, would prefer to see national governments rather than the EC pay for the subsidies.

The free flow of labor has provided cheap labor but has resulted in social problems.

Free flow of labor. The free flow of labor has been instrumental in the rebuilding of Europe. To compensate for a tight labor supply and to provide unskilled workers for assembly lines and some manual service industries, the EC has also opened the doors to immigrants from other countries such as Yugoslavia, Turkey, and Greece. The original idea was that the itinerant workers would move in without families and work on a short-term basis of one to three years. However, many of these unskilled workers have brought in their families and become permanent residents, causing problems in integration, citizenship, housing, education, and welfare.

Free flow of capital requires better information about companies for investors, employees, and governments.

Free flow of capital. Two important aspects of the free flow of capital are *information* and *currency convertibility.* If investors are to make wise decisions, they need high-quality comparable financial information. As will be pointed out in Chapter 19, EC member countries vary considerably in their attitude toward accounting principles and practices. Consequently, the EC passed the Fourth Directive, which takes positive steps standardizing the presentation of financial statements. Additional directives have been issued in the areas of consolidation of financial statements and the qualifications and duties of auditors. The EC also is trying to get companies to present more information about their employees and about investment and disinvestment plans so that employees can have a say before, not after, the fact.

The EMS provides more stability in currency values for EC member countries.

The currency problem is no easier to solve than the uniformity of financial statements. Initially, the EC hoped to have a single Eurocurrency by 1981. However, the intervening steps have proved formidable. In March 1979 the EC member countries created the **European Monetary System (EMS)** in hopes of stabilizing their own exchange rates. This union will be discussed in more detail in Chapter 9.

Latin American Cooperation

Latin America needed economic cooperation to enlarge its market size.

Economic integration in Latin America has taken some interesting twists over the years. As Fig. 7.3 shows, two of the original groups, LAFTA and CARIFTA, changed names and focus. In spite of the evolution the initial reason for integration remains. The post-World War II strategy of import substitution to resolve balance of payments problems was doomed because of Latin America's small national markets. Therefore the feeling was that some form of economic cooperation was needed to enlarge the potential market size so that national firms could achieve economies of scale and be more competitive worldwide.

Initial efforts on free trade areas in Latin America were not very successful.

A study by the **Inter-American Development Bank (IDB)** identified three types of integration in Latin America: a free trade area, a common market, and a partial economic preferences model.[10] The free trade model is best illustrated by LAFTA and CARIFTA. LAFTA was formed in 1960 during the time when the EEC was being organized, and CARIFTA was formed in 1965. However, neither of these efforts endured.

Common market groups arose due to failure of free trade areas and had modest success.

The second model came into existence in Latin America because of the failure of the free trade area model. The Andean Group was formed by several members of LAFTA close to each other geographically who felt that it was necessary to have more than just free trade. Consequently, they included a common external tariff, restrictions on the inflow of foreign investment, and the integration of economic and social policies. These resembled the objec-

Figure 7.3

Integration Systems in Latin America

Source: "Inter-American Development Bank Predicts Renewed Push for Economic Integration in Latin America," *IMF Survey,* December 10, 1984, p. 375.

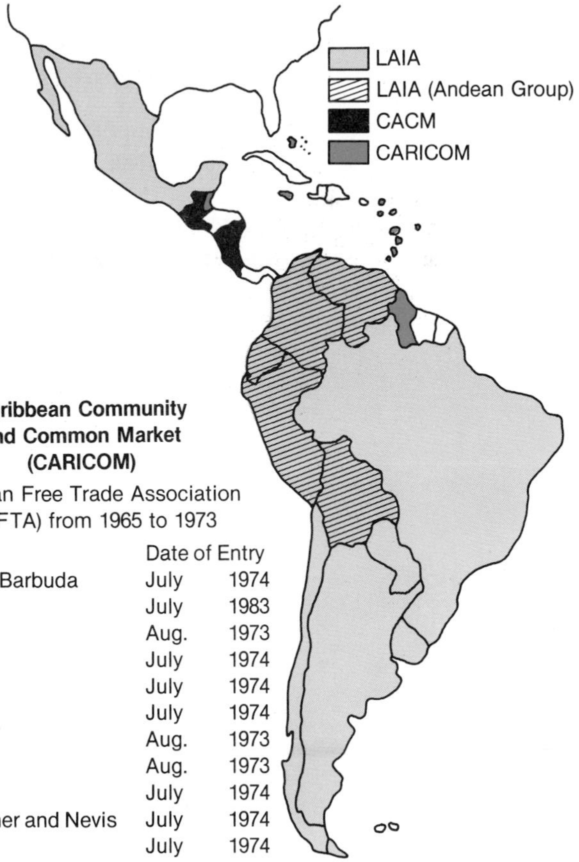

LAIA
LAIA (Andean Group)
CACM
CARICOM

Latin American Integration Association (LAIA)

Latin American Free Trade Association (LAFTA) from 1960 to 1980

Members	Date of Entry	
Argentina	Jan.	1981
Bolivia	Mar.	1982
Brazil	Nov.	1981
Chile	May	1981
Colombia	May	1981
Ecuador	Mar.	1982
Mexico	Feb.	1981
Paraguay	Dec.	1980
Peru	Nov.	1981
Uruguay	Mar.	1981
Venezuela	Mar.	1982

Cartagena Agreement, Andean Group

Members	Date of Entry	
Bolivia	Nov.	1969
Chile	Sept.	1969 (withdrew Oct. 1976)
Colombia	Sept.	1969
Ecuador	Nov.	1969
Peru	Oct.	1969
Venezuela	Nov.	1973

Central American Common Market (CACM)

Members	Date of Entry	
Costa Rica	Sept.	1963
El Salvador	May	1961
Guatemala	May	1961
Honduras	Apr.	1962 (withdrew Jan. 1971)
Nicaragua	May	1961

Caribbean Community and Common Market (CARICOM)

Caribbean Free Trade Association (CARIFTA) from 1965 to 1973

Members	Date of Entry	
Antigua and Barbuda	July	1974
Bahamas	July	1983
Barbados	Aug.	1973
Belize	July	1974
Dominica	July	1974
Grenada	July	1974
Guyana	Aug.	1973
Jamaica	Aug.	1973
Montserrat	July	1974
St. Christopher and Nevis	July	1974
St. Lucia	July	1974
St. Vincent	July	1974
Trinidad and Tobago	Aug.	1973

tives of the **Central American Common Market (CACM)** and CARICOM. The Andean Group decided to develop subregional industries and allocate these industries among the members of the group, which would in turn enable more even development. However, the problems of the region have kept it from achieving the full benefits of integration: Less than 5 percent of its total trade is intrazonal.

Partial preferences are a series of bilateral trade agreements designed to be flexible.

The third model of partial economic preferences is best illustrated by LAIA, the countries originally in LAFTA that decided against joining the Andean Group. LAIA gives countries an opportunity to establish a series of bilateral agreements that may be extended to other countries if desired. This allows countries with common interests to progress faster than might be the case when disparate members have to compromise, thereby diluting the effectiveness of the agreement. However, less than 20 percent of the trade of LAIA countries is intrazonal. Instead of across-the-board tariff cuts, LAIA set up a more flexible regional tariff preference and other forms of economic cooperation, but it did not set a timetable for the full establishment of a common market.[11]

Less than 20% of trade is intrazonal.

Other Regional Efforts

Economic cooperation is taking place in three other regions including Eastern Europe, Asia, and Africa.

Intrazonal trade is 60 percent, the highest of any group.

The Soviet Union dominates in size and influence

Eastern Europe. The **Council for Mutual Economic Assistance (CMEA or COMECON)** was formed in 1949 to assist in the economic development of the member nations. The current members as listed in Table 7.1 include Mongolia, Cuba, and Vietnam, which were admitted in 1962, 1972, and 1978, respectively. Albania, an original member of COMECON, ended its affiliation in 1961.

COMECON is interested in integrating economic activities and planning economic specialization within the region. As noted earlier in the chapter, COMECON's intrazonal trade of 60 percent is the highest of any of the regional forms of integration.[12] Table 7.1 shows that COMECON is the most heavily populated of the regional groups. This is deceiving, however, because the Soviet Union has 60 percent of the population and over 70 percent of the GNP of the group. No other regional economic group has such economic dominance by a single member of the group. Two other major problems faced by COMECON are: (1) the lack of a convertible currency for trade between member nations and (2) the difficult procedures involved in dealing with state trading organizations.

ASEAN is a major form of integration in Asia that is beginning to cooperate; it is not a free trade area.

Association of South East Asian Nations. The major form of integration in Asia is the **Association of South East Asian Nations (ASEAN),** which was organized in 1977. ASEAN, which includes Brunei, Indonesia, Malaysia, the Philippines, Singapore, and Thailand, is trying for cooperation in many areas, including industry and trade. In industry, ASEAN countries are attempting to enter into joint projects and set up medium-sized industries in different countries. These industries would be 60-percent owned by the host country and 40-percent owned by the other members of ASEAN. The two initial projects approved and under construction were urea (fertilizer) projects in Indonesia and Malaysia; other start-up projects were plagued by a series of problems.

Although ASEAN countries have not opted for a free trade area at this point, they are cooperating in reducing tariffs in a variety of areas. Their Basic Agreement on the Establishment of ASEAN Preferential Trade Arrangements was approved by the General Agreement on Tariffs and Trade and has resulted in some trade liberalization. However, only 2 percent of intra-ASEAN trade consists of preferentially traded items; in addition, less than 20 percent of ASEAN's total trade is intrazonal.[13]

Africa has more different forms of integration than any other continent.

Africa. Although only one form of African integration is listed in Table 7.1, several forms actually exist, and these are not necessarily mutually exclusive. The Ivory Coast, for example, is in six different organizations in Africa related to political and/or economic development. The major African groups are the West African Economic Community (Ivory Coast, Mali, Mauritania, Niger, and Senegal); the Entente Council (Benin, Ivory Coast, Niger, and Togo); ECOWAS (countries listed in Table 7.1); the Organisation Commune Africaine et Mauricienne (Benin, Central African Republic, Ivory Coast, Mauritius, Niger, Rwanda, Senegal, and Togo); the Organisation of African Unity (nearly every country in Africa); and the Southern African Development Co-Ordination Conference (Angola, Botswana, Lesotho, Malawi, Mozambique, Swaziland, Tanzania, Zambia, and Zimbabwe). In addition to these specific groups, there is also an African Development Bank.

Most levels of integration are quite low due to agricultural base.

Clearly, there is considerable overlap among the groups. Most groups try to cooperate in some form of economic integration, although it tends to be at a fairly low level. In general the countries are so poor and economic activity is so low that there is an insignificant base for cooperation. Most African countries rely heavily on agriculture as a major source of export revenue, so there is not much reason to lower the barriers to the primary products. Major industrial effort is fairly low-level and still needs protection before opening the doors to competition, which retards the development of a free trade area. In large part, the groups also are seeking cooperation in other areas, such as transportation and other forms of infrastructure, small industrial projects, and the like.

Some groups are heavily political.

ECOWAS is attempting to become a customs union.

The ECOWAS is featured in Table 7.1 because it is the largest of the groups, with the exception of the **Organization of African Unity (OAU),** which is a more political than economic organization. The OAU's original goals were oriented more toward the elimination of colonialism and racism in Africa than toward economic growth. The ECOWAS has four commissions: one for trade, customs, immigration, monetary, and payments; one for industry, agriculture, and natural resources; one for transport, telecommunications, and energy; and, finally, one for social and cultural affairs. Major efforts are being made to eliminate all internal tariffs and set up a common external tariff, which will make the ECOWAS a customs union in the same sense as the EC. However, it is doubtful that the ECOWAS can achieve the other types of integration accomplished by the EC.

Problems of Integration

Major problems of integration include: nationalism, nontariff barriers, economic divergence, cost, and expansion.

Although arguments in favor of some form of economic integration among neighboring countries appear overwhelming, there are some definite problems. The IDB report on Latin America referenced earlier noted that LAFTA eventually disbanded for the following major reasons: It lacked a common external tariff; there were no provisions for coordinating domestic and external policies of member countries; regional industrial production was not addressed; and there was no mechanism to ensure that economic benefits would be spread out evenly among member countries.[14] These issues loomed large in the Latin American context, but there are a variety of other problems facing nearly all of the groups. Among the most important are nationalism, nontariff barriers, economic divergence, cost, and expansion.

Importantly, the problems that keep regional groups from achieving the desired level of harmonization often create uncertainty for firms that want to invest within the group. This doubt complicates a firm's decisions about the site of operations. Many firms, for example, have built large operations in Ireland to serve the entire EC, but these operations would be too large to serve just Ireland. Thus firms must have confidence in the success of a regional economic integration effort.

Nationalism keeps some countries out of regional groups and hinders goals.

Nationalism. Most regional economic groups disintegrate, or at least accomplish less than desired, because of nationalistic pressures. President Charles de Gaulle of France essentially barred the United Kingdom from the EC until he died. Spain and Portugal's political and economic instability also postponed their entrance into the EC. Countries find it difficult to surrender sovereign power to a supernational body, which explains why many of the EFTA countries have never cared to enter the EC and many lofty EC goals have never been achieved. Chile left the Andean Group to pursue a different course from the one set by the other member countries. The Central American Common Market is not as effective as it could be due to war and insurrection in Central America.

Nationalism sometimes creates problems for companies trying to do business in the regional bloc. Cable News Network (CNN) has had difficulty breaking into the European market, largely because of nationalistic attitudes. Europeans strongly fear that the national perspective of a news program could be replaced by an international perspective and further that the U.S.

point of view might prevail. Thus CNN has had to make major changes in its product to gain access to European markets. Moreover, broadcasts in English hinder access to countries where English is not widely spoken.[15]

Regional groups abolish tariffs but have difficulty reducing nontariff barriers.

Nontariff barriers. All of the regional economic groups focus on eliminating tariff barriers so that goods can flow freely from country to country. In most cases, tariffs have been reduced significantly or eliminated altogether, but nationalism keeps trade from flowing as freely as it should. Subsidies are a large problem in the nontariff barrier controversy. As noted earlier, Spain used nontariff barriers to hinder computer firms from getting access to the Spanish market. Over 80 percent of the quantitative restrictions in Europe are estimated to be related to textiles. But there are also quantitative restrictions on autos, and Italy has a variety of quantitative restrictions on outboard motors, ball bearings, and motorcycles dating from the 1950s.[16] Portugal was forced to lift quotas on imports of European autos in early 1988, but it then imposed a new tax on autos based on engine capacity (aimed at curbing consumption of foreign autos),[17] raising the price of some autos by as much as 88 percent.

Although these problems are more acute during periods of region-wide recession, they have characterized regional economic groups since their inception. Governments have replaced tariffs with other measures to protect industries. True integration will never exist as long as these nontariff barriers remain.

Differences in economic strength make it difficult for countries to establish goals in regional groups.

Economic divergence. Another problem is linked to differences in the economic makeup of the members of the group. In LAIA, for example, Brazil has a population of 135.5 million people and a GNP of $222.0 billion compared with Paraguay, which has a population of 3.4 million and a GNP of $3.2 billion. ASEAN ranges from Indonesia with a population of 162.2 million and a GDP of $86.6 billion to Singapore with a population of 2.6 million and a GDP of $19 billion. The absolute size of the Soviet Union compared with other members of COMECON was mentioned earlier.

Size disparity makes it difficult for member countries to agree on long-term development strategies because there are too many differing points of view on how to achieve economic growth. Many of the regional groups have tried to coordinate their development strategies, with differing degrees of success.

A major source of contention in the EC revolves around this disparity in size and economic strength. As noted in Fig. 7.4, the EC has divided along north–south lines, with the exceptions that Ireland is more like the developing south, and Italy is a country of contrasts with wealth in the north and relative poverty in the south. The southern countries in the EC want more expenditures by the EC on social programs and investment, whereas the more wealthy north refuses to contribute more money.[18]

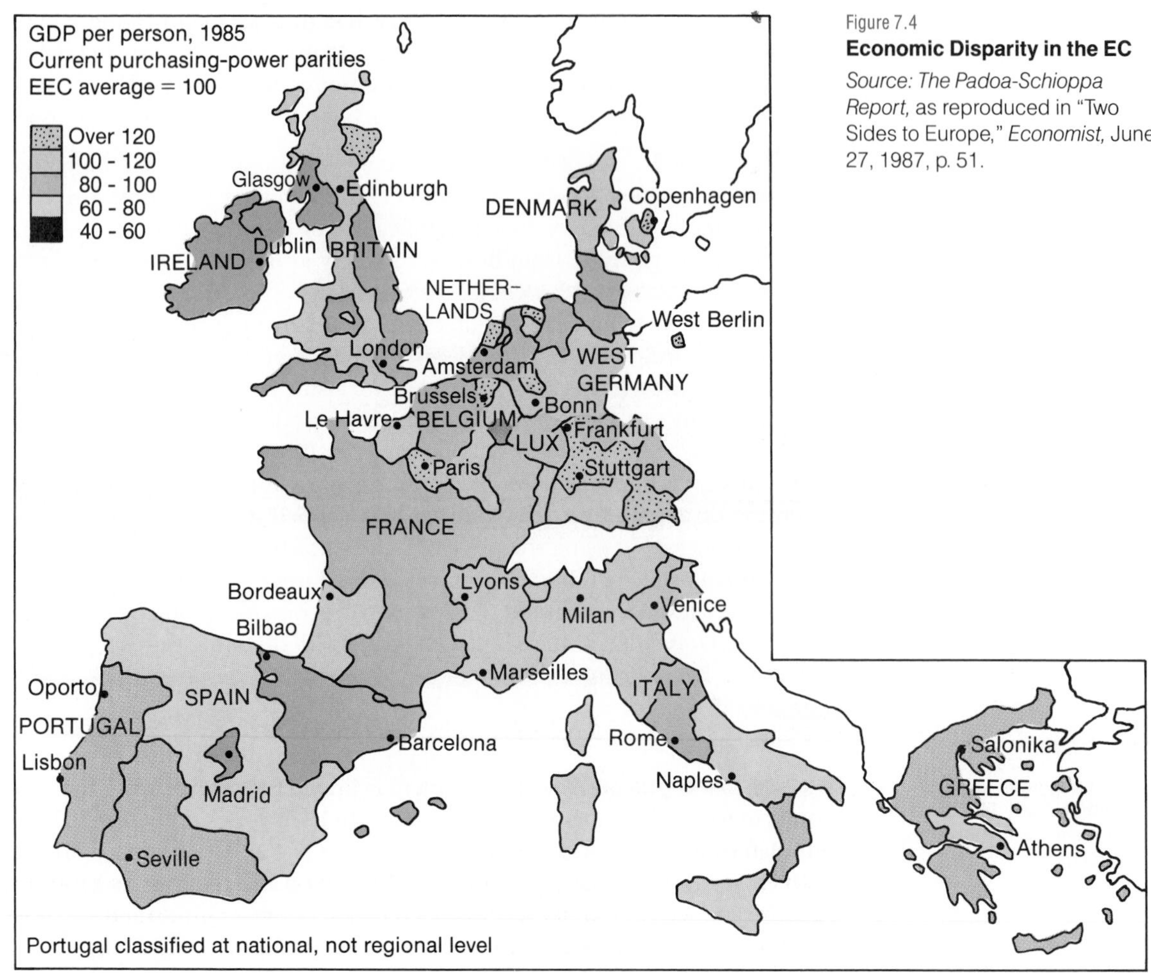

Figure 7.4
Economic Disparity in the EC
Source: The Padoa-Schioppa Report, as reproduced in "Two Sides to Europe," *Economist,* June 27, 1987, p. 51.

Common markets have larger budgets than do free trade areas and customs unions.

Cost. The more complicated the form of integration, the more difficult it is for countries to maintain an equitable budget. Free trade areas and customs unions do not have too much to worry about since they are concerned with expanding internal trade. Other more ambitious forms of regional economic integration, however, cannot put their programs into effect without proper finances. This has been a major source of concern in the EC. In 1988, the budget of the EC increased by one-third over its level in 1987, and it is expected to increase an additional 19.5 percent in 1989.[19]

Expansion. As shown in Fig. 7.3, the composition of the Latin American integration systems is fairly stable. Usually, the countries desiring to affiliate with a system did so when the system was initiated. A major exception is

Venezuela's entry into the Andean Pact in 1973, four years after the other countries had joined.

There are problems over Spain's entry to the EC.

Earlier in the chapter we mentioned the additions to membership in COMECON and in the EC. The addition of Greece, Spain and Portugal to the EC was not easy due to the wide disparity between those economies and the economies of the other members of the EC. Spain found that its trading patterns shifted significantly when it finally joined the EC. A larger percentage of both exports and imports involving other EC and Third World countries resulted in Spain's acquiring more natural resources from those countries than with other Third World countries (notably Latin America) than had been the case. In addition, industries such as steel that were subsidized heavily by the government in the past found competition keen.[20]

There are potential problems over Turkey's application for admission to the EC.

Turkey, which has had associate member status since 1963, would like to join the EC. Several problems are related to Turkey's possible membership: a large population that would have to be given access to Europe; an Islamic (versus Christian) tradition; a land mass primarily in Asia rather than Europe; an unstable political system; relatively high tariffs; and a local economy that might not be ready to compete with Europe.[21] Other countries that will consider seriously the EC in the near future are Malta, Cyprus, Austria, and Norway. Two major requirements for membership in the EC are that the countries be European and Democratic: The first requirement has kept Morocco, a North African nation, from gaining acceptance, and the second kept out Greece, Portugal, and Spain for several years.[22]

Regional Economic Groups vis-à-vis the Rest of the World

Regional economic groups can benefit outsiders as well as insiders as was pointed out in the opening case. However, problems also can develop. For example, when the Andean Pact instituted its investment policies, it met with some resistance. The goal of Andean Pact policy in the areas of foreign capital, trademarks, patents, licenses, and royalties was to gradually reduce the extent of foreign ownership and control so that all businesses eventually would be majority-owned and controlled by local investors and receive greater benefits from the use of intangibles than MNEs would ordinarily grant. However, these stringent policies, considered by some to discourage foreign investment, caused Chile to drop out of the Andean Pact in 1976. Since then, some of the policies have been moderated slightly.

EC countries deal as a group with outside countries on trade issues.

Europe faces difficulties in coping with import competition from Japan and the United States. Formally, the EC is represented in trade negotiations by one representative rather than by representatives from the individual nations; in practice, however, nationalism continues to hold sway. European problems with U.S. industry are potentially more difficult because of the importance of the two markets to each other. Recently, the major sources of contention have been in steel and agricultural products.

Regional economic integration can slow the movement to international economic integration.

A final major problem of regional economic integration is that it can slow down the movement to international economic integration. The objective of GATT is to lower trade barriers worldwide, not just on a regional basis. Regional groups such as the EC liberalized trade for the member countries at the expense of the rest of the world. Proponents of regional economic integration maintain that it is easier to reach a consensus for a smaller group of more homogeneous countries, but the static and dynamic effects of free trade would be more beneficial if applied on a worldwide basis. Unfortunately, if free trade existed worldwide, all of the problems discussed in the previous section on regional economic integration would be magnified globally.

COMMODITY AGREEMENTS

Key factors led to commodity price fluctuations.

Most of the developing countries traditionally have relied on the export of one or two commodities to supply the hard currencies needed for economic development. Unhappily, many short-run factors have caused price instability, leading to fluctuations in export earnings. The most important factors are:

1. natural forces such as floods, droughts, and weather;
2. relatively price-insensitive demand;
3. relatively price-insensitive supply (in the short run); and
4. business cycles in advanced industrial countries that can cause sudden changes in quantities demanded.

Commodity prices have fallen in recent years due to weak demand and abundant supply.

World commodity prices have fluctuated dramatically in recent years. Figure 7.5 illustrates how much non-fuel primary commodity prices fell between 1980 and 1986. By the end of 1986, both demand and supply conditions drove prices to their lowest levels since the 1930s. The major reasons for weak commodity prices were as follows: (1) relatively low rates of economic growth in the industrial countries leading to weak demand; (2) a reduction in the use of commodities due to structural changes in the world economy also leading to weak demand; (3) and abundant supplies of commodities. Although some commodities, notably coffee, have experienced periods of price increases in recent years, the general trend has been downward.[23]

Types of commodity agreements include: buffer stocks, price ranges, export/import quotas.

A **commodity agreement** is an agreement between producing and consuming countries designed to stabilize prices. Some commodities, such as copper, operate in a relatively free market. Wild price fluctuations result from supply and demand as well as speculation. However, consumers and producers alike often would prefer a more stabilized pricing system that allows for predictions of future costs and earnings and thus facilitates planning. The types of commodity agreements most frequently adopted are buffer stocks, price ranges, and export/import quotas.

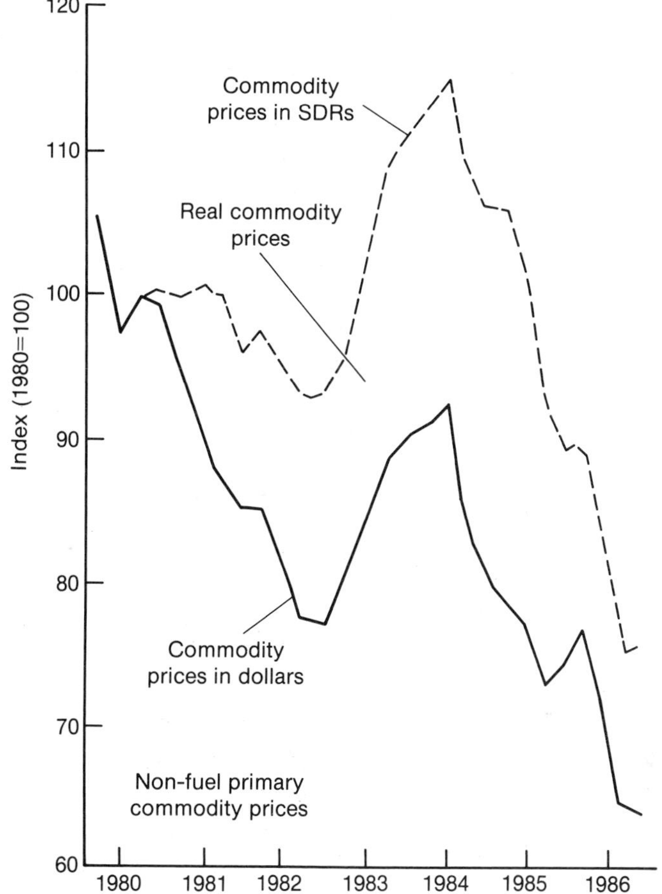

Figure 7.5
Non-Fuel Primary Commodity Price Trends—1980–1986
Source: IMF Survey, July 13, 1987, p. 209.

Buffer stock is a commodity system that utilizes stocks of commodities to regulate prices.

The **buffer stock system** provides a partially managed system monitored by a central agency. Free market forces are allowed to determine prices within a certain range, but outside of that range a central agency buys or sells the commodity to support the price. The signatory countries, those linked to other countries by a signed agreement, to the commodity agreement provide funds that the buffer stock manager can use to purchase commodities.

Net seller range is the price range in which the buffer stock manager must sell more of the commodity than is bought in order to keep the price from rising too high.

The buffer stock manager needs to be concerned on two levels about prices: the **net seller range** and the **net buyer range.** Prevailing theory is that once the price enters the "net seller" range, the buffer stock manager is required to sell the commodity in order to drop the price. When the price enters the low "net buyer" range, the buffer stock manager is required to buy the commodity in order to increase the price.

At one time, the tin market was managed on a buffer stock system. In the early 1980s, however, the Malaysian government began to buy tin secretly in hopes of increasing the world market price. It then began an aggressive

Net buyer range is the price range in which the buffer stock manager buys the commodity in order to keep prices from falling too low.

campaign to corner the market. However, the fund manager was forced to intervene in the market to defend the artificially high floor price of tin, and the fund eventually ran out of funds, thus resulting in the disintegration of the tin agreement.

Currently, the only two commodities operating in buffer stock agreements are cocoa and rubber, and neither is very successful.[24] In fact, the cocoa agreement also has run into difficult times. In 1977, cocoa prices reached $5,500 per ton. At that point, several countries increased their plantings of cocoa trees, and a significant increase in supply hit the market. As the price fell, the buffer stock manager in London tried to purchase more for the buffer stock, but its supply in storage finally reached the limit agreed on by the members of the cartel. At that point, prices fell dramatically, dropping below $1,600 per ton in mid-1988.[25]

Treatment of price ranges varies.

Price ranges can be handled in many different ways. In some of the metal markets, such as zinc, lead, and platinum, prices are fixed at the smelters by producers. Although most purchases are made at the smelters, a free market with prices parallel to the smelter prices but usually at a premium or discount satisfies marginal needs. Bilateral price agreements often are negotiated between two countries to guarantee maximum and minimum prices.

Quotas occur when producing and consuming countries divide total output and sales.

Quota systems occur when producing and/or consuming countries divide total output and sales in order to keep up prices. Quota systems have been used for such products as coffee, tea, and sugar, and they are applied often in conjunction with a buffer stock system. For the quota system to work, countries must develop close ties to prevent sharp fluctuations in supply. The quota system also is most effective when a single country has a large share of world production or consumption. Two of the best examples from a production standpoint are wool, which is controlled by Australians, and diamonds, which are controlled by DeBeers Company in South Africa.

The ICO uses a quota system to keep prices in a range.

Another example of a quota system traditionally has been the International Coffee Organization (ICO). The ICO has decided to set up a quota system in which world producers would limit their exports to keep coffee prices between $1.15 and $1.55 per pound, with the quotas to be loosened or tightened as prices neared the upper or lower limit. This plan involved negotiations by producing and consuming nations alike. Two problems emerge with the quota system, however, as illustrated by the ICO: First, the quotas can be perceived as too low by some of the countries, especially those that rely on coffee as their main (and maybe only) major export cash crop; second, a surplus or shortage of coffee might sabotage quantity and price controls. The quota-regulated price range of $1.15–1.55 is a far cry from the $3.40 per pound price that coffee carried in 1977 after the infamous Brazilian frosts.

The global quota for coffee exports was increased in 1984–1985, but the price was maintained at the same level to allow total revenues to rise for exporting countries. However, two problems faced the members of the

Coffee Agreement: (1) sales to nonmembers of the Agreement are not covered, and (2) countries continue to complain about their allocations. The first point is important because of the temptation to transship coffee from a nonmember importer to a member importer. The second problem is faced by all producer cartels, as will be seen in the discussion of OPEC later in this chapter. The quota system was suspended in 1986 largely because of price increases resulting from Brazilian drought. Some countries, notably nonmember Indonesia, held out for membership in the Organization and a reimposition of the quota system, but at significantly higher levels.[26]

The Multifibre Arrangement

The MFA established rules concerning trade in textiles and garments.

The **Arrangement Regarding International Trade in Textiles,** more commonly known as the **Multifibre Arrangement (MFA)** originated in 1974 and has been renewed three times, most recently in 1986. The MFA is an agreement among the governments of over forty countries establishing rules concerning trade in textiles and garments made of cotton, wool, and man-made fibres. The MFA establishes rules, sanctioned by the General Agreement on Tariffs and Trade (GATT), by which quotas can be levied against producer countries. The MFA initially was signed to assist the textiles industries in developed countries that were facing significant foreign competition. These industries, which tend to be labor-intensive, also have formed a strong political bloc in industrial countries, and are exerting significant governmental influence. The MFA was directed to help the textile industries gain "breathing space" in competing with the industries in developing countries and then provide for a gradual liberalization of trade. Liberalization has not occurred, however, due to the strong political force of the developed-country industries.

The MFA operates on quotas and is sanctioned by GATT.

Unlike the commodities agreements described earlier, the MFA operates primarily on quantitative restrictions. In addition, it allows discriminatory treatment by importers against exporter nations. GATT rules require a most-favored-nation (MFN) status for countries so that all countries in the MFN category are treated similarly in terms of tariffs or quotas. The MFA, however, allows the importer countries to apply differential sanctions against exporter countries.

The major beneficiaries to the MFA are the import-competing textile industries in the developed countries as well as the quota-holding producers. Many of these producers have shifted production into higher value-added products or have sold those quotas to others. Significant graft and corruption also have accompanied some of the quota-holding countries. In 1987, a U.S. garment manufacturer established an assembly facility in Mexico to exploit low wage rates and favorable tariff arrangements between Mexico and the United States. The manufacturer also had quotas from the Mexican government to export the product to the United States, but when the manufacturer attempted to ship the finished goods to the United States, U.S. Customs would not allow the goods to enter. Customs keeps track of the quota allotted to Mexico by product category and the value of shipments made to the United States, and when the value of shipments equals the allotted quota, other shipments are disallowed. Apparently, more quotas had been allotted by the Mexican government than were permitted under the agreement with the United States. Either someone made a mistake, or quotas were sold illegally.

According to U.N. estimates, the textile and garment industry is the largest employer in the developing countries. As a result, developing countries are endeavoring to loosen the MFA to allow entry of more goods to industrial countries, such as the United States, the world's largest textile importer. Quota-holding companies and the import-competing industries in the developed countries have set up strong barriers to liberalization.[27]

The Organization of Petroleum Exporting Countries

Members of OPEC include: Saudi Arabia, Kuwait, Qatar, the United Arab Emirates, Iraq, Libya, Algeria, Iran, Indonesia, Nigeria, Gabon, Venezuela, and Ecuador.

In 1972 the director of the U.S. State Department's Office of Fuels & Energy boldly predicted that the average price of Middle East crude oil, then at $2.25 per barrel (bbl), might rise to $5.00 or even higher by 1980. As an aside, the director mentioned that these figures would translate into higher gasoline prices, heating bills, and industrial cost.[28] The **Organization of Petroleum Exporting Countries (OPEC)** comprises the Middle East Arab countries of Saudi Arabia, Kuwait, Qatar, the United Arab Emirates, Iraq, Libya, Algeria, the Islamic Republic of Iran, Indonesia, Nigeria, Gabon, Venezuela, and Ecuador. OPEC's effectiveness in controlling prices and production first was illustrated by the political and economic events of 1973 and 1974, when the price of crude oil increased from $3.64/bbl to $11.65/bbl within one year. OPEC was able to accomplish this because:

1. It produced over 50 percent of the world's oil in 1973;
2. Demand for oil was high;
3. Consuming countries were not able to supply their own oil needs; and
4. Substitutes were not readily available.

World oil prices dropped slightly in the 1975–1978 period, but they rebounded in 1979–1980, when they peaked at about $35 per barrel.

However, OPEC's resolve began to weaken in the early 1980s. Although oil consumption increased steadily over most of the 1970s, the oil price rise in 1979–1980 resulted in a drop in demand for oil in the industrial countries. The major reasons for the drop in decline in consumption were: the world recession, the increase in crude oil prices, the substitution of other fuels for oil, the effectiveness of national energy policies aimed at conservation, and the changing structure of industry with a decline in the importance of energy-intensive industries.[29]

Key trends in oil since 1973 include:

Some interesting trends developed in the oil industry. First, consumption of oil as a percentage of total energy consumption in the world declined from

- Decline of consumption in oil as a percentage of energy use
- Decrease in American and Western European oil consumers.
- Decrease in importance of OPEC as a supplier.

48 percent to 40 percent by 1983: Natural gas, coal, hydroelectric power, and nuclear energy increased at the expense of oil. Second, the percentage of world oil consumption decreased for North America and Western Europe, whereas it increased for the centrally planned economies and the rest of the world. Finally, the output of OPEC actually decreased by 50 percent over the past decade. Part of the decrease was due to the fall in demand for oil in general, but part of it was traced to the increase in oil supply by non-OPEC members. The major non-OPEC increase came from the USSR (in the centrally planned economies category), Mexico, and the United Kingdom.[30]

Because of these trends, OPEC has been losing its grip. After successive price increases over the period 1973–1980, OPEC was forced to cut prices several times after 1983. These price cuts, along with the drop in demand, have devastated the economies of the larger OPEC countries such as Nigeria, Indonesia, Venezuela, and Iran. It was estimated that OPEC countries as a group suffered balance of payments deficits during the 1982–1985 period. Consequently, foreign exchange reserves began to slip: Saudi Arabia's reserves, which were at $150 billion in 1982–1983, had fallen to less than $100 billion by early 1985.[31]

Clearly, OPEC, which had been considered the model producer cartel, was facing some serious difficulties. In late 1986, OPEC was able to fashion an agreement on production quotas. The key country was Iran, who agreed to stick to a quota even if the agreement were violated by Iraq, its warring neighbor. Prices stayed at low but firmer levels during 1987. Despite OPEC's difficulties, about three-quarters of the Free World's oil reserves are held by OPEC countries. Saudi Arabia and the Persian Gulf nations hold 65 percent of the world's surplus oil production capacity, whereas OPEC as a whole holds 95 percent.[32]

By late 1987 and early 1988, OPEC began to loosen its grip even more. Prices stayed low, and producer countries could not agree to slow down production in order to stabilize prices. By 1986, oil imports fell to 31 percent of total consumption in the United States. Low prices continued to devastate the U.S. oil industry, and oil exploration ceased. Low oil prices resulted in increased consumption and a rise in oil imports in 1987, with further rises predicted for the remainder of the 1980s. But overall world demand remained weak, keeping prices down and weakening OPEC's ability to control production and prices.

OTHER MULTILATERAL INSTITUTIONS

The United Nations

The U.N. has several key purposes.

Of the numerous other bilateral and multilateral organizations, treaties, and agreements in existence, the United Nations (U.N.) is one of the most visible and extensive. Its major purposes are: (1) to maintain international peace and security, (2) to develop friendly relations among nations, (3) to achieve international cooperation in solving international problems of an economic, social, cultural or humanitarian nature, and (4) to be a center for harmonizing national efforts in these areas.

The U.N. comprises a Secretariat, General Assembly, Security Council, and Economic and Social Council. The Economic and Social Council is responsible for economic, social, cultural, and humanitarian facets of U.N. policy. This group organized a Commission of Transnational Corporations to secure effective international arrangements for the operations of transnational corporations and to further global understanding of the nature and effects of their activities. The commission has studied a variety of topics, such as transfer pricing, taxation, and international standards of accounting and reporting.

The U.N. has also established several regional economic commissions to study economic and technological problems of different regions of the world and recommend courses of action for resolving these problems.

A number of other bodies have been established by the U.N., some dealing with issues relating to MNCs. Two such groups are the United Nations Conference on Trade and Development (UNCTAD) and the **International Sea-Bed Authority.** UNCTAD, as discussed in Chapter 2, has been especially active in dealing with the relationships between developing and industrial countries with respect to commodities, manufacturing, shipping, and invisibles and financing related to trade.

The International Sea-Bed Authority, organized in October 1986 following discussions that began in 1973, is aimed at determining coastal water rights and setting policy on the exploitation of resources on the sea bed. Unfortunately, only twenty-nine countries had ratified the Convention by late 1986, and sixty are required for the Convention to be established formally. The United States and other industrial countries refuse to ratify the Convention because of restrictions on the exploitation of resources.

Finally, the U.N. has organized a number of specialized agencies to influence the world economy: the General Agreement on Tariffs and Trade; the World Bank; the International Labor Organization; the International Monetary Fund; and the World Intellectual Property Organization. Each of these groups is discussed in greater detail elsewhere in this text.

The Organization for Economic Cooperation and Development

OECD is a multilateral organization that helps industrial countries formulate social and economic policies.

The U.N. currently is the world's most comprehensive form of multilateral cooperation. The **Organization for Economic Cooperation and Development (OECD)** was described briefly in Chapter 2. Like the U.N., OECD is a multilateral form of cooperation, distinguished by its primarily industrial country makeup. OECD was organized in 1961 to assist member governments in formulating policies aimed at promoting economic and social welfare and to stimulate and harmonize members' assistance to developing countries.[33] It has over 200 different committees that deal with economic issues: Three committees, the Trade Committee, the Executive Committee

Special Session, and the Development Assistance Committee, deal with specific trade issues.

The Trade Committee provides a forum for considering long-range trade policies of member nations and for discussing current problems as well. The Executive Committee Special Session deals with the coordination of national economic policies. This discussion has taken on increased significance over the past few years as inflation has dropped and currencies have come under pressure owing to the fluctuating U.S. dollar. The final committee is concerned about the transfer of financial resources to the developing countries.

The OECD has issued a code of conduct relating to the operations of MNEs to ensure that the MNEs operate in support of economic and political objectives of the individual member nations. In addition, the OECD issued a set of guidelines dealing with the disclosure of financial and operating information of MNEs (mentioned again in Chapter 19).

The U.N. and the OECD are multilateral institutions with broader appeal than the narrower trade or economic issues described earlier in the chapter. All of these organizations, however, have a useful purpose: They provide a forum where nations can discuss political, economic, and social issues of mutual benefit and, it is hoped, come to a cooperative consensus.

SUMMARY

- After a period of economic isolation in the 1930s and World War II, many efforts toward intergovernmental cooperation emerged.
- Regional economic integration emerged strongly after World War II as countries began to realize the benefits of cooperation and larger market sizes. The major types of economic integration are the free trade area, customs union, common market, economic union, and complete economic integration.
- In its most limited sense, economic integration allows countries to trade goods without tariff discrimination (i.e., free trade area). In a more complex arrangement, all factors of production are allowed to move across borders, and some degree of social, political, and economic harmonization is undertaken (i.e., complete economic integration).
- The static effects of economic integration improve the efficiency of resource allocation and affect both production and consumption. The dynamic effects involve internal and external economies that arise because of changes in growth of market sizes.
- The European Community (EC) is an effective common market that has abolished most of the restrictions on factor mobility and is moving toward the status of an economic union by attempting to harmonize national economic policies to a limited extent. It includes Belgium, Denmark, France, Greece, West Germany, Ireland, Italy, Luxembourg, the Netherlands, Spain, Portugal, and the United Kingdom.

- Some of the EC's major goals are: (1) abolishment of intrazonal restrictions on the movement of goods, capital, services, and labor; (2) a common external tariff; (3) a common agricultural policy; (4) harmonization of tax and legal systems; (5) a uniform policy concerning antitrust; and (6) a harmonization of national currencies.
- Other forms of economic integration have occurred in other parts of the world, notably in Latin America and among the communist countries. Various forms of free trade areas and customs unions also exist in Africa and Asia.
- Many developing countries rely on commodity exports to supply the hard currencies needed for economic development. Instability in commodity prices has resulted in fluctuations in export earnings. Commodity agreements, utilizing buffer stocks, price ranges, quotas, or combinations of the three, are often sought in the hope of stabilizing prices.
- The Multifibre Arrangement (MFA) was established to protect textile and garment manufacturers in developed countries from manufacturers in developing countries. It allowed the importing countries to establish quotas to protect domestic producers.
- The Organization of Petroleum Exporting Countries (OPEC) was successful as a producer cartel in the 1970s and effectively forced historic increases in crude oil prices. However, the drop in demand worldwide and the entrance of major non-OPEC producers has reduced OPEC's influence.
- The United Nations (U.N.) has become deeply involved in international business through the World Bank Group, the International Monetary Fund, the Commission on Transnational Corporations, and the Conference on the Law of the Sea.
- The Organization for Economic Cooperation and Development (OECD) is an association of the major industrial countries of the world whose major objective is to foster economic and social development.

CASE: A NEW COMMON MARKET: THE UNITED STATES, CANADA, AND MEXICO[34]

In the late 1970s, many people were looking at the possibility of establishing a common market in North America similar to the EC but involving Canada, Mexico, and the United States. Such a market would have all of the earmarks of a common market with the abolishment of all tariffs and quotas in intrazonal trade, a common external tariff, and mobility of factors of production. Its major objective would be to help the United States lessen its dependence on OPEC by giving it free access to oil and natural gas in Canada and Mexico.

The new market would be large with much of its economic strength coming from the United States. Some of the demographics are as follows:

DEMOGRAPHIC DATA, 1985

	Population (millions)	Gross national product (billions of U.S. dollars)	Per capita GNP (U.S. dollars)
Canada	25.4	$ 347.5	$13,680
Mexico	78.5	163.9	2,080
United States	239.3	3,994.0	16,690

Intrazonal trade currently is as follows:

EXPORTS FROM/TO (in billions of U.S. dollars), 1985

	United States	Canada	Mexico
United States		74.3	8.9
Canada	90.3		0.235
Mexico	14.1	0.393	

A common market involving these three countries could make them totally self-sufficient in energy. In addition, manufacturers in the three countries would have unrestricted access to each other's markets. Canadian and Mexican agricultural and industrial sectors would benefit from U.S.-developed technology. The infusion of modern technology could be especially beneficial to Mexico in helping aleviate high unemployment.

As the table shows, the three countries already enjoy a large amount of intrazonal trade. Trade between the United States and Canada is by far the largest bilateral trading relationship in the world, and this would likely increase in the future. Because of negotiations completed under the Tokyo Round of GATT in 1979, 80 percent of all Canadian exports to the United States and 65 percent of all U.S. exports to Canada were duty-free by the end of

1987. Another 15 percent of Canadian exports entered the United States at tariffs of 5 percent or less. However, Canada's average tariff on dutiable U.S. imports is 8.5 percent, more than double the average U.S. tariff on dutiable imports from Canada. This illustrates the slightly more protectionist policy of the Canadian government in comparison with that of the United States.

U.S.–Canadian Cooperation. Recently a variety of forms of economic cooperation have emerged between the United States and Canada. Since 1965 an Automotive Products Trade agreement has existed between the two countries. It provides for qualified duty-free trade in specified automotive products between the United States and Canada. In the early 1980s there was discussion about developing free trade in specific sectors, such as steel and textiles, which gave way to a broader discussion of free trade. Negotiations were held in 1987 to open up trade more freely between the United States and Canada. The United States was concerned over the amount of governmental subsidies given Canadian businesses and also over greater access to investment in Canada. The Canadians, on the other hand, sought exemptions from laws relieving U.S. producers of unfair Canadian competition. They preferred an international tribunal to deal with trade disputes rather than having to deal with antidumping and countervailing duty legislation. Canadian manufacturers would be able to cut costs by an estimated 20 percent due to economies of scale that would follow from freer access to the U.S. market.

Preliminary discussions gave way to the Canada–U.S. Free Trade Agreement, which was signed on January 2, 1988, by Prime Minister Brian Mulroney and President Ronald Reagan and expected to go into effect on January 1, 1989. Although the treaty was to be ratified in both countries in 1988, serious concerns lingered over its possible impact. Canadians were concerned that Canada would: (1) lose its cultural identity, (2) be too closely integrated with a violent society, (3) be hitching its star to a declining economic power, (4) forfeit its independence in the area of foreign policy, and (5) be overwhelmed politically and economically by the United States. Some U.S. politicians, especially in the Midwest, worried that their states would lose production to Canada. However, the dynamic effects of the expansion of the two markets in a freer environment were expected to create an additional 750,000 jobs in the United States and 150,000 in Canada. Some experts predicted that high-volume production lines would be shifted to the United States, and small-volume specialty lines would be shifted to Canada. The expansion of these two markets, with fewer trade barriers than exist currently in the EC, actually will result in a market that is 15 percent larger than the EC.

U.S.–Mexican Cooperation. Mexico exports a significantly greater amount of goods to the United States than it does to Canada. As far as Mexico's exports to the United States are concerned, tariffs on 40 percent of the total exports (essentially oil and coffee beans) are nonexistent, and tariffs on other goods average 6.03 percent. Mexico, on the other hand, only joined GATT in 1986. Prior to that, goods imported into Mexico entered at tariff rates ranging from 35 to 100 percent; under GATT provisions, these tariffs gradually are being reduced. Mexico's entry into GATT was delayed by its protectionist posture. Consequently, Mexico's complex licensing system discourages many foreign manufactured goods. When Mexico came under severe pressure in the 1970s due to the drop in oil revenues, it was forced to choke off imports and significantly expand exports of goods and services in order to meet its international obligations. However, part of the price that it had to pay for continued assistance from the industrial countries was to liberalize its trade situation.

U.S. Investments in Canada and Mexico. The United States is the largest foreign investor in Canada and Mexico. Mexico varies slightly from Canada, however, because it went through a period of not allowing majority foreign ownership on new investments. Although the Mexican government lifted its restrictions on foreign ownership in 1984, few foreign firms were willing to risk large investments initially in such an unstable economic environment. However, some U.S. companies set up assembly operations in Mexico close to the U.S. border to exploit low Mexican labor rates. These assembly operations supplied more foreign exchange to the Mexican economy than tourism did.

In 1978, U.S. companies provided 79.4 percent of all foreign direct investment in Canada. Then in 1979, U.S. companies controlled forty-five of the one-hundred largest companies in Canada. Canadian-based subsidiaries of U.S. companies accounted for 43 percent of all Canadian manufacturing and 58 percent of all oil and natural gas companies. For a few years under the leadership of Prime Minister Pierre Trudeau the Canadian government tried to force many U.S. companies to divest ownership, especially in the oil and gas industries. However, such a negative climate for investment began to develop in Canada that the government was forced to back off from some of its demands. In contrast to Trudeau, Prime Minister Mulroney voiced considerable interest in encouraging foreign investment. Despite this, the U.S. investment picture in Canada began to weaken: By 1988, U.S. MNEs controlled only 17 percent of corporate assets in Canada. The U.S.–Canada Free Trade Agreement has resulted in a large number of U.S. acquisitions by Canadian firms, and many observers feel that Canadians will soon own as many corporate assets in the United States as do U.S. investors in Canada.

Labor costs are considered to be lower in Mexico than in either Canada or the United States; however, the productivity level in Mexico is also lower.

Although all three countries have some degree of unemployment, the problem is most acute in Mexico. In fact, Mexico's unemployment is so high that workers consistently cross the U.S. border in search of jobs. This trend on the one hand has given the United States a large pool of low-skilled, cheap labor but on the other has created tension between the U.S. and Mexico. If the free flow of goods and capital were to be extended to labor, the level of migration might increase dramatically, leading to a variety of social and economic problems. In spite of these problems, the United States and Mexico began to discuss the possibility of a free trade agreement in 1987.

QUESTIONS

1. List the benefits that would accrue to all three members of the new common market.
2. List the major economic problems that could arise from such a union.
3. Discuss the political and nationalistic ramifications of such a union.

4. How would this union compare with some of the others that we discussed in this chapter?
5. If you were a U.S. businessperson looking at this newly created market, what strategies might you employ to serve all three markets? What factors would you consider in making your choice?

NOTES

1. The information in this incident is from the following sources: various issues of the Ford Motor Company's *Annual Reports; Forbes,* July 1, 1972, pp. 22–26; *Forbes,* April 2, 1979, pp. 44–48; Roger Cohen, "Ford-Fiat: How Their Contest of Wills Prevented a 'Perfect Marriage' in Europe," *The Wall Street Journal,* November 21, 1985, p. 34; James B. Treece, Richard A. Melcher, Cheryl Debes, Neil Gross, John Templeman, and Susan Benway, "Can Ford Stay on Top?" *Business Week,* September 28, 1987, pp. 78–86.

2. Bela Balassa, *The Theory of Economic Integration* (Homewood, Ill.: Richard D. Irwin, 1961), p. 1.

3. *Ibid.,* p. 40.

4. *Ibid.,* p. 2.

5. Paul Hemp, "Pan-European Ventures Face Difficulties," *The Wall Street Journal,* April 1, 1986, p. 34. Also, see Ian Rodger, "Why European Marriages Keep Turning Sour," *Financial Times,* June 26, 1985, p. 6.

6. Richard L. Hudson, "Europe's Computer Software Industry Is Being Reshaped by Series of Mergers," *The Wall Street Journal,* March 31, 1988.

7. For data on intrazonal trade, see the descriptions of the different regional groups in *Europa Yearbook, 1987.*

8. R. Bourguignon-Wittke, E. Grabitz, O. Schmuck, S. Steppat, W. Wessels, "Five Years of the Directly Elected European Parliament: Performance and Prospects," *Journal of Common Market Studies,* Volume XXIV, No. 1, September 1985, pp. 39–59, and "Enter the Iberians," *The Economist,* January 18, 1986, p. 40.

9. Business International, *Business Europe,* August 10, 1987, p. 6.

10. "Inter-American Development Bank Predicts Renewed Push for Economic Integration in Latin America," *IMF Survey,* December 10, 1984, pp. 369, 374–376.

11. *Europa Yearbook, 1987,* p. 170.

12. *Economist,* October 17, 1987, p. 63.

13. *Europa Yearbook, 1987,* pp. 103–105.

14. "Inter-American Development Bank . . . ," *op. cit.,* p. 374.

15. Mark M. Nelson, " 'Ugly American' CNN Snubbed in Europe," *The Wall Street Journal,* September 28, 1986, p. 20.

16. Business International, *Business Europe,* January 25, 1988, pp. 6–7.

17. *Ibid.*

18. "Two Sides to Europe," *Economist,* June 27, 1987, pp. 50–51.

19. "The Lady Turned," *Economist,* February 20, 1988, p. 50.

20. Augusto Lopez-Carlos, "Spain's Membership in European Community Entails Adjustment in Key Economic Sectors," *IMF Survey,* March 9, 1987, pp. 65–68.

21. Philip Revzin, "Europe Cool to Turkey's EC Entry Bid," *The Wall Street Journal,* April 22, 1986, p. 34.

22. "Still Pulling Them," *Economist,* May 23, 1987, p. 45.

23. "Sustained Price Weakness Forecast for Non-Fuel Primary Commodities," *IMF Survey,* July 13, 1987, pp. 209, 218–220.

24. Raphael Pura, "Malaysia's Tin Scheme Stuns the Industry," *The Wall Street Journal,* September 25, 1986, p. 38, and "Uncommon Fund," *The Economist,* August 15, 1987, p. 55.

25. Jeffrey Ryser and David Zigas, "Bitter Times for Cocoa Growers," *Business Week,* April 4, 1988, p. 83.

26. "Indonesia Will Push for Seat on Board of Coffee Cartel," *The Wall Street Journal,* May 26, 1987, p. 16.

27. Good background on the MFA can be found in the following book: Ying-Pik Choi, Hwa Soo Chung, and Nicolas Marian, *The Multi-Fibre Arrangement in Theory and Practice* (London: Frances Pinter, 1985).

28. "The Middle East Squeeze on Oil Giants," *Business Week,* July 29, 1972, p. 56.

29. "International Oil Market Prospects," *Currency Profiles* (New York: The Henley Centre for Economic Forecasting and Manufacturers Hanover Trust Company, December 1984), p. 6.

30. *Ibid.,* pp. 6–7.

31. Ronald Taggiasco and William Glesgell, "OPEC Still Hasn't Faced Up to Reality," *Business Week,* February 11, 1985, p. 29.

32. Deloitte Haskins & Sells, *DH&S Review,* June 8, 1987, p. 2.

33. *Europa Yearbook,* p. 184.

34. Most of the material for this case comes directly from Herbert E. Meyer, "Why a North American Common Market Won't Work—Yet," *Fortune,* September 10, 1979, pp. 118 ff. © 1979 Time, Inc. All rights reserved; "Why Only a Few Companies Are Betting On Mexico's Future," *Business Week,* October 1, 1984, pp. 78–82; Earl H. Fry and Lee H. Radebaugh, eds., *Regulation of Foreign Direct Investment in Canada and*

the United States (Provo, UT: Brigham Young University, 1983); Lee H. Radebaugh and Earl H. Fry, eds., *Canada/U.S. Trade Relations* (Provo, UT: Brigham Young University, 1984); Lee H. Radebaugh and Earl H. Fry, eds., *The Canada/U.S. Free Trade Agreement: The Impact on Service Industries* (Provo, UT: Brigham Young University, 1988); Edith Terry, Bill Javetsky, and John Pearson, "Why Brian Mulroney Is up against a Trade Wall," *Business Week,* June 15, 1987; Sections on Mexico, the U.S., and Canada in *Europa Yearbook, 1987;* World Bank, *World Development Report, 1987;* Edith Terry, William J. Holstein, Wendy Zellner, and Zachary Schiller, "Getting Ready for the Great North American Shakeout," *Business Week,* April 4, 1988, pp. 44–46.

4

PART

WORLD FINANCIAL ENVIRONMENT

A company that operates internationally must work within the framework of diverse financial systems and yet measure and report its worldwide performance in terms of some common frame of reference. Since different nations have distinct currencies, transactions among countries must be conducted in more than one currency.

Chapter 8 defines the terms used in international currency transactions and explains how the foreign exchange markets work.

Chapter 9 explains how different currencies' values are determined. The emphasis is on the exchange rate arrangements that exist within the international monetary system, the theories that explain the determination of exchange rates, methods used to forecast exchange rate movements, and the effects that values and movements have on business operations.

A company operating internationally faces a more diverse group of financial institutions than is found in a domestic situation. These institutions and their scopes and limitations are described in Chapter 10.

8

CHAPTER FOREIGN EXCHANGE

All things are obedient to money.
—English proverb

- To discuss the terms and definitions of foreign exchange.
- To describe how the foreign exchange market works for immediate and long-term transactions.
- To explain the role of convertibility in transactions.
- To illustrate how countries control limited supplies of foreign exchange through licensing, multiple rates, import deposit requirements, and quantity controls.
- To show how the foreign exchange market is used in commercial and financial transactions.

CASE:
THE BRAZILIAN CRUZADO[1]

Brazil moved from revolution, despair, and hyperinflation in the 1960s to the economic miracle of the late 1960s and early 1970s. During the mid- to late-1970s, however, the economic miracle was beset with problems of spiraling oil prices, debt, and a renewed outburst of inflation. By the early 1980s, Brazil's economy was again struggling to generate enough foreign exchange to pay off its debts and pay for imports necessary to fuel an economic recovery and, it was hoped, a repeat of the miracle.

The Brazilian cruzado (Brazil's currency, which was known as the cruzeiro prior to February 28, 1986) is not freely convertible into other currencies because of restraints and restrictions imposed on it by the Central Bank of Brazil. Since 1968 the government has allowed the value of the cruzado to change relatively frequently in relation to the U.S. dollar. Because of controls, however, the law of supply and demand is not allowed to operate freely. Most foreign exchange transactions are taken care of by the Central Bank of Brazil, the Banco do Brasil, S.A., and banks and tourist agencies authorized to deal in foreign exchange.

Despite the frequent devaluation of the cruzado, its value is not always what it would be in a free market. In fact, there is a black market where the cruzado is traded at a substantial discount. One day before the cruzeiro was changed into the cruzado in 1986, the black market value of the cruzeiro was Cr$ 23,000 per dollar compared with the official rate of Cr$ 12,000.

Because of the shortage of foreign exchange, the Central Bank is very concerned about how foreign exchange is used. In most cases, imports require licenses, or import certificates, for foreign exchange allocation to take place. The Foreign Trade Department of the Banco do Brasil (CACEX) establishes an annual import plan (subject to revision). As a result of this plan, importers must anticipate their foreign exchange requirements and convince the Brazilian government that their imports are essential to the nation's long-term viability.

During the mid-1980s the Brazilian government regulated its citizens who were temporarily living abroad. Citizens were permitted to convert cruzados into the currency of the country where they were living, but the government allowed the equivalent of only U.S. $300 per month. Brazilian tourists were allowed to exchange cruzeiros for $1,000 worth of another currency without prior approval, except on trips to Central and South America, where they were permitted only $500.

Some firms were given special dispensation from these controls. For example, a special travel and representation allowance of $20,000 a year was available for firms whose annual exports totaled at least $200,000. In addition, firms that exported products and earned foreign exchange got import certificates more easily than those that did not.

Most of the currency transactions mentioned above occur in the spot market, the market on a given day for foreign exchange. However, forward contracts are available for commercial transactions. These contracts are usually between an importer and the Banco do Brasil to provide for the conversion of cruzados into dollars or some other foreign currency to settle an obligation due at some point in the future. These contracts are often entered into when the Banco do Brasil issues the importer a letter of credit, a document specifying that the Banco do Brasil will pay for the imports when the imports arrive or at some point in the future after arrival. The importer often is required to deposit a large percentage of the contract to guarantee that the Banco do Brasil will have the cash necessary to convert into the foreign currency.

The change from the cruzeiro to the cruzado occurred in 1986 as a result of severe economic pressure in Brazil. By the end of 1985 inflation had been running at 225 percent, but inflation in February 1986 was running at 400–500 percent. The cruzado plan involved lopping three zeros off the value of the cruzeiro and starting off with a value of Cr$ 12 per dollar. The cruzado plan involved daily devaluations of the cruzado, price controls, and the elimination of indexation. The plan began to disintegrate in 1987, and a new plan was implemented involving a hefty devaluation of the cruzado over and above the daily changes, a 90-day wage and price freeze, cutbacks in public spending, and a deflator for nonindexed financial instruments. Clearly, the problems of the cruzado were not over.

INTRODUCTION

As the Brazilian example shows, there is a fundamental difference between making payment in the domestic market and making payment for goods, services, or securities purchased abroad. In a domestic transaction only one currency is used, whereas two or more currencies may be used in a foreign transaction. For example, a U.S. businessperson who exports $100,000 worth of textile machinery to a Zurich textile producer will ask the Swiss buyer to remit payment in dollars unless the U.S. firm has some specific use for Swiss francs. (If the firm has a Swiss subsidiary, for instance, it may wish to make the funds acquired available to this subsidiary and would accept payment in Swiss francs.)

Assume that the situation just described is not the case and that you are a U.S. importer who has agreed to purchase a certain quantity of French perfume and to pay the French exporter 20,000 francs for it. How would you go about paying? First, you would go to the international department of your local bank to buy 20,000 French francs at the going market rate. Let's assume that the dollar/franc exchange rate is FF 6 = $1. Your bank then would debit your demand deposit by $3,333 plus transactions costs and give you a special check payable in francs made out to the exporter. The check then would be sent to the exporter, who would deposit it in a Paris bank. The bank in turn would credit the exporter's account with 20,000 francs, and the transaction would be complete.

Foreign exchange includes currencies and other instruments of payment denominated in other currencies.

The special check and other instruments for making payment abroad are referred to collectively as **foreign exchange.** Although the major purpose of this chapter is to provide essential information about the nature of foreign exchange, Chapters 9 and 10 form an integral part of this discussion. Chapter 9 focuses on what gives exchange rates their value and what causes those rates to change. Chapter 10 looks at the international capital markets in which foreign exchange is traded.

To be effective, MNEs as well as small import and export firms must understand exchange rates. The exchange rate can influence where a wholesaler or retailer buys products from and sells products to an end consumer as well as where a manufacturing firm acquires raw materials or components and produces products. In addition, the rate of exchange affects the location of capital that a firm needs to access in order to expand. A change in exchange rates can force a purely domestic firm into one heavily involved in the international marketplace.

TERMS AND DEFINITIONS

An exchange rate is the number of units of one currency to acquire one unit of a currency of another country.

The spot rate is the exchange rate involved for immediate delivery.

An **exchange rate** can be defined as the number of units of one currency that must be given to acquire one unit of a currency of another country. It is the price paid in the home currency to purchase a certain quantity of funds in the currency of another country. For example, on June 6, 1988, it took only $0.005960 to purchase one Brazilian cruzado. The exchange rate, then, is the link between different national currencies that makes international price and cost comparisons possible.

The interbank market includes the foreign exchange markets between and among banks.

The forward rate is the rate quoted for future delivery.

If the rate is quoted for current foreign currency transactions, it is called the **spot rate.** The spot rate applies to **interbank transactions** for delivery within two business days or immediate delivery for over-the-counter transactions that usually involve nonbank customers. If the rate is quoted for delivery of foreign currency in the future, it is called the **forward rate.** The forward rate is a contractual rate between the foreign exchange trader and the trader's client.

The Spot Market

The spread in the spot market is the difference between the bid (buy) and offer (sell) rates quoted by the foreign exchange trader.

Since most foreign currency transactions take place with foreign exchange traders, the rates are quoted by the traders. Whether the traders quote prices in the spot or the forward market, they always quote a **bid** (buy) and **offer** (sell) rate. The bid is what the trader is willing to buy foreign exchange for, and the offer is what the trader is willing to sell foreign exchange for. The **spread** in the spot market, the difference between the bid and offer rates, is the margin on which the trader earns a profit on overall transactions. Thus the rate quoted by a trader for the British pound might be $1.8005/15. This implies that the trader would be willing to buy pounds at $1.8005 and sell them for $1.8015. Obviously, the trader would want to buy low and sell high.

The direct quote is the number of units of the domestic currency for one unit of the foreign currency.

The indirect quote is the number of units of the foreign currency for one unit of the domestic currency.

As just noted in the example, the pound is quoted by the U.S. bank at the number of U.S. dollars for one unit of the foreign currency (the British pound). This is also known as the **direct quote** or **normal.** If the rate were quoted in terms of the number of units of the foreign currency for one unit of the domestic currency, it would be known as the **indirect quote,** or **reciprocal** because it is the inverse of the direct quote. For example,

$$\frac{1}{\$1.8005} = 0.55554 \text{ British pounds (£) per U.S. dollar (\$).}$$

U.S. terms represent the direct quote.

European terms represent the indirect quote.

Both the direct and indirect quotes are used. In the United States it is common to use the direct quote for domestic business. That is often referred to as **U.S. terms** (also referred to as American system). For international business, however, banks often use **European terms** (also referred to as Continental terms), which would be the indirect quote. The rate quoted for the Brazilian cruzado earlier was the direct rate. The indirect rate at that same time was 167.79 cruzados per dollar. It is customary to use the U.S. dollar as the **base currency** for international transactions; the other currency in the transaction would be the **quoted currency.**

Most large newspapers, especially those devoted to business or with business sections, quote exchange rates on a daily basis. The *Wall Street Journal,* for example, provides the direct and indirect rates for forty-four different currencies in every issue, as shown in Table 8.1. The rates are the selling rate of Banker's Trust for interbank transactions of $1 million and more. In addition to the spot rates of each of those currencies, the forward rates are provided for the British pound, the Canadian dollar, the French franc, the Japanese yen, the Swiss franc, and the West German mark.

The cross rate is an exchange rate computed from two other exchange rates.

A final important definition for the spot market is the **cross rate,** which is an exchange rate computed from two other rates. Since most foreign currency transactions are denominated in terms of U.S. dollars, it is common to see two nondollar currencies related to each other in the cross rate. To simplify this discussion, we will use the European quotes of the Swiss franc and West German mark and figure the cross rate with the Swiss franc as the quoted currency and the West German mark as the base currency. In Table 8.1 the spot rates for West German marks (DM) and Swiss (SwF) francs on Thursday, June 6, 1988, were:

DM 1.7145 per U.S. dollar and SwF 1.4285 per U.S. dollar.

TABLE 8.1

THE *WALL STREET JOURNAL'S* LISTING OF DAILY FOREIGN EXCHANGE RATES

FOREIGN EXCHANGE

Monday, June 6, 1988

The New York foreign exchange selling rates below apply to trading among banks in amounts of $1 million and more, as quoted at 3 p.m. Eastern time by Bankers Trust Co. Retail transactions provide fewer units of foreign currency per dollar.

	U.S. $ equiv.		Currency per U.S. $	
Country	Mon.	Fri.	Mon.	Fri.
Argentina (Austral)	.1350	.1429	7.405	7.00
Australia (Dollar)	.7924	.8075	1.2620	1.2384
Austria (Schilling)	.08271	.08244	12.09	12.13
Bahrain (Dinar)	2.6525	2.6525	.377	.377
Belgium (Franc)				
Commercial rate	.02782	.02774	35.95	36.05
Financial rate	.02769	.02762	36.11	36.21
Brazil (Cruzado)	.005960	.006006	167.79	166.50
Britain (Pound)	1.8005	1.7993	.5540	.5558
30-Day Forward	1.7995	1.7986	.5557	.5560
90-Day Forward	1.7958	1.7952	.5569	.5570
180-Day Forward	1.7894	1.7891	.5588	.5589
Canada (Dollar)	.8119	.8118	1.2317	1.2318
30-Day Forward	.8109	.81077	1.2332	1.2335
90-Day Forward	.8085	.8083	1.2369	1.2372
180-Day Forward	.8053	.8052	1.2417	1.2419
Chile (Official rate)	.004057	.004060	246.47	246.31
China (Yuan)	.2687	.2687	3.7220	3.7220
Colombia (Peso)	.003404	.003422	293.79	292.19
Denmark (Krone)	.1528	.1523	6.5460	6.5655
Ecuador (Sucre)				
Official rate	.004008	.004008	249.50	249.50
Floating rate	.002099	.002099	476.50	476.50
Finland (Markka)	.2446	.2437	4.0890	4.1040
France (Franc)	.1726	.1715	5.7935	5.8300
30-Day Forward	.1726	.1716	5.7915	5.8290
90-Day Forward	.1726	.1716	5.7905	5.8275
180-Day Forward	.1728	.1717	5.7860	5.8240
Greece (Drachma)	.007262	.007257	137.70	137.80
Hong Kong (Dollar)	.1279	.1280	7.8170	7.8150
India (Rupee)	.07342	.07348	13.62	13.61
Indonesia (Rupiah)	.0005970	.0005977	1675.00	1673.00
Ireland (Punt)	1.5555	1.5510	.6429	.6447
Israel (Shekel)	.6309	.6353	1.5850	1.574
Italy (Lira)	.0007849	.0007794	1274.00	1283.00
Japan (Yen)	.007948	.007941	125.81	125.93
30-Day Forward	.007972	.007966	125.43	125.54
90-Day Forward	.008019	.008014	124.70	124.78
180-Day Forward	.008087	.008082	123.65	123.73
Jordan (Dinar)	2.7739	2.7778	.3605	.3600
Kuwait (Dinar)	3.6284	3.6443	.2756	.2744
Lebanon (Pound)	.002755	.002699	363.00	370.50
Malaysia (Ringgit)	.3871	.3871	2.5833	2.5830
Malta (Lira)	3.0994	3.0994	.3226	.3226
Mexico (Peso)				
Floating rate	.0004405	.0004405	2270.00	2270.00
Netherland(Guilder)	.5196	.5163	1.9245	1.9370
New Zealand (Dollar)	.6926	.7000	1.4438	1.4286
Norway (Krone)	.1593	.1589	6.2780	6.2950
Pakistan (Rupee)	.05621	.05653	17.79	17.69
Peru (Inti)	.03030	.03030	33.00	33.00
Philippines (Peso)	.04757	.04758	21.02	21.015
Portugal (Escudo)	.007117	.007092	140.50	141.00
Saudi Arabia (Riyal)	.2663	.2666	3.7555	3.7505
Singapore (Dollar)	.4947	.4948	2.0215	2.0210
South Africa (Rand)				
Commercial rate	.4477	.4476	2.2336	2.2341
Financial rate	.3378	.3389	2.9600	2.9500
South Korea (Won)	.001364	.001365	733.20	732.80
Spain (Peseta)	.008807	.008778	113.55	113.92
Sweden (Krona)	.1664	.1661	6.0100	6.0210
Switzerland (Franc)	.7000	.6949	1.4285	1.4390
30-Day Forward	.7029	.6978	1.4226	1.4330
90-Day Forward	.7088	.7036	1.4109	1.4212
180-Day Forward	.7175	.7124	1.3938	1.4038
Taiwan (Dollar)	.03500	.03500	28.57	28.57
Thailand (Baht)	.03968	.03976	25.20	25.15
Turkey (Lira)	.0007520	.000761	1329.81	1313.72
United Arab(Dirham)	.2723	.2723	3.671	3.671
Uruguay (New Peso)				
Financial	.002941	.002950	340.00	339.00
Venezuela (Bolivar)				
Official rate	.1333	.1333	7.50	7.50
Floating rate	.03183	.03367	31.42	29.70
W. Germany (Mark)	.5833	.5794	1.7145	1.7260
30-Day Forward	.5853	.5814	1.7086	1.7200
90-Day Forward	.5893	.5854	1.6970	1.7082
180-Day Forward	.5950	.5912	1.6807	1.6915
SDR	1.35932	1.35860	0.735664	0.736053
ECU	1.20535	1.20289	....	....

Special Drawing Rights are based on exchange rates for the U.S., West German, British, French and Japanese currencies. Source: International Monetary Fund.

ECU is based on a basket of community currencies. Source: European Community Commission.

z-Not quoted.

Source: *Wall Street Journal*, June 7, 1988, p. 60. Reprinted by permission of *Wall Street Journal*,

The cross rate would be:

$$\frac{\text{SwF } 1.4285}{\text{DM } 1.7145} = \text{SwF } .833 \text{ per DM}$$

which means that one West German mark equals 0.833 Swiss francs. It is common to see the cross rate quoted as 83.3. West German and Swiss managers keep track of the cross rate, since they trade extensively with each other and any material shifts in the cross rate could signal a change in prices of goods. For example, assume that a German exporter sold a product costing DM 100 to a Swiss importer for SwF 83.3 as shown in the cross rate illustration. If the cross rate were to move to SwF .850 per DM, the German exporter and Swiss importer would have to make some interesting decisions. If the exporter kept the price to the importer at DM 100, the importer would now have to come up with SwF 85 to buy the product. The exporter could lower the price to DM 98.0 so that the product would still cost SwF 83.3 or keep the price the same. If the exporter decided to keep the price at DM 100, the Swiss importer would have two options: (1) increase prices to reflect the higher cost of the import and thus keep profit margins the same as before, or (2) keep prices the same and end up with a smaller profit margin due to the higher cost of the product. If the product were especially price-sensitive, the exporter and importer would not want to see the price rise in Switzerland.

The Forward Market

The forward spread is the difference between the spot and forward exchange rates.

As defined at the beginning of the chapter, the forward rate is the rate quoted by foreign exchange traders for the purchase or sale of foreign exchange in the future. As was noted in Table 8.1, there is a difference between the spot rate and the forward rate known as the **spread in the forward market.** The difference between the spot and forward rate is explained in the following chapter, but now we want to determine the amount of the spread and consider two perspectives on the spread: as points and as a percentage premium or discount.

In a discount the forward rate is less than the spot rate.

In the illustration below we compute the points for 90-day contracts for the Canadian dollar and the Swiss franc quoted in U.S. terms:

	Canadian dollars	Swiss francs
Spot	\$0.8119	\$0.7000
90-day forward	0.8085	0.7088
Points	−34	+88

A premium occurs when the forward rate exceeds the spot rate.

The spread in Canadian dollars is 34 points; because the forward rate is less than the spot rate, the Canadian dollar is at a **discount** in the 90-day forward market. The spread in Swiss francs is 88 points, and since the forward rate is greater than the spot rate, the Swiss franc is at a **premium** in the forward market.

The premium or discount can also be quoted in terms of annualized percent. The formula to determine the percentage follows:

$$\text{Premium (discount)} = \frac{F_0 - S_0}{S_0} \times \frac{12}{N} \times 100,$$

where F_0 is the forward rate on the day the contract is entered into, S_0 is the spot rate on that day, N is the number of months forward, and 100 is used to convert the decimal to percent amounts (e.g., 0.05 × 100 = 5%).

Using Canadian dollars,

$$\text{Discount} = \frac{0.8085 - 0.8119}{0.8119} \times \frac{12}{3} \times 100 = -1.6751\%,$$

which means that the Canadian dollar is selling at a discount of 1.6751 percent under the spot rate. Using Swiss francs,

$$\text{Premium} = \frac{0.7088 - 0.7000}{0.7000} \times \frac{12}{3} \times 100 = 5.0286\%,$$

or the Swiss franc is selling at a 5.0286 percent premium over the U.S. dollar.

As shown in Table 8.1, there is no forward market for the Brazilian cruzado, although the opening case mentioned that an importer could get a forward contract from the Banco do Brasil. This discrepancy occurs because a forward contract in cruzados generally is not available in the interbank market. There is an excess of cruzados, and it would be practically impossible for the interbank market to balance off its purchases of cruzado contracts with its sales of cruzado contracts. The market is too thin (i.e., does not have enough transactions) to warrant the forward market in the interbank market.

HOW THE FOREIGN EXCHANGE MARKET WORKS

Basic Spot and Forward Markets

The determinants of exchange rates will be discussed in Chapter 9, but now we need to see how foreign exchange is traded. In addition to being the most important trading currency in the international monetary system, the dollar is also the major reserve asset held by most countries.

A 1986 survey conducted by the Bank of England, the Federal Reserve Bank of New York, and the Bank of Japan, determined that the daily foreign exchange volume conducted in London was \$90 billion, compared with \$50 billion in New York and \$48 billion in Tokyo. The London market is pivotal because of its position in the trading hours with the rest of the world and its greater transaction opportunities. London trading increased to \$90 billion daily in 1986 from \$49 billion daily in 1984 and \$25 billion daily in 1979. It is estimated that one-fourth of the world trading volume occurs in London. The largest volume of transactions in London involves sterling and U.S. dollars (30 percent), followed by West German mark-dollar trades (28 percent).

Daily foreign exchange trading in the United States increased from \$26 billion in 1983 to \$50 billion in 1986. The most actively traded currencies in order of importance were the West German mark, Japanese yen, British pound, Swiss franc, and Canadian dollar.[2]

Brokers are specialists who facilitate transactions in the interbank market.

A swap is an exchange of currencies in the spot market with the agreement to reverse the transaction in the future.

The majority of the foreign exchange transactions are carried out by the commercial banks, with the rest conducted by foreign exchange brokers. **Brokers** are specialists who facilitate transactions between banks rather than have the banks work directly with each other. In addition, over 60 percent of all foreign exchange trading is conducted in the spot market, primarily the interbank market. For transactions not carried out in the spot market, 33 percent were in **foreign currency swaps**, and only 4 percent were in the forward and futures markets, according to a study conducted by the New York Federal Reserve Bank in 1983.

International transactions. The foreign exchange market is based on the economic law of supply and demand. Sometimes governments intervene to control the flow of currency; however, the central action in the foreign exchange market revolves around the commercial banks in the major money centers of the world.

> *The world's communication networks are now so good, and so many countries have fairly unrestricted markets that we can talk of a single world market. It starts in a small way in New Zealand around 9:00 A.M. New Zealand time, just in time to catch the tail end of the previous night's New York market. Two or three hours later, Tokyo opens, followed an hour later by Hong Kong and Manila and then half an hour later by Singapore. By now, with the Far East market in full swing, the focus moves to the Near and Middle East. Bombay opens two hours after Singapore, followed after an hour and a half by Abu Dhabi, with Jeddah an hour behind, and Athens and Beirut an hour behind still. By this stage trading in the Far and Middle East is usually thin and perhaps nervous as dealers wait to see how Europe will trade. Paris and Frankfurt open an hour ahead of London, and by this time Tokyo is starting to close down, so the European market can judge how the Japanese market has been trading by the way they deal to close out positions. By lunch-time in London, New York is starting to open up, and as Europe closes down, so positions can be passed westward. During the afternoon in New York, trading tends to be quiet. The problem is that there is nowhere to pass a position to. The San Francisco market, three hours behind, is effectively a satellite of the New York market. Very small positions can be passed on to New Zealand banks, but the market there is extremely limited.*[3]

Most foreign currency transactions are handled by traders in the commercial banks.

Most transactions are handled in the interbank market. Even in interbank dealings, the majority of the transactions are done by traders in the home offices of the major money center banks. Typically these traders are responsible for a single currency, and they end up dealing with the traders of that currency worldwide. Each money center bank, such as Chase Manhattan or Manufacturers Hanover Trust, has a trading room where the currency traders are housed, allowing them contact with each other as well as with the major traders worldwide.

Sometimes the bankers go through brokers instead of working directly with traders of other banks. A few major brokers and several minor ones in the United States deal in foreign exchange transactions. These brokers typically try to link traders of different banks in foreign exchange transactions. Brokers sometimes work the corporate market as well, but that is rare in comparison with their major area of speciality.

Even though the money center banks trade most of the foreign exchange in the world, companies that are not located in these money centers still can go through regional or local banks for foreign currency transactions. But their banks generally work through a money center bank as demonstrated in Fig. 8.1.

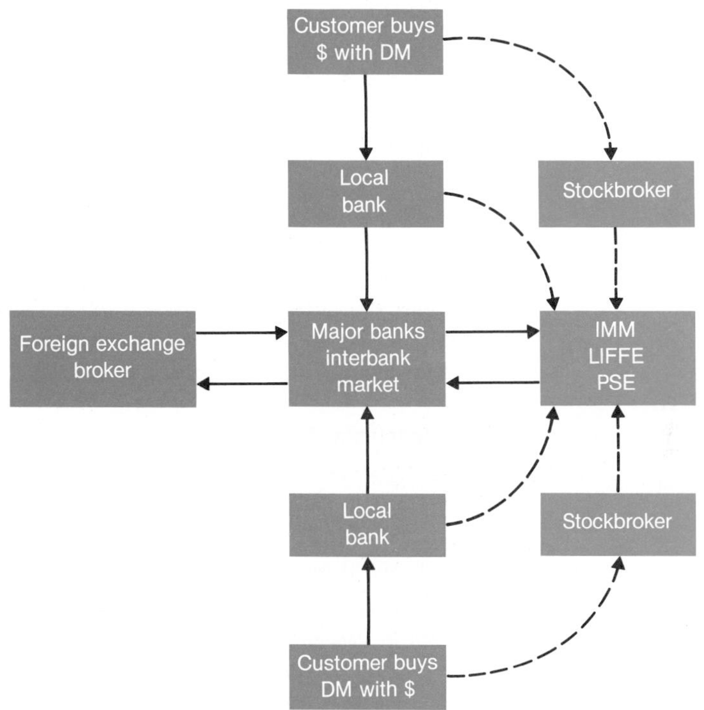

Figure 8.1
Structure of Foreign Exchange Markets

Note: As will be described below, the International Money Market (IMM) Chicago trades foreign exchange futures and DM futures options, the London International Financial Futures Exchange (LIFFE) trades foreign exchange futures, and the Philadelphia Stock Exchange (PSE) trades foreign currency options.

Source: K. Alec Chrystal, "A Guide to Foreign Exchange Markets," *Bulletin* (Federal Reserve Bank of St. Louis, March 1984), p. 9.

Specialized Markets

Certain specialized institutions and markets deal in futures and options and offer some variety from the banking sector: the International Monetary Market (IMM) in Chicago; the London International Financial Futures Exchange (LIFFE); and the Philadelphia Stock Exchange (PSE). As noted in Fig. 8.1, a customer operates in these three markets through a broker, who then has access to the major money markets.

The IMM deals primarily in the futures contracts, which are contracts for forward delivery of currencies for specific amounts with a specific maturity date.

The International Monetary Market. The **International Monetary Market (IMM)** was opened in 1972 by the Chicago Mercantile Exchange to deal primarily in futures contracts for the British pound, the Canadian dollar, the West German mark, the Swiss franc, and the Japanese yen. These contracts are for specific amounts and have a specific maturity date. The "Futures Prices" section of the *Wall Street Journal* provides quotes of the contracts each day.

Although the contracts have a fixed maturity date, there is a ready market for the contracts at the IMM. Brokers make deals on the trading floor rather than over the telephone as is the case with the forward markets for banks. Futures contracts at the IMM also tend to be small relative to the transactions normally encountered in the interbank market. The IMM also limits how much the futures prices can vary from one day to the next, whereas there are no such restrictions in the banking market. Finally, the IMM requires a margin or deposit equal to about 4 percent of the contract to be made by the purchaser of a contract.

The LIFFE deals in futures transactions similar to the IMM.

The London International Financial Futures Exchange. The **London International Financial Futures Exchange (LIFFE),** which opened in September 1982, deals in futures contracts in British pounds, West German marks, Swiss francs, and Japanese yen in fixed contract sizes. The market also deals in Eurodollars and should provide an alternative to the interbank market in Europe for foreign exchange risk protection.

An option is the right to buy or sell foreign exchange within a specific period or at a specific date.

The Philadelphia Stock Exchange. The **Philadelphia Stock Exchange (PSE)** represents a fairly recent concept in foreign exchange trading, that of **options.** In the examples given earlier, there was a contract to buy or sell foreign exchange between a foreign exchange trader or broker and the customer. An option, however,

> *is a contract specifying the right to buy or sell—in this case foreign exchange —within a specific period (American option) or at a specific date (European option).... The buyer of an option has the right to undertake the contract specified but may choose not to do so if it turns out to be unprofitable. The seller of the option must fulfill the contract if the buyer desires.*[4]

The PSE initiated a foreign exchange options market in the United States for several currencies.

The PSE offers foreign exchange options for the Australian dollar, the British pound, the Canadian dollar, the West German mark, the French franc, the Japanese yen, the Swiss franc, and the European Currency Unit (a basket of currencies involving most of the members of the European Community). Since the PSE opened the options market, other bankers entered it, and many bankers feel that the options market in foreign exchange could revolutionize foreign exchange risk protection if the transactions costs decrease.

CONVERTIBILITY

Convertible currency allows residents and nonresidents of a country to exchange that country's currency for other currencies.

The difficulty involved in exchanging one currency for others is a measure of its **convertibility.** The more difficult it is to exchange French francs for U.S. dollars, West German marks, or Japanese yen, the more inconvertible French francs become in relation to these other currencies.

Convertibility has essentially two parts. Most countries today have nonresident, (or external), convertibility. For example, all nonresidents with deposits in French banks may at any time exchange all of their franc deposits for the currency of any other country. In other words, a U.S. exporter to France can be paid in francs and be assured that those francs can be converted to dollars or some other currency. Not all countries permit nonresident conversion, as was noted in the case of Brazil. Thus export sales to Brazil denominated in cruzados create export earnings that cannot be spent easily except in Brazil. Even when an exporter or other nonresident has foreign bank balances denominated in the native currency, there may be problems in the absence of nonresident convertibility.

In 1982, many foreigners with dollar deposits in Mexico had those deposits converted into pesos by the Mexican government because of an acute shortage of foreign exchange. In that case, not even nonresidents could enjoy convertibility status. In Western Europe the trend toward convertibility was accelerated in 1958 when fourteen countries agreed to establish external convertibility for their currencies meaning that nonresidents of these countries as well as all exporters from these countries were free to use the proceeds of their overseas sales anywhere in the world.

A hard currency is a currency that is usually fully convertible and strong or relatively stable in comparison with other currencies.

Full convertibility means that both residents and nonresidents can purchase unlimited amounts of any foreign currency. Currently, thirty countries are free from payments restrictions, defined as basically "official actions directly affecting the availability or cost of exchange, or involving undue delay."[5] **Hard currencies** are usually fully convertible. They are also relatively stable in value or tend to be rather strong in comparison with other currencies. They are desirable assets to hold.

A black market is a free market for a currency that operates outside of the control of the government.

In the absence of full convertibility, there is often a **black market,** which is essentially a *parallel market* with the official market and is usually outside of the sanction and control of the government. However, not all parallel markets are black markets: For example, Venezuela has an official exchange rate and a floating rate parallel to the official rate; both are sanctioned by the government but the rates are very different, as noted in Table 8.1.

EXCHANGE RESTRICTIONS

Governments impose various exchange restrictions to control their limited supplies of foreign exchange. Some of the devices they use are import licensing, multiple exchange rates, import deposit requirements, and quantity controls.

Licensing

Licensing occurs when the government requires that all foreign exchange transactions be regulated and controlled by it through application.

The exchange rate is usually fixed by governmental **licenses,** which require all recipients, exporters, and others who receive foreign exchange to sell it to the central bank at the official buying rate. The central bank or some other agency then rations the currency it acquires by selling it at fixed rates to those needing to make payment abroad for goods considered essential. The test of essentiality is made by the government or some agency acting for the government, such as the central bank. This system allows for the purchase of foreign exchange only if the importer has obtained a license for the importation of the goods in question. For example, purchases of raw materials and basic foodstuffs would likely be regarded as essential; thus foreign exchange would be sold to importers of these commodities.

In New Zealand, for example, imports are controlled through an Import Licensing Schedule. However, only about 18 percent of New Zealand's imports are affected by the schedule. Generally, consumer goods and some manufacturing goods are covered by the schedule with the intent of encouraging import competition.[6]

Multiple Exchange Rates

A multiple exchange rate is where a government sets different exchange rates for different transactions.

Another way to conserve foreign exchange is to allow more than one rate of exchange: This is known as a **multiple exchange rate system.** For example, as of June 6, 1988, there were two exchange markets for the Venezuelan currency, the Bolivar. In the official market the Central Bank of Venezuela maintained a selling rate of Bs 7.50 per U.S. dollar. Note that some official transactions are carried out at the official rate, whereas the remaining transactions take place at the free market rate, which fluctuates in accordance with supply and demand. The exchange rate in the free market, however, is subject to occasional Central Bank intervention. On June 6, 1988, the free market selling rate was Bs 31.42 per U.S. dollar.

If a Venezuelan importer wished to purchase a piece of U.S.-made machinery valued at $1000, the Central Bank would charge the importer Bs 7500 for the funds. If, on the other hand, the importer was importing nonessential goods, the cost to the importer would be Bs 31,420, an additional cost of Bs 23,920 over the official rate. Interestingly, multiple exchange rate arrangements have been rather common. In the 1986 IMF survey on exchange rate arrangements, twenty-eight countries used more than one exchange rate for imports, twenty-five used more than one rate for exports, and thirty-three used a different rate for exports and imports.

Import Deposit Requirement

An import deposit requirement takes place when the government requires a deposit prior to the release of foreign exchange.

Advance import deposits are another form of foreign exchange control. For example, Greece has used import deposits on occasion. In 1985, the government put into effect a temporary six-month advance deposit policy requiring importers to deposit with intermediary banks an amount equal to either 40 percent or 80 percent of the value of certain categories of goods. The deposits were redeposited with the Bank of Greece and could not be redeemed before the end of a six-month period.[7] According to the 1986 IMF report on exchange arrangements, nineteen IMF-member countries (all developing countries with the exceptions of Greece and Israel) used advance import deposits of one form or another.

Quantity Controls

In quantity controls, the government limits the amount of foreign exchange that can be used in a specific transaction.

Governments may also limit the amount of exchange for specific purposes. The types of control, called **quantity controls,** are often used in conjunction with tourism. In Chile, for example, the limit for Chilean tourists going abroad is the equivalent of U.S. $500 per month for travel to Latin American and Caribbean countries and U.S. $1500 a month to other countries. For travel by land to adjacent countries, 20 percent of the allowance is provided in the form of foreign exchange, and the rest is provided in money orders.[8]

THE USES OF THE FOREIGN EXCHANGE MARKET

The major uses of foreign exchange are: commercial transactions, making the market, arbitrage, and risk bearing/risk reduction.

So far, we have defined the key terms and concepts involved in foreign exchange. Now we will discuss the four major uses of foreign exchange: commercial transactions, making the market, arbitrage, and risk bearing or risk reduction.[9]

Banks collect foreign exchange, lend foreign exchange, and buy and sell foreign exchange.

The major facilitators of these transactions, as mentioned earlier in the chapter, are the international departments of the commercial banks, which perform three essential financial functions: (1) collections, (2) lending, and (3) the buying and selling of foreign exchange. The collection function involves the bank in serving as a vehicle for making payments between its own resident customers and foreign nationals.

The purchase and sale of foreign exchange are undertaken by a commercial bank for many purposes. For instance, travelers going abroad or returning from a foreign country will want to purchase or sell foreign currency. Residents of one country wishing to invest abroad also would need to purchase foreign currency from a commercial bank.

Suppose that a Canadian exporter is to receive payment from a U.S. importer in U.S. dollars, and the exporter wishes to use the funds to make payment for raw materials purchased in Norway. The bank in this case simultaneously serves as a collector and acts as a dealer in foreign exchange.

Commercial Transactions

Our focus in this book is on commercial transactions—that is, those that involve the buying and selling of foreign exchange to facilitate the trade of goods and services. These transactions are assumed to take place in the spot market. The forward market is more valuable in terms of risk bearing, which will be discussed under "Risk."

Making the Market

"Making the market," another important use of foreign exchange, refers to transactions between brokers and traders at banks or directly between the traders at different banks. Normally these transactions are undertaken to provide sufficient foreign exchange balances for the banks to conduct their normal commercial transactions as well as to bear risk in the foreign exchange market.

Arbitrage

Arbitrage is the buying and selling of foreign exchange at a profit due to price discrepancies.

Arbitrage is the process of buying and selling foreign exchange at a profit due to price discrepancies. **Triangular arbitrage** involves, for example, selling U.S. dollars for Swiss francs, Swiss francs for West German marks, and West German marks for U.S. dollars, the goal being to end up with more dollars at the end of the process. For example, assume that a trader converts $100 into SwF 150 (Swiss francs) when the exchange rate is SwF 1.5 = $1.00. The trader then converts the francs into DM 225 (West German marks) at an exchange rate of DM 1.5 = SwF 1.00, and finally converts the marks into $125 at an exchange rate of DM 1.8 = $1.00. Thus arbitrage yields $125 from the initial sale of $100.

The process of arbitrage is very difficult because of today's sophisticated information systems in bank trading rooms. Sometimes triangular arbitrage can occur when dealing with foreign exchange traders in different countries.

Interest arbitrage involves investing in interest-bearing instruments in foreign exchange and earning a profit due to interest rate and exchange rate differentials.

Interest arbitrage involves investing in debt instruments in different countries. For example, a trader could take $1000 and invest it in the United States for 90 days, or take the $1000, convert it into British pounds, invest the money in Great Britain for 90 days, and then convert the pounds back into dollars. The investor would pick the highest-yielding alternative at the end of 90 days.

Risk

Speculators take positions in foreign exchange with the major objective of earning a profit.

Foreign exchange transactions can be sought in order to speculate for profit or to protect against risk. Both types of transactions are related to risk but in different ways. **Speculators** are important actors in the foreign exchange market because they spot trends and try to take advantage of them. They can become an important source of the supply of and demand for a currency. Speculation is the taking of a position in a foreign currency for a profit. In speculation, for example, an investor would hold West German marks in anticipation of the strengthening of the mark against other currencies. If the mark strengthens, the investor earns a profit; if the mark weakens, the investor incurs a loss.

On the side of protection against risk are foreign exchange transactions designed to **hedge** against a potential loss due to an exchange rate change. Hedges will be discussed in more detail in Chapter 20, which deals with the international finance function.

THE DETERMINATION OF EXCHANGE RATES—A PREVIEW

It is impossible to grasp foreign exchange without stepping back from the detail and studying the international monetary system in which exchange rates function. Chapter 9 examines how exchange rates obtain and maintain their values. The roles of international institutions, national institutions, and other important factors will be viewed from the standpoint of the law of supply and demand and the underlying forces that affect exchange rates. For example, why is the Brazilian cruzado constantly weakening against the dollar? Do Brazil's high inflation and large foreign debt have an effect? Next we will learn how to predict the direction, magnitude, and timing of an exchange rate change and examine what the fluctuating U.S. dollar has done to international firms in recent years.

SUMMARY

- A major distinction between domestic and international payments for goods and services is that more than one currency is used for international transactions.
- An exchange rate is the value of one currency in terms of another. A spot exchange rate is the rate quoted for current transactions, whereas the forward rate is a rate quoted by a foreign exchange trader for a contract to receive or deliver foreign currency in the future.
- The difference between the spot and forward rates at the time of a contract is the forward spread. The foreign currency is selling at a discount if the spread is negative and at a premium if the spread is positive.
- Most foreign exchange transactions take place through the traders of commercial banks, with the majority of the transactions occurring in the spot market rather than the forward market. Also most of the foreign exchange transactions are interbank transactions rather than between banks and nonbanking institutions.
- The International Monetary Market (IMM) is a specialized market that deals in futures contracts in the British pound, the Canadian dollar, the West German mark, the Swiss franc, the Japanese yen, the Mexican peso, the French franc, and the Dutch guilder. Other specialized markets include the London International Financial Futures Exchange (LIFFE) and the Philadelphia Stock Exchange (PSE).
- A convertible currency can be freely traded for other currencies. Some countries' currencies are partially convertible in that residents are not allowed to convert to other currencies but nonresidents are.

- Some governments control access to their currencies through import licensing, multiple exchange rates, import deposit requirements, and quantity controls.
- The four major uses of foreign exchange are: commercial transactions, making the market, arbitrage, and risk bearing or risk reduction.

CASE:
THE MEXICAN PESO[10]

On August 31, 1976, the Mexican peso was cut loose from its exchange rate of 12.5 pesos to the dollar, which was established in 1955. From 1955 to 1976 the exchange rate had been maintained artificially through a variety of mechanisms. Import controls and market intervention were used extensively to allow the peso to appear stabler than it was, thereby frustrating firms operating in Mexico. Many companies established manufacturing operations in Mexico only to find that the government eventually would phase out their ability to import needed raw materials and components.

During the 1970s pressure began to build for a change in the value of the currency. Tourism, a major source of foreign exchange, began to taper off because of rising prices resulting directly from general inflation in the economy.

Mexico began importing more than it was exporting, which resulted in an outflow of pesos to buy the excess imports. Exporters to Mexico did not want to hold onto pesos, preferring instead to convert them into dollars. To give so many dollars in order to buy back the pesos would have depleted Mexico's holdings of dollar reserves severely if Mexican authorities used these existing reserves to make the conversion. Instead Mexico chose to maintain its level of reserves by increased short-term external borrowing of dollars which would eventually result in principal and interest payments that could rob Mexico of what little foreign exchange it could gather.

Because of these and other pressures, officials agreed to devalue the peso on August 31, 1976, to 20.5 pesos to the dollar in the hope that this devaluation would absorb some of the excess supply of pesos in the market and allow the economy to stabilize. Even though devaluation was the initial solution to the problem, the government also considered establishing more elaborate foreign exchange controls so that spot transactions could be allocated according to governmental priorities. Finally, Mexico decided on devaluation rather than establish an elaborate bureaucracy to administer the foreign exchange controls.

Unfortunately, the solution to the problem was short-lived. From 1976 to mid-1981 the peso held its post-devaluation level, but inflation and other forces that had created the problems leading up to the 1976 devaluation reemerged. The country began to develop a devaluation psychosis, imports again exceeded exports, tourism fell steadily, foreign credit became tight and expensive, and world oil prices and demand softened considerably. The Central Bank of Mexico steadfastly maintained that a relatively modest devaluation of 15–20 percent would correct the imbalances in the economy, and officials appeared to be in no hurry to make any changes.

Meanwhile, the situation worsened. In the absence of capital controls, wealthy Mexicans spent their money abroad on consumer durables and investments that would shelter them against another possible devaluation. With the government continuing to exude confidence up to the last hour, a devaluation of over 40 percent was announced on February 17, 1982, bringing the new rate to 38.50 pesos to the dollar. At the same time the government announced that it hoped to keep the exchange rate to a level of 38–43 pesos during the rest of the year. In an interesting move, a subsequent devaluation was announced on February 26, 1982, to 47.25 pesos, rendering obsolete the prediction of slightly a week earlier.

The two devaluations were not successful. In August 1982, after another devaluation, the government decided to establish two exchange rates: a preferential rate and a free market rate. The official rate was only 49 pesos, unfortunately, and the free market rate shot up to 105 pesos.

In September 1982, the government nationalized all private banks and instituted currency controls. Among the currency controls were the following:

1. Only the Banco de Mexico can import or export foreign exchange.
2. Foreign currency is not legal tender in Mexico and all obligations denominated in foreign currency and payable in Mexico must be paid in pesos at the rate determined by the Banco de Mexico.
3. All foreign currency is to be exchanged at the Banco de Mexico at rates indicated by the Bank.
4. The Banco de Mexico will set rules for maximum amounts to be sold to individuals for foreign travel. Foreign visitors must declare and convert to pesos all foreign currency when entering Mexico and repurchase foreign currency when they leave, all at ordinary exchange rates.

In addition to these rules, the government established a fixed priority list for determining who will get foreign exchange:

1. Public sector obligations.
2. Parastatal companies in the order determined by the Finance Ministry.
3. Mexican Government dues and quotas in international organizations and expenses for Mexico's diplomatic corps.

4. Obligations of credit institutions, including insurance and finance companies.
5. Imports of high-priority basic food items, intermediate goods, and basic capital goods.
6. Imports of capital and intermediate goods to maintain the functioning of existing industrial facilities.
7. Imports of equipment, intermediate products, and capital goods for plant expansions.
8. Financial obligations of the private sector contracted before September 1, 1982.
9. Needs of entities in the border and free-trade zones.
10. Payment of licensing and royalty fees and other commitments of companies with foreign ownership (presumably dividends, but not specifically mentioned).
11. Travel needs for business or health reasons.
12. Travel needs for tourism.

A preferential rate of 50 pesos was established for imports of basic foods and capital goods needed to produce food, intermediate products and capital goods needed to keep industry functioning, and capital goods for industrial expansion.

Importers faced obstacles in getting foreign exchange, even when they were high enough on the priority list to be eligible for foreign exchange. However, the controls did recognize the contribution of exports to the generation of foreign exchange. For materials imported and incorporated in export products the preferential rate could be used even if such materials were not on the preferential list if the exported product generated more foreign exchange than the cost of the import.

QUESTIONS

1. Assume that you manage the Mexican subsidiary of a U.S.-based company that has set up its operation to manufacture products that will supply the Mexican market. Currently, you are importing from the United States approximately 50 percent of the total cost of production. Each month you are required to travel to corporate headquarters in East Rutherford, New Jersey, and you are about to leave for your September 25, 1982, meeting with top management. Briefly outline what you will tell them about the implications of the foreign exchange controls on your operations, and give them some recommendations on what you think they can do to get by. One of the problems that you might want to address is the nature of the competition. With all of these exchange rate changes, you

need to do a little research on how the Mexican spot rate has changed in relation to some of the countries that are your most formidable competitors. In January 1982 you had considered exporting to Brazil, Argentina, West Germany, the United Kingdom, and Canada. However, the exchange rate was not very favorable for exporting at that time. Below are some exchange rates quoted in the *Wall Street Journal* in U.S. terms that might be helpful to you.

	1981	1982			
Currencies of	Dec 31	Mar 31	June 30	July 30	Sep 15
Mexico	0.0381	0.0220	0.0212	0.0205	0.0133
Canada	0.8435	0.8140	0.7725	0.7968	0.8117
Great Britain	1.9170	1.7850	1.7340	1.7410	1.7080
West Germany	0.4460	0.4145	0.4060	0.4072	0.3975
Brazil	0.00801	0.00687	0.0059	0.005587	0.0053
Argentina	0.000103	0.000089	0.000065	0.0000488	0.000025
90-day forward rate quoted on the IMM on the above dates for the Mexican peso	0.03574	0.01955	0.01838	0.01926	0.00815

2. Given the above information, what was the premium or discount that the peso was selling for in the forward market? Would you have expected the market to be very active in terms of the volume of transactions completed on the IMM? Be sure to explain your answer.

NOTES

1. Most of the information about the different controls is taken from the *Annual Report on Exchange Arrangements and Exchange Restrictions, 1986* (Washington, D.C.: International Monetary Fund), pp. 134–140. Other information is found in the following articles: Art Pine and Michael Kepp, "Brazil to Unveil Steps Curbing High Inflation," *The Wall Street Journal,* February 28, 1986, p. 29; "Brazil's Plano Cruzado II," *Business International Money Report,* June 22, 1987, p. 193.

2. John Marcom, Jr. and Charles W. Stevens, "Foreign Exchange Trade Volume Soars," *The Wall Street Journal,* August 20, 1986, p. 20.

3. Julian Walmsley, *The Foreign Exchange Handbook* (New York: John Wiley & Sons, 1983), pp. 7–8.

4. K. Alec Chrystal, "A Guide to Foreign Exchange Markets," *Bulletin* (St. Louis, Mo.: Federal Reserve Bank of St. Louis, March 1984), p. 12.

5. *Annual Report, op. cit.,* p. 573.

6. *Ibid.,* p. 380.

7. *Ibid.,* p. 250.

8. *Ibid.,* p. 164.

9. Chrystal, *op. cit.,* pp. 11–16.

10. Richard Moxon, "The Mexican Peso" in Robert S. Carlson, H. Lee Remmers, Christine R. Hekman, David K. Eiteman, and Arthur I. Stonehill, eds., *International Finance Cases and Stimulation,* (Reading, Mass.: Addison-Wesley Publishing Co., 1980), pp. 22–32; "Acme Do Mexico, S.A.," a case by Ingo Walter, Graduate School of Business, New York University, 1983; "Mexico Lists Priority Items for Imports," *Wall Street Journal,* September 20, 1982, p. 28; Lawrence Rout, "Mexican Firms May Be Able to Get Dollars . . . ," *Wall Street Journal,* September 16, 1982, p. 35; Lawrence Rout, "Mexico Names New Central Bank Head and Tightens Currency Rules Further," *Wall Street Journal,* September 3, 1982, p. 3; Lawrence Rout, "Mexicans Start Picking up the Pieces after Last Week's 30% Devaluation," *Wall Street Journal,* February 23, 1982; p. 30; Lawrence Rout, "Mexico Seeking to Hold Peso at 38 to Dollar," *Wall Street Journal,* February 22, 1982; Lawrence Rout, "Mexico Ponders the Peso's Problems," *Wall Street Journal,* January 28, 1982, p. 27; "Mexico Eases down the Peso," *Business Week,* August 31, 1981, p. 79.

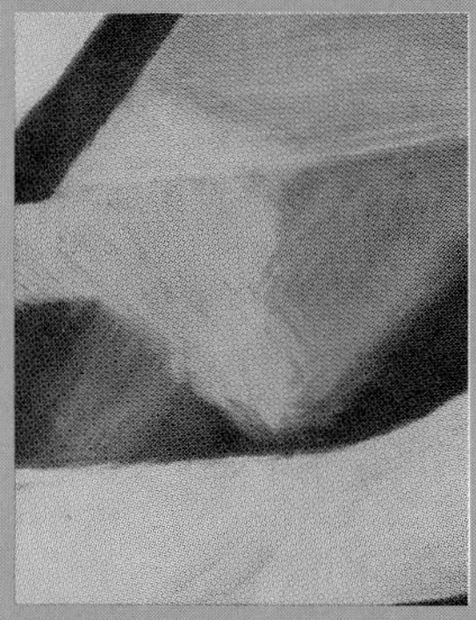

9

CHAPTER

THE DETERMINATION OF EXCHANGE RATES

A fair exchange brings no quarrel.
—Danish proverb

- To describe the International Monetary Fund and its role in the determination of exchange rates.
- To discuss the major exchange rate arrangements under which the currencies of the world function.
- To identify the major determinants of exchange rates in the spot and forward markets.
- To show how to forecast exchange rate movements.
- To explain how exchange rates influence business decisions.

CASE:
THE TINY BOLIVIAN PESO[1]

Bolivia, one of the poorest countries in Latin America, is situated high in the Andes. In the early 1980s its relative geographic elevation was exceeded only by its economic inflation. In 1983, prices increased by 329 percent and soared to 2700 percent in 1984 and 40,000 percent in 1985. Inflation was so high in January 1985 that it represented an increase of 116,000 percent on an annual basis, undoubtedly the highest in the world. Prices in Germany increased 10 billionfold during the 1920s, but Bolivia's experience outdistanced that of Argentina, Chile, Israel, and Brazil, the inflation leaders at one time or another in the 1970s and early 1980s.

Bolivia's political and economic situation has been highly unstable. The government in power in early 1985 was the 189th in 159 years of independence. President Siles Zuazo was elected President in 1980, but the military refused to let him take office for three years. By then the government was spending in huge deficit terms, increasing inflation through loose monetary and fiscal policy. Victor Paz Estenssoro became president late in 1985.

Bolivia's largest export is the coca paste used in making cocaine; its second largest export is tin, the price of which was very depressed on world markets during the early 1980s; and its third largest export is natural gas. However, in late 1985, its major customer for natural gas, Argentina, was having problems of its own and was not a good market for the product.

Skyrocketing inflation has affected Bolivia in a variety of ways. One way is the constant change in prices. In 1984, an egg costing 3000 pesos one week sold for 10,000 pesos the next. A candy bar sold for 35,000 pesos one day and 50,000 the next. Youngsters standing in the back of the line to see a movie paid 20,000 pesos for a ticket; those at the front of the line beat the price increase and had to pay only 4000 pesos. The number of pesos that it would take to buy three boxes of aspirin in 1985 would have bought a luxury Toyota in 1982. A 100-peso bill was of so little value that three of them were required to gain entrance to a public toilet in 1985.

Another problem in Bolivia is the difficulty in having banknotes be of sufficiently large denomination to enable transactions to be completed easily. Four people dining in a restaurant one evening late in 1984 gave the waiter a 48-inch high stack of bills weighing over two pounds to settle the bill, which came to 200,000 pesos, or approximately $22. Until the government began issuing 50,000-peso and 100,000-peso notes in November 1984, the largest banknote was the 10,000-peso note, worth about $1.10 on the official market and 30 cents on the black market. One bank customer brought in 700 million pesos in 50- and 100-peso notes that took six tellers until 1 A.M. to count, and the total was worth only $77,000.

It was also very difficult for wages to keep up with prices, which meant that workers' purchasing power could barely keep up in real terms. As a result, labor unrest in Bolivia is very high; strikes are common as workers struggle to keep up with the staggering cost of living. This is true of white collar professionals, such as doctors, as well as in traditional blue collar areas. People are often left temporarily without enough resources to purchase the basic necessities of life. Food shortages occur often, since the pricing mechanism has become ineffective in allocating scarce resources.

With inflation increasing so rapidly, credit cards are not used, and checks are not allowed. People want to receive cash immediately so that they can use it before its value declines. Because of the situation in Bolivia, a new occupation, the *changador*, has arisen: A *changador* carries stacks of banknotes to and from banks for companies making deposits or withdrawals. The absence of credit cards and checks coupled with the small denominations of banknotes makes such individuals indispensable.

Since Bolivia does not print money, it must import money from other countries, primarily West Germany and Great Britain. In 1984, money was the third largest import into Bolivia, after wheat and mining equipment.

As noted in an exchange rate forecast published by Manufacturers Hanover Trust in the fourth quarter of 1984:

> *Reflecting on Bolivia's worsening economic, political, and social problems, last summer, in a matter of weeks, the peso plunged from around 3,500/$ to 10,000/$ on the parallel market. In response, the government, on August 16, replaced the fixed exchange rate with a two-tiered system. The "official" rate of 2,000/$ was retained for essential imports, while a rate of 5,000/$ was established for non-essential imports. Most transactions, however, continue to be based on the parallel rate.*
>
> *Although the "official" peso was devalued by 60% last November and by another 75% in April (the cost of purchasing dollars in Bolivia has increased tenfold in less than a year), the devaluation pace has not kept up with the country's soaring inflation rate. Inflation, which is also being fueled by food shortages, uncontrolled government spending, and runaway money supply growth, was recorded at 1,041% in the year to June and is likely to reach 1,700–2,000% by year-end.*
>
> *Because authorities have not been able to stem the plunge of the "parallel" rate (currently at 15,100/$ or almost 8 times the official rate), Bolivia's soaring inflation and acute foreign exchange shortage will force additional devaluations and possibly a merging of the official rates. An exchange rate of 20,000/$ next year is not inconceivable.*

The interesting aspect of this forecast is that the key linkage is made between inflation and a change in the exchange rate. In addition, the key determinants of inflation—factors that should be monitored—are identified. The instability in the economy and foreign exchange markets also have resulted in multiple exchange rates and a black (parallel) market.

In late 1984 and early 1985, President Siles, who took office in early 1983, issued 1-million, 5-million, and 10-million peso notes, which rapidly became the most commonly used currency. By Spring 1985, inflation had gotten so far out of hand that it was running at 25,000 percent on an annual basis.

However, President Siles stepped down in 1985, and President Paz was appointed to the presidency following a deadlocked election. President Paz began to turn around the economy by lifting controls on prices, interest rates, imports, and exports. He also freed the official exchange rate and legalized the black market. By mid-1986, President Paz had reduced inflation to an annual rate of only 20 percent, one of the lowest in Latin America. The average for the year was 66 percent, with the last half of the year at only 13 percent. In 1987, Bolivia replaced the peso with the boliviano, worth 1 million pesos, and inflation stayed in the 15–20 percent range.

INTRODUCTION

As discussed in the preceding chapter, an exchange rate represents the number of units of one currency needed to acquire one unit of a currency of another country. The definition seems simple, but how is that exchange rate initially determined, and what causes it to change? This chapter takes a closer look at exchange rates and how they are determined. In addition, it focuses on some of the key management decisions that are influenced by exchange rate changes. Management must make decisions about the sourcing of raw materials and components, the location of manufacturing and assembly, and the location of final markets. Exchange rates can exert a strong influence on any of these decisions.

THE INTERNATIONAL MONETARY SYSTEM

The International Monetary Fund

The IMF was organized to promote exchange rate stability and facilitate the international flow of currencies.

The Depression, economic isolation, and trade war of the 1930s were followed by the global conflict of World War II. At the close of the war the major governments met to determine what international institutions were needed to bring relative economic stability and growth to the free world. As a result of the meetings, the **International Monetary Fund (IMF)** was organized.

The IMF was signed into existence in 1944 by 30 nations at Bretton Woods, New Hampshire; the agreement now covers 148 countries. IMF's basic objectives were to promote exchange stability, maintain orderly exchange arrangements, avoid competitive currency devaluation, establish a multilateral system of payments, eliminate exchange restrictions, and create standby reserves.

The **Bretton Woods** system operated under a principle of fixed exchange rates by which each member country established a par value for its

Par value is the benchmark value of a currency in terms of gold and the U.S. dollar.

currency based on gold and the U.S. dollar. This **par value** became a benchmark by which the country related its currency to the currencies of the rest of the world. Currencies were allowed to vary within 1 percent of par value (extended to 2.25 percent in December 1971), depending on supply and demand conditions. Further moves from par value and formal changes in par value (through devaluation or revaluation) were made with the IMF's approval.

Because of the strength of the U.S. dollar during the 1940s and 1950s, member currencies were denominated in terms of gold and dollars. By 1947 the United States held 70 percent of the international official gold reserves. Because of this, countries bought and sold dollars rather than gold. It was understood, although not formalized, that the United States would redeem gold for dollars, and the two became fixed with respect to each other. The dollar thus became the benchmark of the world trading currency.

Problems with liquidity. The problem with the system as envisioned by the IMF was that, in practice, rigidity replaced stability. Countries did not allow an exchange rate alteration to occur until a crisis developed. It became more and more evident that, as the world's reserve currency, the dollar was in a difficult position. As other countries' economies began to strengthen, it appeared that gold and internationally acceptable currencies (initially known as the **official reserves**) could not handle the reserve requirements of a country. The freer flow of goods and capital put increasing pressure on a country's reserve assets. Also, the growing accumulation of dollars outside of the United States during the 1960s threatened to wreck the stability of the system of fixed exchange rates. The problem was that governments became increasingly uneasy about the currency (i.e., dollar) component of their reserves. Thus they tended to want to replace these currencies with gold. As trade increased, the ratio of reserves to trade decreased sharply.[2]

Special Drawing Right (SDR) was:

- A unit of account developed by the IMF
- Designed to increase world liquidity.

To help increase international reserves during the period when the United States was expected to be able to reduce its balance of payments deficit, the IMF created the **Special Drawing Right (SDR).** The first SDR allocation was made in 1970. On January 1, 1981, the IMF began to use a simplified basket of five currencies for determining valuation; the U.S. dollar (42 percent); West German mark (19 percent); and the Japanese yen, French franc, and British pound sterling (13 percent each). These specific weights were chosen because they broadly reflected the relative importance of the currencies in international trade and payments, which in turn are based on the value of the export of goods and services by the countries issuing these currencies.

Currencies in the SDR included: U.S. dollar, West German mark, yen, French franc, pound sterling.

The SDR has become a unit of account (benchmark) for official IMF transactions.

The SDR has not taken over the role of gold or the dollar as a primary reserve asset. However, it has become a **unit of account.** This means simply that the SDR has become a benchmark or reference point for a variety of transactions. The IMF uses the SDR rather than a specific national currency in most of its official reports.

Evolution to floating exchange rates. As just mentioned, the IMF's initial years involved fixed exchange rates. Because the U.S. dollar was the cornerstone of the international monetary system, its value remained constant with respect to gold. Other countries could change the value of their currencies against gold and the dollar, but the value of the dollar remained fixed.

Partly because of the inflationary pressures that began to build in the United States in the mid-1960s, the traditional U.S. trade surplus began to shrink. Continued outflow of private and governmental long-term capital, coupled with the diminishing trade surplus, caused an increasing deficit in the basic balance. As it became apparent that 1971 would see the first U.S. **balance of trade deficit** in the twentieth century, it was clear something needed to be done.

Exchange flexibility was widened from 1 percent to 2.25 percent on either side of par value in 1971.

On August 15, 1971, President Nixon announced a new economic policy that included the suspension of exchanging gold for dollars and the institution of an import surcharge. These moves were an attempt to force the other industrial countries to the bargaining table in hopes of restructuring the world monetary order. The Smithsonian Agreement of December 1971 resulted in an 8 percent devaluation of the dollar, a revaluation of some other world currencies, a widening of exchange rate flexibility (from 1 to 2.25 percent on either side of par value), and a commitment on the part of all countries to reduce trade restrictions.

This restructuring of the international monetary system did not last. World currency markets remained unsteady during 1972, and the dollar was devalued again by 10 percent in early 1973. Major currencies began to float against each other instead of relying on the Smithsonian Agreement.

Because the Bretton Woods Agreement was based on the system of fixed exchange rates and par values, the IMF had to change its Articles of Agreement in order to permit floating exchange rates. The Jamaica Agreement of 1976 provided the amendment to the original Articles of Agreement that permitted greater flexibility in exchange rates. There was some concern that the world monetary system would collapse under the freedom of flexible exchange rates, so the agreement reiterated the importance of pursuing exchange stability.

Exchange Rate Arrangements

The IMF classifies exchange rate systems.

The Jamaica Agreement formalized the break from fixed exchange rates. As part of this move, the IMF permitted countries to select and maintain an exchange arrangement of their choice, as long as they properly communicated their arrangement to the IMF. Each year the IMF receives information from the member countries and classifies each country into one of three broad categories.

1. currencies that are pegged to a single currency or to a composite of currencies;

2. currencies whose exchange rates have displayed limited flexibility compared with either a single currency or group of currencies; and
3. currencies whose exchange rates are more flexible.[3]

Table 9.1 identifies the countries that fit in each category: Note that the countries in each category are subject to change each year. In 1983, for example, there were thirty-eight countries pegged to the U.S. dollar, compared with only thirty-one in 1985 and thirty-eight again by the end of 1987; there were only thirty-three countries in the more flexible category in 1983, compared with forty-six in 1987.

Currencies fix their values to another currency or composite of currencies.

Pegged rates. Countries that fit in this category **peg,** or fix, the value of their currency with zero fluctuation margins (in this case, of countries that peg to a single currency) or very narrow margins of 1 percent or less in the case of pegs to the SDR or other composite currency. The "other composite" category means that the country has selected a basket of currencies that is different from the SDR. An example of this is the Swedish krona:

> *In managing the exchange rate of the krona, the Sveriges Riksbank (the central bank) is guided by a trade-weighted index based on a basket of 15 currencies of Sweden's most important trading partners. In constructing the index the Swedish authorities established two criteria to be met by each country and currency included in the basket: (1) the country had to account for at least 1 percent of Sweden's total foreign trade (exports plus imports) during the previous five-year period and (2) each currency had to be quoted daily on the foreign exchange market in Stockholm.*[4]

In 1986 the three most important currencies in the basket were the U.S. dollar (20.7 percent), the West German mark (15.9 percent), and the British pound sterling (12.9 percent).

Flexibility increases to 2.25 percent around the reference point.

Limited flexibility. As noted in Table 9.1, there are two subcategories in the "limited flexibility" category. In the first of these, "limited flexibility to a single currency," the exchange rates fluctuate within a 2.25 percent margin. In all four cases the U.S. dollar is the benchmark for the currencies. The 2.25 percent margin is consistent with the Smithsonian Agreement signed in 1971 that increased the flexibility in the par value system from 1 percent to 2.25 percent.

The EMS was designed to promote exchange stability in the EC.

The other subcategory, "cooperative agreements," refers to the **European Monetary System (EMS).** The EMS was created in 1979 as a means of creating exchange stability within the members of the European Community (EC). The major reason for this movement was to facilitate trade among the members of the EC by minimizing exchange rate fluctuations. The EMS links the currencies of all EC members except the United Kingdom, Greece, Spain, and Portugal through a parity grid. A central exchange rate is determined for

TABLE 9.1

EXCHANGE RATE ARRANGEMENTS AS OF DECEMBER 31, 1987[1]

Currency Pegged to					
U.S. dollar		**French franc**	**Other currency**	**SDR**	**Other composite[2]**
Afghanistan	Panama	Benin	Bhutan (Indian rupee)	Burma	Algeria
Antigua & Barbuda	Paraguay	Burkina Faso	Kiribati (Australian dollar)	Burundi	Austria
Bahamas, The	Peru	Cameroon	Lesotho (South African rand)	Iran, I.R. of	Bangladesh
Barbados	St. Kitts & Nevis	C. African Rep.	Swaziland (South African rand)	Jordan	Botswana
Belize	St. Lucia	Chad	Tonga (Australian dollar)	Libya	Cape Verde
Djibouti	St. Vincent	Comoros		Rwanda	Cyprus
Dominica	Sierra Leone	Congo		Seychelles	Fiji
El Salvador	Somalia	Cote d'Ivoire		Vanuatu	Finland
Ethiopia	Sudan	Equatorial Guinea			Hungary
Grenada	Suriname	Gabon			Israel
Guatemala	Syrian Arab Rep.	Mali			Kenya
Guyana	Trinidad and Tobago	Niger			Kuwait
Haiti	Uganda	Senegal			Malawi
Honduras	Venezuela	Togo			Malaysia
Iraq	Viet Nam				Malta
Lao People's Democratic Rep.	Yeman Arab Rep.				Mauritius
Liberia	Yemen, People's Democratic Rep.				Nepal
Mozambique	Zambia				Norway
Nicaragua					Papua New Guinea
Oman					Poland
					Sao Tome & Principe
					Solomon Islands
					Sweden
					Tanzania
					Thailand
					Zimbabwe

[1]Excluding the currency of Democratic Kampuchea, for which no current information is available. For members with dual or multiple exchange markets, the arrangements shown is that in the major market.

[2]Comprises currencies which are pegged to various "baskets" of currencies of the members' own choice, as distinct form the SDR basket.

Source: International Monetary Fund, *International Financial Statistics* (Washington, D.C.: IMF, January 1988), p. 20.

the currency of each country participating in the EMS by the use of a **European Currency Unit (ECU).** The ECU is similar to the SDR in concept, except that the basket includes the currencies of all countries in the EC, including those not actually part of the EMS.

Once the central exchange rate is determined for the currency of each country in the EMS, a parity exchange rate is determined for each pair of

Flexibility Limited in Terms of a Single Currency or Group of Currencies		More Flexible		
Single currency[3]	**Cooperative arrangements[4]**	**Adjusted according to a set of indicators[5]**	**Other managed floating**	**Independently floating**
Bahrain	Belgium	Brazil	Argentina	Australia
Qatar	Denmark	Chile	China, P.R.	Bolivia
Saudi Arabia	France	Colombia	Costa Rica	Canada
United Arab Emirates	Germany	Madagascar	Ecuador	Dominican Rep.
	Ireland	Portugal	Egypt	Gambia, The
	Italy		Greece	Ghana
	Luxembourg		Guinea-Bissau	Guinea
	Netherlands		Iceland	Japan
			India	Lebanon
			Indonesia	Maldives
			Jamaica	New Zealand
			Korea	Nigeria
			Mauritania	Philippines
			Mexico	South Africa
			Morocco	United Kingdom
			Pakistan	United States
			Singapore	Uruguay
			Spain	Zaire
			Sri Lanka	
			Tunisia	
			Turkey	
			Western Samoa	
			Yugoslavia	

[3]Exchange rates of all currencies have shown limited flexibility in terms of the U.S. dollar.
[4]Refers to the cooperative arrangement maintained under the European Monetary System.
[5]Includes exchange arrangements under which the exchange rate is adjusted at relatively frequent intervals, on the basis of indicators determined by the respective member countries.

countries. For example, there would be a parity rate for the French franc and West German mark, for the Italian lira and French franc, for the Dutch guilder and Italian lira, and so on. With the exception of the Italian lira, which is permitted a fluctuation of 6 percent, bilateral rates are allowed to deviate from the central parity rates by only 2.25 percent before the respective central banks must intervene to protect the integrity of the central rate.

Frequent changes to value of currency or total freedom to float according to supply and demand are the hallmarks of "more flexibility."

More flexibility. The final major category of currencies is that of "more flexibility." In those countries whose currencies are floating independently, government intervention occurs only to influence but not neutralize the speed of movement of the exchange rate change. In the "other managed floating" category, governments usually set rates for short intervals, such as a week at a time, and buy and sell the currency at that rate for that period. The final subcategory includes currencies that are managed according to a set of indicators. The Brazilian cruzado, for example, is adjusted on a daily basis in terms of the U.S. dollar. The degree of adjustment depends on a variety of factors, including the movement of prices in Brazil relative to its trading partners.

Parallel markets. As can be noted in Table 9.1, only 18 of the 148 countries of the IMF that reported their exchange rate arrangement have currencies that are floating independently. Many of the other countries control their currencies fairly rigidly. Some of them license their exchange, as noted in Chapter 8, so that residents and nonresidents alike do not enjoy full convertibility.

Black markets closely approximate real supply and demand.

In many of these cases a black market parallels the official market. The less flexibility there is, the likelier there is to be a black market. However, even Brazil, a country in the "more flexible" category, has a black market for its currency. There, the black market is aligned more closely with the forces of supply and demand than is the official controlled market. The black market exists because the government buys dollars for less than the market thinks they are worth. Thus the black market attempts to put a more realistic price on the dollar value of the local currency.

The Role of Central Banks

Central banks often control the value of their currencies through intervention.

Each country has a central bank responsible for the policies that affect the value of its currency on world markets. The central bank in the United States is actually the Federal Reserve System (or, the Fed), a system of twelve banks, each representing a region of the United States. The New York Federal Reserve Bank handles the system's intervention in the foreign exchange markets. Intervention policies are determined by the Federal Open Market Committee. However, the Fed does not act independently of the rest of government; in particular, the Secretary of the Treasury is legally responsible for stabilizing the exchange value of the dollar.[5]

In spite of the unique nature of the central bank system in each country, there is some semblance of international cooperation through the **Bank for International Settlement (BIS)** in Basel, Switzerland. One of the functions of the BIS is to act as a central banker's bank. It gets involved in swaps and other currency transactions between central banks in the major industrial countries. In addition, central bankers can gather there to discuss monetary cooperation.

THE DETERMINATION OF EXCHANGE RATES

As noted earlier, exchange rates are either freely floating or they are fixed to something. The following sections explain how rates change under three major types of exchange rate systems: freely fluctuating, managed fixed, and automatic fixed. In addition, the roles of purchasing power parity, the Fisher Effect, and other factors related to the relationships between currencies are discussed.

Major Types of Exchange Systems

Demand for a country's currency is a function of the demand for goods, services, and financial assets of that country.

Freely fluctuating. To understand the law of supply and demand as it relates to foreign exchange, we will use a two-country model involving the United States and Bolivia. Figure 9.1 illustrates the concept of equilibrium in the market and then a movement to a new equilibrium level as situations change. The demand for dollars in this example is a function of the Bolivian demand for: (1) U.S. goods and services and (2) dollar-denominated financial assets. An example of the former would be the Bolivian demand for dollars to buy U.S.-made machinery; an example of the latter would be Bolivian demand for dollars to buy U.S. treasury bonds. The supply of dollars (which is tied to the demand for bolivianos, the Bolivian currency, in this illustration) is a function of U.S. demand for: (1) Bolivian goods and services and (2) boliviano-denominated financial assets. Initially, the supply of and demand for dollars in Fig. 9.1 is at the equilibrium exchange rate e_0 and the quantity of dollars Q_1.

Assume that there is a drop in demand for Bolivian goods and services by U.S. consumers because of, say, high Bolivian inflation. This would result in a reduction in the supply of dollars in the foreign exchange market, causing the supply curve to shift to S'. Simultaneously the rapidly increasing prices of Bolivian goods might lead to an increase in demand for U.S. goods and services by Bolivian consumers, which would lead to an increase in demand for dollars in the market, causing the demand curve to shift to D', and finally leading to an increase in the quantity demanded and an increase in the exchange rate. Thus the new equilibrium exchange rate will be at e_1. From a boliviano standpoint we could say that the increase in demand for U.S. goods would lead to an increase in supply of bolivianos as more consumers tried to trade their bolivianos for dollars, and a reduction in demand for Bolivian goods would result in a drop in demand for bolivianos. This would result in a reduction in the price of the boliviano, indicating a weakening or devaluation of the boliviano.

Governments buy and sell their currencies in the open market as a means of influencing price.

Managed fixed exchange rate. In the preceding example, Bolivian and U.S. authorities allowed changes in the exchange rates between their two currencies to occur in order to reach a new currency equilibrium. In fact, however, one or both of the countries might not want exchange rates to change. For

Figure 9.1
Equilibrium Exchange Rate

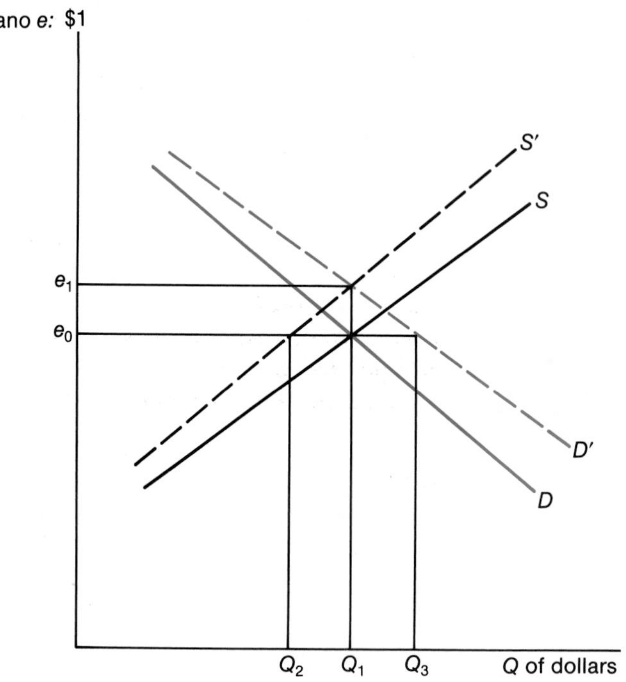

example, Bolivia might not want its currency to weaken because its industrialists would be able to buy less U.S. machinery, which is needed for development. The United States might not want the dollar to strengthen because it would mean unemployment in the machinery-building industry. But how can they keep the values from changing when Bolivia is earning too few dollars? Somehow the shortage between dollars wanted and dollars available must be alleviated. In a managed system the Bolivian central bank would hold foreign exchange reserves, which it had built up through the years for this type of contingency.

Another important factor is that the central bank in Bolivia controls transactions in foreign exchange. Assume that some of these reserves are in dollars. The Bolivian central bank would sell enough of its dollar resources (make up the difference between Q_1 and Q_3) at the fixed exchange rate to maintain the exchange rate. Or the U.S. central bank might be willing to accept bolivianos so that Bolivians can buy U.S. goods. These bolivianos would then become part of the U.S. reserves.

The fixed rate can continue as long as Bolivia has reserves and/or as long as the United States is willing to add bolivianos to its holdings. Unless something changes the basic imbalance in the currency supply and demand, though, the Bolivian central bank will run out of dollars and the U.S. central bank will stop accepting bolivianos because it fears that it holds too many. At this point it would be necessary to change the exchange rate so as to lessen the demand for dollars.

Devaluation occurs when the government reduces the value of the currency relative to a foreign currency.

Revaluation takes place when the government strengthens the value of the currency relative to a foreign currency.

Once a government decides that intervention will not work, it must adjust the value of its currency. If the currency is freely floating, the exchange rate will seek the correct level according to the laws of supply and demand. However, a currency that is pegged or fixed to another currency or to a group of currencies usually is changed on a formal basis with respect to its reference currency or currencies. This formal change is termed more accurately a **devaluation** or **revaluation**, depending on which direction the change takes. If the foreign currency equivalent of the home currency falls (or the home currency equivalent of the foreign currency rises), then the home currency has devalued in relation to the foreign currency. The opposite would happen in the case of a revaluation.

Automatic fixed rate system. As in the managed system just discussed, let us assume that the countries have agreed to maintain fixed rates by setting their domestic money supply on the basis of the amount of reserves held by the central bank and by denominating their currency value in terms of the reserve asset. Historically, the major reserve asset has been gold. In the latter part of the nineteenth century, most countries were on a gold standard.

Consider the Bolivian situation in which Bolivia has a shortage of dollars. Under an automatic fixed rate system it would now sell gold to get the needed dollars. However, unlike the managed system just described, there would be automatic adjustments to prevent Bolivia from running out of gold. As Bolivia sold off some of its gold, its money supply, which is tied to the amount of gold, would then fall. This would lead to higher Bolivian interest rates as well as lower Bolivian investment, followed by increased unemployment and lower prices. Meanwhile, the increase in gold in the United States would be having an opposite effect. The higher interest rates in Bolivia than in the United States and the decrease in Bolivian prices relative to U.S. prices would cause an increase in the supply of dollars in Bolivia as funds flowed in for investments and to purchase Bolivian goods and services. This would result in a strengthening of the boliviano and a weakening of the dollar.

Purchasing Power Parity

If home country inflation is lower than that of the foreign country, the home country currency should be stronger in value.

Purchasing power parity (PPP) is the key theory that explains the relationships between currencies: In essence, it claims that a change in relative inflation must result in a change in exchange rates in order to keep prices of goods in two countries fairly similar. The discussion accompanying Fig. 9.1 illustrates this point. According to the PPP theory, if U.S. inflation, for example, were 500 percent lower than Bolivian inflation, we would expect the value of the boliviano in U.S. dollars to fall by 500 percent. That means that the boliviano would be worth fewer dollars than was the case before the adjustment. Another way to express this boliviano devaluation would be to say that the bolivano value of the dollar would rise by 500 percent, meaning that a dollar would yield more bolivianos than it would have before the adjustment.

The PPP theory is very useful in explaining the relationship between exchange rates, but it is not perfect. We need to make assumptions about equilibrium exchange rates at some starting point and recognize that currencies are rarely related accurately in a two-country world. When several currencies are involved, it is difficult to use prices to determine an equilibrium rate. Also, exchange rates are essentially a function of traded goods, whereas inflation relates to all goods whether traded or not. Throughout the period since 1973 when the world was essentially on floating exchange rates, those rates have not conformed to the PPP theory very accurately. In 1986, for example, the market exchange rate for the Japanese yen was 168 yen per dollar. However, the exchange rate equalized for PPP should have been 223, a difference of 24.2 percent. The West German mark was 12.5 percent weaker than it should have been, and the British pound was 19.3 percent stronger than it should have been against the U.S. dollar.[6]

Interest Rates

If the nominal interest rate in the home country is lower than that of the foreign country, we would expect the home country's inflation to be lower so that real interest rates would be equal.

To relate interest rates to exchange rates, we must first relate interest rates to inflation. This is accomplished through the **Fisher Effect.** According to the Fisher Effect, the nominal interest rate is a combination of the real rate of interest and inflation. For example, it assumes that if interest rates in Country A were 500 percent higher than those in Country B, inflation in Country A would also be 500 percent higher: Thus, the real interest rates (nominal rate minus inflation) would be the same. If inflation in the two countries were the same (zero differential) and interest rates in Country A were 500 percent higher than in Country B, investors would place their money in Country A, where they could get the higher real return.

The International Fisher Effect implies that the currency of the country with the lower interest rate will strengthen in the future.

The bridge from interest rates to exchange rates can be explained by the **International Fisher Effect (IFE).** According to the IFE, the **interest rate differential** is an unbiased predictor of future changes in the spot exchange rate. An **unbiased predictor** is one that is neither consistently above nor below the actual future spot exchange rate. That does not mean that the interest rate differential is an accurate predictor, just that it is unbiased.

Using the United States and Bolivia as an example, the IFE states that if interest rates in the United States are 500 percent lower than those in Bolivia, the value of the boliviano should fall by 500 percent in the future. The fall in the value of the boliviano indicates a weakening or devaluation of the boliviano. Remember from the Fisher Effect that nominal interest rates are 500 percent lower in the United States than in Bolivia because inflation is also lower. Thus if inflation is lower in the United States than in Bolivia, the boliviano is expected to be 500 percent weaker as well. That flows from the discussion that accompanies Fig. 9.1, in which consumers would demand U.S. goods rather than Bolivian goods, causing an increase in demand for dollars and a contraction in supply of dollars. This would lead in turn to a strengthening of the dollar or a weakening of the boliviano.

Forward rates are determined primarily by interest rate differentials.

The interest rate differential is also the most important factor in the determination of forward exchange rates. For example, if exchange rates between the United States and Switzerland were to remain constant but the interest rates in the United States were significantly greater than the interest rates in Switzerland, investors would always invest in the United States. In theory, the forward rate would be the rate that exactly neutralizes the difference in interest rates between the United States and Switzerland. If U.S. interest rates are 5 percent higher than Swiss interest rates, the forward exchange rate for the U.S. dollar would be 5 percent lower than the Swiss franc so that the yield in dollars on the U.S. investment would equal the yield in dollars of the Swiss franc investment converted at the forward rate.

Thus the forward rate allows investors to freely trade currencies for future delivery at no exchange risk and without any differential in interest income. If a difference were to exist, traders would take advantage of this and earn income until the difference were eliminated.

Although the interest rate differential is the critical factor for a few of the most widely traded currencies, the expectation of future spot rates is also very important. Normally, a trade will compute automatically the forward rate through the interest rate differential and then adjust it for future expectations where deemed necessary. Some forward rates are quoted strictly on future expectations rather than on interest rate differentials. This is especially true for currencies that are not traded very widely and for which total convertibility does not exist.

Other Factors

Currencies that are safe havens in troubled times tend to be strong currencies.

A variety of other factors could cause exchange rates to change. One important determinant in a world of political and economic uncertainty is that of **confidence.** During times of turmoil, people prefer to hold currencies that are considered safe haven currencies. During the early 1980s the U.S. dollar was considered a safe haven currency, and this perception was an important source of its strength. Conversely, when the Mexican peso began to slide in the early 1980s, local investors transferred large amounts of pesos out of Mexico via dollar transfers until the Mexican government clamped down. The investors had no confidence in the peso and preferred to hold dollar balances outside of Mexico.

In addition to the basic economic forces and confidence in leadership, a number of **technical factors** influence exchange rates, such as the release of national economic statistics, seasonal demands for a currency, and a slight strengthening of a currency following a prolonged weakness or vice versa.

FORECASTING EXCHANGE RATE MOVEMENTS

In the previous section we looked at the general law of supply and demand, showed how governments intervene to manage exchange rate movements, and explained how inflation and interest rates can be important determinants of exchange rates. In this section we survey data that can be monitored in order to get an idea of what will happen to exchange rate values.

Businesspeople need to be concerned with timing, size, and direction of an exchange rate movement.

As the preceding discussion elaborates, a variety of factors influence exchange rate movements. Businesspeople must be able to analyze these factors in order to have a general idea of the timing, size, and direction of an exchange rate movement. However, prediction is not a precise science, and many things can cause the best of predictions to differ significantly from reality.

For freely floating currencies, the law of supply and demand determines market value. However, very few currencies in the world are freely floating; most are managed to a certain extent, which implies that governments need to make political decisions on the value of the currency. Assuming that governments use a rational basis for managing the value of their currencies (an assumption that may not be realistic in all cases), businesspeople can monitor some of the same indicators which they do in order to try to predict values.

The following factors have been identified as ones that should be monitored when analysts are trying to predict an exchange rate change or a free market movement in rates:

1. balance of payments statistics;
2. interest rate differentials;
3. inflation differentials;
4. governmental fiscal (expenditures) and monetary policies (growth in the money supply) that are important indicators of inflation;
5. the trend in exchange rate movements;
6. an increase in the spread between official and free exchange rates;
7. the politics of the exchange rate change;
8. business cycles;
9. changes in international monetary reserves; and
10. governmental policies that treat symptoms rather than causes.[7,8]

Most of these factors have been discussed in one form or another in the chapter as major determinants of exchange rates. Others are fairly obvious.

However, it is important to understand how balance of payments statistics are determined and how they can be used to help forecast exchange rate changes.

The Balance of Payments

A country's **balance of payments** summarizes international transactions between domestic and foreign residents. A more comprehensive definition follows:

> *The balance of payments is a statistical statement for a given period showing (a) transactions in goods, services, and income between an economy and the rest of the world, (b) changes of ownership and other changes in the economy's monetary gold, special drawing rights, and claims on and liabilities to the rest of the world, and (c) unrequited transfers and counterpart entries that are needed to balance, in the accounting sense, any entries for the foregoing transactions and changes which are not mutually offsetting.*[9]

In double entry accounting each transaction has two entries of equal value.

The concept of double entry accounting holds true in the balance of payments. This implies that each transaction has two entries of equal value that must be accounted for. Debit entries have a negative arithmetic sign, and credit entries have a positive arithmetic sign. The debit entries reflect payments by domestic to foreign residents, and credit entries reflect payments by foreign to domestic residents. Although this appears simple, unfortunately transactions are not recorded as they are in elementary accounting. In balance of payments statistics, export data may come from customs records, and the payment may come from a different source. In addition, errors may occur in recording transactions, and many items must be estimated, such as expenditures by tourists. Thus the balance-of-payments statistics include an account called "Errors and Omissions," which is used to balance the total debits and credits.

Table 9.2 provides balance of payments data for the United States.[10] The intent in providing this table is not to explain each item, but rather to provide an idea of the information that needs to be analyzed in the balance of payments.

Types of Transactions

The current account balance includes merchandise trade, services, and unrequited transfers.

Current account. The **current account balance** is very important because it summarizes the real transactions that occur in a country. The current account balance includes merchandise trade; other goods, services, and income; and unrequited transfers. The **merchandise trade balance** is critical because of the sheer volume of transactions that takes place. The export of merchandise is a credit because it results in the receipt of payment from abroad. An import is a debit because it results in making payment to the

TABLE 9.2
U.S. BALANCE OF PAYMENTS STATISTICS

Aggregated Presentation: Transactions Data, 1980,1986
(in Billions of SDRs)

	1980	1986
A. Current Account, excl. Group F	**1.45**	**−120.30**
Merchandise: exports f.o.b.	172.38	191.28
Merchandise: imports f.o.b.	−191.95	−314.12
Trade balance	−19.57	−122.85
Other goods, services, and income: credit	90.84	126.57
Reinvested earnings	*13.06*	*16.34*
Other investment income	*42.66*	*59.01*
Other	*35.12*	*51.22*
Other goods, services, and income: debit	−63.99	−110.70
Reinvested earnings	*−3.96*	*1.03*
Other investment income	*−28.41*	*−58.53*
Other	*−31.62*	*−53.20*
Total: goods, services, and income	7.28	−106.98
Private unrequited transfers	−.79	−1.42
Total, excl. official unrequited transfers	6.49	−108.40
Official unrequited transfers	−5.04	−11.90
Grants (excluding military)	*−3.63*	*−10.03*
Other	*−1.41*	*−1.87*
B. Direct Investment and Other Long-Term Capital, excl. Groups F through H	**−6.53**	**58.23**
Direct investment	−1.81	−3.20
In United States	*12.99*	*21.04*
Abroad	*−14.80*	*−24.24*
Portfolio investment	2.20	65.84
Other long-term capital		
Resident official sector	−4.50	−.62
Disbursements on loans extended	*−6.69*	*−5.92*
Repayments on loans extended	*3.11*	*4.80*
Other	*−.92*	*.50*
Deposit money banks	−2.42	−3.79
Other sectors	—	—
Total, Groups A plus B	**−5.08**	**−62.08**

Source: *Balance of Payments Statistics,* Vol. 39, Number 2 (Washington, D.C.: International Monetary Fund, February 1988), p. 33.

seller abroad. The **balance on goods and services** involves an exchange where a buyer in one country and a seller in another country exchange something of equal value. An unrequited transfer (or unilateral transfer) occurs when consideration is provided to only one party, such as aid to a drought-stricken country.

The key transactions accounted for in the services account are travel and transportation, tourism, fees and royalties, and income on investments. U.S. tourists going abroad result in a debit entry because they are transferring

TABLE 9.2 (*cont.*)

Aggregated Presentation: Transactions Data, 1980,1986
(in Billions of SDRs)

	1980	1986
C. Other Short-Term Capital, excl. Groups F through H	**−21.07**	**13.03**
Resident official sector	1.35	−.47
Deposit money banks	−21.02	22.30
Other sectors	−1.41	−8.80
D. Net Errors and Omissions	**19.19**	**20.81**
Total, Groups A through D	**−6.96**	**−28.23**
E. Counterpart Items	**.80**	**1.46**
Monetization/demonetization of gold	−.14	−.20
Allocation/cancellation of SDRs	.87	—
Valuation changes in reserves	.07	1.66
Total, Groups A through E	**−6.16**	**−26.77**
F. Exceptional Financing	**.90**	**—**
Security issues in foreign currencies	.90	—
Total, Groups A through F	**−5.26**	**−26.77**
G. Liabilities Constituting Foreign Authorities' Reserves	**11.45**	**27.96**
Total, Groups A through G	**6.19**	**1.19**
H. Total Change in Reserves	**−6.19**	**−1.19**
Monetary gold	.13	.21
SDRs	.02	−.22
Reserve position in the Fund	−1.29	1.29
Foreign exchange assets	−5.06	−2.46
Other claims	—	—
Use of Fund credit	—	—
Conversion rates: U.S. dollars per SDR	**1.3015**	**1.1732**

funds abroad to pay for the vacation. Income received from a foreign investment is treated as a credit, much like merchandise exports, because the income results in receipt of payment from foreign sources.

Direct and portfolio investments and loans are the major forms of long-term capital.

Long-term capital. The major categories in long-term capital are: **direct investment, portfolio investment,** and **loans.** Note that a balance is given for the current account and long-term capital in Table 9.2. That balance is often referred to as the **basic balance** because it measures the long-term international economic stability of a country. Supposedly it indicates productivity, factor endowments, buyer preferences, international competition, perception of the economy as a haven for investment, and the like.

Short-term capital supports real transactions, long-term investments, short-term investments.

Short-term capital. The short-term capital account represents funds that flow as a result of real transactions, such as the payment for exports and imports, as well as the flow of long-term capital transactions, such as the outflow to pay for direct investments or the inflow to recognize the receipt of investment income. In addition, it also represents speculative flows that exploit short-term interest rates and flows that respond to, say, political uncertainty.

Other items. The net errors and omissions category in Table 9.2 was defined earlier as the amount necessary to make the debits equal the credits. The items below the line (including categories E to H) represent official financing in the balance of payments. Counterpart items relate to certain changes within the official reserves and need not be discussed in detail here. Category G in Table 9.2 refers to claims that foreign official agencies have on the assets of the country. The final balance is that of the reserve position of the country.

Major balances are merchandise trade, current account, and basic.

Surplus and deficit. The terms **balance of payments deficit** or **balance of payments surplus** are often mentioned in the press. As was noted earlier, the balance of payments must always be in balance because of the concept of double entry accounting. Thus the idea of a surplus or deficit must be in conjunction with a specific component of the balance of payments. The balances most often cited are the merchandise trade balance, the current account balance, and the basic balance.

Ways to correct an imbalance in the balance of payments include:

- Disrupting trade and capital flows
- Correcting internal economic imbalances
- Forcing or allowing the exchange rate to change.

If there is a material surplus or deficit in the balances just mentioned, there are three major ways to correct the situation: (1) Disrupt trade and capital flows; (2) correct internal economic imbalances; and (3) force or allow the exchange rate to change. It would be illogical to assume that market forces are the sole determinants of trade and capital flows. Governments can and do provide incentives and disincentives in response to their own objectives and pressure from lobbyists. Even at a given level of governmental intervention, disequilibrium still can occur, leading to even more intervention. This approach, which is a cosmetic solution to disequilibrium, requires specific identification of the determinants of the surplus or deficit and the policies to achieve equilibrium. Chapter 5 discussed many ways to restrict trade and capital flows, such as subsidies, tariffs, quotas, and restrictions on the repatriation of dividends. Earlier in this chapter we showed how governments can intervene to support their currencies by buying and selling foreign exchange, using multiple exchange rates, and so on.

The second major way to restore equilibrium is to correct internal economic imbalances. As noted earlier, inflation is one of the major sources of a deficit in the balance of payments. Inflation can be reduced through strict monetary and fiscal policies, high interest rates, and wage and price controls. However, this approach can lead to an economic slowdown and unemployment, both of which are very unpopular politically. Exports can also be diversified through industrialization and by shifting resources to products that are more competitive in export and import markets. Import-competing industries, where economically feasible, also can be encouraged.

In the final analysis it may be impossible to stave off a change in the exchange rate in order to try to restore equilibrium in the balance of payments. Brazil monitors its balance of trade as a factor that it considers in changing the value of its currency. Analysts feel that a devaluation will make domestic products less expensive in international markets, thereby leading to an increase in exports. Simultaneously the devaluation will make imports more expensive, resulting in a reduction in demand and thus a reduction in imports.

In looking at balance of payments data, especially the balance of trade, it is important to understand what is really causing a surplus or deficit. The United States has been beset with significant balance of trade deficits in the past few years. Interestingly, imports as a percentage of GNP have not changed significantly since 1980, when imports were 10.5 percent of GNP; however, exports as a percentage of GNP dropped steadily from 10.0 percent in 1980 to 6.7 percent in 1986.[11] Exports of goods and services finally began to improve in 1987, when they jumped to 12.8 percent of GNP. Growth in the United States has exceeded that of most other nations, especially those that trade with the United States, so that imports have climbed in relation to economic growth. Coupled with the drop in exports as a percentage of GNP, it is obvious that the United States has some real problems. It would be too simplistic to assume that a weakening of the dollar would solve all of the trade problems of the United States.

BUSINESS IMPLICATIONS OF EXCHANGE RATE CHANGES

Exchange rates can affect business in production, marketing, and financial decisions.

Exchange rates can affect businesses in three major ways: market decisions, production decisions, and financial decisions.

Market Decisions

A devaluation could help exports become less expensive and imports more expensive.

On the marketing side, exchange rates can affect demand for a company's products at home and abroad. We already mentioned that a country such as Brazil will devalue its currency if its exports become too expensive owing to relatively high inflation. Even though inflation would cause the cruzado value of the Brazilian products to rise, the devaluation means that it would take less foreign currency to buy the cruzados, thus allowing the Brazilian products to remain competitive.

When a currency changes in value, companies need to decide whether or not to change prices.

A good example of the marketing impact is the problem that Japanese car manufacturers were having selling to the United States in 1986 and 1987 due to the sharp rise in the value of the yen. As the dollar fell 47 percent against the yen in the sixteen months ending in December 1986, Japanese car companies found that their cost advantage had disappeared, prices had to be increased, and profit margins had to be trimmed in order to be competitive. In addition, Korean cars were making inroads due to the low costs and prices of Korean products.[12]

On the other hand, a devaluation could result in foreign products being so expensive in Brazil that Brazilian products soon would pick up market share from imports. The key is whether or not the percentage of devaluation exceeds the relative increase in inflation.

One interesting ramification of a cruzado devaluation is the impact of the cheaper Brazilian goods on exporters from other countries. For example, the cheaper Brazilian goods flooding the market in Argentina might take away market share from Italian exporters, thus affecting the Italian economy.

Production Decisions

Firms might invest in weak currency countries because they are:

- Relatively cheap for initial investment
- Good base for inexpensive exports.

Production decisions also could be affected by an exchange rate change. A manufacturer in a country with high wages and operating expenses might be tempted to locate production in a country such as Argentina (where the austral is rapidly losing value) because a foreign currency could buy lots of australs, making the initial investment relatively cheap. Another reason for locating in a country such as Argentina is that goods manufactured there would be relatively cheap in world markets. However, a firm could accomplish the same purpose by going to any country whose currency is expected to remain weak in relation to that of the parent country currency. The attractiveness of a weak currency country must be balanced with the potential problems of investing there.

Financial Decisions

Exchange rates can influence the sourcing of financial resources, the remittance of funds, and the reporting of financial results.

The final business area where exchange rates make a difference is in finance. This subject will be discussed in more detail in Chapters 19 and 20. The areas of finance that are most affected are the sourcing of financial resources, the remittance of funds across national borders, and the financial statements. There might be a temptation to borrow money where interest rates are lowest. However, we mentioned earlier that interest rate differentials often are compensated for in the money markets through exchange rate changes.

In the area of financial flows, a parent company must convert local currency into the parent's own currency when exchange rates are most favorable so that it can maximize its return. Also, countries with weak currencies often have currency controls, making it difficult to manage the flow of funds optimally.

Finally, exchange rate changes also can influence the reporting of financial results. This complex topic is best left for Chapter 19. However, a simple example can illustrate the impact that exchange rates can have on income. If the Brazilian subsidiary of a U.S. company earns 100 million cruzados when the exchange rate is 200 cruzados per dollar, the dollar equivalent of income is $500,000. If the cruzado devalues to 300 cruzados per dollar, the dollar equivalent of income falls to $333,333. The opposite would occur if the local currency appreciates against the parent currency.

SUMMARY

- The International Monetary Fund (IMF) was organized in 1944 to promote exchange stability, maintain orderly exchange arrangements, avoid competitive currency devaluation, establish a multilateral system of payments, eliminate exchange restrictions, and create standby reserves.
- The Special Drawing Right (SDR) was instituted by the IMF to increase world liquidity.
- The currencies of countries that are members of the IMF are divided into three different categories: those that are pegged (fixed in value) to a single currency or to a composite of currencies; those that have displayed limited flexibility compared with either a single currency or a group of currencies; and those that are more flexible.
- Many countries that strictly control and regulate the convertibility of their currencies have a parallel, or black, market that maintains an exchange rate more indicative of supply and demand than is the official rate.
- The Bank for International Settlements (BIS) in Switzerland acts as a central banker's bank. It facilitates discussion and transactions among the central banks of the world.
- The demand for a country's currency is a function of the demand for that country's goods and services and financial assets denominated in that currency.
- A central bank intervenes in currency markets by creating a supply for its currency when it wants to push the value of the currency down or creating a demand for its currency when it wants to strengthen its value.
- A devaluation of a currency occurs when formal governmental action causes the foreign currency equivalent of that currency to fall (or that currency's equivalent of the foreign currency to rise).

- The major factors that determine the value of a currency are purchasing power parity (relative rates of inflation); real interest rates (nominal interest rates reduced by the amount of inflation); confidence in the government's ability to manage the political and economic situation of the country; and certain technical factors that are a result of trading.
- The major determinant of the forward exchange rate is the interest rate differential between currencies.
- The major factors that businesspeople should monitor when trying to predict the direction, magnitude, and timing of an exchange rate change are the balance of payments statistics, the country's reserve position, relative rates of inflation, interest rate differentials, trends in spot rates, and the forward exchange rate. Also, they must look at the political situation.
- A country's balance of payments statement summarizes all international transactions by government, business, and private residents during a specified period of time (usually one year).
- In the system of double entry accounting, each transaction, as represented by a debit or credit, is offset by an entry that represents the financing or settling of the transaction.
- The major balances in the balance of payments that require close monitoring are the merchandise trade balance, the balance on goods and services, the current account balance, and the basic balance (the current account balance plus long-term capital flows).
- Exchange rates can affect businesses in three major ways: market decisions, production decisions, and financial decisions.

CASE: CATERPILLAR AND THE FLUCTUATING DOLLAR[13]

Caterpillar, one of the world's largest heavy equipment manufacturers, recently has been beset by two major problems: competition from Komatsu Ltd. of Japan and a fluctuating U.S. dollar. Because of a dollar that strengthened against the yen by approximately 50 percent between 1980 and 1985, Komatsu increased its market share in the United States from 15 percent to 25 percent, largely at the expense of Caterpillar. Now Caterpillar is trying to fight back.

Caterpillar concentrates in the worldwide production and sale of heavy equipment and engines. It manufactures product in fifteen plants in the United States, Brazil, Canada, France, the United Kingdom, Australia, Belgium, Indonesia, and Mexico. It also has contract manufacturers in the

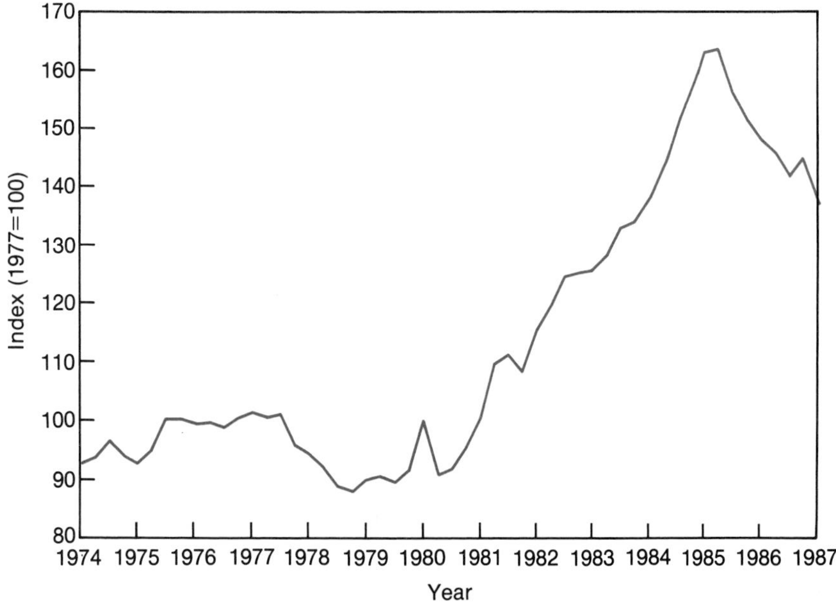

Figure 9.2
Index of Foreign Currency Price of the Dollar Against Twenty-two OECD Countries
Source: Various issues of the *Survey of Current Business.*

United States, Canada, France, Norway, South Korea, the United Kingdom, and West Germany. Parts warehouses and distribution facilities are located in the United States as well as in eight foreign locations. Parts and components are shipped worldwide for final assembly in combination with other parts and components manufactured or purchased locally.

The Dollar Prior to the 1980s. As noted earlier in the chapter, the U.S. dollar operated under a fixed exchange rate system until 1973. As Fig. 9.2 shows, the two dollar devaluations of 1971 and 1973 resulted in a dollar exchange rate that was considerably below that of the pre-1971 era. The effective exchange rate, which is the value of the dollar against its major trading partners weighted for the importance of trade with them, reached a low point in 1973 and again in late 1978 and early 1979.

Several reasons account for the weakening dollar in the 1970s. An overvalued dollar and relatively strong U.S. economy, especially in the late 1960s, led to a growth in imports, a weakening of exports, and a balance of trade deficit. This deficit was magnified by the rise in oil prices and a worldwide recession in the mid 1970s. As the world began to pull out of the recession later in the 1970s, the U.S. economy rebounded quickly, leading to strong demand for imports and an increasingly wider trade deficit.

However, the deficit began to turn around in 1978 and 1979 as the declining dollar finally began to take hold. In particular, there was a marked increase in the exports of U.S.-manufactured goods as foreign customers continued to purchase these products because of sustained economic growth abroad, especially in Western Europe and Japan.

The Dollar in the Early 1980s. In 1980 the dollar began a substantial turnaround. Higher U.S. interest rates attracted marginal capital from abroad. The trend continued in 1981 as a tight monetary policy resulted in higher interest rates and as the current account continued to improve. Several factors were given credit for the strength: relatively low inflation in the United States, relatively high nominal interest rates, the perception of the United States as a safe haven from the crises in the world, a strong U.S. stock market, and demand for dollars by multinational corporations.

The strong dollar had good points and bad points both domestically and abroad. It was hurting U.S. exporters but helping U.S. importers. Foreign exporters liked the strong dollar because it gave them cheaper access to the U.S. market and helped them to compete with U.S. companies abroad. But, the strong dollar was sapping many of the industrial economies. The huge federal budget deficit in the United States kept interest rates high, which created a strong incentive for European investors to invest in the United States rather than Europe. These capital inflows helped offset the trade deficit outflows so that the dollar stayed strong. However, high interest rates kept the European countries from lowering their interest rates to stimulate their weak economies: These countries feared that lower interest rates would force even more of their capital to the United States and thus strip their countries of capital needed for investment.

The developing countries had difficulties because their debt burdens were denominated largely in dollars. High interest rates increased the amount of interest that needed to be paid, and the strengthening dollar meant that they had to come up with more of their own currencies to purchase the dollars to pay off the debt. Both industrial and developing countries found that the strong dollar made raw materials imports (especially oil) more expensive.

Caterpillar's Problems. During this period of the rising dollar, Caterpillar experienced severe competitive pressures. Traditionally Caterpillar has relied extensively on U.S. export of components and products to service world markets, so the strong dollar made it difficult for them to compete. In addition, Komatsu was challenging Caterpillar seriously in the United States and other markets for market share due to the cost advantage and weak exchange rate that the Japan-based company enjoyed.

Another problem for Caterpillar was that some of its major markets were experiencing serious difficulty. Collapsing oil prices and soaring Third World debt made it difficult for Caterpillar to sell machinery to mining and energy-related projects, especially in developing countries.

To tackle these and other issues, Caterpillar embarked on an interesting strategy. The first prong of the strategy was to lobby for a weaker dollar. Management pointed out in Caterpillar's 1985 *Annual Report* that they were hopeful that a weak dollar would "ultimately strengthen the competitiveness of U.S. exporters, cut the huge trade deficit, and reduce the protectionist fever which now infects Congress."

A second prong of Caterpillar's strategy was to cut costs. This was accomplished initially by closing plants and laying off workers. Employment was reduced 40 percent (35,000 workers) to a level of 53,000 workers. Factory space was reduced by one-third through the closing of nine plants.

In the third aspect of the strategy, related to the strong dollar and the desire to cut costs, Caterpillar got involved in contract manufacturing and expanded production capability abroad. Contract manufacturing has given Caterpillar more flexibility to respond to swings in the economy. Caterpillar began producing abroad specifically to take advantage of the strong dollar. At the time, many independent distributors in the United States were buying Caterpillar products abroad at cheap prices, importing them into the United States, and undercutting Caterpillar in its own market. So management decided to have foreign manufacturers make Caterpillar-branded products and also replace U.S. suppliers with foreign ones. Foreign production of Caterpillar's own products jumped from 19 percent in 1982 to 25 percent in early 1987; sourcing of parts overseas increased fourfold during the same time period.

The Weakening U.S. Dollar In the fall of 1985, however, the dollar began to weaken. As noted in Fig. 9.2, the fall was steep, but not uniform. Against some currencies, notably those of the Asian NICs, the dollar remained fairly stable; against the major OECD countries, however, the fall was fairly pronounced. The major concerns seem to be the continuing large U.S. trade deficit, concerns about possible trade protectionism in the United States, the large federal budget deficit, and strong pressures on several currencies in the European Monetary System, especially the West German mark.

Although the dollar was falling, U.S. exports were not increasing dramatically largely due to weakness in other industrial economies and the fact that foreign competitors were willing to absorb the difference in smaller profit margins. In addition, imports have continued to climb due to the strong U.S. economy and the reluctance of importers to raise prices and thus lose market share. However, most experts were looking for a gradual improvement in the trade balance in 1988 as the weak dollar began to take hold.

QUESTIONS

1. What are the major factors that have influenced the value of the dollar over the past fifteen years?
2. What are the key factors that you would monitor if you wanted to have a clear idea of the future direction of the dollar? Be sure to explain how those particular factors might influence the dollar.

3. Evaluate the strengths and weaknesses of Caterpillar's strategy to counteract the strong U.S. dollar in the mid-1980s. Be sure to discuss the potential implications of that strategy as the dollar began to weaken.

NOTES

1. Eduardo Gallardo, "The 'Tiny' Bolivian Peso Can't Keep Pace with Galloping Price Increase," *Deseret News,* December 2, 1984, p. 6M; "Nicaragua, Bolivia Devalue Currencies to Avert Crises," *Arizona Republic,* February 10, 1985, p. A10; Sonia L. Nazario, "When Inflation Rate Is 166,000%, Prices Change by the Hour," *The Wall Street Journal,* February 7, 1985.

2. "The Institutional Evolution of the IMF," *Finance & Development,* September 1984, p. 8.

3. International Monetary Fund, *Annual Report on Exchange Arrangements & Exchange Restrictions—1986* (Washington, D.C.: IMF, 1987), pp. 6–7.

4. *Ibid.,* p. 481.

5. Julian Walmsley, *The Foreign Exchange Handbook* (New York: John Wiley & Sons, 1983), pp. 84–90.

6. *International Economic Conditions* (Federal Reserve Bank of St. Louis, August 1987), p. 1.

7. David K. Eiteman and Arthur I. Stonehill, *Multinational Business Finance,* 4th ed. (Reading, Mass.: Addison-Wesley Publishing Co., 1986), pp. 135–139.

8. Michael Jilling and William R. Folks, Jr., "A Survey of Corporate Exchange Rate Forecasting Practices," Working Paper No. 3, Center for International Business Studies (Columbia: University of South Carolina, 1977).

9. International Monetary Fund, *Balance of Payments Statistics* (Washington, D.C.: IMF, 1984), p. XIV.

10. There are a variety of sources of balance-of-payments statistics. Each country usually publishes its own statistics in its currency. The Survey of Current Business published by the U.S. Department of Commerce is the best source of U.S. balance of payments statistics. The International Monetary Fund publishes balance of payments statistics in two different sources: the *Balance of Payments Yearbook* and *International Financial Statistics.* The former publication provides extensive detail about every member of the IMF. The latter publication does not provide as much information as does the *Balance of Payments Yearbook,* but the data is provided in U.S. dollar terms, and it is accompanied by a variety of other types of data.

11. *International Economic Conditions* (Federal Reserve Bank of St. Louis, April 1987), p. 1.

12. Paul Ingrassia and Damon Darlin, "Japanese Auto Makers Find the Going Tough Because of the Yen's Climb," *The Wall Street Journal,* December 15, 1986, p. 1.

13. Data for the case were taken from Hans H. Helbling, "International Trade and Finance under the Influence of Oil—1974 and Early 1975," Federal Reserve Bank of St. Louis *Review,* May 1975, p. 13; *Wall Street Journal,* February 27, 1978, p. 1.; *Wall Street Journal,* April 21, 1978, p. 1; *Federal Reserve Bulletin,* April 1981, p. 270; various

issues of *Survey of Current Business;* "Strength of the Dollar Is Explained by a Mix of Economics, Psychology," *Wall Street Journal,* December 14, 1983, p. 33; "The Superdollar," *Business Week,* October 8, 1984, pp. 164–174; Caterpillar *Annual Report,* 1985 and 1986; Alex Kotlowitz, "Weaker Dollar Isn't a Boon for Caterpillar," *The Wall Street Journal,* February 20, 1987, p. 6; Harlan S. Byrne, "Track of the Cat," *Barron's,* April 6, 1987, p. 13; Barry Stavro, "Heavy Equipment," *Forbes,* January 12, 1987, p. 146.

10

CHAPTER

FINANCIAL MARKETS FOR INTERNATIONAL OPERATIONS

They were bowing to you when borrowing, but you are bowing to them when collecting.
—Russian proverb

- To show different ways in which firms can acquire outside funds for normal operations and expansion.
- To examine local debt markets, the Eurocurrency and Eurobond markets, and equity markets worldwide.
- To discuss the functions of the international banking community in facilitating the flow of funds.
- To highlight the role of development banks and similar institutions.

CASE:
HYPOTHETICAL SCRIPT FOR COLLAPSE[1]

Scene 1: On December 2, 1988, a small Hong Kong lending company, Global Vista Finance Co., quietly closes its doors. For months it aggressively plunged most of its $7 million in borrowed money into the Hong Kong real estate market, which is now collapsing.

The next day, crowds of depositors begin to form outside the main office of a middle-sized Hong Kong bank, Gresham Bank Ltd. It had enjoyed a tidy business of borrowing money from bigger banks and re-lending it at high interest rates to little, unregulated firms like Global Vista. Suddenly, business was no longer so tidy. Gresham was discovering that other banks were refusing to lend it any more cash.

Scene 2: While there is no central bank in Hong Kong, an informal agreement among banks calls for the huge $30 billion Eastern Imperial Bank of Hong Kong to bail out a sister bank that gets into trouble. After lengthy negotiations that result in a hefty interest rate for a line of emergency credit to little Global Vista, Eastern Imperial comes to the rescue. As it does so, however, Eastern Imperial suddenly finds that it is having trouble. Many depositors, worried about the possibility that Eastern Imperial could have major exposure in loans to real estate developers, begin moving their money elsewhere. When Eastern Imperial looks for new sources of cash, it finds that other major banks are demanding higher-than-usual rates of interest.

Scene 3: Huge sums of money begin to move electronically around the world as banks, big investors, multinational companies, and Arab governments shift their dollars to safe havens, primarily to major banks in New York. By December 6, banks in places considered less safe in a crisis—Panama, Singapore, the Bahamas, and Canada—have become shaky.

Scene 4: The first U.S. bank to falter is the $15 billion Heartland National Bank of Chicago. It is a relatively healthy, conservatively run bank with a number of prosperous branches in Illinois. But it is owned by the now-shaky Eastern Imperial Bank of Hong Kong. This connection is extremely unsettling to Heartland National's largest depositors—three major money funds—which begin yanking millions out of the bank on December 8. The Federal Reserve Bank of Chicago moves quickly to inject new funds.

Scene 5: The following day the $3 billion Transamericana Investment Bank of London runs out of funds. It had been a major lender of Eurodollars to credit-hungry Latin American countries. After 24 hours of often-heated discussions, Transamericana can obtain no more credit from the consortium of eight private banks that owns it (one U.S., one Swiss, one West German, and four Latin American banks and Eastern Imperial of Hong Kong). The central

[1] Source: *Wall Street Journal,* November 10, 1982, p. 1. Reprinted by permission of *The Wall Street Journal*, Dow Jones & Company, Inc., 1982. All rights reserved.

bank of Switzerland has agreed to provide one-eighth of the needed bailout funds, but its counterparts in the United States, West Germany, and Great Britain say they have no legal or moral commitment. The Latin American central bankers say that they are strongly behind the bank but that they have no funds to back it up with. So Transamericana fails.

Scene 6: On December 11, Hector Aquinas-Marx, the finance minister of Argentina's new Socialist-Labor government, assembles a group of foreign bankers and announces that Argentina is repudiating its $55 billion of foreign debt. This is a profound shock to the bankers, who, for one thing, thought that Argentina had borrowed only $40 billion. As Mr. Aquinas-Marx explains, Argentina's rationale for the move is rather simple. For weeks it had been unable to obtain the new loans necessary to make interest payments on its old loans. The mishandling of the Transamericana failure, he says, is the last straw. From now on, Argentina, which has a small trade surplus, will pay for what it needs with cash. "We never needed you anyway," Mr. Aquinas-Marx tells the foreign bankers. "It was you who needed us."

Scene 7: On December 12, gloom spreads through the world banking community as banks begin to fall like bowling pins following the Argentine announcement. There is gloom in the New York headquarters of Megabank, a $54 billion institution that had pioneered the lending to Argentina. Megabank had parceled out pieces of the Argentine debt to dozens of other banks throughout the country and had lent $1 billion itself.

But there is joy in Megabank's currency-trading office in Zurich. There, Rennie Zitz, a 23-year-old trader, has made Megabank more than $1 billion by holding a "short position" in Swiss francs for several weeks. He had borrowed the currency and sold it, then reaped an enormous profit by later buying an equal number of francs back after the Swiss currency dropped sharply against the dollar.

The dollar went up because some Swiss investors were converting their Swiss bank accounts to dollars and then wiring the money to New York, where they would be protected by the Federal Deposit Insurance Corporation (FDIC). Swiss banking regulators did not spot Mr. Zitz's transaction because he had booked it through Megabank's branch on the South Pacific island of Vanuatu, an office consisting of one clerk, one desk, and a telex machine.

Scene 8: On December 13, Youngstown (Ohio) Hope & Trust Bank joins the mounting pile of bank corpses in the United States. Neither its officers nor the federal banking authorities have been able to repair the damage caused by a run on the bank when it became known that Youngstown had participated in Megabank's lending foray into Argentina.

But Joe Lunchpail, a shop foreman at Youngstown Tube & Prong, goes to the bank anyway. He feels sure that he can rescue the $898.42 in his checking account because the bank is insured by the FDIC. Sure enough, the man from the FDIC is there, and Mr. Lunchpail takes his cash home to bury it in a dry place under one corner of his garage. With a sense of great relief, he flips on his Japanese TV set and opens a can of Dutch beer to sip as he watches the evening news report of the economic chaos that seems to be going on elsewhere. Then he learns that Youngstown Tube & Prong is closing. There is no longer an export market for prongs.

INTRODUCTION

This hypothetical case is meant to demonstrate the interdependence of capital markets and industrial growth worldwide. It may seem farfetched to assume that events in Hong Kong could influence a steelworker's job in Ohio, but stranger things have happened. Economic problems in Brazil certainly have had a strong influence on the activities of the large multinational banks.

The small firm involved only tangentially in international business may be concerned only about the functions of the foreign exchange section of its commercial bank. The larger MNE investing and operating abroad cares about access to capital in local markets as well as the large global capital markets. These capital markets and the institutions set up to make them run are primarily in the private sector. However, banks in some countries are owned by the government, and some lending institutions, such as the World Bank, are either government-owned or receive most of their funding from governments.

This chapter examines the financial markets and institutions that allow firms to grow globally and service customers around the world. Initially, the focus will be primarily on the markets themselves, especially concerning the Eurocurrency, Eurobond, and equity markets. In the section on banking, we discuss the institutions and the services. Then we concentrate on the financial institutions distinct from banks that make the securities markets work. We close with a discussion on development banks and their contribution to corporate finance.

LOCAL DEBT MARKETS

Firms have learned to be creative in gaining access to local credit markets.

As corporations expand into foreign frontiers, they must adjust to local debt markets, both short term and long term. Since each country has different business customs, firms need to abandon strict operating procedures developed in other countries. When Caterpillar Tractor went to Brazil for the first time (see Chapter 9) it was accustomed to operating through one bank for all of its transactions. Very quickly, however, it became clear that the tight credit market in Brazil required different operating procedures. So Caterpillar opened accounts in several banks, allowing it to tap several different credit sources. Caterpillar liked this so much that it exported its Brazilian policy back to Peoria.

Commercial paper is an IOU that used to be backed up by standby lines of credit.

In the United States it is customary for U.S. companies needing cash to sell **commercial paper,** a form of IOU that used to be backed up by standby lines of bank credit. When U.S. subsidiaries of foreign corporations began to issue such paper, the market required that the paper be guaranteed by the parent company. Some giants, like Shell Oil, did not need to rely on their parent, but most companies did. Those practices seem to be changing.

Local debt markets are influenced by political and economic pressures.

Even though domestic and international markets are becoming more and more like a single market—at least in the case of the industrial countries—local markets still depend a great deal on internal political and economic pressures. In Latin America, for example, high inflation has created problems for a number of firms. In some other countries, efforts to control inflation have curtailed the money supply and thus the availability of funds.

Spain's preparations for entry into the European Community (EC) revolutionized the local credit market. Before 1981 the only source of medium-term financing was from capital markets outside of Spain. When loans were denominated in currencies other than the Spanish peseta, the borrowers were exposed to a foreign exchange risk when they had to pay off their loans. However, several changes in Spanish banking laws in 1981 opened up the local peseta financial market. The major source of influence has been the international banks, long accustomed to creative financing. Now multinationals can borrow locally without having to worry about exchange risk.[2]

Foreign companies sometimes are treated differently from domestic companies when it comes to access to the credit markets. In Brazil in the early 1980s, for example, subsidiaries of foreign-owned companies were excluded from local credit markets in order to help attract hard currency borrowings.[3]

If a U.S.-based MNE decides to use foreign credit markets to finance foreign operations, it must take into consideration interest rate differentials and exchange rate risks. As noted in Chapter 9, interest rates differ from country to country, primarily because of inflation differentials. During Bolivia's hyperinflationary period, as discussed in Chapter 9, interest rates were running at 50 percent per month. If the Bolivian subsidiary of a U.S. company decided to borrow in dollars at lower interest rates rather than pay 50 percent per month, it would be exposed to an exchange rate risk. If the boliviano were to devalue against the dollar (which it certainly would during a period of relatively high inflation) the Bolivian subsidiary would have to come up with more bolivianos to purchase dollars to pay principal and interest.

From these illustrations it is obvious that MNEs need to weigh several factors as they look at the local credit markets: (1) availability of funds; (2) cost due to interest rates and foreign exchange risk; and (3) local customs and institutions. Because situations and events are dynamic, corporate treasurers must be able to react quickly.

EUROCURRENCIES

A Eurocurrency is a currency (primarily in U.S. dollars) banked outside of its country of origin.

The Eurocurrency market is an important source of debt available to the MNE. A **Eurocurrency** is any currency that is banked outside of its country of origin. Eurodollars, which constitute a fairly consistent 70–80 percent of the market, are dollars banked outside of the United States. Similar markets exist for Euro-Japanese yen, Euro-German marks, Euro-Swiss francs, and other currencies, such as British pounds and French francs. The Eurocurrency market is worldwide. Large transactions take place in Asia (Hong Kong and Singapore), the Caribbean (the Bahamas and the Cayman Islands), and Canada, as well as in London and other European centers.

The major sources of Eurodollars are: (1) foreign governments or businesspeople who want to hold dollars outside of the United States; (2) multinational corporations with cash in excess of current needs; (3) European banks with foreign currency in excess of current needs; and (4) the reserves of countries such as Japan and some of the OPEC countries that have large balance of trade surpluses. The demand for Eurocurrencies comes from individuals, firms, and governments that require funds for operating capital, investment, and the payment of principal and interest on debt.

Eurodollar Expansion

Fractional reserve concept says that very little of the deposit is held back as a precaution; most of it is loaned and reloaned to users.

The key to Eurodollar expansion is the **fractional reserve concept.** The total size of the Eurodollar market is much greater than the actual cash deposited. Once a dollar deposit is made in a London bank, the bank may use that asset as a basis for making a dollar-denominated loan to someone else. The fraction of the original deposit not loaned out is called the *fractional reserve.* Since there are no reserve requirements on Eurodollar deposits, it is up to the individual bank to determine how much protection it requires in the form of reserves. The expansion occurs when the initial loan is spent, deposited in another bank, or used as a basis for another loan.

Market Size

The size of the market is difficult to determine and depends on whether the gross or net size is being discussed (the net size eliminates transfers between banks). Gross liabilities usually are just over twice as great as the net size of the market. In 1971 the total gross Eurocurrency market size was about $150 billion. As Fig. 10.1 shows, the market grew to $3.992 trillion by June 1987. Interestingly, Fig. 10.2 illustrates that the dollar portion of the Eurocurrency market has remained in the 70–80 percent range over the past decade, although the importance of the dollar has diminished in recent years, especially as the dollar has fallen in value. By 1987, the dollar portion had slipped to 70 percent.

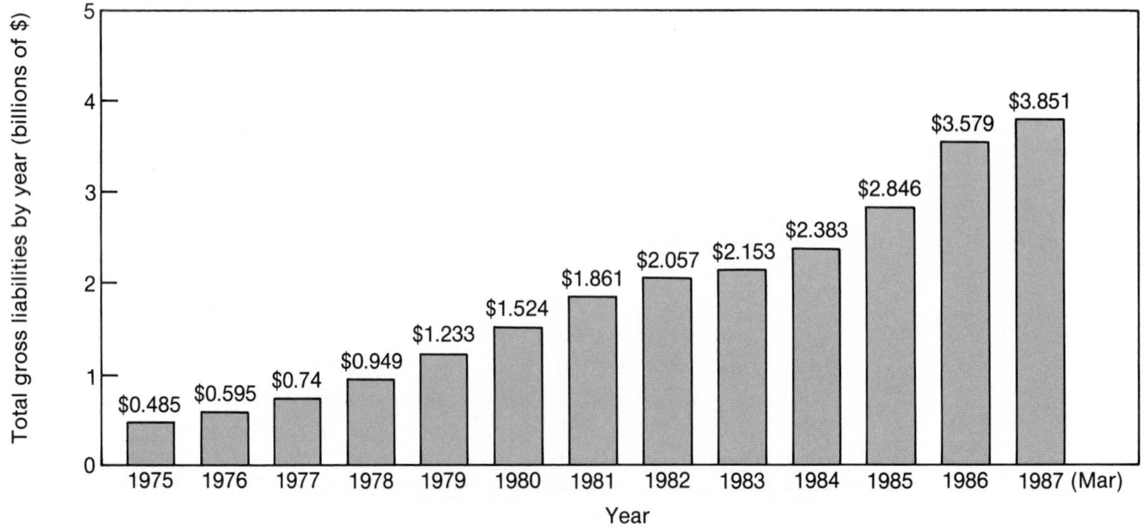

Figure 10.1
Eurocurrency Market Size (Total Gross Liabilities)
Source: The Federal Reserve Bank of St. Louis, *International Economic Conditions,* various issues.

Figure 10.2
Percentage of Eurodollars to Total Eurocurrencies
Source: The Federal Reserve Bank of St. Louis, *International Economic Conditions,* various issues.

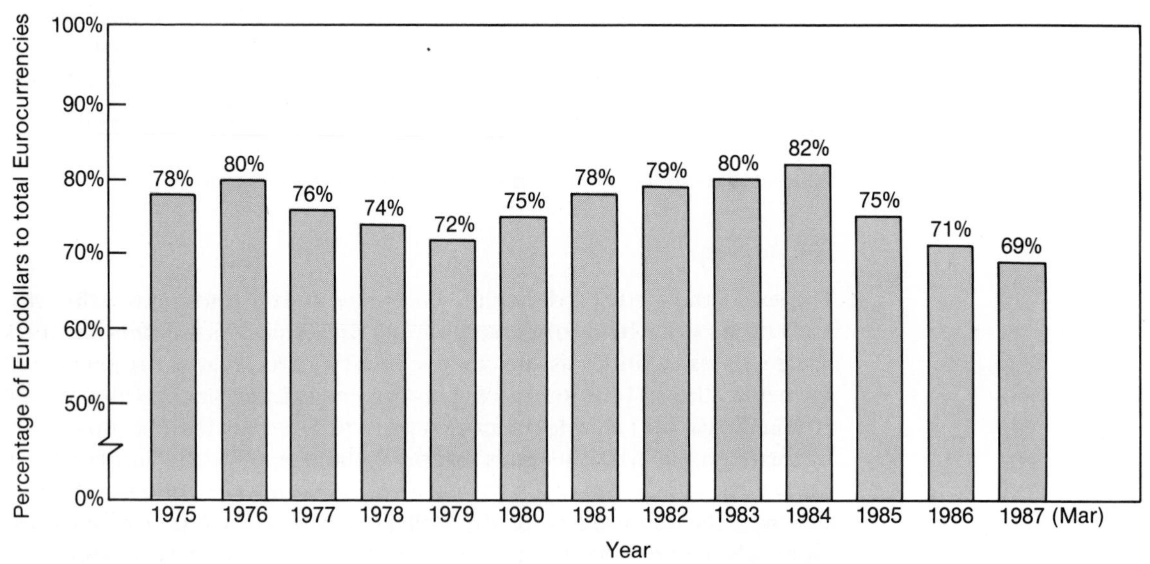

Characteristics of the Eurocurrency market are: large size; dollar-based; big corporate transactions; unregulated; short-term; time rather than demand deposits

Eurocurrency market. The Eurocurrency market has several interesting characteristics. First, it is a wholesale rather than retail market, which means that transactions involve governments, banks, and large corporations. As such, the transactions tend to be very large. Public borrowers such as governments, central banks, and public sector corporations tend to borrow most of the funds. Second, the market is essentially unregulated.

Third, deposits are primarily short term. About one-third of the deposits by nonbanking institutions mature in eight days or less, and 90 percent have maturities of less than six months.[4] This leads to concern about risk, since most Eurocurrency loans are for longer periods of time. Fourth, the Eurocurrency market exists for savings and time deposits rather than demand deposits. That is, institutions that create Eurodollar deposits do not draw down those deposits for expenditures. Instead, they usually convert their Eurocurrency deposits into a particular national currency in order to buy goods and services. Fifth, as shown in Fig. 10.2, the Eurocurrency market is primarily a Eurodollar market.

Eurocredit consists of loans that mature in one to five years.

The Eurocurrency market, excluding the Eurobond market, which will be discussed later in this chapter, has short- and medium-term characteristics. Short-term Eurocurrency borrowing has a maturity of less than one year. Anything over one year is considered a **Eurocredit.** These Eurocredits may be loans, lines of credit, or other forms of medium- and long-term credits, including **syndication,** in which several banks pooling resources to extend credit to a borrower.

Syndication occurs when several banks pool resources to make a large loan in order to spread the risk.

LIBOR is the interest rate that banks charge each other.

Traditionally, loans are made at a certain percentage above the **London Inter-Bank Offered Rate (LIBOR),** which is the interest rate banks charge one another on loans of Eurocurrencies. The interest rate above LIBOR depends on the credit worthiness of the customer and must be large enough to cover expenses and build reserves against possible losses.

INTERNATIONAL BONDS

Many countries have very active bond markets available to domestic and foreign investors. One good example is the United States: In the 1980s, given the high real interest rates, relative political and economic stability, and governmental desire to finance its high budget deficits with borrowing, the U.S. market has been ready for foreign investors. A major influence on foreign investors to take more U.S.-issued bonds was the repeal of the withholding tax on interest in 1984. Many experts feel that the elimination of the withholding tax has taken business away from some of the bond markets in the Caribbean that have existed partly because of the lower yield in the United States.[5]

Foreign Bonds and Eurobonds

Foreign bonds are sold outside of country of borrower but in the currency of country of issue.

Eurobonds are sold in countries other than the currency of issue.

The international bond market can be divided into foreign bonds and Eurobonds. **Foreign bonds** are sold outside of the borrower's country but are denominated in the currency of the country of issue. For example, a French corporation floating a bond issue in Swiss francs in Switzerland would be floating a foreign bond. A **Eurobond** is usually underwritten, or placed in the market for the borrower, by a syndicate of banks from different countries and placed in countries other than the one in whose currency the bond is denominated. If the French firm floated a bond issue in West German marks in Switzerland, Luxembourg, and London, the issue would be a Eurobond.

The Eurobond Market

Eurobonds are sold in different centers simultaneously.

Although the Eurobond market is centered in Europe, it has no national boundaries. Unlike most conventional bond issues, Eurobonds are sold simultaneously in several financial centers through multinational underwriting syndicates and are purchased by an international investing public that extends far beyond the confines of the countries of issue.

Occasionally, Eurobond issues may provide currency options, which enable the creditor to demand repayment in one of several currencies and thereby reduce the exchange risk inherent in single-currency foreign bonds. More frequently, however, interest and principal on the bonds are payable in U.S. dollars. Over the last several years the Eurobond market has become a market for dollar-denominated obligations of foreign as well as U.S. borrowers that are purchased by non-U.S. investors.

In an effort to broaden investor appeal, corporate borrowers increasingly have shifted from straight debt issues to bonds that are convertible into common stock. The option of conversion rests with the holder of the convertible issue. For the nonresident investor, one of the main attractions of a convertible issue is that it usually offers a larger current return than does the dividend of the underlying stock.

Growth in the 1980s brought liberalization of capital markets and strength of the yen.

Recently, the Eurobond market has grown explosively, due to a variety of reasons—primarily the deregulation of markets. The weakening of the dollar in 1985 also caused a shift out of dollars toward Euro-Yen and Euro-Deutschemark issues. The control of inflation in the industrial countries also has resulted in a big demand for financial assets, allowing companies to issue bonds like never before, and in a variety of currencies. In 1985, for example, 140 U.S. firms issued nondollar Eurobonds.[6]

The benefits of the Eurobond market are unregulated, untaxed, and more flexible.

The major benefits of the Eurobond market are that: It is relatively unregulated; its income is essentially untaxed; and there appears to be greater flexibility in making issues than is the case in purely national markets. In addition, it is an important step toward a fully integrated European capital market. However, the yen is potentially the largest source of funds for the Eurobond market, due to the huge trade surpluses that Japan has enjoyed in recent years.

OFFSHORE FINANCIAL CENTERS

Offshore financial centers provide funds other than those of their own country; markets are not regulated in the same ways as domestic markets.

So far we have alluded to the major financial centers of the world. The countries with large markets, such as the major OECD countries, have large domestic financial markets. This does not mean that they have large financial markets that deal in foreign currencies, however; neither does it mean that they have large offshore centers.

Market Characteristics

Offshore financial centers are cities or countries that provide large amounts of funds in a currency other than their own. Generally these markets are regulated in a different, and usually more flexible, way than are the domestic markets. They have one or more of the following characteristics as well:

1. There is a large foreign currency (Eurocurrency) market for deposits and loans (e.g., London).
2. The market is a large net supplier of funds to the world financial markets (e.g., Switzerland).
3. The market is an intermediary or pass-through for international loan funds (e.g., Bahamas, Cayman Islands).[7]

In addition, a good offshore center must provide the following to be especially attractive to banks:

> *(1) economic and political stability; (2) an efficient and experienced financial community; (3) good communications and supportive services; and (4) an official regulatory climate favorable to the financial industry, in the sense that it protects investors without unduly restricting financial institutions.*[8]

Certainly the absence of official regulation and taxation are critical for the fourth point.

These centers can be considered as operational (functional) centers or booking (accounting) centers. London is an example of an operational center, and the Cayman Islands is an example of a booking center. Although there are many offshore financial centers, the seven most important ones are London, the Caribbean (servicing especially Canadian and U.S. banks), Switzerland, Singapore, Hong Kong, Bahrain (for the Middle East), and New York.

Specific Markets

London is a crucial market because it offers a variety of services and has a large domestic as well as offshore market. The Caribbean centers (primarily the Bahamas, Cayman Islands, and Netherlands Antilles) are essentially offshore locations for the New York banks. Switzerland has been a primary source of funds for decades, offering stability, integrity, discretion, and low costs. Singapore has been the center for the Asian dollar market since 1968, thanks to a variety of government regulations that have facilitated the flow of funds, its strategic geographic location, and its strong telecommunications links with the rest of the world. Hong Kong is critical because of its unique status with the United Kingdom and China and its geographic proximity to the rest of the Pacific Rim. Bahrain, an island nation in the Persian Gulf, is the financial center of the petrodollars generated in the Middle East. Even though oil prices had a period of weakness in the mid-1980s, a tremendous amount of revenue is generated by the oil producers.

Some of the offshore centers, especially those in the Caribbean, are going through a period of transition. In 1987, the Tax Treaty between the United States and the Netherlands Antilles lapsed over a disagreement on what the treaty should look like in the future.[9] Many U.S. firms were expected to retire their bonds early, which could reduce the confidence that foreign lenders have in U.S. borrowers.

EQUITY SECURITIES

The three largest international stock exchanges are Tokyo, New York, and London.

In addition to the debt instruments represented by the Eurodollar and Eurobond markets, the equity capital market is another source of financing. The three largest international stock exchanges in the world in terms of market capitalization are the Tokyo, New York, and London stock exchanges. Market capitalization is the total number of shares of stock listed on the stock exchange times the market price per share. Prior to 1987, the New York market was by far the largest in the world. In 1984, Wall Street controlled 55 percent of the world's equity market, three times as much as Tokyo and eight times the size of the London market.[10] As shown in Table 10.1, however, the gap narrowed quickly from 1984 to 1986. By 1986, the market capitalization of U.S. equities was down to 43 percent of the world total, whereas the Japanese had increased from 20.1 percent to 29.1 percent. However, the soaring yen and rapid increase in Japanese equity prices caused Tokyo to surpass New York in the spring of 1987 to become the world's largest equity market.[11]

Reasons for U.S. markets include: size and speed of offerings and good disclosure.

The U.S. market is important for U.S. companies looking for more equity capital as well as for foreign companies. A partial explanation for the popularity of the U.S. market is the size and speed of offerings. For example, the large pension funds in the United States can take large blocks of stock at relatively low transaction costs. In the past few years, pension fund managers have looked at foreign stocks as a good form of portfolio diversification. Many companies go to the United States because the depth and breadth of the market enable firms to raise funds there easily.

TABLE 10.1
MARKET CAPITALIZATION OF THE WORLD'S STOCK MARKETS (Billions of U.S. Dollars)

Country	1986	1984	1982	1980	1978
United States	$2,556	$1,714	$1,481	$1,391	$ 870
Japan	1,746	617	410	357	327
United Kingdon	440	219	182	190	118
West Germany	246	78	69	71	83
Canada	166	116	105	113	67
France	150	40	29	53	45
Italy	141	23	20	25	10
Switzerland	132	43	41	46	41
All Others	418	216	188	226	124
Total:	$5,995	$3,066	$2,525	$2,472	$1,685

Source: Deloitte, Haskins, Sells, *Review* (New York: DH&S) September 14, 1987, p. 2.

Many foreign firms list their securities on U.S. stock exchanges, prompting the Securities and Exchange Commission (SEC) to set up stringent registration and accounting provisions. This was done under the assumption that efficient capital markets would dictate that foreign firms should operate under the same guidelines as U.S. firms. According to SEC rulings, foreign firms may issue financial statements according to their own accounting standards, but material differences from U.S. standards should be disclosed.

The Big Bang in London

The big bang brought deregulation of London's securities market.

The major event to occur in international equity markets in recent years was the "big bang," which occurred in London on October 27, 1986. Prior to that time, the City of London (the financial district in London) operated on two different sides. The first side was the domestic front, home to the U.K. financial firms that controlled the U.K.'s financial system. Custom basically kept this side from keeping up with financial services developed elsewhere.

The other side was the Eurocurrency market, which was dominated by foreign institutions. The abolishment of exchange controls in 1979 by the British government blurred the differences between the domestic and international sides of the City of London. However, the big bang resulted in a dismantling of the trading system, a liberalization of requirements on who can have membership in the Stock Exchange, and an opening of the market to foreign competition.[12] These changes have resulted in a significant liberalization of one of the largest capital markets in the world.

One side effect of deregulation has been the modernization of stock exchanges around the world. New technologies are being employed by nearly every major exchange worldwide, and the exchanges are beginning to link together in various ways. Both the Stockholm and Amsterdam stock exchanges have announced formal links with U.S. exchanges, primarily in the Midwest. There are similar links between Amsterdam and Tokyo and between London and the United States. These are just a few examples of dozens of linkages that exist and are being planned worldwide.[13]

The Euroequity Market

Euroequity refers to shares sold outside of national boundaries of the issuing company.

Another significant recent event is the creation of the Euroequity market. The **Euroequity market** is the market for shares sold outside of the national boundaries of the issuing company. Prior to 1980, few companies thought of offering stock outside of the national boundaries of the headquarters. Since then, over 60 companies from all over the world have issued stock simultaneously in two or more countries. When Black & Decker issued 4.5 million shares of stock in 1983, it looked strictly at the domestic market. In 1985, it decided to use the Euroequity market for another issue, so 2 million of the 8.5 million shares that it issued were in that market.[14]

The issuing firms and investment bankers considered that the Euroequity market holds a number of benefits. First, more investors are identified through multiple syndication, and second, price can often be increased through boosting demand. In 1983, 4 firms worldwide issued stock on the Euroequity market for a value of only $116.6 million. In 1984, the market began in earnest and has tripled in size every year. In 1986, over $11 billion was raised by 119 corporations, banks, and sovereign nations. The first three quarters of 1987 also saw significant growth, but the stock market crash on October 19, 1987 slowed the action somewhat.[15]

Other Exchanges

In addition to the big markets just described, there are a number of emerging markets in the developing countries. There are three levels of emerging markets: (1) established markets, such as Greece, Spain, Mexico, and Brazil, that have been in existence for a long time, although their volume has not been tremendous; (2) emerging markets, such as Hong Kong and Singapore, that have arisen because of special situations; and (3) markets, such as South Korea, that were specifically organized more recently to foster or accelerate economic growth.[16] These markets are not destined to take over the big three in the industrial world, but they are becoming more important as their economies experience industrial growth.

INTERNATIONAL BANKS

An essential aspect of the growth of international business has been the increase in international banking services. Firms would have been unable to

TABLE 10.2
RANKINGS OF THE TOP TEN BANKS IN 1987

Bank	Country	Rank		
		1987	1986	1985
Dai-Ichi Kangyo Bank	Japan	1	1	2
Sumitomo Bank	Japan	2	3	4
Fuji Bank	Japan	3	2	3
Mitsubishi Bank	Japan	4	4	5
Sanwa Bank	Japan	5	5	7
Industrial Bank of Japan	Japan	6	8	13
Credit Agricole	France	7	9	8
Citicorp	United States	8	6	1
Norinchukin Bank	Japan	9	7	11
Banque Nationale de Paris	France	10	10	6

Source: *The Banker*, July 1987, p. 113.

expand as they have without the timely flow of money and other resources provided by the international banks. Not only do banks facilitate the flow of existing corporate resources, they also provide debt financing from local and international markets. A Canadian bank, for example, could loan funds to a Canadian corporation that is attempting to acquire a U.S. business, or it could provide that financing through the Eurodollar market.

Leading World Commercial Banks

U.S. MNEs are among the world's largest, but U.S. banks are not. Table 10.2 illustrates that the only U.S. bank in the top ten in 1987 was Citicorp, which ranked eighth, compared with first in 1985. The six largest banks and seven of the top ten in 1987 were Japanese banks.

There has been a rise of Japanese banks and a fall of European banks.

The strong emergence of the Japanese banks is startling. In 1980 there was only one Japanese bank in the entire list, and it was number ten; that same bank was first in the world in 1987. In 1980, Citicorp was number one, Credit Agricole was number three, and Banque Nationale de Paris was number four. The strength of the yen and Japan's large trade surpluses have boosted the power of Japanese banks worldwide.

However, the comparisons are complicated by exchange rate volatility. Citicorp was number one in 1985 and number seven in 1987, but its growth in dollars exceeded the growth of the largest Japanese bank in yen. Thus there are likely to be significant fluctuations in the top rankings each year, depending on what happens to the dollar–yen exchange rate. As pointed out by *The Banker*, Citicorp may be ranked seventh, but that does not make it any less

TABLE 10.3

COUNTRY OF REPRESENTATION OF THE TOP 500 BANKS IN THE WORLD IN 1987

Country	Number of Banks
Japan	107
United States	87
West Germany	44
Italy	33
France	20
Switzerland	15
United Kingdom	15
Spain	13
Taiwan	11
Korea	10
Austria	9
Belgium	9
Denmark	8
Australia	7
Canada	7
India	7
Sweden	7
Yugoslavia	6
Luxembourg	6
	421 of 500

Source: *The Banker,* July 1988, pp. 113–130.

influential in international banking; its relative strength in different markets remains significant.[17]

Foreign banks in the United States are a good source of funds.

The emergence of foreign banks has influenced the U.S. market strongly and has opened avenues for funding for MNEs that did not exist only a few years ago. Japanese banks, in particular, are aggressively moving into the market and offering loans at lower rates than are U.S. banks. Typically foreign banks operate in the wholesale market (i.e., the market for corporations rather than individuals). On December 31, 1986, more than 250 foreign banks were operating in the United States in one form or another, accounting for about 20 percent of all commercial and industrial loans to firms operating in the United States.[18]

Table 10.3 shows the country representation of most of the top 500 banks in the world in 1987. Although the United States had the largest representation of banks in 1986, it is interesting to note that from 1983 to 1986, there was a drop in U.S. banks from 119 to 104 and an increase in Japanese banks from 66 to 82. By 1987, the United States had slipped into second place after Japan. Table 10.3 includes only those countries with more than five banks.

Structure of International Banking

MNEs find that their banks offer a variety of services worldwide through a variety of different operational modes. U.S. banks have increased their influence abroad through establishing branches in order to service their domestic clients; now they are using those branches to attract local business as well. In countries where they choose not to establish branches, U.S. banks can enter into correspondent relationships with local banks, allowing them to service their clients through the correspondent while servicing the correspondent's client in the United States.

Some banks also have entered into more formal relationships with banks at home and abroad in order to service clients better. A **consortium bank,** for example, occurs when several banks from different countries pool their resources to form another bank that engages in international transactions. This enables the banks to draw on the strengths of its partners, such as foreign currency deposits, branches in different countries, or expertise in specific types of banking transactions.

Domestic U.S. banks can also establish **Edge Act Corporations** in different cities in the United States in order to get involved in international transactions. By law, a bank is allowed to establish an Edge Act company in different cities outside of its home state, as long as the Edge Act bank is involved in international and not domestic banking activities.

Important Developments in International Banking

Although international banks must face a variety of issues and even though a number of key developments that have taken place in recent years, we will focus on the following areas that have an impact on MNEs and their operations worldwide: the expansion of services, communications breakthroughs, and foreign loans.

Expansion of services. The market for financial services virtually has exploded for banks in recent years. The three major functions that are especially suited for the offshore banks are:

1. Money transfer and foreign exchange, which includes international money arbitrage. An ancillary activity is foreign exchange dealing and servicing.
2. International treasury. This category includes providing the source for funds, allocating funds to end users, converting funds, and providing for the reconversion of funds.
3. International loan and credit. This includes the analysis and approval of credit, monitoring loans, and establishing and revising country loan limits.[19]

A good example of the variety of services offered by a large international bank is BankAmerica, which once was the largest bank in the world. BankAmerica divides its services into three categories: international trade support, international financing services, and international money management services. International trade support includes commercial letters of credit, acceptance financing (providing bankers' acceptances), collections of international accounts, remittances and money transfers, and international trade information. International financing services include direct financing, loan syndications, government-sponsored trade financing programs, lease financing, project financing, standby letters of credit, Eurobond transactions, international trust and investment services, private placements of debt and equity capital, and merger and acquisition advisory services. International money management services include international cash management services, foreign exchange trading, foreign exchange advisory services, and international treasury services (including project consulting services, educational services, and treasury management systems).[20] This impressive list of services allows BankAmerica to provide a variety of services in order to meet the needs of its corporate clients.

Multinational banks allow faster transfer of funds and information.

Communications. One of the major services offered by multinational banks is the movement of funds across national boundaries. Nonetheless, this service was not developed adequately until the early 1970s; prior to that, transfers of funds between European countries could take several days to several weeks, even when cable transfers were used.

SWIFT is a cooperative arrangement of banks worldwide to transfer funds instantaneously.

In an effort to eliminate the time lag in carrying out international money transfers by mail or telex, a number of banks organized the **Society for Worldwide Interbank Financial Telecommunication (SWIFT)** in 1973. SWIFT has grown from an initial membership of 239 banks in fifteen countries to over 1200 banks in more than fifty countries. SWIFT services primarily involve processing transactions such as customer transfers, foreign exchange confirmations, bank transfers, and documentary credits. A special message text language allows banks to "talk" to each other by computer in a common language. This added capability greatly facilitates information transfers.[21]

CHIPS is a clearing mechanism for domestic and foreign currency transactions in the United States.

Another important institution is the **Clearing House Interbank Payment System (CHIPS),** an international electronic check transfer system that moves money between major U.S. banks, branches of foreign banks, and Edge Act subsidiaries of out-of-state banks. The system handles a large volume of transactions per day and most of the foreign exchange trade and Eurodollar transactions. CHIPS has speeded up the settling of its transactions to the close of each business day rather than the next business day as was the custom.[22]

TABLE 10.4

THIRD WORLD DEBT (In Billions of Dollars, as of December 31, 1986)

Debtor Nations	Total Foreign Debt	Estimated Bank Debt
Brazil	$108.0	$77.3
Mexico	100.3	76.7
Argentina	49.8	34.3
Venezuela	35.3	30.0
Philippines	26.7	15.0
Chile	21.4	14.8

Source: Peter Truell, "Citicorp's Reed Takes Firm Stance on Third World Debt," *The Wall Street Journal,* February 4, 1987, p. 6.

Foreign loans. Banks have been affected by loans to developing countries because many of them are holding loans on which no principal and interest are being paid. New banking regulations in the United States require banks to identify the amount of their nonaccrual loans at the end of each quarter. A **nonaccrual loan** is one for which principal or interest is 90 days past due or for which payment of interest or principal is determined to be doubtful of collection. The nonaccrual concept relates to domestic as well as foreign loans, and many banks have had more problems with domestic loans than they have with foreign loans.

A nonaccrual loan is at least 90 days overdue in paying principal or interest.

There has been a lot of criticism of the commercial banks for lending several hundred billion dollars to the developing countries. During the late 1970s the banks received large deposits from OPEC countries, which it then tried to lend. During the recession of the late 1970s and early 1980s, when interest rates also began to rise, corporate borrowing in the United States was very soft. However, the developing countries continued to demand loans and appeared to be willing to pay the high interest rates. The pressure on the banks began as the loans from the developing countries came due and the debtors found that they were not earning sufficient foreign exchange to make the payments.

Table 10.4 identifies the debt levels of Third World countries with the largest amount of debt. While not all of the debt indicated is held by the international banks, much of it is. The major issue facing the banks is whether or not the principal and interest will ever be repaid. For some banks, that could be a key issue. For example, Citicorp's loans to Third World countries make up over 90 percent of its primary capital (total equity, plus loan loss reserves plus notes and debentures subordinated to deposits).[23]

Establishment of loan loss reserves protect banks from country default.

As a result of this large exposure, the major U.S. banks gradually have been building huge loan loss reserves in order to protect themselves from a major default. The major move against default was made by Citicorp on May 19, 1987, when it added $3 billion to its loan loss reserves. (In 1986, it had added less than $.5 billion dollars.) The formula Citicorp used boosted its reserves to 25 percent of Latin American loans and 100 percent of its nonperforming loans.[24]

Citibank's move initiated a rash of reserve additions, including $1.7 billion by Manufacturers Hanover, $1.6 billion by Chase Manhattan, $1.1 billion by Chemical Bank, and $1.1 billion by BankAmerica. Many experts consider this inadequate, since loans by U.S. banks to Latin American countries and the Philippines totaled approximately $85 billion in 1987, and the reserves established by the banks were only about 20 percent of that total. Many banks were selling their loans on the open market at discounts of up to nearly 50 percent of their value.[25] This exposure could make it difficult for MNEs to get loans for operations in debt-troubled countries. In addition, any major defaults could reduce the capital base of the banks and tighten up the funds available for MNEs.

NONBANKING FINANCIAL SERVICES FIRMS

Different rules worldwide separate banking and securities functions.

So far we have discussed debt and equity markets available to MNEs as well as the international banks that provide financial services. But there are a number of other financial services firms in addition to banks that provide financial services for MNEs. Sometimes the distinction between banks and financial services firms that deal in the securities markets (both debt and equity) is unclear because of differences in different countries' regulations. For example, the United Kingdom does not require a separation of commercial and investment banking, whereas both Japan and the United States do. As Table 10.5 shows, there is only one British firm among the twenty-five largest securities and financial services firms. This is so partly because of the blurred distinction between commercial and investment banking.

Firms often behave very differently abroad than they do at home. Thus Japanese and American commercial banks get heavily involved in securities work abroad, although that is prohibited at home.

U.S. and Japanese firms dominate the financial services and securities markets.

In looking at Table 10.5, note the importance again of the U.S. and Japanese firms. They dominate the list as they do in the banking industry, but the power is distributed more evenly. When looking at brokerage houses per se, the comparisons usually are made between the Japanese big four (Nomura Securities, Daiwa Securities, Nikko Securities, and Yamaichi Securities) and the American big four (Salomon, Merrill Lynch, Shearson Lehman, and Goldman Sachs).

The Japanese are moving aggressively into the financial markets, just as they have into banking. Nomura Securities is now the largest issuer of Eurobonds, and nearly 20 percent of all Eurobonds are denominated in yen. In addition, Nomura and Daiwa Securities are primary dealers in the U.S. government securities market. The Japanese securities firms are able to charge high fixed commissions in the Japanese market, which has not yet undergone deregulation, so they can accumulate massive profits there allowing them to engage in price cutting elsewhere in the world.[26]

TABLE 10.5

THE TWENTY-FIVE LARGEST SECURITIES AND FINANCIAL SERVICES FIRMS (In Millions of U.S. Dollars at Dec. 31, 1986, Exchange Rates; Percent Change Based on Home Currency)

Rank 1986	Rank 1985	Company (Country)	Capital *	Change from 1985	Assets	Net Income
1	1	American Express (U.S.)	$14,126	31%	$99,476	$1,250
2	2	Salomon Inc. (U.S.)	8,273	15	78,164	516
3	3	Merrill Lynch (U.S.)	7,662	26	53,013	454
4	5	Orient Leasing (Japan)	6,399	23	13,825	62
5	7	Nomura Securities (Japan)	6,000	34	18,320	1,383
6	6	Compagnie Bancaire (France)	4,841	7	21,590	104
7	9	Nippon Shinpan (Japan)	4,798	29	24,064	61
8	10	Orient Finance (Japan)	4,651	26	21,919	74
9	4	Beneficial (U.S.)	4,487 †	−10	7,274	−172
10	12	Daiwa Securities (Japan)	3,551	40	19,474	700
11	14	Yamaichi Securities (Japan)	2,880	36	13,317	518
12	8	Union Discount Co. of London (U.K.)	2,753	−14	3,590	16
13	11	Commercial Credit (U.S.)	2,208	−22	4,864	46
14	13	Nikko Securities (Japan)	2,133	−10	14,358	574
15	16	Japan Securities Finance (Japan)	2,010	33	17,245	18
16	15	Trilon Financial (Canada)	1,999	18	15,733	93
17	—	Drexel Burnham Lambert (U.S.)	1,846	N.A.	38,583	N.A.
18	17	Goldman Sachs (U.S.)	1,526	27	38,794	N.A.
19	18	E.F. Hutton (U.S.)	1,505	32	25,921	−90
20	19	First Boston (U.S.)	1,364	31	48,618	181
21	25	Morgan Stanley (U.S.)	1,337	99	29,190	201
22	22	Integrated Resources (U.S.)	1,096	41	5,137	18
23	21	Japan Consumer Credit Society (Japan)	1,078	9	4,057	7
24	23	PaineWebber (U.S.)	1,037	43	14,726	72
25	—	Bear Stearns (U.S.)	949	85	26,939	132

* Defined as owner's equity, reserves, minority interest, preferred stock, and long-term debt.

† Includes short-term debt.

Source: "Global Finance and Investing: A Special Report," *The Wall Street Journal*, September 18, 1987, p. 260.

Impact of deregulation on British securities firms has been severe.

As noted earlier in the chapter, the British government opened up the British securities market to international competition through deregulation, which has helped increase competition and the volume of securities work in London. However, British bankers and brokers are suffering. There are too many firms for the market, and many are being taken over by foreign firms. They were simply not prepared for the financial boom that accompanied the big bang. Most of the British firms are of the midsize variety that may not have a future in the global securities market.[27]

DEVELOPMENT BANKS

Although MNEs tend to go to private capital markets for financing, there is also a significant amount of funding available from development banks. The funds are usually directed for specific types of projects, so the firms have to qualify for those projects. However, these development banks can provide funding as well as guarantees for projects that might grant the firms access to funds in the private capital markets.

The World Bank

The World Bank is organized under the U.N. charter; the major subunits are the IBRD, IDA, and IFC.

The **World Bank Group,** an autonomous U.N. agency, is composed of three major organizations: the **International Bank for Reconstruction and Development (IBRD),** the **International Development Association (IDA),** and the **International Finance Corporation (IFC).**

International Bank for Reconstruction and Development. The International Bank for Reconstruction and Development was organized in 1945 along with the IMF to aid in rebuilding the world economy. It is owned by the governments of 150 countries, and its capital is subscribed by those governments; it provides funds to borrowers by borrowing funds in the world capital markets. At its founding, the bank's major objective was to serve as an international financing facility to function in reconstruction and development. With the Marshall Plan providing the impetus for the European reconstruction, the bank was able to turn its efforts toward development.

The IBRD lends money to governments for hard currency needs for infrastructure development.

Generally the IBRD lends money to a government for the purpose of developing that country's economic infrastructure, such as roads and power-generating facilities. Funds are lent only to members of the IMF, usually when private capital is unavailable at reasonable terms. Loans are made at low rates of interest for periods of time that depend on the nature of the project and the country involved.

Now the bank's major concern is the development of infrastructure in less-developed countries. This foundation is essential for future industrialization. The impact of the bank's activities is less direct than that of the Eximbank, for example. However, the projects receiving IBRD assistance usually require importing heavy industrial equipment, and this provides an export market for many U.S. goods. Generally, bank loans are made to cover only import needs in foreign convertible currencies and must be repaid in those currencies at long-term rates.

IDA provides infrastructure loans for the poorest countries at very favorable terms.

International Development Association. The International Development Association was formed in 1960 as a part of the World Bank Group to provide financial support to LDCs on a more liberal basis than could be offered by the IBRD. The IDA has 134 countries. IDA's funds come from subscriptions from its developed members and from the earnings of the IBRD. Credit terms usually are extended to fifty years with no interest. Repayment should begin after a ten-year grace period and can be paid in the local currency, as long as it is convertible.

Although the IDA's resources are separate from the World Bank, it has no separate staff. Loans are made for the same types of projects as those carried out by the World Bank, but at easier and more favorable credit terms.

As mentioned earlier, World Bank/IDA assistance historically has been for developing infrastructure. The present emphasis seems to be on helping the masses of poor people in the developing countries become more productive and take an active part in the development process. Greater emphasis is being put on improving urban living conditions and increasing productivity in small industries.

International Finance Corporation. Although the IBRD was providing assistance to the LDCs, it recognized limitations to what it could do. Some of the major problems were: (1) All loans had to be guaranteed by the member government of the country receiving the loan; (2) the bank could only provide loans, not purchase stock; (3) the bank financed only the foreign exchange requirements for a project and was not concerned with local expenditures or working capital; and (4) the bank usually financed large projects of public importance and reached small projects in the private sector only indirectly by means of the development banks.

IFC activities are oriented primarily toward helping corporations in productive projects.

These problems led to the development of the International Finance Corporation (IFC) in 1956. Its main responsibilities are: (1) to provide risk capital in the form of equity and long-term loans for productive private enterprises in association with private investors and management; (2) to encourage the development of local capital markets by carrying out standby and underwriting arrangements; and (3) to stimulate the international flow of capital by providing financial and technical assistance to privately controlled finance companies. Loans are made to private firms in the developing member countries and are usually for a period of seven to twelve years.

The key feature of the IFC is that its loans are all made to private enterprises and its investments are made in conjunction with private business. In addition to funds contributed by IFC, funds also are contributed to the same projects by local and foreign investors.

IFC investments are for the establishment of new enterprises as well as for the expansion and modernization of existing ones. They cover a wide range of projects, such as steel, textile production, mining, manufacturing, machinery production, food processing, tourism, and local development finance companies. Some projects are wholly locally owned, whereas others are joint ventures between investors in developing and developed countries. In a few cases, joint ventures are formed between investors of two or more developing countries.

Regional Development Banks

IDB provides development loans to companies in the Western Hemisphere.

Although the World Bank Group can be considered a development bank, there are other smaller regional and local development banks. The **Inter-American Development Bank (IDB)** was organized in 1959 to give countries in the Western Hemisphere (principally the United States and Latin America) the same types of services the World Bank provides. However, the IDB projects are wider in scope and tailored for the member countries. Loans are made from ordinary capital resources to private and public entities of member nations. These loans are generally made at favorable rates of interest and are repayable in the currencies lent. Procurement sources of goods and services are limited to those countries that contribute funds to the IDB. Many development banks similar to the IDB have been instituted in other regions of the world.

In addition to regional development banks, there are also many national development banks. In the past twenty to twenty-five years, the World Bank has been involved in the creation of over fifty development banks, primarily national banks in member countries. These banks assist profitable investment activities and small entrepreneurs and stimulate investment in areas deemed critical by the government that are unaffected by market forces. This activity is concentrated in a specific country rather than in a larger region, as is the goal of a regional development bank.

SUMMARY

- Local debt markets, which vary dramatically from country to country owing to local business customs and practices, are important sources of funds for MNEs.
- A Eurocurrency is any currency that is banked outside of its country of origin. The dollar comprises the bulk of the Eurocurrency market and is thus referred to as the Eurodollar.
- Eurodollars are expanded through the fractional reserve concept, whereby a bank reserves only a fraction of each Eurodollar deposited and loans the remainder of the deposit, thus "creating" more Eurodollars.
- A Eurobond is a bond issue sold in a currency other than that of the country of issue. A foreign bond is one sold outside of the country of the borrower but denominated in the currency of the country of issue.
- Offshore financial centers such as London, the Caribbean, Singapore, Hong Kong, Bahrain, and now New York City deal in international transactions that are not regulated in the same way as domestic markets.
- Most industrial countries and some developing countries have stock exchanges in which equity capital can be raised by firms. However, the three major international equity markets for the sale and purchase of securities by individuals from many countries are in New York, Tokyo, and London.
- The Japanese stock market has overtaken the U.S. stock market as the largest in the world. This occurred as a result of the strengthening yen and rising Japanese securities prices.

- Because of the strong Japanese yen and large Japanese trade surpluses, the Japanese banks are achieving international dominance.
- The major operational modes used in international banking are branches, consortia, correspondents, and Edge Act corporations.
- International banks are faced with a number of challenges, such as providing adequate cash management and funds flow services, coping with increasingly risky loans, and dealing in a highly competitive environment.
- U.S. and Japanese securities and financial-services firms dominate world markets. The Japanese brokerage houses now do the greatest volume in the Eurobond market.
- The World Bank Group includes the International Bank for Reconstruction and Development (IBRD), the International Development Association (IDA), and the International Finance Corporation (IFC). These multilateral lending institutions are designed to provide financial support for LDCs on a private as well as public basis. The IFC is especially active in providing debt and equity financing in private sector projects.

CASE: LSI LOGIC CORP[28]

In the late 1970s, Wilfred Corrigan, the British-born chairman and president of Fairchild Camera & Instrument Corp., sold the company to Schlumberger Ltd. Approximately one year later, in November 1980, he started LSI Logic Corp., a manufacturer of custom-made microchips based in Milpitas, California. Although Mr. Corrigan's idea of custom-made microchips sounded unconventional at the time, he was able to use his record at Fairchild to convince some U.S. venture capitalists in January 1981 to invest nearly $7 million in the new firm.

The company had only four employees at this point, but since Corrigan had now solved two key issues—the nature of the product and the initial infusion of cash—there was a solid foundation for growth. Corrigan now had to decide how LSI Logic should service its customers worldwide, and how and where it would raise capital to keep expanding.

Global Strategy. Mr. Corrigan learned from his experience at Fairchild that a producer of microchips had to think globally in terms of the location of production and the consumer. He quickly decided that in order to be successful, he needed to concentrate on being in three key geographic areas—Japan, the United States, and Europe. He coined this his "global triad strategy." The key organizational strategy was to establish firms incorporated in the producing and consuming countries that would be jointly owned by LSI Logic and local investors. However, LSI Logic would hold a controlling interest in the firm. Although the operations in each country would be relatively independent of each other, they would still be linked by technology, money, and management. This would allow the synergy of interdependence to take place, but it would also permit local freedom in meeting the demands of the market.

Initial European Thrust. Once Corrigan got operations underway, he began to look for more cash. The key was to find the right amount, at the right price, with the least number of problems. In Februry 1982, slightly more than a year after U.S. venture capital gave the company a start, LSI Logic turned to Europe in search of venture capital. It found a European investing community hungry for U.S. high-tech stock, so it was able to raise $10 million, mostly—but not exclusively—in Britain. That offering brought LSI Logic an average of $7 a share, compared with only $0.90 per share when it was set up only a year earlier.

At this point LSI Logic was growing rapidly. In May 1983, Corrigan took the firm public in the United States and raised over $162 million, an average now of $21 a share. That was a significant improvement over its European experience and demonstrated the size of the appetite in the United States for new high-tech companies.

The Japanese Strategy. In spite of the success in Europe and in the United States, Corrigan still had not been able to complete the third part of his triad—Japan. However, Corrigan learned that Nomura Securities, the largest brokerage house in Japan and subsequently the world, had purchased large blocks of LSI stock for its clients in Japan. Encouraged by this information, Corrigan traveled to Japan to meet with Nomura officials and try to decide what LSI Logic's next move should be. As a result of the visit and discussions, Corrigan decided that the time was right for starting operations in Japan. Following the strategy he had used elsewhere, Corrigan established a Japanese subsidiary of LSI Logic (called LSI Logic Corp. K.K.) in which the parent company owned 70 percent, and 25 local Japanese investors owned 30 percent. The investors were not small operations, however. Nippon Life Insurance Company, the third largest insurance company in the world, just behind Prudential and Metropolitan Life, became a major shareholder in the new venture. The new investment was just right for LSI Logic. Not only did Corrigan now have access to the Japanese consumer market, but he also had access to the Japanese capital market. As a Japanese company, LSI Logic Corp. K.K., and its manufacturing affiliate, Nihon Semiconductor Inc., could now establish lines of credit with Japanese banks. In order to help LSI Logic penetrate the capital markets better and to develop more of a local image in Japan, Corrigan hired Keiske Awata, a senior executive of NEC Corp. who was working outside of Japan at the time. Mr. Awata gave a Japanese image to LSI Logic in Japan and helped open the right doors to the financial world. LSI Logic was able to get a local line of credit at only 6 percent, compared with 9 percent in the United States at the time.

Second European Thrust. Now that business in Japan was underway, Corrigan turned his attentions again to Europe. He was planning to set up a new European company and he needed to decide on its structure. The company could be set up as a branch of the U.S. parent that would use U.S. capital and be totally controlled and protected by the parent; or it could be set up as a European company. Corrigan decided to do the latter, so he used Morgan Stanley & Co., the large U.S.-based securities firm, to set up LSI Logic Ltd. The parent company retained an 82 percent stake in the new company, and the rest was sold to European investors in a private offering. One of the investors was the venture capital arm of five West German banks. Corrigan was convinced that by setting up a European company, he was able to get more money by selling shares at a higher price than would have been possible otherwise and that LSI Logic Ltd. was better placed to service European customers than a branch of the parent company would have been.

Convertible Bonds. In 1985 and again in 1987, Corrigan returned to European capital markets, but this time LSI floated a bond issue. The first issue of $23 million was put together by Swiss Bank Corp., one of the largest banks in the world. The second issue, a bond issue with securities convertible into common stock, was floated by Morgan Stanley and Prudential-Bache Capital Funding. There were two main attractions to the bond market for LSI Logic: a decent price (lower interest rates than would have been offered in the United States), and a quicker time frame. Since LSI didn't have to worry about all of the listing regulations of the Securities and Exchange Commission in the United States, it was able to get the offering together faster and out to the investing public.

Although significant amounts of funds were raised in foreign markets (over $200 million since 1982), there was no real exchange risk. LSI Logic operations worldwide were earning revenues that could be used to pay off the financial obligations. In addition, LSI Logic subsidiaries had access to local credit markets because they were organized as local corporations rather than branches of a foreign corporation.

QUESTIONS

1. What were the different ways that LSI Logic used international capital markets? Discuss specifically the nature of the instruments (i.e. local, foreign, euro, etc.).
2. Why did it use those markets rather than just the U.S. market?
3. How did its organizational strategy fit with its capital acquisition strategy?

NOTES

1. John J. Fialka, "Script for Collapse," *Wall Street Journal,* November 10, 1982, p. 1.

2. "A New Credit Market in Pesetas," *Business Week,* June 15, 1981, p. 102.

3. Rodrigo Briones, "Latin American Money Markets," in *International Finance Handbook,* Abraham M. George and Ian H. Giddy, eds. (New York: John Wiley & Sons, 1983), p. 4.9.4.

4. "The Debate over Regulating the Eurocurrency Markets," Federal Reserve Board of New York *Quarterly Review,* Winter 1979–1980, p. 20.

5. Linda Sandler and Matthew Winkler, "Bond Firms Try Harder to Sell American Debt to Overseas Investors," *Wall Street Journal,* August 31, 1984, p. 1.

6. Charles Grant, "Mapping a Route through the Euromarket Chaos," *Euromoney,* January 1986, p. 29; Matthew Winkler, "U.S. Move to End Antilles Tax Treaty Alarms Many Investors and Borrowers," *Wall Street Journal,* July 1, 1987, p. 2.

7. Maximo Eng and Francis A. Lees, "Eurocurrency Centers," in *International Finance Handbook,* Abraham M. George and Ian H. Giddy, eds. (New York: John Wiley & Sons, 1983), p. 3.6.3.

8. *Ibid.,* p. 3.6.4.

9. "Death of a Tax Haven: Revisiting the Dutch Antilles," *Business International Money Report,* July 6, 1987, pp. 209–210.

10. "Why the Big Apple Shines in the World's Markets," *Business Week,* July 23, 1984, p. 101.

11. Barbara Buell, William Glasgall, Richard A. Melcher, and Jonathan B. Levine, "The Tidal Wave That's Sweeping International Finance," *Business Week,* July 13, 1987, p. 57.

12. "Flinging Open the Doors of Change," *Euromoney Supplement,* August 1986, p. 2.

13. "Big Bang Rumbles across Europe," *The Banker,* May 1987, p. 82.

14. Ann Monroe, "U.S. Firms Offering Stock Look Overseas," *Wall Street Journal,* June 16, 1986, p. 15.

15. Rosamund Jones, "Americans Move into Equities," *Euromoney,* March 1987, p. 52.

16. Vitrang R. Errunza, "Emerging Markets: A New Opportunity for Improving Global Portfolio Performance," *Financial Analysts Journal,* September–October 1983, pp. 51–52.

17. Michael Blanden, "The Risen Sun," *The Banker,* July 1987, pp. 74, 76.

18. E. Gerald Corrigan, "A Perspective on the Globalization of Financial Markets and Institutions," *Federal Reserve Bank of New York Quarterly Review,* Spring 1987, p. 4.

19. Eng and Lees, *op. cit.,* p. 3.6.4.

20. *International Services* (San Francisco: Bank of America, 1981), pp. 3–21.

21. "Banking Tomorrow—Communications," *The Banker,* October 1984, pp. 73–77.

22. "CHIPS: Goodby to Next-Day Settlements," *Business Week,* March 23, 1981, p. 98.

23. Peter Truell, "Citicorp's Reed Takes Firm Stance on Third-World Debt," *Wall Street Journal,* February 4, 1987, p. 6.

24. G. Christian Hill, Richard B. Schmitt, Peter Truell, and Robert Guenther, "BankAmerica Raising Reserve $1.1 Billion; Manufactures Hanover Mulls Similar Step," *Wall Street Journal,* June 9, 1987, p. 3.

25. Richard B. Schmitt and G. Christian Hill, "Banks to Post Record $10 Billion Loss," *Wall Street Journal,* July 20, 1987, p. 2.

26. William Glasgall, Barbara Buell, Richard A. Melcher, and Mike McNamee, "Japan on Wall Street," *Business Week,* September 7, 1987, p. 82; Barbara Buell, William Glasgall, Richard A. Melcher, and Jonathan B. Levine, "The Tidal Wave That's Sweeping International Finance," *Business Week,* July 13, 1987, pp. 56–57.

27. Richard A. Melcher, "The City of London Wanted Competition—But Not This Much," *Business Week,* August 10, 1987, p. 37.

28. Sources for case: Udayan Gupta, "Raising Money the New-Fangled Way," in "Global Finance & Investing: A Special Report," *Wall Street Journal,* September 18, 1987, p. 14D; Nick Arnett, "LSI Lands Former NEC Chief to Head Affiliated Company," *Business Journal—San Jose,* January 14, 1985, p. 17 (1); "LSI Gets A Circuit-Supply Pact," *Wall Street Journal,* January 6, 1987, p. 7.

5

PART

INTERNATIONAL BUSINESS IN INTERNATIONAL CONFLICTS

Although the international mobility of production factors and finished goods by multinational firms may allow the world's consumers to use products that would otherwise not be available and to consume others at a lower cost, all countries seek to influence factor mobility. Chapter 11 analyzes the economic and noneconomic motives and methods by which nation-states seek to influence the flow of direct investment. Chapter 12 examines the approaches by which international firms and governments may deal with each other in order to satisfy the objectives of each and to attempt to strengthen the bargaining position relative to that of the other party. Chapter 13 concludes with an illustration of the effects and uncertainties of international business between market and centrally planned economies as political and economic objectives and policies become intertwined.

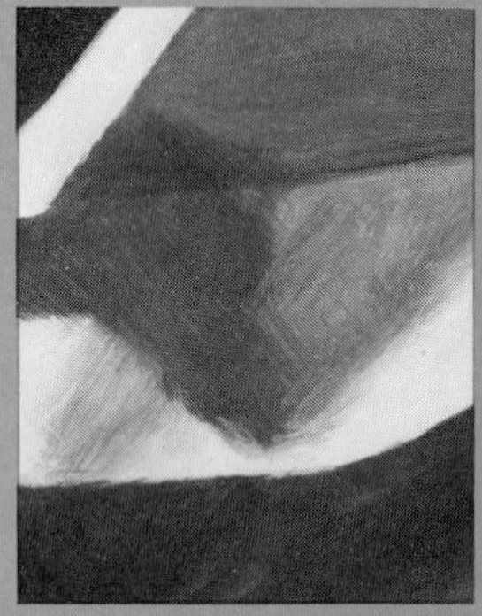

CHAPTER 11
THE IMPACT OF THE MULTINATIONAL

If a little money does not go out,
great money will not come in.
—Chinese proverb

- To examine the conflicting objectives that MNEs face.
- To discuss problems in evaluating MNE activities.
- To evaluate the major economic impacts (balance of payments and growth) of multinational firms on donor and recipient countries.
- To analyze the discussions of multinational companies' activities.
- To introduce the major criticisms asserted about multinational firms.
- To give an overview of the major political controversies surrounding MNE activities.

CASE:
MNEs IN CANADA[1]

Prime Minister Brian Mulroney was elected in late 1984 and soon thereafter replaced the eleven-year-old Foreign Investment Review Act (FIRA) with a new agency called Investment Canada. Whereas the FIRA's purpose was to limit foreign control of the Canadian economy, Investment Canada's intent is to persuade foreign firms to invest in Canada. Investment Canada reduced substantially the number of investment applications that are subject to scrutiny: Under it, direct takeovers of Canadian firms with assets of less than C$5 million and indirect takeovers of less than C$50 million need not be examined. The old review board criterion of "significant benefit" has been replaced with a loosely defined "net benefit" to Canada.

The birth of Investment Canada did not mark the first time Canada had changed its stance toward foreign investors. In 1972, after decades of luring foreign capital to Canada, it was estimated that of the $58 billion of total corporate assets in Canada, $43 billion, or 74 percent, were foreign-owned. No other advanced economy was so dominated by foreign ownership; such a degree of foreign control was unusual even among developing countries. The U.S. ownership was $35 billion, or about 60 percent, of the total corporate assets in Canada.

The evolving public opinion at that time was that foreign ownership should be restricted. This does not imply that Canada had heretofore allowed unrestricted entry of foreign firms. There were already limitations on foreign ownership in certain industries considered to be particularly sensitive to national sovereignty, including banks and other financial institutions, newspapers and magazines, broadcasting, and the uranium industry. Given these existing restrictions, what difference did it make that other firms were controlled outside of Canada? Would operations or decisions be any different than if the ownership were held by Canadians? Obviously, many Canadians thought they would be.

One such allegation concerned the level of positions and type of production taking place in Canada. The Science Council, a governmental advisory board, contended that even in high-technology industries, very little research and development was being performed by the Canadian subsidiaries of foreign firms. Furthermore, very little of the production of newer sophisticated products was being done in Canada. Canadian subsidiaries depended primarily on manufacture of mature products and components. These generally had a lower profit margin and employed a higher portion of lower-skilled people than the more innovative output taking place in the MNEs' home countries. Furthermore, since the corporate headquarters of the MNEs were located abroad, Canadians could aspire to upper-level management positions only by leaving Canada. Given the high education level of the Canadian population and the shrinking advancement opportunities in Canada, there was a net flow abroad of technical and managerial persons with high skills—a so-called brain drain. Many of these workers joined the parent companies' operations, meaning that Canada then had to import the costly technical advancements that its own citizens helped to develop abroad. Many Canadians thus expected that greater Canadian control would bring increased opportunity in Canada for using their skills and would make the country less dependent on foreign technology.

There also was widespread agreement among critics of foreign ownership that in conflict situations the investors would do what was best for the home, rather than the Canadian, situation. Many observers believed that, if given a choice of exporting from Canada or the parent country, the MNEs would choose the latter. Critics were particularly upset that the U.S. government had prevented the Canadian subsidiaries of U.S. firms from exporting to China during the period before the United States opened trading relations with the country. These export limitations contributed to drains on Canadian foreign exchange, which proved substantial because of dividend remittances to parents that exceeded the flow of foreign exchange into Canada.

Because of these contentions about foreign investment the FIRA was passed in late 1973. It provided that any foreign takeover of an existing company would have to be screened by the Foreign Investment Review Agency, which would recommend to Parliament whether or not the investment was of "significant benefit" to Canada. The procedure applied to Canadian companies with assets of at least $250,000 or annual sales exceeding $3 million. A takeover would involve acquisition of 5 percent or more of the Canadian company. By the end of 1974 the law was extended to cover new investments and expansion of foreign-controlled companies into new areas of business.

The term *significant benefit* was never defined specifically: Some of the factors that were considered were the effects on employment, exports, competition, productivity, and industrial efficiency. Approval also depended on the degree of Canadian participation in a venture, although no quota of Canadian representation in the management of a company has been spelled out. After Pierre Trudeau's election as Prime Minister in 1980, a ten-year National Energy Program was announced to reduce foreign ownership in the energy industry to 50 percent. This program led to the "benefit" of an 8-percent drop in foreign control of oil and gas but sparked a two-year outflow of direct and portfolio investment. This in turn led to downward pressure on the Canadian dollar and upward pressure on Canadian interest rates.

The simultaneous occurrence of costs and benefits is one explanation for the historic disagreement within Canada on the question of foreign investment. Some critics have claimed that restrictions have not been sufficient; others have felt that controls should be eased on the foreign ownership of Canadian enterprises. Even when FIRA was passed, Premier Gerald Regan of

Nova Scotia said, "We want all the foreign investment we can get." At the time, 10 percent of Nova Scotians were out of work.

While FIRA was operating, some people favored greater control, contending that FIRA had a positive impact but did not go far enough. These critics showed that although foreign firms increased their research and development (R&D) in Canada, the amount they undertook has been less than their share of the economy. The percent of GNP spent on R&D in Canada is still small in comparison with the percentage in some other industrial countries (e.g., about 60% of that in Switzerland). Critics feel that Canadian control will produce increases in R&D: They point to the Canadian takeover of de Havilland from Britain's Hawker Siddeley Group in 1974 and of Canadair from General Dynamics of the United States in 1976. With Canadian ownership and management these firms have greatly increased R&D, developed new products, increased employment, and are competing internationally. Observers believe that Canadian takeovers of other industries will lead to similar growth in Canada's technical capabilities.

Those who wanted fewer controls questioned whether Canada could fulfill its technological and capital needs if controls result in a lowering of direct investment flows into Canada. First, they questioned whether indigenously controlled firms will undertake in Canada the kind of R&D that foreign firms were critized for not undertaking. These analysts have cited the fact that Northern Telecom, Canada's telecommunications giant, itself maintains an R&D facility with 500 people in the United States. Second, they have shown that technology flows more quickly, more cheaply, and with fewer restrictions between a parent and subsidiary than by license among independent companies. In terms of restrictions, for instance, there is a high incidence of limiting output only for sale in Canada under the licensing arrangements. Among controlled operations, however, a number of investors have transferred technology so that Canada serves as the production base for worldwide sales (e.g., Westinghouse, steam turbines; Motorola, mobile radios; Honeywell, hydronic valves). In terms of capital they pointed to a Royal Bank of Canada estimate that by the year 2000, Canada will need $1.4 trillion for energy investment alone, of which $300 billion will have to come from foreign sources. The capital-need argument became particularly pervasive as unemployment stayed high from the recession in the early 1980s.

It was because of the aforementioned arguments that Investment Canada replaced the FIRA. But how liberal has Canada become toward foreign investors? On one hand Canada permitted the biggest foreign takeover in Canadian history during 1986, the purchase of 51 percent of Hiram Walker by Britain's Allied-Lyons. On the other hand, Canadians are worried about foreign (especially United States) domination. In 1988 four of Canada's ten largest companies were U.S. direct investments. The New Democrats, a party highly critical of U.S. policies, was leading the polls for the first time in history. Canadians are particularly concerned about protection of their culture. In 1987, estimates were that 70 percent of English language television and 80 percent of movies viewed by Canadians were from the United States. About 75 percent of book publishers were foreign-owned. The president of Investment Canada, Mr. Paul Labbé also said, "More non-Canadian control in cultural industries is not welcome."

INTRODUCTION

Pressure groups push to restrict MNE movements at home and abroad.

In Canada as well as in other countries, the rapid growth of international companies in recent years has been controversial. In fact, there are powerful pressure groups in both home and host countries that have pushed their governments to implement policies restricting the movement of multinational firms. These critics are sure to play an even greater role in the future expansion of world business.

This chapter examines the major contentions regarding the practices of MNEs and the main evidence supporting or refuting the contentions. Chapter 12 analyzes the methods by which companies and countries react to criticisms and attempt to strengthen their positions.

Fear size of MNE
- Economically larger than many countries
- Executives deal with heads of state.

The sheer size of many MNEs worries the countries with which they come in contact. For example, the sales of General Motors and Royal Dutch/Shell exceed the GNP of such medium-sized economies as Austria and Argentina.[2] Large MNEs therefore have considerable power in negotiating business arrangements with nation-states that may be of greater consequence than many treaties among countries. Executives of MNEs frequently deal directly with heads of state in small, lesser-developed countries that approve of private ownership as well as in large industrialized nations such as the Soviet Union that favor state ownership of productive facilities.

CONFLICTS AMONG CONSTITUENCIES

The Domestic Conflict

Firms must satisfy
- Stockholders
- Employees
- Customers
- Society at large

A firm must satisfy different groups—stockholders, employees, customers, and society at large—if it is to survive. In the short run, the aims of each group are in conflict. Stockholders, for example, want additional sales and productivity increases, which result in higher profits to be passed on to them in the form of increased dividends or appreciation in equity. Employees would like additional compensation. For customers, lower prices are the priority, and for society at large increased corporate taxes or company involvement in social functions are important. In the long run, all of these aims must be achieved adequately or none will be attained at all, since each group is powerful enough to cause the demise of the organization.

Management must be aware of these various interests but serve them unevenly at any given period. At one moment, most gains may go to consumers; at another time, stockholders may benefit most. Making necessary trade-offs is a difficult task domestically; abroad, where corporate managers are relatively unfamiliar with customs and power groups, the problem of choosing the best alternative is compounded; this is particularly true when dominant interests differ from country to country. For example, Ford Motor Company faced quite different priorities in various countries of the world in the early 1970s. In Great Britain, labor clearly dominated, while prices rose and profits suffered; in the United States, society as a whole (whether consumers or not) demanded more safety and pollution-abatement equipment on automobiles, while wage and price freezes were enforced. Simultaneously, Ford announced that it would build very inexpensive cars in Southeast Asia for the Asian market. There, safety standards and employee compensation gave way to stockholder profits and consumer prices.

Cross-National Conflicts

Decisions made in one country have repercussions elsewhere.

The most cumbersome problem in overseas relationships is not so much one of trying to serve conflicting interests within countries, but rather one of handling cross-national controversies in a manner that will achieve worldwide business objectives. The international company operates in a nationalistic world: Constituencies in any given country seek to fulfill their own, rather than global, objectives. This complicates management's task, since decisions made in one country may have repercussions in another country as well. Among the many decisions managers must make are the location of production, decision making, and research and development (R&D); the method of acquisition and operation; the markets to be served from production; the prices to charge; and the use of profits. In the opening case, for example, many Canadians were concerned about such issues. Assume that a U.S. investor has production facilities in both the United States and Canada: Which facility will export to Venezuela? Clearly the decision will determine where the profits, taxes, employment, and capital flows will be located. Interests in either country, as well as in Venezuela, may claim they should have jurisdiction over the sales.

EVALUATION PROBLEMS

Isolated versus Systems Effects

Effects of MNE's activities may be positive for one national objective and simultaneously negative for another.

An MNE's actions may affect a wide range of economic, social, and political objectives. A positive influence on one objective, such as full employment, may be concomitant with a negative effect on another objective, such as domestic control over economic matters. In other words, there must be trade-offs. Nations find it difficult to prioritize objectives, since they naturally want only benefits without costs, which is seldom possible. Despite the widespread effects on various parts of the social system, much of the literature analyzing MNEs is written to attempt to isolate effects to a single given objective, sometimes because a solution is needed for a given problem, such as a balance of payments deficit for a country. Very often, however, proponents or opponents of an MNE choose to publicize those activities that may win over support to their way of thinking. One must therefore be careful to analyze effects in terms of a systems perspective rather than an isolated one. One should also be aware that it is no simple task to evaluate overall effects when difficult value judgments on trade-offs must be made between, for example, a quantifiable economic objective and a political or social effect that must be argued qualitatively.

Cause–Effect Relationships

It is hard to determine whether societal conditions are caused by MNE actions.

Simply because two factors have moved in relationship to each other does not prove an interconnection between them. Yet because of the growth of MNEs, a number of events in recent years have been attributed to them. Opponents of MNEs have linked inequitable income and power distribution, environmental debasement, and societal deprivation to the growth of international firms; proponents have related tax revenues, employment, and exports to the existence of MNEs. Although the data are often accurate and convincing, it is not certain what would have happened had MNEs not operated or followed certain practices. Technological developments, competitors' actions, and governmental policies are just three of the variables that encumber a cause–effect analysis.

Individual and Aggregate Effects

The philosophy and actions of each MNE are unique.

One astute observer has said, "Like animals in a zoo, multinationals (and their affiliates) come in various shapes and sizes, perform distinctive functions, behave differently and make their individual impacts on the environment."[3] Thus it is difficult to make general statements about impacts. Yet much of the literature, from the viewpoints of both protagonists and antagonists, takes isolated examples and presents them as typical. The examples chosen usually make interesting reading because of their spectacular or extreme nature; there is some danger that policies may be set on the basis of the exceptional rather than the usual.

Some countries have tried to evaluate MNEs and their activities individually. Although this might lead to greater fairness and control, it is a cumbersome and costly process. Many of the policies and control mechanisms therefore are applied to all MNEs. Although this eliminates some of the bureaucracy, it risks throwing out some "good apples" with the "bad apples."

Relative and Absolute Gains or Losses

In an international transaction
- Both parties may gain
- Both parties may lose
- One party may gain while the other loses

In international transactions involving MNEs people sometimes erroneously assume that if one party gains, the other must lose. While that may happen, it is also possible that both parties will either gain or lose in economic transactions. No party would participate willingly in a cross-national transaction in the belief that the deal would harm its priorities. Controversies develop because things do not work out as anticipated, because the precedence given to the trade-offs among objectives changes, and because of disagreements over the distribution of gains when it is acknowledged that both parties have benefited overall. The last problem is at the heart of most controversies. As described in the opening case, Canada has tried to encourage foreign investment but to secure more benefit from it. This was done with the FIRA and later with different approaches through Investment Canada.[4]

Even when both parties gain, they may disagree over share gain.

Countries want greater share of benefits from MNE activities.

Allegations against International Business Activities

The relationship between international firms and societies has generated so many allegations and controversies that they all cannot be examined in this chapter. A number of these deal not so much with whether international business should take place but rather with some specific practices. These latter allegations apply to specific operational areas of management and can, fortunately, be examined in later chapters of the text. They are no less important than the overall areas to be discussed in this chapter and are listed as follows so that students are aware of the wide range of criticisms:

1. In transferring technology to LDCs, prices are set too high and sales restricted too stringently (Chapter 15).
2. If a country attempts regulation, MNEs merely divest and move where regulations are less stringent (Chapter 16).
3. The centralization and control of key functions by MNEs in their home countries perpetuate a neocolonial dependence of LDCs (Chapter 17).
4. Sensitive information about countries is disseminated internationally by MNEs' global intelligence networks (Chapter 17).
5. MNEs introduce superfluous products that do not contribute to social needs and perpetuate class distinctions (Chapter 18).
6. MNEs avoid paying taxes (Chapter 19).
7. Through artificial transfer pricing, MNEs undermine attempts by governments to manage their economic affairs (Chapter 20).

8. The best jobs are given to citizens of the nation in which MNEs have their headquarters (Chapter 21).
9. Inappropriate technology is introduced by MNEs to LDCs (Chapter 21).
10. National labor interests are undermined because of the global activities of MNEs (Chapter 21).

ECONOMIC IMPACT

Balance of Payments Effects

Place in the economic system. Of international economic relationships few topics elicit as much discussion as the balance of payments effect of trade and investment transactions.[5] Discussion itself leads often to incentives, prohibitions, and other types of governmental interference as countries try to regulate the capital flows that parallel trade and investment movements.

One country's surplus is another's deficit, but long- and short-term goals are different.

The distinction between balance of payments arguments and cross-national problems is that gains are a **zero sum,** meaning that one country's surplus shows up as another country's deficit. If both countries were looking only at a limited time period and if both were interested only in the balance of payments effect of international transactions, then one country might be described justifiably as a winner at the expense of the other. In fact, objectives are not this limited. A country may be willing to endure deficits in order to achieve other aims, such as price stability or growth, or it also may be willing to forego short-term surpluses in favor of long-term ones or vice versa.

May be positive or negative

Effect of individual direct investment. Two extreme hypothetical examples illustrate the need to evaluate each activity separately if a person wants to determine the effect on the balance of payments. In the first case, a foreign firm purchases a Haitian-owned company by depositing dollars in a Swiss bank for the former owners. No changes are made in management or operations, so profitability remains the same. Dividends now are remitted to the foreign owners rather than remaining in Haiti, so that there is a net drain on foreign exchange for Haiti and a subsequent influx to another country. In the next case a foreign firm purchases unemployed resources (land, labor, materials, and equipment) in Haiti that it converts to the production of formerly imported goods. Because of rising demand, all earnings are reinvested in Haiti, so the entire import substitution is a gain in foreign exchange.

Formula to determine effect is simple, but figures to put in formula are questionable.

Most investments or nonequity arrangements (such as licensing or management contracts) fall somewhere between these two simplistic and extreme examples and are not evaluated so easily, particularly when policymakers attempt to apply regulations to fit aggregate investment movements. There are numerous measurement difficulties, but guidelines are gradually emerging and are being used by both recipient and donor countries. A basic equation for making an analysis is

$$B = m + x + c - (m^1 + x^1 + c^1),$$

where

B = balance of payments effect,
m = import displacement,
m^1 = import stimulus,
x = export stimulus,
x^1 = export reduction,
c = capital inflow for other than import and export payment, and
c^1 = capital outflow for other than import and export payment.

Although the equation is simple, the problem of choosing the proper values to assign is formidable. Take the case of the **net import change** ($m - m^1$) that results from the direct investment. To determine the value of m, we would need to know how much would be imported in the absence of the foreign production capability. Clearly, the amount the firm has produced and sold locally is only an indication, since the selling price and quality of products may be different from what would otherwise be imported. Furthermore, some of the local sales may have been at the expense of local competitors. The value of m^1 should include equipment, components, and materials brought in for manufacturing the product locally. It should also include estimates of import increases due to upward movements in national income caused by the capital inflow. For instance, if national income were assumed to have risen $2 million from the investment and the marginal propensity to import were calculated to be 10 percent, imports should have risen by $200,000.

The **net export effect** ($x - x^1$) is particularly controversial in donor countries, since conclusions vary widely depending on the assumptions made. The argument is much like the riddle of whether the chicken or egg came first. For example, some critics in the United States have argued that when U.S. firms develop foreign production capabilities they merely substitute for what would otherwise be produced in the United States. These critics have argued that the foreign output sometimes is a substitute for U.S. exports and sometimes imported to displace domestic output. MNEs' response to the critics has been that moves abroad are defensive—that is, restrictions of foreign governments and shifts in cost advantages make foreign production inevitable. By moving abroad, U.S. MNEs pick up business that would otherwise go to foreign firms. MNEs have argued further that the investments stimulate exports from the United States because of the purchase by foreign subsidiaries of equipment, materials, components, and complementary products. Figures show, in fact, that perhaps as much as 70 percent of U.S. exports are by foreign direct investors and that this portion is growing.[6] Again we must make assumptions about the amount of these exports that could have materialized had the subsidiaries not been established.

The **net capital flow** ($c - c^1$) is the easiest figure to calculate because of controls at most central banks. The problem in using a given year for evaluation purposes is the time lag between the outward flow of investment funds and the inward flow of remitted earnings from the investment. Thus what appears at a given time to be a favorable or unfavorable capital flow may in fact prove to be the opposite over a longer period. The payback period (the time it takes to recoup the capital outflow) is affected by differences in company philosophy, type of industry, ability to borrow locally, the host country's balance of payments situation, and the perception of relative risk in the recipient country. Consequently, the capital flows may vary widely from one project to another. A further complication arises because of the ability of international companies to transfer funds in disguised forms (see Chapter 19), thus misstating the real consequences of the investments.

Although the equation is useful for broadly evaluating the balance of payments effects of investments, it should be used with caution. In addition to some of the data problems mentioned earlier, an investment movement might have some indirect effects on a country's balance of payments that are not quantifiable readily. For example, an investor might bring new technological or managerial efficiencies that are then emulated by other firms. What these other firms do may affect therefore the country's external economic relations.

Balance of payments effect of direct investments usually is:
- Positive initially for recipient country and negative for donor
- Positive later for donor country and negative for recipient.

Aggregate assumptions and responses. In spite of the formidable task of evaluating investments from a balance of payments standpoint, there is near consensus that, while investments are initially favorable to the recipient country and unfavorable to the donor country, the situation reverses after some time. This occurs because nearly all investors plan to remit eventually to the parent organization more than they send abroad. If the net value of the foreign investment continues to grow through retained earnings, dividend payments for a given year ultimately may exceed the total capital transfers required for the initial investment. The time period before reversal may vary substantially, and there is much disagreement as to the aggregate time span needed.

Donors and recipients set policies to try to improve short- or long-term effects
- Donors set outflow restrictions
- Recipients set repatriation restrictions, asset valuation control, and conversion to debt as opposed to equity.

In the case of U.S. firms' direct investment abroad, for example, more than half of the net value increase in recent years typically has come from the reinvestment of funds earned abroad. This means that the increase in claims on foreign assets has been coming primarily *not* from a flow of capital to the foreign operations. It also means that the return flow of funds to the United States from earnings greatly exceeds the outward flow to increase investment abroad.

From the standpoint of donor countries, restrictions on the outflow of capital improve short-term deficits, since there should be an immediate improvement in the capital account of the balance of payments. Such restrictions should be effective until repatriation in the absence of restrictions would begin to exceed the capital flow that is restricted. After this period, capital outflow restrictions would merely aggravate a deficit problem. Consequently, the restrictions only buy the possible time needed to institute other means for solving payments difficulties.

Governments also have sought to attract inflows of long-term capital as a means of developing production that will either displace imports or generate exports. This has been particularly true of LDCs. They have sought locally manufactured production in order to ease dependence on the traditional agricultural products and raw materials that have not comprised as important a part of world trade. The problem for recipients, then, is how to take advantage of the benefits of foreign capital while also minimizing the long-run adverse effects on their balance of payments.

Many countries have tried to ease their dilemmas by regulating inflows to assure that short-term positive impacts are maximized and to restrict longer-term capital exports. Sometimes countries have required that new foreign investment be made in the form of freely convertible currencies, industrial equipment, and other physical assets but not in the form of goodwill, technology, patents, trademarks, and other intangibles. These requirements are tied into regulations on maximum repatriation of earnings, which are stated as a percentage of investment; by holding down the stated amount of investment, eventual repatriation is minimized. In this respect, greater control is exerted over the prices of equipment brought in, especially when the investor is also the equipment supplier, so that the investment value is not overstated. Governments also are becoming more interested in receiving part of the capital contribution in the form of loans and in local holdings of equity so that the future outward capital flow is reduced and has an upward limit.

Growth and Employment Effects

Growth and employment effects are not a zero-sum game because:

- MNEs may use unemployed or underemployed resources
- Healthiest domestic firms own the bulk of foreign direct investment.

Unlike balance of payments, the growth and employment effects of MNEs are not necessarily a zero-sum game among countries. Early economists assumed that production factors were at full employment; consequently, a movement of any of these factors abroad would result in an increase in output abroad and a decrease at home. Even if this assumption were true, the gains in the recipient country might be greater or less than the losses in the donor country.

The argument that both the donor and recipient country may gain from direct investment is premised partly on the assumption that resources are not necessarily fully employed and partly on the industry-specific and complementary nature of capital and technology. A farm machinery manufacturer may, for example, be producing maximally for its domestic and export market. This firm may not move easily into other product lines or use its financial resources to effect domestic productivity increases. By participating in the establishment of a foreign production facility the firm may be able to develop foreign sales without decreasing the employment of resources domestically. In fact, the firm may hire additional domestic personnel to manage the international operations. The firm may receive dividends and royalties from its capital and technology being used abroad, thus further increasing domestic income. The foreign facility even may stimulate export sales because of a need for components and replacement parts along with the ability of the foreign operation to sell the companies' related products.

Home country labor claims that jobs are exported through direct investment.

Donor country losses. As the largest donor country for foreign licensing and direct investment, the United States understandably has some of the major critics of outward movements. One such critic is organized labor, which argues that foreign production often displaces what would otherwise have been U.S. exports. They cite many examples of highly advanced technology that has been at least partially developed through governmental contracts and then transferred abroad. In fact, U.S. MNEs are now moving some of their most advanced technologies abroad and are even, in some cases, producing abroad before they do so in the United States. An example is the transfer of aerospace technology by General Dynamics to Japan to produce fighter planes. According to critics, if General Dynamics did not transfer the technology, Japan would purchase the products in the United States, thus increasing employment and output. On the other hand, Japan might have developed technology itself had General Dynamics not made the sale, even though this would have delayed Japan's acquisition of this aircraft.[7]

Recipient countries may gain through:

- More optimum use of production factors
- Utilization of ideal resources
- Upgrade of resource quality.

Recipient country gains. Most observers agree that an inflow of foreign resources by international firms can initiate increased local development through a more optimum combination of production factors and the utilization or upgrading of idle resources. The most common types of resource transmission are capital and technology, which investors may transfer simultaneously. The firm is motivated to move these resources because of the higher return in an area of shortage than in an area of abundance.

International firms may enable idle resources to be used. The mere existence of resources is no guarantee they will contribute to output: Oil production, for instance, requires not only the underground deposits, but also the knowledge of where to find them and the capital equipment to bring the oil to the surface. Production is useless without markets and transport facilities, which an international investor may be able to supply. The access to foreign markets, particularly the investor's home market, may be particularly important to developing countries that lack the knowledge and resources necessary to sell there. An example is the sale of Mexican asparagus in the United States under the recognized Green Giant label. U.S. consumers associate the brand with known quality; it might be prohibitively expensive for Mexican producers to gain the same brand recognition on their own.[8] Another less tangible aspect of this relationship may lead to greater resource utilization: Through exposure to new consumer products, the local labor force may develop new wants, encouraging them to work longer and harder to acquire the new goods and services.

The upgrading of resources by the international firm may be brought about through the education of local personnel to utilize equipment, technology, and modern production methods. Even such seemingly minor programs as those promoting on-the-job safety may result in a reduction of lost worker time and machine down time. The transference of work skills increases efficiency, thereby freeing time for other activities.

Recipient countries may lose if MNE investments:

- Merely replace local firms
- Take best resources
- Destroy local entrepreneurship.

Recipient country losses. Some critics have claimed that there are examples in which MNEs have made investments that domestic firms otherwise would have undertaken. The result may be the bidding up of prices without additional output or the displacement of local entrepreneurship.

Observers argue, for example, that by its ability to raise funds in various countries, the foreign firm can reduce its capital cost vis-à-vis local firms and apply the savings either to attracting the best personnel or to enticing customers from competitors through added promotional efforts. However, evidence is inconclusive. Frequently, international firms do pay higher salaries and spend more on promotion than local firms; however, it is uncertain whether this results from external advantages or a required added cost of attracting workers and customers when entering new markets. Added compensation and promotion costs may negate any advantages from access to cheap foreign capital. Additionally, in many instances, the local competition also has access to cheap capital.

Critics also contend that foreign investment destroys local entrepreneurship drives, which have an important effect on development. Since expectation of success is necessary for the inauguration of entrepreneurial activity, the collapse of small cottage industries when confronted with the consolidation efforts of large foreign enterprises may make the local population feel incapable of competing. However, the presence of multinational firms may either increase or decrease the level of competition in host country markets.[9]

First, the foreign firm may itself serve as a role model that local talent can imitate. Furthermore, foreign enterprises buy many services, goods, and supplies locally and may thus stimulate local entrepreneurship. For example, the Bougainville Copper Limited (BCL) in Papua New Guinea established a development foundation to help set up new businesses. BCL has used local sources of goods and services and has contracted out many things that had formerly been done with company personnel.[10] In fact, the real entrepreneur will find areas in which to compete; consequently, in any country there are success stories that can be emulated.

Finally, it is frequently contended that the international firm sops up local capital, either by borrowing locally or by receipt of investment incentives. This raises the cost of funds and/or makes insufficient funds available to local firms. Although subsidiaries have borrowed heavily in local markets and have exploited investment incentives, this link and the ability of local firms to finance expansion is unclear. In order for international firms to have a noticeable effect on the ability of local firms to secure capital, the amount of funds diverted to foreign investors would have to be larger in relation to the size of the capital market than is probably the case. Furthermore, there are few examples of international firms that acquire all resources locally; thus the additional resources brought in should usually yield a gain for the economy.

Host countries have not only at times prohibited the entry of foreign companies that were believed to inhibit local firms, but they also have restricted local borrowing and have provided incentives for firms to locate in depressed areas where resources are idle rather than scarce. Of particular concern to many countries are foreign investments involving the purchase of local companies. Canada's Foreign Investment Review Act and its Investment Canada Act, discussed in the opening case of this chapter, typify policies in many countries in that they treat acquisitions more carefully than foreign investments started from scratch.

General conclusions. Clearly not all MNE activities will have the same effect on growth in either the home or host country, nor are the effects easily determined. While there are dangers in attempting to categorize, the following generalizations are helpful in understanding the circumstances in which foreign investment is most likely to have a positive impact on the host country.[11]

Direct investment more likely generates growth:

- In LDCs
- When product or process is highly differentiated
- When foreign firms have access to scarce resources
- When investment is in the more advanced of the developing countries.

1. *Developed versus LDCs.* Developed areas such as Western Europe or Canada are more likely than LDCs to have domestic firms capable of undertaking similar investments to those in which foreign investors engage. Foreign investment in developed countries is therefore more likely to be merely a substitute for domestic investment, thus yielding less growth than in developing countries.
2. *The degree of product sophistication.* When the foreign investor undertakes production of highly differentiated products or process technologies, it is less likely that local firms in the host country could undertake similar production on their own. The differentiation may come from product style, quality, or brand name in addition to technology.
3. *Access to resources.* When the foreign investor has access to resources that firms in the host country cannot easily attain, it is more likely to generate growth rather than just substituting for what local firms would otherwise do. Some of the resources would be capital, management skills, and access to external markets.
4. *Degree of development of a developing country.* Foreign investors are more likely to transfer technology and serve as role models for growth in

the more economically advanced of the developing countries. In the least developed LDC the investment may have a negative impact on growth if the investment merely exploits cheap labor that would otherwise be subsisting.[12]

POLITICAL CONFLICTS

Nation-states have concern that:

- MNE is foreign policy instrument of home government
- MNE is independent of any government
- MNE is pawn of host government.

Because of the size of many MNEs, there is considerable concern that they will undermine through political means the sovereignty of nation-states. At the forefront of the concern is that the MNE will be used as a foreign-policy instrument of its home government.[13] Since the home countries for nearly all MNEs are industrial countries, it is understandable that there has been relatively more (but not sole) concern in LDCs. Two other sovereignty questions are raised less frequently. One is that the MNE may become independent of both the home and host country, thus making it difficult for either to do certain things considered to be in the best societal interest. The other is that the MNE might become so dependent on foreign operations that a host country can then use it as a foreign policy instrument against the home or another country.

Home Country Control

Extraterritoriality occurs when governments apply their laws to companies' foreign operations.

Extraterritoriality. When governments extend the application of their laws to the foreign operations of companies, the term used to describe the situation is **extraterritorality.** Host countries generally abhor these occurrences, since they weaken the countries' own sovereignty over local business practices. Companies likewise fear situations in which the home and foreign laws conflict, since settlement inevitably must be between governmental offices, with companies caught in the middle.

Trade restrictions. The U.S. government has attempted to apply its Trading with the Enemy Act to the foreign affiliates of U.S. firms to keep them from selling to certain communist countries. This puts subsidiaries in such countries as France and Canada in a dilemma because the laws in those countries require that the sales be made.[14] More recently, a number of countries have agreed to prohibit shipments of certain goods to South Africa because of racial policies. The same racial policies have led many states and institutions within the United States to hold only "South Africa-free" stocks within their portfolios, which has contributed directly to divestment of South African investments by U.S. MNEs. Through a series of presidential orders, foreign affiliates of U.S. firms have been prevented from making sales to such countries as South Africa, Libya, and Nicaragua even though the orders violate the laws of some of the countries where the affiliates are operating. U.S. firms' subsidiaries also are restricted from participating in the Arab boycott of Israel even though the boycott is a foreign policy instrument of the countries where the subsidiaries are located.[15]

Antitrust. In the case of antitrust the United States has at various times delayed its companies' acquiring facilities in foreign countries (e.g., Gillette's purchase of Braun in West Germany), forced firms to sell their interest in foreign operations (e.g., Alcoa's spin-off of Alcan), and restricted entry of goods produced by foreign combines in which U.S. firms participated (e.g., Swiss watches and parts).[16] The policies for which firms have been restrained have been legal in the countries where the actions took place. The Canadian cabinet, the British House of Lords, and the Australian parliament even enacted laws that forbade Gulf Oil, Rio Tinto Zinc, and Westinghouse from supplying information to the U.S. Justice Department about their participation in a uranium cartel outside the United States. The Canadian government was particularly outraged because it had been one of the principal organizers of the cartel.[17] From a reverse standpoint, the United States objected to the European Community's (EC) antitrust prosecution of IBM because it felt the EC did not have jurisdiction.

One of the cumbersome problems for U.S. firms has been the vagueness with which the U.S. Justice Department views their associations abroad. This has been mitigated partially with publications on foreign merger guidelines including case situations on how antitrust enforcement principles would be applied.[18] Included in the associations that might be subject to challenge are the participation in cartels to set prices or production quotas, the granting of exclusive distributorships abroad, and the forming of joint research and/or manufacturing operations in foreign countries. The United States also has signed a number of bilateral treaties with other industrialized countries so that they consult with each other on restrictive business practices.

An emerging antitrust question is the possible competitive advantage that firms gain through ownership of foreign investments. Once a firm has investments in place in a number of foreign countries, it is in a better position to recognize new market opportunities in those countries.[19]

Other issues. Laws need not be in complete conflict for extraterritoriality to exist. Laws requiring companies to remit earnings or to pay taxes at home of foreign earnings certainly have affected foreign expansion and local governments' control over the expansion. When Moet-Hennessy bought California vineyards, French law prevented the use of the term *champagne* for the sparkling wine the French company planned to produce.[20]

There are a number of areas in which legal differences among countries enable or even require firms to operate differently among these countries. When home country constituents hold ethical or moral values that vary greatly from those abroad, there has been a growing concern as to whether home country governments should regulate their MNEs in order to institute those values abroad. As is true of most ethical and value controversies, the arguments are frequently highly emotional. A number of these issues may lead to future extraterritorial application, such as additional pressures on MNEs to terminate operations in South Africa.[21]

Frequently, regulations in a foreign country are less stringent than those at home because: (1) The foreign country has not yet faced certain problems; (2) it is less sophisticated at anticipating the adverse effects of certain policies, or (3) it believes that the gains outweigh the adversities. A growing controversy in the United States is whether products withdrawn from U.S. sales after being found too hazardous can be exported for sale abroad. On one hand, people argue that the standards are designed for the U.S. and should not be imposed on other countries, which can freely block the entry of hazardous products; on the other hand, critics maintain that there is no biological or ethical reason for treating people differently on safety issues and that "Made in America" should be a sign of quality and not a warning.[22] Pharmaceutical firms have been criticized for conducting tests on humans abroad that were not allowed in the United States and for selling items abroad that were not yet approved by the U.S. Food and Drug Administration. On the other hand, they have also been faulted for being too cautious in what they do abroad. For example, the U.S. State Department criticized Eli Lilly and Company's refusal to sell its herbicide, tebuthiuron, to the U.S. government to use for eradicating coca plants in Peru. Lilly was concerned because the product was considered too potent to use on U.S. cropland, had not been tested in Peruvian soil conditions, and was still being tested as to health effects.[23] These situations involve not only the possible problems of extraterritoriality already discussed, but also of whether home country governments or international firms should try to impose their own standards on other countries.

Key Sector Control

Political concerns include:

- Fear of influence or disruption of local politics
- Foreign control of sensitive sectors of the local economy.

Closely related to the extraterritoriality concept is the fear that if foreign ownership dominates key industries, then decisions made outside of the country may have extremely adverse effects on the local economy or may exert an influence on local politics. This suggests two questions: (1) Are the important decisions actually made outside the host countries? (2) If so, are these decisions different from those that would be made by local companies?

There are numerous examples of decisions that can and have been made centrally, such as what, where, and how much to produce and sell and at what prices. These decisions might cause different rates of expansion in different countries and possible closing of plants with pursuant employment disruption. Furthermore, by withholding resources or accepting strikes the international firm may affect other local industries adversely as well.

Some observers argue that governments generally have more control over companies that are headquartered in their own countries than they have over a subsidiary of a foreign firm. Since home country operations usually comprise the largest single portion of activity for companies, generally they will go to further lengths to protect their home position than their foreign ones. Furthermore, since virtually all board members, upper-level corporate officers, and stockholders are home country nationals, the firm will tend to favor home country objectives more than foreign country objectives in conflict situations.

Political fears are based on the beliefs that international companies may serve as instruments of foreign policy for their home governments and that they also may be powerful enough to disrupt or influence local politics. The former fear is largely a carryover from colonial periods, when such firms as Levant and the British East India Company very often acted as the political arm of their home governments. There are no examples of recent official cooperation of this type. However, there is fear that powerful foreign firms, by withholding resources at the request of the home government, might influence the political process. In the mid-1970s, for example, the U.S. State Department requested that Gulf Oil suspend its Angolan operations in an effort to weaken Soviet-backed factions that were taking control of the government. Several months later Gulf received State Department permission to deal directly with the leftist government in order to resume operations. In the mid-1980s, the story was repeated for other U.S. firms operating in Libya and Nicaragua. Then in 1988 the U.S. government urged U.S. firms not to pay taxes or debts to the Panamanian government,[24] because of its alleged drug dealings. Not only have newly emerging nations been concerned: The French and British have worried, for example, that if U.S. computer companies were to withhold output, they could create havoc in the governmental administrations, companies, and research laboratories dependent on them.

Aside from establishing policies that generally restrict foreign investment entry, countries have prevented selectively foreign domination of a so-called **key industry,** one that might affect a very large segment of the economy by virtue of its size or influence on other sectors. Examples of such protection are the various nationalizations of foreign-owned mining, utility, and transportation companies. In other cases, the government has required management by local personnel in order to ensure that the entities can survive, if necessary, without foreign domination. Some sensitive areas, such as radio and television transmission stations in the United States, are simply off limits for foreign investment. In a few cases, governments have supported the development of competitive local firms, such as consortia of computer manufacturers (for example, ICL in Britain; Telefunken and Nixdorf in West Germany; and Siemens, CII, and Philips in West Germany and the Netherlands) and consortia of aircraft producers (for example, Messerschmitt-Boelkow-Blohm in West Germany; British Aerospace in Britain; Aeritalia in Italy; and Construcciones Aeronauticas in Spain).[25]

State-owned enterprises. There are many state-owned enterprises, of which some are MNEs. The political concern about home country control of these enterprises is different only in degree from other MNEs. Both may in time of conflict give in to the home country interests; however, the state enterprise may be more prone to do so and do so more quickly. Home government officials may be able to influence these firms more easily. Renault, for example, did not hesitate to transfer production from Spain to France in order to avoid employment reductions in the home country whereas a private French MNE may not have made this decision as easily.[26]

MNE Independence

International firms can play one country against another but are reluctant to abandon fixed resources.

The discussion thus far has centered on the fear that international firms are unduly influenced by their home governments. Many observers also fear that these companies can avoid, by playing one country against another, coming under any unfavorable restrictions. For instance, if they do not like the wage rates, union laws, fair employment requirements, or pollution and safety codes in one country, they can move elsewhere or at least threaten to do so. In addition, they can develop structures to minimize the payment of taxes anywhere. However, the fact that companies generally are reluctant to abandon fixed assets in one country to move abroad indicates that these charges probably are exaggerated. Furthermore, the country from which a firm moves can easily restrict the importation of the goods produced abroad under the more favorable conditions. Specific types of conflicts concerning the movement of resources will be discussed in subsequent chapters.

Political Involvement

Historically foreign firms exert a great influence on local politics.

There is concern that the foreign firm will meddle in local politics to foster its own objectives rather than local ones. As recently as 1949, an association of six European firms handled 66 percent of Nigeria's imports and 70 percent of the exports; other European firms had a virtual monopoly on shipping and banking. Because of this economic power, the foreign companies, through forced regulations, forbade Nigerian competition and employment except in the more menial and lower-paying activities. Despite the headline examples, such as the discovery in 1972 of offers by ITT to support a group that planned to overthrow the Chilean government, most evidence shows that international firms have avoided local political involvement in recent years. Even in the ITT situation, the argument could be made that the action was no different than that taken by many locally controlled firms facing nationalization. Nevertheless, such instances kindle fears of a return to earlier periods when some foreign investors did manage to pick local leadership supportive of their firm's activities, regardless of the effect on the local population.

Bribery

Payments to government officials are widespread:

- To secure business from competitors
- To facilitate services
- To assure safety.

Extent. No discussion of the impact of MNEs would be complete without mentioning the disclosures in the 1970s of payments to government officials variously described as "scandalous," "improper," "extorted," "unauthorized," "questionable," and "illegal." Inquiries by the Securities and Exchange Commission (SEC) revealed that such payments amounted to several hundred million dollars.[27]

While much of the criticism has been vented against MNEs (especially those from the United States), it is interesting to note how widespread the practice has been. The investigations showed that officials in industrial as well as developing countries, foreign as well as U.S. nationals, communists as well as noncommunists, have all participated in bribery.[28] Bribery is simply common in many countries, and international firms have conformed.

Motives. By far the biggest motive for the outlays was to secure business that otherwise might not be forthcoming at all or to get it at the expense of competitors. These were mainly for governmental contract sales, and some of the higher fees were in the area of aerospace. Second in importance were expenditures to facilitate governmental services that firms were entitled to receive but that officials otherwise would have delayed. These included such things as product registrations, construction permits, and import clearances. Some firms acknowledged payments in order to reduce tax liabilities, and one (General Tire) paid to keep a competitor from operating in a specific country (Morocco). A group of rubber companies made payments through the Chamber of Rubber Manufacturers in Mexico to get the government to approve price increases that were controlled. Some companies reported payments because of extortion: These included Mobil's payments to forego the closing of its refinery in Naples, Italy, and expenditures by Boise Cascade, IBM, and Gillette to protect the safety of their employees. Some of the payments were contributions to political parties, a practice that is legal in certain foreign countries but not allowed in the United States.

Methods. Most payments were in cash, but in some cases they included products made by the company, such as ITT's gift of a color television set to the managing director of Belgium's state telephone system. Some payments were made directly to governmental officials by the firms; however, most involved the use of intermediaries and/or organizations in third countries. The methods were diverse: For instance, a person influential in a purchasing decision or a relative of that person was sometimes put on the firm's payroll as a consultant; in other cases that person was paid as a middleman at a fee that exceeded normal commissions. Another common practice was to overcharge a middleman or governmental agency and rebate the overcharge to an individual, usually in a foreign country, in order to evade taxes or exchange control.

One firm (Pullman) even used its auditor to effect payment to a governmental official.

Some consequences. Bribery scandals resulted in the replacement of chiefs of state in Honduras, Japan, and Italy. Prince Bernhard of the Netherlands resigned all his public functions after charges that he had accepted a $1.1 million payoff. Officials were jailed in a number of countries, such as Venezuela, Iran, and Pakistan. Sri Lanka cancelled orders for Lockheed aircraft because of that firm's scandals elsewhere. Many observers contend that these disclosures have helped the political parties in many countries that have opposed large defense outlays.

The present legislation is controversial because:

- Some payments are legal to expedite compliance with law, but others are not
- Extraterritoriality issues emerge
- Business may be lost.

Foreign Corrupt Practices Act. In 1977 the United States passed controversial legislation making certain payments to foreign officials illegal. Part of the controversy surrounding this legislation has been its vagueness and seeming inconsistencies. The vagueness stemmed from the fact that two different U.S. agencies could prosecute firms; however, the Justice Department since has published its interpretations of the laws and the Securities and Exchange Commission (SEC) has ceded its enforcement to the Justice Department.[29] One of the seeming inconsistencies is that it is perfectly legal to make payments to people to expedite their compliance with the law but illegal to make payments to other governmental officials who are not directly responsible for carrying out the law. For example, a $10,000 payment to a customs official to clear legally permissible merchandise would be legal, but even a small payment to a governmental minister to influence the customs official would be illegal.[30] The reason for allowing the expediting payments is that in many countries the governmental officials will delay compliance of laws indefinitely until they do receive payments, although these payments may themselves be illegal in the country where they are paid.

Some of the objections are more fundamental. For the United States to impose its standards on its firms operating in other countries may be viewed in some cases as just another extraterritorial infringement. In fact it may be viewed as a double standard in that U.S. governmental aid frequently is given as a bribe, with the understanding that the recipient country will grant political concessions in return. Furthermore, there is little effort to blame donors or suspend these government-to-government programs when it is discovered that officials in recipient countries have siphoned off aid funds for themselves.

Although the actions of U.S. MNEs have been highly publicized, U.S. MNEs did not invent bribery. At present there are still at least two unknowns: (1) To what extent do domestic firms and MNEs of other countries engage in the activities for which U.S. MNEs have been criticized? and (2) To what extent is business lost to those other firms as U.S. MNEs are heavily regulated in their activities abroad?

Host Country Captives

Critics have made allegations that MNEs may become so dependent on foreign operations that they begin to try to influence their home government to adopt policies favorable to the foreign countries although those policies may not be in the best interests of the home government. Such assertions are difficult to support because there is always disagreement on what policy will lead to the "best interests." However, there are certainly many examples of lobbying efforts by MNEs seeking the adoption of policies that are more palatable to the people abroad with whom they are doing business. For instance, they have lobbied for different U.S. treatment toward governments in Angola, Nicaragua, and South Africa.

SUMMARY

- Management must understand the need to compromise and satisfy the conflicting interests of stockholders, employees, customers, and society at large. Internationally, the problem is more complex because the relative strength of competing groups will vary by country. Furthermore, the satisfaction of interests in one country may cause dissatisfaction in another country.
- The effects of MNEs are difficult to evaluate because of conflicting influences on different societal objectives, intervening variables that obscure cause–effect relationships, and the differences among MNE practices. Countries are interested not only in their absolute gains or losses, but also in their performance relative to other countries.
- Since a balance of payments surplus in one country must result in a deficit elsewhere, trade and investment transactions have been scrutinized closely for their effects. However, countries often are willing to accept short-term deficits in favor of a long-term surplus or to achieve other economic gains.
- The basic effects on the balance of payments of a foreign investment theoretically can be determined, but there are disagreements about many assumptions that must be made concerning the relationship to trade. Projects are so different that it is difficult to generalize and set effective policies to apply to large groups of investors.
- Governments have attempted to utilize investment to improve their own balance of payments positions by such devices as regulation of capital flows, requirements of partial local ownership, limitation of local borrowing by foreign investors, and stipulations that a part of capital inflows be in the form of loans rather than equity.
- The growth and employment effects of MNEs do not necessarily benefit one country at the expense of another. Much of the effect is due to the relative resource employment with and/or without the MNE's activities.

- MNEs may contribute to growth and employment by enabling idle resources to be used, by using resources more efficiently, and by upgrading the quality of resources.
- Among the factors affecting growth and employment results are the location where MNEs operate, the product sophistication, the competitiveness of local firms, governmental policies, and the degree of product differentiation.
- The political concerns about MNEs center around the possibilities that they might be used as foreign policy instruments of home or host governments or that they avoid the control of any government.
- Extraterritoriality is the application of home country laws to the operations of companies abroad. This sometimes leads to conflicts with host countries and may put the international firm in the untenable position of having to violate the laws of one country or the other.
- Countries are most fearful of foreign control of key sectors in their economies since decisions made abroad may disrupt local economic and political stability. Furthermore, foreigners then may have enough power to adversely affect local sovereignty. There have been numerous moves to restrict foreign ownership in these sectors.

CASE: FOREIGN REAL ESTATE HOLDINGS IN THE UNITED STATES[31]

In comparison with other countries the United States has been relatively free of restrictions on foreign investors. There are few industries, primarily certain types of transportation and communication, in which foreign control is prohibited. These prohibitions have been based on the sensitivity of these areas in informing the public and moving essential commodities in time of crisis. Historically, the only period in which there was a widespread concern about foreign ownership occurred in the late 1800s, when temporary prohibitions were placed on foreign ownership of agricultural land. This does not imply that direct investment cannot be prohibited. In 1987, for example, the U.S. Commerce and Defense Departments mustered sufficient complaints about national security that Fujitsu (Japan) cancelled its bid to acquire Fairchild Semiconductor. However, at about the same time two British firms (British Aerospace and Plessey) each acquired U.S. firms with large defense contracts. The United States has also been a relatively safe place to invest. The only confiscations have been of properties held by interests from enemy countries during the two world wars and the seizure of Iranian assets during the hostage crisis. More recently the use of Libyan assets has been frozen, but not expropriated. (One may also argue that the Revolutionary War was a confiscation of thirteen English investments.) No wars have been fought on U.S. land for over one-hundred years; thus the loss of property through political unrest has been negligible.

After World War II, direct investment flows were almost all out of the United States as U.S. companies took advantage of a strong dollar and a welcome by foreign governments to establish foreign facilities and position themselves well during the pursuant growth period. Foreign firms simply lacked the resources to make the equivalent reverse flows to the United States. In the late 1960s the U.S. Department of Commerce established offices to lure investors to the United States, and several states began including foreign firms as part of their industrial promotion efforts. Although direct investment into the United States accelerated, the movement was largely unnoticed by the general public. One of the reasons was that no approval by U.S. authorities was necessary before the establishment of an investment. Furthermore, it was not even necessary to register anywhere that a foreign investment had been made. Many of the investors maintained a low profile and were not known, even by governmental officials, to be foreign investors.

The Arab oil embargo of 1973 and publicity attendant on the substantial influx of direct investment to the United States during the next few years led to Congress's adoption of the International Investment Survey Act of 1976. Although studies were carried out to assess the nature of direct investment in the United States and although a number of bills have been introduced to restrict foreign ownership, the United States basically has maintained an open-door policy. Subsequent legislation requiring a foreign direct investor to report the establishment of a new U.S. business or acquisition of an interest in an existing U.S. business became effective in 1979. This has not been enough to soothe people who are concerned about the foreign influx. A 1988 poll showed that 78 percent of the people in the United States favor "a law to limit the extent of foreign investment in American business and real estate."

Some of the criticism about foreign investment in the United States is in response to the more stringent control of investment in other countries. The attitude is one of "why don't we treat them as harshly as they treat us?" Much of the concern, though, has focused on specific key sectors deemed vital to the national interest including banking, food, computers, high technology, oil, and coal. One of the areas that has been singled out has been real estate, especially agricultural land.

Some investment critics have argued that the source of investment may be as critical as the amount. They have pointed out that because of the lack of disclosure requirements, the Soviet Union nearly completed the purchase of three banks in California's Silicon Valley to obtain information on high tech companies.

The Agricultural Foreign Investment Disclosure Act of 1978 now requires the reporting of agricultural land transfer to foreigners. The interest in real estate has evolved for a number of reasons: To begin with, it is a sector with an historical emotional tie among Americans: The country was largely settled by landless persons who were able to better themselves economically because of the availability of free or cheap land. Any threat of foreign control traditionally has been viewed negatively. Even with the so-called decline of the western frontier, Americans have placed a high priority on relatively cheap agricultural products and on housing. Numerous reports have alleged that large foreign real estate purchases tended to inflate prices. Many Americans have feared that the rising prices will put land out of reach of the average American. There also has been fear that agricultural output will flow abroad rather than be sold to Americans.

But how widespread is foreign ownership? The U.S. Department of Agriculture estimates that less than one-half of 1 percent of American farmland is owned by foreign investors. Much of this has been acquired by foreign paper companies such as Bowater of Britain and Abitibi of Canada. Considerable publicity also has been given to foreign purchases of housing and office buildings in Miami, Honolulu, and Los Angeles, three areas of considerable activity by foreign purchasers. Capital flight from developing countries, particularly from corrupt dictatorships, has been embarrassing. Although no federal restrictions have been enacted, twenty of the fifty states have restrictions on ownership of property by aliens. Only three states (Iowa, Missouri, and Minnesota) have singled out agricultural property for special treatment. This was done in the late 1970s because of fear that foreign purchases would cause agricultural land prices to jump. But in the 1980s, the prices plummeted. By 1988 U.S. landowners, real estate brokers, and investment bankers were seeking out foreign buyers.

QUESTIONS

1. In the interests of the United States, should restrictions be placed on the foreign acquisition of real estate?
2. If restrictions were to be put in place, what should be restricted (e.g., type of land, nationality of purchaser, use of land, size of holdings)?
3. Should foreign ownership be restricted in sectors other than real estate?
4. What are the likely consequences if the United States does or does not place new limitations on foreign investment?

NOTES

1. Data for the case were taken from "Limits Proposed to Canada Operations," *Wall Street Journal,* February 4, 1972, p. 8; "Canadian Brain Drain, *Wall Street Journal,* May

22, 1973, p. 1; "Canada Passes Law to Screen Investments Made There by Foreigners Starting in '74," *Wall Street Journal,* December 14, 1973, p. 21; Mitchell C. Lynch, "Canada to Tighten Foreign Ownership Rein Further as Economic, Job Pictures Improve," *Wall Street Journal,* May 4, 1973, p. 24; Edward Carrigan, "Canada Must Control Own Industry If It's to Progress, *Citizen* (Ottawa), June 27, 1980, p. 6; John Urquhart, "Canada Drive," *Wall Street Journal,* February 18, 1981, p. 1ff.; Herbert E. Meyer, "Trudeau's War on U.S. Business," *Fortune,* April 6, 1981, pp. 74–82; Harold Crookell, "The Future of U.S. Direct Investment in Canada," *Business Quarterly,* Vol. 48, No. 2, Summer 1983, pp. 22–28; "Canada Takes 'Positive' Step to Attract Foreign Investment," *American Banker,* January 2, 1985, p. 2; "Investment Canada: Invitation to Foreign Capital," *Mergers & Acquisitions,* Vol. 20, No. 4, March–April 1986, pp. 84–85; "America's Half-Open Door," *The Economist,* Vol. 302, No. 7481, January 17, 1987, p. 66; John Urquhart and Peggy Berkowitz, "Northern Angst," *Wall Street Journal,* September 22, 1987, p. 1+.

2. For country data see *The World Bank Atlas, 1987* (Washington, D.C.: The World Bank, 1987); and for company data see "The World's 50 Largest Industrial Corporations," *Fortune,* Vol. 114, No. 3, August 4, 1986, p. 171.

3. John H. Dunning, "The Future of Multinational Enterprise," *Lloyds Bank Review,* July 1974, p. 16.

4. Crookell, *op. cit.,* p. 22.

5. The following discussion draws on problems reported in several studies that attempted to assess the balance of payments effects of direct investments. For a good example of opposing arguments and conclusions see Richard Bernal, "Foreign Investment and Development in Jamaica," *Inter-American Economic Affairs,* Vol. 38, No. 2, Autumn 1984, pp. 3–21; and Ciaran O'Faircheallaigh, "Foreign Investment and Development in Less Developed Countries," *Inter-American Economic Affairs,* Vol. 39, No. 2, Autumn 1985, pp. 27–35.

6. Raymond Vernon, "Multinationals Are Mushrooming," *Challenge,* Vol. 29, No. 2, May–June 1986, p. 42, cites estimates for 1965 and 1977.

7. Stephen Kreider Yoder, "U.S. Defense Chief Approves an Accord with Japan for Joint Production of Jet," *Wall Street Journal,* June 6, 1988, p. 10.

8. David M. Henneberry, "U.S. Foreign Direct Investment in the Developing Nations: A Taxonomy of Host-Country Policy Issues," *Agribusiness,* Vol. 2, No. 1, 1986, p. 97.

9. Emilio Pagoulatos, "Foreign Direct Investment in U.S. Food and Tobacco Manufacturing and Domestic Economic Performance," *American Journal of Agricultural Economics,* Vol. 65, No. 2, May 1983, pp. 405–412.

10. O'Faircheallaigh, *op. cit.,* p. 31.

11. U.S. Department of Commerce, *The Multinational Corporation: Studies on U.S. Foreign Investment,* Vol. 1 (Washington, D.C., 1972), p. 61.

12. Jonghoe Yang and Russell A. Stone, "Investment Dependence, Economic Growth, and Status in the World System: A Test of 'Dependent Development'," *Studies in Comparative International Development,* Vol. 20, No. 1, Spring 1985, pp. 98–120.

13. For a good discussion of various means of gaining political objectives through economic dependency, see Adrienne Armstrong, "The Political Consequences of

Economic Dependence," *Journal of Conflict Resolution,* Vol. 25, No. 3, September 1981, pp. 401–428.

14. "Review & Outlook: Exporting Leadership," *Wall Street Journal,* April 9, 1984, p. 28, gives recent examples of disagreements.

15. See, for example, "Anti-Boycott Charges Are Settled by Fines for Nine Companies," *Wall Street Journal,* October 13, 1983, p. 16; and Elizabeth Weiner and Laurence J. Tell, "Out of South Africa: Divestment Hits a Snag," *Business Week,* July 6, 1987, p. 53.

16. These are but a few of the types of antitrust actions. See J. Townsend, "Extraterritorial Antitrust Revisited—Half a Century of Change," Paper presented at the Academy of International Business, San Francisco, December 1983.

17. "Extraterritorial Trouble," *Wall Street Journal,* December 20, 1979, p. 7; and "Down Under with the U.S. Courts," *Wall Street Journal,* May 1, 1961, p. 24.

18. "Antitrust Guide for Overseas Is Set for Firms," *Wall Street Journal,* January 27, 1977, p. 2; Eleanor M. Fox, "Updating the Antitrust Guide on International Operations—A Greener Light for Export and Investment Abroad," *Vanderbilt Journal of Transnational Law,* Vol. 15, Fall 1982, pp. 713–766.

19. Vernon, *op. cit.,* pp. 44–45.

20. "A Delicious Irony," *Wall Street Journal,* July 17, 1973, p. 44.

21. Robert S. Greenberger, "Business Group Lobbies to Stop Congress from Imposing Sanctions on South Africa," *Wall Street Journal,* April 28, 1988, p. 52.

22. Irvin Molotsky, "Exporting Products Recalled in the U.S.," *New York Times,* April 3, 1984, p. A17.

23. "Lilly Won't Sell Herbicide to U.S. for Anti-Coca Use," *Wall Street Journal,* May 25, 1988, p. 36.

24. "Gulf Oil Seeks Talks to Resume Operations under Angola Regime," *Wall Street Journal,* February 24, 1976, p. 17; Rose Gutfeld, "U.S. Urges Firms Not to Pay Taxes, Debts, to Noriega," *Wall Street Journal,* April 1, 1988, p. 30.

25. Tim Carrington, "Europe's Plan to Build New Fighter Plane Puts Western Firms on Cutthroat Course," *Wall Street Journal,* May 23, 1988, p. 10.

26. Renato Mazzolini, "Government Policies and Government Controlled Enterprises," *Columbia Journal of World Business,* Fall 1980, pp. 47–54.

27. "Questionable Payments Total Put at $412 Million," *Wall Street Journal,* January 21, 1977, p. 2.

28. See, for example, Richard H. Heindel, "American Business Bribery Shakes the World—Can Americans Remake It?" *Intellect,* April 1977, p. 313.

29. Jerry Landauer, "Agency Will Define Corrupt Acts Abroad by U.S. Businesses," *Wall Street Journal,* September 21, 1979, p. 23; Stan Crock, "SEC to Clarify Ban on Foreign Payoffs, Would Cede Power to Justice Department," *Wall Street Journal,* June 16, 1981, p. 10.

30. John S. Estey and David W. Marston, "Pitfalls (and Loopholes) in the Foreign Bribery Law," *Fortune,* October 9, 1978, pp. 182–188.

31. Data for the case were taken primarily from "Foreign Share of Farms, 0.5%," *New York Times,* January 28, 1980, p. D1; *International Report,* International Chamber of Commerce, August 29, 1980, p. 3; *International Report,* July 25, 1979, p. 3; "Overview

of Restrictions on Foreign Ownership of Agricultural Land in the United States," unpublished report of the law offices of Dechert Price & Rhoads, submitted to the International Business Forum of Pennsylvania Briefing Courses, 1980; Cindy Skrzycki and Maureen Walsh, "America on the Auction Block," *U.S. News & World Report,* Vol. 102, No. 12, March 30, 1987, pp. 56–58; Pat Houston, "Buy Your North 40 While It's Dirt-Cheap," *Business Week,* No. 2995, April 20, 1987, p. 92; Martin Tolchin and Susan Tolchin, "Foreign Money, U.S. Fears," *New York Times Magazine,* December 13, 1987, pp. 63–68; Walter S. Mossberg, "Most Americans Favor Laws to Limit Foreign Investment in U.S., Poll Finds," *Wall Street Journal,* March 8, 1988, p. 28; Cynthia F. Mitchell, "Buying America," *Wall Street Journal,* April 28, 1988, p. 1; Elisabeth Rubinfien, "The Price Is Right," *Wall Street Journal,* June 15, 1988, p. 1+.

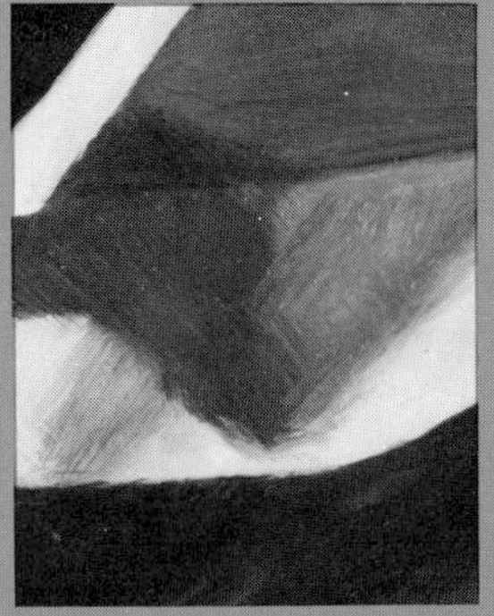

12

CHAPTER INTERNATIONAL BUSINESS DIPLOMACY

Without trouble there is no profit.
—African (Hausa) proverb

- To show that the interests of nation-states and multinational firms may be complementary rather than antagonistic.
- To illustrate the importance and nuances of negotiations between business and government in an international context.
- To trace the changing involvements of home country governments in the settlement of MNE disputes with host governments.
- To highlight the collective means by which firms and/or governments may seek to strengthen their positions vis-à-vis the other.
- To clarify the role of external relations in international business–governmental conflicts.

CASE: ARAMCO[1]

Saudi Arabia has one-quarter of the world's known reserves, is the largest exporter, and second largest producer (after the Soviet Union) of petroleum. One company, Aramco, accounts for about 97 percent of the Saudi production. Aramco's ownership, policies, and division of earnings from the outset have depended on interactions among: (1) the private oil companies participating in Aramco; (2) the U.S. government; and (3) the Saudi government. As the objectives and power of these three parties have evolved, so have the operations of Aramco. To understand these changing relationships we will review some events that preceded Aramco's first oil output in 1939.

U.S. policy toward U.S. oil firms historically has seemed contradictory because governmental objectives have involved trade-offs as well as changing priorities among the objectives. These objectives have included desires to prevent domestic monopolistic practices by oil firms, ensuring sufficient and cheap oil supplies for U.S. needs, and strengthening the U.S. political position in strategic areas worldwide. On the one hand, U.S. action dismembered the Standard Oil Trust in order to stimulate domestic competition; on the other hand, the U.S. government allowed, even encouraged, joint actions abroad by oil firms when the actions would help achieve the latter two objectives.

At least as far back as 1920 the United States realized that in the long run it would have insufficient domestic oil supplies. In interim periods, though, worldwide oil supplies could not easily be sold as fast as they could be produced. In this environment, U.S. oil firms were in a position to serve both U.S. and Middle East interests. In the 1920s and 1930s the U.S. government wanted U.S. oil companies to gain concessions in the Middle East with the result that "representatives of the industry were called to Washington and told to go out and get it." Concessions would help assure a long-term U.S. supply, and an American presence would weaken the relative positions of the British and French. The U.S. firms were welcomed in the Middle East as competitors to Shell Oil Company, British Petroleum (BP), and Compagnie Française des Pètroles (CFP) from Britain and France. They also were welcomed because they offered some sales in the United States that would otherwise be impossible.

During the 1920s and 1930s, some of the U.S. oil companies also made secret arrangements abroad that proved unpopular with the U.S. public. For example, Exxon (formerly called Esso or Standard Oil of New Jersey) agreed with BP and Shell to a system of world prices based on the U.S. price of oil. Exxon's chief executive was forced to resign in 1942 after exposure of his restrictive agreements with I. G. Farben, a major participant in Hitler's World War II efforts. In situations such as these, the oil companies were not acting as instruments of American foreign policy as they were originally conceived to do; instead, they were acting independently of any government. Later they were accused of becoming captive to Middle Eastern Arab policies.

The first two companies to participate in Saudi Arabian oil production were Socal (Standard Oil of California) and Texaco; they formed a joint venture and negotiated large concessions. The U.S. government had no representatives in Saudi Arabia at this time, and the two companies conducted some quasi-U.S. official diplomacy that continued throughout World War II. They organized construction of a pipeline to the Mediterranean in 1945 and received permission from the U.S. government to use steel, which was in very scarce supply. In 1948, Exxon and Mobil joined the original Socal and Texaco in what became known as Aramco. Mobil owned 10 percent; and each of the others held a 30 percent interest.

These four firms, along with three others (Gulf, Shell, and BP), were known as the Seven Sisters. Before the 1970s they collectively controlled such a large share of the world's oil from multiple sources that they were nearly invulnerable to the actions of any single country. By 1950 the United States was entrenched in the Cold War, and although it held military supremacy over the Soviet Union, the Truman Administration wished to maintain cordial relationships with strategic countries. When King ibn-Saud demanded substantial revenue increases from Aramco, the U.S. government became directly involved in the negotiations. A plan was devised in 1951 whereby the oil companies would maintain their ownership but would pay 50 percent of Aramco's profits as taxes to Saudi Arabia. The companies then could deduct those taxes from their U.S. tax obligations so that, in effect, the increase in revenue to Saudi Arabia was entirely at the expense of the U.S. Treasury.

In 1952, Saudi Arabia learned from Iran's experience what might happen if demands on Aramco were pushed further. Iran expelled Shah Reza Pahlevi and nationalized British oil holdings. All major oil companies boycotted Iranian oil and brought the Mossadegh government to the brink of economic collapse. With CIA support, the Shah returned, and the Seven Sisters shared in 95 percent of the ownership of the new Iranian oil company.

Both Presidents Eisenhower and Kennedy proclaimed the importance to U.S. foreign policy of the oil firms' Middle East activities and intervened to prevent antitrust action against them in their joint dealings abroad. In addition to preventing Soviet entry to the Middle East, the United States was able to sidestep certain Arab–Israeli conflicts by being publicly pro-Israel and having the Aramco partners perform most of the direct interactions with Saudi Arabia. Saudi Arabia was unhappy with U.S. policies toward Israel but could not influence them.

When the Seven Sisters gained 95 percent of the Iranian oil holdings, the other 5 percent went to smaller independent U.S. companies that previously had depended on the Seven Sisters for supplies. This marked the beginning of greater competition among distributors; it also meant that countries could make agreements with the independents to gain a greater portion of the spoils. Yet as late as 1960 the producing countries still were unable to prevent the major firms from unilaterally abrogating concessions by reducing the price they paid for oil. This price decrease, which reduced government revenues of petroleum-exporting countries, led to a meeting in Caracas by five governments and the resultant formation of the Organization of Petroleum Exporting Countries (OPEC). OPEC's purposes were to prevent companies from unilaterally lowering prices, to gain a greater share of revenues, and to move toward domestic rather than foreign ownership of the assets. Still in the early 1960s, OPEC lacked the power to flex its muscles.

In the 1960s, three new trends weakened the Seven Sisters and strengthened Saudi Arabia's position in Aramco. First was the continued emergence of other oil companies that made concessions in countries previously not among the major suppliers, such as Occidental in Libya and CFP in Algeria. These smaller companies lacked the Seven Sisters' diversification of supplies; thus they were less able to move to other supply sources if a country tried unilaterally to change agreement terms.

Second, because of rapidly expanding industrial economies, oil demand was growing faster than supply; the earlier oil glut was quickly becoming an oil squeeze. Not even the Seven Sisters could afford any longer to boycott major supplier countries as they had done earlier in Iran.

Third, there was a lessened threat of military intervention to protect oil investors. The failure of the United States to support the abortive efforts of the British and French to prevent the Egyptian takeover of the Suez Canal demonstrated that the major Western powers were unlikely to unify their efforts. Although it had invaded Lebanon successfully in 1958, the United States was less prone to intervene again in the Middle East because the Soviet Union had grown stronger since 1958, thus presenting a greater risk of a major war resulting from intervention. The United States also was increasing its military involvement in an unpopular war in Vietnam, so it was less able to lend military support to its oil firms in the Middle East.

In 1970, Muammar el-Qaddafi of Libya demanded increased prices from Occidental. Since Occidental was almost completely dependent on Libya for crude, the company relented. Qaddafi then confronted the major firms that no longer had sufficient alternative supplies and gained concessions from them as well. Libya's success was noted in other countries, which used OPEC to further strengthen their negotiating positions by dealing collectively with the oil firms. The Teheran Agreement of 1971 immediately increased prices. The embargo by Arab OPEC members in 1973 demonstrated that they had sufficient power to gain further economic demands and to cause Western powers to modify their political positions, particularly in relation to Israel. OPEC now had eleven members and controlled about 93 percent of the world's oil exports.

As the largest OPEC producer, Saudi Arabia has been able to utilize its new-found strengths in several ways. Between 1972 and 1980 the government of Saudi Arabia bought a 100 percent ownership in Aramco operations. As smaller firms gained a larger share of the world oil sales and as national governments in Sweden, West Germany, Japan, and France began buying directly from oil-producing countries, Saudi Arabia has increased the number of customers for its crude from the original four Aramco partners.

How has Aramco's government-owned status affected Exxon, Texaco, Socal, and Mobil's operations in Saudi Arabia? The companies have been able to exploit their many assets successfully in order to maintain a profitable presence vis-à-vis Saudi Arabia. They have realized that Saudi Arabia's increased oil revenues enable the Saudis to be a lucrative customer; they also know that Saudi Arabia is a vehemently anticommunist country that depends on the West, particularly the United States, for technical and defense assistance.

The four oil companies continue to manage the Saudi oil industry because they can make contributions that the Saudi's cannot acquire easily from other sources. As the major employer before government purchase into Aramco, the American partners had demonstrated an ability to attract qualified personnel from abroad, to train Saudis, and to run an efficient operation. As Aramco has expanded and moved into new activities, the oil firms have been able to continue these efforts through lucrative contract arrangements. By 1988 almost half of Aramco's 42,000 employees were non-Saudi workers. The number and percentage of foreigners within Aramco has been falling though, as Saudis have replaced foreigners in production and managerial positions. Between 1986 and 1988, for example, the number of Americans fell from about 4000 to about 2500. During this period Saudis replaced Americans in nearly all top managerial positions, including that of chief executive. Still, there is a near consensus that foreigners will be needed in increasingly technical positions. By the early 1980s, Saudi Arabia was for the first time pumping more petroleum than it replaced with new discoveries. More advanced technology is needed to find and extract oil.

The oil firms' contributions to Aramco's success thus include some continued day-to-day management, the contracting of foreign workers, the infusion of technology, the training of Saudi personnel, and the marketing of crude oil exports when sales are not made directly to a foreign government. The marketing contribution has taken on more importance since the mid-1980s when there was suddenly a glut brought about by new supplies (e.g., from Mexico) and by decreased demand. The war between Iran and Iraq has also threatened Saudi Arabia's ability to sell. To assure future sales, in 1988 Saudi Arabia proposed joint ventures in the United States with the four former Aramco partners to refine and market its oil.

The oil firms also have been important in molding U.S. foreign policy through lobbying and advertising campaigns that proclaim, "We would like to suggest that there is only one realistic possibility: if the United States were to adopt a neutral position on the Arab-Israeli dispute and a pro-American rather than a pro-Israel policy in the Middle East." Given these contributions to Saudi Arabia, the oil companies have been able to sell their Aramco interest at prices reported to be above the net book value of assets. They have successfully secured a continued source of crude oil, although sometimes at a contract price above the world spot price, and have profited from management and technical contracts.

INTRODUCTION

Operating terms of international firms:

- Are influenced by home and host governments
- Shift as priorities shift and as strengths of parties change.

The Aramco case illustrates that the terms under which companies operate abroad are greatly influenced by both home- and host-country policies and that the terms change over time as governmental priorities shift and the relative strengths of the parties evolve. The relative strengths were shown to be affected by such factors as competitive changes, the resources that parties have at their disposal, validating public opinion, and joint efforts with other parties.

As discussed in Chapter 11, companies' foreign operations may have diverse effects on home and host countries, but there is substantial disagreement as to what these effects are and how to deal with them. There is, however, agreement on the point that governments and businesses frequently attempt to follow conflicting courses. In fact, a discord, if carried to the extreme, may result in a cessation of the particular business–government relationship, as either: (1) Firms refuse to operate in the locale; or (2) governments refuse to grant original or continued operating permission. Short of the extreme are practices that, although not deemed ideal by either party, nevertheless are sufficiently satisfactory to permit an evolving relationship. This chapter examines the means by which international business and governments attempt to improve their own positions vis-à-vis each other.

NEEDS AND ALTERNATIVES FOR FULFILLMENT

Nature of Assets

Investor firms and host countries have mutually useful assets.

The international firm and the host country each may control assets that are useful to the other. There is thus an inducement to agree on the establishment of operations and to ensure the operations continue functioning. As Chapter 11 showed, the foreign firm may be able to bring in locally scarce resources in the form of capital, management talent, raw materials, and technology. These resources, in turn, may be used to foster local growth, employment, and balance of payments objectives. The foreign investor also may have access to or control of foreign markets through the ownership of the facilities that make import purchases. International firms may use these multiple facilities to contribute positively to the export development of countries in which they do business. They also may negatively affect the exports of domestic firms by denying them sales access to their operating facilities in other countries, by aggressively competing with them, or by pressuring home-country governments to erect barriers to the importation of foreign-made production. Finally, MNEs may be able to take on commercial risks that governments otherwise might have to undertake with funds borrowed in international markets.

Countries likewise have assets to offer foreign investors. First, they offer access to their own markets, which may be available only by the establishment of local production. The country also offers unique resources in the form of land needed for agricultural production, raw materials, port facilities, cheap or specialized labor, and reasonable interest rates on funds. In fact, the acquisition of some of these resources may be a prerequisite for the company to maintain a viable competitive position elsewhere in the world.

Strengths of the Parties

Alternative sources for acquiring resources affect company/country bargaining strengths.

If either a company or country has assets that the other strongly wishes to acquire and if there are few (if any) alternatives for acquiring these, negotiated concessions may be very one-sided. For example, when a few large oil companies dominated the extraction, processing, shipment, and final sale of an oversupply of petroleum, developing countries with oil deposits could do little but take what the oil firms offered. If a government refused, a firm easily could find another country that would accept a similar proposal. As the supply of petroleum diminished and petroleum-producing countries found alternative means for exploiting their resources, the terms of the concessions gradually evolved more in favor of the oil-producing countries. But shifts are not always in favor of countries: Mexico, for example, was such a growing economy during the 1970s that it could require foreign firms to accept a minority position when establishing operations. However, oil prices plummeted, and capital left Mexico because of fear of the economy during the 1980s. Mexico loosened its regulations to allow majority and even 100 percent foreign ownership.[2] As expected, there are vast differences in bargaining strength among countries, among industries, and among firms.

Strongest company bargaining assets include:

- Technology

Company bargaining strength. Although companies have a variety of assets that they can contribute to their foreign operations, some of these have traditionally put them into better bargaining positions than others. Retailers

- Product differentiation
- Ability to export output
- Local product diversity

often have had more difficulty gaining concessions than manufacturers because local governments believe (sometimes falsely) that local people can do equally well in retailing but that foreign help is needed in manufacturing. Foreign ownership in such areas as agriculture and extractive industries is not very welcome in many countries because of historical foreign dominations of these sectors and beliefs that the land and subsoil are public resources.

The bargain struck between the foreign investor and host country is influenced by the resources brought in by the investor and the number of firms offering similar resources.[3] Foreign investors are more likely to be able to gain a high percentage of ownership in foreign operations when they have few competitors and when they control certain types of assets. One of these assets is technology: For example, IBM has been allowed 100 percent ownership in a number of countries because of the local need for its unique technology, whereas other firms were refused. Another asset is the control of a well-known branded product: Coca Cola, for example, apparently has been able to gain local consumer allies who believe its differentiated products are superior. A third asset is the ability to export output from the foreign investment, especially when exports go to other entities controlled by the parent. These investments gain foreign exchange that might otherwise not be forthcoming. General Motors, for example, has been allowed 100 percent ownership of its Mexican maquiladora operation but shares ownership in its facility, which serves Mexican consumers. Finally, the greater the product diversity, the more foreign ownership allowed. This is probably because a variety of products offers a greater future opportunity to save foreign exchange through import substitution.

Surprisingly, the amount of capital needed to set up operations usually has not affected investors' bargaining power. At least two factors have influenced this: First, a large investment may be examined much more closely than a small one because of the potential impact (positive or negative) it might have on the economy; Second, the government may be more prone to borrow funds externally to invest in large enterprises. However, the ability to contribute large amounts of capital may improve future bargaining strengths of companies. As many Third World countries have encountered debt-servicing problems since the mid-1980s, they must depend more on direct investment for their future capital needs.[4]

Biggest bargaining strengths for countries are:

- Big markets
- Stability

Country bargaining strength. Generally speaking, firms prefer to establish investments in highly developed countries, which offer large markets and a high degree of stability. On a national basis, countries such as the United States, Canada, and West Germany make few concessions to foreign investors; they are large recipients of investment without having to make special arrangements. In all three of these countries, however, there are differences in treatment between advanced and depressed areas.

Home-Country Needs

The home-country government:

- Has similar economic objectives as the host country
- Has direct political relations with the host country.

Thus far we have implied that terms of operations are highly dependent on the interplay of needs between the MNE and host country. Although this is true, it overlooks the role of the home country, which seldom takes a neutral position in the relationships. Like the host government, the home-country government is interested in certain economic objectives and may give incentives to or place constraints on the foreign expansion of its firms in order to gain what it sees as its due share of the rewards. The home government has direct political interests in the host government that also temper its position.[5]

The influence of home governments is illustrated by efforts when France was selling off interests in its government-owned companies during the mid-1980s. The U.S. government interceded to pressure the French government to accept the bid by AT&T to take over CGCT, the French government-owned switchmaker, by threatening to bar U.S. government purchases of French equipment. Chancellor Helmut Kohl of West Germany personally lobbied France's then-Prime Minister Jacques Chirac on behalf of Siemen's bid for CGCT. Caught between two powers, the French government accepted the bid of the Swedish firm, Ericsson.[6]

Other External Pressures

Decision makers in business and government must consider opinions of other affected groups.

The complementary nature of the assets that international firms and countries control would seem, at first, to dictate a mutual interest in finding means to ensure that mutual benefits are developed. While there are pressures to do this, there are other constraints as well, particularly on governmental decision makers, who may have to act in ways not in the best interests of their country. Pressure may come from local companies with which the foreign investor is presently or potentially competing, from political opponents who seize the "external" issue as a means of inciting an unsophisticated population against present political leadership, or from critics who reason that more benefits may accrue to the country through alternative means. Managers also may face pressures from stockholders, workers, consumers, governmental officials, suppliers, and other interest groups outside the country who are concerned with their own interests rather than the achievement of worldwide corporate objectives. These stresses may result in a business–host country relationship quite different from what might be expected from a purely economic rationale. Each party should understand the types and strengths of these external groups, since they affect the extent to which either side may be able to give in on issues under discussion.

NEGOTIATIONS IN INTERNATIONAL BUSINESS

Terms for investments and licensing are often two-tiered.

Increasingly, negotiations are used as a means of deciding the terms by which a company may function or terminate operations in a foreign country. At one time these negotiations prevailed only for direct investments; more recently, however, sometimes they have been extended to other operating arrangements, such as licensing agreements, debt repayment, and large-scale export sales. Although the following discussions highlight investment negotiations, most of the points apply to other forms of operations as well. The negotiation process often leads to two-tiered bargaining: An MNE must first come to an agreement with a local firm in order to purchase an interest in it, sell technology or products to it, or loan money to it; once that accordance is set, a governmental agency may approve, disapprove, or propose an entirely different set of terms.

Bargaining Process

In the bargaining process, agreement occurs only if there are overlapping acceptance zones.

Acceptance zones. Before becoming involved in overseas negotiations a manager usually will have some experience in a domestic bargaining process that is somewhat similar to those in the foreign sphere. For example, collective bargaining negotiations with labor, as well as agreements to acquire or merge facilities with another firm, usually start with an array of proposals from both sides, just as in negotiations with a foreign country. The total package of proposals undoubtedly includes provisions on which one side or the other is willing either to give up entirely or to compromise. These are used as bargaining means, permitting each side to claim that it is reluctantly giving in on some point in exchange for compromise on the part of the other, as well as face-saving devices, which allow either side to report to interested parties that it managed to extract concessions. On certain other points, it is unlikely that compromise can be reached.

As in a domestic situation, the foreign negotiation will rely partly on other recent negotiations to serve as models. The domestic model may be the economy as a whole, the industry, or recent company experience. Abroad, what has transpired recently between other companies and the government or between similar types of companies or the same firm in similar countries may serve as a common reference, and negotiations are not likely to stray too far from established precedent. Finally, there are zones of acceptance and nonacceptance on the proposals presented. If the acceptance zones overlap, there is a possibility of a resulting agreement. If there are no overlapping zones, there is no hope for positive negotiations. For example, if General Motors insisted on 100 percent ownership in Japan and the Japanese insisted on 51 percent local ownership, there would be no zone in which to negotiate. If, on the other hand, Chrysler insisted on a "controlling" interest in Mexico but would take as much as it could get, and the Mexicans required "substantial" local capital and wanted to maximize it, there is probably a wide zone of ownership that would be acceptable to both parties. Assume that Chrysler is willing to go as low as 25 percent and the Mexican government let Chrysler go as high as 90 percent. The final decision will be based on the negotiating ability of each company, their strengths, and other concessions that each makes in the process. Since each side can speculate only on how far the other is willing to go, the exact amount of ownership may fall anywhere within the overlapping acceptance range. Even after an agreement is reached, it is uncertain whether the maximum concessions have been extracted from the other party.

Provisions. The major difference in investment negotiations abroad and the domestic experience is a matter of degree. Negotiations may continue over a much longer period of time abroad and may include many provisions unheard of in the home country.

Most countries in recent years have given incentives to attract foreign investors. These incentives usually are available to local firms as well; however, they often may lack the resources to be in a strong bargaining position. For example, when the Hyster Corporation announced that it would build a $100 million factory in Europe, the company was wooed by representatives of various European governments. The company finally decided on Ireland, whose government agreed to pay for employee training, made an R&D grant, and set a maximum income tax rate of only 10 percent until the year 2000.[7] Other recent incentives have included tax holidays, accelerated depreciation, low-interest loans, loan guarantees, subsidized energy and transportation, and the construction of rail spurs and roads. Governments also provide indirect incentives, such as the presence of a tranquil, trained labor force.

When companies negotiate to gain concessions from a foreign government, they should understand some of the problems that the incentives might bring. First, companies may encounter more domestic labor problems because of claims that they are exporting jobs in order to get access to cheap labor. Second, the output from the foreign facility may be subject to claims of dumping because of the subsidies given by the host government. Third, it may be more difficult to evaluate management performance in the subsidized operation.[8] Finally, it should be noted that there is always a risk that promises will be broken as situations change.

Negotiations are seldom a one-way street; companies agree to many different performance requirements. Those requirements on foreign investment which companies find most troublesome are foreign exchange deposits to cover the cost of imports and capital repatriation, limits on payments for services, requirements to create a certain amount of jobs or exports, provisions to reduce the amount of equity held in the subsidiaries, and price controls. Requirements considered less bothersome include minimum local inputs into products manufactured, limits on the use of expatriate personnel and on old or reconditioned equipment, control on prices for goods imported or exported to controlled entities of the parent firms, and demands to enter joint ventures.[9]

Renegotiations

Agreements evolve after operations begin; the company position is usually stronger before entry, but not always.

For early foreign investments in developing countries it was common to get concessions on fixed terms for a long period of time or to expect that the original terms would not change. This type of expectation has almost ceased to exist. Not only may the terms of operations be bargained before setting up operations, but the same terms also may be re-bargained any time after operations are underway.

Generally, a company's best bargaining position exists before it begins the specific operations in a foreign country. Once the capital and technology have been imported and local nationals have been trained to direct operations, the foreign firm is needed much less than before.[10] Furthermore, the company now has assets that are not moved easily to more favorable locales. The result is that the host government may be in a better position to extract additional concessions from the company. For instance, after Peru already had received loans from Britain's Midland Bank, it was in a much stronger position to renegotiate the repayment in the form of copper and other raw materials, rather than cash.[11] However, a company that is aware of and responsive to the changing needs and desires of the local economy can maintain or even improve its bargaining position by offering the infusion of additional resources that the country needs. One tactic is the promise of bringing in (or withholding) the latest technology developed abroad. Another is to use plant expansion or export markets as bargaining weapons. A host government also may be restrained from pushing too hard against established companies for fear this will make the country less attractive to other firms with which the government would like to do business.

Still another renegotiation is to offer quick compliance with something a government wants badly in exchange for other concessions. For example, Chesebrough-Ponds reduced its wholly owned Indian operation to a 40 percent equity holding. Since "Indianization" was the prime governmental interest, Chesebrough-Ponds was able to get new licenses to expand.[12]

A specific type of renegotiation that has been growing in importance is the valuation of company properties that have come under governmental ownership. The shift may be gradual, as in the case of the Saudi Arabian increased ownership in Aramco, or immediate, such as Libya's nationalization of Exxon and Mobil holdings.[13] In either type of situation the amount of funds to be received by the foreign investor may depend on the negotiated valuation.

The Chilean nationalization of the ITT telephone company indicates some of the price issues that can arise.[14] The Chilean government offered about one-third of the book value of the properties, based on the argument that the equipment was run-down, causing customers to complain about service. ITT countered that the book value understated the value because a high return on assets had been earned and could be expected to continue in the future. The government responded by saying that the return on assets was due to the rates charged to customers in the monopoly industry rather than to the equipment value. Each party proposed outside appraisal of the value, but each wanted to select appraisers and valuation criteria favorable to its position.

Behavioral Characteristics Affecting Outcome

Misunderstandings may result from differences in:

- Nationalities
- Professions
- Languages

Since negotiations are between companies from one country and governmental officials of another country, there is a great possibility of misunderstanding due to cross-country cultural variances as well as possible language differences. Since the individuals involved may react on the basis of how they think their own performances are being evaluated, and since the background and expertise of governmental officials may be quite distinct from that of businesspeople, the intended direction of talks may be uncertain from the start. Finally, it is always possible that one side or the other wishes to terminate bargaining but is hesitant to do so for fear of alienating future relationships.

Some cultural differences among negotiators are evident:

- Some negotiators are decision makers; some are not
- Some take a pragmatic view; others take a holistic view
- Some use gifts and flattery
- Some expressions do not translate well.

Cultural factors. Back in the 1930s, Will Rogers quipped, "America has never lost a war and never won a conference." Many participants and observers agree with this assessment of Americans in business negotiations abroad. Much of the problem stems from cultural differences that lead to misunderstandings and mistrust across the conference table. While we cannot delineate all the possible differences (recall Chapter 3), a few are sufficiently important to warrant mention. U.S. negotiators are more apt to have the power to make decisions than their counterpart negotiators from some other countries; they lose confidence when other negotiators have to keep checking at the head office. U.S. negotiators want to get to the heart of the matter quickly, whereas some others want to develop rapport and trust before getting to business details. Americans attempt to separate the issues into pragmatic parts, whereas some nationalities view the negotiations holistically.[15] U.S. executives often find it very difficult to know how to establish rapport with governmental officials through gifts, which are not considered bribes by the recipients, or through the flattery of asking advice and opinion.[16]

There may be a problem of finding words to express the exact meaning in another language, requiring occasional pauses while translators resort to dictionaries. Furthermore, facial reactions are difficult to judge because of the time lag between the original spoken statement and receipt of the statement in a second language. Since English is so widely understood worldwide, people with a different native language may understand quite well most of the comments and discussions in English, giving them the opportunity to eavesdrop on confidential comments and to reflect on possible responses while remarks are being translated into their language. The degree of precision in language desired by both groups also may be complicated by cultural factors.

The importance of these factors may change during renegotiations because the parties get to know each other. There is much less of a risk if a track record has been established. If the relationship has been amicable, this quality is apt to be carried over. However, if the past relationship has been hostile, the renegotiation may involve even more suspicion and obstruction than occurred during the original process.[17]

Business and governmental officials may mistrust each other and may not understand each other's objectives.

Personal conflict of negotiators. Governmental and business negotiators may start with mistrust of each other due to historic animosity or the different status of the two professions in each other's country. The investors may come armed with business and economic data that are not well understood by the governmental officials, who may counter with sovereignty considerations that are nearly incomprehensible to the businessperson. Thus it may take considerable time before each understands and empathizes with the other's position. Even then, there is a possibility that neither will attempt to develop a type of relationship designed to assure the achievement of long-run objectives: They may see their rewards as dependent on immediate results and perhaps expect not to be closely connected with longer-run problems.[18]

Negotiators should find a means to reinstitute future contacts.

Termination of negotiations. For a variety of reasons, one or both parties may wish to terminate serious consideration of proposals. The method of cessation may be extremely important as it may affect the negotiators' positions vis-à-vis their superiors and the future transactions between the given country and firm, the company in other parts of the world, and the country with other foreign firms. Since termination is an admission of failure to achieve the objectives originally set forth, negotiators of organizations are prone to place blame publicly on others in order to save face themselves.[19] Statements by company officials may make it harder for the country to deal with other foreign firms. Statements by governmental officials might make it more difficult for the company to negotiate and operate in other countries. For fear of adverse consequences from terminations, negotiations sometimes drag out until a proposal eventually dies unnoticed. Although termination is stressful, the parties should attempt to find means whereby each can save face and to avoid publicity as much as possible when talks are terminating.

Simulation can be done to anticipate other's approach but it is hard to simulate stress situations.

Preparation for negotiations. Role-playing is a valuable technique for training negotiators for projects requiring approval of a foreign-government. By practicing their own roles and those of the government's negotiator and researching the culture and history of the country to determine its attitudes toward foreign companies, business executives may be much better able to anticipate responses and plan their own actions.

Choice of negotiators depends on

- Importance of deal
- Functions involved.

The use of simulation presupposes that an MNE knows who will be doing the negotiations. The choice of negotiators will depend in part on the importance of the project, the functional areas being considered, and the level of government involved. Commonly MNEs use a team approach so that persons with legal, financial, and operations responsibility are involved in the decision making. One or more of these aspects might be altered as the need arises. One factor not easily simulated is the possible stress effect of being abroad and away from family and co-workers for an extended period. The location of negotiations may thus give one side or the other an advantage in reaching the final agreement.

HOME-COUNTRY INVOLVEMENT IN ASSET PROTECTION

The Historical Background

In the nineteenth century the home country ensured through military force and coercion that prompt, adequate, and effective compensation would be received for investors in cases of expropriation, a concept known as the **international standard of fair dealing.**[20] The host countries had little to say about this standard. As late as the period between the two world wars, the United States on several occasions sent troops into Latin America to protect investors' property.[21] The 1917 Soviet confiscations without compensation of Russian and foreign private investment led the way to noncoercive interference by home countries in cases of expropriation. In conferences attended by developing countries at The Hague in 1930 and at Montevideo in 1933, participants concluded a treaty stating that "foreigners may not claim rights other or more extensive than nationals."[22] On the basis of this doctrine, Mexico used its own courts in 1938 to settle disputes arising from expropriation of foreign agricultural properties in 1915.[23] This same doctrine formed the precedent for later settlements and, in the absence of specific treaties, remains largely in effect today.

Except for the abortive attempt by British, French, and Israeli forces to prevent Egypt's takeover of the Suez Canal, there have been no major attempts since World War II at direct military intervention to protect property of home-country citizens. (There have been, however, threatened or actual troop movements by large powers to developing countries during this period. Property protection possibly was a surreptitious factor in the movements.) The concept of nonintervention has been strengthened by a series of U.N. resolutions. Of probably greater importance than the resolutions has been the East–West political schism. Western nations have feared that excessive intervention into the affairs of developing countries would result in alliance of these countries with (or intervention by) the Communist Bloc. A secondary factor has been that most expropriations have been selective rather than general—that is, involving a few rather than all foreign firms. In these cases it is thought that intervention might lead to further takeovers and jeopardize settlements for affected foreign firms.

The Use of Bilateral Agreements

Bilateral agreements improve climates for investments abroad, but they:

- Usually lack settlement mechanisms
- Do not protect against gradual changes.

To improve the foreign investment climates for their investors, many industrial countries have established bilateral treaties with foreign governments. Although these agreements differ in detail, they generally provide for home-country insurance to investors to cover losses from expropriation, civil war, and currency devaluation or control and to exporters to cover losses from nonpayment in a convertible currency. The recipient country, by approving a contract, agrees to settle payment on a government-to-government basis. In other words, Gillette could insure its Chinese investment against expropriation because of the bilateral agreement between the United States and the People's Republic of China. If China expropriated Gillette's facilities, the U.S. government would pay Gillette and then seek settlement with China. Other types of bilateral agreements include treaties of friendship, commerce, and navigation as well as prevention of double taxation. All these efforts help promote factor mobility for MNEs.

A major problem with these agreements to protect foreign investments is that they do not normally provide a mechanism for settlement. The host governments simply may lack the financial resources to settle in an appropriate currency, for example. Even if they have the resources, it is unclear whether the amount of payment should be settled in local courts, in external courts, or through negotiations. Many recipient countries resist treaties because they imply the abrogation of sovereignty over business activities conducted within their borders and provide more protection for alien property than for that of their own citizens.[24] Another problem is that the agreements do not protect against gradual changes in operating rules, which can reduce substantially the profit of foreign operations. Revere Copper and Brass, for example, was forced by Jamaica to make payments greater than those provided by the original investment agreement. The result was an operating loss that the investment insurance did not cover.[25]

Home-Country Aid as a Weapon

Home countries may improve terms for their investors by

- Suspending aid to countries that nationalize property
- Offering aid in exchange for better investor treatment.

Home countries have used the promise of aid or the threat to withhold it as a means of effectively extracting from host governments terms that are more acceptable to their investors. The Hickenlooper Amendment of 1961, in response to Brazilian nationalizations, provides for the suspension of aid to any country that nationalizes properties of U.S. citizens or that has moved to nullify existing contracts and fails within a given period of time to take appropriate steps for settlement. The Hickenlooper Amendment has been officially used only once—after Ceylon (now Sri Lanka) nationalized certain Esso and Caltex properties in 1962. Ceylon countered by expropriating additional assets of the same companies. However, in the elections of 1965, the opposition party, which promised to settle the dispute, was elected. One day after the new government took office, a settlement was worked out. The effectiveness of the amendment in the Sri Lankan situation as well as in the other instances is difficult to assess. In several cases, aid has been reduced after takeovers, and the consequences have varied.

Rather than withholding aid and loans, home governments have promised that one or both would be made available if conflict is either avoided or resolved on terms more acceptable to the home-country foreign investors. Perhaps the best known example of this was an accord in which France agreed to give Algeria economic aid over five years in exchange for continued operations by French enterprises in Algeria.[26]

The use of aid and loans, either as a means of averting takeovers of properties by foreign investors or as a force in settling valuation disputes, certainly may be an effective weapon at times, especially since a country may depend heavily on funds from foreign governments and international agencies as either a supplement for or an alternative to foreign private investment. However, the problems are numerous: From the host-country viewpoint, threats or promises from a foreign country may place leaders in a position of seeming manipulation by foreign powers, possibly forcing them to be even more adamant as public opinion becomes increasingly antiforeign. On the home-country side, governments may be inconsistent in their application of financial weapons, since their concerns are primarily with political alliances and concessions rather than with the properties of a few of their citizens. They thus may be willing to give aid in exchange for favorable votes on a U.N. resolution or for permission to locate foreign military bases, or simply through fear that public opinion among nonaligned countries would shift against the country trying to "buy" favorable treatment for its companies. A further problem may occur when home-country taxpayers rightfully object to their payments' going abroad in order to assure the safety and continued profitability of investments of a few of their fellow citizens.

Before a home government comes to the assistance of its firms abroad, it must consider several objectives and possible consequences. This is well illustrated by one of the leading authorities on multinational firms:

> *When Exxon's Peruvian subsidiary, the International Petroleum Company, was threatened with expropriations in Peru during the 1960s, U.S. policymakers had to ask many thorny questions before they could decide how to react. Would a U.S. response hurt American fishing interests operating off the Peruvian shores? Would it push the Peruvian government to choose French planes for its air force? Would it precipitate a clamp-down on the 600 other American firms then operating in Peru? Would it lead Peru to vote against a variety of U.S. projects in United Nations organizations and elsewhere?*[27]

MULTILATERAL SETTLEMENTS

Multilateral settlements of disputes may be done by a neutral country or group or courts in third countries.

When international firms or home governments are unable to reach agreement with a host country, they may agree to have a third party settle the dispute. In cases of trade disputes, the International Chamber of Commerce in Paris, the Swedish Chamber of Commerce, and specialized commodity associations in London frequently are asked to assist the parties. Since the trade transactions are generally among private groups, the disputes do not create the type of widespread emotional environment often attendant upon foreign investment disputes.

Examples of active involvement by third parties in settling investment questions are extremely rare, for such involvement requires a relinquishment of sovereignty by host governments over activities within their own borders. Among the notable uses of external organizations have been the World Bank's agreement to arbitrate the compensation and to act as transfer agent for payments involving the Suez Canal nationalization. Another involved a World Bank nonbinding arbitral award that was accepted by both French bondholders and the City of Tokyo.[28] The Center for the International Settlement of Investment Disputes operates under the auspices of the World Bank and provides a formal organization for parties wishing to submit their disputes. However, both parties must agree to its use, and countries have been reluctant to do so. In 1974, Jamaica refused to use the center after seizing foreign bauxite holdings, although the investors and the Jamaican government had agreed in earlier years to use the center in case of disputes. As yet there is no effective means of imposing international law on nations. However, as a result of the Center's failure to offer potential investors sufficient confidence about LDCs, the World Bank established the Multilateral Investment Guarantee Agency in 1988. This agency offers insurance against expropriations, war, and civil disturbances.

A notable example of multilateral settlement involved claims between the United States and Iran. This situation differed from many other attempted settlements inasmuch as each country had large amounts of investments in the other's territory. In fact when the two governments froze each other's assets, Iran had substantially more invested in the United States than the United States did in Iran. The two countries agreed to appoint three arbitrators each to an international tribunal at The Hague, and those six selected three more. Part of the assets that the United States had held were set aside for the payment of arbitrated claims.[29]

In limited cases, courts in third countries may be used by international firms or by governments as leverage. In 1972 Kennecott Copper, whose investments in Chile had been nationalized, successfully contested in French courts payment from French importers to the Chilean government on the grounds that Kennecott still owned the operations.[30] In 1987 Britain's High Court ruled that the Libyan government could withdraw $292 million from the London facility of Bankers Trust, even though $161 million of this was on deposit in New York and the U.S. government had frozen Libyan assets in U.S. banks at home and abroad.[31]

After expropriation of their Libyan facilities, California Standard, Texaco, and Arco placed notices in the leading newspapers and periodicals of the major oil-consuming countries warning that they might file lawsuits against purchasers of Libyan oil that the oil firms claimed for themselves. They also had arbitrators appointed by the International Court of Justice at The Hague who ruled in the firms' favor and set an amount of compensation.[32] A problem with the International Court of Justice (the World Court) is that there have been many examples of a country failing to consent to a judgment. As a result, the Court handles few cases.[33]

CONSORTIUM APPROACHES

In a consortium, companies or countries join together to strengthen their bargaining positions, e.g., OPEC, oil firms, ANCOM, Arab boycott, codes of conduct, cross-organization production.

As mentioned earlier, a company may at times be able to play one country against another, or a government may be able to do the same with international firms. When in a relatively weak position, companies or countries may be able to join together in a **consortium** to present a united front when dealing with the previously more powerful entity.

Petroleum

The Aramco case at the beginning of the chapter offers a good example of how companies have banded together on one side and countries have joined forces on the other side. The unity has strengthened both sides and at different points has helped to give advantages to one over the other.

ANCOM

ANCOM, as discussed in Chapter 7, sought a common policy toward foreign capital, trademarks, patents, licenses, and royalties. By unifying the policy the aim was to limit the role of MNEs and to prevent them from serving all the member countries by locating in a country with less stringent regulations. This attempt to get ANCOM members to adhere to the common stance has been less than successful; nevertheless it contrasts to the approach of the EC, which has not had a common policy. During the 1960s when France wished to restrict the growth of MNE penetration within its market by withholding ownership permission, that country was helpless. MNEs could serve the French market through production in Belgium, where they were welcome.

Arab Boycott

A loose arrangement whereby Arab countries may cease business with firms doing business with Israel.

In the Arab boycott, efforts have been made to weaken Israel by boycotting purchases of Israeli goods and by refusing to do business with firms that sell strategic tools and certain resources to Israel.[34] This is a loose agreement among participants rather than a highly structured agreement; the looseness of the boycott is in some ways a strength in that it has allowed Arab countries to buy from some firms selling to Israel when they desperately needed the goods themselves. The prevention of trade between Israel and Arab states is not an unusual type of practice, nor does it have much impact on MNEs. What is different about this arrangement is that it often forces MNEs headquartered in other countries to make a choice of selling either to the Arab countries or in Israel, but not in both. (China at times has also retaliated by disallowing certain business with a given country whose firms did sensitive business with Taiwan.)[35] By banding together, the Arab countries represent a very formidable market. Although it is impossible to measure the precise impact of the boycott activities, the big difference in market size undoubtedly has caused many MNEs to think twice about doing business with Israel.

Another distinguishing feature is the nature of a so-called **secondary boycott.** For example, Ford Motor Company is boycotted by the Arab League. Ford was involved in negotiating a joint venture in the United States with Toyota; however, Saudi Arabia threatened retaliation against any firm that concluded a joint venture or production-licensing agreement with Ford. Since Saudi Arabia was the world's second largest importer of Japanese cars, the Saudi warning had to be considered seriously.[36] Toyota subsequently broke off the negotiations with Ford but did not indicate that the threatened boycott was a factor.

Codes of Conduct

Collective attitudes toward MNE activities are:

- Clarified by a number of organizations
- Usually fairly vague
- Involve voluntary compliance
- May make it easier for countries to legislate.

The first widespread attempt to regulate direct investment on a multilateral basis was made in 1929 by the League of Nations. At that time the attention was on foreign exploitation of the tropical commodity industry. Proposals were discarded quickly, however, when the Great Depression occurred. Since World War II there have been several attempts at agreements that would deal in part with the relationship between foreign investors and governments. Among these were the International Trade Organization (ITO) of 1948, which never became operative, attempts in 1951 by the U.N. Economic and Social Council (ECOSOC) to regulate antitrust, and the 1961 Code for Liberalization of Capital Movements established by the Organization for Economic Cooperation and Development (OECD).[37] None of these appears to have had much effect on MNE operations.

In 1975 the newly created Center on Transnational Corporations first met at the United Nations as a result of complaints issued by a large group of poor countries. (The so-called Group of 77 now comprises more than 100 LDCs). The Center provides for the collection of information on MNE activities, is a forum for publicizing common complaints, and is considering the adoption of several codes of conduct for the activities of MNEs. Meanwhile, the OECD, which is composed of industrial countries, approved its own code in 1976. The codes requested by the Group of 77, as well as the code set by the OECD, are necessarily vague so that consensus may be reached among various nations as well as among groups within the nations. The codes are also voluntary; thus adoption does not guarantee enforcement. The codes may, however, clarify a collective attitude toward specific practices of MNEs that will make it easier to pass restrictive legislation at the national level without fear that the legislation is greatly out of step with external public opinion.[38]

Joint Company Activities

Joint company activities are used by countries to strengthen national capabilities vis-à-vis strong foreign competitors and

- To spread risk
- To deal more strongly with governments.

To counter production dominance by firms from other countries, countries have fostered consolidation among their own manufacturers. They have given governmental assistance to R&D and preferred their own firms in governmental contracts. Two of the most notable efforts have been the development of a consortium in Europe to compete against Boeing in aircraft production and the development of various cooperative arrangements in Europe to counter IBM's dominance. Other European cross-national efforts have occurred in such fields as consumer appliances, medical electronics, telecommunications, and television. One of the more notable efforts has been the EC's Esprit program of $1.3 billion to fund electronics research.[39]

Another approach has been for two or more firms from different countries to band together, not so much to strengthen the initial negotiating terms, but rather to improve positions in possible later negotiations. By investing a smaller amount in a given locality, each firm can invest in more countries, thus reducing the impact of loss in one. Furthermore, a host government may be more hesitant to deal simultaneously with more than one home government in conflict situations.

Companies also may ban together to exert pressure on a government to take action against a competitor. For example, when IBM proposed an exemption of shared ownership for a new Mexican venture, forty-three computer-related firms, including Hewlett-Packard and Apple, successfully joined to advertise and to lobby so that IBM would not be treated preferentially.[40]

EXTERNAL RELATIONS APPROACHES

The Need by Countries

Through external relations, countries make themselves known to attract investors and give their viewpoint when controversies with MNE arise.

Countries that wish to attract more foreign investment sometimes have found either that they are inadequately known to investors or that investors have false impressions of business possibilities within their borders. Some potential investments thus are overlooked rather than rejected. An investment in a small country such as Mauritius may not be undertaken simply because the investment decision makers do not think of that country. Other countries may be victims of publicity attendant on conditions in neighboring countries: For example, there is a tendency to stereotype African or Latin American nations. Investment flows to Costa Rica thus may suffer because of a war between El Salvador and Honduras, anti-U.S. sentiment in Nicaragua, nationalization programs in Peru, or political unrest in Guatemala.

To overcome either bad publicity or no publicity at all, many countries have established public relations programs abroad. Their activities are extremely varied: Some include participation in world fairs and exhibits so that the country becomes better known; some advertise to give data on the economy. For example, it is common to see full-page advertisements in the *Wall Street Journal* on such subjects as "Reasons to Invest in the Dominican Republic." In order to become better known, Morocco waged a campaign using advertisements with the slogan, "Invest in Morocco. It may never have crossed your mind." Countries also have used advertising media to overcome the problems of adverse publicity.

Company Approaches

Companies publicize good citizenship activities that

- Business conduct satisfies social objectives
- Nonbusiness functions help society.

Many firms strongly believe that by acting as a good corporate citizen abroad they will remove local animosities and concern that might affect their short- or long-term competitive ability. Some have even gone so far as to set their own published codes of conduct. The behavior itself may not be sufficient, however, since employees, governmental officials, consumers, and other groups may not know or understand what the company is doing. W. R. Grace's chairman, J. Peter Grace, has said, "No matter how responsibly a corporation behaves, it will be viewed with skepticism unless it effectively communicates its activities, its plans, and its goals to its many publics.[41]

Because of conflicting pressures on the international firm from different groups, the investor almost always can be accused of bad behavior by someone. For instance, if the company offers higher wages, it may be accused of monopolistic practices and aiding inflation by attracting workers from competitors. If it pays only the going wage, the contention may be that workers are exploited. By understanding the relative power of competing groups served by the firm, management at least may be able to emphasize

GROUPS OF ECONOMIES

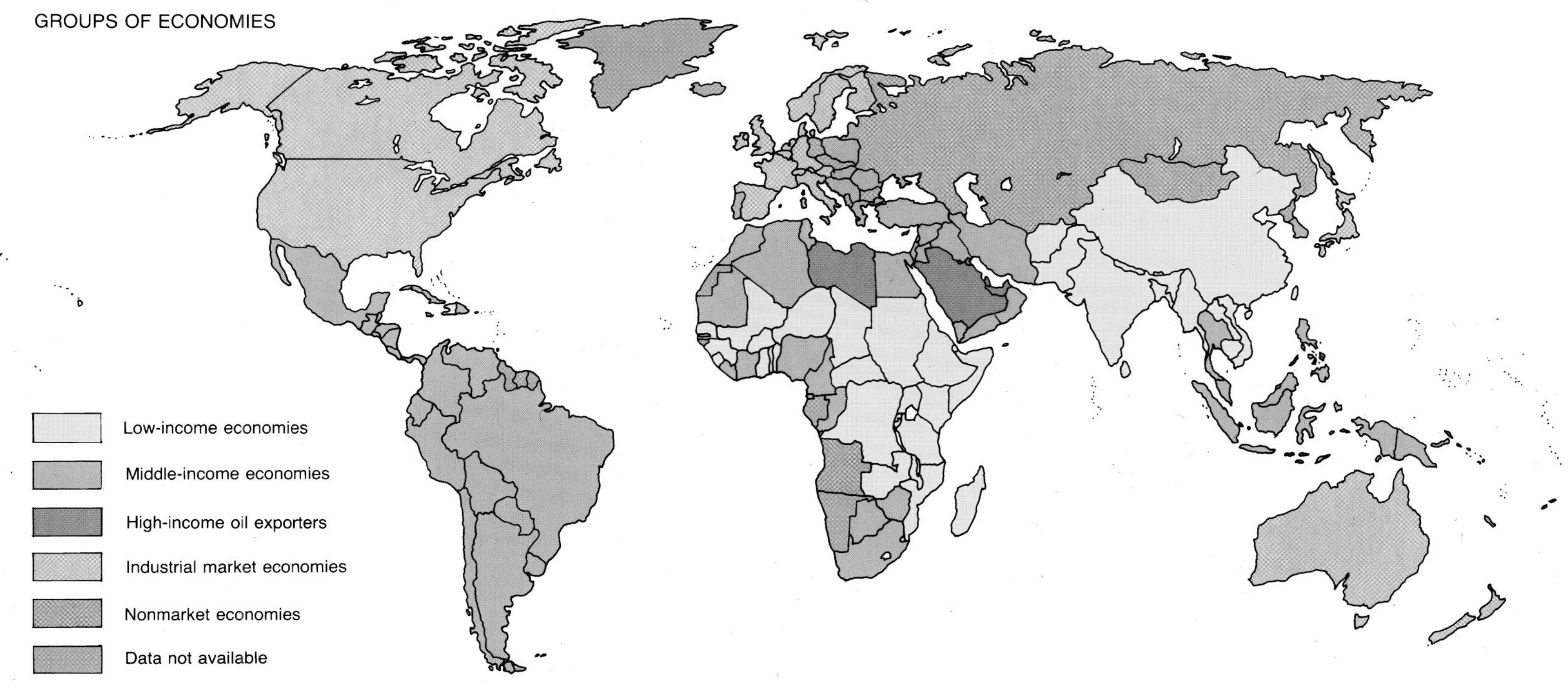

Data from *World Development Report, 1987* (New York: Oxford University Press, 1987).

WORLD VIEW, 1989

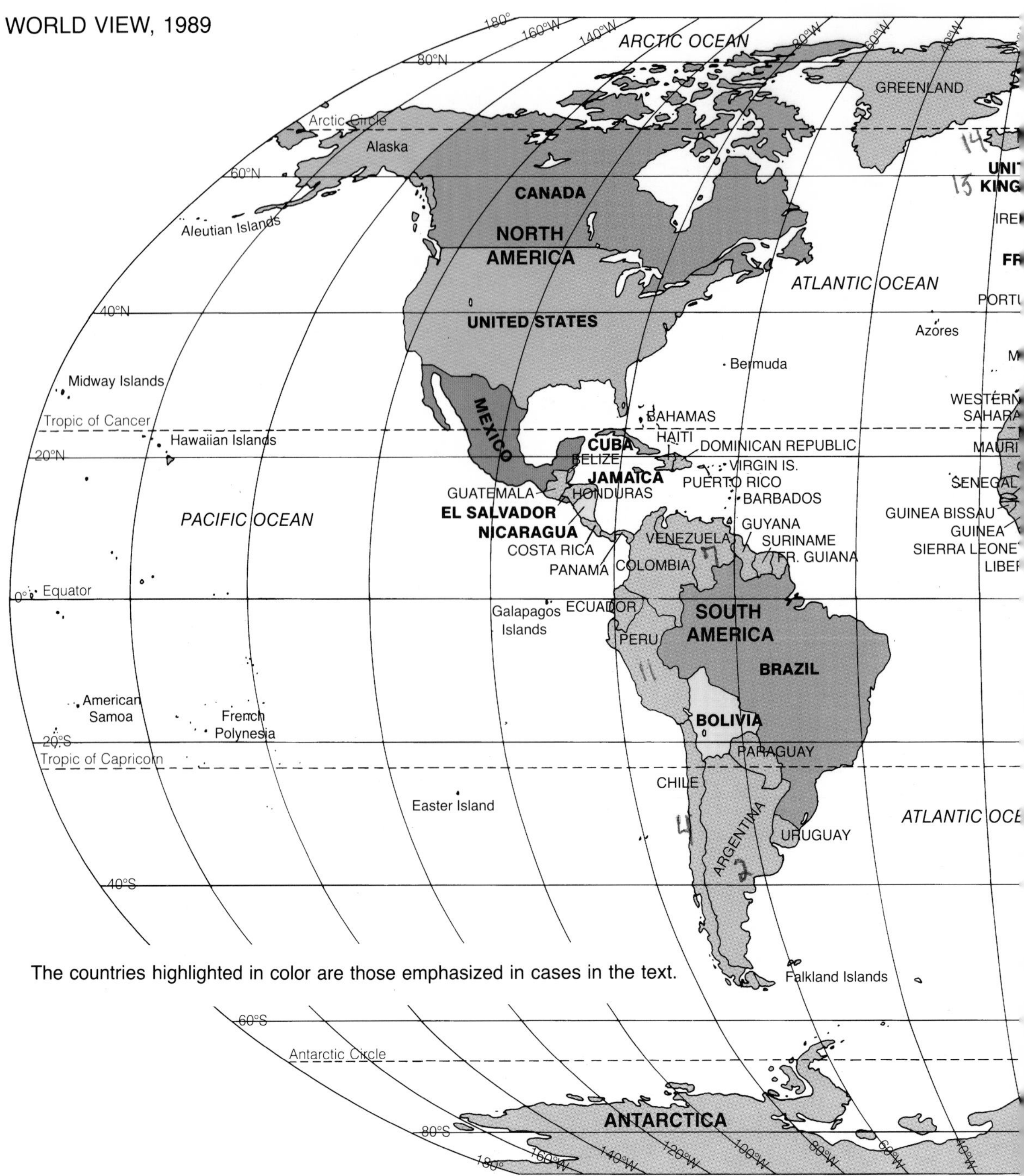

The countries highlighted in color are those emphasized in cases in the text.

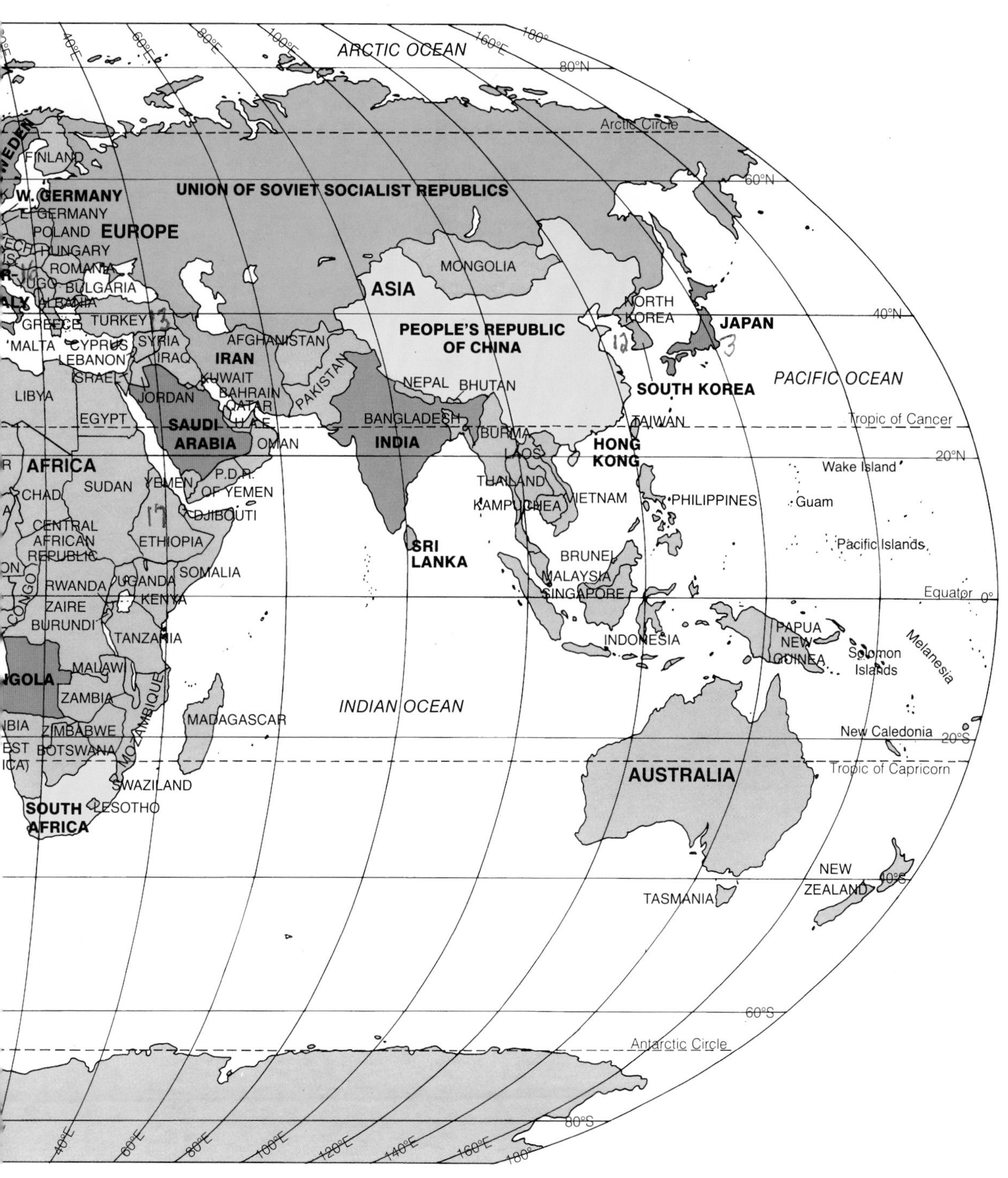

ARCTIC OCEAN
40°E
60°E
80°E
100°E
160°E
180°
80°N
Arctic Circle
FINLAND
60°N
W. GERMANY
UNION OF SOVIET SOCIALIST REPUBLICS
E. GERMANY
POLAND
EUROPE
HUNGARY
ROMANIA
MONGOLIA
BULGARIA
ASIA
ALBANIA
NORTH KOREA
TURKEY
40°N
JAPAN
GREECE
MALTA
CYPRUS
SYRIA
AFGHANISTAN
PEOPLE'S REPUBLIC OF CHINA
LEBANON
IRAQ
IRAN
ISRAEL
KUWAIT
PAKISTAN
NEPAL
BHUTAN
SOUTH KOREA
PACIFIC OCEAN
LIBYA
JORDAN
BAHRAIN
QATAR
EGYPT
U.A.E.
BANGLADESH
Tropic of Cancer
SAUDI ARABIA
TAIWAN
OMAN
INDIA
BURMA
HONG KONG
AFRICA
LAOS
20°N
Wake Island
SUDAN
YEMEN
P.D.R. OF YEMEN
THAILAND
CHAD
VIETNAM
PHILIPPINES
Guam
KAMPUCHEA
DJIBOUTI
CENTRAL AFRICAN REPUBLIC
ETHIOPIA
SRI LANKA
Pacific Islands
BRUNEI
SOMALIA
UGANDA
MALAYSIA
RWANDA
KENYA
SINGAPORE
Equator 0°
CONGO
ZAIRE
BURUNDI
INDONESIA
PAPUA NEW GUINEA
TANZANIA
Melanesia
Solomon Islands
MALAWI
ZAMBIA
MOZAMBIQUE
INDIAN OCEAN
MADAGASCAR
ZIMBABWE
New Caledonia
20°S
BOTSWANA
Tropic of Capricorn
AUSTRALIA
SWAZILAND
SOUTH AFRICA
LESOTHO
NEW ZEALAND
40°S
TASMANIA
60°S
Antarctic Circle
80°S
40°E
60°E
80°E
100°E
120°E
140°E
160°E
180°

POPULATION

Data from *World Development Report, 1987* (New York: Oxford University Press, 1987).

practices that benefit most of the groups that are in a position to substantially help or hurt the firm. A good rule for serving a given group is to try to maximize benefits without excessively disrupting the local situation. Within any given economy there usually is a range of prices, wages, and returns on investment. The international company thus may be able to be among the leaders (e.g., have wage rates or investment returns among the top quarter of firms) without being accused of disruptive practices, while still satisfying the groups directly involved.

Management should avoid direct confrontation whenever possible, since confrontation merely may force opponents to be adamant in their views. When government accusations against a foreign company in India were leaked to the press, the company countered by refuting charges in newspaper advertisements, a tactic that merely served to challenge authority and publicly tarnish the government's credentials. Conversely, in response to newspaper criticism about a U.S. pharmaceutical firm's labeling in Europe, the company decided to work with the Health Ministry, since criticisms affected not only the company but also the ministry's supervision of the matter. By jointly answering the charges, the firm maintained rapport with the ministry, its major regulator and consumer.[42]

Saint Augustine recounted that in his youth he used to pray, "Give me chastity and continence, but not yet." Like Saint Augustine, many companies try to put their efforts off as long as possible. As in the above examples, much of the public relations efforts of companies are defensive—that is, done in response to public criticism. Once a company is on the defensive, efforts may be too little, too late. Gulf & Western, for example, reacted to adverse criticism, primarily in the United States, about its labor relations practices in the Dominican Republic by committing $100 million over a ten-year period to improve worker welfare through such things as housing construction and education programs. Several years later, however, the criticism had not subsided measurably, and Gulf & Western announced it would cease operations in the Dominican Republic.[43]

Firms should organize means to increase the number of local proponents and dampen potential criticism. Opinion surveys of such interested parties as customers and workers can be conducted through various means so as to allay misconceptions, anticipate criticism, and thereby head off potentially more damaging accusations. Many MNEs use advocacy publicity at home and abroad in an aggressive effort to win support for their international activities.[44] For example, Mobil has used newspaper and magazine advertisements to support its international vertical integration. Both Rohm and Haas and Caterpillar have made films to support the positive effects their activities have on home- and host-country societies. MNEs also have set systematic means to identify and react to external conditions that may adversely affect their operations abroad.[45]

While it may not always be possible to dispel criticisim, the international firm can do several things to mitigate it. One method is to consider those things that are important to people in the host country; or it may be something as fundamental as having the new manager continue a policy initiated by previous domestic management. On the question of what to centralize and what to decentralize, there is much to be said for permitting the local manager to determine policies concerning local customs and social matters. On such sensitive issues as employment and worker output, changes should be made only after consultation regarding the attitudes of locally interested parties. Headquarters personnel also may serve a useful public relations function on the local scene. Since they have higher status than local managers, they may be better received by higher governmental authorities.

Allies through Participation

The MNE might increase number of local proponents through:

- Ownership sharing
- Avoiding direct confrontation
- Local management
- Local R&D

The foreign company also may foster local participation designed both to reduce the image of foreignness and to develop local proponents whose personal objectives may be fulfilled by the foreign investor's continued operations. The parent company can follow a policy that involves its subsidiary in purchasing local supplies and raw materials whenever possible. It might be feasible for the local subsidiary to subcontract part of its assembly operations. In the case of purchasing component parts or subcontracting, it may be possible for the parent or the subsidiary to make a loan or give technical assistance to help the local supplier initiate or expand a plant. If it is economically reasonable, R&D activities may be undertaken within the host country.

Another possibility for local participation would be a stock option plan for country nationals employed by the subsidiary. A company interested in improving its image in the host country also may establish a specific program for gradually replacing home-country personnel with local nationals. If local union officials are informed directly by management of possible company actions, they may cooperate with management rather than confront it.

If carried to extremes, local participation can mean that the host country becomes less dependent on the foreign firm. The company strategy might be to hold out on some resources so that the company still is needed. For instance, a centralized R&D laboratory might be in charge of new product development, whereas the local R&D facility can handle the adaptations for local market and production conditions.

Some companies have taken on additional social functions to build local support. For example, Dow Chemical financed a kindergarten in Chile, Citibank participated in a reforestation program in the Philippines, and McDonald's sponsored a telethon in Australia to raise funds for disabled children.[46]

Firms sometimes have been permitted greater latitude in their operations when they have agreed to invest in priority operations outside their normal line of business. These have been negotiated accords, such as a mining firm's agreement to lay out two plantations in Nigeria in exchange for relative freedom in operating its mining venture.[47]

Good corporate citizenship and the attendant publicity may not be enough to guarantee the continued conduct of business activity. If public opinion is directed against foreign private ownership in general, such as in the Cuban expropriations, everyone loses out. If a firm is doing business as a key firm in a key sector, criticisms may come simultaneously from so many directions that the company defense gradually loses strength. Even in these exceptional situations, an external affairs department may identify problem areas. If this is done sufficiently in advance, the company may forestall adverse actions and establish policies to prevent or minimize losses, such as decreasing new parent obligations, selling ownership to local governments or private investors, and shifting into less visible types of local enterprises.

On occasion, an MNE may find it advantageous to be uncompromising in its dealings with a government, even when the adversary positions are reported publicly. The firm may assess its bargaining position as being sufficiently strong to afford to be adamant, or it may perceive that compromises will weaken its position in other countries. Even in these instances, however, the MNE should attempt to keep the government from losing face. Gulf & Western, for example, negotiated for five years with the Thai government for a zinc mine and refinery without coming to an agreement. Then the firm closed its office in Bangkok, which was widely reported as an effort to bully the government into accepting terms. Within a week, the Thai government did accept an agreement, but Gulf & Western announced that the office closing was simply a cost reduction measure during a transition period.[48]

SUMMARY

- Although host countries and international firms may hold resources that, if combined, should achieve objectives for both, conflict may cause one or both parties to withhold resources, thus preventing the full functioning of international business activities.
- Both the managers of international firms and the host-country governmental officials must respond to interest groups that may see different advantages or no advantage at all to the business–government relationship. Therefore the final outcome of the relationship may not be the one expected from a purely economic viewpoint.
- Negotiations increasingly are used to determine the terms under which a company may operate in a foreign country. This negotiating process is

similar to the domestic processes of company acquisition and collective bargaining. The major differences in the international sphere are the much larger number of provisions, the general lack of a fixed time duration for an agreement, and the need to agree on company property values in cases of nationalization.

- The terms under which an international firm may be permitted to operate in a given country will be determined to a great extent by the relative degree to which the company needs the country and vice versa. As the relative needs evolve over time, new terms of operation will reflect the shift in bargaining strength.
- Generally, a company's best bargaining position is before it begins operation. Once resources are committed to the foreign operation, the firm may not move elsewhere easily.
- Since negotiations are conducted largely between parties whose cultures, educational backgrounds, and expectations differ, it is very difficult for negotiators to understand sentiments and present convincing arguments. Negotiation simulation offers a means to anticipate responses and to plan an approach to the actual bargaining.
- Historically, developed countries ensured through military intervention and coercion that the terms agreed upon between their investors and recipient countries would be carried out. The East–West political schism and a series of international resolutions have caused the near demise of these methods for settling disputes. The promise of giving or withholding aid has been used more recently by developed countries as a device for influencing host governments.
- A number of bilateral treaties have been established whereby host countries agree to compensate investors for losses from expropriation, civil war, and currency devaluation or control. These agreements are not clear about the mechanism or place of settlement for the losses.
- Although international organizations or groups in third countries frequently are used to arbitrate trade disputes among individuals from more than one country, this method has been used very rarely to settle investment disputes because governments are reluctant to relinquish sovereignty over matters occurring within their borders.
- To prevent companies from playing one country against another or vice versa, groups of governments or companies occasionally have banded together to present a unified front in order to improve the terms received.
- External relations may be used by both companies and countries to develop a good image, overcome a bad one, and create useful proponents for their positions. If successful, this strategy may result in better terms of operation for either side.

CASE:
JAMAICA LURES FOREIGN HOTELS[49]

A 1987 poll showed that only 10 percent of Jamaicans thought that their Prime Minister Edward Seaga was doing a good job, and 56 percent thought that his predecessor, Michael Manley, would do a better job. This perception concerned President Ronald Reagan of the United States, especially since Seaga was the first head of state to be invited to the Reagan White House in 1981. One of the Reagan Administration's major foreign policy concerns was communist influence in the Caribbean area. (See Fig. 12.1.) Jamaica had voted out of office the pro-Cuban regime of Michael Manley; thus Seaga offered the "great right hope" to the new U.S. administration. One of the major items of ongoing discussion between Reagan and Seaga was how to spur U.S. private assistance to Jamaica, especially in the tourist industry. The two countries reached agreement whereby a private group of Americans and Jamaicans would seek development of joint projects in Jamaica. A second accord allowed Americans to hold tax-deductible business conventions in Jamaica, a move designed to spur tourism but criticized by Puerto Rican officials who feared that their country's tourism industry would suffer as a result. The political objectives of future U.S. business involvement in Jamaica were highlighted by Curt Strand, President of Hilton International: "It's one of our few recent foreign policy victories. It's yanked out of the jaws of Cuba. If we can't help a little country like that, what credibility do we have as proponents of private enterprise?"

Because of Seaga's diminishing popularity in Jamaica, the Reagan Administration sought other ways to promote tourism and U.S. investment to Jamaica. Donna F. Tuttle, the U.S. Undersecretary of Commerce, announced that the United States would consider various plans to help Jamaica, such as assisting in manpower and training needs, helping to develop interisland transport services, aiding the development of standards of service, and participating in bilateral investment treaties. Yet she cautioned that, "Tax laws and investment codes must be pro-business if investment is to take place. It is important to ensure that policies foster tourism development, not fetter it. In a nutshell, there won't be investment in Caribbean tourism unless a good investment climate exists and there is a perception of potential profitability."

When Seaga was first elected in 1980, the once-thriving tourist industry was floundering. Despite the appealing climate, location, and natural beauty, the situation had become so drastic that the government during the Manley regime was forced to assume control of fourteen hotels whose owners were unable to continue mortgage payments. These government hotels comprised the largest chain in the Caribbean and half the hotel rooms in Jamaica. In the

Figure 12.1
Jamaica's Place in the Caribbean

thirty-three months before Seaga took office, the hotels lost over $100 million. Therefore, increased tourism not only would be a potential source of funds for the economy, but it would also help alleviate the current drain on governmental budgets that was necessary to cover the loss.

Tourism also involved high visibility both inside and outside Jamaica; thus successes in tourism might build investor confidence. Mr. Seaga said, "Every segment is vital because we took over such a rotten state of affairs. But tourism has an important special spin-off: people coming here, liking it and investing in the future of the country."

Not everyone has been of the same opinion about the place of international tourism in development. Most of the local jobs generated by tourism are low-level service positions catering to foreigners who expect luxury and who spend more per day than the worker earns in a month. Considering Jamaica's history of slavery, its 90-percent black population, and recent (1962) independence, the juxtaposition of affluent white tourists suggests neocolonialism.

There are economic arguments against tourism as well. Several studies have indicated that tourism tends to reduce agricultural production in two ways: First, many agricultural workers merely shift employment to nonagricultural areas without being fully replaced; second, foreign tourists want familiar, rather than local, foods. So instead of serving ackee and codfish and curried goatbelly soup, the tourist industry imports other foods, which eventually are demanded by the local population, thereby supplanting local products. This leakage of earnings to buy imports is further carried over in buying other hotel and restaurant supplies and stocking duty-free shops, where tourists make most of their purchases.

Hotels were not the only enterprises socialized under Manley. Once Seaga took office, Jamaica began a major desocialization program. Because of the losses that the government was incurring, hotels were considered to be a good first sector in which to move to private participation. Large foreign hotel chains were in a better position to infuse efficient management systems and to attract tourists, (1) because of their sales and reservations networks and (2) because many people prefer to stay in well-known chains.

Foreign hotel organizations were reluctant to invest in Jamaica because the outlook for foreign tourism was mixed. Uncertainty remained about the international perception of Jamaica, which had suffered violence in which over 700 people (but no tourists) had died in 1980. Unlike many other Caribbean areas, Jamaica did not permit gambling. If tourists could be persuaded to come back initially, their negative impressions might cause another downturn. Many of the hotels had fallen into bad repair during the Manley years, and development of infrastructure had fallen behind. Tourists might find less-than-posh accommodations, crumbled roads, and frequent power outages. To counter these problems, the government launched a widely publicized advertising campaign highlighted by slogans of "Jamaica is smiling again" and "Come back to Jamaica." The number of tourists did increase—in fact, the upsurge was so great that foreign exchange earnings from tourism more than doubled between 1980 and 1984, putting tourism ahead of alumina as the major foreign exchange earner.

The overall political–economic outlook also was mixed. Seaga inherited a 30 percent inflation and a 35 percent unemployment rate. The country also was saddled with huge foreign debts and needed substantial foreign exchange for such necessities as oil and food. Sugar yield was going steadily down because of soil depletion and plant disease. Yet Seaga gained breathing time by more than tripling foreign debt by 1987. This action was not totally well received in Jamaica. A business leader said, "Every time Mr. Manley borrowed a dollar, everybody said, 'Oh my God!' Now Mr. Seaga is borrowing everywhere, and everybody says, 'What a great guy!' "

Another problem in Jamaica has been labor. Substantial numbers of talented people emigrated in the late 1970s. From 1977 to 1980 nearly 60 percent of Jamaica's graduates of professional and technical schools left to live in North America. There have been substantial constraints against work permits for non-Jamaicans. A U.S. Embassy report cautioned that "investors seeking skilled labor for their factories may run into problems. Skilled labor is, in general, scarce and relatively expensive.... Labor relations in Jamaica can be turbulent."

In Seaga's first seven years in office, the unemployment rate dropped to 25 percent and inflation was slashed to 14 percent; but since per capita incomes fell during the same period, people remained discontent. The *Daily Gleaner* newspaper, which had been vehemently anti-Manley, wrote, "The honeymoon with the Seaga government is fast coming to an end.... So far, he has shown us that he is a good bookkeeper.... We are still looking for a prime minister."

But what about foreign hotel expansion? The Jamaican government first offered to lease eight of its fourteen hotels under agreements that would guarantee returns to the government. The government wished to use a leasing arrangement in order to get an immediate positive rather than negative return, yet hold on to properties whose values it believed would increase substantially during the next few years. Since this drew little response, the Jamaican government later offered ten- to fifteen-year income tax concessions based on the size of the hotel. This has not been enough to attract the necessary amount of additional investment.

QUESTIONS

1. What types of concessions might foreign hotels request of Jamaica as a requisite for entry?
2. What things might Jamaica do to improve its bargaining stance with foreign hotels?
3. If a foreign hotel group were to invest, what practices should it follow to strengthen its position after commencing operations?
4. To what extent might or should home governments (especially the United States) become involved in promoting or discouraging foreign hotel entry into and subsequent operations in Jamaica?

NOTES

1. Data for the case were taken from Louis Morano, "Multinationals and Nation-States: The Case of Aramco," *Orbis,* Summer 1979, pp. 447–468; "Oil: New Power Structure,"

Business Week, December 24, 1979, pp. 82–88; "Saudi Takeover of Aramco Looms," *Wall Street Journal,* August 6, 1980, p. 21; Douglas Martin, "Aramco's Tough Oil Search," *New York Times,* February 10, 1982, p. D1; "Yamani Reportedly Loses Seat on Aramco's Board," *Wall Street Journal,* April 16, 1987, p. 8; Ted D'Affisio, "Aramco Long-Term Contract with Saudis May Pressure Oil Company Earnings," *The Oil Daily,* February 9, 1987, p. 3; "New Aramco Chief Named," *New York Times,* April 7, 1988, p. 32; "Saudis Reportedly Map Changes for Aramco," *New York Times,* May 10, 1988, p. 34.

2. Richard J. Meislin, "Mexico Relaxes Rules on Foreign Ownership," *New York Times,* February 17, 1984, p. D1.

3. Nathan Fagre and Louis T. Wells, Jr., "Bargaining Power of Multinationals and Host Governments," *Journal of International Business Studies,* Vol. 8, No. 2, Fall 1982, pp. 9–23, studied ownership percentages of foreign investors in Latin America.

4. Michael R. Sesit, "Foreign Investment Playing Bigger Role in Poorer Countries," *Wall Street Journal,* March 29, 1984, p. 3.

5. Many of these conflicts are discussed in "The Multinationals: An Urgent Need for New Ties to Government," *Business Week,* March 12, 1979, pp. 74–82.

6. Thane Peterson, Frank J. Comes, Jonathan Kapstein, Steven J. Dryden, and John J. Keller, "The Swedes Give AT&T and the U.S. Painful Black Eyes," *Business Week,* No. 2997, May 4, 1987, pp. 44–45.

7. Niles Howard, "The World Woos U.S. Business," *Dun's Business Month,* Vol. 120, No. 5, November 1982, pp. 38–45. For effects on locational patterns, see Raymond Vernon, "Multinationals Are Mushrooming," *Challenge,* Vol. 29, No. 2, May–June 1986, pp. 43–44; for examples of competition among the states in the U.S., see Martin Tolchin and Susan Tolchin, "The States' Global Hustlers," *Across the Board,* Vol. 25, No. 4, April 1988, pp. 14–22.

8. Robert Weigand, "International Investments: Weighing the Incentives," *Harvard Business Review,* Vol. 61, No. 4, July–August 1983, pp. 146–152; Stephen E. Guisinger, "Do Performance Requirements and Investment Incentives Work?" *The World Economy,* Vol. 9, No. 1, March 1986, pp. 79–96.

9. R. Hal Mason, "Investment Incentives and Performance Requirements: A Case Study of Food Manufacturing," a paper presented to the Academy of International Business, San Francisco, December 29, 1983, which was a summary of a larger report submitted to the World Bank.

10. William A. Stoever, "Renegotiations: The Cutting Edge of Relations between MNCs and LDCs," *Columbia Journal of World Business,* Spring 1979, pp. 6–7.

11. Eric Berg, "Peru to Pay Part of Debt in Goods," *New York Times,* September 17, 1987, p. 25+.

12. Dennis J. Encarnation and Suchil Vachani, "Foreign Ownership: When Hosts Change the Rules," *Harvard Business Review,* Vol. 63, No. 5, September–October 1985, pp. 152–160.

13. "Exxon Agrees to Sell Oil and Gas Assets in Libya to Government for Net Book Value," *Wall Street Journal,* January 6, 1982, p. 2; and Youssef M. Ibrahim, "Mobil Negotiating Pullout from Libya, Duplicating Exxon's Decision Last Year," *Wall Street Journal,* April 13, 1982, p. 2.

14. Stoever, *op. cit.*

15. These and other differences are noted in John L. Graham and Roy A. Herberger, Jr. "Negotiators Abroad—Don't Shoot From the Hip," *Harvard Business Review,* Vol. 61, No. 4, July–August 1983, pp. 160–168.

16. Ashok Kapoor and J. J. Boddewyn, *International Business–Government Relations: U.S. Corporate Experience in Asia and Western Europe* (New York: American Management Association, 1973), p. 67.

17. Stoever, *op.cit.,* pp. 12–13.

18. Kapoor and Boddewyn, *op. cit.,* pp. 67–71.

19. Ashok Kapoor, *International Business Negotiations: A Study in India* (New York University Press, 1970), p. 284.

20. George Schwarzenberger, "The Protection of British Property Abroad," *Current Legal Problems,* Vol. 5, 1952, pp. 295–299; Oliver J. Lissitzyn, *International Law Today and Tomorrow* (Dobbs Ferry, N.Y.: Oceana Publications, 1965, p. 77); and Gillis Wetter, "Diplomatic Assistance to Private Investment," *University of Chicago Law Review,* Vol. 29, 1962, p. 275.

21. James M. Perry, "Gunboat Diplomacy Is Older than U.S., and Its Purpose Hasn't Changed Much," *Wall Street Journal,* October 26, 1983, p. 24.

22. Ian Brownlie, *Principles of Public International Law* (Oxford, England: Oxford University Press, 1966), pp. 435–436.

23. Green H. Hackworth, *Digest of International Law* (Washington, D.C.: U.S. Government Printing Office, 1942), pp. 655–661.

24. David R. Mummery, *The Protection of International Private Investment* (New York: Praeger Publishers, 1968), p. 49.

25. "OPIC Contends Levy against Revere Copper Wasn't Expropriation," *Wall Street Journal,* June 15, 1977, p. 35.

26. Mummery, *op. cit.,* p. 98.

27. Raymond Vernon, "The Multinationals: No Strings Attached," *Foreign Policy,* Winter 1978–1979, p. 126.

28. Mummery, *op. cit.,* p. 74.

29. William A. Stoever, "Issues Emerging in Iranian Claims Negotiations," *Wall Street Journal,* May 7, 1981, p. 26; James B. Stewart and Peter Truell, "U.S. Firms Win Some, Lose Some at Tribunal Arbitrating $5 Billion in Claims against Iran," *Wall Street Journal,* November 15, 1984, p. 38.

30. "Chile Halts Shipments to France of Copper from El Teniente Mines," *Wall Street Journal,* October 17, 1972, p. 12.

31. John Marcom, Jr., "U.K. Court Says U.S. Bank Owes Money to Libya," *Wall Street Journal,* September 3, 1987, p. 12.

32. "Arco Unit Awarded Payment from Libya's Takeover of Assets," *Wall Street Journal,* April 4, 1977, p. 4; and "California Standard, Texaco Win Ruling Against Libya Takeover of Oil Holdings," *Wall Street Journal,* March 3, 1977, p. 4.

33. Burton Yale Pines, "Hollow Chambers of the World Court," *Wall Street Journal,* April 12, 1984, p. 30.

34. For further discussions of the subject see Jack G. Kaikati, "The Challenge of the

Arab Boycott," *Sloan Management Review,* Winter 1977, pp. 83–100; Dan S. Chill, *The Arab Boycott of Israel* (New York: Praeger Publishers, 1976).

35. Barry Kramer, "China Warns Dutch on Selling Subs to Taiwan," *Wall Street Journal,* January 14, 1981, p. 31.

36. "Saudis Warn Toyota on Ford," *New York Times,* June 24, 1981, p. D5.

37. Don Wallace, Jr., *International Regulation of Multinational Corporations* (New York: Praeger Publishers, 1976), pp. 5–26.

38. For a discussion of how codes may harbinger national regulations, see Richard L. Rowan and Duncan C. Campbell, "The Attempt to Regulate Industrial Relations through International Codes of Conduct," *Columbia Journal of World Business,* Vol. 18, No. 2, Summer 1983, pp. 64–80.

39. John Tagliabue, "I.B.M. Turns up the Heat in Europe," *New York Times,* June 10, 1984, p. F1; John Templeman, "Hands across Europe: Deals that Could Redraw the Map," No. 2999, May 18, 1987, pp. 64–65.

40. Charles T. Crespy, "Global Marketing Is the New Public Relations Challenge," *Public Relations Quarterly,* Vol. 31, No. 2, Summer 1986, pp. 5–8.

41. "Corporate Citizenship: Outstanding Examples Worldwide," *Top Management Report,* 1979, p. 2.

42. Kapoor and Boddewyn, *International Business–Government Relations,* p. 32.

43. Belmont F. Haydel, "Case Study of a Social Responsibility Program: Gulf & Western Industries, Inc. in the Dominican Republic in Employee Health, Housing, Education, Sports, and General Welfare, and Other Assistance to the Dominican Republic," paper presented to the Academy of International Business, New York, October 7, 1983; Pamela G. Hollie, "G. & W. to Sell Dominican Holdings," *New York Times,* June 13, 1984, p. D1.

44. For a discussion of the advertising part of the promotion, see S. Prakash Sethi, "Advocacy Advertising and the Multinational Corporation," *Columbia Journal of World Business,* Fall 1977, pp. 32–46.

45. Douglas Nigh and Philip L. Cochran, "Issues Management and the Multinational Enterprise," *Management International Review,* Vol. 27, No. 1, 1987, pp. 4–12.

46. "Corporate Citizenship: Outstanding Examples Worldwide," *Top Management Report,* 1979, p. 2.

47. Frans G. J. Derkinderen, "Transnational Business Latitude in Developing Countries," *Management International Review,* Vol. 22, No. 4, 1982, p. 58.

48. "Thailand Zinc Talks by Gulf and Western Unit Run into Snag," *Wall Street Journal,* February 25, 1977, p. 22, and "Gulf and Western Thailand Unit Accepts Plan for $90 Million Zinc Mine, Refinery," *Wall Street Journal,* March 2, 1977, p. 12.

49. Data for the case were taken from Jo Thomas, "Tourism up, Violence off, Jamaica Says," *New York Times,* November 25, 1980, p. A3; John Huey, "Going Private," *Wall Street Journal,* May 29, 1981, p. 1ff.; John Huey, "Money Returns to Troubled Jamaica," *Wall Street Journal,* April 27, 1981, p. 27; Ann Crittenden, "Jamaican Economy Is Speeding Exodus," *New York Times,* September 30, 1979, p. 9; "Jamaica: A U.S. Boost in Luring Overseas Investors," *Business Week,* February 23, 1981; Frank Long, "Tourism: A Development Cornerstone that Crumbled," *Ceres,* September–October 1978, pp.

43–45; Edward Seaga, Helping Developing Nations Help Themselves," *Management Review,* May 1985, pp. 11–12; Canute James, "U.S. Maps CBI Tourism Plan," *Journal of Commerce,* June 17, 1986, p. 4A; and Pete Engardio, "Seaga Plays for Time in Jamaica," *Business Week,* No. 2995, April 20, 1987.

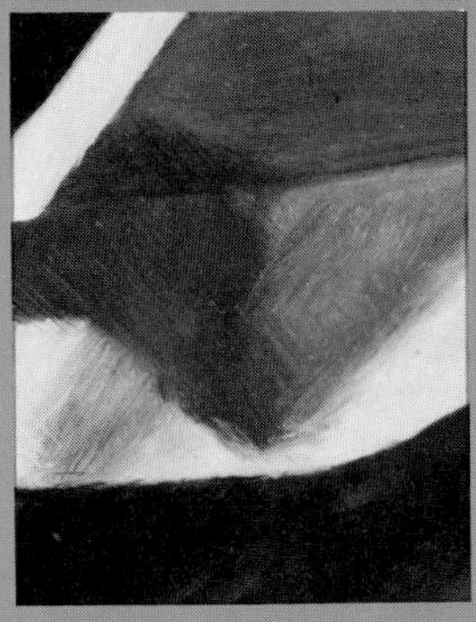

13

CHAPTER

BUSINESS WITH CENTRALLY PLANNED ECONOMIES

Whether you buy or not, you can always barter a little.
—Russian proverb

- To contrast business between communist and noncommunist countries during periods of friendly and unfriendly political relationships.
- To survey the major problems inherent in expansion of business between market and centrally planned economies.
- To describe the various methods of commerce between the communist and noncommunist countries.
- To demonstrate the factors that may affect the future of U.S. business with centrally planned economies.

CASE:
KAMA RIVER TRUCK FACTORY[1]

The participation of U.S. firms in the Kama River project in the Soviet Union illustrates the vacillation of U.S. policy regarding sales to communist countries. The project involved construction of the largest truck factory in the world. Because the Soviets had no automobile supply system as in Western industrial countries, every part has to be forged, machined, and assembled in one location—a plant site covering nine square miles and larger than the combined capacity of all U.S. heavy truck manufacturing. The capacity is 150,000 trucks and an additional 100,000 replacement engines per year. In addition to the manufacturing facilities, the site included housing for about 300,000 people.

When the Soviets announced plans for the project in 1969, they indicated that only three basic truck models of Soviet design would be produced, in order to reduce the requirements for skilled labor and cut costs through automation. The Soviets considered the possibility of manufacturing all the production equipment themselves but preferred extensive cooperation with Western firms for three reasons: (1) The effort would require designing and building specialized production equipment that the Soviets lacked and which would severely tax their limited resources; (2) they lacked experience in the large-scale manufacture of heavy vehicles; and (3) reliance on domestic sourcing would delay truck production by several years.

From mid-1970 through mid-1971, several U.S. firms became involved in negotiating sales for the project. However, sales to the Soviet Union required U.S. governmental approval, and none was forthcoming even when agreements were reached between U.S. firms and Soviet authorities. For example, Henry Ford II visited Moscow to discuss providing technical assistance; while he was there, the U.S. Secretary of Defense made public statements against Ford's participation, resulting in Ford's withdrawal. Mack Truck signed a protocol agreement on prime responsibility for both plant and product at the Kama River facility, which would have involved the sale of between $700 million and $1 billion of machinery and technology for U.S. firms. After three extensions to the expiration dates on the protocol agreement, Mack withdrew in September 1971 because the U.S. government had not granted permission.

Meanwhile, several things were occurring that foreshadowed the eventual participation of U.S. firms. The United States had begun to open trade with China and was anxious to demonstrate to the Soviet Union that the Chinese trade would not be at the expense of Soviet trade. At the same time, the U.S. machine tool industry was in a depressed state and facing added foreign competition. Permission to sell $88 million of machine tools to the

Soviets was granted in June 1971; and by October, approval was given for over $400 million in sales. These sales were unrelated to the Kama River project, but they provided a precedent of equipment exports by U.S. firms to the USSR.

Once Mack stepped aside the Soviet Union had to look elsewhere for a prime contractor. Within days they announced the signing of a contract with Renault of France for an estimated $300 million. Other French firms as well as a host of European companies also were expected to provide much of the necessary machinery for the project. For example, the West German company Liebherr Verzahntechnik negotiated a contract for $144 million worth of machine tools and other equipment for truck transmissions.

U.S. firms were now in a position to convince government authorities that the Soviet Union could get what it wanted from someone else if U.S. companies were denied the sales opportunities. The logjam was broken in October 1971 when the Swindell-Dressler Division of Pullman received approval for a $10 million contract for foundry equipment for the Kama River facility, the first of several of its contracts. To gain approval, Swindell-Dressler had shuttled between the Commerce and Defense Departments and even had a Soviet delegation visit the Senate Commerce Committee and the Senate minority leader.

Certain negotiating problems arose between Swindell-Dressler and the Soviets: One involved a translation error that caused Swindell-Dressler to make a proposal far beyond the scope of what was wanted; another was related to comparing efficiencies of two different furnace systems when electricity and transportation were not treated as part of total expenses by the Soviets. The Americans also were denied permission to visit the plant site. The contract was much more detailed than a comparable one in the United States because the Soviets left little to "good faith." Many other U.S. firms followed with contracts: Carborundum supplied shot-blasting equipment; Hallcroft, thermal equipment; and American Chain and Cable, aluminum foundry equipment. By 1974, sixty-five U.S. firms had signed contracts, and eight firms were doing over $10 million in business each.

Once the United States began allowing firms to sell to the Kama River project, it began helping to finance sales. By 1974 the Export-Import Bank had financed $164.6 million in exports. Payment guarantees also were given to a number of large private bank loans to the Soviet Union which were used to make U.S. purchases. George S. Shchukin, chairman of the Kama Purchasing Commission, said that probably not more than 20 percent of the facility could have been built from U.S. sources without the Export-Import Bank's assistance.

In 1976 the Soviet press agency, Tass, reported that the first vehicles had been manufactured. At that time the output was between thirty and forty vehicles per day, but output exceeded 3,000 per day by 1981. In 1979 a CIA officer reported that the plant was producing engines for military vehicles. This accusation led to hearings by the House Armed Services subcommittee;

however, Defense and Commerce Department officials testifying before that committee said that they knew of no violation of any existing trade understanding.

In early 1980, many members of the U.S. Congress were openly critical of the fact that, in its invasion of Afghanistan, the Soviet Union was using trucks built at the Kama River plant through assistance by U.S. companies. The Chairman of Ingersoll Milling Machine, which built the machines to produce the engine blocks, responded:

> *To sell our machinery to the Kama River plant, we were in competition with the French and German machine builders, and the technology we offered was competitive. The Russians already had similar machines running in their country. We won the competition because of our cost effectiveness and because we had the most experience.*

The United States nevertheless tightened controls on American exports of high-technology products to the Soviet Union in such areas as computers and software, manufacturing technology, and materials critical to the manufacture of high-technology defense goods. Export permission was revoked on spare computer parts for the plant.

INTRODUCTION

The centrally planned economies (CPEs), as discussed in Chapter 2, are sometimes referred to as Second World countries or as members of the Communist or Eastern bloc. Table 13.1 profiles the CPEs. (Note that this list varies slightly from the World Bank categorization in Table 2.1.) Commercial transactions between CPEs and the rest of the world, particularly with developed capitalist countries, are often called East–West business. Four factors primarily set this business apart from other international business transactions.

1. Opinion varies widely on how much and what form this business should take; thus there has been more international business volatility than among other parts of the world.
2. The large collective size of the CPEs helps the CPE's policies of relative self-sufficiency from the West, thus limiting the potential of East–West business by more than what would be expected based on the sizes of the economies.
3. The East–West economic systems are at opposite extremes; and a firm's competitive advantage and method of operating within its own system must be adjusted radically to succeed in the other system.

TABLE 13.1
CENTRALLY PLANNED ECONOMIES

Country	Population (in Millions)	Membership in COMECON
Albania	2.9	no
Bulgaria	9.0	yes
China (People's Republic of)	1,041.1	no
Cuba	10.1	yes
Czechoslovakia	15.5	yes
Germany (Democratic Republic of)	16.7	yes
Hungary	10.7	yes
Kampuchea (Democracy of)	n.a.	no
Korea (Democratic People's Republic of)	20.4	no
Lao People's Democratic Republic	3.6	no
Mongolia	1.9	yes
Poland	37.3	yes
Rumania	22.9	yes
Union of Soviet Socialist Republics	277.6	yes
Vietnam	61.4	yes
Yugoslavia	23.1	no

Source: Population information is taken from *The World Bank Atlas 1987* (Washington, D.C.: The World Bank, 1987), pp. 6–9.

4. Disagreements exist among Western governments on the proper amount and type of business to undertake with CPEs, which leads to (1) strains among Western nations that adversely affect their international business with each other and (2) constraints on what countries are willing to do if their allies have different opinions.

In addition to these factors, the CPEs have some characteristics, such as severe shortages of foreign exchange, which make them more similar to Third World than to industrial countries in their ability to participate in international business.

Yet business does take place. After discussing the factors that make the business different, this chapter will examine methods by which firms enter into East–West transactions and the outlook for future growth.

BUSINESS VOLATILITY

Causes

Volatility of East–West trade has occurred when
- Communist actions changed

The Kama River Truck case is an example of business volatility because of changing political attitudes. The business has been compared to a "light switch;" it turns on and then off.[2] The changes sometimes have been in response to unpopular actions by communist countries (such as the Soviet

• Different U.S. decision makers are in power.

invasion of Afghanistan) or to the ascendency of political decision makers who hold different philosophies about business interactions with communist countries. The change in decision makers sometimes has been the result of elections, but not always. Within the same U.S. administrations there have been many examples of in-fighting among people with opposite views that resulted in policy swings. A good example was in late 1983, when Secretary of State George Shultz sought closer economic ties with the Soviets while Secretary of Defense Caspar Weinberger fought for tighter controls. This difference was characterized as: "There are theological positions on both sides. To the hawks any trade helps the Russians and zero is already too much. To the doves, trade leads politics, and more trade will improve relations."[3]

Within the ideology of a restrictive trade position, three different motives sometimes have been pursued. The first is a punitive one, focusing on controls to damage an unfriendly country economically and militarily in a type of economic warfare. The second is to try to remedy a situation through the withholding of trade, such as trying to coerce the Soviet Union into allowing the emigration of Jews to Israel. The third is to make a public declaration in order to register displeasure over certain activities, for example, the shooting down of a Korean passenger plane by the Soviet Union.[4]

Within the ideology of a more liberal trade position in the United States it is argued that: (1) Restrictions merely penalize U.S. exporters and help firms from other Western countries; (2) the benefits to CPEs from getting more U.S. products is of limited strategic benefit to them anyway; and (3) closer economic ties will lessen political tensions.

It is not only the policies of the United States or even Western countries that cause the shifts in East–West business relations. Communist countries also have altered their attitudes and practices substantially. In both the Soviet Union and the People's Republic of China, for example, changes in leadership and planning cycles have resulted in wide swings in how much each country depends on foreign business, with whom the foreign business occurs, what products are involved, and what forms of business are allowed.

Risk to Business

Trade volatility makes businesspeople reluctant to expend resources.

Most companies prefer to invest their capital and human resources in endeavors that are expected to continue for a long period of time. There is a great deal of uncertainty about the future of East–West political relationship; consequently, many firms hesitate to commit their resources to developing East–West ties.[5] On one hand, businesspeople have witnessed increased peaceful political interactions, such as visits by political leaders, joint efforts to secure peace in the Middle East, and arms reduction discussions. On the other hand, they also realize that the experience thus far in this century shows how rapidly business volumes can alter because of politics and how it can continue to fluctuate over time.

Examples of Change: Especially in the United States

East–West trade fluctuations have been substantial since World War I due mainly to political relationships.

The twentieth century began with peaceful trading operations between the United States and what was then Russia. The two countries were neither allies nor enemies, so there was no official governmental effort to expand or retard the volume of trade. When the two countries became allies in World War I, U.S. exports to Russia jumped more than eighteen-fold, due largely to war-related credits. When the Bolsheviks came to power, Soviet foreign trade became a state-controlled monopoly, credits nearly disappeared, and U.S. exports to the country became negligible. A formal trade agreement between the countries in 1935 resulted in the Soviet Union's becoming the biggest customer for the United States during the Depression. In 1939 the German–Russian treaty and subsequent invasions of Poland and the Baltic states brought certain U.S. export embargoes, which were dropped in 1941 when the two countries again became allies. From then until the war ended in 1945 the United States exported over $9 billion in goods to the Soviet Union. In the post-World War II period the advent of the Cold War resulted in a drop in U.S. exports to the Soviet Union from $149 million in 1947 to $19 million in 1953.[6] U.S. sales to the Soviet Union have climbed since 1953 but have been marked by substantial year-to-year changes because of political relationships and agreements. The most notable agreements were the special wheat sales and growth in credit, which caused exports to jump in the 1970s.

East–West trade fluctuated abruptly immediately after the establishment of communist governments in countries other than the Soviet Union. When the Eastern European countries formed a communist bloc with the Soviet Union, U.S. exports to those nations fell from $400 million in 1948 to only $2 million in 1953. Exports from the United States to China and Cuba fell to nearly zero after the communist takeovers in 1949 and 1958, respectively. As long as Mao Tse Tung headed the People's Republic of China (PRC), the United States traded little with that country; but with new Chinese leadership, trade has grown rapidly. Figure 13.1 illustrates U.S. export fluctuations to the Soviet Union and six Eastern European countries in the recent 1970–1986 period. The average yearly change in export values from the U.S. was over 44 percent.

Exports from other Western industrialized countries have followed varied patterns, reflecting once again the diverse political relationships. For example, in the critical period from 1948 to 1953, when U.S. exports to communist countries fell so sharply, the exports of Canada, the United Kingdom, and Sweden to the Eastern bloc took sharp declines as well, whereas the exports of Austria, Finland, France, and West Germany shot upward. When the United States cut exports in response to the Soviet invasion of Afghanistan, exports from Canada and the United Kingdom increased substantially to the Soviet Union and Eastern Europe.[7]

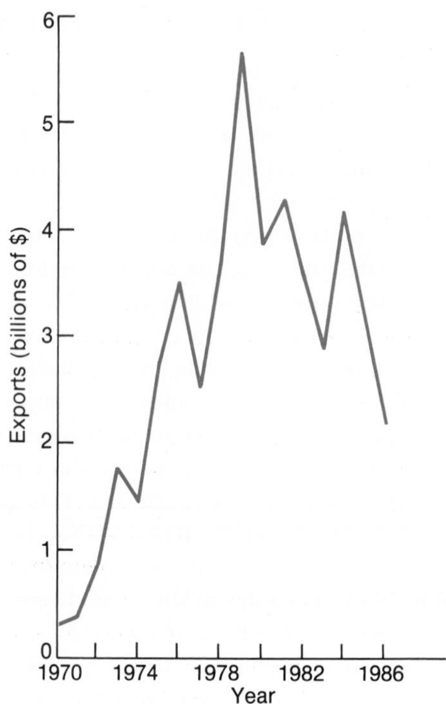

Figure 13.1
U.S. Exports to Selected CPEs (1970–1986, in billions of U.S. dollars)
Source: Economic Commission for Europe, *Economic Survey of Europe in 1986–1987* (New York: Secretariat of the Economic Commission for Europe, Geneva, 1987), p. 355. The CPEs include Bulgaria, Czechoslovakia, German Democratic Republic, Hungary, Poland, Rumania, and the Soviet Union. The 1986 figure is preliminary.

SELF-SUFFICIENCY

Large size means big market

The combined population of Eastern countries is a major factor in the optimism of Western businesses as to their future opportunities in communist countries. A spokesman for Monsanto Chemical summed up this attitude about China by stating, "You just can't look at a market of that size and not believe that eventually a lot of goods are going to be sold there. One aspirin tablet a day to each of those guys, and that is a lot of aspirin."[8] The communist world comprises approximately one-third of the world's population and about one-quarter of world income. China alone accounts for about one-fifth of the world population, or roughly two-thirds of the people in communist countries. The Soviet Union has a population slightly larger than the United States, and the other communist areas have a combined population that is slightly smaller.

Large size also means more self-sufficiency

COMECON countries seek to trade highest proportion with each other

China trades little with other communist countries

Although the large size of the communist countries indicates possible opportunities, it is in some ways a deterrent to expanded East–West business. The Soviet Union and China rank as the first and third largest countries of the world in terms of land mass. Their natural resources are extremely diverse and, when coupled with the large populations, give them the potential of developing a wide variety of production. They, like the United States, might be expected to be much more nearly self-sufficient than would a smaller country. The size is further enhanced by the existence of the **Council for Mutual Economic Assistance (COMECON).** COMECON is made up of ten communist countries: the Soviet Union, Poland, Czechoslovakia, Hungary, Bulgaria, Rumania, East Germany, Mongolia, Vietnam, and Cuba. As noted in Chapter 7 the group has embarked upon far-reaching economic integration by coordinating the long-term production plans of its members.[9] The USSR conducts over 60 percent of its foreign trade and the Eastern European COMECON members almost 70 percent of their foreign trade with other communist countries.[10] The PRC, however, conducts less than 5 percent of its trade with other communist countries; and Japan, Hong Kong, the United States, and West Germany all sell more to the PRC than the Soviet Union does.[11] The size and desired mutual interdependence, when coupled with the geographic proximity of most of the member countries, makes trade within the Eastern bloc more natural than trade between Eastern and Western nations. Geographic proximity also should, in East–West transactions, favor Western European sales to Eastern European and Soviet markets, Japanese sales to China, and U.S. sales to Cuba.

One of the striking features of communist countries is their relatively small portion of world trade. The absolute amount is smaller than might be indicated from population figures: They account for less than 10 percent of the world's share of imports and of exports, including the trade they conduct with each other, and this share has been declining.[12] Table 13.2 shows the imports and populations of the major CPEs and compares these with countries of similar populations and of similar imports. Part of the lag in export share by these countries is their level of income, part is due to some factors brought about by the system of central planning that will be discussed in the next section, and part seems self-imposed. The self-imposition is due to Eastern countries' policies of attaining maximum self-sufficiency because they fear that supplies from other communist countries may arrive late or be of poor quality.[13]

TABLE 13.2
LARGEST CPE IMPORTERS COMPARED WITH SELECTED COUNTRIES, 1985

CPEs	Population in Millions	Imports in Billions of US $	Countries with Similar Population	Population in Millions	Imports in Billions of US $	Countries with Similar Imports	Population in Millions	Imports in Billions of US $
USSR	277	83	US	239	362	Italy	57	91
PRC	1,041	43	India	765	15	Belgium	10	56
GDR	17	25	Australia	16	26	Singapore	3	26
Czechoslovakia	16	18	Netherlands	15	65	Denmark	6	18
Poland	37	11	Spain	39	30	Norway	4	16

Source: *World Bank Report 1987* (New York: Oxford University Press, 1987), pp. 203–221.

DIFFERENT ECONOMIC SYSTEMS

The CPE Method

In the CPE method, prices are set arbitrarily.

The differences in economic systems underlie the differences between Eastern and Western ways of conducting business. As opposed to the free-market systems of the West, the communist countries do not rely much on the market to determine what to produce or what price to charge. In the Soviet Union, for example, 95 percent of prices have been changed only twice since 1955, in 1967 and in 1982. Prices therefore bear little resemblance to what prices or costs would be in a market economy. Currencies are not convertible, and their values are set arbitrarily in relation to Western ones. Since the countries decide centrally what will be produced and consumed domestically, they plan certain production to be in excess of domestic consumption and certain production to be less. Those excesses and shortages in turn are their planned exports and imports, respectively. These then are varied only on an emergency basis because of supply problems.[14]

Export Problem

When CPEs sell abroad, their inability to know what their costs and prices would be in a market situation makes it difficult for them to sell. For primary products, such as fuels and minerals, this is less of a problem because there is usually an established world market price that can be referenced. Most Soviet exports, for example, are of this type. However, Eastern European exports are much less so. The problem manifests itself even in trade among CPEs. Since prices of consumer and industrial manufactures are determined centrally and since exchange rate values are set arbitrarily, CPE governmental buyers worry that the prices from other CPEs are too high. The result often is that the buyers look to similar Western products to get an indication of value, which is a very cumbersome and inexact process. Or buyers may try to settle accounts as much as possible on a bilateral basis, in effect bartering among themselves. Recall from Chapter 9 that the ability to settle deficits on a multilateral rather than a bilateral basis is a major advantage for increasing the volume of trade. The Eastern countries' balancing of accounts as much as possible among themselves does not permit them as much discretion in using surpluses with one country to offset deficits with others.

In selling to the West, CPEs largely view exports as a necessary nuisance to pay for imports. Eastern sellers are effectively price-takers, lacking the competitive experience to get higher prices through such market economy mechanisms as product differentiation. In contrast to their sales with other CPEs, the Eastern sellers often are accused of dumping their products into Western markets. For example, in the late 1970s the Soviets were charged with selling such products as automobiles and trucks in the West for a fraction of their costs in order to earn foreign exchange.[15] But since costs are not calculated the same way, it is impossible to determine whether they are sold at below what the costs would be if computed on a market basis.

The pricing situation also has hampered sales from Western firms to CPEs. Since the Eastern currencies are not convertible, the ability to sell depends largely on the ability of the CPEs to gain access to hard currencies. However, the Eastern countries have had chronic difficulty in getting hard currency to buy imported goods because they have lacked products marketable to the West in sufficient quantity to gain the exchange needed for imports. The methods for handling balance of payments deficits used by the Eastern countries are substantially different from those of Western countries. While Western countries use price mechanisms (e.g., import tariffs, currency devaluations, or development of competitive viable export industries to alleviate trade imbalances) to solve exchange problems, the Eastern countries halt foreign buying by decree or sell some commodity abroad without much regard for what it does to availability at home. Between 1980 and 1982, for example, Rumania cut its imports from the West by 56 percent, resulting in consumer austerity that would cause turmoil in countries with market economies. Since CPEs can curtail imports quickly, this is an added uncertainty for potential sellers. Poland canceled a proposed $1 billion truck-manufacturing venture that General Motors was to build, and China cancelled $1.5 billion in contracts with Japanese groups, both largely because of foreign currency shortages.[16]

Design of Competitive Products

CPE products often lack consumer orientation. Eastern countries lack expertise in Western selling.

The lack of internal competition within CPEs also makes it difficult for communist countries to react to competitive market demands when they attempt to sell in the West. For many products that they have sold, there have been reports of a lack of responsiveness to users' needs, poor maintenance, and poor after-sales support services.[17] The Eastern countries also have encountered problems in selling goods in the West because of unfamiliarity with the prevalent sophisticated advertising methods. Even though these countries have relied on Western advertising agencies, the agencies have only slowly been able to convince them of the need for such things as marketing segmentation and the targeting of budgets toward key products.[18]

Marketing to CPEs

Western countries lack reliable and comparable statistics on CPEs.

A major competitive advantage of Western firms in world markets is their ability to assess potential demand and then develop products and promotional campaigns to fit the assessment. Such advantages are largely diminished in selling to Eastern countries. The first stumbling block is the lack of reliable and comparable statistics on Eastern economies. Income figures must be taken from national account statistics of individual countries. Because pricing systems differ substantially from those in the West, the comparability to Western figures is immediately suspect. Since the national account figures are calculated in local currencies, they must be converted at official exchange rates, which may bear little resemblance to either purchasing power or to an exchange rate that might prevail if natural market factors were allowed to operate. In spite of these formidable obstacles, some researchers have developed means of converting Eastern figures so as to get cumbersome, but better, approximations of the value equivalents.[19]

Even reliable economic statistics for Eastern countries are of little use in demand assessment, since basic buying decisions are not determined by market forces familiar to Western exporters. The Eastern countries plan their economies and allow purchases only of products included in the plans. Although these countries make detailed long- and short-range economic plans, the details are not available to outsiders.[20] The result is that it is difficult to determine not only what will be consumed, but also how much of which products will be imported. The centralized nature of planning and importing makes it difficult to create demand among end users of products. Many Western firms that do sell to Eastern countries shy away from advertising because they feel that the real decisions are made by planning authorities and industrial ministries rather than by the ultimate consumers that the advertising would reach. When they do advertise, usually they cannot target their messages or use flamboyant appeals. On Soviet television, for example, there are fifteen-minute advertising blocks, which broadcast such messages as "Vacuum cleaners can be bought at electrical appliance shops" while displaying on the screen a photograph of a row of vacuum cleaners.[21]

The profit motive is undergoing change in some centrally planned economies, as discussed later in this chapter in the section, "CPE Reforms." Nevertheless, the low importance of profit within CPEs remains a difficult concept for many Western businesspeople to grasp. For export sales to Western countries, sales can be promoted to the import decision maker on the basis of what the product and terms will do for the decision maker's profit or profit center, since it is assumed that the importer is motivated largely by and evaluated on profits. For Eastern decision makers, motivation is less clear. Certainly, the communist negotiators will act on the basis of how they view a transaction vis-à-vis their own positions within the bureaucratic structure. Decisions are often political rather than economic and vary by country and product. There is usually little reward for the bureaucrat who makes a "good" purchase, but penalties for the one who makes a "bad" one. In view of this, should the Western exporter try selling a tried and true product rather than an innovative one? Should the exporter emphasize price, specifications, durability, delivery time, labor- or material-saving properties, payment terms, or what? The situation is complicated further by the fact that the properties of many products are difficult to describe except in terms of cost savings in the production process. How do you describe these properties to someone who does not price inputs in the same manner, does not use depreciation accounting, and assesses no cost to transportation?

WESTERN REGULATIONS

Export Controls

Export controls:
- Differ according to communist country
- Differ by product
- Involve strategic control problems

The United States and several other Western countries maintain export controls to ensure national security, promote foreign policy objectives, and prevent the exports of certain raw materials that are in short supply. While these controls may be applied to any other country, sales to the Communist Bloc have been most affected, especially those from the United States. Cuba, Kampuchea, Vietnam, and North Korea receive practically no goods from the United States. Nicaraguan trade embargos were instituted in 1984. Rumania and China, on the other hand, are treated quite leniently, with restrictions on only a limited number of products that could be of strategic military importance and few procedural requirements. Poland was treated like Rumania until 1981 and again after 1987. The other Eastern bloc countries fall somewhere in between in terms of severity of U.S. export restrictions. These restrictions vary by product in addition to varying by destination. The Office of Export Control maintains a list of products for which special permission must be given before an export license is granted. The licensing requirements apply as well to controlled foreign affiliates of U.S. firms.

Many potential U.S. exporters, as in the Kama River Truck case, have argued that, when permission to export certain goods is withheld, the communist countries simply buy from other countries or develop technology independently. This argument is sometimes effective in obtaining a license; very often, though, it does not suffice, and groups of American companies estimate that the United States loses large amounts of export sales because of these restrictions.[22]

Although the United States, Japan, and allied Western European countries belong to the **Coordinating Committee on Multilateral Export (Cocom),** which agrees not to export high-technology goods with potential military use to the Eastern bloc, countries have increasingly gone around Cocom when it seemed in their national interests to do so. The United States, for example, protested the French delivery of a sophisticated telephone exchange to the Soviet Union. France and West Germany, in turn, complained of the 1984 U.S. trade liberalization with the People's Republic of China.[23] There has been very little dispute on military and atomic-energy products but considerable disagreement on civilian sales that could have military or strategic applications. One of the biggest controversies in recent years concerned a West German contract to build the West European–Soviet pipeline.[24] As West European, U.S., and Japanese firms joined as subcontractors, the United States sought to have the agreement abrogated. The allies refused to do so, and the United States ultimately allowed its firms to participate. Another thorny issue has been that restricted goods (e.g., sophisticated Digital computers) have been exported to countries where they can be sold legally and then reexported from those countries to communist nations where the sale is not allowed by the U.S. government. This has led to U.S. export restrictions that worry many firms because of the greater difficulty they have in selling to countries such as West Germany, Austria, and Norway. In fact about 90 percent of U.S. export licenses are sought for goods to other Western countries.[25]

By no means are high-technology products the only ones affected. After the Soviet invasion of Afghanistan, the United States limited exports to the Soviet Union of an array of products. The most important limitation was a very controversial one involving the reduction in sales of feed grains. On one hand, some argued that the restriction was successful because it raised the price the Soviets had to pay for grain and reportedly caused them to slaughter vast herds of beef cattle prematurely at the very time that Soviet consumers had grown to expect greater meat supplies. On the other hand, observers said the Soviet Union has developed new sources of grain, such as Argentina, and has perhaps been pushed to achieve greater self-sufficiency.[26]

There also have been attempts in the United States to prevent certain exports to the Eastern bloc by firms from other countries. For example, the Japanese firm, Toshiba, and the Norwegian firm, Kongsberg, exported militarily useful equipment to the Soviet Union. Some U.S. Congressmen then included economic sanctions against Toshiba and Kongsberg (i.e., restricting their sales in the United States) in a trade bill.[27]

Import Controls

Import controls:

- Are not the same for all communist countries.
- Are affected by the most-favored-nation status.

In addition to virtual embargoes on goods from Vietnam, Kampuchea, North Korea, and Cuba, the United States uses the 1930 tariff rates (the highest in U.S. history) on goods coming from most Eastern countries. This failure to grant most-favored-nation status puts most Eastern-made goods at a competitive disadvantage in the U.S. market. Although the Soviet Union also has two tariff schedules and charges duty on U.S. goods at the higher of the two rates, the tariffs mean little: First, the prices of Soviet products are not based on what costs would be if calculated in the West; second, since purchases are made by governmental buying agencies, they can effectively prevent the importation of any foreign-made good, regardless of price differential, by simply not purchasing it.

Since U.S. import controls are not the same for all communist countries, problems sometimes emerge if goods are transshipped from one communist country to another so that they arrive in the United States from a country for which there are few import restrictions. For example, the United States has an embargo on imports from Cuba: The United States ceased importing nickel from the Soviet Union because of claims that Cuban nickel was reaching the United States via the Soviet Union.[28]

METHOD OF EAST–WEST BUSINESS

Thus far we have focused on differences in East–West business. Yet in spite of these differences many firms have adjusted to the nuances that have let them expand their business in communist countries.

Negotiations

Each Eastern country buys independently.

The Eastern countries operate independently of each other in making their foreign purchases. The fact that a Western firm has sold successfully to one Eastern country is seldom much of an advantage in obtaining sales contracts in others. Within most CPEs (Hungary is the primary exception) are numerous **foreign trade organizations (FTOs)** that operate autonomously. The Soviet Union, for example, has over fifty of these groups organized along product lines and rivaling large Western firms in size. If a Western negotiator goes directly to an FTO to try to make sales, the negotiator must be certain that it is the right organization for the particular product line; otherwise, information is likely to be greatly delayed in reaching the proper destination, if it gets there at all. Salespeople may contact FTOs directly or through foreign trade missions or commercial offices abroad, such as the Soviet purchasing office (Amtorg) in the United States. There is some disagreement as to whether sales can be developed effectively through Amtorg or whether they should be sought directly via an FTO in the Soviet Union. The FTOs maintain technical staffs that constantly research prices and technical developments in their field. The purchases tend to be large; thus it is difficult for small firms to take part in sales.[29] In 1986 the Soviet Union began decentralizing trade decisions by allowing production ministries and some individual enterprises to deal directly with foreigners.

The FTOs are known as very shrewd negotiators that attempt to secure the lowest possible prices from foreign producers. Although profit is not the motive, the CPE bureaucracies apparently favor negotiators who can extract low prices. Once a company has sold to an FTO satisfactorily, it usually faces less negotiation and delay to secure repeat sales. Eagerness of Western firms and governments to penetrate Eastern markets has led to transactions with FTOs and other communist agencies that are often one-sided in favor of the Eastern countries. For example, in the European pipeline arrangement, sellers were so eager for the business that they sold equipment at "basement rate" prices.[30] U.S. wheat sales to the Soviets in 1973 were at so low a price that the Soviets resold much of the supply in world markets at a profit. The Soviets appear to have made very good analyses of supply–demand conditions and to have known when political officials were vulnerable or eager to come to some type of agreement.

These examples do not imply that Western firms regard profit as less important in their Eastern transactions. It simply means that some arrangements have turned out to be very disadvantageous for the West. If there are more of these examples in the future, Western companies will not be as interested in such business.

Much of today's Western business with Eastern countries is not export of products but rather exports of technology through other types of agreements, which enable Eastern countries to produce the products themselves. The Eastern negotiators usually insist on a long list of clauses in the contracts, such as penalties for late delivery, resulting in negotiations that are much lengthier than similar ones in the West. Bargaining for less than one year is unusual, and three to four years is not uncommon when several Western firms are competing for the contract. The Soviets and the Chinese usually opt for attaining production capabilities at a set fee. Eastern European countries have been prone to seek out longer-term arrangements that include a continual transfer of new technology because of the greater dependence of these countries on international markets in which they need to be competitive.

Financial Arrangements

Sales may be financed by credit, cash, or some type of barter arrangement.

Although balance of payments problems in the Eastern countries have inhibited the ability of these countries to buy goods in the West, sales may be financed in several ways. When an exporter sells to a communist country, it may be for credit, cash payment in a convertible currency, or it may be through some type of barter arrangement.[31] Vneshtorbank, the Soviet Foreign Trade Bank, has correspondent relations with over 1300 banks in over 100 countries and owns banks in Western Europe. Through this network, one can export by means of letters of credit or bills of exchange, which function substantially the same as the instruments used in exports to other Western countries. Since World War II, the credit reliability of the FTOs that handle import purchases, especially in the Soviet Union, has been noteworthy.

Many sales to communist countries are so large that long-term credit arrangements through domestic governmental agencies may be necessary. All Western industrial countries have some type of export credit insurance, which enables their exporters to raise the required credit funds from government or private sources. Except for the United States, the credit insurance arrangements have been the same for the communist countries as for the rest of the world. The United States has at times allowed and at other times disallowed the Export-Import Bank to grant credit or credit guarantees to certain communist countries. As was shown in the Kama River Truck case, credit may be essential in order to make sales. One of the more recent concerns is that some Eastern countries have so extended their debt that they may be economically unable to repay on schedule. Of concern, too, has been the fact that many loans are subsidized.

Rarely, a Western exporter may demand and receive a cash payment in a convertible currency when selling to Eastern countries. Because of the shortage of convertible currencies, Eastern European countries frequently will, and the Soviet Union and China occasionally, try to pay for imports through some type of barter arrangement similar to those discussed in Chapter 20. These arrangements are most likely to be required when the Western export is of a low-priority consumer item, products not included in five-year plans, very large projects, and industrial imports without sophisticated technology. Barter arrangements are also popular for payment in licensing and joint venture arrangements. For example, Combustion Engineering is paid in oil for its control system joint venture in the Soviet Union.[32]

Marketing Methods

Western firms assess demand through examination of economic plans, bilateral treaties.

Occasionally, a Western firm has a product or technology that is so well known or so desired by Eastern FTOs that no marketing effort is needed to secure sales. Rarely, there are also firms that manage to develop business by simply sending catalogs, price lists, and specifications to FTOs and Eastern trade missions. Most firms have to develop an active approach to assessing and creating demand.

They create demand through:

- Trade fairs
- Straightforward advertising
- Frequent visits
- Being subcontractors.

Although the assessment of communist import requirements is a formidable task, a number of information sources give some indication. Even though the country plans do not include published import projections by product, the overall investment and production figures by industry do signify priorities. Consequently, for example, a firm may learn of an increased need to supply the steel industry or a decreased need to service farm machinery production. Also a company may examine Eastern foreign trade statistics in a number of different sources, such as the *IMF Statistical Yearbook* and the *OECD Foreign Trade Statistics, Series C,* which indicate recent import needs. Examination of bilateral trade treaties with various Western countries will indicate broadly the anticipated import needs for the near future. Western consular offices in the communist countries are a very good source of information for firms both on the degree of need for a given product and on the names of other Western firms that are negotiating for a contract.

Probably the major means of creating demand for products in the Eastern countries is through exhibitions at trade fairs. The fairs sometimes are general in nature and sometimes specialize in products or goods from specific countries. Some producers have acted as consultants, giving lectures and demonstrations to officials of research institutes in Eastern Europe, which has led to personal contacts, critical for sales in communist countries. Many firms believe that they must send managers to visit Eastern countries at least twice a year if they are to maintain market growth.

Advertising in communist countries lacks some of the flamboyance found in the West. Almost every industrial branch has specialized publications in which advertising may be placed, and these advertisements must be as straightforward and give as much technical information as possible. A French chemical company was criticized because it did not mention how much and what kind of residues would remain in the soil from using its herbicides.

A typical sequence of East–West transactions is as follows: One Western firm receives a contract to supply most of the equipment needed for an industrial product in an Eastern country; this firm then sets out to find subcontractors to supply much of the needs. There is usually considerable publicity attendant on the signing of such a contract, with the result that potential subcontractors may easily contact the prime contractor to solicit sales. The ultimate suppliers are often companies from a number of different countries.

Cooperative Arrangements

Forms of cooperative agreements include

- Licensing
- Turnkey operations
- Management contracts
- Co-production agreements
- Joint ventures.

Because they want to gain Western products and services with high-technology and management skill inputs and, at the same time, minimize the outflow of hard currencies, Eastern countries increasingly are entering into arrangements by which they license Western technology for a fee or have a Western firm build and/or run the establishment for them under turnkey or management contracts.[33]

Of particular interest are the co-production arrangements, which involve having a Western firm provide equipment, technical input, or management for a plant owned by Eastern partners in exchange for a portion of the output or output from another Eastern plant. For instance, Siemens, a West German equipment manufacturer, receives telephone relay equipment in Bulgaria in exchange for providing a telephone system.

CPEs are beginning to allow Western direct investments in the form of joint ventures, as they have realized the package of assets that the foreign firms can contribute. Although there are still substantial obstacles to the investments, such as currency convertibility, this change is noteworthy because it is contrary to their traditional ideology and practice.

The transfer of assets on a cooperative basis need not be paid for in the form of merchandise but may, instead, be in any one of the payment forms discussed earlier in the chapter. The types of asset transfers have been extremely varied: For instance, Kodak granted permission to Czechoslovakia to make its Super 8 movie film cartridges; Claret, a manufacturer of refrigerators in France, built a refrigerator plant for the Soviets; and Holiday Inn is providing training and reservations services for motels in Eastern Europe.

Most cooperative arrangements in China have been established primarily to get resources for or output from China. Much of this goes through and shows up in Hong Kong's trade figures. In 1979, China enacted legislation allowing foreign firms to set up joint ventures in China with Chinese partners to serve the Chinese market. Thus far the number of these ventures has been small because of (1) the long negotiations involved; (2) concerns about the Chinese legal system; (3) difficulties in getting state-run enterprises to relinquish personnel for the ventures; and (4) many firms taking a "wait and see" attitude. In addition, many of the foreign investors have been required to sell a certain percentage of the output in export markets to earn foreign exchange to cover their remittances.[34]

Planning the Exports to CPEs

The steps needed to develop profitable business with CPEs can be long and expensive. For example, McDonald's negotiated with Soviet authorities for twelve years before reaching a joint venture agreement. Furthermore, there are many examples of firms that have expended considerable effort without reaching their business objectives.[35] Table 13.3 outlines the major steps that a U.S. manager would have to undertake to export profitably to a CPE. Note that each step is effectively a decision point. For example in step one, if there are insurmountable objections within the company for doing business with CPEs, it would be fruitless to incur the costs inherent in the other steps.

TABLE 13.3

EXPORTS TO CPEs: A PLAN FOR U.S. MANAGERS*

1. Internal Political Obstacles
   a. If they exist, try to overcome them.
2. Validated Export License
   a. Find out if one is needed.
   b. Get nonbinding opinion from the U.S. Department of Commerce on likelihood of receiving one.
3. Contact with Buying Agency
   a. Find out which FTO or production ministry handles product in target country from U.S. Department of Commerce or from foreign consular office.
   b. Make contact in person, through intermediary, by mail or by phone, to ascertain if proposition might be entertained.
4. Competitive Situation
   a. Ascertain who they likely are.
   b. Ascertain your competitive advantages in terms of such factors as price, quality, technology, delivery time, and payment receipt methods.
5. Counterpurchase
   a. Discover what products might be available from CPE for counterpurchase.
   b. Determine any limits for resale.
   c. Analyze if and under what terms your firm might undertake a profitable counterpurchase arrangement.
   d. Investigate internal versus external handling of arrangements.
6. Sale
   a. Negotiate an agreement.
   b. Obtain validated license, if required.
7. Growth
   a. Analyze after a year or two if continued sales look promising.
   b. Consider setting up a special operating unit in a "gateway city," such as Vienna or Hong Kong.
   c. Consider establishment of local representation in the target CPE and investigate feasibility of being granted permission by the CPE authorities.

*The authors wish to acknowledge the assistance of Paul Marer in conceptualizing these steps.

FUTURE OF U.S. BUSINESS IN THE EAST

Lagging U.S. Trade Share

Several OECD countries sell more than the United States sells to Eastern Europe and the Soviet Union. Furthermore, almost all OECD countries sell a larger portion of their exports to Eastern Europe and the Soviet Union than the United States does.[36] Although part of the difference is attributable to location, U.S. restrictions have been a major retarding factor. The United States has fared much better with China.

The Need for U.S. Products

The composition of imports by Eastern countries from the West indicates the industrial emphasis of state planners. Nearly one-third of imports are classified as engineering products, and the Eastern countries have been particularly eager to expend their resources on importing advanced machinery and equipment. From numerous examples it is obvious that the communist negotiators want to get the most advanced technology, which should give an advantage to U.S. firms, whether exporting or licensing, because of their R&D expenditures. However, the CPEs also want proven technologies, and it is difficult to get both at the same time.[37]

Of particular importance is the need for replacement machinery over the next several years. The Eastern countries generally have expanded the stock of equipment and machinery in order to bring additional workers into the labor force, rather than increased the output of existing workers through the introduction of replacement capital. There is a near-consensus that the communist countries practically have reached their limits of increasing output by simply adding to the work force. The recent five-year plans confirm this, as there is a new emphasis on technological innovation to save labor, materials, and fuels that involves the replacement of antiquated machinery with more productive capital.

U.S. firms have not only the technology needed in the Eastern countries; they also have the greatest experience in operating plants of the size needed for the amount of output required by the large Soviet and Chinese markets. Recall the Kama River truck plant discussed earlier.

Aside from machinery for industrial use, it is anticipated that the Eastern countries will have a greater need for agricultural machinery, including food-processing and distribution equipment. About one-third of the Soviet labor force is in agriculture, compared to only about 5 percent in the United States, yet the Soviet farmer can feed many fewer people than the U.S. counterpart. The difference in productivity is due partially to natural geographic conditions, but the major culprit appears to be the lack of modern machinery. The Eastern bloc countries also lag behind in the ability to preserve foods once they are produced. The lack of agricultural productivity also points to a continued need for U.S. agricultural products, which make up over half the U.S. sales to the Soviet Union.[38]

There are indications that some emphasis will shift to the production and importation of consumer goods. One of the ways the communist countries have produced growth is to force savings and investment by having few consumer goods available. In Rumania, for instance, the goal has been to plow between 30 and 35 percent of gross national product into investment. The inevitable result of these longstanding policies has been consumer resentment, followed by decisions to produce and market more of the goods that consumers want. If the trend toward consumer orientation continues, then many U.S. firms selling consumer goods that were scorned by decision makers in the past may find new markets in communist countries. Already such products as Pepsi-Cola and Coca-Cola are licensed for production in some Eastern countries. Some observers believe the United States should foster promotion of consumer products to the communist countries, arguing that there will be added pressures in those countries to divert funds from investment and military spending, thus making the United States relatively stronger.

Traditionally, service firms such as banks and advertising agencies have followed their production clients abroad in order to provide them with the same types of services as at home and to help them in coordinating worldwide strategies. The volume of East–West business activity now has reached the level that warrants many service investments.

Two-Way Flows

The Eastern bloc is now selling technology to the West.

Trade must inevitably be two-way to succeed. For some time, basically because of ideological differences, U.S. nationals have assumed that all communist-made products are inferior, pointing to a few items that are, in fact, of lower quality than their Western counterparts. This stance is similar to having outsiders view recent U.S. railroad operations as being typical of all U.S. industries. The reality is that perhaps as many as 25 percent of all scientists in the world are employed in the Soviet Union and that there are many technical areas in which they are now leaders. There has been an upsurge of Soviet patent registrations in the United States and sales of their technology to U.S. firms. In 1988 Payload Systems became the first U.S. firm to contract to have experiments aboard the Soviet space station. In 1987 the Soviets granted their first nonindustrial license to a U.S. company—from the House of Zaitzev to Tanner Companies—providing for U.S. production of high-fashion Soviet-designed clothing aimed at affluent American women.[39] Communist countries conceivably could sell many products in greater abundance abroad.

This two-way flow need not necessarily be on a bilateral basis. The Eastern countries have tried in recent years to alleviate their difficulties in buying from OECD countries by building trade surpluses with LDCs. Given the debt problems of developing countries, however, it may become increasingly difficult to sustain and be paid for surpluses with the LDCs.

Debt-Servicing Problems

On the subject of foreign earnings by communist countries, there are a number of question marks: One of the biggest is what will happen to commodity prices. During part of the 1970s the Soviet Union was able to mitigate its payments problems largely because of the high world prices of oil, gold, diamonds, and platinum. Since then the prices of these commodities have fallen considerably. Furthermore, a study financed by the National Science Foundation of the United States focuses doubt on the Soviet's ability to take advantage of its rich storehouse of minerals. The remoteness of the bulk of these resources often make them more expensive to the Soviets even than imported ones.[40]

The Chinese have begun to bid on labor-intensive construction projects abroad as a means of alleviating foreign exchange shortages. The state-run companies pay workers less than the amount they receive on contracts; additionally, workers send part of their salaries to their families in China. They have worked on such projects as highway construction in Ethiopia, the construction of a power station in Hong Kong, and the building of model farms in Algeria. Labor contracts now bring the Chinese about $1.5 billion a year.[41]

Interaction of Economic and Political Ties

Future interaction depends in part on:

- Whether closer economic ties ease animosity
- What other countries do.

Much of the easing of economic restrictions by the U.S. government has been based on the premise that closer economic ties will ease political animosities. There is little evidence to either support or reject this premise; consequently, events in the world power struggle over the next several years will determine to a great extent what occurs in East–West business.

The United States is, of course, not the only trader with the East, or even the major one. Some of the change in U.S. policy has been due to the realization that, if U.S. firms do not sell, someone else will. What such major Western nations as Japan, West Germany, and the United Kingdom do will undoubtedly help mold U.S. policy. Japan and Europe, for example, have been hurt in the past by raw materials shortages from LDCs and may thus turn more to the East for supplies and sales. West Germany has followed a policy called "ostpolitik," which was designed to increase economic relations with communist countries, particularly East Germany, in an effort to bring about German reunification.

In the late 1980s the schism between China and the Soviet Union showed signs of easing. As long as the rift existed, the two countries traded very little with each other; thus there could be considerable trade diversion from the West if their political animosities lessen.

CPE Reforms

Reforms could increase East–West business.

In the mid-1980s Mikhail S. Gorbachev introduced a policy known as "glasnost," or openness, aimed at improving quality and productivity by opening up more ties with the West. This is an extension of domestic policies of promoting more decentralization, flexible prices, production incentives, market research, and competition. As a further extension, Mr. Gorbachev proposed Soviet membership in GATT, the World Bank, and the IMF. Similar moves have been taking place in other CPEs as well, where profitability is now one of several indicators by which managerial performance is judged. In fact, the Soviet moves were largely in response to the policies already undertaken in Hungary and China. If successful, these changes could make more Eastern products more competitive in the West and ease adverse Western attitudes toward business with CPEs. These changes have also brought more Western optimism; for example, more Western firms are visiting the Soviet Union to explore joint venture formations.[42]

Yet there has been considerable internal opposition to the reforms that could lead to more restrictions. This opposition evolves because of the greater uncertainty created by competition: Most workers in CPEs have been accustomed to full employment and cradle-to-grave social benefits that they fear losing.

Attitudes toward East–West Business

Even if governmental policies do not change, changes in public opinion may make it difficult to expand East–West business. For instance, in spite of official movements to encourage East–West business, ideological differences frequently lead to U.S. boycotts of merchandise produced in the East, to harassment of companies selling to communist countries, and to legislative stipulations that restrict the growth of East–West business. Leaders of these movements usually contend that expanded business relations will strengthen the Eastern countries in relation to the United States. Among the boycotts have been refusals by longshoremen to unload goods of communist origin and campaigns by citizen groups to prevent purchases of Polish hams, Czech glass, and Yugoslav tobacco. Both Firestone and Ford Motor Company bowed to public pressure against their proposed transactions with communist countries. Lobbyists have successfully amended the National Defense Education Act to prevent governmental purchases of teaching equipment from communist countries. They also have blocked most-favored-nation treatment for the Soviet Union until Soviet Jews are allowed to emigrate en masse to Israel.

OTHER TYPES OF COOPERATION

As Western companies continue to develop cooperative arrangements with state-owned Eastern enterprises, increased realization of the complementary nature of their resources may result. By combining these resources in other countries, Western companies may gain considerable economic advantages. For example, Soviet, West German, and Austrian firms have constructed jointly a power station in Iceland; Siemens of West Germany already is teaming up with East German partners to sell electric rail cars in Greece and control systems in developing countries. Chrysler's joint venture with local partners in Egypt assembles Belarus tractors for a Soviet firm.[43]

The United States and the Soviet Union could:

- Cooperate in third countries
- Combine basic with applied research capabilities
- Combine natural resource holdings with management of projects
- Combine transportation with marketing

Several areas are logical complements for U.S. and Soviet interests. One of these could involve more research collaboration, since Soviet firms are strong in basic technology but weak in applying that technology to new products, an area in which U.S. firms are strong. Another is the combination of vast Soviet natural resources with U.S. firms' ability to manage extraction in large projects. Still another is the Soviet strength in transporting goods over long distances, which could be complemented by U.S. abilities to market such goods.[44]

Ventures eventually could develop in which East and West each supply resources for projects in LDCs. This might overcome some of the resentment against foreign exploitation, prevent the East and West from being played against each other, and reduce the dumping of expensive military hardware into poor countries.[45]

SUMMARY

- As political relationships have varied in this century between what is now the Communist Bloc and the Western countries, business relationships have fluctuated substantially. This has been especially true of trade between the United States and the Soviet Union. Trade flourished during the two world wars when the two countries were allies but fell when animosities arose.
- Trade controls have been instituted to hurt an unfriendly country, to try to make a country change some policy, or to make a public statement of displeasure about another country's actions.
- One of the major factors inhibiting the expansion of East–West business since World War II has been the communist countries' lack of products that could be marketed in the West in sufficient quantity to gain the exchange needed for imports.

- When trade is out of balance, command and market economies use different means of restoring equilibrium. Command economies simply may terminate certain imports or sell abroad below cost.
- Many products for which U.S. producers might find sales in Eastern countries cannot be exported because of U.S. controls. Many potential exporters have argued that these policies result not in keeping things from the communists, but rather in diverting their purchases to other sources.
- The fact that the communist countries contain about one-third of the world's population indicates a large market potential. However, the large land mass and the desire to be as independent as possible from the West mean that the Eastern bloc is more nearly self-sufficient than other areas of the world.
- It is difficult for Western firms to assess potential demand for their products in communist countries because of the lack of comparable economic indicators and the secrecy surrounding communist countries' import plans. Since most purchase decisions are made by planning authorities and industrial ministries, it is difficult to effect sales by creating a demand among the ultimate consumers of products.
- The agencies that handle import and service purchases in Eastern countries are shrewd negotiators who are frequently able to get the best possible terms by playing one Western firm against another and by bargaining over a very protracted period of time.
- When an exporter sells to a communist country, it may be for credit, for cash payment, or in exchange for merchandise. All Western industrial countries have some type of export credit insurance, which helps their firms to make large sales to the Eastern bloc.
- A general analysis of Eastern import requirements may be determined by examining recent trade statistics and bilateral trade treaties. Two of the major means of creating demand are through exhibitions at trade fairs and by soliciting sales to other Western firms that have become major contractors for building plants and facilities in Eastern countries.
- An increasing amount of Western business in communist countries is in the form of licensing of technology or building plants or facilities to be run and owned by Eastern governments. Frequently, the Western firm is paid by receiving part of the merchandise, which is then sold in the West.
- The U.S. share of East–West business generally has been small in recent years. Certain factors indicate a possible future growth in the U.S. share. These include the communist countries' desire for products encompassing the most recent technology, plants producing on a very large scale, a need for agricultural products, and an increase in consumer goods, all areas in which U.S. production excels.

CASE:
U.S. TRADE EMBARGO ON CUBA

In 1988 there was speculation about future trading relations between the United States and Cuba. The United States recently had permitted Cuban athletes to travel to the Pan American Games in Indianapolis in charter planes. U.S. amateur baseball players later played in Cuba. Cuba said it would drop its demand for access to American radio frequencies if the U.S. would stop using the name, Radio Martí (named for Jose Martí, the leader of Cuban independence) for its transmissions to Cuba. The two countries agreed to a new immigration pact allowing the deportation of 2,600 Cuban criminals from the United States in exchange for entry to the United States of about 27,000 Cubans per year. Both the Carter and Reagan Administrations had met with Fidel Castro or his intermediaries to discuss the normalization of relations between the two countries.

Background: The Embargo. The fact that virtually no trade had taken place between the two countries since 1961 underscores some of the emotional issues on both sides that have plagued the reestablishment of commercial activities. The United States could boast that some of its best friends (e.g., China) were communist, but apparently it could not accept a communist country in its own neighborhood. Cuba, in turn, was buying well over $1 billion a year from Western industrial countries, including over $200 million from both Canada and Spain, but was unwilling to make direct overtures for trade with the United States.

Several factors led up to the 1961 embargo. After the Batista government was overthrown in 1959, Fidel Castro reportedly spent several months practicing his English before traveling to Washington to visit with the Secretary of State, John Foster Dulles. Dulles then refused to meet with him. Castro returned to Havana and made pronouncements about exporting his type of revolution elsewhere in Latin America. The United States countered by canceling its agreements to buy Cuban sugar, and Cuba retaliated by seizing U.S. oil refineries. The oil companies then refused to supply Cuba with crude oil, and Cuba turned to the Soviet Union for supplies. Since this occurred at the height of the Cold War, when the United States and the Soviet Union had few business relations, the United States quickly severed diplomatic relations with Cuba.

The incidents that further strained relations during the next twenty years were too numerous to detail. Some were so serious that they threatened peace; others were almost ludicrous. They included the U.S. sponsorship of an invasion by exiles at the Bay of Pigs, the placement and removal of Soviet missiles in Cuba, the deployment of Cuban forces to overthrow regimes that the United States supported, and post-Watergate exposés that the CIA had tried to airlift someone to assassinate Castro and had spent thousands of dollars to develop a powder to make his beard fall out. There also were incidents that indicated an improving relationship. The countries have agreed on antihijacking measures and in 1977 established diplomatic interest sections in each other's capitals. Many travel restrictions have been removed, but in 1983 the United States imposed restrictions on taking money to Cuba.

The Future of Cuban–U.S. Trade. By the early 1980s a number of prominent people in the United States had indicated publicly that they favored trade with Cuba. These people included some senators from both parties, the head of the United Auto Workers, and several heads of major firms. The primary rationale was that the embargo had not succeeded: Cuba was able to buy elsewhere. Among Latin America countries, nearly all had abandoned the 1964 Organization of American States embargo, from which only Mexico had abstained. Since Cuba had been able to turn to other countries for goods, trade proponents have reasoned that the United States has lost market opportunities. Before the Castro takeover, 80 percent of Cuba's imports were from the United States.

Others have been pessimistic about U.S. export possibilities if trade restrictions are eased. Since Cuba is short of foreign exchange, they say, it may have to sell in the United States if it is to buy from the United States. Over 80 percent of Cuba's recent exports have been sugar, and the possibility of selling large amounts of sugar to the United States may be unlikely since it would have to be sold either at the expense of U.S. domestic sugar producers or at the expense of other countries' production. U.S. firms have strong lobbies; if the United States reduced purchases from such countries as Mexico, the Dominican Republic, or the Philippines, there would be political repercussions.

Proponents of trade believe that Castro might be less of a threat if trade with Cuba increases. Cuba once again would be dependent on the United States for spare parts; and Cubans, they argue, would become aware again of the benefits of capitalism to consumers. Furthermore, such countries as Nicaragua might not be so isolated from the United States if their Cuban benefactor were closer. Overtures toward Cuba also might counter some of the Soviet efforts to trade with and to openly court governments in Latin America.

The United States intermittently has raised a number of issues as prerequisites to commercial relations. One of these is that Cuba agree to stop sending troops, advisors, and propaganda to other countries, such as Angola and Nicaragua. Cuba's position is that as a sovereign nation it has as much right as the United States to become involved in other countries. Another U.S. objection is that the Soviet Union maintains a submarine base in Cuba; Cuba, in turn, objects to the U.S.-maintained military base at Cuba's Guantanamo Bay. Another possible hurdle is compensation for seized properties of U.S. investors. However, Cuba has settled with investors from France, Canada, Switzerland, and Liechtenstein. Furthermore, the United States trades with a number of countries that have not settled for property seized from U.S. parties.

Neither country seems willing to be the first to propose trade formally. If the United States were to do so, then Cuba could propagandize that the embargo has not worked and that Cuban policies have removed some of the shackles of dependence on the United States. If Cuba were to make proposals, the propaganda advantage would fall to the United States, which could then publicize to other developing countries that "even Cuba needs us."

QUESTIONS

1. Should the United States seek to open trade with Cuba? If so, under what terms?
2. What types of commercial relations with the United States would be in Cuba's best interest?
3. Does the Cuban situation warrant a different U.S. policy than that employed with such countries as China, the USSR, Poland, and East Germany? Why?

NOTES

1. Data for the case were taken from many articles, with particular reference to Herbert E. Meyer, "What It's Like To Do Business with the Russians," *Fortune,* May 1972, pp. 67–69ff; and Edson I. Gaylord (Chairman of the Board and President, The Ingersoll Milling Machine Company), "Soviet Trucks and Technology Transfers," *Wall Street Journal,* March 10, 1980, p. 27.

2. This term was used by R. D. Schmidt, Vice Chairman of Control Data, in "U.S.–USSR Trade: An American Businessman's Viewpoint," *Columbia Journal of World Business,* Vol. 18, No. 4, Winter 1983, p. 36.

3. Clyde H. Farnsworth quoting Gary C. Hufbauer, senior fellow of the Institute for International Economics, in "The Doves Capture Control of Trade," *New York Times,* October 23, 1983, sec. 3, p. 1

4. Michael V. Forrestal and James H. Giffen, "U.S.–Soviet Trade: Political Realities and Future Potential," *Columbia Journal of World Business,* Vol. 18, No. 4, Winter 1983, pp. 29–31.

5. In a study of large U.S. firms not doing business with Eastern Europe or the Soviet Union, for example, one of the main reasons given for their reluctance to get involved was that there would be a high initial investment without assurance of return. Robert D. Hisrich, Michael P. Peters, and Arnold K. Weinstein, "East–West Trade: The View from the United States," *Journal of International Business Studies,* Winter 1981, pp. 109–121.

6. See James Henry Giffen, *The Legal and Practical Aspects of Trade with the Soviet Union* (New York: Praeger, 1969), pp. 139–142; Committee for Economic Development, *A New Trade Policy toward Communist Countries* (New York: Committee for Economic Development, 1972), pp. 54–59; John E. Felber, *Manual for Soviet–American Trading* (New Jersey: International Intertrade Index, 1967), pp. 7–9.

7. Economic Commission for Europe, *Economic Survey of Europe in 1986–1987* (New York: Secretariat of the Economic Commission for Europe, 1987), p. 355.

8. Jonathan Kwitny, "U.S. Concerns Export Mainland-Bound Goods as Embargo Loosens," *Wall Street Journal,* March 11, 1971, p. 1.

9. Seth Mydans, "Comecon Leaders Back Closer Economic Ties," *New York Times,* June 15, 1984, p. D1+; and H. Stephen Gardner, "Soviet Foreign Trade Decision-Making in the 1980's," *Columbia Journal of World Business,* Vol. 18, No. 4, Winter 1983, pp. 17–23.

10. Central Intelligence Agency, *Handbook of Economic Statistics 1986,* September 1986, pp. 98–101.

11. *Ibid. CIA Report on China Economy,* released by Joint Economic Committee of Congress of the United States, August 22, 1984, p. 11.

12. Economic Commission for Europe, *op. cit.,* pp. 350–351.

13. Daniel Franklin and Edwina Moreton, "A Little Late in Learning the Facts, *The Economist,* April 20, 1985, p. 5.

14. Franklyn Holzman, "Systemic Bases of the Unconventional International Trade Practices of Centrally-Planned Economies," *Columbia Journal of World Business,* Vol. 18, No. 4, Winter 1983, pp. 4–9.

15. "Britain Jumps on Russia over Dumping of Trucks," *Wall Street Journal,* February 24, 1977, p. 24.

16. Franklin and Moreton, *op. cit.,* p. 16.

17. George D. Holliday, *East–West Technology Transfer,* Part II, "Survey of Sectoral Case Studies" (Paris: OECD, 1984), p. 75.

18. Larissa Oleson, "Soviet Advertising Techniques in the U.S.," *Columbia Journal of World Business,* Vol. 18, No. 4, Winter 1983, pp. 63–66.

19. See, for example, Elizabeth Goldstein and Jan Vanous, "Country Risk Analysis: Pitfalls of Comparing the Eastern Bloc Countries with the Rest of the World," *Columbia Journal of World Business,* Vol. 18, No. 4, Winter 1983, pp. 10–16; and Paul Marer, *Dollar GNPs of the USSR and Eastern Europe* (Baltimore: The Johns Hopkins University Press for the World Bank, 1985).

20. Lyman E. Ostlund and Kjell M. Halvorsen, "The Russian Decision Process Governing Trade," *Journal of Marketing,* April 1972, p. 10.

21. David K. Shipler, "Soviet Ads—Why Try Zip and Flair When a Fact Will Do?" *New York Times,* January 30, 1977, p. 27.

22. Raymond Bonner, "U.S.–Soviet Trade Bars Said to Cost $10 Billion," *New York Times,* May 25, 1984, p. D1; *Common Sense in U.S.–Soviet Trade* (Washington, D.C.: American Committee on East–West Accord, 1983).

23. Frederick Kempe and Eduardo Lachica, "Cocom Feuds over Trade to East Bloc," *Wall Street Journal,* July 17, 1984, p. 27.

24. D. A. Loeber and A. P. Friedland, "Soviet Imports of Industrial Installations under Compensation Agreements: West Europe's Siberian Pipeline Revisited," *Columbia Journal of World Business,* Vol. 18, No. 4, Winter 1983, pp. 51–62.

25. Jon Zonderman, "Policing High-Tech Exports," *New York Times,* November 27, 1983, pp. 100+; "U.S. Sets Trade Curb for Digital," *New York Times,* March 19, 1984, p. D1; Eduardo Lachica, "U.S. Effort to Stiffen Export Licensing Is Costly and Confusing, Industry Says," *Wall Street Journal,* March 20, 1984, p. 10; and "Export Controls," *The Economist,* January 17, 1987, pp. 33–34, quoting information from a National Academy of Science publication.

26. David Brand, "Soviets See Pluses in Grain Embargo," *Wall Street Journal,* February 26, 1981, p. 31; and Everett G. Martin, "Commodities," *Wall Street Journal,* May 7, 1981, p. 46.

27. Steven J. Dryden, Larry Armstrong, and Jonathan Kapstein, "Congress Wants Toshiba's Blood," *Business Week,* No. 3006, July 6, 1987, pp. 46–47; Clyde H. Farnsworth, "Trade Conferees in Congress Agree on Toshiba Curbs," *New York Times,* April 1, 1988, p. 1+.

28. Clyde H. Farnsworth, "U.S. Bars Soviet Nickel," *New York Times,* November 22, 1983, p. D1.

29. Jonathan Kwitny, "Moscow Missions," *Wall Street Journal,* December 30, 1986, p. 1+.

30. Gordon Crovitz, "Europe Pays for Its Pipedream," *Wall Street Journal,* December 13, 1983, p. 30; "Paying the Piper," *Wall Street Journal,* September 30, 1983, p. 28.

31. Paul Marer (ed.), *U.S. Financing of East–West Trade* (Bloomington, IN.: International Development Research Center, Indiana University, 1975).

32. U.S. International Trade Commission, *Analysis of Recent Trends in U.S. Countertrade* (Washington, D.C.: U.S. Government Printing Office, March 1982); Felicity Barringer, "To Russia, for Partners and Profits," *New York Times,* April 10, 1988, p. 3F+.

33. Jerzy Cieslik, "Western Firms Participating in the East–West Industrial Co-operation: The Case of Poland," *Management International Review,* Vol. 23, No. 1, 1983, p. 69. "China: How Trade Zones Are Luring Foreign Investors," *Business Week,* January 11, 1982, pp. 50–51; and OECD, *East–West Technology Transfer–Draft Synthesis* (Paris: OECD, 1984), pp. 348–350.

34. John D. Daniels, Jeffrey Krug, and Douglas Nigh, "U.S. Joint Ventures in China," *California Management Review,* Vol. XXVII, No. 4, Summer 1985, pp. 46–58; Lucian W. Pye, "The China Trade: Making the Deal," *Harvard Business Review,* No. 4, July–August 1986, pp. 74–84; Adi Ignatius, "Foreign Firms Hiring Workers in China Hit a Catch 22: Obstinate Ex-Employers," *Wall Street Journal,* March 30, 1988, p. 15.

35. For a good discussion of this point see Stephen Telegdy, "Doing Business in Eastern Europe: A Manager's Perspective on the Practical Aspects," in Paul Marer and Pieter Van Veen (eds.), *East European Economic Trends and East–West Trade: U.S., West and East European Perspectives* (Greenwich, CT: JAI Press, 1987), pp. 99–106. For information on McDonald's see Peter Gumbel, "Golden Arches to Rise Near Kremlin As McDonald's Sets a Moscow Venture," *Wall Street Journal,* May 2, 1988, p. 14.

36. Stephen Marris, "East–West Economic Relations: A Longer-Term Perspective," *OECD Observer,* No. 128, May 1984, p. 15.

37. Holliday, *op. cit.,* p. 65.

38. Hertha W. Heiss, "The Framework for U.S.–Soviet Trade," *Columbia Journal of World Business,* Vol. 18, No. 4, Winter 1983, pp. 25–28.

39. Oleson, *loc. cit.,* quoting data in *U.S. News and World Report,* January 17, 1983; "U.S. Firm Plans Project on Soviet Space Station," *Wall Street Journal,* February 22, 1988, p. 6. Thomas H. Naylor, "Fashion Gives Life to Soviet Reforms," *New York Times,* September 13, 1987, p. D20.

40. Robert C. Jensen, ed., *Soviet Natural Resources in the World Economy* (Chicago: University of Chicago Press, 1983).

41. Christopher S. Wren, "China's Growing Export: Its Workers," *New York Times,* June 3, 1984, p. 3.

42. Barringer, *loc. cit.*

43. John Tagliabue, "Bonn Innovating in Trade with East," *New York Times,* March 19, 1984, p. D8; Tony Horowitz, "U.S.S.R. Tractors, U.S. Cars Roll Out of Egyptian Plant," *Wall Street Journal,* March 28, 1988, p. 12.

44. Forrestal and Giffen, *op. cit.,* p. 35.

45. Samuel Pisar, "East West Are Business Partners," *Wall Street Journal,* August 31, 1973, p. 4.

6

PART
CORPORATE POLICY AND STRATEGY

Whether a firm is heavily engaged in foreign markets or supply sources or is merely in the initial process of developing them, many interrelated alternatives must be considered. In this part we will discuss those operational alternatives that normally transcend decision making within functional disciplines. These alternatives include where to go, what form the foreign operations should take, and how to organize the corporate structure to accommodate the international operations.

In Chapter 14 we discuss the different strategic dimensions of global production and import/export operations.

Chapter 15 examines some of the major means and activities by which foreign involvement may be approached in order to ration the allocation of scarce resources.

Chapter 16 discusses methods of comparing countries when choices have to be made in terms of where to go to sell or produce.

Chapter 17 elaborates strategies that top management can follow to make the necessary changes for foreign operations while, at the same time, maintaining order and control for the organization as a whole.

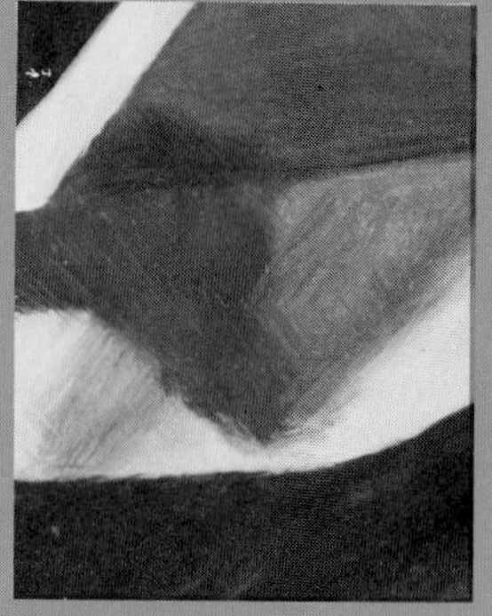

14

CHAPTER GLOBAL SOURCING, PRODUCTION, AND EXPORT STRATEGIES

Right mixture makes good mortar.
—English proverb

- To gain an overview of the different dimensions of a global production strategy.
- To describe the major differences in ways that firms can source materials and components and manufacture and assemble products for international use.
- To identify the key elements of import and export strategies.
- To understand the role of the government in the mechanics of trade, especially export promotion.

CASE:
THE AUTO INDUSTRY AND WORLDWIDE SOURCING[1]

The auto industry, significant in terms of production and employment in the industrial economies, has changed dramatically over the past two decades because of international competition.

U.S. Automakers' Strategies. Historically, the U.S. market has been dominated by the major U.S. producers: General Motors, Ford, and Chrysler. Until 1960, imports held less than 1 percent of the U.S. market share. By 1970, however, that share had risen to 14.7 percent, and Japanese producers held 3.7 percent of the market. For the auto industry, the 1970s were revolutionary, resulting in a strong shift in demand from large cars to small, more fuel-efficient cars and an increase in imports.

As the share of imports rose, U.S. automakers scrambled to solve their problems. Their strategies involved downsizing their regular line of cars, importing parts and cars produced by them abroad or by foreign producers, entering into new production arrangements, and developing whole new production technologies. Without innovations, U.S. automakers would be forced to concede the market entirely to foreign competition.

In addition to servicing some markets with exports, the U.S. industry adopted a strategy of supplying the market outside of the United States with production in foreign locations. Part of that was due to tariff structures: Latin American tariffs made it nearly impossible to sell cars produced in the United States, except to the very wealthy. Post-World War II tariffs designed to encourage growth within the EC forced the automakers to set up production facilities in Europe.

The U.S. market, however, has been relatively open to foreign competition, and the size of the market made it an attractive market for foreign producers. The Japanese strategy has been to develop economies of scale at home and use that production as an export base to supply the U.S. market. By the mid-1980s, however, the Japanese began investing significantly in the United States.

The U.S. government has maintained a relatively free trade attitude toward auto trade since World War II. In 1965 an Automotive Agreement was negotiated with Canada, which allowed automakers to **rationalize** operations in North America. To rationalize is to specialize production of components or assembly of products to achieve economies of scale. This enables a company to avoid having to produce all components or products in each country where it operates. Exports of automobile components and finished products from Canada to the United States rival those from Japan, although U.S. companies also export a great deal to Canada. The integration of the industry in the two countries became evident in the early 1980s and again in 1987, when the United Auto Workers in Canada went on strike. Delays in Canadian production eventually crippled production in some U.S. plants before the strikes were finally resolved.

Because of extreme loss of U.S. market share by U.S. companies, the U.S. government entered into a voluntary quota arrangement with the Japanese in 1980. During the time of the quota, U.S. companies were expected to retool and become more competitive. As a partial measure of effort, the U.S. companies spent $50 billion on new plant and equipment during the 1979–1983 period, compared with $23 billion in the preceding four years. During the 1980–1983 period, U.S. companies cut $4 billion from inventory costs, trimmed management ranks by 15 percent, and nearly doubled the number of vehicles produced per employee per year.

As a result of the problems caused by import competition, U.S. car manufacturers now are developing new production strategies involving foreign and domestic locations. Although these strategies are similar for all of the companies, each company is stressing something slightly different. One of Ford's strategies, for example, is to assemble cars in Hermosillo, Mexico, and ship them to the United States. The cars are designed by the Japanese company Toyo Kogyo Co. (Mazda) and use some Japanese parts.

Chrysler sells Mitsubishi cars through its domestic dealers (it owns 15 percent of Mitsubishi's stock), and it plans to have Mitsubishi build the Omni and Horizon models for sale in the United States.

General Motors' Program. General Motors expanded its production in Mexico significantly toward the end of 1987. It hoped to nearly double the 2,060 employees employed in its Ramos Arizpe plant that produces midsized autos. General Motors is embarked on a multifaceted program to remain competitive internationally. GM's strategy involves overseas production to service overseas markets, the importation of Japanese and Korean cars sold through GM dealer networks, and the importation of parts and technology. According to GM, its overall strategy can be summarized as follows:

> *to remain the Number One automaker in the USA and become Number One in the world by making massive investments in new technologies, product development, and automated facilities to create a broad line of sophisticated, fuel efficient cars capable of competing successfully in all major markets.*

GM also has set a number of substrategies to accomplish these lofty goals. In purchasing and manufacturing, it wants to

> *build new plants for new model types and components; maximize global commonality and centralize production in single divisions; locate facilities in or near target markets; increase the level of automation rapidly; overtake the Japanese in fit and finish quality; develop "flexible" tooling to allow rapid changes in product mix; source components from overseas/low cost countries (engines from Japan, Australia, Mexico, Brazil); and integrate European operations under Opel.*

GM's operations in Europe traditionally had been headed up by the Adam Opel AG subsidiary in West Germany. It never has been a major player in a market historically dominated by Ford, Renault, Fiat, Volkswagen, and Peugeot. However, the European market differs radically from the U.S. market, where one company (GM) controls slightly under 50 percent of the market. In 1986, GM decided to scrub its Opel strategy and established a European headquarters in Zurich to coordinate its European strategy. GM felt that it would have more freedom to run its operations in Zurich, since its Opel operations were required to have workers make up half of the board of directors according to German law.

In the U.S. market GM's strategy is clearly international in scope. Because of the huge cost differentials in Asia, GM has adopted a so-called Asian strategy. It has entered into a variety of agreements with Japan's Suzuki Motors, Isuzu Motors Ltd., and Toyota and with Korea's Daewoo Corp. The object is to step up **outsourcing** of cheaper foreign-made components as well as finished products. Outsourcing means that the company purchases parts and components from abroad rather than from domestic sources. Currently it is selling small cars made by Suzuki Motor Co. and Isuzu Motors Ltd. This outsourcing strategy is a serious concern to the United Auto Workers, which has seen employment in the auto industry shrink dramatically in recent years.

The Daewoo Operation. GM's most ambitious Asian strategy from the standpoint of overseas production is the Daewoo operation in Korea. The Korean operation is interesting because its wages are so much lower than those for U.S. and Japanese workers. The Daewoo operations will be using technology developed by Adam Opel AG, which is contributing $310 million in new equipment to the project as well as advice on the design and construction of new engine, stamping, and assembly facilities. In addition, the company is putting $10 million into a separate parts venture. Additional assistance is being provided in the form of production technology, for which it will be paid a royalty on every unit produced. The new car, using the Pontiac LeMans name, is being sold by the Pontiac division and provides an important product in the market that GM cannot supply from domestic production due to high U.S. labor costs. The parts operation could eventually have important ramifications for GM's entire production line.

The Toyota Venture. The joint venture between Toyota and GM was approved in 1983–1984. The basic idea is to use a Toyota design and parts to assemble approximately 240,000 subcompacts a year in a GM assembly plant in Fremont, California. The plan uses Japanese manufacturing concepts such as a team assembly system, "the just-in-time inventory method of ordering and storing parts, non-adversary labor-management relations, management flexibility in assigning jobs, and an emphasis on building quality into a car at every stage of production." Thus parts and technology from abroad are being combined with capital and dealer networks in the United States to attempt to further penetrate the small car market.

Ford's Program. Ford's international strategy is no less aggressive. Donald E. Petersen, Chairman of the company, wants Ford to become the first truly global auto company. He would eventually like to develop a specific car or component in whichever Ford technical center worldwide has the greatest expertise for that specific product or component. The project would then be done once for the entire world. This concept is being tested with the production of the Ford Sierra, which is being planned in Europe with input from the United States. The plan is to design the Sierra so that the U.S. counterparts, the Ford Tempo and Mercury Topaz, could use the basics of that same design, which would reduce development and production costs and lead to greater profits.

Asian Strategies. Asian producers have adopted interesting strategies for servicing the North American market. As mentioned earlier, Asian producers traditionally have expanded domestic production and serviced North American markets through exports. However, fears of protectionism in the United States and a strengthening yen against the dollar have forced Japanese producers to look to North America as a locus of production. Hyundai, for example, is planning to produce autos in Canada and ship them to the United States as part of a strategy to head off U.S. protectionism. Japanese and other foreign ownership of North American capacity is expected to increase from 5 percent in 1986 to 11 percent in 1990. For a variety of reasons, however, much of that increase in production capacity is expected to go to Mexico and Canada rather than the United States. The Japanese companies also are considering using their North American production as a base for exports back to Japan and to Europe. The strategy for servicing Europe is to circumvent trade legislation that restricts Japanese imports. However, Japanese cars with at least 70 percent U.S. content can be shipped to Europe as U.S. rather than Japanese cars. There are no restrictions against U.S. imports comparable with those against Japanese imports.

INTRODUCTION

A Global Sourcing and Production Strategy

Most firms have the option of where they want to source production for worldwide sales. As was shown in the auto case, for any given market the MNE can manufacture the product itself, or it can buy the product from someone

Firms' options include:

- Buy versus manufacture
- Manufacture in domestic or foreign plants
- Sell products produced at home or in foreign locations.

else. If it decides to manufacture the product itself, it can either manufacture it in the local market or manufacture it in another country and import it into the market. The firm also has the option of buying the product from another manufacturer, which can produce the product locally or in another country and import it into the market.

Obviously, the true MNE is involved in fairly sophisticated forms of production sharing, in which it may produce and/or assemble components in one or several countries for markets all over the world. The virtual explosion of this form of business operation in the past few years has increased the complexity of the production and operations functions dramatically. Separating manufacturing and exporting is almost impossible. Formerly a firm would either export finished goods or manufacture in a particular country for that market. The lines are becoming increasingly blurred, however, and the percentage of total exports coming from intraenterprise trade appears to be growing.

This concept of multinationality is very different from that of a decade ago. In a study of 156 of the world's largest multinationals, it was found that the Swiss and Benelux countries had a significantly higher proportion of their production outside of their parent countries because of the small size of the home market and lack of local resources. At that time, U.S. firms exhibited a very low ratio of exports to total parent firm production because of the large home market in the United States and the commitment to serve foreign markets through production abroad rather than through exports. The Japanese, on the other hand, tended to export more and produce less abroad.[2] Now, however, international trade is becoming a more important part of the GNP in the United States, U.S. firms are beginning to integrate their operations worldwide in a production sense, as was noted in the GM case, and Japanese firms are becoming large investors worldwide. Their expansion into North American auto production is a good example of this movement.

Strategic Alternatives

From an international standpoint this global production and sourcing strategy can be better understood by looking at Fig. 14.1. Figure 14.1 illustrates the options available by country (the home country or any foreign country) and by stage in the production process (raw materials sourcing, manufacture and assembly of parts and components, and sale of products).

To use the auto case, Ford can purchase components manufactured in Korea and ship them to the United States for final assembly and sale in the U.S. market, or it can have the components shipped to Mexico for final assembly and sale in the United States and Mexico. If the components are manufactured in Korea, many of the raw materials were probably imported. In the case of Mexican assembly, some of the components would come from the United States, some from Korea, and a small percentage from Mexico.

Figure 14.1
Global Sourcing and Production Strategy

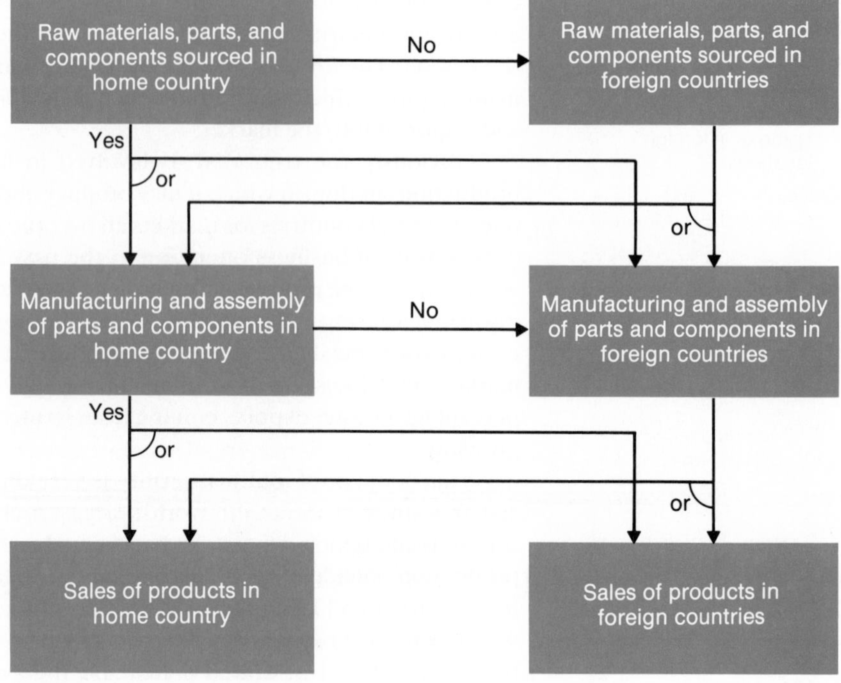

INTERNATIONAL SOURCING—THE IMPORT STRATEGY

Before components can be manufactured, raw materials must be procured. For a country such as Japan, this can be critical, since nearly all of its uranium, bauxite, nickel, crude oil, iron ore, copper, and coking coal and approximately 30 percent of its agricultural products are purchased from abroad. Trading companies came into being to acquire the raw materials necessary to fuel the manufacturing process.

Imports involve problems nonexistent to the same extent in domestic sourcing: language, distance, currency, wars and insurrections, strikes, political problems, and tariffs, to name a few.

Trends in Global Sourcing

One of the difficult problems faced by firms as they devise global sourcing strategies is to deal with changing world economic events. The strong dollar from 1980–1985 was thought to contribute to firms' stepped-up outsourcing, as demonstrated in the auto industry case. It would seem to follow that a weakening of the dollar would drive sourcing back on shore; however, it is more complex than that.

Foreign sourcing has increased as a percentage of total purchases by U.S. firms.

A 1987 survey of 107 major U.S.-based manufacturers revealed a number of interesting trends in global sourcing. In the study, it was pointed out that foreign sourcing as a percentage of total purchases by U.S. firms increased from 8 percent in 1980 to 15 percent in 1985–1986. There seems to be a difference of opinion in the report, however, over whether or not this share of foreign purchases will increase over the next decade.

Outsourcing is due to lower costs and better quality.

The major reasons for outsourcing tend to be lower costs and improved quality. Many manufacturing firms find that materials costs are a significant percentage of total costs of manufacturing, and overhead as a percentage of total cost is falling. That would imply that firms need to continue to search for the most economic source of supply of materials.

Three major risks of outsourcing are:

- Length of supply lines
- Inventory levels
- Currency fluctuations

In spite of the benefits of sourcing abroad, firms find that their three major risks are: the length of supply lines, inventory levels, and currency fluctuations. **Just-in-time (JIT)** manufacturing systems are becoming increasingly popular among U.S. manufacturers, and it is important that firms have quick access to components in order to make that system work.

Just-in-time systems deliver parts and components as they need to be used in production.

The concept behind JIT is that parts and components must be delivered to the production process just in time to be used. As a result, firms do not carry large inventories, thereby saving financing and storage costs. This means that parts must have few defects and must arrive on time to be used. Foreign sourcing can create big risks for JIT, since interruptions in the supply line can cause havoc. JIT implies that inventories need to be small, but foreign sourcing almost requires large inventory levels in order to counteract the risk. Exchange rates are problematic, since they directly influence costs, but within a certain range, firms tend to ignore exchange rate fluctuations in order to establish stable sources of supply and enter into long-term relationships with suppliers.

In spite of the many advantages of sourcing abroad, the problems listed above and other factors have caused many firms to return to domestic sources of supply for products. Besides fluctuating exchange rates and the rising use of JIT, many firms have noted improvements in quality, design, and cost of U.S. producers as key reasons to return to the domestic market. Nearly half of the firms surveyed said that they had decided to return to the domestic market for some of their purchases;[3] however, many suppliers also disappeared in the early 1980s when their customers moved abroad to take advantage of cheaper sources of supply.

An Import Strategy

Procedural issues are the rules and regulations involved in imports.

There are two different types of considerations for potential importers: procedural and strategic. Procedural considerations relate more to the rules and regulations of the customs office of a country. U.S. Customs, for example, suggests eight key points that must be considered for faster customs clearance.[4] These points deal with accurate documentation and with a familiarity with special U.S. laws relating to such products as food, drugs, cosmetics, and alcoholic beverages.

An import broker is a specialist in import institutions and documentation.

Importation clearly requires a certain degree of expertise in dealing with institutions as well as documentation that a firm may prefer to avoid. As a result, the importer may wish to work through an **import broker.** The broker obtains the customs release, foreign release, and other clearances before forwarding necessary paperwork, such as a **bill of lading,** to the carrier that is to deliver the goods from the dock to the importer. The function of the bill of lading is threefold: It serves as (1) a receipt for goods delivered to the common carrier for transportation, (2) a contract for the services to be rendered by the carrier, and (3) a document of title.[5]

Strategic issues include the long-run decision to source at home or abroad.

The strategic considerations are more critical in the long run. In the case at the beginning of this chapter it was noted that the strong U.S. dollar in the early 1980s forced GM and other auto companies to consider sourcing more of their purchases abroad. These felt that they needed to do so to help achieve cost parity in competing with foreign manufacturers. Although it is easy to say that a company chooses a foreign over a domestic supplier because of a cheaper price, the reasons given for foreign sourcing are more complex than that.

Domestic companies often choose foreign goods over domestic ones for nine basic reasons: price; quality; unavailability of items domestically; faster delivery and continuity of supply; better technical service; more advanced technology; a marketing tool (especially in conjunction with offset, where firms are required to import products from a country in order to be able to sell to consumers in that country); a tie-in with foreign subsidiaries (such as when GM decides to buy parts produced by its foreign operations in Korea or Japan); and competitive clout (to convince local suppliers to keep their prices low).[6]

As just noted, in spite of the benefits a number of problems result from using foreign suppliers: location and evaluation of reputable vendors abroad; lead/delivery time; difficulty of expediting delivery and direct contact with foreign personnel; political and labor problems; currency fluctuations; payment methods; quality of merchandise; rejects and the problem of returns; tariffs and duties; paperwork costs due to the extra documentation needed to clear goods from customs, etc.; legal problems; transportation; language; and cultural and social customs.[7]

Companies must consider a variety of factors in developing a foreign sourcing strategy. Obviously, the set of important variables varies from industry to industry and country to country. But in some MNEs, such as electronics, instrument, and automotive, a wide variety of factors other than cost have influenced sourcing decisions in recent years.

The movement toward JIT has forced firms to focus more on quality, prompt delivery, low incidence of defects, and strong technical capacity.[8] In some cases, this restricts the use of traditionally low-cost labor areas and forces firms to look to countries that can emphasize quality and reliability. The use of countries such as Japan and West Germany can solve the quality and reliability problems, but the strength of their currencies against the dollar during 1987 and 1988 made them prohibitively expensive as a source of U.S. supply. As a result, firms are looking more to the NICs, such as Brazil and South Korea. As these countries increase their technical capability, they can combine cost factors with reliability to result in a strong source of supply.

The Role of Customs Agencies

The major roles of Customs are collecting fees and enforcing laws.

When importing goods into any country, the firm must be totally familiar with the governmental customs operations. The primary duties of the U.S. Customs Service, for example, "include the assessment and collection of all duties, taxes, and fees on imported merchandise, the enforcement of customs and related laws, and the administration of certain navigation laws and treaties." As a major enforcement organization, it "combats smuggling and frauds on the revenue and enforces the regulations of numerous other Federal agencies at ports of entry and along the land and sea borders of the United States."[9] The importer needs to know how to clear goods, what duties must be paid, and what special laws exist.

Sometimes goods are imported into a country and are immediately exported or assembled into an intermediate or final product and exported. Such action may allow the firm to get a total or partial refund of any import duties.

Foreign Trade Zones

Foreign trade zones are special zones designated by the government where tariffs can be delayed or avoided.

In recent years, **foreign trade zones (FTZs)** have become more popular as an intermediate step in the process between import and final use. Oftentimes, the final use is for export; however, the zones are good for making use of foreign sourcing.

> *FTZs, established by federal grants [in the United States] primarily to state and local government agencies, provide areas where domestic and imported merchandise can be stored, inspected, and manufactured free from formal customs procedures until the goods leave the zones. The intended purpose of the zones is to encourage the domestic location of firms by affording them opportunities to defer duties, pay less duties, or to avoid certain duties completely.*[10]

FTZs have been used primarily in the United States as a means of providing greater flexibility as to when and how customs duties are to be paid. However, their use in export business has been climbing. In the United States, FTZs used for exports are in one of the following categories:

- Foreign goods transshipped through U.S. zones to third countries
- Foreign goods processed in zones, then transshipped abroad
- Foreign goods processed or assembled in U.S. zones with some domestic materials and parts, then reexported
- Goods produced in zones wholly of foreign content and exported
- Goods produced in zones from a combination of domestic and foreign materials and components then exported
- Domestic goods moved into a zone to achieve export status prior to their actual exportation.[11]

In 1975, there were only twenty-seven general-purpose zones and subzones for individual plants. By 1987, the number of zones had increased to 247 in forty-seven states and Puerto Rico. Imports flowing through zones increased sixty-twofold during that same time period to nearly $40 billion.[12]

An example of how a foreign trade zone can be used is a Coastal Corp. subsidiary that refines oil in Texas at a foreign-trade subzone. If the subsidiary exports refined oil products, it pays no duty at all. If it sells the products domestically, it saves over $250,000 a year in areas such as interest saved on duties postponed until the products leave the zone.[13] Smith Corona used a FTZ facility to import parts into the United States for its typewriter manufacturing facilities. After the parts were manufactured into typewriters, they would be imported officially into the United States at a zero duty, something that was not possible for the parts due to a ruling in the customs code.[14]

INTERNATIONAL MANUFACTURE

Once the manufacturer has decided on the source of raw materials and components, it must determine where the components are to be manufactured and where the final goods are to be assembled. This judgment depends on complex factors such as the cost of transportation, duties on components versus finished goods, the need to be close to the market, foreign exchange risk, economies of scale in the production process, and national image.

Production possibilities include: single plant; multiple plants; manufacturing interchange (various assembly locations using common components); and rationalization (specialization by product or process).

A firm may choose one of many manufacturing systems. It may try to serve all markets from one single plant. Economies of scale, transportation charges, tariffs, and the like may render this system infeasible. Firms also can specialize production by product or process so that a particular plant produces a product or range of products or produces all products using a particular process and services all markets. Or it could have several plants specializing in the same product or process so that the firm gets a larger geographical spread. The process of manufacturing interchange involves plants producing a range of components and interchanging them so that all plants assemble the finished product for the local market. Obviously, there is no best way to set up the production process. For a particular product or line of products a firm may use a single-plant strategy and depend on exports to serve world markets. This essentially would be a worldwide product and production strategy. For other products or groups of products a multiplant strategy such as rationalization or manufacturing interchange might be best.

Offshore Manufacturing

Offshore manufacturing outside of the United States is done in low-cost locations for importing into the United States and other markets.

In recent years, offshore manufacturing has provided a useful alternative to giving up the local market to low-cost foreign competitors. Offshore manufacturing escalated sharply in the 1960s and 1970s in the electronics industry worldwide as one firm after another set up production facilities in the Far East, principally in Taiwan and Singapore. Those locations were chosen because of low labor costs, the availability of cheap materials and components, and proximity to markets. Now these countries are beginning to give way to the newer "low-cost" countries of Asia (Indonesia, Thailand, Malaysia, and South Korea) and Latin America.

The maquiladora, or in-bond industry, is an industry concept developed by the Mexican government in which U.S.-source components are shipped to Mexico duty-free for assembly and reexported to the United States.

Maquiladora Industry. Mexico has become one of the newest centers for offshore production for U.S. firms through the **maquiladora industry,** also known more formally as the **in-bond industry.** The Mexican government estimates that the industry, which already earns more foreign exchange than does tourism, could employ one million people by the year 2000. Under the maquiladora concept, U.S.-sourced components are shipped to Mexico duty-free, assembled by Mexican workers, and reexported to the United States or other foreign markets under favorable tariff provisions. U.S. duties are levied on the imports only to the extent of the value added in Mexico. Since labor is so cheap, the value added is not great. This industry allows U.S. firms to assemble products more cheaply than would have been the case in the United States and provides employment for Mexicans.[15] Japanese firms also are investing significant capital in Mexico for assembly and export into the United States.

Many firms are combining the maquiladora concept with free trade zones being established in the Caribbean Basin countries. Some of the countries being used most frequently are Costa Rica, the Dominican Republic, El Salvador, Guatemala, Haiti, Honduras, Jamaica, Panama, and Puerto Rico. The major attractions of these countries are low labor costs, tax incentives, tariff concessions, and access to U.S. markets through specially negotiated agreements or provisions 806 and 807 of the U.S. tariff schedule. In Jamaica, for example, the minimum salary for skilled workers is $16 per week, investors are exempted from sales and profit taxes, some imports and exports are duty free, and there is free repatriation of profits.[16]

Although the maquiladora plant is a fairly recent phenomenon, MNEs have been investing abroad for a long time. In the case of U.S.-based MNEs, a surge in investment activity occurred in 1984–85 as a result of the strong dollar. Firms cut costs and consolidated operations as much as they could to combat import competition, but many of them decided to expand abroad significantly to service both the domestic and foreign markets. It was estimated that 25 percent of U.S. exports during that period were to service U.S. manufacturing abroad. As the dollar began to weaken in 1985, the strategy of the previous two years seemed a little risky. However, the commitment to produce abroad had been made, and it is difficult to reverse those investments in the short run.[17]

Inventory Control

The greater the interchange of products and components, the more difficult the inventory control process. The problems of distance and time and the uncertainty of the international political and economic environment can make it difficult to determine correct reorder points. For example, if a manufacturer in a country with a weak currency imports a lot of inventory from a country with a strong currency, management may wish to stockpile inventory in anticipation of a devaluation despite large carrying costs and the risk of damage or pilferage. Also, the firm may wish to stockpile inventory in anticipation of political chaos or legislation slowing down imports. Rapidly changing international events can ruin a smoothly running inventory control system.

In recent years a lot of press has been given to the concept of just-in-time inventory management, which the Japanese have fine tuned. As mentioned earlier, the basic idea of JIT is to produce the items needed just in time to be used or sold. In order for companies in other countries to implement such a system, the following modifications in manufacturing systems and production processes have been suggested: smooth and stable production schedules; more flexibility in manufacturing; higher quality of inputs and throughputs; better cooperation between workers and management; the development of relationships with dependable suppliers; greater concentration geographically for suppliers and manufacturers; more appropriate plant configuration; and strong management commitment and support.[18]

EXPORT STRATEGY

So far we have concentrated on foreign countries as a source of supply for products assembled and/or sold in the domestic market. We also have discussed how foreign sourcing can take place through investment in a foreign country and the shipping of products to the domestic market. Many of these exports are parts and components to company-owned plants in foreign locations for final assembly and sale. Caterpillar, for example, adopted a strategy after World War II of manufacturing key components in its domestic plants and shipping them around the world for final assembly, which allowed them to maintain tight quality control. Thus the export strategy also is part of the larger sourcing and manufacturing strategy of the MNE as well as a sales strategy for servicing final markets around the world.

Exports take place for a number of good reasons. Raw materials must be exported to the manufacturer, components need to be exported to the assembly operation, and finished goods need to be exported to foreign distributors and consumers. Sometimes this process occurs within the confines of a vertically integrated company so that the exporter can sell directly to the next level through an intracompany transaction. However, the sale may be to an outsider; in that case the exporter may decide to sell directly to the buyer or indirectly through an intermediary.

Factors Favoring Exportation

The most common means by which firms begin international activity is through exportation. Even firms with sizable foreign contractual arrangements and investments usually continue to export to achieve their overall objectives.

Exporting:
- Achieves economies of scale in production
- Alleviates excess capacity
- Is less risky than direct investment.

The decisions to define a market as larger than that contained within domestic boundaries usually will add to a firm's potential sales volume. Export sales also may be a means of alleviating excess capacity in the domestic market. Some firms export rather than invest abroad due to the perceived high risk in foreign environments. Finally, many firms export to a variety of different markets as a diversification strategy. Since economic growth is not the same in every market, broadly based exports allow a firm to take advantage of strong growth in one market to offset weak growth in another.

Export Functions and Facilitating Intermediaries

A company engaged in exportation or planning to export must decide whether certain essential activities are to be handled by its own staff or through contracts with other firms. The following functions must be carried out:

1. stimulate sales, obtain orders, and do market research;
2. make credit investigations and perform payment collection activities;
3. handle foreign traffic and shipping functions; and
4. function as support for the overall sales, distribution, and advertising staff of the firm.

Nearly all firms can benefit at one time or another from using the services of an intermediary organization that will assume some or all of these

There are four major classifications of exporters.

functions. A variety of different intermediaries can facilitate exports. The most important types may be grouped into four major classifications: agents acting for the exporter who is the principal; agents purchasing for themselves as principals; agents undertaking a specialized aspect of the export cycle; and agents acting for other buyers as principals. Export management companies and trading companies are prominent examples of the first two types, and the freight forwarder is an example of the third type. Trading companies illustrate the fourth type as well.

Because of the cost of these different services and the expertise required, most firms tend to use specialists initially. They may develop in-house capability somewhere down the road, but it is still often useful to utilize specialists for this type of activity.

Direct selling involves sales representatives, agents, distributors, or retailers.

Direct selling. **Direct selling** is undertaken to give the exporter greater control over the marketing function and to earn higher profits. When selling direct, the manufacturer normally sells directly to the foreign market. The manufacturer may sell to a sales representative or agent who normally operates on a commission basis rather than taking actual title to the product. A foreign distributor takes title to the product and earns a profit on the final sale to the consumer. Foreign retailers are outlets for consumer goods primarily and can be serviced by company traveling salespeople or by purchases from catalogs or trade fairs. When manufacturers deal in high-technology goods or expensive machinery manufactured to specification, the sale is made directly to the end user. This would be a common practice in industrial as opposed to consumer marketing.

If a firm decides to export directly rather than work through an intermediary, it must set up a solid organization. As noted in Chapter 17, firms can organize in a number of ways, from setting up a separate international division, to a separate international company, to a full integration of international with domestic activities. There is commonly a sales force separate from the domestic force so that a firm can concentrate its expertise in one area.

Indirect selling. **Indirect selling** implies that the manufacturer deals through another domestic firm before entering the international marketplace. The domestic firm may act as a **commission agent** for the manufacturer and not take title, or it may choose to purchase the product from the manufacturer and sell the merchandise abroad. The latter option is common for the **export management company (EMC).**

Export management companies are firms that buy merchandise from manufacturers for international distribution or that sometimes act as agents for manufacturers.

Although EMCs originally operated on a commission basis and assumed no risks, they now operate largely on a buy-and-sell basis and provide financing for export shipments. The primary function of the EMC is to obtain orders for its clients' products through the selection of appropriate markets, distribution channels, and promotion campaigns. The EMC collects, analyzes, and furnishes credit information and advice regarding foreign accounts and payment terms. Other services the EMC may handle include documentation; arrangement of transportation (including the consolidation of shipments to reduce costs); arrangement of patent and trademark protection in foreign countries; and counseling and assistance in establishing alternative forms of doing business, such as licensing or joint ventures.[19]

EMCs, which can deal in imports as well as exports, operate on a contractual basis, usually for two to five years, and provide exclusive representation in a well-defined overseas territory. The contract specifies such things as pricing, credit and financial policies, promotional services, and the payment basis. EMCs usually concentrate on complementary and noncompetitive products so that they can present a more complete product line to a limited number of importers. There are over 2,000 EMCs in the United States, and most of them are small operations. As a result, they tend to specialize by product, function, or market area. Although EMCs perform an important function for firms that need the export expertise, the manufacturer may lose control over foreign sales. Thus the manufacturer needs to balance the desire for control with the cost in performing the export functions directly.[20]

Export trading companies. In the fall of 1982 the U.S. government enacted legislation that removed some of the antitrust obstacles to the creation of **export trading companies** in the United States. It was hoped that these ETCs, which are a form of indirect selling that a manufacturer can take advantage of, would lead to greater exports of U.S. goods and services. ETCs are similar to EMCs, but they tend to provide a broader range of services and often take title to goods. There are four major types of ETCs: newly formed ETCs that received antitrust certification; ETCs organized by state and local governments; ETCs created by commercial banks; and ETCs organized by U.S. companies initially to handle their own exports.

ETCs can be formed by competitors and exempt from antitrust.

The first category involves business enterprises that would like to cooperate for foreign sales but have difficulty cooperating for domestic sales because of antitrust concerns. The government set strict guidelines on how firms would qualify for exemption from antitrust considerations: Cooperation must not lessen competition in the United States.

ETCs can be formed by state and local governments.

One example of ETCs organized by state and local governments is the Port Authority of New York and New Jersey. Their ETC, known as XPORT, is courting smaller firms with high-technology products that have an export potential.

ETCs can be formed by money center banks.

Most of the large money center banks have applied for permission to establish ETCs. These applications must be approved by the Federal Reserve Board before the bank can start export operations. Many of the banks are concentrating on customers in their geographical market and in parts of the world where they already have a good banking network.

ETCs can be formed by major corporations.

Some major corporations, such as Control Data, have also set up ETCs. Initially, they were designed to handle the firm's own business, but they are now expanding to include products produced by other companies as well. In the case of Control Data, its ETC first was established to handle countertrade agreements for sales of products to Eastern European countries as well as developing countries. Now the ETC of Control Data is aggressively seeking products of other companies.

From the time the Export Trading Company Act was signed in October 1982 until the end of 1987, nearly 700 ETCs had been formed, of which forty-three were affiliated with banks. Over $1 billion in sales had been generated by those ETCs. The lack of significant success of the ETC concept in the United States is the result of a number of factors, not the least of which were the strong dollar, weak economies of the major trading partners of the United States, and the debt situation in Latin America, a major market area for U.S. firms. In addition, the antitrust dimension of the Act had not been tested in court, and many U.S. firms were hesitant to establish an ETC until those provisions could be tested. This has now taken place, and the U.S. government hopes that the ETC concept will spark the same degree of success as have the Japanese sogo shosha, which will be discussed in the next section.[21]

Sogo shosha are Japanese trading companies that import and export merchandise.

Japanese trading companies. EMCs and ETCs are essentially new, untested trading companies. When one thinks of trading companies, the giants such as Mitsui, Mitsubishi, and Marubeni of Japan come to mind. The **sogo shosha,** the Japanese equivalent word for trading company, can trace their roots back to the late 1800s, when Japan embarked on an aggressive modernization process. The sogo shosha took the primary role of acquiring raw materials for the industrialization process and then finding external markets for goods. Although there are more than 6,000 trading companies in Japan, the sixteen major sogo shosha control about 55 percent of Japan's exports and 65 percent of its imports. In addition, their annual sales are slightly greater than one-third of Japan's GNP, a tremendous economic concentration.[22] Table 14.1 identifies the major sogo shosha in Japan.

When the sogo shosha were first organized, their primary functions were: handling paperwork for import and export transactions, financing imports and exports, and providing transportation and storage services. However, their operations expanded significantly to include the following: investing in production and processing facilities, establishing fully integrated sales systems for certain products, expanding marketing activities, and developing large bases for the integrated processing of raw materials.[23]

An example of how a sogo shosha can help a client involves Marubeni and Bridgestone Tire. Marubeni is one of the top three trading companies in Japan. For years, Marubeni supplied Bridgestone with carbon black used in the manufacture of tires. The business had been modest, but Bridgestone was a valued client. One day, Yasushi Kawahara, the manager in charge of the

TABLE 14.1
THE SIXTEEN MAJOR SOGO SHOSHA

1. Chori Co. Ltd.
2. C. Itoh & Co., Ltd.
3. Itoman & Co. Ltd.
4. Kanematsu-Gosho Ltd.
5. Kawasho Corp.
6. Kinsho-Mataichi Corp.
7. Marubeni Corp.
8. Mitsubishi Corp.
9. Mitsui & Co., Ltd.
10. Nichimen Corp.
11. Nissho Iwai Corp.
12. Nozaki & Co., Ltd.
13. Okura & Co., Ltd.
14. Sumitomo Corp.
15. Toshoku Ltd.
16. Toyo Menka Kaisha Ltd.

Source: *The Banker,* January 1984, p. 84. These sixteen large trading companies are known as sogo shosha, and they comprise the Sogo Shosha Committee in Japan. The five largest companies in total sales are Mitsubishi, Mitsui, Marubeni, C. Itoh, and Sumitomo.

Bridgestone account, received a request for help in building a unique test track for Bridgestone tires that would mirror Belgian road conditions.

Bridgestone could not solve the problem because it lacked staff in Belgium, but Marubeni did have the needed resources. Kawahara contacted one of his staff in Brussels, who hunted around until he found cobblestones that met the proper specifications. The shipment was prepared to meet export requirements in Belgium and import requirements in Japan, areas in which Marubeni had expertise. Finally, 100,000 stones were shipped to Japan and used to build the test track.

Because Bridgestone was an old and valued client, Kawahara did not price the transaction to earn a significant profit. However, he was able to develop a thriving and profitable cobblestone business for other Japanese auto and tire companies trying to emulate Bridgestone's project.[24]

The sogo shosha faced a variety of challenges in the decade of the 1980s, many of which have been brought on by changes in the domestic Japanese economy as well as the international economy. Their role in trade financing, for example, is being disputed by the banks, which are more internationally oriented than they used to be. Many of the marketing functions are being questioned by the manufacturers themselves. The transition appears as follows:

> *First, the larger and more significant the market, the sooner the manufacturer turns away from the GTC [general trading company or sogo shosha] (e.g., C. Itoh still handles auto marketing for Toyota in Saudi Arabia, a small market).*

> *Second, the more complex the technology involved, the sooner the manufacturer turns away from the GTC [because of the difficulty of the GTC dealing with the technical requirements of the product]. Third, the more specific and involved are the marketing and service requirements, the sooner the manufacturer turns away from the GTC.*[25]

Finally the sogo shosha are beginning to get more involved in foreign investment. Historically the Japanese have preferred to sell abroad through exports rather than through direct investment, as has been the strategy of U.S. companies. (Compare the strategy of Ford with that of Toyota or Nissan.) However, the nature of the international marketplace is causing the trading firms to consider more direct investments because many of the trading companies have developed their own manufacturing niches and have decided to expand these operations abroad.[26] This not only illustrates a change in locational strategy but also shows how the trading companies have diversified their revenue base.

A foreign freight forwarder is an export/import specialist dealing in the movement of goods from producer to consumer.

Foreign freight forwarders. As was mentioned in the section of the chapter on international sourcing, dealing in ocean transportation involves a number of different institutions and documentation with which the typical exporter does not have expertise. This is true even if the manufacturer is exporting components to a foreign subsidiary controlled by a common parent corporation. Commonly the services of a **foreign freight forwarder** are employed. Even export management companies and other types of trading companies often use foreign freight forwarders for their specialized services.

The foreign freight forwarder is the largest export intermediary in terms of value and weight handled; however, the services offered are more limited than those offered by an EMC. Once a foreign sale has been made, the freight forwarder acts on behalf of the exporter in recommending the best routing and means of transportation based on space availability, speed, and cost. The forwarder secures such space and necessary storage, reviews the letter of credit, obtains export licenses, and prepares necessary shipping documents. Other services that may be provided include advice on packing and labeling, purchase of transport insurance, and repacking shipments damaged en route.

The freight forwarder usually is paid by the exporter on a percentage of the shipment value, with a minimum charge dependent on the number of services provided. In addition, the forwarder receives a brokerage fee from the carrier. The use of a freight forwarder still is usually less costly than providing the service internally, since most firms find it difficult both to utilize a traffic department full-time and to keep up with shipping regulations. The forwarder can get space because of its close relationship with carriers and can consolidate shipments in order to obtain lower rates.

Governmental Role in Exporting

The ITA is the major U.S. government agency that assists exporters.

The government plays a variety of roles in the export process, some of which support exporting and others of which appear to retard it. The **International Trade Administration (ITA)** of the U.S. Department of Commerce offers a variety of services to firms. There are offices in every state where trade specialists can help firms develop export strategy and get access to commercial officers overseas as well as to a variety of data services. The ITA also sponsors and promotes trade shows.

Eximbank. A major federal source of assistance to U.S. exporters is the **Export-Import Bank (Eximbank).** The Eximbank is the oldest federal agency specializing in foreign lending. As a fully owned government corporation, it has been in existence since 1934 with the specific objective of financing U.S. foreign trade. The Eximbank provides assistance in the form of loans, guarantees, and insurance.[27]

The loans can be made directly to foreign buyers of U.S. exports or to intermediary parties that provide loans to foreign buyers of U.S. exports. The guarantee program is designed to provide security for firms that provide loans to purchasers of U.S. exports. The guarantee also can be accompanied by an intermediary loan as described earlier. Guarantees can be for political and commercial risks, but they also are available for political risk only.

Another way that an exporter can reduce risk is through the **Foreign Credit Insurance Association (FCIA).** An exporter that secures a policy with the FCIA is insured against loss resulting from failure of the exporter's customers to pay because of commercial or political reasons. Political risks include currency inconvertibility, expropriation, cancellation of import licenses, or other actions taken by foreign governments that prevent payment by the buyer. Also, the policyholder can arrange favorable financing of export receivables because of the security brought about by the insurance.

One example of an Eximbank project involved the sale of locomotives to Brazil arranged in 1984 by GM and GE. The project involved the Brazilian import of parts produced by GM and GE; final assembly took place in Brazil. The Brazilian importer made a 15-percent cash payment of $9.47 million and arranged for the rest of the financing for the U.S. purchases through private financial institutions. The loans are guaranteed by the Eximbank. It was estimated that the exports will create 832 man-years of employment for GM and 768 man-years of employment for GE.

Building an Export Strategy

As mentioned earlier, many firms enter into exporting by accident rather than by design. When that happens, many of the problems described in exporting tend to happen. In addition, the firm never gets a chance to see how important exports could be. That is why it is important to develop a good export strategy. Before developing the strategy, however, the firm must understand some of the major problems that firms face in exporting.

Problems in Exporting. In addition to the problems already mentioned, a number of others are quite common to international business in general and are not unique to exporting. These include language and other culturally related factors.

Ten mistakes are frequently made by firms new to exporting:

1. Failure to obtain qualified export counseling and to develop a master international marketing plan before starting an export business.
2. Insufficient commitment by top management to overcome the initial difficulties and financial requirements of exporting.
3. Insufficient care in selecting overseas agents or distributors.
4. Chasing orders from around the world instead of establishing a basis for profitable operations and orderly growth.
5. Neglecting export business when the U.S. market booms.
6. Failure to treat international distributors on an equal basis with domestic counterparts.
7. Unwillingness to modify products to meet other countries' regulations or cultural preferences.
8. Failure to print services, sales, and warranty messages in locally understood languages.
9. Failure to consider use of an export management company or other marketing intermediary when the firm does not have the personnel to handle specialized export functions.
10. Failure to consider licensing or joint venture agreements. This factor is especially critical in countries that have import restrictions.[28]

Changing governmental policy also creates problems.

Another problem faced by exporters relates to the changing nature of governmental policy. Although the government can provide incentives for firms, it also can withdraw those incentives at any time. In the case of the United States, for example, the Export-Import Bank at one time faced extinction due to governmental budget pressures. However, the rapid increase in the trade deficit made lawmakers realize that Exim Bank operations were essential to help restore a healthy trade picture.

The Strategy. The design of a strategy involves a series of steps. First, a firm must assess its export potential. This involves taking a look at opportunities and resources. It would not be smart to make commitments to export if the firm did not have the production capacity to deliver the product.

Next, the firm needs to get expert counseling. For U.S. firms the best place to start is with the ITA office of the U.S. Department of Commerce in the exporter's area. Such assistance is invaluable in helping the exporter get started. In addition, the Small Business Administration can be useful in helping the firm to develop an export business plan and secure financing. As the export plan increases in scale, the exporter probably will want to secure specialized assistance from banks, lawyers, freight forwarders, export management companies, ETCs, and so forth.

The next important step is to select a market or markets. This step often occurs by default if the exporter is responding to requests from abroad that result from trade shows, advertisements, or articles in trade publications. However, the firm must pick a market or markets in which to concentrate a push strategy. It should develop expertise in a variety of factors when dealing with foreign consumers; it is best to focus on a few key markets rather than try to develop global expertise all at once.

Once the markets have been targeted and the decision has been made to expend corporate resources in the export effort, the firm should formulate an export strategy, which usually involves dealing with the following four factors: (1) export objectives, both immediate and long-term; (2) specific tactics that the firm will use; (3) a schedule of activities and deadlines that will help the firm achieve its objectives; and (4) the allocation of resources to accomplish the different activities.

Finally, the firm needs to select a channel-of-distribution technique from the major techniques mentioned earlier in the chapter: using sales representatives or agents; distributors; foreign retailers; direct sales to end users; EMCs; or export trading companies. The key in the export plan is to approach exporting from an organized point of view rather than just to sit back and let it happen.

SUMMARY

- A global production strategy involves the storage and movement of goods from the source of raw materials to the production of components, to the assembly of goods, to the distribution to consumers.
- The international firm differs from the domestic one in that goods in intermediate or final form may move from country to country rather than remain in one particular country.
- International sourcing of goods—primarily in the area of purchasing—differs from domestic sourcing in terms of language, distance, currency, wars and insurrections, strikes, political problems, and tariffs.

- Foreign sourcing is often undertaken to exploit lower costs and higher quality. However, U.S. firms are beginning to compete with foreign firms in both dimensions.
- Three major risks in foreign sourcing are: the length of supply lines, inventory levels, and currency fluctuations.
- Firms must be involved in procedural as well as strategic decisions in order to import successfully. Familiarity with customs procedures is necessary and firms often require the help of specialists.
- Foreign trade zones (FTZs), long popular outside of the United States, are being used increasingly as a place to import and assemble goods for domestic consumption as well as final export.
- Manufacturing strategies include servicing the world from one production facility or from many by using multiple plants that specialize in products or processes or by interchanging components for eventual assembly.
- Many firms are using offshore manufacturing centers to take advantage of cheap labor and materials. Then the finished goods are sold in the local market, shipped to the United States, or sold in third country markets.
- The Japanese have perfected the concept of just-in-time (JIT) inventory management, which means that inventory shipments are planned to coincide as closely as possible with their use. This cuts down the size of inventories held and therefore the carrying costs. JIT is being used increasingly by U.S. firms and is having a dramatic impact on sourcing decisions for raw materials and components in the manufacturing process.
- Exporters may deal directly with agents or distributors in a foreign country or indirectly by using export management companies or other types of trading companies.
- Trading companies, such as the Japanese sogo shosha, can perform many of the functions that manufacturers lack the expertise to do. In addition, exporters can use the services of other specialists, such as freight forwarders, to facilitate exports.
- Governments provide a variety of services for exporters. The U.S. government operates through the International Trade Administration (ITA) of the U.S. Department of Commerce.
- Firms new to exporting (and also some experienced exporters) often make lots of mistakes. One way to avoid making those mistakes is to develop a comprehensive export strategy that includes an analysis of the firm's resources as well as market opportunities.

CASE:
BLACK & DECKER[29]

Black & Decker (B&D), once known almost exclusively as a manufacturer of power tools for professionals, is now involved in "the manufacturing, marketing and servicing of a wide range of power tools, household products, and other labor-saving devices generally used in and around the home and by professional users." In the 1970s, before broadening its base to include a larger segment of the household market, B&D was flying high. It had captured a large share of the world's power tool market, and financial analysts were betting strongly on the company's future.

By 1981, however, the picture began to change. Earnings had begun to slip, and a worldwide recession caused a significant downturn in the power tools segment of B&D's business, its bread and butter. In addition, other events in the world economy added to B&D's problems. A strong U.S. dollar eroded B&D's competitive position in export markets and made B&D vulnerable to competition from abroad.

While these events were taking place, Japan's Makita Electric Works Ltd. began to erode B&D's market share. Makita adopted a global strategy for its products that allowed it to become the lowest-cost producer in the world. It decided that consumers in different countries really did not need significantly different products; then it combined its cost advantage with aggressive marketing, took advantage of the relatively weak yen compared with the U.S. dollar and B&D's mistakes to make serious inroads in the power tools market. By the late 1970s and early 1980s, Makita was able to nearly equal B&D's 20 percent market share in professional tools worldwide.

B&D's problems were partly a result of its own strategy. By 1982, B&D operated twenty-five manufacturing plants in thirteen countries on six continents. It had three operating groups as well as the headquarters in Maryland. Each group had its own staff, which led to duplication and overstaffing. In addition, individual B&D companies, such as B&D of West Germany, operated autonomously in each of the more than fifty countries where B&D sells and services products. The company's philosophy had been to let each country adapt products and product lines to fit the unique characteristics of each market. The Italian firm produced power tools for Italians, the British subsidiary made power tools for Britons, and so on.

As a result, countries did not communicate well with each other. Successful products in one country often took years to introduce in others. For example, the highly successful Dustbuster, which was introduced in the United States in the late 1970s, was not introduced in Australia until 1983. When efforts were made to introduce B&D home products into European markets, the European managers refused to comply. Even though sales were stagnating, B&D held a large percentage of the power tools market in the early 1980s—over 50 percent on the Continent and 80 percent in the United Kingdom. They felt that home appliances and products were uniquely American and would not do well outside of the United States.

In order to meet the tailor-made specifications of different markets, design centers were not being used efficiently. At one point, eight design centers around the world had produced 260 different motors, even though it was determined that the firm needed fewer than ten different models. Plant capacity utilization was quite low, employment levels were high, and output per employee was unacceptable.

For several years, B&D split its consumer and professional tools into two different groups. Because each group did not work together to develop new product lines, Makita was able to spot a market niche that it could exploit, the mid-priced tools. In addition, B&D had begun to stagnate in new product development. It appeared that the company had decided to concentrate on its top lines and sell them aggressively.

As B&D moved into the mid-1980s, management realized that something had to be done. One area where the Japanese had not made significant inroads was the housewares and small appliances market. Japanese consumers were not fond of those items, so Makita and other competitors had not established a strong home market that it could use as an export base. B&D was having trouble introducing its own line of housewares because of its image as a power-tool manufacturer. As a result, B&D acquired the small appliances division of General Electric in 1984 in order to give it more shelf space in housewares and also a large enough line of products to provide economies of scale in manufacturing.

QUESTIONS

1. What are the major reasons why Black & Decker has gotten itself into its current dilemma?
2. What should it do to solve those problems?

NOTES

1. Data for the case were taken from the following sources: various issues of the General Motors *Annual Report;* Lawrence Ingrassia, "Europe's Auto Makers, Hurt by Low Volume, Make Dismal Showing," *Wall Street Journal,* November 5, 1984, p. 1; Douglas R. Sease, "South Korea Will Vie in U.S. Auto Market to Spur Its Economy," *Wall Street Journal,* November 16, 1984, p. 1; "Drastic New Strategies to Keep U.S. Multinationals Competitive," *Business Week,* October 8, 1984, pp. 168–172; "Showdown in Detroit," *Business Week,* September 10, 1984, pp. 102–110; Jonathan Tasini, Maralyn Edid, and John Hoerr, "The GM–Toyota Linkup Could Change the Industry," *Business*

Week, December 24, 1984, p. 71; "The All-American Small Car Is Fading," *Business Week,* March 12, 1984, pp. 88–95; Mark B. Fuller, "Note on the World Auto Industry in Transition," 9-382-122 (Boston: HBS Case Services, 1982); Anne B. Fisher, "Can Detroit Live without Quotas?," *Fortune,* June 25, 1984, pp. 20–25; Patricia Sellers, "General Motors Reshuffles in Europe," *Fortune,* March 3, 1986, p. 11; Lance Ealey, "Seoulmates: Pontiac Pulls off a Korean Coup," *Automotive Industries,* January 1987, pp. 62–63; "GM Plans to Ship to U.S. Cars Built at Mexican Plant," *Wall Street Journal,* April 6, 1987, p. 13; James B. Treece, et al., "Can Ford Stay on Top?" *Business Week,* September 28, 1987, pp. 78–86; James B. Treece, "Detroit Is Bracing for a One-Two Punch," *Business Week,* November 16, 1987, pp. 136–144.

2. Peter J. Buckley and Richard D. Pearce, "Overseas Production and Exporting by the World's Largest Enterprises: A Study in Sourcing Policy," *Journal of International Business Studies,* Spring/Summer 1979, pp. 11, 13.

3. "U.S. MNCs Increase Global Sourcing Despite Contrary Trends," *Business International,* September 21, 1987, p. 302. This information is from a report, "Global Sourcing as a Corporate Strategy—1987," issued by the Washington-based Machinery & Allied Products Institute.

4. Department of the Treasury, *Importing into the United States* (Washington, D.C.: Superintendent of Documents, U.S. Government Printing Office, May 1984), p. 6.

5. Philadelphia National Bank, *International Trade Procedures* (Philadelphia, 1977), p. 30.

6. Michael Leenders, Harold E. Fearon, and Wilbur B. England, *Purchasing and Materials Management* (Homewood, Ill.: Richard D. Irwin, 1985), pp. 350–353.

7. *Ibid.,* pp. 353–358.

8. "MNCs Adapt to Weak Dollar with Sourcing Strategies for Enhanced Flexibility," *Business International,* April 6, 1987, p. 105.

9. Department of the Treasury, *Importing into the United States* (Washington, D.C.: Superintendent of Documents, U.S. Government Printing Office, May 1984), p. 28.

10. *Ibid.*

11. John J. DaPonte, Jr., "Foreign-Trade Zones and Exports," *American Export Bulletin,* April 1978.

12. Ken Slocum, "Foreign-Trade Zones Aid Many Companies but Stir up Criticism," *Wall Street Journal,* September 30, 1987, p. 1.

13. *Ibid.,* p. 31.

14. *Ibid.*

15. Roger Turner, "Mexico's In-Bond Industry Continues Its Dynamic Growth," *Business America,* November 26, 1984, p. 26.

16. "Caribbean Basin FTZs Offer Low-Cost Production and Entries to New Markets," *Business Latin America,* February 2, 1987, pp. 35–37.

17. Lynn Adkins, "New Wave of Offshore Plants," *Dun's Business Month,* July 1985, p. 73.

18. G. H. Manoochehri, "Crucial Requirements for Effective Application of Just-in-Time System," unpublished paper, California State University, Fullerton, 1984.

19. Philip MacDonald, *Practical Exporting and Importing,* 2nd ed. (New York: Ronald Press, 1959), pp. 30–40.

20. "Basic Question: To Export Yourself or To Hire Someone To Do It for You?" *Business America,* April 27, 1987, pp. 14–17.

21. Charles E. Cobb, Jr., "Export Trading Companies: Five Years of Bringing U.S. Exporters Together," *Business America,* October 12, 1987, pp. 2–9.

22. "Sogo Shosha," *The Banker,* January 1984, pp. 78–84.

23. Marubeni Corporation, *The Unique World of the Sogo Shosha,* (Tokyo: Marubeni Corporation, 1978), p. 14.

24. Marubeni Corporation, *The Japanese Edge* (Tokyo: Marubeni Corporation, 1981), pp. 85–93.

25. Kichiro Hayashi and Stefan H. Robock, "The Uncertain Future of the Japanese General Trading Companies," *Kajian Ekonomi Malaysia,* December 1982, p. 61.

26. Masaaki Kotabe, "Changing Roles of the Sogo Shoshas, the Manufacturing Firms, and the MITI in the Context of the Japanese 'Trade or Die' Mentality," *Columbia Journal of World Business,* Fall 1984, pp. 33–42.

27. Susan Rodes, "U.S. Export–Import Bank Changes with World Trading Environment," *Business America,* November 9, 1987, pp. 2–9.

28. "Ten Most Common Mistakes of New-to-Export Ventures," *Business America,* April 16, 1984, p. 9.

29. Sources for case are various issues of the Black & Decker *Annual Report;* Bill Saporito, "Black & Decker's Gamble on 'Globalization,'" *Fortune,* May 14, 1984, pp. 40–42, 44, 48; Christopher S. Eklund, "How Black & Decker Got Back in the Black," *Business Week,* July 13, 1987, pp. 86, 90; "How Black & Decker Forged a Winning Brand Transfer Strategy," *Business International,* July 20, 1987, pp. 225, 227.

15

CHAPTER SOME MORE FORMS OF FOREIGN INVOLVEMENT

When one party is willing, the match is half made.
—American proverb

- To explain the major motives that should guide firms in their choice of form for global business activities.
- To differentiate the major forms of operations by which firms may tap the potentials of international business.
- To describe how international agreements affect the protection of proprietary rights on assets that firms might exploit internationally.
- To describe the considerations that firms should explore when entering into contractual international arrangements with other companies.
- To emphasize that multiple forms of international operations may exist simultaneously and that firms must develop means by which to coordinate these diverse activities.

CASE:
GRUPO INDUSTRIAL ALFA[1]

By 1973 Mexican import restrictions had enticed most of the world's large multinational manufacturers to establish facilities there to produce goods that Mexico otherwise might have imported. At that time the government sought to counter foreign control by setting restrictions on foreign equity in new ventures and on the expansion of existing investments with large foreign ownership.

At that time, one of the largest Mexican-owned firms was a family enterprise in Monterrey controlled by the Garza and Sada families. This firm had been affected only slightly by foreign competition because of its major lines of business such as steel, beer, and banking. These products and services were not imported easily into Mexico because of import restrictions on steel and the need of the others (usually) to locate near customers. There were also prohibitions against foreign ownership in these sectors. Although the Garza and Sada families were relatively immune from foreign competition, the outlook was for slow growth.

The Garza-Sada families saw in the 1973 Mexicanization laws the opportunities to diversify into growth industries that foreigners would henceforth find more difficult to control. They reasoned that they might be able to buy some subsidiaries of foreign companies from firms unwilling to accept a minority ownership. They also reasoned that they were in a good position to share in cooperative arrangements with foreign firms that sought business activities involving Mexico. The owners felt that to capitalize on these possibilities, they would be better off to shed the family image. Additional shares could raise capital, and good professional management could be attracted to them. In 1974 they divided the enterprise into four different companies and went public by issuing shares in each of them.

One of the firms that emerged from the 1974 split is Grupo Industrial Alfa, which inherited the steel facilities and several smaller businesses. At the time of the split, Alfa's assets were estimated at $315 million (U.S.), of which 75 percent was in steel. Management of the new company, with help from some of the top international consulting groups, agreed that diversification should be based on objectives of minimizing cyclical changes in earnings, getting into growth industries, and utilizing resources for which Mexico had advantages.

During the 1974–1976 period, Alfa expanded much less than had been anticipated but did manage to acquire the television production facilities of three U.S. brands: Philco, Magnavox, and Admiral. Through these acquisitions Alfa got 35 percent of Mexico's market for television sets as well as the continued use of the three trade names for sales in Mexico.

Alfa subsequently became Mexico's largest private company. By 1980 it had assets of $1.9 billion, sales representing 1.2 percent of Mexico's gross domestic product, 157 subsidiaries, and 49,000 employees. Two events external to Alfa contributed to the growth: The first was the discovery of huge oil and natural gas reserves in Mexico; The second was the election of a pro-private enterprise president, Jose Lopez Portillo. Portillo offered many incentives for industry, including nearly free energy. Suddenly there was a rush among foreign firms to find ways of expanding their businesses in Mexico; almost any such expansion had to involve Mexicans. In addition to being Mexico's largest private firm, Alfa had good profitability, and its management had a good reputation so it was in an excellent position to acquire the foreign resources that it wanted. In fact, its biggest problem was in how to choose among the many opportunities.

Alfa established numerous Mexican companies in which it owned a majority interest with a foreign partner holding a minority. The foreign partners came from a number of countries including Japan (Hitachi, electric motors; Yamaha, motorcycles); Canada (International Nickel, nonferrous metal exploration); the Netherlands (AKZO, artificial fibers); and West Germany (BASF, petrochemicals). For two U.S. firms, the joint venture operations involved substantial departures from prior policies. Ford's 25 percent interest in a plant making aluminum cylinder heads for the U.S. and Canadian auto markets was the first minority interest Ford had ever taken in a joint venture. DuPont had taken minority interests before accepting 49 percent to Alfa's 51 percent. However, DuPont had always handled the management of the ventures. In the Mexican synthetic fibers joint venture, Alfa did the managing; the company's policy was to import technology but to maintain management control.

In many of the above situations the Mexican output has been produced by using the trademark developed by the foreign partner, which has helped in gaining Mexican consumer acceptance. In 1979, Alfa bought 100 percent of Massey-Ferguson's tractor operation in Mexico, paying the Canadian company a royalty fee for the use of the Massey-Ferguson trade name.

In the aluminum cylinder head joint venture just described, it was not a captive Mexican market that attracted Ford; rather, it was lower production costs so as to supply the American and Canadian markets. In addition to cheap energy, Mexico had offered an abundance of cheap labor and no taxes on reinvested earnings. The motors built under the Hitachi brand name have been produced in Mexico for 25 percent below the Japanese cost. Alfa has become interested in export markets: A sales arrangement was established by which the Mitsui Trading Company of Japan handles exports of Alfa's polyester chemicals abroad. Alfa opened discussions about Mexican television production with several Japanese firms in order to use known Japanese brands to penetrate the U.S. market. Because of prior contractual arrangements, Alfa could not export its "American" brands (Philco, Magnavox, and Admiral) to the United States.

Alfa developed a method of producing steel by direct reduction, thus bypassing the high capital cost of blast furnaces. To transfer this patented technology to new plants in other countries would require substantial on-site personnel and construction assistance. Alfa lacked personnel that can be spared as well as foreign construction experience. Alfa has transferred its know-how to four foreign engineering firms: West Germany's GHH-Sterkrade, Japan's Kawasaki Heavy Industries, and the United States' Pullman Swindell and Dravo. Those firms have in turn acted as agents on behalf of Alfa and have constructed steel plants in such countries as Brazil, Venezuela, Indonesia, Iran, Iraq, and Zambia. Alfa receives fees for the use of the technology in foreign mills, and the engineering firms receive fees for building the plants in what are known as turnkey projects.

In order for Alfa to expand and to maintain management control during the 1976–1980 period, it had to borrow and recruit managers outside of Mexico. Alfa ended up with debt of almost $3 billion from over 130 different banks; about 75 percent of this was payable in U.S. dollars. Alfa also had to pay highly to attract managers with the backgrounds it wanted. Then oil prices plummeted, and the Mexican peso devalued. By 1981, Alfa was losing so much money that it had to receive Mexican government aid of U.S. $680 million to keep afloat. Between 1980 and 1985, Alfa had to shut down forty of its subsidiaries and reduce the number of its employees by almost 19,000. By 1984, foreign banks had agreed to convert a part of Alfa's debt into a 30-percent stake in the company rather than have loans default. Meanwhile, many of the foreign firms that had made agreements with Alfa in the 1970s found that their expected Mexican expansion (via Alfa) had been put on hold. These included, for example, BASF's and Hercules' joint ventures with Alfa. Alfa simply lacked the resources to carry out so many agreements with so many different foreign companies.

INTRODUCTION

International business may be conducted in a variety of ways. The truly experienced firm with a full global orientation usually makes use of most of the forms available, selecting them according to specific product or foreign operating characteristics.

The preceding case illustrates the use of several different methods of exploiting international opportunities. Alfa made joint ventures with foreign firms, engaged in the acquisition and sale of process and product technology through licensing and turnkey contracts, and paid for goodwill (the favor a company has acquired beyond its tangible assets) by gaining the use of trademarks through licensing agreements. (A type of asset not mentioned in the case is the reproduction right of some marketable asset, most commonly copyrights on such things as books, records, films, and lithographs.)

This chapter discusses the most common means by which companies commit resources to the foreign sector, methods prompted either by their own desire or by external pressures that force them to accept certain parameters. The chapter also covers the problems of control when one company enters an agreement that makes another company responsible for handling its business objectives. For example, BASF and Hercules both lost control of their Mexican expansion plans when Alfa became unable to comply with the agreed-upon plans. The reasons for the use of two forms—trade and direct investment—will be discussed only peripherally in this chapter, since the motives were handled in Chapters 4 and 6. Export operating considerations were taken up in Chapter 14, and one form of direct investment, shared ownership, will be covered in this chapter.

SOME VARIABLES AFFECTING CHOICE

Choice of form may necessitate trade-offs among objectives.

Factors influencing choice include legal, cost, experience, competition, risk, control, and nature of assets.

In terms of resources, the modes of foreign operations differ in terms of both the amount a firm commits to foreign operations and the portion of the resources that is located at home versus abroad. Exports may, for example, result in a lower additional resource commitment than direct foreign investment if there is domestic excess capacity. If a firm must increase capacity, then this increase may take place by investing the resources either at home or abroad. The former involves a substantial commitment to foreign operations, although the assets are not in a foreign location. In exporting, in direct investment, and in some of the other forms of foreign operations a firm may be able to reduce its total resource commitment by making contracts with other companies to conduct activities on its behalf or by sharing ownership in international business endeavors. Before examining these other operational forms it is useful to discuss some of the major factors that firms should consider when selecting a form of operation in a given market. We will cover them more intensively when we discuss specific operational modes.

Throughout this discussion, keep in mind that there are trade-offs. For example, a decision to own 100 percent of a foreign subsidiary will normally increase the parent's fulfillment of the objective of controlling decisions; however, it may simultaneously reduce the parent's fulfillment of the objective of minimizing exposure to political risk.[2]

Legal

Legal factors may be:

- Direct prohibitions against certain forms
- Indirect, e.g., affecting profitability.

As was indicated in the case on Grupo Industrial Alfa, a firm may be constrained in its choice of operating mode regardless of its preferences. Some of the foreign firms discussed, such as Ford, may have preferred a wholly owned Mexican operation but were not legally permitted. In addition to the outright prohibition of certain operating forms, other legal means may influence the choice. These include differences in tax rates, differences in the maximum funds that can be remitted, actual or possible enforcement of antitrust provisions, and stipulations on the circumstances in which a proprietary asset will be in the public domain and available for others to use.

Cost

Sometimes it is cheaper to get another firm to handle work:
- Especially at small volume
- Especially if the other firm has excess capacity.

In order to produce or sell abroad, certain fixed costs must be incurred, so that at a small volume of business it may be cheaper for a firm to contract the work to someone else than to handle it internally. A specialist can spread the fixed costs over services to more than one firm. If business increases enough, a firm may be able to handle the activities more cheaply itself than by buying outside services. Firms should therefore periodically reappraise the question of internal versus external handling of their varied operations.

Another reason that the external contracting of operations may be lower in cost is that another firm may have excess production or sales capacity that can be easily utilized. This utilization also may reduce start-up time and thus result in an earlier cash flow.

Experience

With more experience, companies take on more direct involvement abroad.

In their early stages of international development few companies are willing to expend a large portion of their resources on foreign operations; they may not even have sufficient resources to expand abroad rapidly. As a result, they *usually* move through stages of increased levels of international involvement. In the early stages they attempt to conserve their own scarce resources and to maximize the portion of the resources that are at home rather than abroad. This leads them to operational forms that transfer the burden of foreign commitment to outsiders. As the firms and their foreign activities grow, they will tend to view the foreign portion of their business differently. Then there is a movement toward the internal handling of more operations and locating a larger portion of resources abroad.[3]

Competition

Firms have more choice of form when there is less likelihood of competition.

When a firm has a desired, unique, difficult to duplicate resource, that firm is in a good position to choose the operating form that it would most like to utilize. When there are competitive possibilities, a firm may have to settle on a form that is lower on its priority list; otherwise, a competitor may preempt the market. The possibility of competition also may lead to a strategy of rapid international expansion, which may be possible (because of limited resources) only by developing external arrangements with other firms.

Minimization of competition in given markets also may be achieved through cooperative arrangements that exclude entry, share resources, or divide output. The effectiveness will depend in part on the type of mode selected as well as the permissiveness of governmental authorities to the specific agreement.

Risk

The higher the perceived risk, usually the greater the desire to set external operating forms.

There are many types of risk. However, the possibility of political or economic changes affecting the safety of assets and their earnings is often at the forefront of management's concern in foreign operations. One way of minimizing the loss through the seizure of assets in foreign operations is to minimize the base of assets located abroad. This may dictate external arrangements so that the asset base is shared by others. This move also might make a government less willing to move against an operation in the fear that it might encounter opposition from more than one firm.

External forms allow for greater spreading of assets among countries.

One way of spreading risk is to place operations in a number of different countries. This means less chance that all foreign assets will simultaneously be subject to such adversities as confiscation, exchange control, or even a slowing of sales caused by a local recession. The maximum losses as well as the year-to-year changes in consolidated earnings thus may be minimized. For companies that have not yet attained widespread international operations, operational forms that minimize their own resource expenditures may permit a more rapid dispersion of operations. These forms will be less appealing for companies whose activities are already widely extended or who have ample resources to so extend.

Control

Internal handling usually means more control and no sharing of profits.

The more a firm deals externally, the more likely it will lose control over decisions that may affect its global optimization including where output will be expanded, new product directions, and quality. External arrangements also imply the sharing of revenues, a serious consideration in undertakings with high potential profits. They also risk giving information more rapidly to potential competitors. The loss of control over flexibility, revenues, and competition has been implied by some writers to be the most important variable guiding firms' priorities for a mode of operation.[4]

Product Complexity

There are costs associated with the transfer of technology to another entity. Usually it is cheaper to transfer within the existing corporate family, such as from parent to subsidiary, rather than to another company. The cost difference is especially important when the technology is quite complex because subsidiary personnel are apt to be more familiar with approaches that the firm is using. For this reason, it has been noted that the higher the level of technology, the more likely a company will expand abroad with its own facilities rather than contracting with another firm to produce abroad on its behalf.[5]

Prior Expansion of the Company

When a company already has operations in place within a foreign country, some of the advantages of contracting an external firm to handle production are no longer as prevalent. In other words, the company knows how to operate within the foreign country and may have excess capacity that can be used to add new production. Much depends, however, on whether the existing foreign operation is in a line of business that is closely related to the product or service that is being transferred abroad. When there is similarity, such as a new type of office equipment in a company that already produces office equipment, there is the highest probability of handling the new production internally. In highly diversified companies, the existing foreign facility may be producing goods so dissimilar to what is being transferred that it is easier to deal with an experienced external company.

Similarity of Country

Management is more confident of its ability to operate in those foreign countries which it perceives to be similar to its home environment. U.S. companies, for example, are much more apt to handle operations internally in other English language speaking countries than in countries where the language is different.

LICENSING

MNEs want return from intangible assets.

Under a licensing agreement a firm (the licensor) grants rights on intangible property to another firm (the licensee). The rights may be exclusive or nonexclusive. The U.S. Internal Revenue Service (IRS) classifies intangible property into five categories:

Licensing agreements may be:
- Exclusive or nonexclusive
- Used for patents, trademarks, knowhow, or copyrights.

1. Patents, inventions, formulas, processes, designs, patterns;
2. Copyrights, literary, musical, or artistic compositions;
3. Trademarks, trade names, brand names;
4. Franchises, licenses, contracts; and
5. Methods, programs, procedures, systems, etc.

Usually, the licensor is obliged to furnish technical information and assistance and the licensee to exploit the rights effectively and to pay compensation to the licensor.

Economic Motives

Licensing can have economic motives, such as faster start-up, lower cost, and access to additional resources.

Frequently, a new product or process may affect only a part of a firm's total output and only for a limited period of time. The sales volume may not be large enough to warrant the establishment of overseas manufacturing and sales facilities. Furthermore, during the period of acquiring operations there is a risk that competitors will develop improvements that negate the firm's advantages. As discussed earlier, a firm that is already operating abroad may be able to produce and sell at a lower cost and with less start-up time. Risk of operating facilities and holding inventories is reduced for the licensor. The licensee may find that the cost of the arrangement is less than if the development were accomplished internally. For industries in which technological changes are frequent and affect many different products, such as chemicals and electrical goods, firms in various countries often exchange technology rather than compete with each other on every product in every market, an arrangement known as **cross-licensing.**

Cross-licensing may violate antitrust regulations if it results in the restriction of entry into a market by one of the parties. The regulations in this respect are extremely complex, and good legal assistance is necessary for any type of agreement.[6] Another cross-licensing problem is that some of the parties may produce more innovations than others. American Home Products participated in pharmaceutical arrangements with several foreign drug makers that later terminated the arrangements because American Home produced few important drugs on its own.[7]

A second economic motive concerns the resources a firm has at its disposal. Chrysler's American Motors, for example, has insufficient resources to establish its own facilities everywhere that overseas production is necessary for Jeep sales. For some of the largest markets, such as India and Australia, American Motors has subsidiaries. For some smaller markets, such as Sri Lanka and Pakistan, licensing arrangements are used.

Strategic Motives

Licensing can give return on products not fitting the firm's strategic priority.

Large diversified firms are constantly reevaluating and altering their product lines to put their efforts where their major strengths best complement their assessment of high-profit businesses. This may leave them with products or technologies that they themselves do not wish to exploit but which may be profitably transferred to other firms. Because it does not fit into GE's major lines of business, the company has marketed to other firms its development of a microorganism that destroys spilled oil by digesting it.[8]

Political and Legal Motives

Licensing hinders nonassociated firm from usurping the asset.

Aside from licensing because of restrictions on trade or foreign ownership, licensing may also be a means of protecting an asset. This may come about for two reasons. First, many countries provide very little de facto protection for a foreign property right such as a trademark, patent, or copyright unless authorities are prodded consistently. To prevent the so-called pirating of these proprietary assets, companies sometimes have made licensing agreements with local firms, which then monitor to ensure that no one else uses the asset locally. A second situation is in the type country that provides protection only if the internationally registered asset is exploited locally within a specified period of time. If a firm does not use the registration within the country during the specified period, then whoever does so first will have the right to it. Mexico is one such country: In Mexico City Gucci, Chemise La Coste, and Cartier shops, unrelated to the European houses, are in close proximity. The Cartier shop copies a Cartier watch dial, bracelet, presentation box, and storefront to the smallest detail, but it puts cheap movements and poor-quality gold filling in the watches. This has hurt Cartier's reputation among unsuspecting buyers, who then refuse to buy in the authentic stores in New York and Paris.[9] Had Cartier licensed the use of its name in Mexico early on, it might have preempted the nonassociated use of the name there. Instead, the real Cartier has opened a shop close to the bogus one in an attempt to educate and steer clients to its legitimate products.[10]

In the absence of licensing, a firm may find that another firm can even exclude its market entry at a later date or can compete in certain areas of the world through exploitation of the asset. Western Electric has a liberal licensing policy in order to avoid patent litigation.

Problems and Provisions

Hardly any aspect of international business has been as controversial in recent years as licensing. Given the fact that virtually all royalties are paid to organizations in industrial countries, it is perhaps inevitable that groups within LDCs have criticized the amounts and methods of payments. Since MNEs view their technologies and trademarks as integral parts of their asset bases, it is perhaps just as inevitable that they are skeptical about transferring their use to other organizations. The following discussion highlights the major concerns of licensors, licensees, and host governments that might be incorporated into a formal agreement.

Asset transference can create control problems such as
- license inadequately worked
- poor quality
- development of competitor

Control and competition. By transferring rights to another firm the owner undoubtedly loses some control over the asset. There are a host of potential problems with the lack of control that should be settled in the original licensing agreement. Provisions should be made for the termination of the agreement if the parties do not adhere to the directives. The agreement should specify methods of testing of quality, the obligations of each party concerning expenditures on sales development, and the geographic limitations on the use of the asset. Without these provisions the license may be inadequately worked, the two parties may find themselves in competition with each other, or a poor-quality product in one country may jeopardize product image and sales elsewhere. A good example of how the lack of specification led to legal suits is the case between Oleg Cassini Inc. and the U.S. subsidiary (Jovan) of the Beecham Group from the United Kingdom. Cassini licensed Jovan to promote and extend sales throughout the world of various Cassini fragrances, cosmetics, and beauty aids. Then Jovan introduced Diane Von Furstenberg products instead and denied Cassini the right to license the Cassini name to other firms. This case was settled when Jovan agreed to market the Cassini products; however, Cassini won an award in a later suit because of image injury through sales in discount stores.[11]

Some firms have well-known trademarked names that they license abroad for the production of some products that they have never produced nor have had expertise with themselves. The Pierre Cardin label, for example, is used by over 800 licensees in 93 countries to produce hundreds of different products, from clothing to sheets and from clocks to deodorants. Monitoring and maintaining control of so much diversity is very difficult. Two U.S. firms, Saks Fifth Avenue and Eagle Shirtmakers, dropped arrangements with Pierre Cardin labeled products because the lack of policing for quality on some licensees' products adversely affected the image of others.[12]

Depending on the nature of the asset, either the licensor or licensee stands the risk of developing a future competitor after the agreement expires. If a brand or trademark is involved, the licensee may develop consumer preferences and have to turn the market over to the licensor. If know-how or patents are involved, the licensee may be able to exploit the assets long after the agreement is terminated. Even before an agreement is terminated, the two parties may come into competition with each other because one has made improvements on the licensed technology that make the original patents obsolete. Therefore it has become common for firms to make provisions in the original contract for the possible use and sharing of superseding technology built on knowledge from the original transfer.

In licensing agreements:

- Seller does not want to give information without payment assurance
- Buyer does not want to pay without evaluating information.

Secrecy. The value of many technologies would diminish if they were widely known or understood. Provisions that a licensee will not divulge this information historically have been included in agreements. Some licensors have, in addition, held onto the ownership and production of specific components so that licensees will not have the full knowledge or capability to produce an exact copy of the product. Coca-Cola, for example, licenses its trademark and a portion of the production techniques to bottlers worldwide; however, the production of Coca-Cola concentrate is carried on by Coca-Cola itself. The Indian government required Coca-Cola to divulge the contents of the concentrate or lose its right to receive trademark royalties there. Rather than risk losing control over this asset, Coca-Cola chose to abandon the market.[13]

Secrecy arises as a problem for negotiating agreements to transfer process technology. Many times a firm has developed techniques that it has not yet used commercially but which it wishes to sell. A buyer is reluctant to "buy a pig in a poke," but a licensor who shows the potential licensee the process risks having the process used without payment. It has become common to set up preagreements in order to protect all parties.

An area of growing controversy is the degree of secrecy in the financial terms of licensing agreements. Within some countries, for example, governmental agencies now must approve royalty contracts once the contracts have been negotiated by the parties involved. Sometimes these authorities consult with their counterparts in other countries regarding similar agreements in order to improve their negotiations with MNEs. Many MNEs object to this procedure because they believe that contract terms are proprietary information of competitive importance and that market conditions usually dictate the need for very different terms in different countries.

Licensing payments vary by:

- Fixed fee versus usage
- Exclusive versus nonexclusive
- Market size
- How long assets will have value
- How taxes are assessed
- Cost to transfer.

Payment. There is a wide variation in the amount and type of payment under licensing arrangements, and each contract tends to be negotiated very much on its own merits. The amount requested by the licensor will depend in part on whether the firm views this type of income as simply a residual for which little or no additional investment is required or whether the firm seeks to cover its R&D costs by selling to other firms. The uniqueness of the technology and the other resources that a potential licensor has at its disposal will, in addition, dictate in part the possibilities of exploiting a market in the absence of a licensing contract. The potential licensee will, of course, consider alternative possibilities. The value of a license to the licensee will depend in part on the potential sales based on market size, degree of exclusivity within that market, the time frame before the asset becomes obsolete, and the possibility of ongoing relationships through new or cross-licensing arrangements.

One of the thorny issues as seen by LDCs is that licensees are usually prevented by contract from exporting; thus small-scale production may cause high full costs to the consumers. MNEs have countered that extending sales territories would necessitate high royalties because MNEs could not sell exclusive rights to parties in other countries. They also have argued that the development of process technologies for small-scale production would often be too costly but is done when economically feasible.[14]

Taxes may be assessed quite differently depending on the methods of arranging payments under the agreement—for example, as income or as a capital gain. If the taxes on capital gains are different from those on income, the after-tax receipts will be different. Payment schedules also may be deferred in order to defer the payment of taxes. Fees to be paid for the use of an asset may be made in a lump sum, on a percentage of sales value, on a specific rate applied to usage, or on some combination of these methods.

There has been a trend in recent years to negotiate a "front-end" payment to cover the cost of transfer and to follow this with another set of fees based on actual or projected usage. The reason for this is the realization that few technologies may be moved abroad simply by transferring publications and reports. The negotiation process is itself expensive and must be followed by engineering, consultation, and adaptation. The early stages of production usually are characterized by low quality and slow productivity.[15] The substantial costs in the transfer process increasingly are charged to the licensee so that the licensor is motivated to assure a smooth adaptation.

Sales to controlled entities are common because they:

- Are separate legal entities
- Protect value when ownership is shared
- Provide a way to avert payment or exchange limitations

Sales to controlled entities. Many licenses are given to companies connected in ownership with the licensor. A license may be needed to transfer technology abroad because operations in a foreign country, even if 100 percent owned by the parent, usually are separate firms from a legal standpoint. When there is a present or potential shared ownership, a separate licensing arrangement also may be a means of compensating for contributions beyond the mere investment in capital and managerial resources.

The price at which MNEs sell to foreign operations they control is very controversial. Since much of what is transferred among controlled entities of a multinational company is unique to that company, it is highly difficult to estimate what the competitive price would be if the company were selling the same thing to a noncontrolled entity.[16] Yet by altering the price of product, components, patents, and so on, MNEs effectively may transfer more of their profits from one country to another. Critics in donor countries have contended that too little is charged, and thus profits are transferred to low tax countries.[17] LDCs with low tax rates have contended the opposite, arguing that MNEs have minimized artificially their profits in LDCs in order either to move funds to countries with a stronger currency or to gain certain host governmental concessions.[18] Obviously MNEs cannot be shifting profits simultaneously to both the home and the host country; nevertheless, the criticisms have made it more difficult for MNEs to establish licensing contracts with their controlled affiliates. Tax authorities in home countries ask for pricing justifications. Governmental authorities in LDCs are increasingly approving transfers on a case-by-case basis.

Positioning the Licensing Unit[19]

Where the responsibility for licensing is handled typically in organizations depends on the motives for licensing. When licensing is an integral part of a company's growth and diversification objectives, a separate licensing department is likely to be in charge of buying and selling. In multidivisional firms there may be more than one of these departments. When the strategy is primarily the safeguarding of existing activities, licensing is apt to be a part of the legal or patents department. When a company combines the above two objectives, it tends to attach licensing to the R&D department.

Protection of Intangible Assets

International treaties and agreements help safeguard patents, trademarks, copyrights.

The poet and essayist, Ralph Waldo Emerson said, "If a man can write a better book, preach a better sermon, or make a better mousetrap than his neighbor, though he builds his house in the woods, the world will make a beaten path to his door." But if someone else gets hold of the design for the same book, sermon, or mousetrap the number of people beating the way on any single path will be divided. Some of the most valuable assets that businesses have are their intangibles, such as patents, trademarks, and copyrights, and millions of dollars can be spent in their development. Improper protection of these assets could lead to limited profitability by the parties that invested in developing the intangible. Given the different attitudes by countries toward property rights, adequate international protection to a firm's intangibles can only come about through international cooperation. Most countries have legal procedures for registering patents, trademarks, and copyrights, but it is extremely expensive for an MNE to duplicate the application process in every country where it operates, which is why international treaties can be so important.

Patents. The first major attempt of cross-national cooperation was the Paris Convention, initiated in 1883 and periodically revised. This convention gave rise to the International Bureau for the Protection of Industrial Property Rights (BIRPI) and involved the protection of patents, trademarks, and other property rights. The general idea behind the Paris Convention was that a nation would grant to foreigners who are members of the Convention the same status accorded its own citizens in the protection of property rights. A second major provision of the Paris Convention is that a registration in one country has a grace period of protection before filing in other member countries. The Inter-American Conference of 1910 on Inventions, Patents, Designs, and Models was initiated among the United States and Latin American countries to accomplish the same objectives as the Paris Convention.

The three most important contemporary cross-national patent agreements are the Patent Cooperation Treaty (PCT) of the World Intellectual Property Organization (WIPO), the European Patent Convention (EPC), and the EEC Patent Convention.[20] The PCT and EPC allow firms to make a uniform patent search and application, which is then passed on to all signatory countries.

Patent infringement battles are both costly and complex, and they may take years to settle. The major problems on the international level are the rapid development of technology and the different patent rules and regulations in different countries. Companies are forced to change their patents from country to country to meet local needs, and patent infringement is often difficult to prove. For example, a company in Italy, where there is no patent protection on drugs, could manufacture a drug patented by a firm in the United States and sell it anywhere in the world. If the U.S. firm were to bring suit, it would have to prove patent infringement but would have difficulty getting the proof in Italy. Owing to the high costs of patent infringement suits, many firms are attempting to settle out of court.

Trademarks. Companies may spend millions of dollars to develop brand names. If the brand names are not protected by a trademark, then other companies may produce under the same brand name. Even if the names have a trademark, they may become generic and thus in the public domain. "Yo-yo" is actually a foreign trademark that has become generic in the United States; although "Ping-Pong" is a registered trademark in the United States, it has become generic in China and is used in place of "table tennis." Since the Japanese have no name for vulcanized rubber, they use "goodyear" to identify the product.[21]

One of the most recent developments in cross-national cooperation for trademark protection is the Trademark Registration Treaty, which was formalized at a diplomatic conference in Vienna. The United States, the United Kingdom, West Germany, and Italy were among the industrial countries that signed initially. The agreement is designed to be more universally acceptable than the Madrid Convention, which provides for the international registration of trademarks but does not include many industrial countries, such as the United States.

Some countries require the use of a trademark before an application of registration can be filed. Codified-law countries (those using statutory law rather than common law) traditionally have not recognized use as a precondition to registration or as a valid protection against infringement. According to the Vienna Convention, a country may not require the use of a mark as a prerequisite to obtain or maintain registration until three years after its international registration. Once the mark has been registered internationally, each country must accept it or provide grounds for refusal within fifteen months so that the firm will have sufficient time to act before its three-year period is completed.

Copyrights. Most large publishing and recording companies have extensive foreign interests and can be influenced easily by foreign competition. If there were no international copyright laws, it would be feasible for a foreign producer to copy a book or tape and then distribute it at cut-rate prices in the country where it was first produced. The Universal Copyright Convention (UCC), the major cross-national agreement, honors the copyright laws of the signatory states.

Piracy. Not all countries are members of the various agreements to protect intangible property rights. Of those that are, some enforce the agreements haphazardly. Many countries simply do not place a high priority on tracking down or prosecuting people who violate these property rights, preferring to put their police efforts on crimes they consider more serious.

The cost to companies that depend on a well-known trademark to merchandise their goods has become enormous. Cashing in on massive advertising by placing well-known trademarked labels on copies of products is tempting for some companies. This has occurred on almost every type of goods; fake labels even go on merchandise that the copied companies do not make, such as the Jordache label on disco bags and caps.

What about consumers? Sometimes they get good-quality merchandise with a prestige label for a fraction of what the legitimate product would have cost. Some firms have even contracted counterfeiters to be legitimate suppliers. Often, though, shoddy or even dangerous merchandise is substituted for the original, legitimate goods. In Britain, defective brake parts turned up in military aircraft; and in the United States, twelve people died from counterfeit tranquilizers.[22]

Sales also are lost when products are copied, although the copier does not use someone else's trademark. For example, the Association of American Publishers estimates the value of pirated books at more than $100 million a year in Korea alone.[23] When the drug company, Pfizer, introduced Feldene, an antiarthritic drug to Argentina, five Argentine firms were already selling generic copies in the market.[24] Television broadcasts of programs from satellites in countries such as Jamaica and Haiti are commonplace. Not only do the original broadcasters receive no fees from this, but the practice also cuts in on sales to movie theaters in those countries, since films may be on television before they are distributed to theaters.[25]

Various associations of manufacturers have sprung up worldwide to deal collectively with the problem of piracy. Among the deterrents that have been proposed are greater border surveillance, criminal penalties for dealing in counterfeit goods, and the cessation of aid to countries that do not join and adhere to international agreements. Companies such as Apple Computer and Union Carbide are also successfully tracking down infringers on their own and bringing cases against them; but it is difficult to prove infringement when slight changes are made in trademarks or product models. At this writing, for example, Lego from Denmark and Tyco from the United States have already spent over $2 million each on Lego's claim of infringement on plastic blocks that snap together, even though Tyco's president said, "We went into this business with the purpose of copying Lego and making a sound profit."[26] Other companies are using high technology, such as holographic images and magnetic or microchip tags, to identify the genuine products. But this has cost them millions of dollars in payments for detecting devices.[27] Vuiton, a French luggage manufacturer, is fighting with a withdrawal strategy: selling registered and numbered goods only in company owned retail outlets. Still other firms are warning the public of imitations and advising on how to tell the genuine product.[28]

FRANCHISING

Franchising includes trademark and continual infusion of necessary asset.

Franchising is essentially a way of doing business in which the franchisor gives an independent franchisee the use of a trademark that is an essential asset for the franchisee's business and in which the franchisor more than nominally assists on a continuing basis in the operation of the business. In many cases the franchisor also provides supplies.[29] For instance, Holiday Inn grants to franchisees the goodwill of the Holiday Inn name and the support service to get started, such as appraisal of a proposed motel site. As part of the continued relationship, Holiday Inn offers reservations services and training programs to help ensure the success of the venture. In a sense the franchisor and franchisee act almost like a vertically integrated firm because the parties are interdependent and each produces part of the product or service that ultimately reaches the consumer.

Some Patterns

Many types of products and countries are involved in franchising.

Franchising goes back at least as far as the nineteenth century and is most associated with the United States, where one-third of retail sales are handled that way. About three-quarters of the sales are in three areas: car and truck dealers, gasoline service stations, and soft drink bottling. By 1984 U.S. franchisors had over 27,000 outlets in foreign countries.[30] Although they are located in all regions of the world, Fig. 15.1 shows that only four countries (Canada, Japan, the United Kingdom, and Australia) account for about two-thirds of the outlets. The fastest growth areas of U.S. firms have been in the areas of food and business services.

Not all franchising is by U.S. firms. Pronuptia, a French bridal wear franchisor, has 250 foreign outlets. Such firms as Wimpy's and Bake 'N' Take from the United Kingdom and Wienerwald from West Germany have been among some of the earliest and most successful food franchisors abroad. In Japan, which has been considered the most lucrative market for food franchising, U.S.-based ventures have only about half the sales.[31]

Operational Modifications

A major type of modification has been in the method of recruiting foreign franchisees because: (1) The franchisor and franchising are relatively less well known and (2) local financing is less readily available abroad. One strategy to overcome this has been to enter a foreign country initially with a direct investment. Another is to contract a major franchisee to commit to

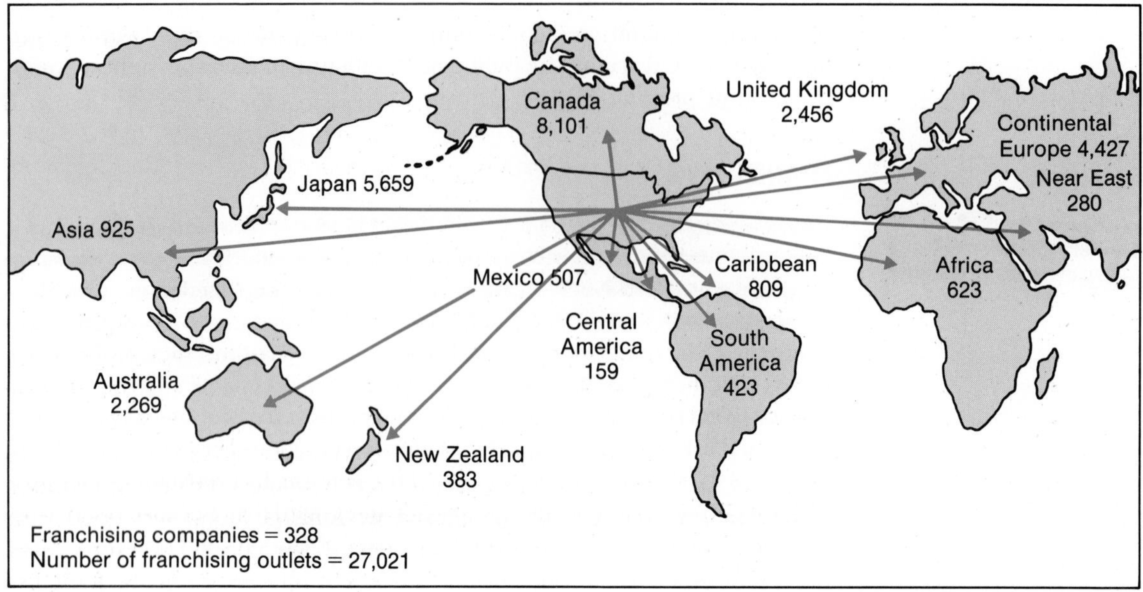

Figure 15.1
International Franchise Operations by U.S. Firms
Source: "U.S. Franchising Industry Promotes Increased Domestic and International Business Activity," *Business America,* March 3, 1986, p. 13, giving data for 1984.

open a large number of operations. Once the feasibility of success is demonstrated, it is much easier to find investors for franchising operations. Finding suppliers can also be an added problem and expense: For example: McDonald's had to invest to build a plant to make hamburger buns in the United Kingdom, and it had to help farmers develop potato production in Thailand.[32] Another concern in foreign franchise expansion has been governmental or legal restrictions that make it difficult to gain satisfactory operating permission.

Dilemma:
- the more standardization, the less acceptance in foreign country
- the more adjustment to foreign country, the less the franchisor is needed.

A dilemma for franchisors is that their success at home has been largely due to three factors: (1) product and service standardization; (2) high identification through promotion; and (3) effective cost controls. When entering many foreign countries, various restraints may make it difficult to conform to home country methods. Yet the more adjustments that are made to the host country's nuances, the less a franchisor has to offer a potential franchisee. The success of franchisors in Japan has been due in great part to enthusiastic assimilation of Western innovations, so firms such as McDonald's have been able to copy their U.S. outlets almost intact. In Italy, however, McDonald's tested the market for two years and then decided not to enter; Wimpy's closed its outlets there after sustaining heavy losses.[33] The conclusion was that it would be too expensive to get Italians to accept the foreign food; yet if firms offered menus that were more acceptable to the Italians, there would be nothing different to offer a franchisee. Even in countries where franchises have been successful, it usually has been necessary to make some operating adjustments. For example, Kentucky Fried Chicken in Japan had to redesign its equipment and stores to save space because of the higher cost of rent: It eliminated mashed potatoes and put less sugar in its cole slaw because of Japanese tastes.

Contract Problems

Some of the problems that plague franchising agreements are no different from those in licensing agreements. Contracts must be spelled out in detail, but if courts must rule on disagreements, both parties are apt to lose something in the settlement. A good example was when McDonald's granted a license for up to 166 stores in France to Raymond Dayan at less than its normal fee because of doubts that the French would ever take to fast-food restaurants. M. Dayan, with the help of McDonald's, found very good Paris locations for fourteen stores, which he opened over a period of several years. He was very successful, but McDonald's had the right to revoke the franchise agreement if its inspection found that the stores were not up to its level of cleanliness. The agreement was cancelled on these grounds, leading to a court case. M. Dayan claimed that McDonald's action was simply a ruse to make him pay McDonald's usual rate. He lost out on further expansion with the McDonald's trademark; but McDonald's lost something too. When M. Dayan took down the McDonald's signs, he immediately replaced them with signs saying O'Keefe's Hamburgers; and he had the clientele, the know-how, and the best locations in Paris. These stores were later sold to the French firm, Quick, the largest fast food chain in France.[34]

MANAGEMENT CONTRACTS

Management contracts are used primarily when:

- The owned operation has been expropriated
- The firm manages a new facility
- The firm manages an operation in trouble.

One of the most important assets a firm may have at its disposal is management talent. Despite huge endowments of capital and technology, many governmental enterprises in LDCs encounter difficulties because of inadequately trained management. The transmission of management internationally has depended largely on foreign investments that deploy expatriate managers and specialists to foreign countries. Management contracts offer a means through which a firm may use part of its management personnel to assist a firm in a foreign country in general or specialized management functions for a specified period of time for a fee.

Management contracts are established in three types of situations.[35] The first, and probably the most common, is when a foreign investment has been expropriated by a foreign government and the former owner is invited to continue supervising the operations until local management is trained. In this case the management structure may remain substantially the same, although board membership changes. A good example of this is the case on Aramco at the beginning of Chapter 12: After the Saudi Arabian government took over the ownership, the former owners continued to supply management. Some advantages of entering into contracts in this type of situation are that this may: (1) facilitate getting resources out of the country in addition to those agreed upon in the expropriation discussions; (2) ingratiate the firm with local authorities so that future business operations are possible; and (3) ensure continued access to raw materials or other resources needed from the country. The second type of management contract is when a firm is asked to manage a new venture, in which case it may sell much of its own equipment to the facility. The third situation occurs when a foreign firm is invited in to manage an existing operation more efficiently.

From the standpoint of the recipient country, the need to receive direct investment as a means of gaining management assistance is removed. From the standpoint of the firm providing management, contracts are appropriate in order to avoid the risk of capital asset loss, when returns on investment are too low and capital outlays are too high. The contracts do have potential problems, not the least of which is the training of future competitors. Additionally, if the firm has differences of opinion on policy with the government, incurs start-up inefficiencies, or does not train local managers quickly, bad feelings may result. Contracts usually are drawn to cover three to five years, and fixed fees or fees based on volume rather than profits are most common.

TURNKEY OPERATIONS

Turnkey operations:

- Most commonly are construction firms
- May develop future competitor.

Turnkey projects involve a contract for construction of operating facilities that are transferred to the owner when the facilities are ready to commence operations, for a fee. Firms performing turnkey operations are frequently industrial equipment manufacturers that supply some of their own equipment for the project. Most commonly, they are construction firms. In addition, they may be consulting firms or manufacturers that do not find an investment on their own behalf in the country to be feasible.

The customer for a turnkey operation is very often a governmental agency that has decreed that a given product must be produced locally and under its auspices. As in the case of the management contract, a firm building a turnkey facility may be developing a future competitor. Yet many firms have chosen to perform design and construction duties, particularly in communist countries and India, where there are restrictions on foreign ownership. In recent years, most of the large projects have been in oil-exporting countries, which are moving rapidly toward infrastructure development and industrialization. Of course, not all turnkey projects are developing potential competitors. Projects to build airports and port facilities, for example, do not lend themselves to competition.

The size of these contracts is one of the things setting this business apart from most other international business operations. Most of the contracts are for hundreds of millions of dollars, and many are for several billion, which means that a few very large firms account for most of the international market. One firm, Kellogg Rust, accounts for about 10 percent of the international market and about one-quarter of the U.S. portion of the market by itself.[36] This also has meant hiring executives with top-level governmental contacts abroad who can gain entry with the right decision makers to negotiate their proposals in foreign countries.

Pullman-Kellogg, for example, secured a large fertilizer plant contract in Nigeria. They sent Andrew Young, a former U.N. Ambassador who enjoys immense personal prestige in Africa, to negotiate the contract.[37] The nature of the large-scale government contracts also has placed great importance on ceremony, such as opening a facility on a country's independence day or getting a head of state to inaugurate a facility in order to build goodwill for future contracts. Although public relations are important, it takes much more to sell contracts of such magnitude. The U.S. Department of Commerce lists the following four factors in order of importance:

1. price,
2. export financing,
3. managerial and technological quality, and
4. experience and reputation.[38]

Payment for a turnkey operation usually is in stages, as a project develops. It is common for 10 to 25 percent to be made as a down payment, another 50 to 65 percent to be paid as the contract progresses, and the remainder to be paid once the facility actually is operating in accordance with the contract. Because of the usual long time periods between conception and completion, the company performing turnkey operations is exposed to possible currency fluctuations for an extended period of time and should be covered, if possible, by escalation clauses or cost-plus contracts. Since the final payment is made only if the facility is operating satisfactorily, it is important to specify very precisely what constitutes "satisfactory." For this reason, many firms insist on performing a feasibility study as part of the turnkey contract in order not to build something that, although desired by local governmental authorities, nevertheless may be too large or inefficient. Although the facility may be built exactly as directed, its inefficiency could create legal problems that hold up final payment.[39]

Many of the turnkey contracts are in remote areas, thus necessitating massive housing construction and importation of personnel (see Chapter 21). They may involve building an entire infrastructure under the most adverse geographic conditions.

If a firm holds a monopoly on certain assets or resources, it will be difficult for other companies to be competitive in building facilities. As the production process becomes known, however, the number of competitors for performing turnkey operations increases. The president of an international consulting engineering firm has listed five stages for developing countries:

1. Expatriates do all the work;
2. Local subcontractors develop;
3. Small local contractors start up;
4. Local contractors take over local work; and
5. Local contractors go abroad.[40]

This series of changes has pushed U.S. firms' involvement in recent years to the high technology end of the spectrum, whereas firms from such countries as India, Korea, and Turkey can compete better for conventional projects where low labor costs are important.[41]

CONTRACT ARRANGEMENTS

Contract arrangements:
- Sometimes give similar advantages as vertical integration
- May spread risk and developmental costs.

Companies that at one time would have integrated vertically by making direct investments for the extraction of raw materials in foreign countries now are finding increased desire for local ownership of the extractive process. Since the local owners frequently continue to need certain resources the foreign firms hold, contracts may be established whereby raw materials are traded for the assets held by foreign firms. For example, as the Saudi Arabian government increased its ownership share of Aramco, it still needed management and exploration assistance, which was traded for commitments of preferred status for oil sales.[42] On the basis of this precedent, several other oil-producing countries have made arrangements whereby the oil firms take all exploration and development risks in exchange for a share of the oil produced.[43]

One of the fastest growth areas for contract arrangements has been for projects that are too large for any single company to take on. This has been apparent in the development of new aircraft and weapons systems. From the inception of a project, companies from different countries frequently agree to take on the high cost and high risk of developmental work for different components needed in the final product; afterward a lead company buys the components from the firms that did a part of the developmental work.

The major aluminum producers have developed swap contracts whereby they can save transport costs. They are all vertically integrated firms, but not in each country where they operate. Alcan might give Pechiney semi-processed alumina in Canada in exchange for the same amount of semi-processed alumina delivered to Alcan in France.

IMPROVING ACCESS TO FOREIGN TECHNOLOGY

Access to foreign technology may help domestic and international competitiveness.

In most of the aforementioned operational forms (licensing, franchising, management contracts, turnkey operations, and other contractual arrangements) an organization in one country gains access to scientific or managerial technology from an organization in another country. By gaining these assets a firm may be in a much better position to compete domestically and internationally. Because of the competitive implications, it is not surprising that many firms are establishing mechanisms whereby they may increase the likelihood of gaining advantages before their competitors.

One of the most used mechanisms has been the establishment of company units to monitor journals and technical conferences. These are not sufficient since very few patent descriptions ever appear in other than the voluminous patent office publications from each different country; therefore, firms must go to these publications as well.[44] This combined monitoring helps assure that the company learns of new developments, thereby enabling decision makers to decide whether to ignore the innovations, to try to counteract them through in-house developments, or to establish an operational link with the individuals or organizations that are apparently leading the field. A second mechanism is to develop formal links with academic and other research organizations at home and abroad so as to determine possible breakthroughs before they are publicized in professional journals. A third means is to increase visibility through participation in trade fairs, the distribution of brochures, and contacts with technical acquisition consultants. This visibility may encourage innovators to think of a particular firm rather than another when they seek out clients. A fourth is the establishment of cooperative research projects with foreign firms, thereby gaining scale benefits and the use of personnel from other organizations. Finally, a company may set up part of its R&D activities in foreign countries in order to utilize foreign talent that would not likely immigrate to the company's home country.[45]

THE LEVEL OF EQUITY OWNERSHIP

When a firm does establish foreign operations, it may own the entire stock or it may share the ownership. There are various types of ownership sharing, just as there are several reasons for selecting an equity amount.

The Argument for 100 Percent

One-hundred percent ownership is:

- Easier to control
- Has no sharing of profits.

Most businesspeople would prefer to have a 100-percent interest in foreign operations in order to ensure control and to prevent the dilution of profits. As long as there are no minority stockholders, corporate management has a greater freedom to enact measures that, although not in the best interest of the particular operations, are in the best interest of the company as a whole. With minority stockholders the parent firm has much less freedom of action, since these minority stockholders may become very vocal to their governments about practices that are not in the best interest of the subsidiaries. In fact, most countries have legislation to protect minority stockholders. Freuhauf-France, for example, received export orders that, although in the best interest of that subsidiary, were not considered by its U.S. majority owners to be in the best interests of Freuhauf's worldwide operations. When Freuhauf-France did not fulfill the export orders, the minority stockholders contested the action in French courts. This left the majority stockholders with the options of either filling the export order or paying damages to the minority holders.[46]

Even when the majority owners act in what they consider to be the best interest of the local company, there may be conflicts with local stockholders because of different opinions as to what businesses should be doing. Some points of possible conflict are dividend pay-out versus the retention of earnings, the degree of public disclosure of activities, and the degree of cooperation with various governmental agencies.

The argument against diluting profits is simple: Many firms contend that if they own all the resources necessary for the successful foreign operation and are willing to contribute these resources, they should not have to share ownership.

Shared Ownership Arrangements

Internal reasons for partial ownership are:

- Faster geographic spread
- R&D over larger base

In spite of the advantages to owning 100 percent in a foreign facility, ownership sharing is popular.[47] The reasons for this are undoubtedly a combination of outside pressures and internal willingness to take partial ownership abroad.

From an internal standpoint there has been a need to bring outside resources into foreign operations. By sharing ownership in some existing foreign operations, many firms have been able to spread geographically at a faster rate. This has prevented competitors from gaining dominant market shares and also allowed maximum sales expansion, which helps to spread such relatively fixed costs as R&D to a larger sales base.

Governments pressure for sharing:

- Because they want local control
- But treat industries differently.

Externally, there has been pressure by many countries for ownership sharing with local shareholders, as countries feel this policy will enhance their economic or political objectives. In addition, many companies feel that by bringing local capital into the organization they take on a local character that decreases governmental and societal criticism (thus reducing the risk of nationalization or expropriation) and may bring captive sales to the participating shareholders.[48] Some industries share ownership much more than others, especially those for which a high capital outlay is necessary for making the investment. The higher capital outlay in these large investments necessitates additional outside resources. Furthermore, local governments exert greater pressure for ownership sharing on those firms having the most significant impact on the economy.

Equity as a control mechanism. As was discussed in Chapter 6, the problem of deciding how much equity is necessary for control is cumbersome. With a few exceptions, the larger the percentage of equity held, the more likely it is that the owner of this equity will control the decisions and policies of the enterprise. Many firms are willing to share ownership but usually will specify whether the sharing is to be with or without control. If, for example, a firm takes only a minority holding in its foreign operations, ordinarily it can still control policies and decisions if the remaining ownership is fragmented widely. After the 1973 Mexicanization law discussed in the Grupo Industrial Alfa case, many foreign firms sought to maintain management control in spite of minority equity positions by selling 51 percent of their shares to a broad ownership market through the Mexican stock exchange. BASF, a German chemical company, maintained management control by transferring a majority interest in its pharmaceutical company to Bancomer, a big Mexican bank. The bank was simply interested in diversifying its investment holdings and had no desire to manage.[49] Another possibility is to divide profits on the basis of shares but to give voting rights only to one class of shareholders. Still another is to stipulate that your own directors will appoint management and key officers.[50]

When no one company has control, the operation may lack a significant direction. In discussing the problems of a company that was jointly owned by a U.S. and a Japanese firm, a Sterling Drug spokesman said, "You must decide right off the bat whether you'll control it or will put confidence in the Japanese organization."[51] This opinion is supported by studies showing that when two or more partners attempt to share in the management of an operation, there is a much higher incidence of failure than when one parent dominates.[52]

Joint ventures:

- Need not be fifty-fifty
- There may be various combinations of ownership.

Joint ventures. A type of ownership sharing very popular among international companies is the joint venture, which occurs when a company is owned by more than one organization. Although it is formed usually for the achievement of a limited objective, it may continue to operate indefinitely as the objective is redefined. Joint ventures are sometimes thought of as fifty-fifty companies, but often more than two organizations participate in the ownership. Furthermore, one organization may frequently control more than 50 percent of the venture. The type of legal organization may be a partnership, corporation, or some other form of organization permitted in the country of operation. When more than two organizations participate, the resultant joint venture is sometimes referred to as a **consortium.**

Almost every conceivable combination of partners may exist in joint ventures. They may include, for example, two firms from the same country joining together in a foreign market, such as Standard Oil–California and International Minerals and Chemicals in India. They may involve a foreign company joining with a local company, such as Sears Roebuck and Simpsons in Canada. Companies from two or more countries may establish a joint venture in a third country—for example, Alcan (Canadian) and Pechiney (French) in Argentina. The ventures may be formed between a private company and a local government (sometimes called **mixed ventures**), such as Philips (Dutch) with the Indonesian government. Even some government-controlled companies have had joint ventures abroad, such as Dutch State Mines with Pittsburgh Plate Glass in the United States. The more firms are involved in the ownership, the more complex the ownership arrangement is. For example, Australia Aluminum is owned by two U.S. companies (American Metal Climax and Anaconda), two Japanese companies (Sumitomo Chemical Company and Showa Denko), one Dutch company (Holland Aluminum), and one West German company (Vereinigte Aluminum Werke).

The arguments for and against the sharing of ownership apply as well to joint ventures. Certain types of firms have a greater tolerance for joint ventures than others.[53] Firms with higher tolerance include those that are new at foreign operations and those with decentralized decision making domestically, very often the multiproduct companies. Since the latter firms are accustomed to extending control downward in their organizations, it is an easier transition to do the same thing internationally.

BUY VERSUS BUILD DECISION

A foreign direct investment may be made by acquiring an interest in an existing operation or by constructing new facilities. Each of these alternatives has advantages and disadvantages, and a firm's preference for one or the other may affect the feasibility of investing in a given country. A firm may, for example, be willing to go only to a country in which it can acquire ongoing operations.

Reasons for Buying

A firm may wish to acquire to:

- Get an ongoing operation with no start-up problems
- Have an easier financial situation
- Not add capacity in market.

A major motive for a firm's seeking acquisitions is that a potential investor may find it difficult either to transfer some resource to a foreign operation or to acquire that resource locally for a new facility. One such resource is personnel, particularly if the local labor market is tight. Instead of paying higher compensation rates than competitors to entice employees away from their old jobs, the buy-in approach gains not only labor and management but also a whole organizational structure through which these personnel may interact. Acquisitions also may be a means of gaining the goodwill and brand identification important for mass consumer products, especially if the cost and risk of breaking in a new brand are high. If a company must depend substantially on local financing rather than on the transfer of capital, it may be easier to gain access to local capital through an acquisition. For one thing, local capital suppliers may be more familiar with an ongoing operation than with the foreign enterprise. Second, an existing company may sometimes be acquired through an exchange of stock, thus circumventing home country exchange controls.

In other ways acquisitions may reduce costs and risks as well as provide quicker results. A firm may be able to buy facilities, particularly of a bankrupt operation, for less than it would cost to build plants at current construction costs. If an investor fears that a market does not justify added capacity, acquisition avoids the risk of depressed prices and lower unit sales per producer that might result from new facilities. Finally, by buying a company an investor avoids the high expenses caused by inefficiencies during the start-up period and gets an immediate cash flow rather than tying up funds for the period of construction.

Reasons for Building

Firms may build if:

- No desired firm is available for acquisition
- Acquisition will carry over problems
- Acquisition is harder to finance.

While the advantages just mentioned may be possible through acquisitions, a potential investor will not be able to gain them necessarily. Since foreign investments frequently are made where there is little or no competition, it may be difficult to locate a company to buy. In addition, governmental restrictions may prevent the purchase of firms because of fears of such things as the lessening of competition or the dominance by foreign enterprises. Those firms that can be acquired may create substantial problems for the investor: Personnel and labor relations may be both poor and difficult to change; bad will rather than goodwill may have accrued to existing brands; or facilities may be inefficient and poorly located in relationship to future potential markets. Finally, local financing may be easier rather than harder if a firm builds facilities, particularly if the investor plans to tap development banks for part of its financial requirements.

Some Experiences

Buy-ins are not usually as successful because

- Half-diversifications result
- They get less-well-run operations.

To date the most extensive study of international acquisitions included 407 made by eighty-four firms in Europe.[54] This study concluded that, although there are some notable success stories, acquisition of an interest in foreign firms gave low payoffs in comparison with other methods of penetration. According to the firms themselves, 50 percent of the acquisitions by U.S. MNEs and 46 percent by European MNEs were "failures or not worth repeating." There was no single reason for this high perceived failure rate. However, several factors were important: One included "half-diversifications," which involved gaining interest in a firm that was much less similar to the MNE than would appear on the surface. In these cases, management sometimes was lulled into a false sense of security when, in fact, the acquisition meant dealing with very different types of customers or in utilizing an unfamiliar technology. Another factor was that companies had a tendency to acquire not very profitable enterprises with the belief that they could turn them around with new management, an assumption that was seldom valid.

MANAGING FOREIGN ARRANGEMENTS

Chapter 17 discusses organization and control strategies for international operations. However, the forms of foreign involvement examined in this chapter have some unique characteristics that warrant discussion.

Contracts with Other Firms

When contracting another firm, a firm must:

- Still monitor performance
- Assess whether to take over operations itself
- Work out conflicts and disputes.

Even though a company may find it beneficial to rely on other firms at home or abroad to carry out a part or all of its foreign business functions, management is not relieved of the responsibility for these functions. Periodically management must assess whether the functions should be carried out internally. Great care should be taken to ensure that the best firms are involved and that they are performing the jobs of making, selling, or servicing the product adequately.

We have already referred to the major reason for getting other companies to perform functions overseas. If an outside firm can perform the same functions (assuming the same quality) at a cheaper rate, a company should give little consideration to taking on the duties itself. If it can do them more cheaply itself, there may still be justification for getting someone else to do the work. Every company has limited resources, which it should use to the best advantage. If the resources can be used to a better advantage in other activities, then it will pay the firm to commit those resources to activities with a higher return and get someone else to commit resources to the pursuit of foreign business, which should yield a return to both firms. Two subjective factors also enter into the analysis: First, management may not feel capable of doing as good a job as an outside firm; second, management also may feel that the commitment of resources abroad would incur too large a risk for the firm. Since situations change, decisions should be reexamined from time to time.

In choosing a firm to handle overseas business, management should consider the firm's professional qualifications, personal attributes, and motivation. Unfortunately, there is no way of precisely measuring these factors, nor is there a magic formula for weighing one qualification against another. The proven ability to handle similar business is one key professional attribute.

Many possible conflicts can develop between the companies. Although any agreement should specify provisions for termination and should include means to settle disputes, these are costly and cumbersome means of achieving objectives. If possible, it is much better for both parties to settle disagreements on a personal basis. The ability to develop a rapport with the management of another firm is thus an important consideration in choosing a representative.

Management also should estimate potential sales, determine whether quality standards are being met, and assess servicing requirements in order to check whether the other firm is doing an adequate job. Goals should be set mutually so that both parties understand what is expected, and the expectations should be spelled out in the contractual agreements.

Multiple Forms

Same firm usually will use different forms simultaneously.

Most firms move through stages of increased involvement: Exporting usually precedes foreign production, and contracting for another firm to handle foreign business generally precedes handling it internally. A firm may be at different stages for different products and for different markets. A firm also may feel that differences in country characteristics necessitate diverse forms of involvement. Because of the multiproduct nature of most companies, diverse stages may accompany the varied products sold in the same country.

Tension may develop internally as a firm's international operations change and grow. For instance, a move from exporting to foreign production may reduce the size of a domestic product division. Various profit centers may all think they have rights to the sales in a country the firm is about to penetrate. Legal, technical, and marketing personnel may have entirely different perspectives on contractual agreements. Under these circumstances a team approach to evaluate decisions and performance may work. A firm also must develop means of evaluating performance by separating those things that are controllable and noncontrollable by personnel in different profit centers.

SUMMARY

- The forms of foreign involvement differ in terms of internal versus external handling of activities and in terms of the portion of resources committed at home versus abroad.
- Although the mode employed for foreign operations should be examined in terms of a firm's strategic objectives, the choice often will involve a trade-off among objectives.
- Among the factors that will influence the choice of operating mode are legal conditions, the firm's experience, competition factors, political and economic risk, and the nature of the assets to be exploited.

- Licensing is granting another firm the use of some rights, such as patents, trademarks, or know-how, usually for a fee. It is a means of establishing foreign production that may minimize capital outlays, prevent the free use of assets by other firms, allow the receipt of assets from other firms in return, and allow for income in some markets where exportation or investment are not feasible.
- Among the major controversies concerning the terms of licensing agreements are the control of use of assets as they may affect future competitive relationships, the secrecy of technology and contract terms, the method and amount of payment, and how to treat transfers to a firm's controlled foreign facilities.
- International agreements have been made to protect important intangible assets such as patents, trademarks, and copyrights. Since millions of dollars are often spent in the development of these assets, worldwide protection is a necessity.
- One of the big problems for firms with intangible assets in recent years has been the pirating of the assets in countries that have not signed international agreements or do not actively enforce their laws on the asset protection.
- Franchising differs from licensing in that a trademark is an essential asset for the franchisee's business *and* the franchisor assists in the operation of the business on a continuing basis.
- Management contracts are a means of securing income with little capital outlay. They are usually used for expropriated properties in LDCs, for new operations, and for facilities with operating problems.
- Turnkey operations involve a contract for construction of operating facilities owned by someone else. In recent years, most of these have been very large and diverse, thus necessitating specialized skills and abilities to deal with top-level governmental authorities.
- In the absence of control of vertical operations through ownership, firms are increasingly achieving similar objectives through long-term contract and output sharing arrangements.
- Companies usually want to own 100 percent of their foreign operations, if possible, in order to secure control and to prevent the dilution of profits. However, sharing ownership is widespread because host countries want local participation and because rapid foreign expansion has necessitated that firms bring in outside resources.
- Joint ventures are a special type of ownership sharing in which equity is owned by a few organizations rather than the public at large. There are various combinations of ownership, including government and private, same or different nationalities, and two or several organizations participating.

- Contracting foreign business does not negate management's responsibility to ensure that company resources are being worked adequately. This involves constantly assessing the work of the outsiders and evaluating new alternatives.
- Firms may use different forms for their foreign operations in different countries or for different products. As diversity increases, the task of coordinating and managing the foreign operations becomes more complex.

CASE: NPC[55]

In 1974 the Northern Petrochemical Company (NPC), a subsidiary of Northern Natural Gas (now named Internorth), decided to get into polypropylene production. The decision was based on an analysis of NPC's production capabilities and on a forecast of future market demand.

From a production standpoint, NPC was already making propylene, which is a precursor of and building block for polypropylene. The parent company could supply many of the raw materials for the new product. From a market standpoint, NPC estimated that, since the introduction of polypropylene in the early 1960s, the compound growth rate of sales had been somewhere between 15 and 20 percent. The firm also estimated that future growth would be even more rapid because of high benzene prices and possible shortages, which would depress sales of polystyrene. In many cases polypropylene could substitute for polystyrene. The polypropylene market could be divided into two segments depending on the properties put into the product: The first, homopolymer, comprised 85 percent of the market and was used for such applications as carpet backing, packaging film, appliance moldings, and fibers; the second, copolymer, included products such as battery cases, luggage, and high-clarity bottles. The copolymer sector was of most interest to NPC because this was a newer technical area in which they could expect growth and less entrenched competition.

NPC felt that further inroads for sales were possible as continued performance and cost-effectiveness were improved. One possibility would be in automotive-component fabrication. An entry into polypropylene production would necessitate a continued commitment to R&D in order to improve both product and process technology. NPC was willing to invest over $100 million in the project but lacked the technical capabilities. To use its own R&D efforts would greatly delay market entry. It also would mean risking legal complications because already there were numerous patent infringement cases pending: Producing companies claimed that others had copied various aspects of their technology.

The total sales for Northern Natural Gas were approximately $1 billion for 1974, of which about 20 percent were accounted for by the NPC subsidiary. About 62 percent of Northern's sales was of natural gas to customers in the United States and Canada. The NPC petrochemical subsidiary was growing faster than the rest of the company and had had successes in such products as antifreeze and LDPE resins. The technology for the resins had been licensed from another firm after NPC had identified markets for use in trash can liners and leaf bags. A commercial success with technology developed externally therefore had been demonstrated.

NPC next set out to find a firm from which it could gain the use of polypropylene technology on acceptable terms. Of the nine producers in the United States, only three were believed to be in an advanced stage of copolymer development. The first of these was Hercules, which dominated the entire polypropylene market. Hercules was interested because some of its customers wanted a secondary supply source in case of supply problems. NPC felt that such an arrangement was incompatible with its strategy, since it would inevitably place NPC in Hercules' shadow. NPC next contacted the Rexene Division of Dart Industries. Rexene rejected outright any sharing of its technology because it did not want another competitor in the market. No agreement could be reached with Phillips Petroleum for two reasons: Phillips had not yet commercialized the aspect of production that NPC considered critical; furthermore Phillips was not enthusiastic about creating another competitor.

Having exhausted domestic possibilities, NPC turned abroad. Identification of possible companies was more difficult because many of those companies were believed to have a bigger lag between product development work and commercial introduction of the products. In other words, management could not depend on looking at what was currently being sold to find all the firms with a current capability. Because of market differences, some of the European and Japanese producers had been known to hold on to a development for several years before commercializing it.

After some preliminary inquiries, five firms from four countries were identified as possibilities: These were Tokuyama Soda and Mitsubishi Petrochemical from Japan, Solvay from Belgium, Montedison from Italy, and BASF from West Germany. NPC contacted all of these companies and learned that none had fully commercialized advanced copolymer production. In order to proceed to some possible agreement, each firm had to share with NPC its R&D data and to make special plant test runs to satisfy requests for further information. Interestingly, each had a very different approach to making the same product.

If NPC were to proceed to negotiations, it must choose the company and method most likely to reach the desired end results. NPC decided that BASF offered the best potential since it was and remains one of the giants among chemical companies with 1974 sales in excess of $8 billion. About 55 percent of BASF's sales were outside of West Germany; in 1973 sales in the United States were $523 million. In addition to exporting to the U.S. market, BASF had substantial U.S. investments, the most notable of which were Wyandotte Chemical, which it fully owned, and a joint venture with Dow Chemical called Dow Badische. Increases in U.S. investment had been running between $45 million and $55 million per year. This was expected to go to $90 million beginning in 1975.

The chairman of BASF, Dr. Matthias Seefelder, announced that he expected no growth in the West German market for 1975 because of a reluctance on the part of consumers to buy. This would make it more difficult to continue to infuse German funds into the U.S. operations, which were saddled with uncompetitive soda ash and chlorine plants. Given this cash flow problem, it was hard for BASF to make commitments for market development of new products. Dr. Seefelder also indicated that the company's main specialties (plastics, synthetic fibers, and dyestuffs) were encountering difficulties and that it would be necessary to give greater attention to other products that BASF had already developed. A strong West German mark was making German products expensive abroad, thus jeopardizing exports.

The early stages of negotiations between the two companies left the parties in opposition as to which technology BASF would share with NPC provided an agreement on other points could be reached. BASF was willing to sell the technology that it had developed already but was not willing to make a commitment to continue copolymer research, which was not now a high priority for them because of their expectation of not being able to get substantial near-term sales in Europe. Nor was BASF yet willing to commit itself to sharing the future technology if and when it was developed. NPC wanted more than the pilot plant advancements and was in a position of having to convince BASF to alter its position if an agreement were to be reached that met NPC's original expectations.

QUESTIONS

1. How likely is it that the two firms will come to a mutual agreement?
2. What type agreement and operating form would be in the best interest of NPC? Of BASF?
3. What should NPC do if BASF is unwilling to share technology beyond the pilot plant stage?
4. What risks have the firms already incurred by going this far in their discussions?
5. In this case, NPC was seeking to obtain technology. How might a search process have differed if NPC had been trying to sell a technology?

NOTES

1. Data for the case were taken from James Flanigan, "The Strategy," *Forbes,* October 29, 1979, pp. 42–52; "Dravo Agrees to Market Type of Plant for Grupo," *Wall Street Journal,* September 23, 1980, p. 38; Hugh O'Shaughnessy, "A Hive of Private Enterprise," *Financial Times,* May 4, 1979, p. 34; Christopher Lorenz, "A Front-Runner in Mexican Industry," *Financial Times,* June 1, 1979, p. 16; "Mexico: Exporting a Cheaper Way of Making Steel," *Business Week,* June 11, 1979, p. 53; Alan M. Field, "After the Fall," *Fortune,* Vol. 135, No. 8, April 22, 1985, pp. 93–95; Keith Bradsher, "Back from the Brink, Mexico's Giant Alfa Slims Down for Hard Times," *International Management,* Vol. 41, No. 9, September 1986, pp. 65–66.

2. For a discussion of the many trade-offs see James D. Goodnow, "Individual Product: Market Transactional Mode of Entry Strategies—Some Eclectic Decision-Making Formats," paper presented at Academy of International Business meetings in New Orleans, October 24, 1980.

3. Ian H. Giddy and Stephen Young, "Do New Forms of Multinational Enterprise Require New Theories?" working paper, no. 322A, Columbia University Graduate School of Business, April 1980; also, R. T. Carstairs and L. S. Welch, "Licensing and the Internationalization of Smaller Companies: Some Australian Evidence," *Management International Review,* Vol. 22, No. 3, 1982, pp. 33–44, found that firms typically export before licensing, which in turn precedes direct investment.

4. Ian H. Giddy and Alan M. Rugman, "A Model of Trade, Foreign Direct Investment and Licensing," working paper, no. 274A, Columbia University Graduate School of Business, December 1979.

5. Leo Sleuwaegen, "Monopolistic Advantages and the International Operations of Firms: Disaggregated Evidence from U.S. Based Multinationals," *Journal of International Business Studies,* Vol. 16, No. 3, Fall 1985, pp. 125–133; W. H. Davidson and D. G. McFetridge, "Key Characteristics in the Choice of International Technology Transfer Mode," *Journal of International Business Studies,* Vol. 16, No. 2, Summer 1985, pp. 5–21, found evidence for this point as well as those that follow in this discussion.

6. See, for example, Marcus B. Finnegan and Brian G. Brunsvold, "Antitrust Problems in Licensing," *Current Trends in Domestic and International Licensing 1977,* Tom Arnold, ed. (New York: Practicing Law Institute, 1977), pp. 263–292.

7. "American Home Plans Drug Venture in U.S. with French Company," *Wall Street Journal,* June 3, 1981, p. 54.

8. David Ford and Chris Ryan, "Taking Technology to Market," *Harvard Business Review,* March–April 1981, p. 118.

9. Alan Riding, "Cartier's Mexican Look-Alike," *New York Times,* October 17, 1980, p. D1+.

10. Michael G. Harvey and Ilkka A. Ronkainen, "International Counterfeiters: Marketing Success without the Cost and the Risk," *Columbia Journal of World Business,* Vol. 20, No. 3, Fall 1985, pp. 37–45.

11. "Oleg Cassini Inc. Sues Firm over Licensing," *Wall Street Journal,* March 28, 1984, p. 5; "Cassini Awarded $16 Million in Fragrance Line Squabble," *Wall Street Journal,* June 2, 1988, p. 28.

12. William H. Meyers, *The New York Times Magazine,* May 3, 1987, pp. 33–35+.

13. *Wall Street Journal,* November 8, 1977, p. 4.

14. See, for example, Samuel A. Morley and Gordon W. Smith, "The Choice of Technology: Multinational Firms in Brazil," *Economic Development and Cultural Change,* January 1977, pp. 240–241.

15. Edwin Mansfield, "International Technology Transfer: Forms, Resource Requirements, and Policies," *American Economic Review,* May 1975, pp. 372–382.

16. The difficulty of choosing a fair price is discussed in Wilson B. Brown, "Islands of Conscious Power: MNCs in the Theory of the Firm," *MSU Business Topics,* Summer 1976, pp. 37–45.

17. Thomas Horst, "American Multinationals and the U.S. Economy," *American Economic Review,* May 1976, pp. 150–152.

18. Claudio V. Vaitsos, *Intercountry Income Distribution and Transnational Enterprises* (Oxford: Clarendon Press, 1974); P. Streeten, "Theory of Development Policy," in *Economic Analysis and The Multinational Enterprise,* J. H. Dunning, ed. (London: Allen and Unwin, 1974); G. F. Kopits, "Intrafirm Royalties Crossing Frontiers and Transfer Pricing Behavior," *The Economic Journal,* December 1976; and Donald R. Lessard, "Transfer Prices, Taxes, and Financial Markets: Implications of Internal Financial Transfers within the Multinational Firm," paper presented for the New York University Conference on Economic Issues of Multinational Firms, November 4, 1976.

19. This is taken from D. W. Fewkes, "Positioning the Licensing Unit," *les Nouvelles,* March 1979, pp. 28–33.

20. William T. Ryan and Doria Bonham-Yeaman, "International Patent Cooperation," *Columbia Journal of World Business,* Vol. 17, No. 4, Winter 1982, pp. 63–66.

21. "Expanded Business Volume Reflected in Trademarks Processed," *Commerce Today,* August 20, 1973, p. 16.

22. Paul Lewis, "Counterfeiting of Goods Rises," *New York Times,* October 10, 1983, p. D9; "U.S. Says Counterfeits Cost Concerns Billions of Dollars in Lost Sales," *Wall Street Journal,* February 27, 1984, p. 35.

23. "Publishers Aim New Weapon at Piracy," *Publishers Weekly,* April 27, 1984, pp. 21–22.

24. Harvey and Ronkainen, *op. cit.,* p. 39.

25. Peter Kerr, "Foreign Piracy of TV Signals Stirs Concern," *New York Times,* October 13, 1983, p. 1A+.

26. Erik Bjerager, "Denmark's Lego Challenges Imitators of Its Famous Toy Blocks across Globe," *Wall Street Journal,* August 5, 1987, p. 14.

27. Louis Kraar, "Fighting the Fakes from Taiwan," *Fortune,* Vol. 107, No. 11, May 30, 1983, pp. 114–116; "Two Who Smuggled Counterfeit Computers Get Prison and Fines," *Wall Street Journal,* May 1, 1984, p. 62; Todd Mason, "How High Tech Foils the Counterfeiters," *Business Week,* May 20, 1985 p. 119.

28. Harvey and Ronkainen, *op. cit.,* p. 43.

29. Jerry H. Opack, "Likenesses of Licensing, Franchising," *les Nouvelles,* June 1977, pp. 102–105.

31. "Japan: A Growing Appetite for U.S. Fast Foods," *Business Week,* April 17, 1978, pp. 48–53.

32. Kathleen Deveny, John Pluenneke, Dori Jones Yang, Mark Maremont, and Robert Black, "McWorld," *Business Week,* No. 2968, October 13, 1986, pp. 78–86.

33. Linda Charlton, "Franchising, Global Venture," *New York Times,* January 27, 1974, p. 30 ff.

34. "Judge Revokes License of Paris McDonald's," *International Herald Tribune* (Zurich), September 11–12, 1982, p. 14; Steven Greenhouse, "McDonald's Tries Paris, Again," *New York Times,* June 12, 1988, p. 1F+.

35. Richard Ellison, "An Alternative to Direct Investment Abroad," *International Management,* June 1976, pp. 25–27.

36. "Where Top 250 Found Business in 1984," *Engineering News Record,* July 18, 1985, pp. 41–53.

37. "Nigeria," *Business Week,* October 1, 1979, p. 60.

38. *Competitive Assessment of the U.S. International Construction Industry* (Washington: U.S. Department of Commerce, International Trade Administration, July 1984).

39. Edgar J. Moor, "Turnkey-Plus Operations," *Business Horizons,* December 1973, pp. 39–44.

40. Louis Berger, "The Construction Scene in Southeast Asia: Who's Getting the Business?" *Worldwide P & I Planning,* January–February 1974, p. 13.

41. Joan Gray, "International Construction," *Financial Times,* April 12, 1985, pp. 13–17.

42. "Mobil Sees Further Role in Saudi Arabia for U.S. Firms after Aramco Take-Over," *Wall Street Journal,* September 25, 1974, p. 7.

43. "Exxon, Dutch-Shell Units and Malysia Reach Initial Pact on Oil Output Sharing," *Wall Street Journal,* November 17, 1976, p. 4.

44. F. A. Sviridov, ed., *The Role of Patent Information in the Transfer of Technology* (New York: Pergamon Press, 1981), p. 137.

45. Robert Ronstadt and Robert J. Kramer, "Getting the Most out of Innovation Abroad," *Harvard Business Review,* Vol. 60, No. 2, March–April 1982, pp. 94–99, and Beth Karlin and George Anders, "Importing Science," *Wall Street Journal,* October 5, 1983, p. 1+.

46. Carl H. Fulda and Warren F. Schwartz, *Regulation of International Trade and Investment* (Mineola, N.Y.: The Foundation Press, 1970), pp. 776–782.

47. Stephen J. Kobrin, "Trends in Ownership of American Manufacturing Subsidiaries in Developing Countries: An Inter-industry Analysis," *Management International Review,* Special Issue 1988, pp. 73–84.

48. Brad Heller, "U.S. Firms Must Propose Joint Ventures to Win a Slice of Huge Saudi Contracts," *Wall Street Journal,* April 13, 1984, p. 31.

49. George Getschow, "Foreign Investment in Mexico Swells," *Wall Street Journal,* May 1981, p. 34.

50. R. Duane Hall, "International Joint Ventures: An Alternative to Foreign Acquisitions," *Journal of Buyout and Acquisitions,* Vol. 4, No. 2, March–April 1986, pp. 39–45.

51. Mike Tharp, "Uneasy Partners," *Wall Street Journal,* November 8, 1976, p. 28.

52. J. Peter Killing, "How to Make a Global Joint Venture Work," *Harvard Business Review,* Vol. 60, No. 3, May–June 1982, pp. 120–127.

53. Lawrence G. Franko, *Joint Venture Survival in Multinational Corporations* (New York: Praeger, 1971); Richard H. Holton, "Making International Joint Ventures Work," in *The Management of Headquarters–Subsidiary Relationships in Multinational Corporations,* Lars Otterbeck, ed. (London: Cower, Aldershot, 1981), pp. 255–267.

54. John Kitching, *Acquisitions in Europe* (Geneva: Business International, 1973); John Kitching, "Winning and Losing with European Acquisitions," *Harvard Business Review,* March–April 1974, pp. 124–136.

55. Data for the case were taken from Ellen Lentz, "Chemical-Group Profits Surge in West Germany," *New York Times,* December 2, 1974, pp. 53–54; Paul Kemezis, "West German Chemical Giants Plan Additional Expansion in U.S.," *New York Times,* February 10, 1975, p. 39–40; Northern Natural Gas Company, *Annual Report,* 1974; Lou Potempa, "Business Technology Choice," *les Nouvelles,* March 1979, pp. 24–27; Steven P. Galante, "How Foreigners Botch Their U.S. Investments," *Wall Street Journal,* June 6, 1984, p. 32.

16

CHAPTER COUNTRY EVALUATION AND SELECTION

If the profits are great, the risks are great.
—Chinese proverb.

- To discuss strategies firms should develop for their penetration sequence by country and for committing their resources.
- To explain how clues from the environmental climate can help limit geographic alternatives.
- To examine the major variables that firms should consider when deciding whether and where to expand abroad.
- To describe some simplifying tools for firms to help decide on global geographic strategy.
- To introduce how final investment, reinvestment, and divestment decisions are made.

CASE:
FORD MOTOR COMPANY[1]

By any standard, Ford is a large company. Its 1986 sales of $62.7 billion made it one of the five largest industrial firms in the United States and one of the ten largest in the world. It is also the world's second largest automobile company, holding about 13 percent of the worldwide market in 1986. Ford also is highly involved internationally. The company began operations in 1903 and exported the sixth car it built. By 1911 the company boasted that a man could drive around the world and stop every night at a garage handling Ford parts. By 1930, Ford was manufacturing or assembling automobiles in twenty foreign countries and had sales branches in another ten. In 1986, about 35 percent of Ford's car and truck vehicles were produced and sold outside of the United States. Yet as large and internationally involved as Ford is, it must allocate its limited financial and human resources to maintain emphasis on those markets and production locations that are most compatible with corporate expectations and objectives.

The present locations of Ford operations are largely due to historical antecedents. Although foreign expansion was a stated objective at Ford's first annual meeting, the company initially was passive about where the emphasis would be. Ford's first foreign sales branches and assembly operations, such as in Canada, England, and France, took place because people in those countries made proposals to Ford.

Ford also made international expansion decisions on a highly decentralized basis. Much of the European expansion was handled through the English operations and the British Commonwealth sales through the Canadian company. Where sales grew most rapidly (e.g., Argentina, Uruguay, Brazil) Ford established assembly operations in order to save on transportation costs by limiting the bulk of shipments. Much of Ford's early expansion, therefore, was not based on scanning the globe to choose the best locations. Instead, Ford took advantage of opportunities as they came along.

Ford's pattern of international activities also has been affected by criteria that management considered essential. One of these policies stated that Ford would not manufacture or assemble anywhere without a controlling interest. The concept of control in this case went beyond that of voting shares. In 1930, for example, a Ford group inspected potential production sites in China and reported back to Henry Ford that the title for any Ford purchase of land in China would have to be in the name of a Chinese citizen because a foreigner cannot own land in China. Henry Ford's response was simply, "No." In the 1950s and 1960s, Ford extended this concept of control to the point that nothing short of 100 percent ownership was acceptable. This further influenced Ford's geographic area of emphasis, causing Ford to expend resources to buy out a minority interest in the British company. It also meant the abandonment of production in India and Spain in 1954 (Ford re-commenced Spanish production in 1976 and no longer adheres to the 100 percent policy) because the governments of those countries insisted on sharing ownership.

Political conditions also have helped to forge Ford's foreign investment pattern. For example, during World War II the French facility was bombed and was not replaced. Assembly facilities were seized by communist governments in Hungary and Rumania in 1946. Not until 1977, however, did Ford establish a separate department to evaluate the external political environment. Changes in governmental regulations often have caused Ford to commit a high proportion of its resources to a given area during a given period. This occurred, for example, when Mexico required a higher portion of local content in vehicles, thus forcing Ford to increase its Mexican investment or lose sales there.

Despite the extended and heavy commitment to foreign operations, Ford's production and sales are highly concentrated in a few countries. Figure 16.1 shows, for example, that about 78 percent of Ford's sales are in just four countries, although these same four countries comprise only about 54 percent of world demand. Because of the heavier commitments in some countries than in others, Ford's competitive position is much stronger in some markets than in others. In the United Kingdom and Spain, where Ford has large investments, its market share in 1986 was 27.5 percent and 16.5 percent, respectively. But in France and Italy, market share was only 6.9 and 3.8 percent, respectively.

One result of Ford's international commitment is that the dependence on multiple markets and facilities has minimized year-to-year sales and profit fluctuations. This has occurred because demand and price levels may move

Figure 16.1
World Vehicle Production. Ford Versus All Manufacturers (percent of market, 1986)

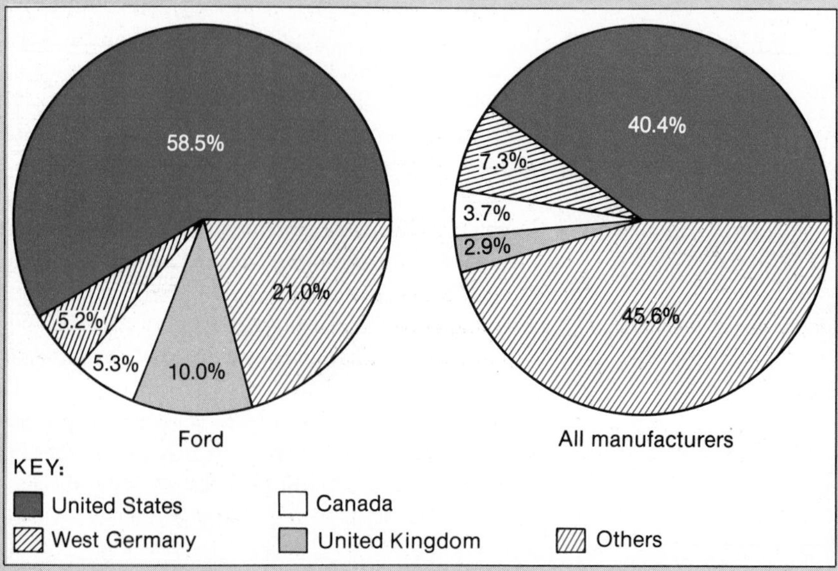

differently in various countries. From 1981 to 1982, for example, Ford's U.S. vehicle production fell by 91.6 thousand. This was largely made up by a 64.9 thousand increase in EC output. In 1980, Ford lost over $2 billion in the United States, earned $775 million in Britain, and lost $200 million elsewhere in the world. This points out not only the positive effect of geographic diversification on the smoothing of earnings, but also the importance of shifting resources in order to exploit areas of greatest profit potential.

With huge amounts of fixed assets already in place, Ford cannot easily abandon countries and then pick them up again. It can, however, compare the attractiveness of each country with actual and potential Ford operations and move toward greater emphasis on those countries with the most promising outlooks. Ford does this separately for each of its major product groups because different market conditions may affect various product groups. In 1979, for example, Ford tractors showed the biggest percentage unit increase in sales of the decade while car and truck sales fell.

One of the tools that Ford uses to aid decision makers in choosing where to emphasize their marketing efforts is a country comparison matrix. Ford staff members rank countries on one axis in terms of how attractive the country appears for sales of a specific type of product being considered, for example, tractors, trucks, or automobiles. On the other axis the same staff members rank the countries in terms of Ford's competitive capabilities for the specific markets. The resultant plotting helps the decision makers to narrow their major considerations primarily to the areas of the world that both look attractive and seem to offer the best fit with Ford's unique capabilities. This is by no means the end of the evaluation process. The exercise does, however, enable the decision makers to concentrate on more detailed analyses of a manageable list of alternatives. It also allows them to progress to interrelated decisions, such as where to locate production for the chosen markets.

INTRODUCTION

Early international expansion tends to be passive.

Later expansion cannot take advantage of all opportunities.

Ford's international expansion is typical of many firms as they become more heavily involved abroad. In the early stages, companies may lack the experience and expertise to devise strategies for sequencing countries in the most advantageous way. Instead, they respond to opportunities that become apparent to them, and many of these turn out to be highly advantageous. As they gain more international experience, however, they come to realize that they seldom have enough resources to take advantage of all the opportunities. They see that the commitment of human, technical, and financial resources to one locale may mean foregoing projects in other areas. Consequently, foreign operations become an integral part of companies' decisions on how to allocate resources.

Choosing Geographic Sites

Main questions:
- Where to sell?
- Where to produce?

There are two interrelated questions concerning geographic areas of emphasis: (1) Which markets should be served and (2) where should production be located to serve these markets? Frequently the answer to these two questions will be the same, particularly if transportation costs or governmental regulations require local production for serving the chosen market, such as in Mexico. In other cases, however, the sales and production may be in different countries. For example, Ford serves the French market in vehicles from its West German production facilities.

The market and production location decisions may be highly interdependent for other reasons as well. For example, a company may have excess production capacity already in place that will influence its relative capabilities of serving different country markets; or a firm may find a given market very attractive but forego sales there because of an unwillingness to invest in needed production locations.

A firm's international objectives should not be substantially different from those that guide domestic actions. Any foreign operations should complement domestic ones, and vice versa, so that fulfillment of overall company goals is enhanced. Because of each firm's uniqueness, the decisions of where to sell and produce can be quite variable. Firms seeking foreign markets, for example, will have different considerations from those that view foreign operations as a means of acquiring scarce or cheaper resources. Furthermore, even if the objectives and situations were similar, differences in patterns would remain because of varying assumptions about such unknown factors as future costs and prices, reactions of competitors, technology, and a host of other internal and external constraints.

Overall Geographic Strategy

The determination of an overall geographic strategy must be dynamic because conditions change, and results do not always conform to expectations. A plan must therefore be flexible enough to let a company: (1) respond to new opportunities and (2) withdraw from less profitable activities. Unfortunately, there is little agreement on a comprehensive theory or technique for optimizing the allocation of resources among countries. Nevertheless, a number of approaches frequently are used.

A firm may expand its international sales by marketing more of its existing product line, by adding products to its line, or by some combination of the two. In this chapter we will assume, for the most part, that the company has decided on its product line or product portfolio. Companies frequently alter their product characteristics to satisfy foreign consumers. But nearly all firms begin with the question, "Where can we sell more of our communications equipment?" rather than, "What new product can we make in order to maximize sales in the Greek market?"[2] The reasons and considerations for altering products and product portfolios will be discussed in Chapter 18.

SCANNING FOR ALTERNATIVES

Without scanning, a company:
- May overlook opportunities
- May examine too many possibilities.

In the opening case, Ford used scanning techniques so that decision makers could perform a much more detailed analysis among a manageable number of geographic alternatives that looked most promising. This is a useful exercise because otherwise a company might consider too few or too many possibilities.

Risk of Overlooking Opportunities

As a company tries to optimize its sales or minimize its costs, it easily can overlook or disregard some promising options. Rather than being rejected, potential projects in many countries may not be carried out simply because managers never think of them. A U.S. manager pondering foreign operations may consider countries such as Canada, Japan, and West Germany while overlooking some very small countries that actually may hold better opportunities.

Even if they are considered, certain locales may be eliminated almost immediately before they are sufficiently examined for expansion possibilities. Whole groups of countries are sometimes lumped together and rejected: Thus Zambia might not be considered because "Africa is too risky."[3]

Risk of Examining Too Many

A detailed analysis of every alternative might result in maximized sales or the pinpointing of a least-cost location; however, the cost of so many studies would erode profits. For a company with 1,000 products that might locate in any of 100 countries, there are 100,000 different situations to be analyzed. Within each of these situations are other alternatives as well, such as whether to export or to set up a foreign production unit. If there are conditions that would greatly enhance the probability of making or not making an investment, a firm should examine those first, before completing a more detailed feasibility study.

The Environmental Climate

In the Ford case at the beginning of the chapter, certain investments were overlooked because Ford could not gain sufficient control of the operation. Decision makers' perceptions of environmental climate will determine whether a detailed feasibility study will be undertaken and the terms under which a project will or will not be initiated. The **environmental climate** refers to those external conditions in host countries that could significantly affect the success or failure of a foreign business enterprise. Certain variables are commonly considered important in many firms' foreign expansion decisions. The environmental analysis is key in limiting alternatives to a manageable number.

INFLUENTIAL VARIABLES

Examining key indicators helps firms:

- Determine order of entry
- Set allocation rate among countries.

The following discussion highlights the factors mentioned most often as influencing where sales and production emphasis will be placed. Some of the variables are more important for the sales allocation decision; others are more important for the production location decision. Some, of course, affect both decisions, especially when foreign investment is necessary for serving a given foreign market.

The ranking or prioritizing of countries is useful for aiding decision makers in (1) determining the order of entry into potential markets and (2) setting the allocation and rate of expansion among the different markets. The former determination assumes that a firm cannot or does not want to go everywhere at once; consequently, it chooses to allocate its resources first to those more desirable locations. The latter assumes that a firm already is selling or producing in many locales, perhaps even in all that are feasible, but wishes to decide how much of its efforts should be expended in one country versus another.

Market Size

Expectation of sales growth is probably the major attraction of a potential location.

The importance of sales potential cannot be overlooked when comparing countries as markets or as production locations. Sales probably are the most important variable in ascertaining which locations will be considered and whether an investment will be made. The assumption, of course, is that sales will be made at a price above cost; consequently, where there are sales, there will be profit.

As was the situation in the Ford case, many firms begin sales to an area very passively. They may appoint an intermediate firm to promote sales for them or a licensee to produce on their behalf; if there is a demonstrated increase in sales, the company may consider investing more of its own resources. The generation of exports to a given country is an indication that sales may be made from production located in that country as well. As long as there is no threat to export sales, however, there is little to motivate a firm to shift to production abroad.

In some cases a firm may obtain past and current sales figures on a country-to-country basis for the type product that the company would like to sell; in many cases, however, such figures are unavailable. Regardless, management must make projections about what will happen to future sales. Such data as GNP, per capita income, growth rates, size of the middle class, and level of industrialization often are used as indicators of market size and opportunity. Methods of projecting demand from the indicators are examined in Chapter 18. There are many problems in comparing these data across countries, a subject that is discussed in Chapter 17.

The triad market of the United States, Japan, and Western Europe accounts for about half of the world's total consumption and an even higher portion of purchases for such products as computers, consumer electronics, and machine tools.[4] It is not surprising therefore that most international firms place a major part of their efforts on these areas.

Ease of Operations/Compatibility

There is a high operating attraction to countries:

- Nearby
- With same language
- With large population and high per capita income.

Geographic, language, and market similarities. Recall in the Ford case at the beginning of the chapter that earnings and vehicle sales were smoothed because of operations in various parts of the world. Because investors generally prefer smoother performance patterns, they are even willing to pay more for assets in internationally diversified firms.[5] Therefore, it might seem that companies would seek to go first to those countries whose economies are least correlated with that of the home country. Evidence, however, suggests the contrary, whether they go abroad in related or unrelated operations in terms of marketing systems, production technologies, or vertical or horizontal products.[6]

Regardless of the industry involved, U.S. firms usually make their first direct investment in Canada; the United Kingdom and Mexico alternate for the second and third locations; West Germany, France, and Australia have most of the fourth, fifth, and sixth ranks.[7] This fairly remarkable similarity in patterns among dissimilar industries seems due to the fact that decision makers perceive a greater ease of operations in these countries that are near the home country. Canada and Mexico rank high because of their geographic proximity, which makes it easier and cheaper for U.S. firms to control these foreign subsidiaries. The common language helps to explain the appeal of Canada, the United Kingdom, and Australia to investors. Managers feel more comfortable in operating at early stages of international expansion in their own language and in similar legal systems evolving from British law. The language and cultural similarity also may lower operating costs and risks. Finally, market similarity tends to exert a considerable influence on the early location of foreign operations. All the leading countries except Mexico have high per capita incomes, and all except Canada and Australia have large populations.

Once companies have sequenced their market entries, they may grow at different rates within those markets. The United States, Japan, and Western Europe share many economic and demographic conditions, which also help to explain the relative emphasis international firms place on these areas.[8]

Negative attraction of countries is not directly measurable.

Red tape. One of the things that companies frequently try to factor into their comparison of country-by-country opportunities is the degree of red tape necessary to operate in a given country. Red tape would include such things as the degree of difficulty in getting permission to bring in expatriate personnel, to obtain licenses to produce and sell certain goods, and to satisfy governmental agencies on such matters as taxes, labor conditions, and environmental conditions. Red tape is not directly measurable; therefore, firms commonly have people familiar with operating conditions in a group of countries rate them as high, medium, or low on this factor.

There is best acceptance of proposal when a location has:

- Size, technology, and other factors familiar to company personnel
- High percentage of ownership
- Easily remitted profit.

Fit with company capabilities and policies. After the alternatives are pared to a reasonable number, firms must prepare much more detailed feasibility studies, which are quite expensive. Firms very often get committed to locations that are far from optimal for them because the more time and money they invest in examining an alternative, the more likely they are to accept that project regardless of its merits.[9] Companies first should examine very carefully their motives for considering a commitment. The project manager should have broad experience so that a corporate point of view is maintained. The feasibility study should have from the start a series of clear-cut decision points so that sufficient information is gathered at each stage and so that, if a study is unlikely to result in an investment, it may be terminated before it becomes too costly.

One way to make the surveys more manageable is to ensure that proposals fit the organization's general framework. These proposals, if presented to management decision makers, will have a higher probability of acceptance.[10] For example, consideration may be limited to locales where such variables as product and plant size will be within the experience of present managers. In fact, so many guidelines and policies may be set up that very few possibilities are investigated for final feasibility. From a policy standpoint, management may find it useful to ensure that its proposal group includes personnel with backgrounds in each functional area—marketing, finance, personnel, engineering, and production. While various factors might cause ultimate decision makers to reject a proposal once a feasibility study is completed, two factors stand out as sufficiently important to sway large numbers of organizations. These are restrictions on the percentage of ownership that can be held and the maximum allowed remittance of profits.[11]

Another concern is the local availability of resources in relationship to the company's needs. A foreign operation requires combining imported resources with local inputs, which may severely restrict the movement by individual companies to given locales. The international company may, for example, need to find local personnel who are sufficiently knowledgeable about the type of technology being brought in. Or the international firm may need to add local capital to what it is willing to bring in. If local equity markets are poorly developed and local borrowing is very expensive, the company may consider locating in a different country.

The fit for a particular country is important regardless of whether the company is thinking of an initial entry or whether it is trying to decide how to allocate resources among countries where it already has operations. Take marketing capabilities, for example. Assume that a company already has developed a product in one country that has been marketed successfully through mass advertising methods. Normally it is far easier and less costly to move that product into a country where product alterations are minimal or unnecessary and where there are few advertising restrictions.

Costs and Resource Availabilities

Cost is more important for production location decision, especially labor cost.

So far the discussion has centered on market-seeking operations. Companies are engaged internationally in the pursuit of foreign resources as well. If this is a resource to be transferred, such as a raw material or technology, the analysis is somewhat simpler than for a resource that will be used in producing a product or component abroad for export into other markets. Eventually a firm must examine the costs of labor, raw material inputs, capital, taxes, and transfer costs in relation to productivity to approximate a least-cost location. Before all of this information is collected within a final feasibility study, there are indicators that will aid decision makers in narrowing the alternatives to be considered.

Employee compensation is the most important cost of manufacturing abroad for most companies, accounting for over 60 percent of costs besides taxes.[12] In most cases, therefore, current labor costs, trends in the costs, and unemployment rates are useful ways to approximate cost differences among countries. Labor, though, is not a homogeneous commodity. If the country lacks the specific skill levels required, the company may have to go through an expensive alternative to use the labor, such as training, redesigning production, or adding supervision. If the country turns out competitive products embodying inputs that are similar to those required in the production being considered, labor costs most likely will be sufficiently low in the planned operation.

Any other important costs should be added into the analysis. If precise data are unavailable, useful proxies on operating conditions may be used, such as the degree of infrastructure development and the openness to imported components.

Firm should consider different ways to produce the same product.

The continual development of new production technologies makes cost comparison among countries more difficult. With increases in the number of ways the same product can be made, a firm must compare, for example, the cost of producing by using a large labor input in Malaysia with the use of robotics in the United States.[13]

RETURN ON INVESTMENT: COUNTRY COMPARISON CONSIDERATIONS

Is a projected rate of return of 9 percent in Nigeria the same as a 9 percent rate in France? Should return on investment be calculated on the basis of the entire earnings of a foreign subsidiary or just on the earnings that can be remitted to the parent? Does it make sense to accept a low return in one country if this will help the firm's competitive position elsewhere? Is it ever rational to invest in a country with an uncertain political and economic future? These are but a few of the unresolved questions that firms must debate when making international capital budgeting decisions.

Risk and Uncertainty: The Concept

Most investors prefer certainty to uncertainty.

Given the same expected return, most decision makers prefer a more certain to a less certain outcome. An estimated rate of **return on investment (ROI)** is calculated by averaging the various returns deemed possible for investments. The result, as shown in Table 16.1, is that two identical projected ROIs may have quite different certainties of achievement as well as diverse probabilities around the expected return. In the table, the certainty of the 10 percent projected ROI is higher for investment B than for investment A. Furthermore, the probability of earning at least 10 percent is also higher (70 percent versus 65 percent) for that alternative. Experience shows that most, but not all, investors would choose alternative B over alternative A. In fact, as uncertainty increases, investors usually require a higher estimated ROI.

Often it is possible to reduce risk or uncertainty, such as by insuring against the possibility of nonconvertibility of funds. However, any such actions are apt to be costly for the firm. In the first process of scanning to develop a manageable number of alternatives, it is useful to give some weight to the elements of risk and uncertainty. At a later and more detailed stage of feasibility study, management should determine whether the degree of risk is acceptable or not without the incurring of additional costs. If it is not, then management would need to calculate an ROI that includes expenditures to increase the outcome certainty of the operation.[14]

Multidomestic versus Global Strategies

The comparison of rates of return among countries as a means of making geographic capital budgeting decisions is most appropriate when operations

TABLE 16.1
COMPARISON OF ROI CERTAINTY

	Investment A		Investment B	
ROI as percentage	Probability	Weighted value*	Probability	Weighted value*
0	.15	0	0	0
5	.20	1.0	.30	1.5
10	.30	3.0	.40	4.0
15	.20	3.0	.30	4.5
20	.15	3.0	0	.0
Estimated ROI		10.0%		10.0%

*Calculated by multiplying ROI as percentage by probability.

in one country have little effect elsewhere. In such a situation, a company may effectively allocate resources among countries from the highest to lowest expected ROI, accounting of course for risk and uncertainty. But as we will show later in this chapter, it is not easy to separate the operating results in one country versus another.

If a firm faces the same competitors in different markets, it may be appropriate to take a low ROI or even a negative one in some markets in order to counteract what would otherwise be a competitor's advantage. Recall from Chapter 6 that firms in oligopoly industries frequently will invest in the same countries at about the same time. Although this strategy may overcrowd the market and lower profits for all firms, it nevertheless prevents any one company from making a high profit that it can use for advantages elsewhere in the world. A similar strategy was used by Caterpillar when it established a joint venture with Mitsubishi in Japan, the home market of Komatsu, Caterpillar's major global competitor. This move lowered Komatsu's profits within the market that had been accounting for 80 percent of its worldwide cash flow.[15]

Competitive Risk

Investors prefer similar operating environments and try to out-guess competitors.

National boundaries play a role in the degree of certainty of return that investors perceive for alternative investments. As long as the investors are conducting business entirely within one country, the alternative investment projects fall within similar political and economic environments. Furthermore, the experience of having already operated within that country as well as operating abroad in general increases the probability of accurate assessments of consumer, competitor, and governmental actions.[16] This is consistent with the earlier discussion that firms generally go first to those foreign environments perceived to be more similar to the home country. It also helps to explain the fact that reinvestments or expanded investments within a country where the company has extensive operations often are evaluated very differently than proposed moves into a country. The reinvestment decision will be discussed later in the chapter.

In Chapter 15 we explained that one of the reasons for using nonequity arrangements was to spread business to many markets rapidly when a firm perceives that its innovative advantage may be short-lived. Even when the firm assesses that it has a substantial competitive lead time, this may vary in different markets. One of the strategies to take advantage of temporary monopoly advantages is known as the **imitation lag,** which holds that a company should move first to those countries most likely to develop local production themselves and later to other countries.[17] Local technology and high international freight costs generally result in a more rapid move to local production. If technology is available, local producers may start manufacturing well before foreign companies are willing to sell the technology. If freight costs are high for exports to the country, a local producer may, despite inefficiencies, be able to gain an advantage in cost over imported goods.

Firms also may develop strategies to find countries where there is least likely to be significant competition. When Japanese automobile producers first began selling in the European market, they shied away from countries with established national producers, such as France and West Germany. Instead, they targeted smaller countries, such as Denmark and Portugal, where they were able to gain significant market shares before the producers in larger European countries were able to react to them. L. M. Ericsson, the Swedish telephone equipment producer, has developed technology aimed at the needs of small countries, partially because this fits its home market and partially because its competitors have concentrated their efforts on larger markets.[18] Ericsson has taken this strategy a step further by putting most of its developing country investments in nations that lack colonial ties to Europe because its major competitors have longstanding distributional advantages and support of the home government where there were colonial relationships.

Monetary Risk

If the firm's expansion is via direct investment, access to and exchange rate on the invested capital and its earnings is a key consideration. The **concept of liquidity preference** is a common theory to help explain capital budgeting decisions in general and can be applied to the international expansion decision.

Investors usually want some of their holdings to be in highly liquid assets, on which they are willing to take a lower return. Part of the liquidity need is for near-term payments, such as dividends; part is for unexpected contingencies, such as to purchase stockpile materials if a strike threatens supply; and part is so that funds may be shifted to even more profitable opportunities, such as purchasing materials at a discount during a temporary price depression.

Aside from types of investments, there are some differences in liquidity by country of investment. One of these involves locating buyers for equity that one owns so that the funds may be used for other types of expansion endeavors. The ability to find buyers varies substantially among countries, depending largely on the existence of a local capital market.

Assuming that a foreign investor does find a local purchaser, chances are the intent is to use the funds in another country. If the funds are not convertible, then the foreign investor will be forced to spend them in the host country. Of more pressing concern for most investors is the ability to convert earnings from operations abroad, since earnings generally are used not only for expansion but also for dividend payment to stockholders in the home country. The discussion in Chapter 8 showed that not only does the ability to convert vary substantially among countries, but so does the cost of convertibility. It is not surprising that most investors are willing to accept a lower projected ROI for projects in countries with strong currencies than they are in countries with weak currencies.[19]

Political Risk

Political risk may come from wars and insurrections, takeover of property, and changes in rules.

One of the major concerns of international firms is that the political climate will change in such a way that their operating positions deteriorate. Political actions may affect company operations adversely through governmental takeovers of property, either with or without compensation; through operational restrictions that impede the ability of the firm to take actions it would otherwise have taken; and by damage to property or personnel. These types of risks were illustrated in the opening case of this chapter. Ford's operation in Hungary was taken over by the government; the one in Mexico was given very different operating requirements; and the one in France was bombed.

The following discussion centers on only one type of political risk—the governmental takeover of foreign facilities—because the methods to evaluate this type of risk are not fundamentally different than those used to make other political risk predictions. Three approaches to predict political risk will be discussed here: the analysis of past patterns; the use of expert opinion; and the building of models based on instability measurements.

Management can make predictions based on past patterns.

Analysis of past patterns. Firms cannot help but be influenced by what has been happening within a country. There are many dangers in predicting political risk on the basis of past patterns, though. Political situations in specific countries may change rapidly for the better or worse as far as foreign investors are concerned. However, the historical evolution is indicative of the broad climate for operations. Studies that have examined large numbers of takeovers in the post-World War II period give some clues about what to expect.[20]

Almost all of the takeovers were in LDCs, with Latin American countries accounting for about half. In terms of percentage of investments affected, however, Africa and the Middle East were riskier whereas Asia was the lowest risk area by all measurements. Even these regional categories obscure country-by-country differences. Approximately fifty countries had no takeovers, and three alone (Argentina, Chile, and Peru) accounted for about one-third of the takeovers.

Governmental takeovers, except in a few countries, have been highly selective and have usually involved land, natural resources, financial institutions, and utilities.[21] Since the early 1970s, however, manufacturing investments have been the most vulnerable. The selectivity is illustrated by the experience of investors in Peru: Cerro's mining interests and ITT's telephone company were nationalized; however, Cerro's manufacturing companies and ITT's hotel were not. Even among manufacturing industries, there are differences. Those most likely are the ones that may have a substantial and visible widespread effect on a given country because of their size, monopoly position, or necessity for national defense or because other industries depend on them.

Both among and within industries variances exist in local need for foreign resources (see Chapter 12). Companies holding assets badly needed in a given country and for which that country has little alternative source are much less vulnerable to political actions, emphasizing the need for internal assessment to design types and places for foreign operations that minimize the risk of governmental control. Thus far, firms with a high technological input that produce a large amount of component parts outside the countries where investments are made have been less prone to takeovers.[22]

The takeover of assets does not necessarily mean a full loss to investors. In fact, most takeovers have been preceded by a formal declaration of intent by the government with a subsequent legal process to determine compensation to the foreign investor. Historical analysis of compensation and continuing relationships (e.g., purchase and management contracts) help indicate possible losses from takeovers of facilities. Although investors receive compensation in more than 90 percent of takeovers, it is difficult to determine how adequate the compensation is.

Firms should:
- Examine views of governmental decision makers
- Get cross-section of opinions
- Use expert analysts.

Opinion analysis. A second approach for political risk analysis is to analyze the opinions of knowledgeable people about a country situation.[23] In this approach one attempts to ascertain the evolving opinions of people who may influence future political events affecting business. The first step involves reading statements made by political leaders both in and out of office to determine their philosophies on business in general, foreign input to business, and the means of effecting economic changes and their feelings toward given foreign countries. Although published statements are readily available, they may appear too late for a firm to have time to react.

Management should analyze the context of statements to determine whether they express true intentions or were made merely to appease particular interest groups or social strata. It is not uncommon, for example, for political leaders to make emotional appeals to the poor based on allegations that foreign business is draining wealth from the country while, at the same time, these leaders quietly negotiate entry and give incentives to new foreign firms. Examination of investment plans offers further insights to the political climate.

Visits to the country under question in order to "listen" are very important for firms in determining opinions and attitudes. Embassy officials and other foreign and local businesspeople are useful for obtaining opinions as to the probability and direction of change. Journalists, academicians, middle-level local governmental authorities, and labor leaders usually reveal their own attitudes, which often reflect changing political conditions that may affect the business sector.

A more systematic method of relying on opinions is to use a panel of analysts with experience in a country and have them rate categories of political conditions over different time frames. For example, they might rate a country in terms of the fractionalization of political parties that could lead to disruptive changes in government at the present time as well as for future periods such as one, five, and ten years.[24]

Political instability does not always affect business.

Instability models. A third method being used to predict political risk is to build models based on instability measurements. The greater the political instability, the greater the possibility of change in the political climate. Although political instability has been found to be one of the major concerns of businesspeople, it is difficult to reach a consensus as to what constitutes dangerous instability or how such instability can be predicted.[25] Political parties may change rapidly at times with little effect on business; on the other hand, sweeping changes for business may occur without a change in government. Nevertheless, there are services to measure and weight different types of political stability, differentiating, for example, among institutionally prescribed elections, the fall of a cabinet, the outlawing of significant groups, the execution of a significant political figure, the assassination of a chief of state, a coup d'état accompanied by a mild amount of violence, and a civil war.[26] Rather than political stability itself, the direction of change in government seems to be very important; takeovers have occurred most frequently within three years after a leftist government has taken office.[27]

One theory, which has been used in predictive models, is that frustration, the difference between the level of aspirations and the level of welfare and expectations, develops and that foreign investment is a scapegoat when a country's frustration level is high.[28] Since frustration, aspiration, welfare, and expectations cannot be measured directly, it is necessary to use substitutes for these. For example, a growth in urbanization, literacy, radios per capita, and labor unionization are all measurable indicators of growth in aspirations; such variables as infant survival rate, caloric consumption, hospital beds per capita, piped water supply per capita, and per capita income are measurable indicators of welfare. Variables such as the change in per capita income and in gross investment rates are indicators of expectations. This approach to predicting actions toward foreign investors has considerable possibilities, since it predicts future trends rather than looking to the past and is predicated on a lead time that might be sufficient for managements to adjust operations in order to minimize losses.

SOME TOOLS FOR COMPARING COUNTRIES

Grids

A grid may be used to compare countries on whatever factors are deemed important. Table 16.2 is an example of a grid with information placed into

TABLE 16.2

SIMPLIFIED GRID TO COMPARE COUNTRIES FOR MARKET PENETRATION

Variables	Weight	Countries I	II	III	IV	V
1. Acceptable (A), Unacceptable (U) factors						
a. Allows 100 percent ownership	—	U	A	A	A	A
b. Allows licensing to majority-owned subsidiary	—	A	A	A	A	A
2. Return (higher number = preferred rating)						
a. Size of investment needed	0–5	—	4	3	3	3
b. Direct costs	0–3	—	3	1	2	2
c. Tax rate	0–2	—	2	1	2	2
d. Market size, present	0–4	—	3	2	4	1
e. Market size, 3–10 years	0–3	—	2	1	3	1
f. Market share, immediate potential, 0–2 years	0–2	—	2	1	2	1
g. Market share, 3–10 years	0–2	—	2	1	2	0
Total			18	10	18	10
3. Risk (lower number = preferred rating)						
a. Market loss, 3–10 years (if no present penetration)	0–4	—	2	1	3	2
b. Exchange problems	0–3	—	0	0	3	3
c. Political unrest potential	0–3	—	0	1	2	3
d. Business laws, present	0–4	—	1	0	4	3
e. Business laws, 3–10 years	0–2	—	0	1	2	2
Total			3	3	14	13

Grids are tools that:
- May depict acceptable or unacceptable conditions
- Rank countries by important variables.

three major categories. Certain countries may be eliminated immediately from consideration because of characteristics decision makers find unacceptable. These are in the first category of variables, where country I can be eliminated. Values and weights are assigned to items so that a country may be ranked according to attributes that are important to the decision maker. In the same table, for example, II is graphically pinpointed as a high return–low risk; III as a low return–low risk; IV as a high return–high risk; and V as a low return–high risk.[29]

Both the variables and weights should vary by product and company, depending on the firm's internal situation and consequent objectives. The grid technique is useful even when comparative analysis is not made because a company may be able to set a minimum score necessary for either investing additional resources or committing further funds to a more detailed feasibility study. Grids do tend to get cumbersome, however, as the number of variables increases. Furthermore, while they are useful in ranking, they often obscure interrelationships among countries.

Opportunity–Risk Matrix

One way of showing more clearly the summary of data that could be included on a grid is to plot risk on one axis and opportunity on the other.[30] Many

With an opportunity–risk matrix, a firm can:

- Decide on indicators and weight them
- Evaluate each country by weighted indicators
- Plot to see relative placements
- Plot size of operations differently
- Plot expected movements.

companies, such as Borg-Warner, use variations of this instrument.[31] Figure 16.2 is an example that is simplified to include only six countries. The grid shows that the company has current operations in four of the countries (all except countries A and E). Of the two nonexploited countries, country A has low risk but low opportunity and country E has low risk and high opportunity. If resources are to be spent in a new area, country E appears to be a better bet than A. In the other four countries there are large commitments in country F, medium in countries C and D, and small in B. In the future time horizon being examined, it appears that only country F will have low risk along with high opportunity. The situation in country D is expected to improve during the studied period. Country C's situation is deteriorating, and country B's is mixed (it has better opportunity but more risk). Note that the averages shift during the period. The importance of the matrix is to reflect the placement of a country *relative* to other countries.

But how are values plotted on such a matrix? It is up to the company to determine what factors are good indicators of risk and opportunity; these factors then must be weighted to reflect their importance. For instance, on the risk axis the company may give 40 percent (.4) of the weight to expropria-

Figure 16.2
Opportunity–Risk Matrix

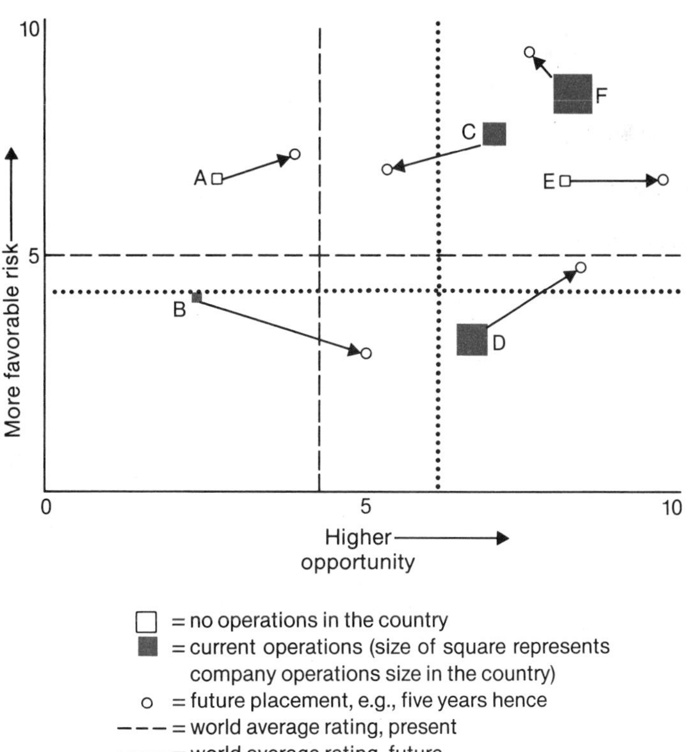

tion risk, 25 percent (.25) to foreign exchange controls, 20 percent (.2) to civil disturbances and terrorism, and 15 percent (.15) to exchange rate change: This makes a total allocation of 100 percent. Each country then would be rated on a scale of 1 to 10 for each of the variables, with 10 indicating the best score and 1 indicating the worst. The score on each item is multiplied by the weight allocated for the variable. For instance, if country A were given a rating of 8 on the expropriation risk variable, the 8 would be multiplied by 0.4 for a score of 3.2. All of country A's risk variable scores are then summed to give the placement of country A on the risk axis. Management would follow a similar procedure to find the plot location on the opportunity axis. Once the scores are determined for each country, management can determine the average score for risk and the average score for opportunity, thereby dividing the matrix into quadrants.

A key element of the sample matrix, and one that is not always included in practice, is the projection of the future country location. The utility of such a placement is obvious if the projections are realistic. Therefore it is useful to have forecasts made by people who are not only knowledgeable about the countries but also knowledgeable about forecasting methods.

Country Attractiveness–Company Strength Matrix

The attractiveness–strength matrix highlights fit of company's product to country.

Another commonly used matrix approach has been devised to highlight a company's specific product advantage on a country-by-country basis. This was briefly explained in the case on Ford: For its tractor operations, for example, Ford uses this type of matrix. On the country attractiveness scale, countries are ranked from highest to lowest attractiveness for tractors specifically; on the other scale, Ford ranks its competitive strength in tractors by country. The method of performing the ranking is the same as for the opportunity–risk matrix. Ford's weighted scale for country attractiveness includes such variables as market size, market growth, price controls, red tape, requirements for local content and exports, inflation, trade balance, and political stability. Ford's competitive strength weighted scale includes market share, market share position, its product fit for the needs of the country, absolute profit per unit, percentage profit on cost, quality of Ford's distribution in comparison with competitors, and the fit of Ford's promotion program for the country in comparison with competitors.[32]

Figure 16.3 illustrates this type of matrix for market expansion before countries are plotted into their positions. The company should attempt to concentrate its activities in the countries that appear in the top left-hand corner of the matrix and to take as much equity as possible in investments there. In this position the country attractiveness is the highest *and* the firm has the best competitive capabilities to exploit the opportunities. In the top right-hand corner, the country attractiveness is also high, but the company has a weak competitive strength for that market, perhaps because it lacks the right product. If it is not too costly, the company might attempt to gain greater domination in those markets by remedying its competitive weakness. Otherwise, it might consider either **divestment** (reducing its investment), or strengthening the position through joint venture operations with another firm whose assets are complementary. Investments ordinarily should not be made in areas in the bottom right-hand corner, and divestment should be attempted. Income may be "harvested" by pulling out all possible cash that can be generated while, at the same time, not replacing depreciated facilities. Licensing still offers potential because it may generate some income without having to make investment outlays. In other areas the company must analyze situations selectively in order to decide which approach to take. These are marginal areas which require specific judgment.

DIVERSIFICATION VERSUS CONCENTRATION STRATEGIES

Strategies for ultimately reaching high commitment in many countries include:

- Diversification—go to many fast and then build up slowly in each.
- Concentration—go to one or a few and build up fast before going to another
- A hybrid of the two.

Ultimately, a firm may gain a sizable presence and commitment in most countries of the world; however, there are different paths to reach that position. At one extreme, in a **diversification strategy** the company may move rapidly into most foreign markets, gradually increasing its commitments within each of them. This could be done, for example, through a liberal licensing policy for a given product so that there are sufficient resources for this initial widespread expansion. The company eventually may increase its involvement by internalizing activities that it initially had contracted to other firms. At the other extreme, in a **concentration strategy** the company might move only to one or a few foreign countries until it developed a very strong involvement and competitive position there. There are, of course,

Figure 16.3
Country Attractiveness–Company Strength Matrix

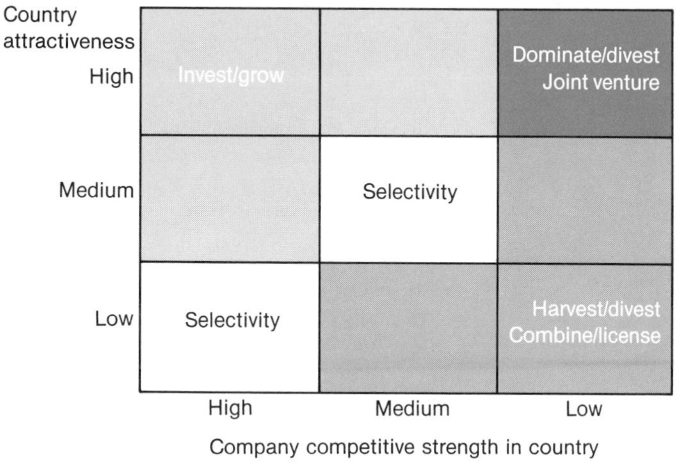

Country attractiveness	High	Medium	Low
High	Invest/grow		Dominate/divest Joint venture
Medium		Selectivity	
Low	Selectivity		Harvest/divest Combine/license

Company competitive strength in country

hybrids of these two strategies: for example, moving rapidly to most markets but increasing the commitment in only a few. The following discussion centers on those major variables a firm should consider when deciding whether to use a diversification or concentration strategy.[33] (See Table 16.3.)

Sales Response Function

An increasing sales response rate favors concentration whereas a decreasing sales rate favors diversification.

The **sales response function** refers to the amount of sales created at different levels of marketing expenditures. If, for example, the first $100,000 of marketing expenditure in a given country yielded $1,000,000 of sales, the next $100,000 yielded $800,000, and the third yielded $600,000, this would be a decreasing response. On the other hand, if the first $100,000 in a country yielded $600,000, the second yielded $800,000, and the third yielded $1 million, it would be an increasing response. There are products that follow each pattern over similar expenditure levels. If the company had $300,000 to spend on a marketing program for which there is the same decreasing response in each country, the company would create more sales by spreading entry over three countries. This would yield $3 million ($1M. + 1M. + 1M.), whereas a concentration on one country would yield only $2.4 million ($1M. + 0.8M. + 0.6M.). If the same $300,000 were spent on a product with an increasing response, however, a concentration strategy would yield better results: $2.4 million ($0.6M. + 0.8 + 1M.) as opposed to $1.8 million ($0.6M. + 0.6M. + 0.6M.).

TABLE 16.3

PRODUCT/MARKET FACTORS AFFECTING CHOICE BETWEEN DIVERSIFICATION AND CONCENTRATION STRATEGIES

Product/Market Factor	Prefer Diversification if:	Prefer Concentration if:
1. Sales response function*	Decreasing	Increasing
2. Growth rate of each market	Low	High
3. Sales stability in each market	Low	High
4. Competitive lead time	Short	Long
5. Spillover effects	High	Low
6. Need for product adaptation	Low	High
7. Need for communication adaptation	Low	High
8. Economics of scale in distribution	Low	High
9. Program control requirements	Low	High
10. Extent of constraints	Low	High

*The terms used in the original article for "decreasing" and "increasing" were "concave" and "S curve," respectively.

Source: Igal Ayal and Jehiel Zif, "Marketing Expansion Strategies in Multinational Marketing," *Journal of Marketing,* Vol. 43, Spring 1979, p. 89. Reprinted by permission of the American Marketing Association.

Growth Rate in Each Market

Fast growth favors concentration because companies must use resources to maintain market share.

When the growth rate in each market is high, it is usually preferable for a firm to concentrate on a few markets because it will cost a great deal to maintain market share, and costs per unit are typically lower for the market share leader. Slower growth in each market may allow the company to have enough resources to build and maintain a market share in a number of different countries.

Growth Stability in Each Market

International diversification has been shown to have an even stronger relationship to profit stability than product diversification.[34] Recall the Ford case at the beginning of the chapter and the earlier discussion that earnings and sales are smoothed because of operations in various parts of the world: This is because there are leads and lags in the business cycles. Additionally, a company whose assets and earnings base are in a variety of countries will be less affected by occurrences within a single nation. A strike or expropriation therefore will affect earnings from only a small portion of total corporate assets. Currency devaluations in some countries may be offset by revaluations in other countries.

The more stable sales and profits are within a single market, the less need there is for a diversification strategy. Likewise the more interrelated markets are, the less smoothing is achieved by selling in each. For example, Ford would seemingly get less of a smoothing effect between France and West Germany (because their economies are so interrelated through the EC) than between either of those two countries and the United States.[35]

Competitive Lead Time

The longer the lead time, the more the firm can use a concentration strategy.

In Chapter 15 we discussed that one of the reasons for using nonequity arrangements as a means of serving foreign markets is to beat competitors into the market. The use of these external arrangements helped the companies to spread into more markets than if they had had to use their own resources. If a company assesses that it has a long lead time before competitors can likely copy or supersede its advantages, then it may be able to maintain control of the expansion by following a concentration strategy and still beat competitors into other markets.

Spillover Effects

Spillover effects refer to situations whereby the marketing program in one country results in awareness of the product in other countries. This can happen, for example, if the product is advertised through media viewed on a cross-national basis. In such situations a diversification strategy has advantages because additional customers may be reached with little additional incremental cost.

Need for Product, Communications, and Distribution Adaptation

Adaptation means additional costs for the firm because it is:
- Hard to spread to many markets
- Hard to gain economies of scale through diversification.

Chapter 18 discusses why and under what circumstances products and the marketing of them may have to be altered for foreign markets. The adaptation process is often costly and, if so, may lead to two factors that favor a concentration strategy: First, the additional costs may limit the resources the firm has for expansion in many different markets; second, the fixed costs incurred for adaptation cannot be as easily spread over sales in other countries as a means of reducing total unit costs.

Program Control Requirements

Diversification often implies external arrangements that may cause control to be lost.

The more necessary it is that the company control what is happening in the foreign country where the product is being sold, the more likely that it should develop a concentration strategy. This is because more of the firm's resources will need to be used to maintain that control. The need for more control could come about for a number of reasons including fear that an external arrangement will create a competitor or that there is a need for highly technical assistance to customers.

Extent of Constraints

Constraints limit resources for going to many places simultaneously.

Constraints on what a firm can do may come about internally or externally. In resource availability, for example, the higher the constraints, the more likely a concentration strategy is. Assume that the key resource for introducing a new product into the foreign markets is the availability of certain specialized technical personnel. If there is a shortage of these personnel both within and outside the company, the company will be constrained in the number of countries to which it can expand rapidly. Or if there are constraints in where they can be moved, the company may find it difficult to expand into many different markets rapidly.

INVESTMENT PROPOSAL EVALUATION

Internal and accounting rates of return are the most popular measurements for precise projections.

Thus far we have examined comparative opportunities on a very broad basis. At some point it is necessary for firms to do a much more detailed analysis of specific projects and proposals in order to make allocation decisions. Firms use a variety of financial criteria to evaluate foreign investments—internal rate of return and accounting rate of return being the most used measurements.[36]

Measurement Problems

The derivation of meaningful rate of return figures is no easy task when foreign operations are concerned. Profit figures from individual operations may obscure the real impact those operations have on overall company activities. For example, if a U.S. company were to establish an assembly operation in Australia, this assembly operation could either increase or decrease exports from the United States. Management would have to make assumptions about the changed profits in the United States and elsewhere as a result of the Australian project. Or perhaps by building a plant in Brazil to supply components to Volkswagen of Brazil, the investor increases the possibility of selling to Volkswagen in other countries.

The preceding discussion assumes that, although overall company returns are difficult to calculate, those for the operating subsidiary are fairly easily ascertained, but this is not the case. A substantial portion of the sales and purchases of foreign subsidiaries may be with units of the same parent company. The prices charged on these transactions will affect the relative profitability of one unit vis-à-vis another. Furthermore, the base on which to estimate the net value of the foreign investment may not be realistically stated, particularly if part of the net value is based on exported capital equipment that is both obsolete at home and useless elsewhere. By stating a high value, the company may be permitted to repatriate a larger portion of its earnings.

Noncomparative Decision Making

Most proposals are decided on a go-no-go basis if they meet minimum acceptance criteria.

Because of the limited resources firms have at their disposal, it might seem that companies maintain a storehouse of foreign investment proposals that may be ranked on the basis of some predetermined criteria. If this were so, management simply could start allocating resources to the top-ranked proposal and continue down the list until no further investments were possible. This is seldom the case, however: About three-quarters of final investment proposals are evaluated separately, and a decision is made on what is commonly known as a **go-no-go decision.**[37] This decision is usually made on the basis that the project meets some minimum threshold criteria. Of course, before this there is a good deal of weeding out of possible projects at various scanning and decision points along the way.

One of the major factors restricting firms from comparing investment opportunities is cost. Clearly, most firms cannot afford to conduct very many investigations simultaneously. Another factor inhibiting comparison of investment opportunities is that feasibility studies are apt to be in various stages of completion at a given time. Assume that the investigation process has been finished for a possible project in Australia but that ongoing research is being conducted for New Zealand, Japan, and Indonesia. Can the company afford to wait until the results from all the surveys are completed? Probably not. The time interval between completions probably would invalidate much of the earlier results, requiring an updating, added expense, and further delays.

There are other time-inhibiting problems as well. Frequently, governmental regulations may require a decision within a given period of time. Another external limitation may be imposed by other companies that have made partnership proposals. If no answer is forthcoming in a short period of time, a proposal may be made to a different potential partner.

Finally, few companies can afford to let resources lie idle or to be employed for a low rate of return during a waiting period. They must answer to both stockholders and employees. This applies not only to financial resources but also to such resources as technical competence, since the lead time over competitors is reduced when a company holds off a decision.

Reinvestment Decisions

A company may have to make new commitments to maintain competitiveness.

Most of the net value of foreign investment has come from the reinvestment of earnings abroad rather than from new international capital transfers. The decisions to replace depreciated assets or to add to the existing stock of capital from retained earnings in a foreign country are somewhat different from original investment decisions. Once committed to a given locale, a firm may find that there is no option to move a substantial portion of the earnings elsewhere because to do so would endanger the continued successful operation of the given foreign facility. For example, the failure to expand might result in a falling market share and a higher unit cost than that of competitors.

Aside from competitive factors, a company may need several years of almost total reinvestment as well as allocation of new funds to one area in order to meet its objectives. Over a period of time, the earnings may be used to expand the product line, the integration of production, and the market served from present output. A further factor for treating reinvestment decisions differently is that once there are experienced personnel within a given country, they may be the best judges of what is needed for their countries; therefore, certain investment decisions may be delegated to them.

DIVESTMENT

Firms must decide how to get out of operations if:

- They do not fit the overall strategy
- There are better alternative opportunities.

In much of the preceding discussions we showed that firms should consider decreasing their commitments to certain areas in order to free resources when they will better fit with corporate objectives. Now it is common to read that a firm is terminating its ownership in an investment in a foreign country. Many of the headlines highlight the conflict between MNEs and nation-states. They emphasize either governmental expropriation or moves by MNEs to gain leverage over host countries in operating terms. These headlined examples are decidedly in the minority;[38] the majority of divestments have involved the selling of operations that have poor performance prospects compared to alternative opportunities. Admittedly, however, some of these have been in anticipation of governmental takeovers if the firms did not move to sell their ownership voluntarily. About one-third of divestments have been neither voluntary sales nor expropriations; instead, they have involved the liquidation of unprofitable operations.

Managers are less apt to propose divestments than investments.

Studies of the divestment experience conclude that most firms might have fared better had they been more experienced and developed divestment specialists. Instead, there has been a tendency to wait too late and to be thwarted by local managers who fear loss of their own positions if the MNE abandons an operation. In fact, this question of who has something to gain or lose is a factor that sets apart decisions to invest from decisions to divest. Both types of decisions should be highly interrelated and geared to the company's strategic thrust. The idea for investment projects typically originates with middle managers or with managers already employed in foreign subsidiary operations who are enthusiastic in collecting information to accompany a proposal as it moves upward in the organization. After all, the evaluation and employment of these people depend on growth. They have no such compulsion to propose divestments. These proposals typically originate at the top of the organization after upper management has tried most remedies for saving the operations.[39]

Use of asset book value has been most common when selling an interest, and firms have sought to smooth their exit in a way that permitted possible reestablishment of operations at a later date. The wish to reestablish operations, along with efforts to salvage as much as possible when divesting, makes it difficult for MNEs to threaten to move to another country in contrast to what is often alleged.

SUMMARY

- Because companies do not have sufficient resources to exploit all opportunities apparent to them, two of the major considerations facing firms are (1) which markets to serve and (2) where to locate the production to serve those markets.
- The market and production location decisions are often highly interdependent because of requirements that markets be served from local production, because firms seek nearby outlets for excess capacity, and because firms may be unwilling to invest in those production locations necessary to serve a desired market.
- Scanning techniques are useful to aid decision makers in considering alternatives that might otherwise have been overlooked. They also help limit the final detailed feasibility studies to a manageable and promising number.
- The prioritizing of countries is useful for determining the order of entry into potential markets and in setting the allocation and rate of expansion among different markets.

- Because each company has unique competitive capabilities and objectives, the makeup of factors affecting each geographic expansion pattern will be slightly different for each. Nevertheless, certain variables have been shown to influence most firms including the relative size of country markets, the ease of operating in the specific foreign countries, the availability and cost of resources, and the perceived relative risk and uncertainty of operations in one country versus another.

- Some tools frequently used to compare opportunities in various countries are grids that rate country projects according to a number of separate dimensions and matrixes on which firms may project one attribute on a vertical axis and another on the horizontal axis, such as risk and opportunity or country attractiveness and company capability.

- By using a similar amount of internal resources a firm may choose initially to move rapidly into many foreign markets with only a small commitment in each (a diversification startegy) or to make a strong involvement and commitment in one or a few locations (a concentration strategy).

- The major variables to consider when deciding whether to diversify or concentrate are: the response of sales to incremental increase in marketing expenditures; the growth rate and sales stability in each market; the expected lead time over competitors; the degree of need for product and marketing adaptation in different countries; the need to maintain control of the expansion program; and the internal and external constraints facing the company.

- ROI figures alone do not tell the full impact a foreign investment may have on total corporate performance. Firms must assess such factors as effects on export and licensing income as well as what advantages competitors would gain in the absence of the investment.

- Rather than ranking investment alternatives, once a feasibiliity study is complete, most investors set some minimum criteria and either accept or reject a foreign project on that basis. The reason for this type of decision is that feasibility analyses seldom are finished simultaneously, and there are pressures to act quickly.

- Reinvestment decisions normally are treated separately from new investment decisions because a reinvestment may be necesssary to protect the viability of existing resources and because there are people on location who can better judge the worthiness of proposals.

- Firms must develop strategies for where new investments will be made and devise the means to deemphasize certain areas and to divest if necessary.

CASE:
MITSUI IN IRAN[40]

In late 1987, Mitsui, one of Japan's largest trading companies, faced a very tough decision. Should it abandon a project in which it had already invested $1.97 billion? The project was a petrochemical joint venture in Iran for which planning began in 1973 and construction in 1976. A Mitsui-led group of five Japanese firms owned 50 percent of the venture, with the remainder held by the Iranian government. By 1980, Mitsui had already invested $930 million directly in the project. Additionally, Mitsui had made indirect investments in the project through two of its partially owned subsidiaries that were part of the Japanese investment group.

From 1980 through 1987, Mitsui was called upon on several occasions to add as much as $60 million to the project. In 1981, Mitsui finally stopped work because it feared the plant would become a "bottomless pit." This led to two years of exhaustive and sharp negotiations and exchanges between Mitsui and the Iranian government. By the end of 1983 the Iranian government proposed that it would put up some additional funds, provided that the future ownership share would be adjusted to reflect the capital contribution and assuming that Mitsui would send a survey team of 100 engineers and experts to the site to get the project rolling again.

Work on the project had been suspended several times. The Iranian revolution first brought work to a halt in March 1979, when it was estimated that completion would be within six months. Construction resumed in the summer of 1980 but was halted again in October because of Iraqi attacks. Although the project escaped extensive damage from the attacks, the facilities were to have depended on naptha supplies from a refinery in Abadan that was almost totally destroyed. (See Fig. 16.4 for facility location.) Work restarted in 1983, but stopped in 1984 after Iraqi attacks. Late that same year construction began anew, when the completion was estimated to be in three and a half years at a project cost in excess of $4 billion as compared with the original budget of $500 million. Then in 1987 Iraq attacked again, and the Iranian government put the site off limits to representatives of Mitsui or the Japanese government.

The scope of the project was significant for Mitsui, Iran, and Japan. If completed, it would be the largest foreign investment anywhere in the world by Japanese interests. For Mitsui, the Iranian venture is a substantial portion of its total investment and even more significant in terms of its foreign assets. At the time of becoming involved in Iran, Mitsui was at an early stage of developing foreign production with only new smaller projects for Chinese coal development and for natural gas in Southeast Asia and Canada.

Meanwhile, Iran has put a very high priority on completion of the facility. Of the Shah's dozen or so billion-dollar projects, it is the only one that

Figure 16.4
Southern Iran

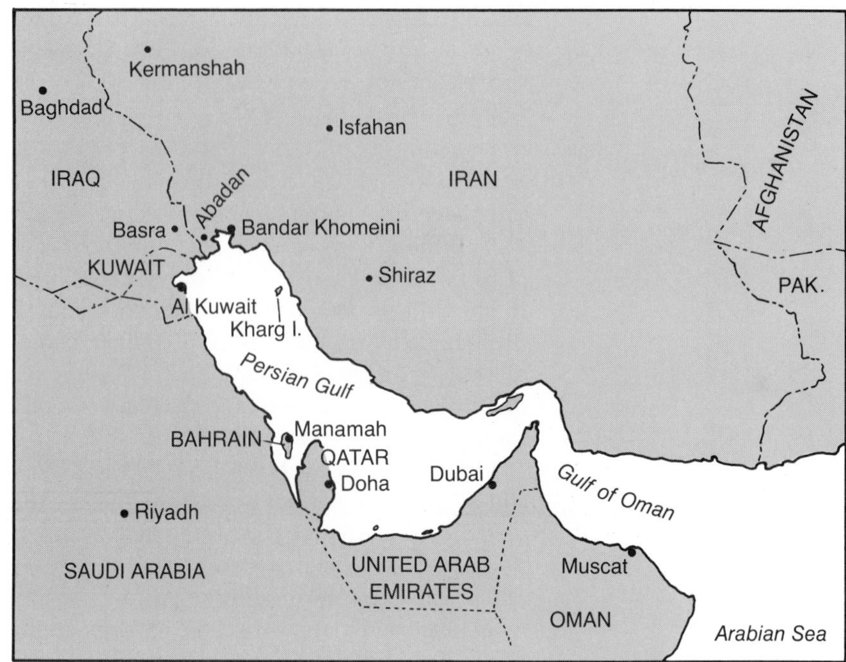

continues under the regime of Khomeini. Iranian governmental officials indicated that Mitsui's decisions on its future participation would affect Iran's overall economic relations with Japan. The Iranian Prime Minister told a Japanese government survey team in Tehran that the Iranian government would ensure stable supplies of crude oil to Japan if the project was completed. The question of oil supplies was a very sensitive issue because of Japan's dependence on foreign sources for over 99 percent of its needs. Japan depended more on Iran than on any other single oil source, but Japan also was dependent on Iraq. An official of Japan's Ministry of International Trade and Industry said, "The project will decide the destiny of the fiduciary relations between Japan and the Middle East and eventually, the destiny of Japan's energy security."

Mitsui had insured against war damage with the Japanese government's export insurance program. This insurance covered the cost of equipment that originated in Japan as well as losses caused by discontinuation of work, but it was due to expire in 1987. Prior to the expiration, Mitsui could apply for the war loss; however, without the ability to inspect the site, settlement could be much less than the damage. This would also mean abandoning ownership in the project. Alternatively, Mitsui could apply for discontinuation of work for six months at an even lower settlement, but keeping its asset ownership. Finally, Mitsui could stall for settlement; however, if the site were to be attacked after the insurance expired but before inspection, it could be claimed that the insurance would not cover the damage. In the meantime, the

Japanese government wanted Mitsui to withhold claims because of its relationship with Iran and because the claims could dry out Japan's export insurance program.

QUESTIONS

1. What should Mitsui do about its Iranian investment?
2. What might Mitsui have done to prevent the Iranian dilemma?

NOTES

1. Data for the case were taken from "Ford in Britain," *The Economist,* February 28, 1981, pp. 66–67; Gilbert D. Harrell and Richard O. Kiefer, *MSU Business Topics,* Winter 1981, pp. 5–15; Mira Wilkins and Frank Ernest Hill, *American Business Abroad: Ford on Six Continents* (Detroit: Wayne State University Press, 1964); Alan Nevins, *Ford: Expansion and Challenge: 1915–33,* Vol. II (New York: Charles Scribner's Sons, 1957); "Ford Annual Report 1986," "How Safe Is It to Invest Abroad?" *International Management,* October 1979, pp. 67–70; *Automotive News: 1987 Market Data Issue,* April 29, 1987.

2. Karen B. Hisey and Richard E. Caves, "Diversification Strategy and Choice of Country: Diversifying Acquisitions Abroad by U.S. Multinationals, 1978–1980," *Journal of International Business Studies,* Summer 1985, p. 52, show that between 70 and 85 percent of foreign acquisitions have been in related businesses.

3. Yair Aharoni, *The Foreign Investment Decision Process* (Boston: Harvard University Graduate School of Business, 1966), pp. 52–53.

4. Kenichi Ohmae, "Becoming a Triad Power: The New Global Corporation," *International Marketing Review,* Autumn 1986, pp. 36–49.

5. Raj Aggarwal, "Investment Performance of U.S.-Based Companies: Comments and a Perspective on International Diversification of Real Assets," *Journal of International Business Studies,* Spring–Summer 1980, pp. 98–104; Rolf Buhner, "Assessing International Diversification of West German Corporations," *Strategic Management Journal,* Vol. 8, January–February, 1987, pp. 25–37.

6. Hisey and Caves, *op. cit.,* pp. 58–62.

7. Irving B. Kravis and Robert E. Lipsey, "The Location of Overseas Production and Production for Export by U.S. Multinational Firms," *Journal of International Economics,* Vol. 12, May 1982, pp. 201–223.

8. Ohmae, *loc. cit.*

9. Rodman L. Drake and Allan J. Prager, "Floundering with Foreign Investment Planning," *Columbia Journal of World Business,* Summer 1977, pp. 66–77.

10. Aharoni, *op. cit.,* pp. 54–56.

11. These were found in studies of reactions to the Ancom investment code by Robert E. Grosse, *Foreign Investment Codes and the Location of Direct Investment* (New York: Praeger, 1980), pp. 122–123.

12. Kravis and Lipsey, *op. cit.,* p. 212.

13. Alan Marshall, "International Facility Planning in Emerging Industries," *Industrial Development,* May–June 1983, pp. 23–25.

14. See, for example, Briance Mascarenhas, "Coping with Uncertainty in International Business," *Journal of International Business Studies,* Vol. 13, No. 2, Fall 1982, pp. 87–98; Philip J. Stein, "Should Your Firm Invest in Political Risk Insurance?" *Financial Executive,* March 1983, pp. 18–22; Pravin Banker, "You're the Best Judge of Foreign Risks," *Harvard Business Review,* Vol. 61, No. 2, March–April, 1983, pp. 157–165.

15. Craig M. Watson, "Counter–Competition Abroad to Protect Home Markets," *Harvard Business Review,* January–February 1982, p. 40.

16. For an analysis of the importance of these variables in the decision-making process, see Joseph La Palombara and Stephen Blank, *Multinational Corporations in Comparative Perspective* (New York: The Conference Board, 1977), pp. x–xii.

17. Robert B. Stobaugh, Jr., "Where in the World Should We Put That Plant?" *Harvard Business Review,* January–February 1969, pp. 132–134.

18. For more information on the Ericsson strategy see Thomas Hout, Michael E. Porter, and Eileen Rudden, "How Global Companies Win Out," *Harvard Business Review,* September–October 1982, p. 102.

19. Marie E. Wicks Kelly and George C. Philippatos, "Comparative Analysis of the Foreign Investment Evaluation Practices by U.S. Based Manufacturing Multinational Companies," *Journal of International Business Studies,* Vol. 13, No. 3, Winter 1982, p. 39.

20. Robert G. Hawkins, Norman Mintz, and Michael Provissiero, "Government Takeovers of U.S. Foreign Affiliates," *Journal of International Business Studies,* Spring 1976, pp. 3–16; David G. Bradley, "Managing against Expropriation," *Harvard Business Review,* July–August 1977, pp. 75–83.

21. See, for example, U.S. Department of State, Bureau of Intelligence and Research, *Nationalization, Expropriation, and Other Takings of United States and Certain Foreign Property since 1960* (Washington, D.C., 1971); J. F. Truitt, "Expropriation of Foreign Investment: Summary of the Post-World War II Experience of American and British Investors in the Less-Developed Countries," *Journal of International Business Studies,* Fall 1970, pp. 21–34.

22. Bradley, "Managing against Expropriation," pp. 81–82, noted this for takeovers by Allende and Velasco in Chile and Peru.

23. Lee C. Nehrt, "The Political Climate for Private Investment: Analysis Will Reduce Uncertainty," *Business Horizons,* June 1972, pp. 52–55; Herbert Cahn, "The Political Exposure Problem: An Often Overlooked Investment Decision," *Worldwide P & I Planning,* May–June 1972, pp. 20–22.

24. F. T. Haner, "Rating Investment Risks Abroad," *Business Horizons,* April 1979, pp. 18–23. This methodology is used by a number of consulting services as well. See, for example, "As the World Twirls: BI's Ratings Show New Risks vs. Opportunities," *Business International,* April 15, 1983, pp. 113–115.

25. National Industrial Conference Board, *Obstacles and Incentives to Private Foreign Investment,* 1967–1968 (New York, 1969); R. S. Basi, *Determinants of United States Private Direct Investment in Foreign Countries* (Kent, Ohio: Kent State University Press, 1963); Franklin R. Root, "Attitudes of American Executives toward Foreign

Governments and Investment Opportunities," *Economic and Business Bulletin,* January 1968, pp. 14–23.

26. Ivo K. Feirabend and Rosalind L. Feirabend, "Aggressive Behavior in Politics: A Cross-National Study," *Journal of Conflict Resolution,* Fall 1966, pp. 249–271.

27. Hawkins et al., "Government Takeovers of U.S. Foreign Affiliates," p. 7.

28. Harold Knudsen, "Explaining the National Propensity to Expropriate: An Ecological Approach," *Journal of International Business Studies,* Spring 1974, pp. 51–69.

29. This classification scheme is adapted from Carl Noble and Virgil Thornhill, "Institutionalization of Management Science in the Multinational Firm," *Columbia Journal of World Business,* Fall 1977, pp. 13–15.

30. The incorporation of risk and opportunity are considered essential elements in any portfolio analysis. Yoram Wind and Susan Douglas, "International Portfolio Analysis and Strategy: The Challenge of the 80s," *Journal of International Business Studies,* Vol. 12, No. 2, Fall 1981, pp. 72–73.

31. See, for example, "How Borg-Warner Uses Country–Risk Assessment as a Planning Element," *Business International,* November 9, 1979, pp. 353–356.

32. Harrell and Kiefer, *loc. cit.*

33. Igal Ayal and Jehiel Zif, "Market Expansion Strategies in Multinational Marketing," *Journal of Marketing,* Vol. 43, Spring 1979, pp. 84–94.

34. Joseph C. Miller and Bernard Pras, "The Effects of Multinational and Export Diversification on the Profit Stability of U.S. Corporations," *Southern Economic Journal,* Vol. 46, No. 3, 1980, pp. 792–805.

35. *Ibid,.* p. 804.

36. Kelly and Philippatos, *loc. cit.,* p. 32.

37. *Ibid.*

38. Jagdish C. Sachdev, "Disinvestment: A New Problem in Multinational Corporation Host Government Interface," *Management International Review,* No. 3, 1976, pp. 23–35; J. J. Boddewyn, *International Divestment* (Geneva: Business International, 1976).

39. Jean J. Boddewyn, "Foreign and Domestic Divestment and Investment Decisions: Like or Unlike?" *Journal of International Business Studies,* Vol. 14, No. 3, Winter 1983, p. 28.

40. Data for the case were taken primarily from *Japan Company Handbook* (Tokyo: The Oriental Economist, 1981), p. 748; Atsuko Chiba, "Mitsui Led Group Must Pay More Money or Pull out of Iran Petrochemical Project," *The Wall Street Journal,* November 25, 1980, p. 30; "Mitsui Halts Iran Plant's Start-Up," *New York Times,* April 24, 1981, p. D1; Henry Scott Stokes, "Mitsui Said to Plan Iran Pullout," *New York Times,* November 12, 1980, p. D1; Steve Mufson, "Iran, Iraq Both Offer Oil to Japan," *The Wall Street Journal,* February 11, 1981, p. 31; James P. Sterba, "Japan Affirms Sanctions Decision," *New York Times,* April 27, 1980, p. 1; Youssef M. Ibrahim, "Japan Threatened by Iran-Iraq War," *Wall Street Journal,* November 8, 1983; Suleiman K. Kassicieh and Jamal R. Nassar, "Revolution and War in the Persian Gulf: The Effect on MNCs," *California Management Review,* Vol. 26, No. 1, Fall 1983, pp. 88–99; "Construction to Resume on War-Damaged Plant," *The Journal of Commerce,* July 11, 1984, p. 22B; and "Japan Foreign Minister to Visit Iran to Query on Gulf Safety, Mitsui's Complex," *Oilgram News,* June 5, 1987, p. 2.

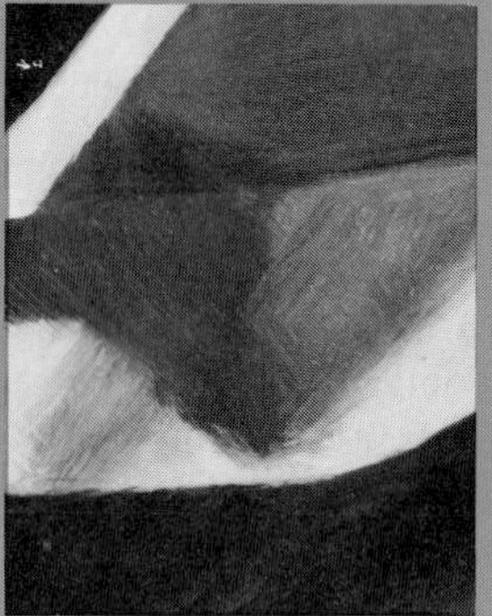

17

CHAPTER CONTROL

Form your plans before sunrise.
—Indian–Tamil proverb

- To explain the special control challenges of foreign operations.
- To indicate the advantages and disadvantages of decision making at the headquarters and foreign subsidiary locations.
- To describe the alternative organizational structures for international operations.
- To highlight both the importance of and the methods for global planning, reporting, and evaluating.
- To give an overview of some specific control considerations affecting international firms, such as the handling of acquisitions, the choice of headquarters location, and the legal structure of the foreign facility.

CASE: NESTLÉ[1]

The former managing director of Nestlé, Pierre Liotard-Vogt, said, "Perhaps we are the only real multinational company existing." Although this may be something of an exaggeration, it is difficult to find other companies with such a high dependence on foreign involvement. The Swiss-based company, one of the fifty largest industrials in the world, was international from the start. Nestlé was formed by a 1905 merger between an American-owned and a German-owned firm. More than 96 percent of Nestlé's sales are outside of Switzerland, and about 40 percent of the top management at the Vevey headquarters is non-Swiss. A Frenchman, an Italian, a German, and a Swiss who took out American citizenship have at various times held the position of chief executive officer. The one area in which the company stays staunchly Swiss is in ownership. Nearly two-thirds of the shares are registered; if sold, they can be bought only by other Swiss. This ownership identification with neutral Switzerland, a country that never colonized, has allowed the company to do business where some of its worldwide rivals have been restricted, such as in Chile under Allende, in Cuba, and in Vietnam.

In 1986 Nestlé's sales from 372 factories around the world were more than $3.5 billion. About 45 percent of the company's plants were in Europe, 20 percent in North America, and 35 percent elsewhere. With such a geographic spread of operations, Nestlé maintains quite clear-cut policies on where decisions will be made and what roles corporate and country managers will play.

A major responsibility of Nestlé's corporate management is to give strategic direction to the firm. To do this, the corporate management decides in which geographic areas and with which products it plans to allocate efforts. For instance, in recent years Nestlé has become less dependent on chocolate and Third World countries by placing more emphasis on culinary products and on the North American market. To maintain this control, Nestlé's headquarters staff handles all acquisition discussions as well as decisions as to which products will be researched at the centralized facilities in Switzerland. To support these functions, each geographic area is expected to provide a positive cash flow to the parent. In fact Nestlé tries to move almost all cash to Switzerland where a specialized staff decides in which currencies it will be held and to what countries it may be transferred.

Headquarters also researches commodity situations and mandates purchase amounts and prices, such as requiring that all overseas companies contract a supply of green coffee for, say three to six months, at some maximum price. Because of a heavy dependence on the introduction of new products that may take several years to become profitable, the company must ensure that the more established products remain sufficiently profitable for generating needed funds. If a new product does not become profitable in a reasonable period of time, such as its mineral water in Brazil, or if it has run its cycle of profitability, such as its Libby's vegetable canning operations, the management in Switzerland decides to divest the business.

The budget that originates from the country area level is the main means used to ensure that each area carries its share within the corporation. Budgets are set up on an annual basis, revised quarterly, and subject to approval in Switzerland. Actual performance reports are sent to Switzerland monthly where they are compared with budgets and the previous year's performance. The market head must explain any deviations satisfactorily or headquarters personnel will intervene. Another corporate function is to serve as a source for information: The successes, failures, and general experiences of product programs in one country are passed on to managers in other countries. Information on the success of a white chocolate bar in New Zealand and on a line of Lean Cuisine frozen food in the United States was disseminated this way.

In spite of the centralized directives described above, Nestlé's area managers have a great deal of discretion in certain matters, especially marketing. Product research is centralized so that duplication of efforts is kept to a minimum. When a new product is developed, the corporate management offers it to the subsidiaries and may urge initial trials. However, they will not force the subsidiaries to launch a new product if the subsidiary managements do not find it acceptable. If the product is introduced, local management is fairly free to adapt it as long as corporate management does not find the changes harmful. One of Nestlé's best selling products, Nescafé instant coffee, is blended and colored slightly differently from country to country.

In addition to budgets and reports, Nestlé relies heavily on information-gathering visits to the local operations. Several things are done to try to bring corporate and country management closer together. One is to alternate people between jobs in the field and jobs at headquarters. Another is the scheduling of meetings to bring large groups of managers together. Still another is to ensure that top management can converse with area management in at least French and English and preferably in German and Spanish as well. The compensation system and management style are established purposely to limit turnover among employees. The combination of these various methods contributes to many long-term interactions designed to break down barriers between headquarters and the field.

The method of making decisions at headquarters has not remained the same. At one point Nestlé sought to balance functional, area, and product viewpoints by putting different people in charge of each activity at headquarters. This meant that the person in charge of each activity would have to agree before a decision could be made, which sometimes meant a slow process. This structure was abandoned in the mid-1980s in order to slim down the corporate staff and speed decision making. This was replaced with a board of seven general managers, five in charge of zones into which Nestlé divides the world and two in charge of some specific functions.

Many company actions necessitate new decisions on where control will be vested. Nestlé's policy of expanding largely through acquisition of existing firms is one type of action that has resulted in situations not quite fitting the established lines of responsibility. The acquisition policy is premised on the belief that it is more prudent to enter an already highly competitive market by buying an existing firm and infusing resources into it. Since acquired firms are unlikely to have the exact product and geographic basis to fit Nestlé's structure, these operations must be accommodated.

For example, Nestlé acquired Libby, McNeill & Libby, a U.S. company with substantial international operations including a subsidiary in the United Kingdom. Nestlé had to iron out not only how Libby, McNeill & Libby would relate to Nestlé's existing U.S. operations, but also whether the U.K. subsidiary should continue to report to Libby or to Nestlé's European operations. Fifteen years later, in 1985, the Libby, McNeill & Libby production facilities and distribution center were closed; however, two other Nestlé divisions took on the manufacture and sale of products using the Libby name. In another case, the acquisition of Stouffer Foods put Nestlé into hotel ownership for the first time. Because Stouffer had been highly profitable and because the Swiss headquarters management lacked hotel experience, many more decisions were initially made at the subsidiary level than would normally be the case. The corporate level learned from the experience and established a European joint venture hotel operation with Swissair.

The most notable Nestlé acquisitions in the United States have been Alcon, a pharmaceutical company bought for $267 million, and Carnation, which for $3 billion made it the largest nonoil merger in history. Acquisitions reported directly to Switzerland until 1981, when Nestlé named a head of North American operations for the first time. This move was designed to centralize much of the U.S. operations. The managing director of Nestlé worldwide supported it so that he could spend time on strategic planning instead of supervising day-to-day operations. Although Carnation reports directly to Switzerland, some of its foreign operations are being integrated with local Nestlé organizations.

Competitive factors have influenced Nestlé's decisions of where to place emphasis. For example, the rapid growth strategy in the United States has been based partially on the realization that the company must maintain a certain size relative to its competitors (who have been growing internally and through acquisition). This size helps in dealing with a few large supermarket chains that account for most of Nestlé's sales, which also led Nestlé into some new products, such as generic brands. Another factor that has influenced decision-making authority has been a need to share subsidiary ownership of some facilities because of host country requirements, as in Venezuela. This in turn has reduced the flexibility of corporate decision making.

INTRODUCTION

Control questions facing all companies include:

- Where are decisions made?
- How can the firm optimize globally?
- How can country units report to headquarters?

International companies take a wide variety of approaches in managing their foreign operations. Many of the problems that they face nevertheless are very similar. The Nestlé case illustrates concerns of where decisions should be made, how country operations should report to headquarters, and how to optimize on a global basis. Behind each of those concerns is a more basic one—that of control. The discussion in this chapter is broader than simply the ownership of sufficient voting shares to direct company policies. **Control** is the planning, implementation, evaluation, and correction of performance in order to ensure that organizational objectives are achieved. Several factors make the control process more difficult internationally:

Foreign control is usually more difficult because of:

- Distance: it takes more time and expense to communicate
- Diversity: country differences make it hard to compare
- Uncontrollables: more outside stockholders and governmental dictates
- Certainty: data problems, rapid changes

1. *Distance.* Both the geographic and cultural distance separating countries will increase the time, expense, and possibility of error in cross-national communications. Inquiries and control systems may not be understood fully by subsidiary managers, and the time and expense of gaining verification may very well hinder the functioning of the control systems.

2. *Diversity.* Throughout most of the text, we have shown the need for firms to adjust operations to find the unique situations encountered in each country in which the international firm has operations. When market size, type of competition, product, labor cost, currency, and a host of other factors differentiate operations from one country to another, the task of evaluating performances or setting standards to correct or improve business functions is extremely complicated.

3. *Uncontrollables.* Performance evaluation is of little importance to control unless there is some means of attaining corrective action. The fact that many foreign operations must contend (1) with the dictates of outside stockholders, whose objectives may be somewhat different from those of the parent, and (2) with governmental regulations over which the firm has no short-term influence for change means that corrective action may be minimal.[2]

4. *Degree of certainty.* Control implies setting goals and developing plans to meet the goals. Economic and industry data are much less complete and accurate for some countries than for others. Furthermore, political and economic conditions are subject to rapid change in some locales. These situations impede the setting of plans, especially long-range ones, and reduce the certainty of results from the implementation of the plans.

Although these factors make control more difficult in the international context, companies do follow procedural and structural practices in an effort to ensure that foreign operations comply with overall corporate goals and philosophies. This chapter discusses seven aspects of the international control process: (1) location of decision making, (2) organizational structure; (3) planning; (4) business research; (5) corporate culture; (6) reporting techniques; and (7) some special situations.

LOCATION OF DECISION MAKING

Centralization implies higher level decisions, especially above the country level.

Any firm must determine where decisions will be made on such diverse questions as product policy, the acquisition of funds, and placement of liquid assets. The higher within the organization that decisions are made, the more they are considered to be **centralized;** the lower, the more they are **decentralized.** The centralization-decentralization question may be addressed from the standpoint of the company as a whole or merely some part of it, such as within a particular subsidiary operation. This discussion will not cover the latter; rather, it will highlight the relationship of the country level operations to other parts of the international company, such as to headquarters, regional offices, or to other subsidiaries. For purposes of this discussion, decisions made at the foreign subsidiary level are considered to be decentralized, whereas decisions made above the foreign subsidiary level are termed centralized. There are opposing pressures for centralization and decentralization; consequently, policies must be adapted to the firm's unique situation.

Complete centralization and decentralization may be thought of as the extremes. In actuality, companies neither centralize nor decentralize all decisions; instead, they vary policies according to the type of question and the particular circumstances involved. The location of decision making may vary within the same company by product, by function, and by country. In addition, actual decision making is seldom as drastic as it may appear on the surface. In other words, although a manager may have decision making authority, that manager may consult and reach consensus with other managers before exercising the authority. In spite of these differences and subtleties, the following section focuses on the rationale for locating decision control at either the corporate or the subsidiary level. Once these motivations are clear, it is easier to comprehend such elements as organization structure, planning, and evaluation, which parallel the basic centralization or decentralization philosophy.

Corporate Efficiency Factors

Firms must consider how long it takes to get help from headquarters in relation to how fast a decision must be made.

Cost and expediency. Although corporate personnel may be more experienced in advising or actually making certain decisions, the time and expense involved in centralization may not justify the so-called better advice. Many decisions cannot be put off for the lengthy period needed to transmit information from one country to another. Other decisions could not effectively be made without on-the-spot observation. To bring in corporate personnel may not be warranted.

The distance of foreign operations from headquarters is also a factor to consider. For U.S. subsidiaries in either Canada or Mexico, the time and cost of communications with the parent are low in comparison with being in a country such as the Philippines. The Philippine managers may be forced to make decisions on matters for which the Canadian and Mexican managers get corporate assistance.[3]

Decisions on moving goods or other resources are more likely to be made centrally.

Resource transference. Both product and production factors may be moved from a company's operations in one country to its facilities in another. The movement may be in the best interest of corporate goals, although individual subsidiaries may not do as well if resources are transferred. Decisions involving these external relationships usually are made centrally because they require information from all operating units and the ability to mesh the various data to achieve overall corporate objectives. While these external relationships may involve many different types of decisions, a few examples should suffice to explain the need for centralization.

Frequently, corporate profits may be improved by moving production factors—capital, personnel, or technology—from one subsidiary to another. First, without some central control point, reports would have to be disseminated from every unit to every other unit to determine the resource from one locale that could be used elsewhere. Second, if exports among subsidiaries are needed to maintain a continual production flow (e.g., vertical integration or interdependent components needed in the company's end product), centralized control may be required to assure this flow. Third, exports to nonaffiliated companies involve jurisdictional questions. For example, if a firm has manufacturing facilities in the United States, Venezuela, and West Germany, which one will export to South Africa? By answering that question centrally, the firm may avoid price competition among the subsidiaries that could result in reduced corporate income. Furthermore, a number of different factors can be considered, including production costs, transportation costs, tax rates, exchange controls, and capacity utilization.

What is best for the company globally may not be best for the country unit.

Economies and interrelationships through standardization. Even though worldwide uniformity of products, purchases, methods, and policies may not be best for an individual operation, the overall gain may be more than sufficient to overcome the individual country losses. Standardization of machinery used in the production process, for example, may result in a more favorable purchasing price for the firm as a whole because of quantity discounts. This also may bring savings in the training of mechanics, in maintaining manuals, and in carrying inventories of spare parts. The firm may consider economies in almost any type of corporate activity, such as advertising programs, R&D, and purchase of group insurances. Uniformity of products also gives a firm greater flexibility in filling orders when supply problems arise because of strikes, disasters, or sudden increases in demand. Production simply can be expanded in one country to meet shortages elsewhere.

Another argument for adhering to like policies globally is to ensure that foreign operations do not veer so drastically from the overall line or method of business that control is completely lost. If units in different countries alter products, policies, and methods even gradually but in different directions, the eventual diversity may be so great that economies are no longer possible and the personnel, products, and ideas can no longer be interchanged easily.

Increasingly, the people with whom a firm must deal (governmental officials, employees, suppliers, consumers, and the general public) are aware of what that firm does in every country in which it operates. Concessions that have been easily granted in one country may then be demanded in other countries, where they are not afforded as easily. Suppose that, for public relations purposes, the management in one country decided to give preferential prices to the government and established a profit-sharing plan for employees. If the governmental officials and employees in a second country were to ask for similar treatment, the result may be reduced profits or poor public relations.

Even internal pricing and product decisions can affect demand in other countries. With the growing mobility of consumers, especially industrial consumers, a good or bad experience with a product in one country eventually may affect sales elsewhere. This is especially true if industrial consumers themselves want uniformity in their end products. If prices differ substantially among countries, consumers even may find they can import more cheaply than buying locally.

Global competitive strategies. A company needs to determine whether it is better off trying to emphasize country-by-country competitive positions or an integrated global one. In addition to the question of standardized versus differentiated products among countries, the firm must consider a number of other factors. One is whether large-scale production of components and finished goods can be exported so that costs can be reduced to buyers in various countries. The nature of the production process, transportation costs, and government import restrictions all affect the production integration advantages.

The present and potential existence of global customers and/or competitors also may dictate decisions to improve global performance at the expense of a particular country's operations. Price concessions to an automobile manufacturer in Brazil, for example, may help gain business for the supplier in other countries where the buyer manufactures automobiles. A company also may attack a competitor by producing and selling where that competitor gains its major resources to compete globally.

Competence Arguments

Since a condition for delegating authority is the belief that those selected will act responsibly, the perception of local managers' competence will determine to a great extent the courses of action they can pursue. Although there are rational factors affecting the belief of relative capability, it has been noted that too often unrealistic attitudes lead to excessive control delegated to either the corporate or subsidiary managers. Unrealistic attitudes include, say, a belief that only the on-the-spot person knows the situation well enough to make a decision or a perception that corporate managers are the only individuals capable of handling decisions.

The more different the foreign environment is from the home country, the more delegation occurs. The more confidence there is in foreign managers, the more delegation occurs.

Calibre and local conditions. Since the local management is usually in a much better position to know what will and will not work locally, they are normally given greater latitude when local conditions are perceived as quite different from the home country's operations. For example, the corporate managers of a U.S. company will probably feel more competent about dictating practices to a Canadian than to a Mexican subsidiary, since the former is presumed to parallel successful U.S. operations more closely. Yet local conditions may be more important for some functions than others. Nestlé, for example, decentralizes most marketing decisions because they need to be adjusted to local needs; however, foreign exchange decisions are centralized because of the importance of examining global conditions.

Other things would seem to dictate differences in approaches to different local managers. Factors that would appear to favor decentralization are: when the local management team is large rather than lean, when local managers have had a long time with the company, and when they have developed a successful track record. These factors seem to dictate advantages in differentiating the location of decision making for operations in different countries.[4]

The more uniform the product is globally, the more centralization occurs.

Product factors. The product itself may determine the relative competence of the centralized staff versus the local managers. For technically sophisticated products there is little need for local adaptations; consequently, at least for marketing policy, decisions may be made that apply to a very broad spectrum of countries. A good contrast is between Nestlé's food products, which depend on geographic differentiation, and GE's power generation and jet engine businesses, which are big-ticket products requiring very little adaptation to local needs. Food products lend themselves much more to decentralization than big-ticket products do. Also many products are first introduced in the largest market and later introduced to smaller markets when the country of original entry is in a later stage of the product life cycle. In such instances the centralized staff often asserts control in order to ensure that the same mistakes are not repeated in more than one country. If product technology changes rapidly, usually there is a greater need for headquarters involvement than if the product technology is stable for a long period of time.

The larger the total foreign operations are, the more likely headquarters has specialized staff with international expertise. The larger the operations are in a given country, the more likely that country has specialized staff.

Time and size variables. Usually, the longer a company operates in overseas markets, the larger its foreign sales and the greater experience it has in dealing with foreign problems. The size of total foreign operations as well as the size of operations in individual foreign countries both exert influence on the location of decision making. Studies of financial as well as marketing decisions have found that increased centralization is feasible when a corporate staff that is large enough and qualified enough has developed.[5] The company with very limited foreign operations cannot afford this centralized expertise and must therefore delegate decisions to the operating managers abroad. However, if the specific foreign country operation is very large, then that operation can afford to have its own specialized staff personnel and be treated differently than operations in some of the smaller countries.

At the advanced stage, both headquarters and subsidiary management have country knowledge and global view.

Firms often go through stages of centralization-decentralization. At an early period they tend to be decentralized because headquarters management does not feel confident about assessing situations abroad. Later, however, the headquarters personnel take more control as they gain capabilities and experience and strive to achieve global objectives. Finally, the decision making often becomes more decentralized again and shared as local managers learn to understand the corporate as well as the local perspective.[6]

Bigger decisions are made at headquarters.

Importance of the decision. Any discussion of authority location must consider the importance of the particular decisions. The question sometimes asked is, "How much can be lost through a bad decision?" The greater the potential loss, the higher in the organization the level of control usually is. In the case of marketing decisions, for example, the local autonomy over product design is not nearly as prevalent as over advertising, pricing, and distribution. Product design generally necessitates a considerably larger capital outlay than the other functions; consequently, the potential loss through a wrong decision is higher. Furthermore, advertising approaches, pricing, and distribution decisions may be more easily reversed if an error in judgment is made. Rather than delineation of the type of decision that can be made at the subsidiary level, limits may be set instead on expenditure amount, thus allowing local autonomy on small outlays while requiring corporate approval on larger transactions.

Miscellaneous Considerations

Subsidiary inputs help global strategy through:

- Information
- Commitment.

Using subsidiaries effectively. The development of standardized practices does not imply that headquarters should generate all the information necessary for decision making. In fact, if the subsidiaries' viewpoints are ignored, the company may not develop the best types of cross-national or standardized programs. Furthermore, good local managers may gravitate to other firms where they feel they can play a more important role. Procter & Gamble (P&G), for example, had allowed its European country operations nearly total autonomy in adapting technology, products, and marketing approaches. In order to capture Europewide scale economies, P&G put one office in charge of the strategy for all of Europe, ignoring local knowledge, underutilizing subsidiary strength, and demotivating subsidiary managers. P&G has since moved to greater standardization with other brand management activities; however, this has been led by teams representing the subsidiary operations. In another case EMI, a U.K. based company, used feedback only from the U.K. market to determine how its central laboratory would seek to improve its CAT scanners—through better image resolution. This ignored the larger U.S. market where a different improvement, shorter scan times, was preferred. When GE came out with a shorter scan time, it captured the U.S. market and got better scale economies than EMI. EMI started losing money and had to accept a takeover bid.[7]

Some operations are isolated from the global situation.

National rather than international strategies. Although the development of a global strategy offers many advantages, there are circumstances in which subsidiaries cannot reasonably be brought into this scheme. This occurs, for example, in products associated with uniquely national taste preferences.[8] In other situations, subsidiaries may be prevented from being a full part of a global network because governmental protectionism isolates them from competitive threats.[9] In such situations, corporate strategic control may be less appropriate than national control.

Centralization may hurt local management because they:

- Cannot perform as well
- Do not get training through more responsibility.

Local performance considerations. Although some decisions clearly can be made efficiently at the corporate level, this technical efficiency must be weighted against morale problems created from taking responsibility away from the local management team. When local managers are prevented from acting in the best interest of their own operation, they tend to think, "I could have done better, but corporate management would not let me." These managers may lose commitment to their jobs and may not gain the experience needed to move into jobs of even greater responsibility. Lack of commitment may be overcome through development of a reward system that does not penalize managers for decisions that are outside of their control. In fact, a compensation system that rewards local managers partially on the basis of the corporation's total worldwide performance may enhance the development of global thinking at each country level.

LDCs argue that centralization keeps them subservient.

Dependency. Many critics within the LDCs have contended that the centralization of decision making by MNEs is leading to an ever-increasing movement of management and technical functions to the home country, leaving the menial and low-skilled jobs in the LDCs. The critics recall colonial eras in which their own people were forbidden responsible positions and depended on the colonial powers for the control of their destinities.[10] They

Decentralization is:

- More likely on adaptive R&D
- May entice highly skilled foreigners.

have been particularly disparaging about the fact that very little R&D by MNEs is done outside their home countries; of that portion done outside, almost all is in other industrial countries.[11]

This presents dilemmas for MNEs. There are some potent arguments for centralizing most R&D in home countries, such as the availability of large numbers of people to work directly for the company, the proximity to private research organizations and universities doing related work, and the general advantages of centralized authority for less duplication of efforts.[12]

Recall that, in the Nestlé case, new product R&D was done in Switzerland to reduce duplication and to be close to the strategic planners who projected product needs further into the future than would country managers, who were more concerned with day-to-day operations. Nestlé did allow country areas the freedom to conduct adaptive R&D but controlled this carefully by requiring corporate approval of the adaptations. Thus even when the corporation allows adaptive or new product R&D to be carried out abroad, the corporate management may exert substantial influence on it. Studies show that MNEs with substantial R&D outside the home country seldom allow the foreign affiliate complete autonomy. The corporate management may allocate budgets, approve plans, and offer suggestions. At the same time there may be substantial input from affiliates for R&D conducted centrally.[13]

By giving groups of overseas employees a great deal of autonomy in certain areas, an international company may be able to attract a high calibre of personnel who might not wish to work in the firm's home country. For example, IBM scientists at its small Zurich laboratory won the Nobel prize for physics in both 1986 and 1987. There are many ways that certain subsidiaries may be given autonomy over certain activities, such as the development of a specific product, a specific technology, or the conduct of certain market testing. Even very small subsidiaries may be used to collect valuable competitive and technical information.[14]

ORGANIZATIONAL STRUCTURE

As a firm develops international business activities, its corporate structure must adapt to the changing environment in order to accommodate foreign operations effectively. The organizational structure that emerges will depend on many factors, including the location and type of foreign facilities, the impact of international operations on total corporate performance, the nature of assets employed in pursuit of business abroad, and the time horizons for achieving international and total corporate goals.

Firms must establish legal and organizational structures at home and abroad to meet company objectives. Within each foreign country these arrangements may differ because of the unique nature of activities and environmental requirements. Layered above the country organizations are additional structures that coordinate activities in more than one country. The form, method, and location of operational units at home and abroad will affect taxes, expenses, and control. Consequently, organizational structure has an important effect on the fulfillment of corporate objectives.

Level of Importance

The larger the foreign operations, the higher they report in the structure.

The more important the specific foreign operations are to total corporate performance, the higher the corporate level to which these units should report. The organizational structure or reporting system therefore should change over time to parallel a company's increased involvement in foreign activities.

At one end of the spectrum is the firm that merely exports temporary surpluses through a middleman who takes title and handles all the export details. Clearly, in this situation few people in the firm are concerned with the conduct of the business. Since no personnel are either overseas or engaged in the export arrangement, there is no need for the firm to devise new personnel policies or training programs. Because the title to goods changes hands in the home country, there are no foreign legal or tax matters to consider. Also, since payment is effected in the home currency, there are no problems of transferring funds or evaluating country-by-country performance. Finally, because no attempt is made to increase foreign sales, the firm does not require new marketing programs. The entire operation is apt to be so insignificant to total corporate performance that top-level management is concerned very little with such transactions. The duties may be handled by anyone in the organization who knows enough and has time to discern whether or not orders can be filled. In this situation, foreign activities should be handled at a low level in the corporate hierarchy.

At the other end of the spectrum is the firm that has passed through intermediate stages and now owns and manages foreign manufacturing and sales facilities. Every functional and advisory group within the company undoubtedly will be involved in the establishment and direction of the facilities. Since sales, investments, and profits are now a more significant part of the corporate total, people very high in the corporate hierarchy are affected by the foreign operations.

Integrated versus Separate International Activities

All of a company's international activities may be grouped together (e.g., international department or division) or gathered by the product, function, or geographic structure the company relies on domestically. Figure 17.1 shows simplified examples of different approaches to the placement of foreign activity within the organizational structure; most companies broadly fit one of these categories.

International division:

- Creates critical international mass
- May have problem of getting resources from domestic divisions.

International division. The separation of international activities allows for specialized personnel to handle such diverse matters as export documentation, foreign exchange transactions, and relations with foreign governments. By combining all international operations, the international activities constitute a large enough critical mass to wield power within the organization. When separated among product or functional units, these activities may be so small in comparison to domestic business that the firm gives little attention to their development. On the other hand, this separation may necessitate dependence of the international division on the domestic divisions for product, personnel, technology, and other resources. Since managers in the domestic divisions are evaluated against domestic performance standards, they may withhold their best resources from the international group in order to improve their own performance.

Part A of Fig. 17.1 is an example of separating international operations. Although this structure is not popular among European multinational firms, it is very common among those based in the United States.[15] One of the apparent causes for the difference is that U.S. firms are typically much more dependent on the domestic market than are European firms; therefore, the international division allows U.S. firms to gain the "critical mass" discussed above.

Worldwide product division is popular among diverse product firms.

Product division. Parts B, C, and D in Fig. 17.1 are types of international operations that are integrated rather than handled separately. The product organization (B) is particularly popular among companies that operate within highly diverse product groups, especially those that have become diverse primarily through acquisitions. Since the product groups may have little in common, even domestically, the groups may be highly independent of each other. Note that different subsidiaries within the same foreign country will report to different groups at headquarters.

Area division is popular when foreign operations are large and are not dominated by a single country or region.

Geographic (area) division. The geographic organization, part C in Fig. 17.1, is used primarily by firms with very large foreign operations, not dominated by a single country or area. This structure is found more commonly among European than U.S. MNEs because of the dominance of the U.S. domestic market. Recall that Nestlé can use this structure because no one region dominates its operations.

Functional division is popular among extractive companies.

Functional division. The functional organization, part D in Fig. 17.1, is popular among extractive companies (such as those involved in oil or bauxite extraction) because of their very homogenous products for which production and marketing methods are relatively undifferentiated from one country to another.

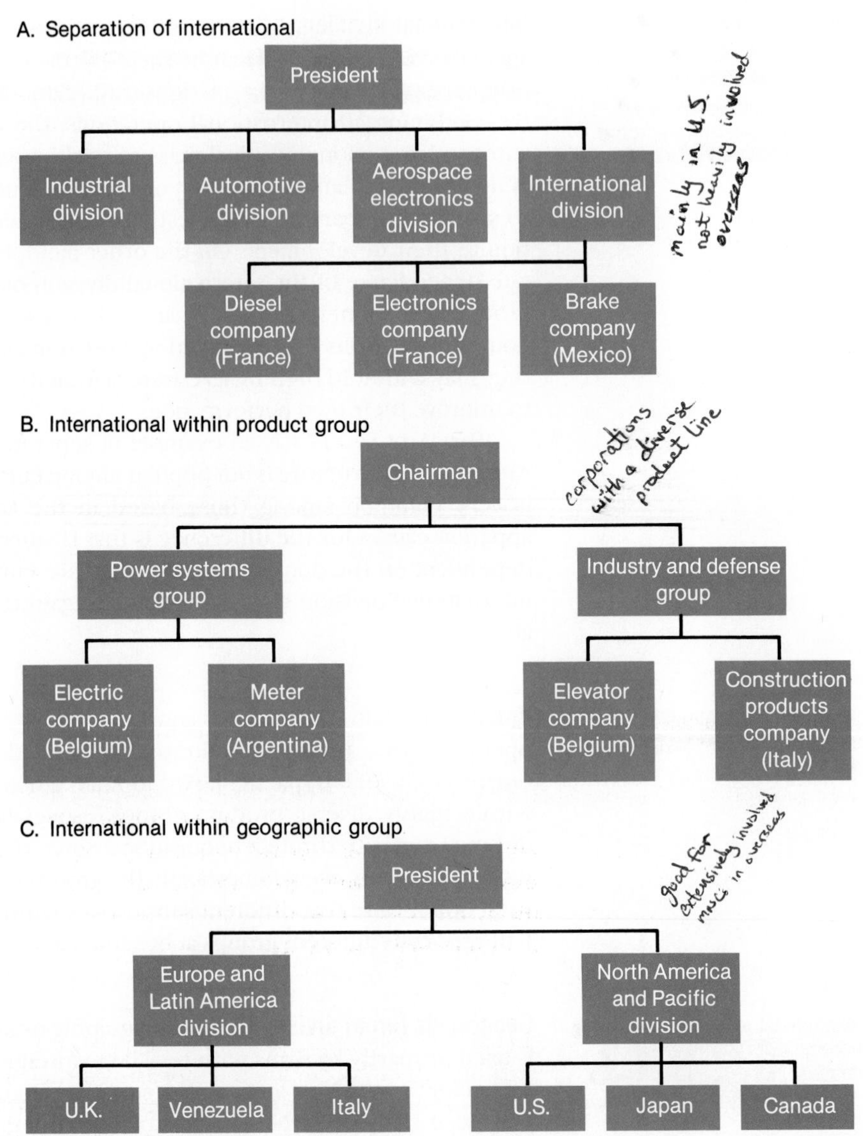

Figure 17.1

Placement of International Activities within the Organizational Structure

D. International within functional area

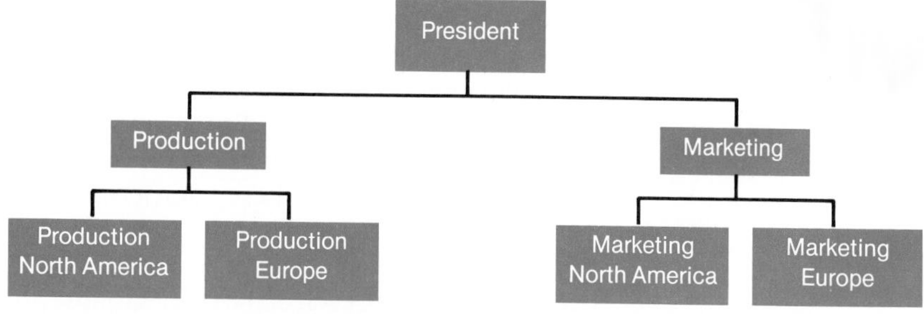

E. International with matrix

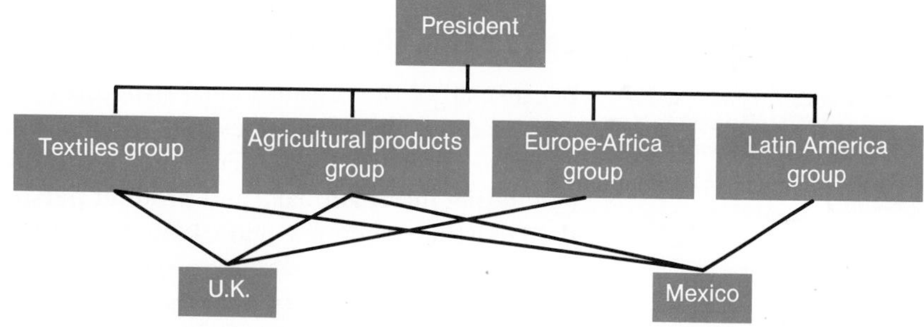

Figure 17.1 (continued)

Matrix gives product, function, and area an even focus.

Matrix. Because of the problems inherent either in integrating or separating foreign operations, some firms are moving toward matrix organizations, E in Fig. 17.1. In these a subsidiary reports to more than one group (product, function, and area). The theory is that, since each group shares responsibility over foreign operations, each group will depend on the others. The groups will become more interdependent, will exchange information, and ultimately take strategic global perspectives as they seek to exchange resources with other groups. For example, product group managers must compete so that R&D personnel responsible to a functional group are assigned to the development of technologies that fall within their product domain. The same product group managers must compete as well to see that area managers put sufficient emphasis on their lines. Not only are product groups competing, the functional and geographic areas also must strive to draw upon resources held by others in the matrix.

Although a matrix form requires that all major perspectives be represented in strategic decision making, this form of organization is not without drawbacks. One of the problems is that groups and coalitions inevitably compete for scarce resources, and a management decision must be made above the group level on how to allocate the resources when lower-level managers fail to reach an agreement. Such elements as faith in a specific executive or business group may result in more decisions being made in favor of those components.[16] As others in the organization see this occurring, they may perceive that the locus of relative power lies with a certain individual or group, which may lead managers in turn to divert most of their energies toward the activities that are perceived as most likely to be accepted, thus perpetuating the difference in relative power. This may not represent the areas that would be the firm's best strategic choices on a global basis. Consequently, some of the advantages sought in a matrix organization may be diminished because of these interpersonal relationships. A number of alternatives may help to alleviate this problem, including the transfer of individuals among groups and the development of additional reporting and control systems reflecting each of the three groups (product, function, and area) on a global basis. However, these alternatives are not without costs.

Coordinating Mechanisms

Rather than changing overall structure, many companies are finding mechanisms to pull product, function, and area together.

Because all of the organizational structures just described have advantages and disadvantages, companies in recent years have developed organizational mechanisms to pull together some of the diverse functional, geographic (including international), and product perspectives without abandoning their existing structures. These have included the strengthening of corporate staffs so that people with line responsibilities are required to listen to different viewpoints whether they take advice or not; the use of more management rotation such as between line and staff and domestic and international in order to break down parochial views; the placement of international and domestic personnel in closer proximity to each other; and the establishment of liaisons among different subsidiaries within the same country so that different product groups can get combined action within an area. Companies also use staff departments (e.g., legal or personnel) to centralize functions common to more than one subsidiary. At Heinz, for instance, one expatriate-transfer-and-compensation policy is used by all the geographic divisions thus minimizing the duplication of effort.[17]

Locating International Headquarters

Locating headquarters staff in "international" center

- Saves travel time
- Provides access to international services.

Once a company develops substantial foreign operations, there may be advantages in shifting part of the headquarters staff to a new location.[18] One reason is to minimize communications and travel expense and time between the staff group and the foreign operations. Another is to be near specialized private and public institutions such as banks, factoring firms, insurance groups, public accountants, freight forwarders, customs brokers, and consular offices, which handle certain international functions. Finally, firms need to hire bilingual or multilingual personnel as well as export documentation people. The international transportation, institutions, and specialized personnel are concentrated in a few locales. For this reason, New York is by far the most popular international headquarters location for U.S. companies that maintain corporate headquarters elsewhere. If foreign operations are sufficient, staff may be segmented on a regional basis. Many U.S. firms maintain Latin American regional offices in Miami, and many have a European headquarters somewhere in Europe.

As transportation and communications have become faster and cheaper, some of the advantages of locating an international group apart from headquarters have lessened. This, when coupled with moves to seek greater integration of international and domestic operations, has meant that more of the international operations are being relocated near the corporate headquarters.

PLANNING

Firms must mesh objectives with internal and external constraints and set means to implement, monitor, and correct.

Throughout this text we have emphasized the firm's need to adapt its unique resources and objectives to the different and changing foreign situations. This is the essence of **planning.** Without planning, it is only by luck that a company picks the best order and method of expansion by country. Without planning, it is again by chance that a company sets policies and practices in a given locale that result in the desired performance. Since planning has been both implicitly and explicitly discussed already, this section presents merely an overview of the process.

The Process

Figure 17.2 indicates that planning must involve the meshing of objectives with the internal and external environment. The details in each planning section include items discussed in the environmental and operational sections of this text. Note that the first step is a self-analysis of internal resources and constraints on the total corporation along with the environmental factors that affect each company differently. Only by taking this first step can a firm set the overall rationale for its international activities. For instance, a company faced with rising domestic costs and expanded competition from imports may validly pursue one of several objectives such as cost reduction, acquisition of resources the competition needs, or diversification into new markets or products. The analysis of the internal resources will help to determine which of these objectives is feasible and most important and aid in selecting alternatives.

Since each country in which the firm is operating or contemplating operations also is unique, the local analysis also will have to be made before the final alternatives can be examined fully. For instance, local marketing factors will determine which product strategies can be considered. Priorities must be set among alternatives so that programs may be added easily or deleted as resource availability or situations change. A company may, for example, prefer and plan to remit dividends from one of its foreign subsidi-

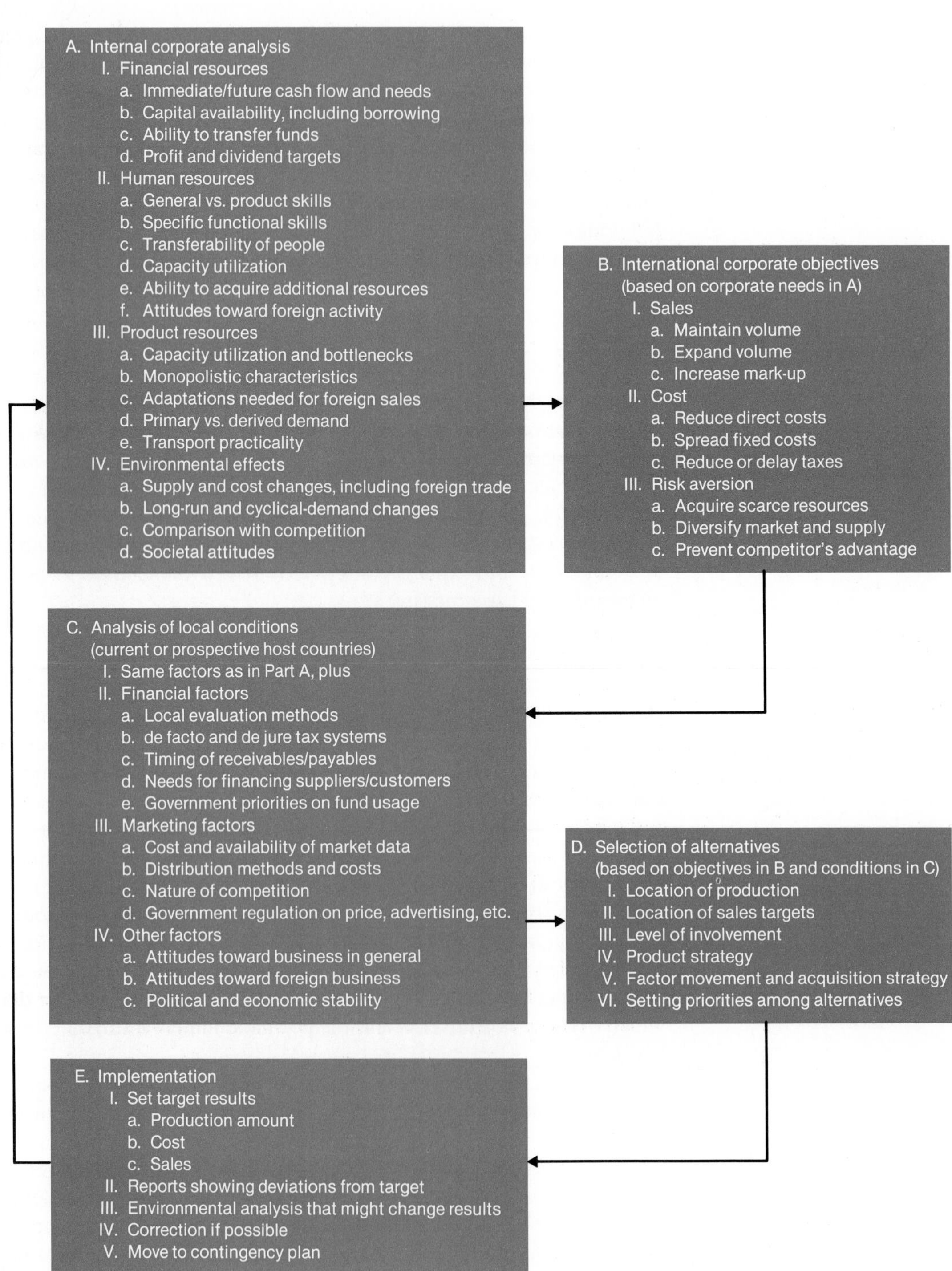

A. Internal corporate analysis
I. Financial resources
a. Immediate/future cash flow and needs
b. Capital availability, including borrowing
c. Ability to transfer funds
d. Profit and dividend targets
II. Human resources
a. General vs. product skills
b. Specific functional skills
c. Transferability of people
d. Capacity utilization
e. Ability to acquire additional resources
f. Attitudes toward foreign activity
III. Product resources
a. Capacity utilization and bottlenecks
b. Monopolistic characteristics
c. Adaptations needed for foreign sales
d. Primary vs. derived demand
e. Transport practicality
IV. Environmental effects
a. Supply and cost changes, including foreign trade
b. Long-run and cyclical-demand changes
c. Comparison with competition
d. Societal attitudes
B. International corporate objectives
(based on corporate needs in A)
I. Sales
a. Maintain volume
b. Expand volume
c. Increase mark-up
II. Cost
a. Reduce direct costs
b. Spread fixed costs
c. Reduce or delay taxes
III. Risk aversion
a. Acquire scarce resources
b. Diversify market and supply
c. Prevent competitor's advantage
C. Analysis of local conditions
(current or prospective host countries)
I. Same factors as in Part A, plus
II. Financial factors
a. Local evaluation methods
b. de facto and de jure tax systems
c. Timing of receivables/payables
d. Needs for financing suppliers/customers
e. Government priorities on fund usage
III. Marketing factors
a. Cost and availability of market data
b. Distribution methods and costs
c. Nature of competition
d. Government regulation on price, advertising, etc.
IV. Other factors
a. Attitudes toward business in general
b. Attitudes toward foreign business
c. Political and economic stability
D. Selection of alternatives
(based on objectives in B and conditions in C)
I. Location of production
II. Location of sales targets
III. Level of involvement
IV. Product strategy
V. Factor movement and acquisition strategy
VI. Setting priorities among alternatives
E. Implementation
I. Set target results
a. Production amount
b. Cost
c. Sales
II. Reports showing deviations from target
III. Environmental analysis that might change results
IV. Correction if possible
V. Move to contingency plan

Figure 17.2
International Planning Process

aries back to the parent; however, this may not be possible. Management also should consider what it will do with earnings if exchange controls are put into effect. Furthermore, what alternatives will then exist for the parent, which has to do without the funds? It may be necessary to borrow more at home, remit more from other subsidiaries, forego domestic expansion, or forego domestic dividends. Without priorities, the firm may have to make hurried decisions to fulfill company objectives even partially.

Finally, very specific objectives should be set for each operating unit, along with ways of measuring both deviations from the plan and conditions that may cause a deviation. Through timely evaluation, management may take corrective actions or at least move to contingency means to achieve the objectives. Evaluation methods are discussed later in the chapter.

A distinction must be made between operating plans and strategic plans. Strategic plans are longer term and involve major commitments depending on which businesses the company will be in and where. Although input for a strategic plan may come from all parts of the organization, only at a corporate level can allocations be made to implement overall planned changes in geographic and product policies. Also it is usual for those of the corporate staff to be the primary people concerned with making strategic plans, since they have information on the firm's worldwide activities, competition, and trends.

Problems

The firm's international operations have more complexity and uncertainty than the domestic ones.

The greater the amount of uncertainty, the more difficult it is to plan. Generally it is agreed that operations in the international sphere involve more uncertainty than those in the domestic one because of the greater complexity of international operations.[19] One type of complexity is caused by the increase in the number of operating environments; another is due to different requirements for different markets in terms of task, because of different products and how they are made.[20]

Generally we would expect that greater complexity and uncertainty would lead to greater need and use for information.[21] However, there is substantial evidence that the higher the uncertainty, the lower the amount of environmental scanning to collect information.[22] This may be due to the relative inaccessibility of accurate information internationally.

BUSINESS RESEARCH

Information is needed at all levels of control.

Business research is undertaken to reduce uncertainties in the decision process, to expand or narrow the alternatives under consideration, and to assess the merits of existing programs. The reduction of uncertainty would include attempts to answer such questions as: Is there a market for the product? Can qualified personnel be hired? Will the economic and political climate allow for a reasonable certainty of operations? Alternatives may be expanding by asking, "Where are possible new sources of funds or sales?" or narrowed by ascertaining, "Where among the alternatives would operating costs be lowest?" Evaluation and control is improved by assessing present and past performance: Is the distributor servicing sufficient accounts? What is our market share? Clearly, there is a myriad of details that, if ascertained, would be useful in meeting the firm's objectives.

How Much Research?

Companies should compare cost of information versus value.

A company can seldom if ever gain all of the information its managers would like. This is due partially to time constraints, since markets or raw materials may need to be secured before competitors gain control of them. Furthermore, contracts that call for bids or proposals usually have deadlines. The cost of information is another factor. The greater area to be considered by a multinational company, of course, amplifies the number of alternatives and complexities. Therefore it is useful to limit extensive information gathering to those projects that seemingly have the highest potential. One method is to estimate the costs of data collection along with the probable payoff from the data in terms of revenue gains or cost savings. In this way a company may prioritize research projects on the basis of expected return from the costs of the collection.

Problems in Data

The lack, obsolesence, and inaccuracy of data on many countries make much research difficult and expensive to undertake. In some countries, such as the United States, the government collects very detailed demographic and purchasing data, which is available very cheaply to any firm or individual. (But in the United States, some economists estimate that GNP figures may be understated by as much as 15 percent; and the Census Bureau official in charge of overseeing the 1980 count was relieved of his duties because of allegations that too many millions of people were not being counted properly.)[23] Using samples based on available information, a firm can draw fairly accurate inferences concerning market segment sizes and locations, at least within broad categories. Also in the United States the fact that so many firms are publicly owned and required to disclose considerable operating information is an advantage in learning competitors' strengths and weaknesses. Furthermore, firms may rely on a multitude of behavioral studies dealing with U.S. consumer preferences and experience. With this available information a firm can devise questionnaires or get acknowledgments from demonstrations that reflect predictable responses. Contrast this situation to that in a country whose basic census, national income accounts, and foreign trade figures are suspect, and where no data are collected on consumer expenditures. In such countries, business is conducted in a veil of secrecy, consumer buying behavior is speculated upon, and middlemen are reluctant to answer questions. Here, expensive primary research may be required before meaningful samples and questions can be developed. (The reasons for the problems in international data are discussed in the Appendix at the end of this chapter.)

External Sources of Information

Specificity and cost of information vary by source.

The number of organizations as well as publications that deal in whole or in part with information on international business is too large to explore in depth here. But in general the main sources are firms that make a living from supplying information, firms that would like to supply services connected with the conduct of international business, governmental agencies, and international organizations.

Individualized reports. In almost any country there are market research and business consulting firms that will conduct studies for a fee. Naturally, the quality and cost of these studies vary widely. Generally, this is the most costly information source because the individualized nature of the study restricts proration among a number of firms. However, the fact that the client can specify the information wanted often makes the expense worthwhile.

Specialized studies. Some research organizations prepare fairly specific studies and then sell them to any interested firm at a cost much lower than for individualized studies. The studies sometimes are printed as directories of firms operating in a given locale, perhaps with financial or other information about the firms. Or they also may be about business in certain locales of the world, such as Brazil; forms of business, such as licensing; or specific products, such as baby food. They may combine any of these elements as well: For example, a title could well be "The Market for Imported Auto Parts in West Germany."

Service firms. Most firms that serve international clients, such as banks, transportation agencies, and accounting firms, publish reports that are available to potential clients. These reports usually are geared toward either the conduct of business in a given area or some specific subject of general interest, such as tax or trademark legislation. Since these are intended to reach a wide market of firms, they usually lack the specificity a firm would like for making a final decision, but much of the data give useful background information. Some of these organizations also are helpful in giving informal opinions about such things as the reputation of possible business associates and the names of people to contact. Management also may discern useful information from other companies operating in a given locale.

Governmental agencies. Governments are another source of information. Statistical reports on many topics vary in the quantity and quality from country to country. When a government or governmental agency has an interest in stimulating foreign business activity, the amount and type of information may be substantial. For example, the U.S. Department of Commerce not only compiles such basic data as news and regulations on individual countries, but will also help set up appointments with businesspeople in foreign countries.

International organizations and agencies. Numerous organizations and agencies are supported by more than one country, such as the United Nations, the International Monetary Fund, the Organization for Economic Cooperation and Development, and the European Community. All of these organizations have large research staffs that compile basic statistics as well as reports and recommendations concerning common trends and problems. Many of the international development banks even will help finance investment feasibility studies.

Trade associations. Many product lines have trade associations that collect, evaluate, and disseminate a wide variety of data dealing with technical and competitive factors in the industry. Much of this information is available in their trade journals whereas other data may or may not be made available to nonmembers.

Information service companies. A number of companies, such as Lockheed Dialog, have information-retrieval services that typically maintain data bases from hundreds of different sources, including many of those just described. For a fee, a firm can access these computerized data by telephone modem and arrange for an immediate printout of studies of interest.

Internal Generation

International firms themselves may have to conduct many studies abroad. Sometimes the research may consist of no more than observing keenly and asking many questions. Investigators can see what kind of merchandise is available, who is buying and where, and uncover the hidden distribution points and competition. In some countries, for example, the competition for ready-made clothes may be from seamstresses in private homes rather than from retailers. The competition for vacuum cleaners may be in the form of servants who clean with mops rather than from other electrical appliance manufacturers. Surreptitiously sold contraband may compete with locally produced goods. Traditional analysis would not reveal such matters. In many countries, even bankers have to rely more on clients' reputations than on their financial statements. Shrewd questioning may yield very interesting results.

Firms frequently set certain minimum criteria on which to base a decision. If a company regards a total market of 35 million as satisfactory, it is fruitless to spend the time and money on determining where within a range of 90 to 100 million the market actually lies.

Often a firm must be extremely imaginative, extremely observant, or both. A soft drink manufacturer wanted to determine the market share it held vis-à-vis its competitors in Mexico. Attempts to make estimates from the points of distribution as management would do at home were futile because of the extremely widespread distribution. The manufacturer hit upon two alternatives, both of which turned out to be feasible: The manufacturer of bottle caps was willing to reveal how many caps were sold to each client; and customs supplied data on the volume of imports of soft drink concentrate used by each of the competitors.

CORPORATE CULTURE

People trained at headquarters are more likely to think like headquarters personnel.

Any corporation has certain common values for employees. These constitute the **corporate culture** and form a control mechanism that is implicit and which helps enforce the explicit bureaucratic control mechanisms that the firm has in place.[24] International firms have more difficulty relying on the corporate culture for control because managers from different countries have different norms of values pertaining to the management of operations. Nevertheless, many firms seek to enhance a worldwide corporate culture by bringing managers from different countries into closer contact with each other. For instance, the degree of control imposed by corporate headquarters on the selection of top managers for foreign subsidiaries may dictate to a great extent how much formal control over the subsidiaries' operations the corporate personnel feel is necessary. The use of parent country nationals in the subsidiary management, or even determining the standards of selection and training, may be perceived as a means of assuring primary loyalty to the corporate rather than subsidiary culture.[25] This may be effective even if the operations are not wholly owned or whether the parent requires long-range planning from the subsidiaries.[26] Frequent transfers of managers among foreign operations develops increased knowledge and commitment so that fewer procedures, less hierarchical communication, and less surveillance are needed.[27]

REPORTS

Need for Reports

Reports must be timely in order to allow firms to respond to them.

Headquarters needs timely reports from all operating units of an international firm so that management can allocate resources properly, correct plans, and reward personnel. First, the decisions on the use of capital, personnel, and technology are almost continuous; consequently, reports must be frequent and show recent situations so that these resources are put to the best of use. Second, plans need to be updated in order to be realistic and to assure that there is a high probability of meeting desired objectives. Feedback of both results and conditions that might affect results are essential so that corrective action, whether in the form of new strategies to meet objectives or in the form of alteration of objectives, may be undertaken. Finally, reports are needed in order to evaluate the performance of personnel in the various operating units of the company. Not only will comparison of performance aid in determining who will receive the rewards of monetary compensation and advancement, but it also will help stimulate personnel to improve their own weaknesses.

The use of written reports is more important in an international than in a domestic setting because subsidiary managers have much less personal and oral contact with line and staff personnel above them. Thus corporate managers miss out on much of the informal communication that can tell them about the performance of the foreign operations.

Types of Systems

Reporting systems are intended first to evaluate operating units and second to evaluate management in units.

Most international firms use reporting systems for foreign operations that are similar to those they use domestically.[28] There are several reasons for this. If the systems have been effective domestically, management often believes that they will be effective internationally as well—particularly if home country management considers its know-how superior to that abroad. Next, there are economies through carrying over the same types of reports; the need to establish new types of reporting mechanisms is eliminated, and corporate management is already familiar with the system. Finally, like reports presumably allow management to compare one operation against another and consolidate the reports without as much fear that they have added "apples to oranges."

The main purpose of MNE's reporting systems is to assure adequate profitability by identifying deviations from plans that would indicate possible problem areas. This focus may be on short-term performance or on longer-term indicators that match the strategic thrust of the organization. The emphasis is on the evaluation of the subsidiary rather than evaluation of the subsidiary manager, although the profitability of the foreign unit is one of the important ingredients in the managerial evaluation.[29]

Not all information exchange is by formalized reports. Within many MNEs, certain members of the corporate staff travel more than 50 percent of their time in order to visit with subsidiaries. Although this may do much to alleviate misunderstandings, there are some inherent dangers if visits are not done properly. If, on one hand, corporate personnel visit the tropical subsidiaries only when there are blizzards at home, the personnel abroad may perceive the trips are mere boondoggles. If, on the other hand, subsidiary managers offer too many social activities and not enough analysis of operations, the corporate staff members may consider the trip a waste of time. Also, if visitors come only when the corporate level is upset about foreign operations, the overseas managers may always be overly defensive.

Reporting Problems

Firms should evaluate managers on things they can control, but there is disagreement on what is in their control.

Management versus subsidiary performance. There is general agreement that subsidiaries should be evaluated separately from the management within subsidiaries. This is so that managers are not penalized for conditions and occurrences outside their control. Beyond this agreement, however, there is a good deal of difference among firms in what they do and do not include in the managerial performance evaluation. For instance, some firms hold managers abroad responsible for gains or losses in currency translation whereas others do not. Most firms deduct interest expenses before measuring the profitability of foreign operations whereas many do not.[30] These are examples of environmental factors that some, but not all, companies consider to be outside the control of the local managers.

Another area of noncontrollables is when centralized decisions are made that will optimize the performance of the total corporation. A particular subsidiary may not do as well as if it had been left to operate independently. In fact, the normal profit center records may well obscure the importance that the subsidiary plays within the total corporate entity.

It is hard to compare countries through standard operating ratios.

Cost and accounting comparability. Different affiliate cost structures may prevent a meaningful comparison of operating results. For example, the percentage of direct labor to sales in one country may reasonably be much higher than in a subsidiary in another country if the former has low labor and high capital costs in relation to the latter. Different accounting practices can also create problems. Most international firms keep one set of books that are consistent with parent principles and another set to meet local reporting requirements.

Firms want higher return in high-risk countries but risks may be outside management's control.

Country risk. Recall from Chapter 16 that, when evaluating foreign investment possibilities, most companies set a higher minimum return to invest in high-risk countries. Having done this, firms logically would expect the performance within the high-risk countries to reflect the expected higher return. Most companies agree that such an analysis would be useful; however, they also agree that they know of no reasonable means of incorporating country risk into the performance evaluation. They feel that the incorporation would penalize managers in risky countries and make them responsible for something outside their control.[31]

Evaluative Measurements

A system that relies on a combination of measurements is more reliable.

Multiple measurements. Every evaluation measurement has shortcomings when applied internationally. Consequently, a system that relies on a number of different indicators may be preferable to one that relies too heavily on one measurement. Financial criteria tend to dominate the evaluation of foreign operations and their managers. Although many different ones are used, the most important for evaluating the operations are budget compared with profit, budget compared with sales, and return on investment. The most common financial criteria for management appraisal are budget compared to profit, budget compared to sales, and return on sales. Many nonfinancial criteria also are employed. The only one commonly given much weight in subsidiary evaluation is market share increase. Several nonfinancial criteria are important for evaluating the managers, though. These include market share increase, quality control, and relationship with the host government.[32]

Firms must evaluate actual budgets in relation to planned ones.

Budget concept. One way of overcoming the problems of evaluating performance is the budget, which can help the MNE differentiate between the worth of the subsidiary and the performance of subsidiary management. The budget should include the goals for each subsidiary that will help the MNE achieve an overall objective. As long as the subsidiary manager is working toward a budgeted goal rather than a measure such as return on investment, there will be fewer problems in dealing with inflation, exchange rate changes, and transfer prices. A further discussion of budget techniques, particularly as they relate to exchange rate changes, is presented in Chapter 19.

Planning Information Acquisitions

Management should reevaluate information needs periodically to keep costs down, assure that information is being used.

Thus far the discussion has centered on information needed to evaluate subsidiary and subsidiary management performance. Although this information is crucial, corporate management requires additional data. The information needs may be categorized as follows:

1. information generated by informal operations for centralized coordination, such as cash balances and needs;
2. information relating to external conditions, such as analyses of local political and economic conditions;
3. information for feedback from parent to local subsidiaries, such as R&D breakthroughs;
4. lateral information between related subsidiaries; and
5. external reporting needs.[33]

Since information needs are so broad, two problems for firms are (1) the cost of information relative to its value and (2) "information glut," which refers to redundancy. One technique used by some firms is Planned Information Acquisition Analysis (PIAA), which involves a periodic reevaluation of each new document or service the firm uses.[34] By comparing the number of times sources have been retrieved and found relevant, the firm may limit acquisition to those items most valuable to the firm.

Local needs and differences in data processing create problems of compatibility.

Compatibility. Another problem is the compatibility of information needed by the subsidiary and by corporate management. Even when different subsidiaries are trying to solve similar problems, their information needs may differ vastly. Consequently, corporate management may be faced with dilemmas of trying to compare unlike data or of requiring different or additional data, which may be expensive. An approach that has been instituted by some firms is to allow diversity but to send copies and analysis to centralized data banks.[35] For many corporate needs, standardization is not necessary, but standardization of coding is. On a centralized basis, personnel may compare the accuracy of subsidiary projects and suggest more refined models by using existing data.

Aside from the problem of data or coding uniformity, a major obstacle to the on-time retrieval of comparable information is the diversity from country to country in a company's approach to data processing, especially in terms of equipment and software packages. Uniformity of approach is hampered by substantial cost differences in personnel, hardware, and data communications.[36]

Information centers may permit choice of centralization or decentralization.

Information centers. With the expansion of multinational telecommunications and computer linkages, managers throughout the world now can share information almost instantaneously.[37] On one hand, this may permit more centralization, since truly global implications of policies may be examined. On the other hand, managers in foreign locations may become more autonomous because of the greater amount of information at their disposal.

Many countries are restricting data flows:

- To preserve personal privacy
- To give economic protection
- Because of strategic implications.

Restrictions on data flows. Over sixty countries have passed or are considering legislation that directly or indirectly affects the flow of data internationally. These have been enacted for three primary reasons. First, there is concern about individual privacy, particularly that the development and transmission of personnel data might give the company an undue advantage over the individual. Such restrictions, however, make it difficult for the international company to maintain centralized personnel records, which assist in making international transfers. Burroughs, for example, could not transfer its personnel records from West Germany to other locations. A second concern is economic: For example, local jobs will be lost if data processing and analysis are done abroad and resource transmission will occur without payment to the country that created the resource. Legislation has included the requirement of local purchases (such as for data-processing equipment, materials, or services); that the local subsidiary maintain copies of anything transmitted, and that local authorities monitor anything transmitted. Companies worry about additional costs and that proprietary information may fall into the hands of competitors. The third reason for legislation is that corporate networks may be used to pirate military and commercial data to be sent abroad.[38]

SOME SPECIAL SITUATIONS

Acquisitions

An acquired firm is usually not a complete fit with the existing organization.

As was noted in the Nestlé case, a policy of expansion through acquisition may create some specific control problems. In the Nestlé situation, some of the U.S. acquisitions resulted in overlapping geographic responsibilities as well as new lines of business with which corporate management had no experience. Another type of problem is that the existing management in the acquired firm is probably accustomed to a great deal of autonomy. Attempts to centralize certain decision-making procedures or to change operating methods may result in distrust, fears, and reluctance to change. This is especially true when a firm acquires another firm in a foreign country. Resistance may come not only from the personnel, but also from governmental authorities. Authorities may use a variety of discretionary means to ensure that decision making remains vested within the country.

Moving from National to Global Strategies

Also it is difficult to pull control from other operations once their managers have become accustomed to a great deal of autonomy. This is a particular problem for companies that attempt to move from a country-to-country to a global strategy. Within Europe, for example, many U.S. firms owned very independent operations for decades in the United Kingdom, France, and West Germany. These firms often have faced difficult obstacles to the integration of these operations because the country managers perceive personal and operating disadvantages through such moves. However, Japanese firms that have invested in Europe more recently have had fewer problems contending with these vested positions.[39]

Branch versus Subsidiary

There are tax and liability implications for branches versus subsidiaries.

When establishing a foreign operation management may often have to decide between making that operation a branch or a subsidiary. A **foreign branch** is legally not a separate entity from the parent; therefore branch operations are possible only if the parent owns 100 percent. A **subsidiary,** on the other hand, is legally a separate company, even though the parent may own all of the voting stock. Because of the legal separateness of the subsidiary, it is generally concluded that liability is limited to the assets of that subsidiary. Creditors or winners of legal suits therefore may not have access to other resources owned by the parent. This limited liability concept is a major factor in the choice of the subsidiary form, since otherwise, claims against a firm for its actions in one country may be settled by courts in another. There is some evidence that the subsidiary concept will not suffice in future liability disputes. At this writing, the government of India is challenging the limited liability concept even further. A case is pending against Union Carbide in an Indian district court over damages in the Bhopal accident for an amount far in excess of Union Carbide's investment value in the Indian joint venture. In the meantime, Union Carbide has been trying to reach an out-of-court settlement in the United States for a lesser amount, but one that also exceeds the book value of the Indian investment.[40]

Since subsidiaries are separate companies, there is also a question of how much and what decisions a parent may be allowed to dictate. Generally, this does not present a problem; however, U.S. courts ruled that Timken was in effect conspiring with another company to prevent competition when Timken dictated which markets its Canadian subsidiary could serve. Another factor related to control is public disclosure: Generally, the greater the control vested by the owners, the greater the secrecy that can be maintained. In this respect, branches usually are subject to less public disclosure because they are not covered by tight local corporate restrictions.

From these examples it should be clear that there are conflicting control advantages with either the branch or subsidiary that should be considered when choosing the legal form of foreign operations. In addition, each form has different tax advantages and implications. Furthermore, each may have different initiation and operating costs as well as abilities to raise capital.

COMPARISON OF LEGAL FORMS

Each legal form has different operating restrictions.

A firm establishing a subsidiary in a foreign country usually has a number of alternative legal forms from which to choose. The variety of these forms is too numerous to list in detail; however, some distinctions warrant mentioning. In addition to differences in liability, forms vary in terms of ability to transfer ownership, the number of stockholders required, the percentage of foreigners who can serve on the board of directors, the amount of required public disclosure, whether equity may be acquired by noncapital contributions, the types of businesses (products) eligible, and minimum capital required. Before making a decision an international firm should analyze all of these differences in terms of its corporate objectives. The nomenclature, "Inc.," in the United States is roughly equivalent to "S.A." in most Romance language countries; "A.G." in Germany and Switzerland; "KK" in Japan; "AB" in Sweden; and "NV" in the Netherlands. The term "PLC" is used in the United Kingdom when companies list their securities, but "Ltd." may be used for privately held companies. However, there are subtle differences from country to country.

Minority Control

Minority control is usually harder, but there are mechanisms that can work.

As we have already discussed, a greater share of equity usually gives a firm a better chance of controlling an operation; however, it is not always possible to gain more than 50 percent of the ownership in a foreign enterprise. Aside from the dispersion of stock not held by the foreign investor, there are several other means of gaining control with only a minority interest. One is to maintain control over some asset needed by the operation abroad, such as patents, brand name, or raw materials. This in fact is a motive for setting separate licensing, franchising, or management contract agreements with the foreign subsidiary.

Another means to gain control is to set up administrative devices. One such device is to separate equity into voting and nonvoting stock so that the minority foreign investor has a majority of the voting stock. Another is to make a side agreement with a majority holder for an operating committee in which the minority foreign investor has majority representation.

Nonequity Forms

As form of operations evolves so must structure.

As Chapter 15 showed, the use of multiple operating forms (e.g., export, license, joint venture) and the move from one to another may create needs to change areas of responsibility in the organization. Also it may mean that different areas in the organization have responsibilities related to the different forms. For example, the legal department may have little day-to-day responsibility with exports but a great deal with licensing to the same foreign market. Organizational mechanisms, such as the planned sharing of information or joint committees, are useful to ensure that the activities complement each other. Also, it is useful for the firm to plan organizational change to minimize obstacles when responsibilities shift from one group to another.

A further consideration is the importance of the nonequity operation to the firm's overall operations. For example, if a firm contracts only one supplier for an essential component, the contract will likely be controlled more closely, and from higher in the organization, than contracts of less strategic dependence.

SUMMARY

- Control is more difficult internationally because of (1) the geographic and cultural distance separating countries, (2) the need for diversity among locales in methods of operating, (3) the larger amount of uncontrollables abroad, and (4) the higher uncertainty due to data problems and rapid change.

- Whether decisions are made at the subsidiary level or by managers above the subsidiary should depend on the relative competence of individuals at the two levels, the cost of decision making at each level, and the effects the decisions will have on total corporate performance.
- Even though worldwide uniformity of policies and other centralized decisions may not be best for an individual operation, the overall company gain may be more than enough to overcome the individual country losses. When top management prevents subsidiary managers from doing their best job, however, they should consider the consequences for employee morale.
- Many critics within LDCs have argued that centralization of key decision making within MNEs continues the dependency that they had in colonial periods, and they are pressuring for increased control at their level.
- Good planning should include environmental analysis, strategies, and contingency strategies with inputs from both top-level and subsidiary managers.
- The amount, accuracy, and timeliness of published data vary substantially from one country to another. A researcher should be particularly aware of varied definitions, collection methods, base years for reports, and misleading responses.
- Sources of published data on international business include consulting firms, governmental agencies, supranational agencies, and organizations that serve international business accounts. The cost and specificity of these publications vary widely.
- The corporate culture constitutes an implicit control mechanism. Although it is more difficult in international companies because of national value differences, bringing managers together enhances the common culture.
- Timely reports are essential for control so that resources can be allocated properly, plans can be corrected, and personnel can be evaluated and rewarded.
- International reporting systems are similar to those used domestically because home country management is familiar with them and because uniformity makes it easier to compare different operations.
- The evaluation of subsidiaries and their managers are separate processes; however, some of the same inputs, including financial and nonfinancial criteria, may be used for both.
- Two of the growing difficulties of getting timely and comparable reports from foreign operating units are the incompatibility of data processing

systems among countries and the restrictions placed on the cross-national flow of data.

- As a firm develops international business activities, the corporate structure must encompass a means for foreign operations to report. The more important the foreign operations, the higher up in the hierarchy they should report.
- Whether a company separates or integrates the international activities, there is usually a need to develop some means by which (1) to prevent costly duplication and (2) to ensure that domestic managers do not withhold the best resources from the international operations.
- International or regional headquarters may be located away from corporate headquarters in order to save transport costs and gain access to specialized international talents.
- Some situations that raise special control problems include acquired operations; operations with historical autonomy; the legal status of foreign operations; the legal organization form allowed in the specific country; and operations with shared ownership and nonequity arrangements.

CASE: WESTINGHOUSE[41]

In 1969, Westinghouse's top management noted with concern that its chief rival, GE, gained 25 percent of its sales abroad, compared to only 8 percent by Westinghouse. Top management was determined to compete more vigorously against GE in foreign markets. At that time, Westinghouse had a separate operation, Westinghouse Electric International Company, located in New York, away from corporate headquarters in Pittsburgh. Between 1969 and 1971, overseas volume increased to 15 percent of sales; and the chairman, Donald C. Burnham, said, "I've set a goal that 30 percent of our business will be outside the U.S. I hope to get there and then set a bigger goal." The spurt in foreign sales was largely the result of the aggressive pursuit of overseas acquisitions. This marked a substantial change in foreign operating practice, inasmuch as Westinghouse had depended almost entirely on exports and licensing agreements for its foreign sales since World War I, when its three European subsidiaries were confiscated.

From 1969 to 1971 the International Company operated alongside four other Westinghouse divisions. These were operated as companies that were each in charge of a group of diverse products. A major complaint of the

International Company was that the four other companies tended to view foreign operations as merely an appendage to which they were unwilling to give sufficient technical or even product assistance. Since the International Company had to depend on the product groups for anything that it was going to export, there were problems of gaining continued assured supplies. The product companies were quite willing to divert output abroad when they had surplus production but were reluctant to do so when there were shortages largely because the International Company rather than the product company got credit for the sales and profits. Likewise, the product groups were reluctant to lend their best personnel to the International Company to assist in exportation of highly technical orders or to lend support to production from foreign licensing and subsidiaries.

Partially resulting from these complaints, Westinghouse eliminated its international division in 1971. The four product-based companies then were put in charge of worldwide control of production and sale of their goods. (Westinghouse produces more than 8,000 different products.) The philosophy was that, because of their access to product technology, the people in those divisions would have a greater capability of selling than the disbanded company. Second, since they would now be evaluated on their foreign successes, they would be willing to divert resources to international development. Another factor that affected the decision to move to a worldwide product organization from that of an international division was that GE had made a similar move with apparent success a few years earlier.

When responsibilities were shifted to the domestic division, many of the managers from the formerly New York-based International Company did not conceal their belief that "those unsophisticated hicks back in Steeltown couldn't be trusted to find U.S. consulates abroad, let alone customers." Although management in each of the four product companies was free to pursue foreign business or not, each chose to do so. Between 1971 and 1976, foreign sales grew to 31 percent of the Westinghouse total. During this five-year period, product diversity continued to grow. Product emphasis was further accentuated in 1976, when the company was reorganized into thirty-seven operating groups known as business units: Each unit was given a great deal of autonomy, including a free hand abroad.

From 1976 through 1978, foreign sales of Westinghouse fell to 24 percent of its total. The extension of responsibility by product units further complicated cooperation among units and created problems of duplication in foreign markets. For instance, a company salesperson called on a Saudi businessman who pulled out business cards from salespeople who had visited him from twenty-four other business units: His question was, "Who speaks for Westinghouse?" In another situation, different units had established subsidiaries in the same country. One had excess cash, whereas another was borrowing locally at an exorbitant rate. In many cases, large projects required the ultimate cooperation among business units to carry out different parts. At times, units could not agree in time to assemble a package and lost out to foreign competitors such as Brown, Boveri from Switzerland and Hitachi from Japan. In a case in Brazil, three different sales groups were calling on the same customer for the same job.

By 1978, Douglas Danforth was the vice-chairman and chief operating officer of Westinghouse. He was highly interested in international expansion, not only because he expected greater sales and growth there, but also because he had previously worked in the Mexican and Canadian subsidiaries. In early 1979 he enlisted a Westinghouse executive to head an exhaustive study of the firm's international operations and to make a recommendation within ninety days. The study group interviewed Westinghouse personnel in the United States and abroad; it also determined how other firms were handling their international operations. The recommendation was to move to a matrix system with a head of international operations. The international operations then were to be organized along geographic lines including three regions: This plan was adopted. To get a consensus among the people in charge of product and geographic areas was a major departure from Westinghouse's product orientation. Danforth told the company's top 220 managers that "Some of you will adjust and survive, and some of you won't."

In 1980, 27 percent of Westinghouse's sales were outside the United States. Danforth announced that he wanted 35 percent of Westinghouse's sales to be coming from abroad by 1984. Seventeen countries were identified as having the highest potential, and these were examined in detail. To carry out the planned growth, Westinghouse has had to mesh country unit plans with product unit plans. In other words, if a product unit wants switchgear in Brazil increased by 40 percent and the Brazilian country manager wants to increase it by 50 percent, they must either work out an agreement or defer the decision upward in the organization to the next higher product and geographic heads. Disagreements can effectively go as high as the top-level operating committee, which consists of the chairman, vice-chairman, three presidents of product groups, the top financial officer, and the president of the international group.

By 1984 foreign sales for Westinghouse had fallen to 19.7 percent of its total, and these recovered to only 20.6 percent by 1987.

QUESTIONS

1. What have been the major organizational problems inhibiting the international growth of Westinghouse?
2. What organizational characteristics may affect the successful implementation of the matrix management at Westinghouse?
3. How can a firm such as Westinghouse go about implementing a goal to increase the percentage of its sales accounted for by foreign operations?

4. Was the failure to reach the 1980 foreign sales goal due to the Westinghouse organization structure?

NOTES

1. Data for the case were taken from "Nestlé: Centralizing to Win a Bigger Payoff from the U.S.," *Business Week,* February 2, 1981, pp. 56–58; "Nestlé—At Home Abroad: An Interview with Pierre Liotard-Vogt," *Harvard Business Review,* November 1976, pp. 80–88; Robert Ball, "Nestlé Revs up Its U.S. Campaign," *Fortune,* February 13, 1978, pp. 80–90; "For the Record," *Advertising Age,* August 2, 1976, p. 8; Robert Ball, "A Shopkeeper Shakes up Nestlé," *Fortune,* Vol. 106, No. 13, December 27, 1982, pp. 103–106; Damon Darlin, "Nestlé Hopes to Bring Its Other U.S. Units up to Level of Its Stouffer Corp. Subsidiary," *Wall Street Journal,* March 15, 1984, p. 33; Maile Hulihan, "Nestlé Plots Aggressive Acquisition Program," *Wall Street Journal,* May 21, 1984, p. 29; James Sterngold, "Nestlé Planning to Pay $3 Billion to Acquire Carnation Company," *New York Times,* September 5, 1984, p. 1+; "Nestlé to Close Libby Units," *New York Times,* September 26, 1985, p. D5; Graham Turner, "Inside Europe's Giant Companies: Nestlé Finds a Better Formula," *Long Range Planning,* Vol. 19, No. 3, June 1986, pp. 12–19; and "Nestlé Enterprises, Inc. 1986."

2. For a good discussion of the difficulty of observing foreign environmental changes and subsequent control of them, see William R. Fannin and Arvin F. Rodrigues, "National or Global?—Control vs. Flexibility," *Long Range Planning,* Vol. 19, No. 5, October 1986, pp. 84–88.

3. For a discussion of the distance factor, see Jacques Picard, "How European Companies Control Marketing Decisions Abroad," *Columbia Journal of World Business,* Summer 1977, pp. 113–121. Also Robert L. Drake and Lee M. Caudill, "Management of the Large Multinational: Trends and Future Challenges," *Business Horizons,* May–June 1981, p. 84, found that Canadian subsidiaries of U.S. firms did not have the same degree of autonomy as subsidiaries in other countries because of their closeness to corporate headquarters.

4. Donna G. Goehle, *Decision Making in Multinational Corporations* (Ann Arbor: University Research Press, 1980).

5. Robert Stobaugh, Jr., "Financing Foreign Subsidiaries of U.S. Controlled Multinational Enterprises," *Journal of International Business Studies,* Summer 1970, pp. 48–55; R. J. Aylmer, "Who Makes Marketing Decisions in the Multinational Firm?" *Journal of Marketing,* October 1970, pp. 27–29.

6. Drake and Caudill, *loc. cit.*

7. Christopher A. Bartlett and Sumantra Ghoshal, "Tap Your Subsidiaries for Global Reach," *Harvard Business Review,* Vol. 64, No. 6, November–December 1986, pp. 87–94.

8. James Leontiades, "Going Global—Global Strategies vs. National Strategies," *Long Range Planning,* Vol. 19, No. 6, December 1986, pp. 98–100, discusses how national strategies may be more appropriate in given circumstances.

9. Yves Doz and C. K. Prahalad, "Controlled Variety: A Challenge for Human Resource Management in the MNC," *Human Resource Management,* Vol. 25, No. 1, Spring 1986, p. 57.

10. Among the many treatments of this subject are Osvaldo Sunkel, "Big Business and 'Dependencia': A Latin American View," *Foreign Affairs,* April 1972, pp. 517–531; Benjamin J. Cohen, *The Question of Imperialism—The Political Economy of Dominance and Dependence* (New York: Basic Books, 1973).

11. Daniel Creamer, *Overseas Research and Development by United States Multinationals, 1966–1975* (New York: The Conference Board, 1976), pp. 35, 79.

12. The arguments pro and con are summarized in Michael J. Thomas, "The Location of Research and Development in the International Corporation," *Management International Review,* No. 1, 1975, pp. 35–41.

13. William A. Fischer and Jack N. Behrman, "The Coordination of Foreign R&D Activities by Transnational Corporations," *Journal of International Business Studies,* Winter 1979, pp. 28–35.

14. Bartlett and Ghoshal, *op. cit.*

15. W. G. Egelhoff, "Strategy and Structure in Multinational Corporations: An Information Processing Approach," *Administrative Science Quarterly,* Vol. 27, 1982, pp. 435–458; John D. Daniels, Robert A. Pitts, and Marietta J. Tretter, "Strategy and Structure of U.S. Multinationals: An Exploratory Study," *Academy of Management Journal,* Vol. 27, No. 2, June 1984, pp. 292–307.

16. C. K. Prahalad, "Strategic Choices in Diversified MNCs," *Harvard Business Review,* July–August 1976, pp. 67–78, explores in depth the problems inherent to the locus of relative power.

17. C. A. Bartlett, "MNCs: Get off the Reorganization Merry-Go-Round," *Harvard Business Review,* Vol. 61, No. 2, 1983, pp. 138–146; Robert A. Pitts and John D. Daniels, "Aftermath of the Matrix Mania," *Columbia Journal of World Business,* Vol. 19, No. 2, Summer 1984, pp. 48–54.

18. For an extensive discussion of various approaches to regional groupings, see Daniel Van Den Bulcke and Marie-Anne Van Pachterbeke, *European Headquarters of American Multinational Enterprises in Brussels and Belgium* (Brussels: Institut Catholique des Hautes Etudes Commerciales), 1984.

19. B. Mascarenhas, "Coping with Uncertainty in International Business," *Journal of International Business Studies,* Fall 1982, pp. 87–98.

20. Egelhoff, *loc. cit.*

21. M. J. Culnan, "Environmental Scanning: The Effects of Task Complexity and Source Accessibility on Information Gathering Behavior," *Decision Sciences,* No. 14, 1983, pp. 194–206.

22. N. R. Boulton, W. M. Lindsay, S. G. Franklin, and L. W. Rue, "Strategic Planning: Determining the Impact of Environmental Characteristics and Uncertainty," *Academy of Management Journal,* Vol. 25, No. 3, 1982, pp. 500–509.

23. "The Underground Economy's Hidden Force," *Business Week,* April 5, 1982, pp. 66–67; Brooks Jackson, "Census Exceeds Projections by Millions," *Wall Street Journal,* October 29, 1980, p. 2; and Robert Reinhold, "Major Census Aide Is Relieved of Post," *New York Times,* February 12, 1980, p. A-1.

24. See B. R. Balliga and A. M. Jeager, "Multinational Corporations: Control Systems and Delegation Issues," *Journal of International Business Studies,* Vol. 15, No. 2, Summer 1984, pp. 25–40; and Vladimir Pucik and Jan Hack Katz, "Information Control, and

Human Resource Management in Multinational Firms," *Human Resource Management,* Vol. 25, No. 1, Spring 1986, pp. 121–132.

25. Samir M. Youssef, "Contextual Factors Influencing Control Strategy of Multinational Corporations," *Academy of Management Journal,* March 1975, pp. 136–145.

26. A. B. Sim, "Decentralized Management of Subsidiaries and Their Performance," *Management International Review,* No. 2, 1977, pp. 47–49.

27. Anders Edström and Jay R. Galbraith, "Transfer of Managers as Coordination and Control Strategy in Multinational Organizations," *Administrative Science Quarterly,* June 1977, p. 251.

28. David F. Hawkins, "Controlling Foreign Operations," *Financial Executive,* February 1965; V. Mauriel, "Evaluation and Control of Overseas Operations," *Management Accounting,* May 1969; and J. M. McInnes, "Financial Control Systems for Multinational Operations: An Empirical Investigation," *Journal of International Business Studies,* Fall 1971, pp. 11–28.

29. Frederick D. S. Choi and I. James Czechowicz, "Assessing Foreign Subsidiary Performance: A Multinational Comparison," *Management International Review,* Vol. 23, No. 4, 1983, p. 15.

30. *Ibid.,* pp. 18–20.

31. *Ibid.,* p. 22.

32. *Ibid.,* pp. 16–17.

33. George M. Scott, *An Introduction to Financial Control and Reporting in Multinational Enterprises* (Austin: Bureau of Business Research, Graduate School of Business, The University of Texas at Austin, 1973), pp. 77–79.

34. J. Alex Murray, "Intelligence Systems of the MNCs," *Columbia Journal of World Business,* September–October 1972, pp. 63–71.

35. James Milano and Phillip D. Grub, "Problems Associated with a Worldwide Information and Control System in the Multinational Environment," paper presented at the Academy of International Business Meeting, New York, December 28, 1973.

36. Martin D. J. Buss, "Managing International Information Systems," *Harvard Business Review,* Vol. 60, No. 5, September–October 1982, pp. 153–162.

37. Leland M. Wooton, "The Emergence of Multinational Information Centers," *Management International Review,* No. 4, 1977, pp. 21–23.

38. The information in this section is taken from Saeed Samiee, "Transnational Data Flow Constraints: A New Challenge for Multinational Corporations," *Journal of International Business Studies,* Vol. 15, No. 1, Spring–Summer 1984, pp. 141–150.

39. James Flanigan, "Multinational as We Know It Is Obsolete," [an interview with Peter F. Drucker], *Forbes,* August 26, 1985, pp. 30–32.

40. William B. Glaberson and William J. Powell, Jr., "India's Bhopal Suit Could Change All the Rules," *Business Week,* April 22, 1985, p. 38; "India Fights Carbide Suit," *New York Times,* June 18, 1988, p. 28.

41. Data for the case were taken primarily from Hugh D. Menzies, "Westinghouse Takes Aim at the World," *Fortune,* January 14, 1980, pp. 48–53; other background information may be found in "Westinghouse's Third Big Step Is Overseas," *Business Week,* October 2, 1971, pp. 64–67; and in several issues of Westinghouse's *Annual Report.*

APPENDIX

Problems of International Data

Inaccuracies result from:

- Lack of ability to collect
- Purposeful misleading.

Reasons for inaccuracies. For the most part, incomplete or inaccurate published data result from the inability of many governments to collect the needed details. Poor countries may have such limited resources that other projects necessarily are given priority in the national budget. Why collect precise figures on the literacy rate, governments of poor countries reason, when the same outlay may be used to build schools to improve that rate?

Education affects the competence of governmental officials to maintain and analyze accurate records. The economic factor likewise hampers the retrieval and analysis of records, since hand calculations may be used extensively instead of electronic data processing systems. The result may be information that is years old before it is public. Finally, cultural factors affect responses. Mistrust of data use may lead the respondent to give erroneous information—particularly if questions seek financial details.

Of equal concern to the researcher is the publication of information designed to persuade the businessperson to follow a certain course of action. While perhaps not purposefully publishing false statements, many governmental and private organizations may be so selective as to create false impressions. Therefore it is useful for firms to consider carefully the source of such material in the light of possible motives or biases.

Not all of the inaccuracies are due to collection and dissemination procedures of governments. A large portion of the studies by academics that purport to describe business practices either by domestic firms in different countries or by international firms abroad are not necessarily accurate. Broad generalizations frequently are drawn on the basis of too few observations, nonrepresentative samples, and poorly designed questionnaires. There is a tendency for academic researchers to describe the unusual because it may make more interesting reading than the typical.

Peoples' desire and ability to cover up data on themselves may distort published figures substantially. Part of the cover-up is attributable to unrecorded criminal activity. Economic data on Colombia, for example, do not include cocaine revenue, yet estimates are that the export earnings from cocaine exceed all other Colombian exports combined.[1] In the United States, illegal income from such activities as drug trade, bribery, and prostitution amount to over $100 billion a year. As much as 25 percent of the GNP in Italy and 30 percent in Israel goes unreported because of tax evasion.[2]

The following illustrates the plight of Argentina:

> *Last year [1986], only 130,000 out of three million people who were supposed to pay the three main taxes actually did. When tax agents hit the streets in search of evaders, they found that 40 percent of the people registered had declared false addresses, including one who claimed to live in the middle of the River Plate, another in a church and a third in a soccer stadium.*[3]

Comparability problems include:

- Collection methods, definitions, differences in base years
- Distortions in currency translations.

Some comparability problems. One important variable when contrasting data from different countries is the year in which collection was made. Censuses, output figures, trade statistics, and base year calculations are published for different periods in different countries; thus it may be necessary for the researcher to make estimates of current figures based on projected growth rates.

There are also numerous definitional differences among countries; a category as seemingly basic as *family income* might represent quite different things. Not only does the average number of children per family vary across national lines, but such relatives as grandparents, uncles, and cousins also may be included in the definition. *Literacy* is defined in some places by some minimum of formal schooling, in others by certain specified standards, and in still others as simply the ability to read and write one's name. Furthermore, percentages may be published in terms of adult population (with different ages used for adulthood) or total population. Another definitional difference concerns accounting rules such as *depreciation,* which can alter substantially the comparability of net national product figures among countries. Accounting differences have also led to debates on whether Japan has a higher savings rate than the United States.[4]

National income and per capita income figures are particularly difficult to compare because of differences in the dispersion of the income. A country with a large middle class will have consumption patterns quite distinct from those in a country where large portions of the population are excluded from the money economy. In Benin, a West African country, for instance, at least half the population effectively earns nothing, which means that the per capita income of the remaining group is at least double what the published figure shows for the country as a whole. Those outside the money economy obviously have consumption patterns that are greater than zero, since they may grow agricultural products and produce other goods, which they consume or barter. The extent to which people in one country produce for their own consumption (e.g., growing vegetables, baking bread, sewing clothes, cutting hair) will distort comparisons with other countries that follow different patterns.

A further problem concerns exchange rates, which must be used to convert country data to some common currency. A 10-percent revaluation of the Japanese yen in relation to the U.S. dollar will result in a 10-percent increase in per capita income of Japanese residents when figures are reflected in dollars. Does this mean that the Japanese are suddenly 10 percent richer? Obviously not, since their yen income, which they use for about 85 percent of their purchases in the Japanese economy, is unchanged and buys no more. Even without the changes in exchange rates, it is difficult to compare purchasing power and living standards, since costs are so affected by climate and habit. Exchange rates constitute a very imperfect means of comparing national data.[5]

NOTES

1. Peter Nares, "Getting a Fix on Colombia's Largest Export," *Wall Street Journal,* November 25, 1983, p. 13.

2. "The Underground Economy's Hidden Force," *op. cit.,* p. 65.

3. Maria E. Estenssoro, "When an Economy Goes Underground," *New York Times,* July 26, 1987, p. F3.

4. Kenichi Ohmae, "Americans and Japanese Save About the Same," *Wall Street Journal,* June 14, 1988, p. 30.

5. Steven Greenhouse, "Comparing Wealth as Money Fluctuates," *New York Times,* August 23, 1987, p. E3, discusses the problem of comparing purchasing power.

7

PART

FUNCTIONAL MANAGEMENT, OPERATIONS, AND CONCERNS

In the preceding part we discussed those alternatives that normally transcend decision making within functional disciplines. In this part we will examine concerns of a more functional orientation. This does not imply that these are of less importance. In fact, they are essential considerations within the firm's global implementation of strategy. Chapter 18 emphasizes the uniqueness of each company, product, and consumer area in international marketing. Chapter 19 discusses the problems of accounting and tax when legal systems, exchange rates, and inflationary conditions vary among countries. Chapter 20 examines the securement and management of funds internationally, the transfer of currencies, and the handling of inflation and exchange rate risks. Chapter 21 deliberates "people problems"—emphasizing management personnel and labor.

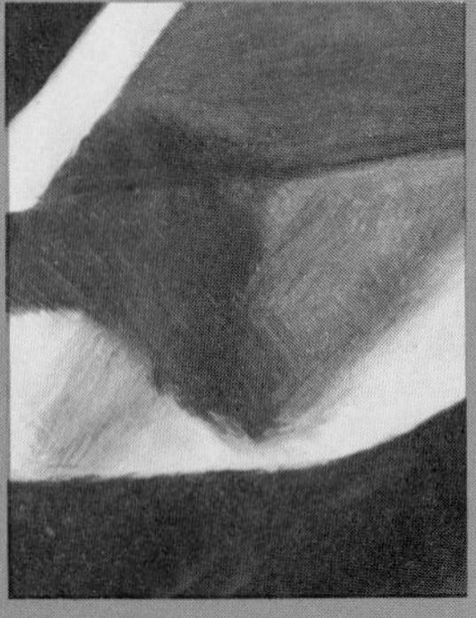

18

CHAPTER
MARKETING

May both seller and buyer see the benefit.
—Turkish proverb

- To postulate the valid marketing philosophies for different firms in varying circumstances.
- To introduce techniques for assessing market sizes for given countries.
- To contrast practices of standardized versus differentiated programs for each country where sales are made.
- To emphasize how environmental differences complicate the management of marketing worldwide.
- To discuss the major international considerations within each of the marketing functions: product, pricing, promotion, and distribution.

CASE:
MARKS & SPENCER[1]

Great Britain often has been called a nation of shopkeepers, and Marks & Spencer (M & S) is undoubtedly the shopkeeping leader. With several hundred stores in the United Kingdom, M & S is its largest retailer and the Marble Arch store in London is in the Guinness Book of Records as the store that takes in more revenue per square foot than any other in the world.

Soft goods (clothes and household textiles) account for 70 percent of the sales, and it is estimated that M & S has about 16 percent of the retail clothing sales in the United Kingdom. For some specific clothing items, M & S supplies over half the British market. M & S added food lines to its stores and is now the fifth largest food retailer in Britain.

How has M & S become so dominant in the British market? The operations were begun in 1884 by a Polish immigrant who believed in selling durable merchandise at a moderate price. Since then, this philosophy has endured. M & S has merchandise made to its specifications. Because of its vast buying power, it can get producers to make cost-cutting investments and to compete by offering low prices on merchandise to be sold under M & S's St. Michael trademark. Because M & S is so well known, it has no need of many of the costly marketing expenses that other stores must undertake. There is practically no advertising, and stores are decorated austerely. There is very little personal service and no dressing rooms or public bathrooms. Customers receive no sales slips for small purchases, but merchandise is returned easily.

Another practice that has paid off for M & S in its home market has been to appeal to the nationalistic attitudes of its clientele. M & S has promoted heavily the fact that about 90 percent of the clothing it sells originates in the United Kingdom. M & S has managed to develop an image that is as British as bed and breakfast or fish and chips. Foreign visitors to England usually do not feel that they have sopped up the local atmosphere without a visit to one of the M & S stores. One of the stores has had to put its warning signs to shoplifters in five languages.

There have been foreseeable problems to attain continued growth in the U.K. market. Not the least of the problems has been the high market share. Being already so dominant, M & S would have to add new products or appeal to new market segments to maintain its growth rate. In the late 1970s the company moved into higher priced clothes by using finer materials for its traditional styles, such as silk blouses and cashmere coats. It also hoped to cash in on publicity that Margaret Thatcher used to buy her suits at M & S before becoming prime minister. This attempt was disastrous: The Harrods-type customer did not switch to M & S, and many M & S customers traded down to even cheaper retailers. As a result, M & S dropped its higher-priced lines; but in 1980, M & S unit sales fell for the first time. By the mid-1980s

M & S began again to target a more fashion-conscious market, this time with lines that moved away from its traditional styles. Because the merchandise needed for the fashion-conscious market changes rapidly, this meant getting supplies within one week from the placement of orders instead of M & S's accustomed deliveries of up to 14 weeks. Although this move offered hope in Britain, an M & S executive summed up the emerging problems by saying, "Because the company is near saturation in the U.K., its growth must be overseas."

The foreign operations of M & S have been slow to achieve success. When Britain joined the EC, management saw an opportunity to expand on the Continent because clothing from M & S suppliers could then enter other common market countries without tariffs. Paris and Brussels were selected as the first locations for stores. Before opening stores in 1975 the company sent a team of observers to Paris for 18 months so that product differences could be targeted to the French-speaking customers.

The team found substantial differences. One was in sizes: They noted that "French girls always seem to wear a size less than they need with everything obviously relying on the buttons, while we [English] go for a half size too large." Frenchwomen wanted skirts that were longer than the English preferences. Frenchmen wanted single instead of double back vents in their jackets, sweaters in a variety of colors (including pastels), and jackets and slacks rather than suits. None of these men's preferences were the norm in the United Kingdom. All of these differences had implications for the merchandise mix and the establishment of supplies.

In spite of the substantial research on product, the company was not well received initially. Many fewer people entered the stores than had been anticipated. M & S believed that, since they were so well known in Britain and since so many foreign tourists visited London stores, their reputation had preceded them. Belatedly, they learned that only 3 percent of the French had even heard of M & S or St. Michael's before the continental stores were opened. Store locations exacerbated the situation: M & S management wanted their first stores to be "flagships" and therefore sought to locate them on the most popular shopping streets. Since store space was at a premium on those streets, they had to settle for a spot in Paris where most pedestrian traffic preferred the other side of the street. In Brussels they accepted a store with a very small frontage that did not give an impression of a vast amount of merchandise on the inside. To get people to visit the stores, M & S had to depend much more heavily on advertising than the firm did in the United Kingdom. This was an added expense that made it difficult to keep prices low.

Another factor influencing costs was that M & S lacked the same kind of buying power as it enjoyed in Britain for its continental stores. Initially, the company contracted nearly 80 percent of its merchandise from continental sources that were unwilling to treat M & S any more favorably than other department stores and retail chains already in the market. Most of the remaining merchandise came from the United Kingdom, where M & S had buying clout. Since much of this was clothing made to specifications to meet the French and Belgian needs (e.g., stronger buttons, single vent jackets, and pastel sweaters), the British producers had to make these items in short production runs. As initial large sales did not materialize, the U.K. manufacturers were reluctant to keep markups very low. Even when merchandise prices were kept low, M & S found the French to be highly suspicious of bargains.

Potential customers were unaccustomed to the starkness and lack of service in the new stores. A French fashion writer summed up the customer reaction to the Paris store as "not madly joyful unless of course one is as impervious to English shopping as one is to English cooking."

To bring customers into its Paris store, M & S has had to make operating adjustments. The primary change surprisingly has been in merchandise, the area where M & S had done so much preliminary research. In trying to copy what the continentals were offering in merchandise, M & S simply could not get a more durable product to customers at a sufficiently cheaper price to attract a mass clientele. However, it discerned fairly quickly that there is a small market segment willing to buy the more English-type merchandise for which M & S can exert its buying power. M & S now buys only 10 percent of its merchandise from continental sources and has differentiated itself from local competitors by capitalizing on its "Englishness." It now concentrates on such items as tan and navy blue sweaters, biscuits, English beer, and even a quiche Lorraine made in the United Kingdom.

The dependence on British supplies necessitates moving thousands of pounds of merchandise across the English Channel each day. Despite the existence of the EC, the goods carried by one truck may be subject to as many as 50 different tariffs. Sanitary inspectors have to check such items as fresh fruit and plants, veterinarians inspect meat for correct storage temperatures, and clothes made of non-U.K. textiles have to conform to import quotas. M & S has been able to streamline the movement and clearance (such as preparing customs entries in advance) so that food products shipped one afternoon can be in the Paris stores by the next afternoon. In deference to French tastes, M & S has carpeted its Paris store.

Unsurprisingly, a large portion of the early customers turned out to be Britishers living in France, but this gradually changed. Parisians learned to like wandering through wide aisles with shopping carts before paying for all merchandise at one cash register. One Paris store now sells more per square meter than any other department store in France, and about 90 percent of its business is to Parisians.

In entering the Canadian market, M & S assumed that the "Englishness" would be a greater advantage there than on the continent. M & S quickly expanded in Canada to 60 stores in order to get nationwide distribution. However, Canadians found the merchandise to be dull, the stores to be "cold and clinical," and they did not like finding food next to clothing. Most stores were placed in downtown locations as is the custom in the United Kingdom.

The Canadians were increasingly going to suburban shopping centers, and only the M & S stores in those centers began to earn an early profit.

In 1979, after eight years of Canadian operations, M & S finally made an overall small profit in Canada, but this was short-lived; losses returned the next year. In deference to Canadian tastes, M & S has added fitting rooms, wood paneling, mirrors, partitions between departments, and wall-to-wall carpeting. There are still complaints about the merchandise, however. A former supplier opined that the British management did things "because that's the way they did it in England." This included the placement of bigger sleeves on clothing and the avoidance of livelier colors of clothing and of advertising. While Canadian stores carrying the Marks & Spencer logo have floundered, M & S has acquired two other Canadian clothing chains, D'Allaird's and Peoples. These acquisitions have kept their Canadian marketing programs and have been profitable. When M & S first entered Canada with its own brand of stores, management had hoped that the operations would serve as a springboard for entry into the U.S. market. In late 1986 it announced that the D'Allaird's chain had signed leases for sites at shopping malls in three cities in New York. In 1987 M & S appointed a top-level team to conduct an in-depth study of the U.S. marketplace to set up stores under the M & S name. One of the firm's executives said, "There is nothing like M & S in the United States, and we believe there could be good potential for us." The 1988 M & S acquisition of Brooks Brothers, a chain concentrating on expensive clothes and a dignified image, seemed contradictory, since M & S indicated it would not change Brooks Brothers' merchandising.

INTRODUCTION

Domestic and international marketing principles are the same but:

- Managers often overlook foreign environmental differences
- Managers often interpret foreign information incorrectly.

The M & S case points out many of the problems a firm may face internationally. Although the company did substantial research before it began its continental operations, it still faced unexpected problems that inhibited rapid sales growth. Marketing principles are no different in the international arena; however, environmental differences often cause managers either to overlook important variables or to misinterpret information. M & S made mistakes in terms of such important marketing variables as the target market segment, the merchandise mix, the degree to which products would need to be altered for the markets, and the importance of the location and appearance of distribution outlets.

Global versus national programs

- Are not an either/or decision
- May take degrees of one versus the other.

This chapter examines alternative approaches to the analysis of market potential among different countries and the selection of product, pricing, promotion, and distribution strategies in international marketing. Within these areas, specific emphasis will be placed on whether firms should follow global versus national marketing programs. The global versus national approaches may be viewed at opposite ends of a spectrum, with the possibility of moving differently along that spectrum for any specific marketing program or decision. The following discussion highlights the circumstances that might enhance movements toward one end or the other of the spectrum.

MARKET SIZE ANALYSIS

Broad scanning techniques:
- Limit detailed analysis to the most promising possibilities
- Are good for LDCs where precise data are less available.

In Chapter 16 we explained the importance of market potential in determining a company's allocational efforts among different countries and discussed some common variables used as broad indicators for comparing countries' market potentials. The following section covers some techniques that can be used to estimate the size of potential markets. These are merely tools to help management estimate market potential, thus helping in the decision of which markets to emphasize.[2] In using any of the techniques, management must keep in mind the problems and limitations of data as discussed in Chapter 17.

To determine the potential demand for a given company, management usually must first estimate the sales of the category of products that the company sells and then base the company's sales on market share potential. For advanced countries, there usually are consumption figures and trained market research personnel, so costly and detailed research studies are feasible. For many LDCs, however, it may be useful to develop inexpensive forecasting methods based on readily available data. Regardless of whether a firm is dealing with industrial or poor countries, there are different informational needs depending on the precision of data required and the commitments that firms have already made in markets. For example, a firm may first scan a large number of potential markets fairly inexpensively by using published data. Only those markets that appear most promising will then be analyzed more closely, such as by test marketing in those areas.

Total Market Potential

Input-output shows the relationship of one economic sector to another.

Existing consumption patterns. **Input-output** is a tool used widely in national economic planning to show the resources utilized by different industries for a given output as well as the interdependence of economic sectors. Through the use of tables showing all sectors on both the vertical and horizontal axes, the production (output) of one is shown as the demand (input) of another. For instance, vehicle output becomes an input to the steel industry, households, government, foreign sector, and even to the vehicle industry itself. Most developed countries as well as many LDCs now publish input-output tables. By comparing these with economic projections for an economy as a whole or with plans for production changes in a given industry, management can project the total volume of sales changes for a given type of product as well as the purchases by each sector. The three major shortcomings of this method are: (1) For many countries the data contained within the input-output tables and in plans or projections of economic changes are too sparse; (2) there is a questionable assumption that the relationships among sectors and resources are fixed; and (3) the tables may be many years old before they are published and readily available.

The relationship between imports and domestic production and consumption of given products is useful in determining both the existing demand for products and the country of origin of the competition. The UNCTAD/GATT International Trade Center has published a manual detailing this information and its use,[3] but this information has the same shortcomings as are found in input-output tables.

Data assume one country will follow similar pattern to that of another country.

Data on other countries. The amount of sales of a product in one country may be based on the same conditions that determine sales in other countries. For example, as incomes change, the demand for a product may change on the basis of that income change. Management thus may collect data on the consumption of a given product in countries with different per capita GNPs and then project sales at different income levels by plotting a path through which average demand changes as incomes change (see Fig. 18.1).

Reasonably good fits for many products have been found by using this method. However, for some products the analysis breaks down in some countries because other variables affect demand. For instance, the consumption of cars in Switzerland is far lower than income would predict because of the public transportation system, difficult terrain, and high import duties.[4] A further problem is that this method is static. With changes in technology and prices, a country may change its consumption pattern much earlier or later than would be indicated by looking at a group of countries in only one time period.

Time series projects future by past trends.

Time series data. Sometimes sales follow a pattern over a historical period. If this is the case and data are available over a period of time, a firm may be able to make future projections based on past values.[5] Figure 18.2 illustrates sugar

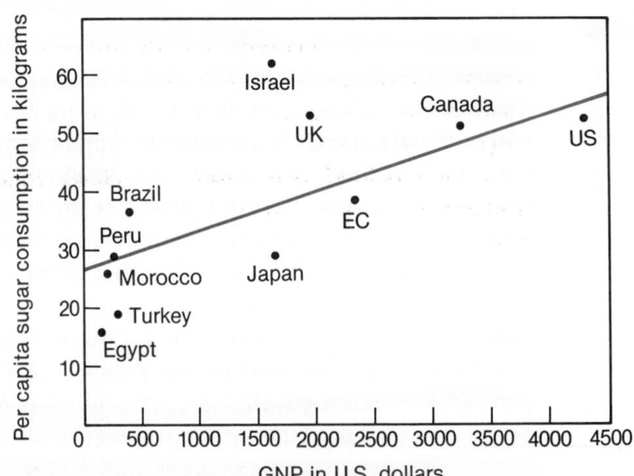

Figure 18.1
Sugar Consumption and per capita GNP for Selected Countries: 1970
Source: U.N. Statistical Yearbook, 1972.

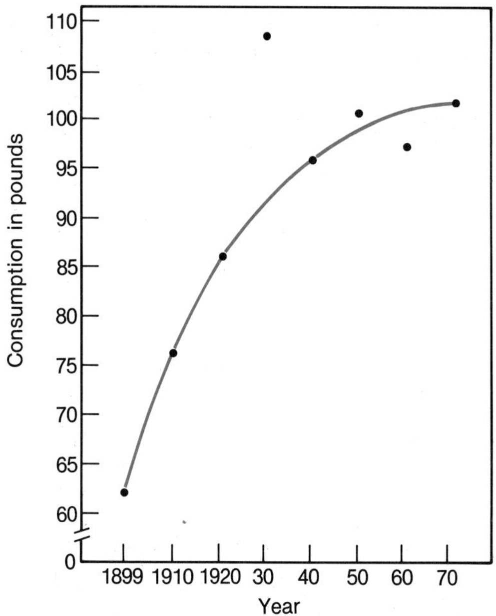

Figure 18.2
Per capita Sugar Consumption of the United States: 1899–1970
Source: Statistical Abstract of the United States, Supplement: 1957 and *Statistical Abstract: 1972.*

consumption in the United States based on time series data. This contrasts with projections of sugar consumption in Fig. 18.1 based on cross-national data. The use of time series and cross-national data also may be combined. For example, between 1899 and 1957 this combination of methods noted that as incomes rose, the portion of textile sales decreased and metal products increased.[6] Such cross-sectional analyses within an economy are useful for predicting total demand and for identifying the economic sectors generating this demand.

As percentage of income changes, product demand may change by a different percentage.

Income elasticity. A common predictive means is to divide the percentage of change in product demand by the percentage of change in income. If the resultant answer is greater than 1, the demand for the product is considered elastic; if the number is less than 1, demand is inelastic. Demand for necessities, such as food, is relatively less elastic than demand for discretionary products, such as automobiles. In other words, upward or downward movements in income ordinarily would affect automobile sales more than food sales. This concept is useful in estimating the expenditures for countries at different levels of income. For instance, in the United States, less than 20 percent of personal income is spent on food, whereas South Koreans spend over 50 percent on food items. The difference is not due to relative appetites but rather to income differences that allow people in the United States to spend more on other types of purchases. Since a large portion of people in South Korea are poor, a change in income levels affects food consumption much more than in a higher-income country.[7] An elasticity of 1.5 would mean that a percentage change in income would result in 1.5 times that percentage change in the demand for the specific product.

As for the methods of demand projection just mentioned, income elasticity measurements must be approached with caution, especially if a firm is making projections in one country based on demand analysis in another. Not only are there the problems of taste but also of price differences that affect the desire of consumers to substitute cheaper for more expensive products. Italy consumes a much higher quantity of fruits and vegetables than Norway, even though Norway's income is higher, because of price differences. When starting clothing sales in Japan, Genesco found (surprisingly) that although Japan's per capita income was only about half of that in the United States, Japan's per capita consumption of suits was double that of the United States.[8] The greater formality and status ascribed to wearing suits in Japan contribute to the divergence in consumer buying behavior between the two countries.

Demand is related to some economic or other indicator.

Regression. Regression is merely a means of refining data collected on numbers of countries, on a historical basis, or as incomes change. By using data based on the historical relationship between demand for a given product and some economic indicator, or between demand and some economic indicator in a given time period, a firm may construct a regression equation that shows the demand (the dependent variable) based on a level of the indicator (the independent variable). This technique allows an amount of consumption that is not directly contributable to changes in the indicator to be taken into consideration. It further allows for the determination of the degree of correlation between the independent and dependent variables. For instance, one study made forty-two observations of demand for radio sets based on per capita GNP and developed an equation that explained 78 percent of the variation in sets among the countries examined. The formula was $y = a + bx$, where y is the amount of product in use per 1,000 population, a is the constant of radio sets in use, and bx is radios times per capita GNP. This resulted in an equation of $y = 8.325 + 0.275x$.[9] In other words, on the basis of observed radios in use, for an expected increase in per capita GNP of $100, radio sets would increase by 27.5 per 1,000 population.

Although this equation indicates a high predictability of present radios where figures are not available on radio sets, a problem of using regression to make future projections is that tastes and technical changes may alter demand. Furthermore, there may be a saturation point in consumption that has not yet been observed. At some point, if incomes are high enough, people may merely buy radios as replacements rather than add to the amount of radios they own. If this is shown to occur, then it is possible to construct a nonlinear regression equation. Although this example used per capita GNP as the independent variable, an equation based on other variables may result in high correlations as well.

Gap Analysis

The difference between total market potential and companies' sales is made up of gaps:

- Usage: less product sold by all competitors than potential
- Competitive: "head-to-head" competition
- Product line: company lacks some product variations
- Distribution: company misses geographic or intensity coverage.

The tools just described may give an estimation of the market potential for a given product. Once this rough determination is made, a firm must calculate how well it is doing within each of the markets. A useful tool for scanning markets and comparing countries in this respect is **gap analysis.**[10] When a company's sales are lower than the estimated market potential for a given type of product, there is a company potential for increased sales, which may be due to a usage, competitive, product line, or distribution gap.

The two largest Swiss chocolate companies, Nestlé and Interfood, have found in recent years very different types of gaps in different countries.[11] This has led them to emphasize different types of marketing programs among nations. In some markets they have found substantial usage gaps: In other words, less chocolate is being consumed than would be expected on the basis of population and income levels. This has led the two companies to try to increase primary demand in those areas for chocolate in general. Industry specialists estimated, for example, that in many countries more than 80 percent of the population have never tasted a chocolate bar. They project, consequently, that if more people can be persuaded to try chocolate bars, the companies' sales should increase with the market increase.

The U.S. market comprises another type of usage gap. Nearly everyone has tried most chocolate products, but per capita consumption fell from 20.3 pounds to 14.3 pounds between 1968 and 1978 because of increasing concern about calories. To increase chocolate consumption in general, Nestlé began promoting chocolate as an energy source for the sports-minded. In markets such as France and West Germany the companies feel that the potential market demand is being fulfilled but that there is a competitive gap: That is, Nestlé and Interfood might increase sales there but only at the expense of competitors. In some hot climates the companies have found that they have product line gaps in terms of the market for sweetened products. By working on new products, such as chocolate products that melt less easily, they may be able to garner a larger share of the present market for sweetened products. They also have found chocolate products with which they do not compete directly. Finally, there are some markets, such as Japan, where they have not yet achieved a sufficient distribution to reach their sales potentials.

PRODUCT POLICY

The Philosophies

International marketing philosophies may be categorized as:

1. We sell what we make,
2. We make what we sell, and
3. We adapt what we make to the needs of foreign consumers.

This frame of reference is useful for understanding the varied approaches firms may validly take in international product policy decisions.

We sell what we make. For some products, particularly raw materials and agricultural commodities, there is little need or possibility of product differentiation from one country to another. Although this is one approach within the philosophy of "we sell what we make," this idea better describes the firm that develops a product for its domestic market and then attempts to sell the product abroad—as it is. There are three circumstances under which this approach may be valid:

1. passive exports, particularly ones that serve as an appendage to the domestic market;
2. the existence of foreign market segments or niches that may resemble either the mainstream or the niche to which the product is aimed domestically; and
3. situations in which product standardization may so lower prices that a large group of consumers from many countries are willing to forego certain nationally differentiated product characteristics in order to get lower prices.

Passive sales occur when:

- Advertising spills over
- Foreign buyers seek new products.

Many firms begin selling abroad very passively. Sometimes for unknown reasons, requests for information on products or even actual orders simply arrive from abroad. Foreign products are discovered through numerous channels, including new developments reported in scientific and trade journals with international circulation, advertising that spills across national boundaries, and demonstration of products that consumers have bought in one country and transferred abroad. Finally, many firms send buyers abroad or actively search for new products. At this point firms do very little if any real adaptation to what consumers abroad might prefer, which suffices for many companies that view foreign sales as an appendage to domestic sales. This same type of company frequently exports only if it has excess inventory for the domestic market. In fact fixed costs may be covered from domestic sales so that lower prices are offered on exports as a means of liquidating inventories without disrupting the domestic market.

The domestic, unaltered product may have appeal abroad.

A company may develop a product aimed at achieving a large share of its domestic market, yet find that there are market segments abroad willing to buy the same product. Recall the M & S sales of English-style clothes and foods within its stores in Paris. Sometimes the product may have a universal appeal, such as Schweppes tonic water or various French wines. In other situations, the company may be able to target to a mass market at home, but to a small niche within foreign locations.[12] For example, Perrier water appeals to a mass French market but to an elitist market in the United States. Another situation involves sales to countries for which the total market potential is assessed to be small regardless of whether changes are geared to unique consumer needs. In small developing countries, particularly, international firms are apt to make few changes because the market size does not justify the expense to them and since competitors are apt to be other international firms who do not make product alterations. Firms may not even adjust electrical voltage and plugs to local standards, leaving the job of conversion to local purchasers. The greatest ability to sell the same product in more than one country occurs when consumer characteristics are similar and when there is a great deal of spillover in product information, such as between the United States and Canada.[13] Improvements in international communications and transportation increasingly are extending the spillover effects to more distant countries so that there are more opportunities to aim the same products to groups of similar consumers in a number of different countries.

Standardization usually reduces costs.

Whether a firm is exporting or has foreign production facilities, it may cut costs substantially by standardizing its products. This usually is done on the basis of the home country experience, since costs associated with product development, promotional programs, and distributional expertise already have been expended there. The transference abroad allows for economies as the outlays are spread over a larger volume of output. As the world moves toward the use of flexible factories with robots, the economic gains through standardization may be diminished.

We make what we sell:

- Is not a common strategy
- Takes geographic area as given.

We make what we sell. In a firm that operates according to the dictum described in the previous section, management is usually guided by such questions as: "Should we send some exports abroad?" "Where can we sell some more of product X?" In other words, the product is held constant, and the location of sales is varied. The type of strategy to be described in this section is one that asks, "What can we sell in country A?" In this case the country is held constant, and the product is varied.

Sometimes a firm wants to penetrate markets in a given country because of the country's size, growth potential, proximity to home operations, currency or political stability, or a host of other reasons. The extreme of this approach would be for a company to move to completely unrelated products. This is not a common strategy, but there are examples: Henkel of West Germany wished to diversify into the United States in order to counter an expected sluggish market at home. But management felt that it would be difficult to compete in the United States in its major product lines, detergents and cosmetics. Henkel chose instead to buy the chemical division of General Mills.[14]

This reactive attitude to consumers does not necessarily mean that a firm has to forego the economies of standardization. A company may well do market research in a number of countries in order to develop and aim a product at a global market segment. Canon's development of a 35-millimeter automatic camera is an example.[15] Instead of merely trying to transfer sales of a domestic product abroad, the firm designs a product to fit some global market segment, which may mean changing what is sold domestically to correspond to the international standard. The possibilities of global products for industrial users may be large as well because the purchasers are apt to be technically trained decision makers. SKF, for example, introduced a line of 20,000 ball bearings to replace 50,000 on a worldwide basis.[16]

As in the preceding philosophy, a firm following a "make what we sell" approach may do so passively. Increasingly there are examples of purchasing agents who set specifications and then seek out contracts for the foreign manufacture of components or finished products. In responding, a firm may make a product that is quite different from what it sells within its home market. In such a situation, the producer is less concerned about choosing the product characteristics than about the pricing and distribution aspects of what it is marketing abroad.

This is the most common strategy:

- Product changes are adaptations, done by degree.

We adapt what we make to the needs of foreign consumers. Most firms that are committed to continual rather than sporadic foreign sales adopt a strategy that combines the production and consumer orientations just described. Refusal to make changes for the needs of foreign markets means that too many sales may be lost. Yet expertise concerning a type of product may be very important, and companies want the foreign operations to be compatible with their product understanding. Product changes are common but tend to occur in degree. Thus a company accustomed to manufacturing electric typewriters is more apt to move into the production of manual typewriters or calculators than tires or detergents. The latter products ordinarily would be too far from the management's area of expertise.

Reasons for Product Alteration

Legal factors are usually related to safety or health protection.

Legal factors. Direct legal requirements are the most obvious reason for altering products for foreign markets, since without adhering to the regulations the company will not get permission to operate. The exact requirements vary widely by country but are usually meant to protect people who come into contact with a given product or service. Pharmaceuticals and foods are particularly subject to regulations concerning purity, testing, and the labeling of contents. Cars imported into the United States must conform to safety and pollution standards not found in many other countries.

When foreign legal requirements are less stringent than those at home, a firm then may not be compelled legally to alter its products for sales in the foreign country. However, the firm will have to weigh such questions as whether foreign sales will be lost if high domestic standards are used abroad and whether there will be domestic ill will if those standards are not used. Firms have been criticized in recent years for selling abroad, especially in

LDCs, such products as toys, automobiles, contraceptives, and pharmaceuticals that did not meet home country safety or quality standards.[17]

A recurring question is to what extent it is possible to arrive at international product standards to eliminate some of the seemingly wasteful product alterations from country to country. Although there has been some progress, such as agreement on the sprocket dimensions on movie film, other things (railroad gauges and electrical socket shapes, for instance) continue to vary. In reality, there is both consumer and economic resistance. The conversion to the metric system for beverages, for example, meant that U.S. consumers had to learn that 236.58 milliliters is the same as the 8 fluid ounce soft drink to which they were accustomed. In an economic sense the changeover was more costly than simply educating people and relabeling. Containers had to be redesigned and production had to be retooled so that dimensions would be in even numbers. At best, international standards will come very slowly.

Less apparent are the indirect legal requirements that may affect product content or demand. In some countries it may be difficult or prohibitively expensive to import certain raw materials or components, thus forcing a firm to construct an end product with local substitutes that may alter the final product substantially. Or legal requirements, such as high taxes on heavy automobiles, may shift sales to smaller models, thus altering demand indirectly for tire sales and gasoline octanes.

Examination of cultural differences may pinpoint possible problem areas.

Cultural factors. Consumer buying behavior is complex. It is difficult to determine in advance if the introduction of new or different products will meet with acceptance. Some U.S. food franchisors, such as McDonald's, have been highly successful in Japan by duplicating most of their U.S. product and distribution—an acceptance attributed to the "enthusiastic assimilation" by the Japanese of Western ways. Yet Western cosmetic firms have been able to garner only very small shares of the Japanese cosmetics market. Among the cultural factors inhibiting their sales are the facts that Western products are unsuited to the Japanese market: Perfume is hardly used in Japan, suntans are considered ugly, and bath oil is impractical in communal baths.[18] In another case, Armstrong World Industries had heard so much about the so-called world car that it reasoned there must be a market for a world gasket. Management found though that consumer and therefore industrial requirements were very different. For example, U.S. car owners are not bothered by an occasional drop of oil on the garage floor, whereas Japanese car owners will complain to the manufacturer.[19]

Personal incomes and infrastructures affect product demand.

Economic factors. If consumers in a foreign country lack sufficient income, they may not be able to buy in sufficient quantity the same product the international firm sells in its home market. The company therefore may have to design a cheaper model or perhaps sell a product with characteristics similar to those sold at an earlier period in the home market. National Cash Register has designed crank-operated machines that are being sold in the Philippines, Latin America, the Orient, and Spain. Where incomes are low, consumers may buy many personal items in smaller quantities, such as one aspirin, one piece of chewing gum, or one cigarette, which usually necessitates new types of packaging.

Even if a market segment has sufficient income for purchasing the same product the firm sells at home, the general level of the economy may be such that products have to be altered. The type of infrastructure (e.g., roads and utilities) in a country may determine the necessary structural composition and tolerances of products. Factory managers will have to consider the low educational levels of machine operators when planning equipment purchases, which may result in product simplification.

LDC criticisms. Within LDCs, labor-saving industrial equipment and luxury goods are criticized for contributing to unemployment problems and to the enhancement of elitist class distinctions. Therefore MNEs are being increasingly pressured to justify their contributions or to design and sell products that are perceived to be more in line with the needs of LDCs. The question of appropriate technology will be discussed more fully in Chapter 21. The question of luxury or superfluous products has been largely answered by MNEs through showing the positive side effects of seemingly unnecessary products. For example, soft drink manufacturers have argued that they are responsible for the establishment of glass bottle-making firms, which are essential for other industries, such as pharmaceuticals.

Cost of Alteration

Some products save costs more than others through standardization.

Cost savings through uniformity may apply to any part of the marketing program; however, product standardization is the area where the greatest savings are possible. If a firm is exporting, longer production runs from a centralized output may result in substantial economies of scale. Total inventories also may be lowered, since domestic and foreign sales come from the same backlog. Even if different production centers in different countries are involved, a standardized approach ordinarily reduces product development costs and should lead to easier and more comparable cost controls. Output in different countries also may be exported to substitute for domestic production when local manufacturing units cannot fill orders, as in periods of unusual demand or during strikes. The cost savings from standardization sometimes have enabled producers to cut prices and improve reliability so that markets have increased in spite of differences in national and regional tastes, such as personal calculators from Malaysia and housewares from Rumania.[20]

There is a wide variance in cost-saving possibilities though. For example, a production that has a need for a high fixed capital input (e.g., automobile manufacture) can gain more through long production runs than one with a high proportion of variable to fixed costs (e.g., pharmaceuticals). If a company must produce abroad in order to serve the foreign market, some of the economies of product standardization, such as from long runs or inventory centralization, will be lost anyway. In this situation, there is less cost pressure to maintain uniformity.

Furthermore, some changes are cheap to effect, yet have an important influence on demand: One such area is packaging. In Panama, Aunt Jemima Pancake Mix and Ritz Crackers are sold in cans rather than in boxes because of the high humidity—a low-cost change with a high potential payoff. Before making a decision a firm should always compare the cost of alteration with the cost of lost sales if no alteration is made.

One strategy a firm can use for compromising between uniformity and diversity is to standardize many components while changing the end characteristics. Coca-Cola, for example, exports concentrates to bottling plants all over the world; then carbonation, color, and sugar are added to conform with local preferences.[21] This type of change is practically costless, since standardization is achieved for the concentrate process and the finished product cannot feasibly be exported. Even when end products appear to be quite different, the standardization of many components is possible. Another strategy is to make product changes less frequently in small markets to spread the fixed costs associated with production over a larger amount of sales.

Extent and Mix of the Product Line

Narrowing of line allows for concentration of efforts.

Most companies produce multiple products. It is doubtful that all of these products would generate sufficient sales in a given foreign locale to justify the expenditures to penetrate the markets. Yet of the remaining products, a company may offer only a portion in order to reduce expenditures. Instead of offering as many models and options as in the United States, GM in Mexico produces and sells a much more limited variety, which reduces the amount of capital investment allowing sales activity to concentrate on fewer products. In other words, a firm may narrow its efforts to a few segments of a given market.

Broadening may gain distribution economies.

A firm also must consider whether any new products need to be added to the line for sale in certain countries. Two primary considerations in reaching these decisions are the possible effects on sales and the relative cost of having one product versus a family of products. Sometimes a firm finds that it must produce and sell some unpopular items if it is to sell the more popular ones. The manufacturer may be forced to go to a few short production runs in order to gain the mass market on other products. If a firm must set up some foreign production if it is to sell in the foreign market, it may be able to produce locally those products in its line with a longer production run and import the other products needed to help sell the local production.

If the foreign market is small in relation to the domestic market, selling costs per unit may be high because of the fixed costs associated with selling. When faced with a situation such as this, the firm can follow a strategy of broadening the product line to be handled. This may be done by grouping sales of several manufacturers or by developing new products for the local market that the same salesperson can handle. Coca-Cola, for instance, has offered a line of bar mixes in South Africa, a lemonade in Australia, a mango drink in Pakistan, a tomato juice in Belgium, and two mixed juice-based drinks in Mexico.[22]

Product Life Cycle Considerations

Product life cycles may differ by country in:

- Time of introduction
- Shape of growth curve.

There may be differences among countries in either the shape or the length of the product life cycle. Thus a manufacturer who faces declining sales in one country may be able to find a foreign market that will have growing or at least sustained sales for a product. For example, the Dixie Canning Company, a producer of home-canning equipment, faced falling demand in the United States but found that sales in some developing countries were growing. In fact, introducing its products earlier in these countries probably would have yielded few sales. Mattel found that its Cheerful Tearful Doll had a much longer sales life span in West Germany than in the United States.[23]

Because of mass communications and transportation coupled with rising income levels, many of the differences among countries in the periods of product introduction are being lessened. The result is that companies are increasingly forced to penetrate international markets quickly with their new products or face the probability that competitors will beat them with products that are close substitutes.

PRICING

Firms generally place only product above price in the ranking of marketing program variables.[24] A price needs to be high enough to guarantee the proper flow of funds to carry on the other activities that bridge the gap between production and consumption. The proper price will not only assure short-term profits, but will also allow the firm to have the resources to build its other elements within the marketing mix that are necessary to achieve long-term competitive viability. Pricing in the international context is more complex than in the domestic arena because of:

1. a different degree of governmental intervention,
2. a greater diversity of markets,

3. price escalation in exporting,
4. the changing relative value of currencies, and
5. differences in fixed versus variable pricing practices.

Governmental Intervention

Governmental price controls:

- May set minimum or maximum prices
- May prohibit certain competitive price practices.

Every country has laws that affect the prices of goods at the consumer level, but these laws may affect different products in different ways at different times. Restrictions may prevent firms from using the strategies they consider optimal in achieving their ends.

A governmental price control may set either maximum or minimum levels to be charged the consumer. Controls against lowering prices usually are intended to prevent firms from eliminating competitors in order to gain monopoly positions. An example of this type of control would be West Germany's Unfair Competition Law, which has been interpreted by the German courts to prohibit such items as coupons, boxtops, and giveaway articles unless these will remain a consistent policy of the company throughout the years. A firm accustomed to relying on such practices as a means of increasing its sales at home must develop new methods in West Germany consistent with the German laws. Mexico sets maximum prices on many products: If costs rise, profit margins necessarily contract. Or price controls may force firms to lower the quality of a product, in which case they may consider changing the brand name in order to reintroduce the higher-quality product at a later date. Price controls even may force firms to abandon formerly lucrative markets. Two Swiss firms, Schwarzenbach and Gessner, which had been selling over $3 million of chadors to Iran per year were forced to pull out of the market because of such controls.[25]

Another type of control that reduces discretionary pricing is directed specifically at imports. The General Agreement on Tariffs and Trade (GATT) has a provision, the Antidumping Code, that permits countries to establish restrictions against imports that come in below the price to consumers in the exporting country. The provision makes it more difficult for firms to differentiate markets through price.

A firm might wish to export abroad at a lower price than that charged at home for several reasons. One might be to test sales in the foreign market. Assume that a firm finds that it cannot export to a given country because tariffs or transportation costs make the price to foreign consumers prohibitively high, but some preliminary calculations show that by establishing foreign production, prices may be reduced substantially to the foreign consumer. Before committing resources to produce overseas, management may wish to test the market by exporting at the price at which goods could be sold if produced in the local market. If sales do not materialize, management will know factors other than price may be preventing product sales. If sales do materialize, management may go ahead and establish an investment or make a second round of exports to determine whether repeat sales develop. Other reasons for charging different prices in different countries involve competitive and demand factors. For example, a firm may feel that prices can be kept high in the domestic market by restricting supply to that market. Excess production then can be sold abroad at a lower price as long as the sales price makes some contribution to overhead.

Greater Diversity of Markets

Consumers in some countries simply like certain products more and are willing to pay more for them.

Although there are numerous ways for a firm to segment the domestic market and to charge differently in each segment, the country-to-country variations create even greater natural segments. Few sea urchins can be sold in the United States, for example, at any price, yet they are exported to Japan, where they are considered delicacies. The Shenandoah Valley Poultry Company exports 2,500 metric tons of turkey yearly from the United States to Europe largely because Europeans like the plump dark meat of turkey thighs. In the United States this meat would be sold for a lower price to cat food suppliers.[26] In some countries a firm may have many competitors and thus little discretion on its prices whereas in others, it may have a near monopoly due either to the stage in the product life cycle or to government-granted manufacturing rights not held by competitors. In near-monopoly situations the firm may exercise considerable pricing discretion, such as using skimming, penetration, or cost-plus strategies.

Another factor differentiating pricing possibilities is that country of origin stereotypes differ among countries. For example, in comparing consumer perceptions for automobiles with their objective ratings, West German cars seem overrated by American consumers in relation to U.S.-made cars, yet Japanese overrate Japanese cars in relation to the West German ones. In effect, West German producers may be able to charge a higher margin above their American competitors in the United States than they can with their Japanese competitors in Japan. Yet any competitor who responds to adverse stereotypes by lowering prices to increase sales actually may reduce the product image even further.[27] This could occur, for example, if the West German automobile producers were to lower their prices in the Japanese market where consumers often equate price with quality.

Cash versus credit buying affects demand.

The total cost that a consumer may pay for a product will be more than the sales price if there are additional charges because of buying on credit. How consumers view these additional charges may thus affect total demand as well as the sales price they are willing to pay. The tax treatment of interest payments as well as attitudes toward being in debt affect whether consumers will pay in cash or by credit. Japanese, for example, are much more reluctant to rely on consumer credit than Americans.[28] In selling to Japanese consumers therefore it is less possible than in the United States to use credit payments as a means of receiving revenue from the sale of goods.

Price Escalation in Exporting

Price generally goes up by more than transport and duty costs.

If standard markups are used within the distribution channels, lengthening the channels or adding expenses somewhere within the system will increase the price to the consumer by a greater amount than the initial increase. Assume that the markup is 50 percent and that a product costs $1.00 to produce: The price of the product would then be $1.50. If the cost of the production were to increase by $.20 to $1.20, the markup of 50 percent would then make the price of the product $1.80 instead of merely $1.70. In export sales, two things happen to escalate the price of goods to the consumer: First, channels of distribution are usually longer because of greater distances and because of the need to engage organizations that know export procedures and/or selling in the foreign market; second, tariffs are an additional cost that may be passed on to consumers in an escalated form.

There are several implications of price escalation. Many seemingly exportable products turn out to be noncompetitive abroad. Furthermore, to become competitive in exporting, a firm may have to sell its product to middlemen at a lower price to lessen the amount of escalation.

Currency Value and Price Changes

Pricing decisions must consider replacement cost.

For firms accustomed to operating with one relatively stable currency, pricing in highly volatile currencies can be extremely problematic. Pricing decisions should be made to assure that sufficient funds are received to replace the inventory that has been sold and still make a profit. If this is not done, a firm may be making a "paper profit" while liquidating itself. In other words, what shows as a profit may result from failure to adjust for inflation while the merchandise is in stock. In addition to the effect of inflation on prices, a company also must consider that its income taxes may be based on the paper profits rather than on real profits. Table 18.1 illustrates a pricing plan to make a target profit (after taxes) of 30 percent on replacement cost. If the firm does not use a procedure similar to this one, it may quickly lack sufficient funds to operate. Westinghouse's subsidiary in Belgium nearly went bankrupt, for example, because inflation was high but payment receipts were slow.[29] The longer the collection period, the more important it is for the firm to use a graduated pricing model.

Two other pricing problems that occur because of inflationary conditions are: (1) the receipt of funds in a foreign currency that, when converted, will buy less of the firm's own currency than had been expected and (2) the constant readjustment of prices necessary to compensate for cost changes. In the first case the firm can sometimes specify in sales contracts an equiv-

TABLE 18.1

EFFECT OF TAX AND INFLATION ON PRICING

Assume: Cost at beginning of 1,000
36% inflation
40% tax rate
30% profit goal on replacement cost after taxes

If Sold and Collected at Beginning of Year		If Sold and Collected at End of Year	
Cost	1,000	Replacement cost	1,360
Markup	500	Markup on replacement	320
Sale prices	1,500	Sales price	1,680
− Cost	1,000	− Original cost	1,000
Taxable income	500	Taxable income	680
Tax @ 40%	200	Tax @ 40%	272
Income after taxes	300	Income after taxes	408

Explanation: The pricing structure for sales or collections at the end of the year is calculated at follows: Replacement cost is cost plus inflation until collection, or 1,000 + 0.36 (1,000) = 1360; income after taxes is profit goal times replacement cost, or 0.30 (1,360) = 408. Since income after taxes is 60 percent of taxable income, taxable income may be calculated by 408 ÷ 0.6 or 680; tax is 0.4 (680) = 272; sales price is original cost (1,000) plus taxable income (680); markup on replacement is sales price (1,680) less replacement cost (1,360), or 320.

alency in some hard currency. For example, a sale of equipment from a U.S. manufacturer to a company in Uruguay may specify that payment be made in dollars or pesos at an equivalent price, in terms of dollars, at the time that payment is effected. Whether a firm can invoke an equivalency clause depends on competitive factors and governmental regulations.

When it is necessary to change prices frequently because of inflationary conditions, it becomes more difficult to quote prices in letters or catalogues. Constant price rises even may hamper what would otherwise be a preferred distribution method. Vending machine sales, for example, make price increases difficult to effect because of the need to change machines in the process and to come up with coins that correspond to the percentage increase in price desired.

Currency value changes also affect pricing decisions for any product with potential foreign competition. For example, when the U.S. dollar becomes stronger, non-U.S. made goods can be sold more cheaply in the U.S. market. In such a situation, U.S. producers may have to accept a lower margin in order to be competitive. When the dollar weakens, on the other hand, foreign producers may have to adjust their margins downward in order to remain competitive.

When companies sell similar goods in more than one country, price differences between the countries must not exceed by much the cost of bringing the goods in from a lower-priced country, or spillover in buying will occur. Soft drink manufacturers easily can vary their prices by a large percentage from country to country, since the cost of transportation would render large-scale movements across borders impractical. However, consumers feasibly could buy abroad and import higher-priced items, such as cameras. For example, importers in the United States and France paid yen to buy Japanese cameras; consequently, the imported price in yen was the same in both France and the United States. But then the franc cheapened in relation to the dollar, so some U.S. dealers scurried to buy inventories located in France rather than buying from the official distributor. U.S. dealers could buy the Olympus OM-10 for $224.95 through the official distributor or for $152 from inventories already in France. Such movements could undermine the longer-term viability of the distributorship system or upset the capacity utilization balance among plants, so camera manufacturers cut camera export prices to the United States to prevent such product arbitrage from taking place. However, some companies take advantage of currency swings by switching exports from one location to another; for example, GAF does this with butane diol, a raw material used in plastic.[30]

Fixed versus Variable Pricing

There are country-to-country differences in

- Whether manufacturers set prices
- Whether prices are fixed or bargained in stores
- What type of establishment has bargaining.

There is substantial variation from country to country in the extent to which manufacturers can or must set prices at the retail level. For instance, in Venezuela, most consumer products must have prices printed on the label, whereas in Chile it is illegal for manufacturers either to suggest retail prices or to put prices on labels.[31] There is also a substantial variation in whether consumers bargain in order to settle upon an agreed price. For instance, bargaining takes place in about 60 percent of the stores in India and Kenya but in less than 5 percent in the People's Republic of China and South Africa. Bargaining is much more prevalent in purchases from street vendors in India than in Singapore, whereas bargaining in high-priced specialty stores is more frequent in Singapore than in India.[32]

PROMOTION

Promotion is the process of presenting messages intended to help sell a product or service. The types and direction of messages and the method of presentation may be extremely diverse, depending on the company, product, or country of operation.

The Push-Pull Mix

Promotion may be categorized as **push,** which involves direct selling techniques, or **pull,** which relies on mass media. An example of the former would be door-to-door selling of encyclopedias; an example of the latter would be

Push is more likely when:

- Self-service is not predominant
- Product price is a high portion of income
- Advertising is restricted.

magazine advertisements for a brand of cigarettes. Most firms use combinations of the two strategies. For each product in each country a company must determine its total promotional budget as well as the mix of the budget between push and pull.

Several factors necessitate differences between push and pull among countries: (1) the type of distribution system, (2) the cost and availability of media to reach target markets, (3) consumer attitudes toward sources of information, and (4) price of the product relative to incomes.

Generally, the more tightly controlled the distribution system, the more likely a firm is to emphasize a push strategy because a greater effort is required to get distributors to handle a product. This is true, for example, in Belgium where distributors are small and highly fragmented, thus forcing firms to concentrate on making their goods available.[33] Another distribution factor affecting promotion is the amount of contact between salespeople and consumers. In a self-service situation, where customers lack the opportunity of asking sales personnel their opinions on products, it becomes more important for the firm to advertise through mass media or at the point of purchase.

Because of diverse national environments, promotional problems are extremely varied. In India, for example, the large number of languages, low literacy rate, and lack of reliable media information make it very difficult and expensive to reach customers. Governmental regulations pose an even greater barrier in many countries. For example, Scandinavian television has long refused to accept commercials. In the Communist bloc, sales must be pushed to the governmental purchasers, since there is little or no opportunity to advertise to final consumers through any media. A less obvious effect of government on the promotional mix is the direct or indirect tax many countries put on advertising.

France and the United States present an interesting contrast of cultural factors affecting the push-pull mix.[34] U.S. housewives spend more time watching television and reading magazines, and they rely more on friends and advertising before purchasing a new product. French housewives spend more time shopping, examining items on shelves, and listening to the opinions of retailers. It is therefore easier to presell the U.S. housewives, whereas discounts to distributors and point-of-purchase displays are more important in France.

Finally, the price of the product relative to the income of consumers is important in the promotional mix. The more critical the purchase is in relation to income, the more time and information the customer usually will want in order to make a decision. Information is best conveyed in a personal selling situation where two-way communication is fostered. In LDCs, more products will have to be pushed.

Standardization of Advertising Programs

Advantages of standardized advertising are:

- Some cost savings
- Better quality at local level
- Rapid entry to different countries.

Just as there are possible economies in standardizing products worldwide, there are economies in using the same advertising programs as much as possible. Although these economies are not as great as those found for product standardization, they may nevertheless be significant. McCann-Erickson claims to have saved $90 million in production costs for Coca-Cola by carrying over certain elements of its advertising program on a global basis over a twenty-year period.[35] Some savings occur in hidden costs of executive time spent in supervising advertising campaigns as well.[36] In addition to cost, standardization takes place to improve the quality of advertising at the local level where local agencies may lack expertise. A second reason for standardizing is to speed the entry of products into different countries.[37]

Standardized advertising usually means a program that is recognizable from market to market rather than one that is identical in each. Some problems in complete standardization relate to translation, legality, credibility or image factors, and media availability. Because of these problems, truly multinational campaigns have been rare; rather, there are degrees of similarity. For example, Coca-Cola's print advertisements for the United States and France used the same concept of "refreshment" and both showed young people who had been playing sports. For the United States the advertisement showed a baseball player and the slogan "Coke is it!" For France the slogan was "Un Coca-Cola pour un sourire" (A Coca-Cola for a smile) and the photograph showed soccer players.

Sometimes the elements of standardization might be regional rather than global. American Express's United States campaign of "Do You Know Me?" aimed at gaining market share from other credit cards. However in Europe the company needed to build credit card usage. A Europe-wide campaign was devised with a common appeal, even though each country's advertisements used different characters and situations.[38]

Obviously, if a firm is going to sell in a country with a different language, messages will have to be translated into that language. On the surface, this would seem to be an easy project; however, the number of ludicrous but costly mistakes firms have made attest to its difficulty. Sometimes what is an acceptable word or direct translation in one place is obscene, misleading, or meaningless in another. One firm described itself as an "old friend" of China, but used the character for "old" that meant former instead of long-term.[39] Even product names may present a problem: GM thought that its model Nova could easily be called the same in Latin America, since it means "star" in Spanish. However, people started pronouncing it "nō vä," which is the Spanish translation for "it does not go." Even within the same language words can mean different things in different countries. For example, United Airlines showed Paul Hogan, star of the *Crocodile Dundee* films, in the Australian

Outback on the cover of its inflight magazine. The caption, "Paul Hogan Camps it Up," meant "flaunts his homosexuality" in Australian slang.[40]

What is allowed legally in one place may not be allowed elsewhere. The basic reasons for the differences are national differences in views on consumer protection, competitive protection, promotion of civil rights, standards of morality, and nationalism.[41] A few examples should illustrate the vast differences that exist. In terms of protection, policies differ on the amount of deception permitted, what can be advertised to children, whether warnings must be given of possible harmful effects, and the degree to which ingredients must be listed. The United Kingdom and the United States allow direct comparisons of competitive brands (e.g. Pepsi versus Coca Cola), whereas the Philippines prohibits them. Only a few countries regulate sexism in advertising. In terms of morality and good taste, advertising of some products (e.g., contraceptives and feminine hygiene products) have been restricted in some locales. Elsewhere restrictions have been placed on ads that might prompt children to misbehave and those that show barely clad women. The nationalism issue has risen in several countries that restrict the use of foreign words, models, or themes in advertisements.

Yet in spite of these differences there is evidence that there are segments of consumers in each country that respond similarly to similar messages. (Companies typically aim different campaigns at different segments within a given country.) The size of each segment as a portion of total potential consumers may differ substantially, though, from nation to nation.[42] Because of this, companies may have to alter the portion of expenditures for different campaigns within each country.

Nationality Images

Images of products are affected by where they are made.

Firms should consider whether to create a local or foreign image for their products. Certain countries, particularly developed ones, tend to have a higher-quality image for their products than do other countries. But images can change. Consider that various Korean firms sold abroad under private labels or under contract with well-known companies for many years. Some of these are now emphasizing their own trade names and the quality of Korean products.[43]

There also are image differences concerning specific products from specific countries. The French firm BSN-Gervais Dannone brews the largest selling bottled beer in Europe, and the firm's director general frankly admits that the Kroenenbourg trademark "sounds German."[44] But the image that will help to sell a product in one country may not have the same effect in another. In a unique approach, Champagne India Ltd. has allowed its importers to choose the name wherever its bubbly wine is sold. It is sold as "Omar Khayyam" in Britain, "Marquise de Pompadour" in West Germany, and "Guatamah Buddha" in Japan.[45]

Generic and Near-Generic Names

If a brand name is used for a class of product, the firm may lose the trademark.

Companies want their product names to become household words but not so much so that trademarked names can be used by competitors to describe similar products. In the United States the names Xerox and Kleenex are nearly synonymous with copiers and paper tissues, respectively, but have remained proprietary brands. Some other names, such as cellophane, linoleum, and cornish hens have become generic, or available for anyone to use.

Internationally, producers sometimes face substantial differences among countries that may either help or frustrate their sales. Roquefort cheese and champagne are proprietary names in France but generic in the United States, a situation that impairs French export sales of those products. A factor impeding international sales of U.S., Canadian, Irish, and Japanese whiskies is the fact that in much of the world whiskey is a synonym for Scotch whiskey.[46]

LDC Criticism

Critics argue that MNE advertising leads to superfluous and dangerous product consumption in LDCs.

Related to arguments that MNEs introduce superfluous products that consumers in LDCs cannot afford is the assertion that advertising for these products has led to their acceptance by people who are not equipped to understand the product implications or their needs.

The most famous case in this respect involved sales of infant formula to developing countries. Infant mortality increased in the poor countries because the rate of bottle feeding increased over breast feeding. Because of low incomes and poor education, mothers frequently overdiluted formula so that it was no longer nutritious and gave it to their babies in unhygienic conditions. Critics argued that the increased bottle feeding resulted from heavy promotion of formula by such firms as Nestlé, Bristol-Meyers, and American Home Products. The firms, in contrast, claimed that increased bottle feeding was due to factors other than promotion of formula—specifically, the firms cited the rise in the number of working mothers and a general trend of providing fewer products and services being made in the home. The promotion, they argued, got people to give up their "home brews" in favor of the most nutritious breast milk substitute available. The World Health Organization overwhelmingly passed a voluntary code for restricting formula promotion in developing countries. The company most hit by criticism was Nestlé because it had the largest market share in developing countries and because it was easy to organize a boycott against Nestlé because of its name-identified products. Although formula sales in LDCs never accounted for more than 3 percent of Nestlé's worldwide business, management was most concerned about how the criticism would affect its image. The company agreed to prohibit advertising that would discourage breast feeding, to limit free formula supplies at hospitals, and to ban personal gifts to health officials.[47]

DISTRIBUTION

Firms may have to devise ways to help distributors so they give attention to their products.

A company may accurately assess market potential, design products or services for that market, and promote to likely consumers; however, it will have little likelihood of reaching its sales potential if the goods or services are not conveniently available to customers. This includes getting goods to where people want to buy them. For example, does a man prefer to buy hair dressing in a grocery store, barber shop, drugstore, or some other type of outlet?

Distribution is the course—physical path or legal title—that goods take between production and consumption. In international marketing, a producer must decide on the method of distribution among countries as well as the method of distribution within the foreign country of sale. Chapters 14 and 15 discussed many considerations for distribution, including the channels of distribution to move goods among countries, how the title to goods gets transferred, and the forms of operations for foreign market penetration. This section does not repeat these aspects of distribution; rather, it discusses distributional differences and conditions within foreign countries which an international marketer should understand.

Difficult Standardization

Distribution reflects different country environments:

- It may vary substantially among countries.
- It is difficult to change.

Different systems. Within the marketing mix, distribution is one of the most difficult functions to standardize internationally for several reasons. First, all countries have their own distribution systems. These are usually difficult to change because they have evolved over time and reflect countries' cultural, economic, and legal environments. Such factors as the attitudes toward owning one's own store, the cost of paying retail workers, labor legislation affecting chains versus individually owned stores differently, legislation restricting the size of stores, the trust that owners have in their employees, the efficacy of the postal system, and the financial ability to carry large inventories are but a few of the factors that influence how goods will be distributed in a given country.

A few examples should illustrate how different the distribution norms are. Finland, for example, has few stores per capita because of the predominance of general-line retailers, whereas Italian distribution is characterized by a very fragmented retail and wholesale structure. In the Netherlands, buyers' cooperatives deal directly with manufacturers. In Japan, there are cash and carry wholesalers for retailers who do not need financing or delivery. An estimated six million people buy by mail in West Germany; however, Portugal has offered little as a market for mail-order development. Companies such as Avon have had success in selling within homes in the United States, but not in Japan.

How do these differences affect companies' marketing activities? One soft drink company, for example, has targeted most of its European sales through grocery stores; however, the method of getting its soft drinks to those stores has varied widely. For the United Kingdom there is one national distributor who has been able to gain sufficient coverage and shelf space so that the soft drink firm can concentrate on other aspects of its marketing mix. For France, a single distributor has been able to get good coverage in the larger supermarkets, but not in the smaller ones; consequently, the soft drink firm has been exploring how to get secondary distribution without upsetting the relationship with the primary distributor. Within the Norwegian market, there are regional distributors; thus the soft drink firm is challenged in getting them to cooperate sufficiently so that national promotion campaigns can be effective. Within Belgium, the company could find no acceptable distributor, so has had to take on the functions itself.

Most distributors are national rather than international.

Domestic rather than international distributors. Whereas most large advertising and public relations firms have become international, few wholesalers and retailers have expanded their services abroad. For advertising and public relations firms this had been an advantage in developing various degrees of global programs. For wholesalers and retailers, there has, of course, been some international movement, such as illustrated in the M & S case earlier. Mostly, though, companies that are marketing abroad must rely on the services of locally controlled distributors. It is extremely difficult, especially if initial sales expectations are not very high, to get these distributors to alter their accustomed practices to adhere to some practice that the producer wishes to standardize globally.

Choosing Distributors and Channels

Internal handling. Chapter 15 discussed the pros and cons of handling foreign operations with a company's own facilities versus using contracts with other firms for handling the operations. The same considerations hold for distribution as well. Usually at a low amount of sales, it is more economical to handle distribution through a contract with another company; but a firm may lose a certain amount of control this way. If a company does use external distributors, management should reassess periodically if sales have grown to the point that they can be handled effectively internally.

Distribution may be handled internally:

- At high volume.
- When there is a need to deal directly with customer due to the nature of the product.
- When the customer is global.
- To gain a competitive advantage.

In addition to a high volume of sales, some other circumstances are conducive to the internal handling of distribution. One of these involves the nature of the product. When the product has any of the characteristics of high price, high technology, and need for complex after-sales servicing (such as aircraft), the producer probably will have to get quite involved in dealing directly with the buyer. In such a situation, the producer nevertheless may use some type of distributor within the foreign country who will serve to identify sales leads. A second situation is when the firm is dealing with global customers, such as an auto parts manufacturer who sells original equipment to the same automobile manufacturers in more than one country; such sales may go directly from producer to the global customer. A third situation is when the company views its main competitive advantage to be in its distribution methods, such as some food franchisors. Eventually they may franchise abroad but maintain their own distribution outlet as well to serve as a "flagship."

Some evaluative criteria for distributors are:

- Financial capability.
- Connections with customers.
- Fit with a firm's product.
- Other resources.

Distributor qualifications. When using external channels of distribution, a company usually can choose from a number of alternatives. Four common criteria for comparing among these are: (1) financial strength; (2) good connections; (3) other business commitments; and (4) personnel, facilities, and equipment.[48] The first is important because of the potential long-term viability of the relationship as well as whether money can be put into such things as the maintanence of sufficient inventory. The second is particularly important if sales must be directed to certain types of buyers, such as government procurement agencies. The third involves whether the potential distributor has time for a firm's product and whether competitive or complementary products now are handled. Fourth, the current status of personnel, facilities, and equipment indicates not only ability to deal with the product, but also how quickly start-up is feasible.

Spare parts and service are important for sales.

Spare parts and repair. Consumers are reluctant to buy products requiring future spare parts and service unless they feel assured that these will be available readily at a good quality and reasonable price. The more complex and expensive the product, the more important after-sales servicing is. In the 1950s, for example, some European automobile producers entered the U.S. market without ample consideration of this factor. After the European firms made some initial sales, consumer "horror stories" followed, such as waiting weeks or months for parts and finding no trained mechanics. Sales dried up as a result. Volkswagen entered later and successfully invested heavily in parts depots and training as well as promotion. Where after-sales servicing is important, it may therefore be necessary for firms to invest in service centers for groups of distributors who serve as intermediaries between producers and consumers. At the same time, sales of parts and service sometimes may be as high as that of the original product sales.

Distributors choose what they will handle. Firms:

- May need to give incentives.
- May use successful products as bait for new ones.
- Must convince distributors that product and firm are viable.

Gaining distribution. Firms must do more than evaluate potential distributors. Distributors also choose which firms and products will get their emphasis. Both wholesalers and retailers have limited storage facilities, display space, money to pay for inventories, and transportation and personnel to move and sell merchandise; therefore they try to carry only those products with the greatest potential profits. If a firm is new to a country and wishes to introduce products that some competitors are already selling, it may be difficult to convince distributors to handle the new brands. Even established firms sometimes may find it hard to gain distribution for their new products, although they have the dual advantage of being known and being able to use existing profitable lines as "bait" for the new merchandise.

If a firm wishes to use existing distribution channels, it may need to develop incentives for those distributors to handle the product. Firms must analyze competitive conditions carefully in order to offer effective incentives. Kodak, for example, noted that a problem prevalent throughout the world was inventory control: On the one hand, distributors had to scrap outdated film or paper because of overordering or shifts in customer demands; on the other hand, there were frequently shortages of given brands or products because of international delivery problems and the inability of distributors to project future demands with sufficient accuracy. By establishing forecasting techniques, weekly sales reports and replenishment shipments, and maintenance of regional inventories, Kodak was able to increase distribution by offering better service than before.[49]

Firms may turn to several other distribution possibilities, including the offer of higher margins, after-sales servicing, and promotional support, which may be on either a permanent or introductory basis. The type of incentive to be offered should depend as well on the comparative costs within each market. In the final analysis, incentives will be of little help unless distributors believe that a firm's products are viable. The company therefore must sell both itself as a reliable firm and its products to the distributors.

Distribution Segmentation

A firm may enter a market gradually by limiting geographic coverage and emphasizing only certain types of middlemen.

Many products and markets lend themselves to gradual development or to different distributional strategies in different areas. In many cases, geographic barriers divide countries into very distinct markets: For example, Colombia is divided by mountain ranges and Australia by a desert. In other countries, such as Zimbabwe and Zaire, very little wealth or few potential sales may lie outside the large metropolitan areas. In still others, advertising and distribution may be handled effectively on a regional basis. For example, when Kikkoman first began selling soy sauce in the United States, the company could not find middlemen willing and able to get the sauce onto the shelves of national supermarket chains; nor did Kikkoman have the resources to bypass the middlemen. However, the firm was able to target its first sales to the San Francisco area, where the product was already well known to much of the large Japanese-American population. Through a local food broker Kikkoman gained access to distribution in neighborhoods with a large Asian population. By advertising the product to the general public on television and by showing sales results from the initial distribution, the company was able to gain distribution in other neighborhoods as well. Two years later, Kikkoman moved into Los Angeles, where it continued to expand. Over the next seventeen years, using food brokers in all cases, it achieved national distribution and over 50 percent of the soy sauce market.[50] It is not uncommon for a firm to use one type of middleman in one area and another elsewhere.

Some Hidden Costs

When companies consider launching products in foreign markets, they must consider what final consumer prices will be in order to estimate a sales potential. Because of different national distribution systems, the cost of getting products to consumers varies widely from one country to another. Three of the areas which often contribute to cost differences in distribution are (1) the number of levels in the distribution system, (2) retail inefficiencies, and (3) inventory stock-outs.

Many countries have small multitiered wholesalers who sell to each other before the product reaches the retail level. This sometimes occurs because wholesalers are too small to cover more than a small geographic area, thus national wholesalers sell to regional ones, who sell to local ones, and so on. Japan is an example of a market in which there are about the same number of wholesalers as in the United States despite the much smaller geographic area and population. Because each intermediary adds a markup, the product prices are driven up.[51]

Because of low labor costs and a basic distrust by owners of all but family employees, it is common to find retail practices, particularly in developing countries, that raise the price of merchandise to the shopper. A typical situation is counter rather than self-service: A customer waits to be served and shown merchandise. If the customer decides to purchase what is shown, the customer is given an invoice to take to a cashier's line in order to pay. Once the invoice is stamped as paid, the customer must go to another line to pick up the merchandise after presenting the stamped invoice. This procedure is followed for purchases as small as a pencil. The use of the added personnel adds to the cost of retailing, and the added time that people must be in the stores means that fewer people can be served in the given space.

SUMMARY

- Although the principles of selling abroad are the same as those in the home country, the international businessperson must deal with a less familiar environment which may be subject to rapid change.
- Some methods for broadly assessing foreign demand for products are: analysis of consumption patterns; estimates based on what has happened in other countries; studies of historical trends; income elasticity; and regression and gap analysis. Some problems with these tools include taste and technology changes that render past observations and observations in other countries invalid for specific countries.
- A standardized approach to marketing implies maximum uniformity in products and programs among the countries of operation. Although this will minimize expenses, most firms make changes to fit country needs in order to increase the volume of sales.

- A variety of legal and other environmental conditions may call for alteration of products in order to capture foreign demand. In addition to determining when products should be altered, businesspeople also must decide how many and which products to sell abroad.
- Because of different demand characteristics, a product may be in a growth stage in one country and a mature, or declining, stage in another. Firms can usually exert more control over pricing during the growth stage.
- Governmental regulations may directly or indirectly affect the prices companies charge. International pricing is further complicated because of changes in the values of currencies, differences in product preferences, and variations in fixed prices versus bargaining.
- For each product in each country a company must determine not only its promotional budget, but also the mix of the budget between push and pull. The relationship between push and pull promotions should depend on the distribution system, cost and availability of media, consumer attitudes, and the product price relative to incomes.
- Some major problems for standardizing advertising in different countries involve translation, legal, media availability, and credibility factors.
- Distribution channels vary substantially among countries. These differences may affect not only the relative costs of operating, but also the ease of making initial sales.

CASE: SOURCE PERRIER[52]

During the strong dollar era of the 1950s to 1960s, when hordes of Americans flocked to vacation in France, one of the tourists' vocal complaints was the impurity of French tap water. When purchasing the alternative, bottled water, they complained about those with bubbles. At that time, the probability that, by 1980, Americans would be importing from France over $65 million per year of Perrier's naturally carbonated water seemed almost impossible. But there was an earlier market for French water in the United States: One of the earliest customers was Benjamin Franklin, who, after returning from being ambassador in Paris, imported his drinking water. Near the turn of the century, Perrier set up U.S. distribution; however, by 1976, sales had reached only 3.5 million bottles per year. The so-called Perrier freaks had to hunt in gourmet shops or a few bars to quench their thirsts. At over $1 for a 23-ounce bottle, the product had gained acceptance among only a small group of high-income people. Thus it was a product with small sales and high retail margins.

By the early 1970s, Source Perrier was having trouble sustaining growth in France given its large share of the bottled drink market. The company sought to increase sales by acquiring related French companies, including firms producing soft drinks, milk, chocolate, and confectionery products. In 1972 Poland Spring, a U.S. firm producing still (noncarbonated) spring water was acquired. None of these ventures fared well under Perrier's leadership.

The Chairman of Source Perrier, Gustave Levin, met Bruce Nevins, who as an executive of Levi Strauss had been instrumental in the upsurge of jeans sales. Nevins believed it would be possible to develop a mass market for a "noncaloric, chic alternative to soft drinks." The U.S. soft drink market at that time was about $10 billion wholesale. Thus the stakes were high—so high, in fact, that Perrier sold off 70 percent of its acquisitions in 1975–1976 (including Poland Spring) to finance a U.S. marketing subsidiary. The new subsidiary, Great Waters of France, was headed by Bruce Nevins.

A number of conditions made Nevins optimistic about the possible acceptance of Perrier water by U.S. consumers. The most important of these was growing consumer diet-consciousness. Miller Brewing had had phenomenal success a few years earlier with the introduction of Lite beer. Since cyclamates had been banned in soft drinks, producers of low-calorie sodas had turned to saccharin, which many people found distasteful. Also there was no popular low-calorie drink considered chic. The use of the adjective "diet" simply announced that the drinker had weight problems. If people could be persuaded that Perrier tasted good, then it could become a preferred low-calorie alternative.

A second trend Nevins observed was toward natural foods for health reasons. Even tap water and the 75 percent of bottled water processed from tap water had become suspect because in the process of purification, cancer-suspect chlorine derivatives were added to water. Furthermore, certain viruses, sodium, and heavy metals still were found in most purified water and soda water. Perrier came from natural springs and contained high levels of calcium, very little sodium, and no additives. It could be promoted as a natural drink with healthy properties, even though some of the bubbles were lost when the water was removed from the springs and put back in during the bottling process.

A third factor was a growing U.S. preference for imports apparent not only in the rising ratio of imports to gross national expenditures, but also in the acceptance of "foreignness." In terms of food, so-called gourmet restaurants, cookbooks, dinner clubs, ingredients, and wines were becoming commonplace, and French items were practically synonymous with the word *gourmet.* Perrier might capitalize successfully on these attitudes.

The marketing program for Great Waters of France got underway in 1977. One of the first questions was in which part of the market to position Perrier.

The three trends just discussed clearly would lead to different price, promotional, and distributional strategies. In seeking the diet market segment, for example, Perrier would come face-to-face with Coca-Cola and Pepsi-Cola, which between them controlled 45 percent of the soft drink market. These firms, along with many others, fought vigorously in the market by keeping prices fairly low, advertising heavily, and clamoring for shelf space in supermarket soft drink sections. The difficulty of competing in this segment is evident from the experience of Schweppes, which despite establishing U.S. bottling facilities and engaging in heavy marketing outlays had failed to get even 1 percent of the market. Competing in this mass market segment also might cause Perrier to lose the snob appeal it held among high-income buyers.

Entering the natural or health foods segment would pit Perrier against other bottled water producers and various tonics that contained healthful additives. This was a very small market compared with that for soft drinks. The 1976 sales of bottled water were $189 million, of which 93 percent was from purified domestic still water, which was sold largely in five-gallon containers at low prices through home or commercial delivery. Less than 20 percent of bottled water was sold in retail stores, and there was little brand identification. To expand retail sales probably would mean concentrating on gaining shelf space in the health food sections of stores. Since bottled water sales were determined to be much more geographically concentrated (about 50 percent in California) than soft drink sales, it would be far easier for Perrier to target its promotion and distribution for this segment.

Source Perrier had been selling to the gourmet market for some seventy years. Undoubtedly there were usage and distributional gaps in this market. The total sales of mineral water in 1976 were only $15 million. Primary demand might be increased, and Perrier might be made more readily available through increased distribution to specialty stores and new distribution to the growing gourmet sections of supermarkets.

Perrier decided to hit the mass market by competing in the soft drink market segment, but price was a problem. Through massive distribution, the retail price could be cut about 30 percent from what it was when the company emphasized the gourmet segment of the market; however, the price was still about 50 percent higher than the average soft drink price partly due to the cost of transporting water across the Atlantic. Furthermore, the price included a retail gross margin of 27.6 percent as compared to 22.6 percent on soft drinks in order to make supermarkets more willing to handle Perrier. Perrier kept its price at a "rock bottom" not only to become more price competitive with domestic soft drinks, but also to dissuade other European firms from exporting to the United States. To get people to pay what was still a high price, the company had to segment the soft drink market differently than anyone had heretofore done: by aiming at an adult population and using the higher price to gain snob appeal.

Great Waters of France felt that distribution was the key to success. A sales force of forty people, almost all of whom were formerly with soft drink firms, was hired. Three cities (New York, San Francisco, and Los Angeles) were picked for the first expansion efforts because they had consumers with the largest penchant for imported food items. The company made a film designed to convey to distributors and supermarket chains that Perrier water had a long-term viability. The film showed that the springs had been popular as far back as 218 B.C., when Hannibal partook of the waters, and that the present firm dates back to 1903, supplies 400 million bottles a year, and outsells the leading cola in Europe by 2 to 1. Perrier sought the most aggressive distributors, including soft drink bottlers, alcoholic beverage distributors, and food brokers in different areas. For Perrier's success, it was essential that distributors be able to get supermarket space in the soft drink sections, replenish stocks frequently, and set up point of purchase displays. One of the first distributors, Joyce Beverage Management, bought fifty-five trucks and hired 100 additional people to handle the Perrier account. In the introductory period, arrangements were made for secondary display stacks and in-store tastings. The company also gave cents-off coupons with purchases. Within a year, Perrier had moved from three to twenty major market areas; this was doubled in the second year.

Perrier developed 11-ounce and 6.5-ounce bottles, the latter sold in multipacks. They also developed a modern logo on the bottles, which was later replaced by the original label design, more in line with the old-world image that the firm wished to project. With initial distribution assured, it was necessary to get sufficient appeal so that the bottles on the shelves would be sold. In Europe the company could make therapeutic claims; however, U.S. law very strictly forbade this. In test marketing, Perrier tried such themes as "Formerly heavy drinkers such as Richard Burton and Ed McMahon are now 'hooked' on Perrier" and Perrier "contains no sodium which causes heartburn."

These claims were abandoned in favor of messages emphasizing the water's qualities as a natural thirst-quencher with no calories and no additives. Initial promotion was regional, relying heavily on the print media. Groups of food and beverage writers were invited for dinners and exhibitions so that they would write about Perrier. The company sponsored marathons so that the product would be associated both with "healthiness" and "thirst-quenching." As distribution became national, Perrier got Orson Welles to appear in television spots on major networks. The advertising budget was set high. Perrier was able to maintain snob appeal by getting tidbits in gossip columns about celebrities being seen sipping Perrier in the "right places."

Sales increased rapidly to 21 million bottles in 1977, 60 million in 1978, over 100 million in 1979, and over 200 million in 1980. The increase did not go unnoticed by either the media or competitors. By 1979 a bottling executive said, "Everyone with water seeping from a rock is buying glass, slapping a label on it, and marketing a new bottled water." Some of the old bottled spring water firms suddenly sought a larger share of the growing market. They promoted blind tasting comparisons to emphasize that U.S. water was just as tasty as the imports. Nestlé's Deer Park brand made a challenge with a spring water priced 35 to 40 percent below Perrier. A Chicago firm, Hincley and Schmitt, introduced Premier in a bottle with a label that unashamedly copied Perrier. Its theme was, "Let your guests think it's imported." Norton Simon's Canada Dry began repositioning its club soda to be more competitive with Perrier. A market research group, SAMI, reported 104 brands of bottled waters in its territory.

By late 1980, Bruce Nevins believed that the "U.S. market for sparkling water is in the process of maturing." Perrier's sales peaked in 1980 and began falling, largely because of competition from domestic seltzer (carbonated tap water) and domestic club soda (carbonated tap water to which mineral salts are added usually). Sales of imported water in the United States fell from 28.1 million gallons in 1979 to 12.1 million in 1982. To combat U.S. domestic competition, Perrier repurchased Poland Spring in 1980. After buying Poland Spring in 1976 for $1 million, Poland Spring's new owners had carbonated the still water, modernized the facilities, and captured 6 percent of the bottled water market. The reported purchase price in 1980 was $10 million. But most of the growth in bottled waters was not for spring waters, which constituted only 11 percent of the bottled water market in 1982. Another problem was that the name Perrier was practically becoming generic as customers increasingly asked for Perrier when they simply wanted some kind of sparkling water.

In 1982, Perrier devised a new U.S. strategy, the handling of specialized imports that could be sold to market segments similar to those to which Perrier seemed to appeal. This segment was described by different Perrier officials as "aspirant people who try to improve their quality of life," as "households with incomes of $30,000 or more," and as "the same people who tend to buy better fashions, better cars and the like." Perrier took on Lindt chocolate from Switzerland in 1982 and Bonne Maman preserves from France in 1983. Both of these firms had been selling previously in the U.S. market with annual sales of $1 million and $1.5 million before the Perrier connection. By 1984 their sales were estimated to be $15 million and $5 million, respectively. In 1985 Perrier began marketing its mineral water with traces of lemon, lime, or orange flavoring to try to shore up its U.S. water sales. Source Perrier also began to look seriously for the first time at the British and German markets where sales were increasing despite little advertising and marketing efforts.

But what had appeared to be a maturing of the U.S. bottled water market turned out to be a mere blip. By the mid-1980s industry sales were growing at between 15 percent and 20 percent annually, the second fastest beverage growth just behind wine coolers; the fastest segment of that growth was for imported mineral water. But the U.S. market has continued to be fragmented. One reason is that the cost and technology to enter the market are low; thus fifty new companies started up in 1986 alone. A second reason is that transportation costs lead to regional distribution. By 1985 only Perrier was distributed nationally because it is actually cheaper to ship the water from France than to ship domestic waters across the United States by truck or rail. By 1988 several industry trends seemed apparent to Perrier's management:

1. Growth in all sectors of the bottled water market would be robust over the next ten years, especially in geographic areas not yet accounting for a large share of the sales.
2. Big competitors increasingly would get involved. Coca-Cola, PepsiCo, Anheuser-Busch, and Japan's Suntory had all recently gotten involved in some aspect of the market through ownership, bottling, or distribution.
3. Because of the capital-intensive nature of distribution (e.g., cost of adding trucks), growth is more apt to come from acquisitions by the bigger competitors than from the start-up of new firms.
4. New importers would attack Perrier through targeting specific U.S. market niches. For example, Rambosa (Sweden) targeted snooty consumers, Eau Canada Sparcal (Canada) played up its high calcium content to appeal to women fearful of developing weak bones, and Heart of Tuscany (Italy) promoted its low mineral content for therapeutic value.

As a result of these trends, Perrier has reemphasized the bottled water market in the United States as opposed to either the expansion of water sales to other countries or to the handling of related products. Frederick W. Zimmer, chairman of Perrier Group of America said, "The U.S. market has far and away the biggest potential. And we're aiming to take the lion's share." This major share is expected to come about largely through acquisitions: Perrier acquired Calistoga in California, Oasis Water in Texas, and Zephyr Hill in Florida. In 1987 it out-bid major competitors to acquire Arrowhead, the market share leader in bottled water, for an estimated $500 million.

QUESTIONS

1. Might Perrier have been better off by positioning itself in a segment other than the soft drink market?
2. Should Perrier have tried a means other than exporting to penetrate the U.S. market?
3. What options are open to Perrier in the U.S.?
4. What lessons were learned in the United States that might help Source Perrier if it expands in Britain and Germany?

NOTES

1. Data for the case were taken from "M & S in Japan," *The Times* (London), August 7, 1978; "M & S Getting Their French Lessons Right," *The Times* (London), August 2, 1976, p. 16; Sandra Salmans, "Britain: How Marks & Spencer Lost Its Spark," *New York Times,* August 31, 1980, p. F3; Barbara Crossette, "British Store Shapes up for Parisians," *New York Times,* June 28, 1975, p. 14; "St. Michael Spreads the Gospel," *The Economist,* September 1977, pp. 68–69; "Super Supermarkets," *The Accountant,* June 26, 1980, pp. 981–983; Carrie Dolan, "Marks & Spencer Finds No-Frills Policy in Retailing Suits the British Just Fine," *Wall Street Journal,* April 14, 1981, p. 35; Alan Freeman, "Marks & Spencer Canada Adheres to Parent's Principles Despite Losses," *Wall Street Journal,* August 4, 1981, p. 39; Patience Wheatcroft, "Marks Looks at Sparks," *The Times,* (London), October 23, 1983, p. 53; Margaret de Miraval, "British Influence Aiding French Department Stores," *Christian Science Monitor,* July 7, 1983, p. 15; "International Corporate Report," *Wall Street Journal,* May 2, 1984, p. 35; "Marks & Spencer Tries Yet Again," *Financial Times,* April 25, 1985, p. 16; Janet Porter, "Marks and Spencer Loves French Customs," *The Journal of Commerce,* May 30, 1986, p. 1 +; Brian Oliver, "M & S Targets U.S.," *Advertising Age,* Vol. 58, No. 9, March 2, 1987, p. 46; Isadore Barmash, "Marks & Spencer Planning Brooks Brothers Expansion," *New York Times,* May 6, 1988, p. 29.

2. For a more extensive coverage of similar techniques, see Susan P. Douglas, C. Samuel Craig, and Warren J. Keegan, "Approaches to Assessing International Marketing Opportunities for Small- and Medium-sized Companies," *Columbia Journal of World Business,* Vol. 17, No. 3, Fall 1982, pp. 26–32.

3. UNCTAD/GATT, *The Compilation of Basic Information on Export Markets* (Geneva: UNCTAD/GATT, 1968). For a more detailed discussion of these procedures, see C. G. Alexandrides and George P. Moschis, *Export Marketing Management* (New York: Praeger Publishers, 1977), pp. 21–25.

4. Reed Moyer, "International Market Analysis," *Journal of Marketing Research,* November 1968, pp. 357–359.

5. Houston H. Stokes and Hugh Neuburger, "The Box-Jenkins Approach—When Is It a Cost-Effective Alternative?" *Columbia Journal of World Business,* Winter 1976, pp. 78–86.

6. Alfred Maizels, *Industrial Growth and World Trade* (Cambridge: University Press, 1963), p. 55.

7. H. Youn Kim, "Estimating Consumer Demand in Korea," *Journal of Development Economics,* Vol. 20, No. 2, 1986, pp. 325–338.

8. Isadore Barmash, "Genesco's Motivation," *New York Times,* November 28, 1971.

9. Moyer, *op. cit.,* pp. 357–359.

10. J. A. Weber, "Comparing Growth Opportunities in the International Marketplace," *Management International Review,* No. 1, 1979, pp. 47–54.

11. "Chocolate Makers in Switzerland Try to Melt Resistance," *Wall Street Journal,* January 5, 1981, p. 14.

12. For a discussion of niche strategy, see James Leontiades, "Going Global—Global Strategies vs. National Strategies," *Long Range Planning,* Vol. 19, No. 6, December 1986, pp. 96–104.

13. The similarity aspects among countries are discussed in Sandra M. Huszagh, Richard J. Fox, and Ellen Day, "Global Marketing: An Empirical Investigation," *Columbia Journal of World Business,* Vol. 20, No. 4, 1968, pp. 31–42.

14. John D. Daniels, "Combining Strategic and International Business Approaches through Growth Vector Analysis," *Management International Review,* Vol. 23, 3, 1983, p. 11.

15. John Thackray, "Much Ado about Global Marketing," *Across the Board,* April 1985, pp. 38–46.

16. Yves L. Doz, "Managing Manufacturing Rationalization within Multinational Companies," *Columbia Journal of World Business,* Fall 1978, pp. 82–93.

17. John S. Hill and Richard R. Still, "Adapting Products to LDC Tastes," *Harvard Business Review,* Vol. 62, No. 2, March–April 1984, pp. 92–101.

18. Andrew H. Malcolm, "On the Battlefield of Beauty," *New York Times,* May 22, 1977, p. 1.

19. William W. Locke, "The Fatal Flaw: Hidden Cultural Differences," *Business Marketing,* Vol. 7, No. 4, April 1986, p. 65+.

20. Theodore Levitt, "The Globalization of Markets," *Harvard Business Review,* Vol. 61, No. 3, May–June 1983, p. 94.

21. *Momentum* (an in-house magazine published by Coca-Cola), 1970, p. 17.

22. *Momentum,* 1970, p. 16, and Coca-Cola Annual Reports, 1982–1984.

23. Mattel, *1979 Annual Report,* p. 10.

24. Saeed Samiee, "Pricing in Marketing Strategies of U.S.- and Foreign-Based Companies," *Journal of Business Research,* Vol. 15, No. 1, February 1987, pp. 17–30.

25. "Swiss Find Iran Market for Chaders Unraveling," *Wall Street Journal,* January 26, 1981, p. 25.

26. "World Report," *Wall Street Journal,* January 20, 1977, p. 1; Patricia Wells, "Peddling Boursin to the French and Pizza to the Italians," *New York Times,* September 16, 1979, p. F3.

27. Johny K. Johansson and Hans B. Thorelli, "International Product Positioning," *Journal of International Business Studies,* Vol. 16, No. 3, Fall 1985, pp. 57–75.

28. John Marcom, Jr., "Consumer Credit Expands in Japan," *Wall Street Journal,* March 3, 1981, p. 35.

29. "The Luster Dims at Westinghouse," *Business Week,* July 20, 1974, p. 58.

30. Ann Hughey, " 'Gray Market' in Camera Imports Starts to Undercut Official Dealers," *Wall Street Journal,* April 1, 1982, p. 29; Douglas R. Sease, "Selling Abroad," *Wall Street Journal,* August 31, 1987, p. 1+.

31. Hill and Still, *op. cit.,* p. 95.

32. Laurence Jacobs, Reginald Worthley, and Charles Keown, "Perceived Buyer Satisfaction and Selling Pressure versus Pricing Policy: A Comparative Study of Retailers in Ten Developing Countries," *Journal of Business Research,* Vol. 12, No. 1, March 1984, p. 67.

33. Seymour Banks, "Cross-National Analysis of Advertising Expenditures: 1968–1979," *Journal of Advertising Research,* Vol. 26, No. 2, April–May 1986, p. 21.

34. Robert T. Green and Eric Langeard, "A Cross-National Comparison of Consumer Habits and Innovator Characteristics," *Journal of Marketing,* July 1975.

35. John A. Quelch and Edward J. Hoff, "Customizing Global Marketing," *Harvard Business Review,* Vol. 64, No. 3, May–June 1986, p. 62.

36. Dennis Chase, "Global Marketing: The New Wave," *Advertising Age,* June 25, 1984, p. 49+; for examples, see Joanne Lipman, "Ad Fad," *Wall Street Journal,* May 12, 1988, p. 1+.

37. "Multinationals Tackle Global Marketing," *Advertising Age,* June 25, 1984, p. 50.

38. John Marcom, Jr., "American Express's Ads in Europe Seek to Leap Borders," *Wall Street Journal,* April 1, 1988, p. 16.

39. Rene White, "Beyond Berlitz: How to Penetrate Foreign Markets through Effective Communications," *Public Relations Quarterly,* Vol. 31, No. 2, Summer 1986, p. 15.

40. John R. Zeeman, "What United Airlines Is Learning in the Pacific," speech before the Academy of International Business, Chicago, November 14, 1987.

41. "High Hurdles," *Wall Street Journal,* November 25, 1980, p. 56; Frank J. Prial, "Very, Very Bad, Pakistani Says as He Confiscates Lingerie Ad," *New York Times,* April 20, 1981, p. A11; Barry Newman, "Watchdogs Abroad," *Wall Street Journal,* April 8, 1980, p. 1+; J. J. Boddewyn, "Advertising Regulation in the 1980s: The Underlying Global Forces," *Journal of Marketing,* Vol. 46, Winter 1982, pp. 27–35; "Regulation of Advertising: Countries Starting to Eye Use of Foreign Languages," *Business International,* May 4, 1979, pp. 142–143.

42. Alfred S. Boote, "Psychographic Segmentation in Europe," *Journal of Advertising Research,* Vol. 21, December 1982/January 1983, pp. 19–25.

43. "Marketing Korean as Korean," *Business Korea,* Vol. 3, No. 5, November 1985, p. 41.

44. William H. Flanagan, "Big Battle Is Brewing as French Beer Aims to Topple Heineken," *Wall Street Journal,* February 22, 1980, p. 16.

45. Anthony Spaeth, "Indian Entrepreneur Exports Bubbly but Will Markets Burst His Bubble?" *Wall Street Journal,* January 4, 1988, p. 8.

46. "Global Report," *Wall Street Journal,* April 26, 1976, p. 6.

47. "Boycott against Nestlé over Infant Formula to End Next Month," *Wall Street Journal,* January 27, 1984, p. 19.

48. Subhash C. Jain, *International Marketing Management* (Boston: Kent Publishing Company, 1984), p. 435.

49. Robert E. Schellberg, "Kodak: A Case Study of International Distribution," *Columbia Journal of World Business,* Spring 1976, pp. 32–38.

50. John E. Cooney, "Selling American," *Wall Street Journal,* December 16, 1977, p. 1.

51. Michael R. Czinkota, "Distribution in Japan: Problems and Changes," *Columbia Journal of World Business,* Vol. 20, No. 3, Fall 1985, p. 66.

52. Data for the case were taken from James F. Clarity, "Perrier, the Snob's Drink, Soon to Come in Six Packs," *New York Times,* April 27, 1977, p. C1+; Louis Botto, "Straight from the Source," *New York Times Magazine,* June 26, 1977, pp. 68–72; Roger B. May, "French Bottler Tries to Replace U.S. Pop with a Natural Fizz," *Wall Street Journal,* April 12, 1978, p. 1+; Maria Anna Ferrara, "Nestlé's Deer Park Challenges Perrier in New York Market," *Wall Street Journal,* November 27, 1978, p. 34; "Deep Chic," *Wall Street*

Journal, December 7, 1979, p. 24; Carolyn Pfaff, "Perrier Fortunes Rest on Whimsical Chief," *Advertising Age,* April 14, 1980, p. 66; Peter C. DuBois, "Perrier Going Flat?" *Barron's,* May 12, 1980, p. 1; "Perrier: Putting More Sparkle into Sales," *Sales & Marketing Management,* January 1979, pp. 16–17; Bob Lederer and Martin Westerman, "How Perrier Became a Soft Drink," *Beverage World,* May 1979, pp. 37–45; "Perrier: The Astonishing Success of an Appeal to Affluent Adults," *Business Week,* January 22, 1979, pp. 64–65; "The Water Treatment," *Fortune,* January 12, 1981, p. 22; "Sales Boon for Bottled Water," *New York Times,* August 8, 1982, p. F27; Marian Burros, "Carbonated Water: More Than a Matter of Taste," *New York Times,* April 27, 1983, p. C1; Steven P. Galante, "Perrier's U.S. Marketing Know-How Put to Use for Other European Brands," *Wall Street Journal,* June 26, 1984, p. 30; Lawrence M. Fisher, "A New Zip to Bottled Water Sales," *New York Times,* May 23, 1986, p. F6; John Roussant, "Perrier's Unquenchable U.S. Thirst," *Business Week,* No. 3005, June 29, 1987, p. 46; Robert Alsop, "New Imports Aiming to Take the Fizz out of Perrier's Sales," *Wall Street Journal,* December 24, 1987, p. 11.

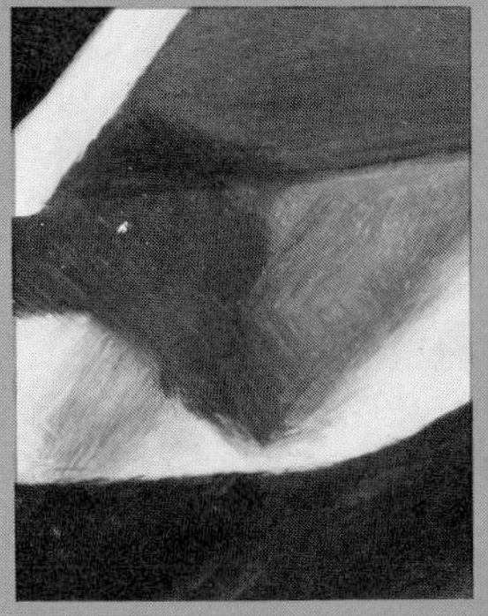

19

CHAPTER MULTINATIONAL ACCOUNTING AND TAX FUNCTIONS

Even between parents and children, money matters make strangers.
—Japanese proverb

- To examine the major factors influencing the development of worldwide accounting objectives, standards, and practices.
- To explain how to account for foreign currency transactions and foreign currency financial statements.
- To show how firms must disclose financial data concerning their international operations.
- To investigate the major aspects of the taxation of foreign-source income in the United States from export activities, branches, and foreign affiliates and subsidiaries.
- To examine some of the major non-U.S. tax practices and to show how international tax treaties can alleviate some of the impact of double taxation.
- To learn what MNEs need to consider in order to properly plan the tax function.

CASE:

COLGATE-PALMOLIVE COMPANY'S INTERNATIONAL OPERATIONS[1]

In 1986, Colgate-Palmolive derived 54 percent of its sales and 48 percent of its operating profits from outside of the United States, and it had 42 percent of its identifiable assets abroad. Although Colgate-Palmolive's 1986 *Annual Report* does not list all of the countries where the firm has manufacturing and sales operations, it discloses the data about the firm's geographic segments shown in Table 19.1.

As noted in Table 19.1, sales dollars increased each year from 1984–1986. In the 1986 *Annual Report,* management stated that a major reason for the 10 percent increase in sales in 1986 was the weak dollar and relatively stronger European currencies. In particular, a 4 percent increase in sales volume in Europe, combined with stronger European currencies, led to a 32 percent increase in sales. This was partly offset by results in Latin America, where the U.S. dollar was strong relative to all Latin American currencies in 1986.

TABLE 19.1

COLGATE-PALMOLIVE GEOGRAPHIC AREA DATA (Thousands of Dollars)

Geographic Segment	1986	1985	1984
Net sales			
United States	2,286,007	2,169,988	2,025,431
Europe	1,384,293	1,039,492	982,936
Western Hemisphere	821,952	843,378	849,344
Far East and Africa	492,324	470,820	511,468
	4,984,576	4,523,678	4,369,179
Operating profit			
United States	188,697	196,205	37,944
Europe	69,770	26,907	(31,976)
Western Hemisphere	82,712	74,839	81,035
Far East and Africa	20,510	30,824	37,823
	361,689	328,775	124,826
Identifiable assets			
United States	1,557,093	1,431,382	1,252,867
Europe	614,124	483,315	409,171
Western Hemisphere	308,550	317,980	346,122
Far East and Africa	225,736	206,801	231,619
	2,705,503	2,439,478	2,239,779

Source: Colgate-Palmolive *Annual Report, 1986.*

However, this has not always been the situation for Colgate-Palmolive. Sales dollars actually declined from 1982 to 1983. However, the 1983 *Annual Report* emphasized that the firm's unit volume increased during that time because of "renewed economic growth" in the United States and certain overseas countries and Colgate-Palmolive's increased market share in a variety of business categories.

In explaining why dollar sales volume fell during 1983 while unit sales volume increased, management pointed out the pressure from the strong U.S. dollar. Had exchange rates remained constant (everything else remaining equal), Colgate-Palmolive actually would have experienced sales growth of a little over 8 percent. As it happened, sales volumes outside of the United States did not increase as rapidly as the local currencies fell in value relative to the dollar. Thus the impact that exchange rates can have on the financial results of a firm from one year to the next becomes clear.

Colgate-Palmolive operates in a variety of countries whose currencies are not U.S. dollars. In order to prepare financial statements, Colgate-Palmolive had to translate the local currency financial statements into U.S. dollars. Table 19.2 provides a consolidated income statement for the firm in dollars. A consolidated statement is one that combines or consolidates the financial information from all of the firm's operations worldwide into one.

Some of the gains and losses that result from the translation of the financial statements into dollars are taken directly to the income statement. In addition, gains and losses arising from foreign currency transactions also are taken to the income statement. In 1986, the company included $6,284,000 of losses in net income; However, it is not clear specifically where that amount is contained. In prior years, Colgate-Palmolive put that amount in general and administrative expenses.

Table 19.3 contains the consolidated balance sheet for Colgate-Palmolive. Each dollar balance represents not only dollars but also the dollar equivalent of foreign currency balances from around the world. Although cash is listed as $24,704,000, there is no way of knowing how much is dollars, German marks, Swiss francs, or Japanese yen. Interestingly, the shareholders' equity section of the balance sheet contains an account entitled "Cumulative translation adjustments." That amount arises when the foreign currency financial statements are translated into dollars. This is the number used to make assets equal liabilities plus stockholders' equity. Notice that the number is negative for Colgate-Palmolive, indicating a reduction in shareholders' equity. In fact, that number is larger than the sum of the capital stock accounts; however, the number at least decreased from 1985 to 1986.

On the income statement in Table 19.2 is a line item called "provision for income taxes." That amount contains income taxes paid to the U.S. government as well as to foreign governments for income earned in other countries. Although the U.S. statutory rate was listed at 46 percent in the footnotes to the Colgate-Palmolive annual report, the rate was different abroad. In fact,

TABLE 19.2

COLGATE-PALMOLIVE COMPANY CONSOLIDATED STATEMENT OF INCOME (Thousands of Dollars Except Per Share Amounts)

	1986	1985	1984
Net sales	4,984,576	4,523,678	4,369,179
Cost of sales	2,892,322	2,680,693	2,616,722
Gross profit	2,092,254	1,842,985	1,752,457
Operating expenses and other items			
Marketing and selling	1,302,262	1,144,623	1,104,330
General and administrative	457,705	421,604	378,043
Provision for restructured operations	—	—	174,000
Interest expense	76,235	53,908	51,061
Interest income	(30,381)	(43,291)	(52,260)
Earnings from equity investments	(10,577)	(9,314)	—
Total operating expenses and other items	1,795,244	1,567,530	1,655,174
Income from continuing operations before income taxes	297,010	275,455	97,283
Provision for income taxes	119,545	107,654	54,615
Income from continuing operations	177,465	167,801	42,668
Discontinued operations			
Income from discontinued operations, net of income taxes	—	4,091	10,920
(Loss) gain on disposal of discontinued operations, net of income taxes	—	(62,450)	17,962
Net income	177,465	109,442	71,550
Earnings (loss) per common share			
Continuing operations	2.52	2.13	.51
Discontinued operations	—	.05	.13
Disposal of discontinued operations	—	(.79)	.22
Total	2.52	1.39	.86
Average number of common shares outstanding (in thousands)	70,230	78,605	82,599

Source: Colgate-Palmolive *Annual Report, 1986.*

the rate varies all the way from zero to significantly higher than 46 percent. Different countries have different rates and different ways to calculate taxable income.

On the balance sheet (Table 19.3) is a liability called "deferred income taxes," which arises because of the different ways that income is computed for tax purposes and financial statement purposes. Even though there are such timing differences for income earned abroad, Colgate-Palmolive does not include those differences if it feels that the income will be invested permanently abroad.

TABLE 19.3

COLGATE-PALMOLIVE COMPANY CONSOLIDATED BALANCE SHEET (Thousands of Dollars)

	1986	1985
Assets		
Current Assets		
Cash	24,704	39,240
Short-term investments	140,432	220,221
Receivables (less allowance for doubtful accounts of $14,705 and $13,735)	553,393	543,880
Inventories	637,098	616,067
Other current assets	128,660	101,907
Net assets of discontinued operations	—	132,256
Total current assets	1,484,287	1,653,571
Property, plant and equipment, net	1,113,728	978,273
Other assets	247,920	182,161
Total Assets	2,845,935	2,814,005
Liabilities and Shareholders' Equity		
Current Liabilities		
Notes and loans payable	129,933	336,323
Current portion of long-term debt	25,636	30,579
Accounts payable	413,722	348,550
Accrued income taxes	59,104	45,656
Other accruals	427,240	374,475
Total current liabilities	1,055,635	1,135,583
Long-term debt	522,023	529,255
Deferred income taxes	140,510	105,045
Other deferred liabilities	147,851	137,074
Shareholders' Equity		
Preferred stock	12,562	12,562
Common stock	83,485	83,211
Capital surplus	121,963	114,070
Retained earnings	1,423,845	1,342,036
Cumulative translation adjustments	(256,198)	(273,582)
	1,385,657	1,278,297
Treasury stock, at cost	(405,741)	(371,249)
Total shareholders' equity	979,916	907,048
Total liabilities and shareholders' equity	2,845,935	2,814,005

Source: Colgate-Palmolive *Annual Report, 1986.*

INTRODUCTION

The accountant is essential in providing information to decision makers.

The finance and accounting functions of Colgate-Palmolive, like those of any MNE, are very closely related. Each relies on the other in fulfilling its own responsibilities. The financial manager of any firm, domestic or international, is responsible for procuring and managing financial resources. But these functions cannot be performed without adequate, timely information from the accountant.

The actual and potential flow of assets across national boundaries complicates the finance and accounting functions. The MNE must learn to cope with differing rates of inflation, changes in exchange rates, currency controls, the risk of expropriation, and different customs, levels of sophistication, and local requirements.

The international controller must be concerned about different currencies and accounting systems.

A firm's accounting or controllership function is responsible for collecting and analyzing data for internal and external users. To manage assets, the corporate treasurer needs accounting information on the nature and extent of those assets. As noted in Chapter 17, local managers and operations are usually evaluated with information provided by the controller's office. Reports also must be generated for internal consideration, local governmental needs, creditors, shareholders, and prospective investors. The controller must be concerned about the impact of many different currencies and varied rates of inflation on the statements as well as be familiar with different countries' accounting systems.

FACTORS INFLUENCING THE DEVELOPMENT OF ACCOUNTING AROUND THE WORLD

Both form and substance of financial statements are different in foreign countries.

One of the problems that Colgate-Palmolive faces is that accounting systems vary around the world. This means that financial statements in France, for example, do not look the same as financial statements in the United States. Some observers argue that this is a minor matter, based in form rather than substance. In fact, however, the substance is also different, such as in Peru, where consolidation of related companies is not allowed; in Sweden, where significant inventory write-downs are allowed; and in France and West Germany, where tax accounting and book accounting are essentially the same. These variations put the MNE in a difficult position because it needs to prepare and understand reports generated according to the local accounting standards as well as prepare financial statements consistent with **generally accepted accounting principles (GAAP)** in the United States in order to generate consolidated financial statements.

Accounting Objectives

The FASB sets accounting standards in the United States.

Accounting is basically a process of identifying, recording, and interpreting economic events, and its goals and purposes should be clearly stated in the

Critical users of information are creditors, stockholders, investors, and employees.

The IASC sets standards internationally.

There is no binding worldwide set of accounting standards and practices.

objectives of any accounting system. The **Financial Accounting Standards Board (FASB)** in the United States stated that financial reporting should provide information useful in: (1) investment and credit decisions; (2) assessments of cash flow prospects; and (3) evaluating enterprise resources, claims to those resources, and changes in them.[2] The users identified by the Board are primarily investors and creditors, although other users might be considered important. The **International Accounting Standards Committee (IASC),** a multinational standard-setting organization comprised of professional accounting organizations from over forty countries, includes employees as well as investors and creditors as the critical users. Also named are suppliers, customers, regulatory and taxing authorities, and many others.

Although the question has been discussed widely, there has been no consensus on whether a uniform set of accounting standards and practices exists for all classes of users worldwide or even for one class of users. To understand the different accounting principles and how they affect the MNE's operations, we must examine some of the forces leading to the development of accounting principles internationally. Figure 19.1 shows these major factors. The top four factors deal with the nature of the enterprise

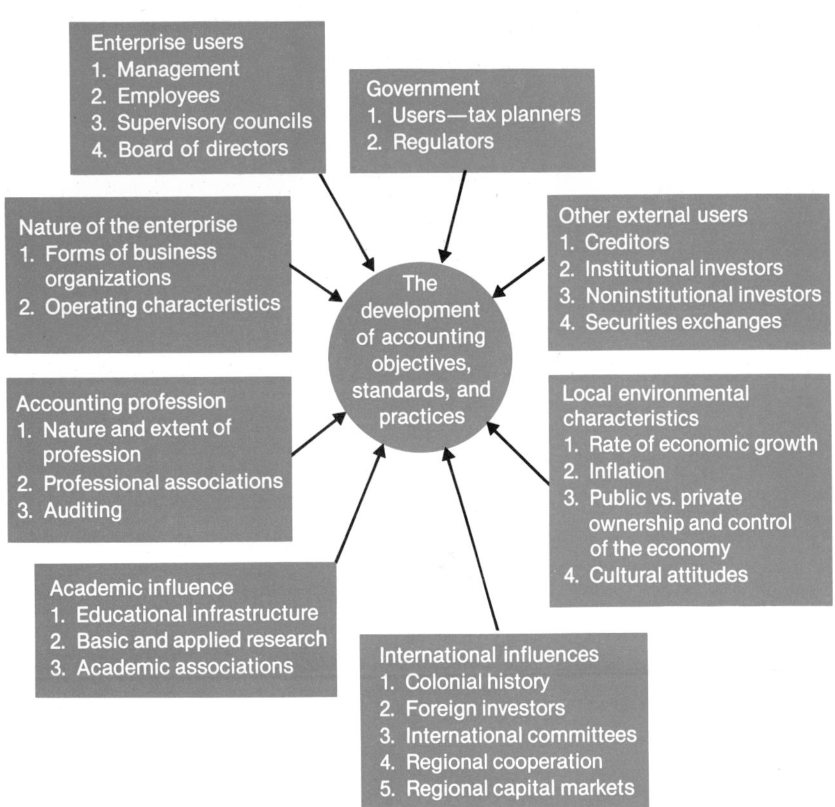

Figure 19.1
Major Domestic and Worldwide Factors Influencing the Development of Accounting Objectives, Standards, and Practices

Source: Lee H. Radebaugh, "Environmental Factors Influencing the Development of Accounting Objectives, Standards, and Practices—The Peruvian Case," *The International Journal of Accounting,* Fall 1975, p. 41.

and the direct users of information. The bottom four represent other major factors that affect accounting objectives, standards, and practices.

Nature of the Enterprise

Businesses all over the world generally are organized into corporations, partnerships, or proprietorships. Ownership of enterprises can be broadly based, as is typical of U.S. businesses; state-owned; or family owned, as is typical of firms in most developing countries. The nature and extent of information required by decision makers also may depend on the size of the organization and the nature of the business.

Enterprise Users

Within every enterprise there are many users of information, such as managers and employees. The quantity and quality of information provided depends on the users' level of sophistication as well as on the accountants' technical competence. Managers require specialized information to assist in decision making, and this has led to the development of managerial accounting. Employees have a vested interest in the enterprise and may have an impact on the disclosure of financial data as they seek better wages and working conditions.

Government

Government is one of the most pervasive forces in the development of accounting objectives, standards, and practices. Government can be divided into two groups: users and regulators. *Users* are tax authorities, planning commissions, and various agencies that compile statistics for general use. *Regulators,* such as the SEC in the United States, respond to the perceived best interests of the general public.

The extent to which the government becomes involved in the setting of objectives, standards, and practices depends on the interaction of all the factors listed in Fig. 19.1. Where the government is an important user of information, does not feel that the accounting profession is meeting users' needs, and does not foresee much change in the near future, it will probably take a much more active role in influencing the development of accounting.

Other External Users

The major external users of information other than those mentioned above are investors and creditors. Investors can work alone or through institutions by way of pension funds, mutual funds, and other such investments. In countries where there is a small equity market, creditors tend to be an important source of financing and thus a strong influence on accounting standards and practices.

Local Environmental Characteristics

This category of factors influencing accounting is probably the broadest and perhaps the most important, including such diverse features as cultural attitudes and the nature and state of the economy. The four factors listed in Fig. 19.1 are by no means exhaustive. Although the characteristics are referred to as "local," they are not independent of the world economy. The rates of economic growth and inflation depend on a country's major trading partners as well as on internal economic conditions.

International Influences

Many international forces that are institutional rather than environmental have influenced accounting principles worldwide. A prime example is the colonial influence of England and France during the past few centuries. Each of these countries carried their business and accounting philosophies to their colonies and instituted similar systems. The United States also has tended to do this as its economic influence has spread through direct foreign investment.

Accounting Profession

As it has done in countries such as the United States, Canada, the United Kingdom, and the Netherlands, the accounting profession itself can influence the development of accounting principles. Three phases of the profession are important: (1) its nature and extent; (2) the existence of professional associations; (3) and the auditing function.

Academic Influence

The *academic infrastructure* refers to the quality of accounting education offered as well as to the accessibility of this education. One of the typical problems in developing countries is the shortage of qualified professors in the accounting field. Since instruction in accounting is not considered a full-time profession and generally is not done at a very high level, little academic research is done.

HARMONIZATION OF DIFFERENCES

Many differences in worldwide accounting standards and practices impede the move to harmonization. Some of the major factors are:

1. the diversity of views regarding the purpose of financial statements;
2. differences in the extent to which the accounting profession has developed in various countries;
3. the influence of tax laws on financial reporting;

4. requirements of company laws;
5. differences among countries in basic economic facts affecting financial reporting;
6. differences among countries in practices recommended by the accounting profession;
7. the failure of professional pronouncements to accord with economic facts; and
8. the lack of an agency to enforce worldwide accounting standards.[3]

The EC is setting accounting directives that must be incorporated into the laws of each member nation.

Despite these differences, some serious efforts have been undertaken to harmonize accounting standards on a regional as well as an international level. Regionally, the most ambitious and potentially most effective efforts are taking place in the EC. The EC's Commission is empowered to set directives, which are orders to the member states to bring their laws into line with the requirements within a certain transition period. The initial directives involved the type and format of financial statements, the measurement bases on which the financial statements should be prepared, the importance of consolidated financial statements, and the requirement that auditors ensure that the financial statements reflect a true and fair view of the operations of the firm being audited.

The IASC is trying to harmonize diverse standards worldwide.

The IASC was organized in 1973 by the professional accounting bodies of nine nations: Australia, Canada, France, West Germany, Japan, Mexico, the Netherlands, the United Kingdom and Ireland, and the United States. Since then, Italy, Nigeria, South Africa, and Taiwan (Republic of China) have been added as board members. Initially, the IASC wanted to develop standards that would have rapid and broad acceptance; thus it seemed to focus mostly on improved disclosure. More recently, it has been interested in tackling some substantive issues.

The IASC has no power or persuasion to help enforce its standards.

The IASC must rely on goodwill for acceptance of its standards since it has no legislative mandate as does the EC. However, a number of countries have used the standards as models for their own legislation. Singapore, for example, has adopted IASC standards successfully.

IASC standards closely resemble U.S. GAAP.

Most IASC standards have been issued after the relevant U.S. standards. In addition, there are few major differences between IASC standards and U.S. GAAP. Apparently the presence of the United States as a founding member of the IASC has allowed it considerable input and influence in the decision-making process. It would be difficult to imagine an IASC standard in substantial conflict with U.S. GAAP.

TRANSACTIONS IN FOREIGN CURRENCY

One of the major problems of international business is that of operating in different currencies. Chapter 20 deals with eliminating or minimizing foreign exchange risk. This section helps explain the proper recording and subsequent accounting of assets, liabilities, revenues, and expenses that are measured or denominated in a foreign currency. These transactions result from the purchase and sale of goods and services as well as the borrowing and lending of foreign currency.

Recording of Transactions

Foreign currency receivables and payables give rise to gains and losses whenever the exchange rate changes.

Any time a U.S. importer is required to pay for equipment or merchandise in a foreign currency, it must trade U.S. dollars for that currency to pay the supplier. Assume that Sundance Ski Lodge buys skis from a French supplier for FF 28,000 when the exchange rate was $0.1700/FF. Sundance would record the following on its books:

Purchases	4,760	
Accounts payable		4,760
FF 28,000 @ $0.1700		

As long as Sundance pays immediately, there is no problem. But what happens if the exporter extends to Sundance thirty days' credit? The original entry would be the same as above; during the next thirty days, anything could happen. If the rate changed to $0.1600/FF, Sundance would record a final settlement as follows:

Accounts payable	4,760	
Gain on foreign exchange		280
Cash		4,480

The merchandise stays at the original value of $4,760, but there is a difference between the dollar value of the account payable to the exporter ($4,760) and the actual dollars that the importer must come up with in order to purchase the French francs to pay the exporter ($4,480). The difference between the two accounts ($280) is the gain on foreign exchange and is recognized as income.

Transaction gains and losses must be included in income in the accounting period in which they arise.

These gains and losses arising from foreign currency transactions must be recognized at the end of each accounting period, even if the payable (in the case of a purchase) or receivable (in the case of a sale) has not been completed. For most U.S. companies this adjustment is made every month. Using the example just given, assume that the end of the month has arrived and Sundance still has not paid the French exporter. The skis continue to be valued at $4,760, but the payable has to be updated to the new exchange rate of $0.1600/FF. The journal entry to record that would be:

Accounts payable	280	
Gain on foreign exchange		280

The liability would now be worth $4,480. If settlement were to be made at the end of the next month and the exchange rate were to remain the same, the final entry would be:

Accounts payable	4,480	
Cash		4,480

If the U.S. firm were an exporter and anticipated receiving foreign currency, the corresponding entries (using the same information) would be:

Accounts receivable	4,760	
Sales		4,760
Cash	4,480	
Loss on foreign exchange	280	
Accounts receivable		4,760

In this case a loss results because the firm receives less cash than if it had collected its money immediately.

Correct Procedures for U.S. Firms

The procedures that U.S. firms must follow to account for foreign currency transactions are found in FASB Statement No. 52, "Foreign Currency Translation," which was adopted in December 1981. Statement 52 requires that firms record the initial transaction at the spot exchange rate that is in effect on that date and record receivables and payables at subsequent balance sheet dates at the spot exchange rate on those dates. Any foreign exchange gains and losses that arise from carrying receivables or payables during a period when the exchange rate changes are taken directly to the income statement.[4] In its 1986 *Annual Report,* for example, Colgate-Palmolive disclosed that it had foreign currency transactions losses that were included in net income that year. However, it did not disclose the actual amount.

TRANSLATION OF FOREIGN CURRENCY FINANCIAL STATEMENTS

Translation is the process of restating foreign currency statements into U.S. dollars.

Consolidation is the process of combining financial statements of different operations into one statement.

Even though Colgate-Palmolive receives reports originally developed in a variety of different currencies, eventually it must end up with one set of financial statements in U.S. dollars in order to help management and investors get an aggregate view of its worldwide activities in a common currency. The process of restating foreign currency financial statements into U.S. dollars is known as **translation.** The combination of all of these translated financial statements into one is known as **consolidation.**

Translation in the United States is a two-step process: The first step involves recasting the foreign currency financial statements into statements consistent with U.S. GAAP; the second step involves translating all foreign currency amounts into U.S. dollars.

FASB Statement No. 52 also describes how firms must translate their foreign currency financial statements into dollars. The complete process of translation is too technical to discuss here; a textbook in international accounting can provide the details.[5]

Translation Methods

Functional currency is the currency of the primary economic environment in which the entity operates.

The current rate method is used when the local currency is the functional currency.

The temporal method is used when the parent's reporting currency is the functional currency.

Every income statement account is multiplied by the average exchange rate.

Statement 52 allows for two methods to be used to translate financial statements: the current rate and the temporal methods. The choice of the translation method depends on the functional currency of the foreign operation. The **functional currency** is the currency of the primary economic environment in which the entity operates. If the functional currency is that of the local operating environment, the firm must use the **current rate method.** If the functional currency is the U.S. dollar, the firm must use the **temporal method.**

Since the current rate method is used more extensively than the temporal method, the following illustration focuses on the current rate method. According to the current rate method, all assets and liabilities are translated into dollars at the exchange rate in effect on the balance sheet date, also known as the current rate. For most U.S.-based MNEs which tend to use a calendar year, that would be the exchange rate in effect on December 31. Capital stock is translated at the exchange rate in effect when the stock is actually issued, and retained earnings is simply the dollar accumulation of income from all prior years.

The income statement is translated into dollars by using the average exchange rate for the year. The exchange rate used to translate dividends into dollars is the rate in effect when the dividends are actually declared.

Table 19.4 shows how to translate a balance sheet using the current rate method, and Table 19.5 does the same for the income statement. Note that the current rate (the exchange rate in effect on December 31, 1988) was $1.30; the rate in effect when capital stock was issued was $1.90; the average rate for the year was $1.40; and the rate in effect when dividends were declared was $1.42.

As noted in Table 19.5, the retained earnings balance at the end of 1987 was $11,560. The retained earnings balance for the end of the year is determined by adding net income for 1988 to the beginning retained earnings balance and subtracting dividends. That amount can then be put into the balance sheet in Table 19.4. The only amount in the balance sheet that is not determined by translating a local currency amount into dollars is the accumulated translation adjustment, which arises because accounts from year to year are translated at different exchange rates. That amount can be determined by subtracting liabilities, capital stock, and retained earnings from total assets.

Disclosure of Foreign Exchange Gains and Losses

Earlier, we mentioned that a company could experience two kinds of foreign exchange gains and losses: those that arise from foreign currency transactions and those that arise from the translation of foreign currency financial statements into dollars. Gains and losses from foreign currency transactions are taken directly to the income statement, but a firm is not required by Statement 52 to show the amount or the location on the income statement. As was noted in Table 19.2, Colgate-Palmolive does not disclose this information in the income statement, but it does mention in the footnotes to the financial statements that transactions losses are included in income.

According to the current rate method, translation gain or loss is taken to stockholders' equity.

The treatment of foreign exchange gains and losses arising from translation depends on how the firm translates its financial statements. If the current rate method is used, the translation gains and losses are taken to the balance sheet and called the accumulated translation adjustment. The amount of $256,198,000 that appears as the December 31, 1986, balance of the cumulative foreign currency translation adjustment in Table 19.3 reflects the cumulative balance on that date for Colgate-Palmolive. One of the footnotes to the financial statements explains more fully the changes in the balance between 1985 and 1986.

In the temporal method, translation gain or loss is taken to income.

If the temporal method is used, the translation gains and losses are taken to the income statement. That has caused a corporation's net income (and,

TABLE 19.4

BALANCE SHEET, DECEMBER 31, 1988

	Local Currency	Current Rate Method: Exchange rate	Current Rate Method: Dollars
Assets			
Cash and receivables	4,000	1.30	$ 5,200
Inventory	4,500	1.30	5,850
Property, plant, and equipment (net)	14,000	1.30	18,200
	22,500		$29,250
Liabilities and Shareholders' Equity			
Current liabilities	5,500	1.30	$ 7,150
Notes payable	5,500	1.30	7,150
Capital stock	5,000	1.90	9,500
Retained earnings	6,500		13,650
Accumulated translated adjustment			(8,200)
	22,500		$29,250

TABLE 19.5

INCOME STATEMENT, 1988

		Current Rate Method	
	Local Currency	Exchange rate	Dollars
Sales	18,000	1.40	$25,200
Expenses			
Cost of Sales	9,000	1.40	12,600
Depreciation	3,000	1.40	4,200
Other expenses	2,100	1.40	2,940
	14,100		19,740
Income before taxes	3,900		$ 5,460
Income taxes	1,900	1.40	2,660
Net income	2,000		2,800
Retained earnings (12/31/87)	5,000		11,560
	7,000		$14,360
Dividends	500	1.42	710
Retained earnings (12/31/88)	6,500		$13,650

therefore, earnings per share) to fluctuate wildly as the exchange rate changes, which is a major reason why firms prefer to use the current rate method where possible.

TAXATION

Tax planning influences profitability and cash flow.

Tax planning is crucial for any business, since it can have a profound effect on profitability and cash flow. This is true in international as well as domestic business. As complex as domestic taxation seems, it is relatively simple in comparison with the intricacies of international taxation. The international tax accountant must be familiar not only with the home country's tax policy relating to foreign operations, but also with the laws of each country in which the client operates.

Taxation has a strong impact on the choice of: (1) location in the initial investment decision; (2) legal form of the new enterprise, such as branch or subsidiary; (3) method of finance, such as internal versus external sourcing and debt versus equity; and (4) method of arranging prices between related entities.[6] This section of the chapter examines taxation for the firm involved in international operations. Emphasis will be placed on U.S. tax policy because of the nature and extent of U.S. foreign direct investment. As any country finds its firms generating more and more foreign-source income, it must decide on the principles of deferral, tax credits versus deductions, and so on. Therefore principles of taxation that U.S.-based MNEs face at home and abroad are, or could be, applicable to firms domiciled in other countries.

TAXATION OF FOREIGN-SOURCE INCOME

When a domestic firm makes the decision to sell its products internationally, it can do so directly through the export of goods and services (including licensing agreements, management contracts, and so on); through foreign branch operations (a legal extension of the parent); and through foreign corporations in which the domestic firm holds an equity interest that could vary from a small percentage to complete ownership.

Export of Goods and Services

Many enterprises, such as public accounting firms, advertising agencies, banks, and management consulting firms, deal in services rather than products. Many manufacturing industries also find it easier and more profitable to sell expertise, such as patents or management services, rather than goods. Generally, payment is received in the form of royalties and fees, and this payment usually is taxed by the foreign government. Since the sale of services is made by the parent, the sale also must be included in the parent's taxable income.

Despite the large amount of foreign direct investment, U.S. firms still export a great deal of merchandise. In 1987, this export figure reached $252.87 billion.[7] Generally, the profits from these exports are taxable immediately to the parent. However, many governments have created tax incentives to encourage exports.

A Foreign Sales Corporation can be used by a U.S. exporter to shelter some of its income from taxation.

In order to gain tax advantages from exporting, a U.S. firm can set up a **Foreign Sales Corporation (FSC)** abroad, according to strict guidelines established by the IRS. If the foreign corporation qualifies as an FSC, a portion of its income is exempt from U.S. corporate income tax. Also, the law provides that any dividends distributed by the FSC to its parent company are exempt from U.S. income taxation as long as that income is foreign trade income.

The FSC must be engaged in substantial business activity.

Certain kinds of economic activity qualify for the FSC legislation: the export of merchandise as well as services such as engineering services or architectural services. Also it is important that substantial economic activity take place outside of the United States. The FSC cannot be a mailbox company in Switzerland that simply passes documents from the United States to the importing country. The FSC must engage in advertising and sales promotion, processing customer orders and arranging for delivery, transportation, the determination and transmittal of a final invoice or statement of account and the receipt of payment, and the assumption of credit risk.[8]

Foreign Branch

Foreign branch income (loss) is directly included in the parent's taxable income.

Deferral means that income is not taxed until it is remitted to the parent company as a dividend.

A foreign branch is an extension of the parent rather than an enterprise incorporated in a foreign country, as is a foreign manufacturing subsidiary. Therefore any income generated by the branch is taxable immediately to the parent, whether or not cash is remitted. One important aspect of taxation of foreign branch income is that if the branch suffers a loss, the parent is allowed to deduct that loss from its taxable income, thus reducing its overall tax liability. There is no such thing as deferral in the case of a branch, since all income or loss is immediately combined with parent income or loss. **Deferral** means that foreign source income generally is not taxed until it is remitted to the parent company. Since the branch also pays corporate income tax to the government of the country in which it is operating, it may take advantage of the tax credit.

Foreign Corporations

In a CFC 50 percent of voting stock is held by "U.S. shareholders."

CFC. From a tax standpoint it is critical to determine first of all whether or not the foreign subsidiary or affiliate is a **controlled foreign corporation (CFC).** A CFC is any foreign corporation in which 50 percent or more of the voting stock or value of the corporation is held by "U.S. shareholders." A U.S. **shareholder** is a U.S. person or enterprise that holds 10 percent or more of the voting stock of the subsidiary. Table 19.6 explains how this might work.

Foreign corporation *A* is a CFC because it meets both tests described above. This is the case when *A* is a wholly owned subsidiary of parent firm *V* in the United States. Foreign corporation *B* is also a CFC because U.S. persons *V*, *W*, and *X* are qualified "U.S. shareholders," and their share of the voting stock exceeds 50 percent. Foreign corporation *C* is not a CFC because only U.S. persons *V* and *W* are qualified "U.S. shareholders," and their combined voting shares do not equal or exceed 50 percent.

TABLE 19.6

DETERMINATION OF CONTROLLED FOREIGN CORPORATIONS

Shareholders and Their Percentage of the Voting Stock	Foreign Corporation A	Foreign Corporation B	Foreign Corporation C
U.S. person V	100%	45%	30%
U.S. person W		10%	10%
U.S. person X		20%	8%
U.S. person Y			8%
Foreign person Z	—	25%	44%
Total	100%	100%	100%

Active income comes from the active conduct of a trade or business.

Passive income is usually from operations in tax-haven countries and results from investments and work of other affiliates.

A tax-haven country is one with low or no taxes on foreign source income.

Once a CFC has been identified, its income must be divided into two categories: (1) active income and (2) subpart F, or passive, income. **Active income** implies that it is income derived from the active conduct of trade or business, whereas **passive income** usually results from operations in so-called **tax-haven countries.** In Chapter 10, we discussed the importance of offshore financial centers. Companies established in these centers are often called *tax-haven subsidiaries.*

The tax-haven subsidiary sometimes has acted as a holding company for its parent of stock in foreign subsidiaries (called *grandchild* or *second-tier subsidiaries,* as illustrated in Fig. 19.2); a sales agent or distributor; an agent for the parent in licensing agreements or an investment company. The tax-haven subsidiary is meant to concentrate cash from the parent's foreign operations into the low-tax country and to use the cash for global expansion. As long as a dividend is not declared to the parent, no U.S. tax must be paid. However, the Revenue Act of 1962 eliminated the deferral concept for tax-haven subsidiaries involved in passive rather than active investments.

Subpart F income is earned by a CFC in a tax-haven country from passive activities outside of the country.

Subpart F income. As noted earlier, subpart F income is passive income, in that the company earning it is not actively seeking it. Subpart F income basically is earned by CFCs in a tax-haven country from activities outside of that country. That type of income comes from the following major sources.

1. **Holding company income:** primarily dividends, interests, rents royalties, and gains on sale of stocks.
2. **Sales income:** income from foreign sales subsidiaries that are separately incorporated from their manufacturing operations. The product is either manufactured, produced, grown, or extracted outside of and sold for use outside of the CFC's country of incorporation. Any CFC performing significant operations on the property is excluded, such as when personnel in the CFC are heavily involved in selling the product.
3. **Service income:** income from the performance of technical, managerial, or similar services for a related person and performed outside the country in which the CFC is organized.

Figure 19.2
The Tax-Haven Subsidiary Acting as a Holding Company

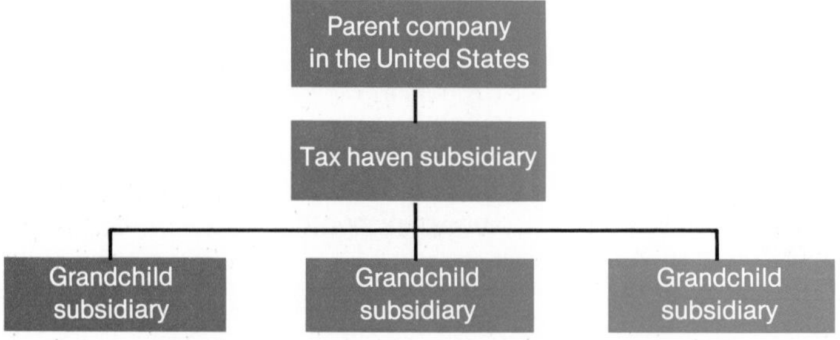

Figure 19.3
Deferral for Different Legal Forms

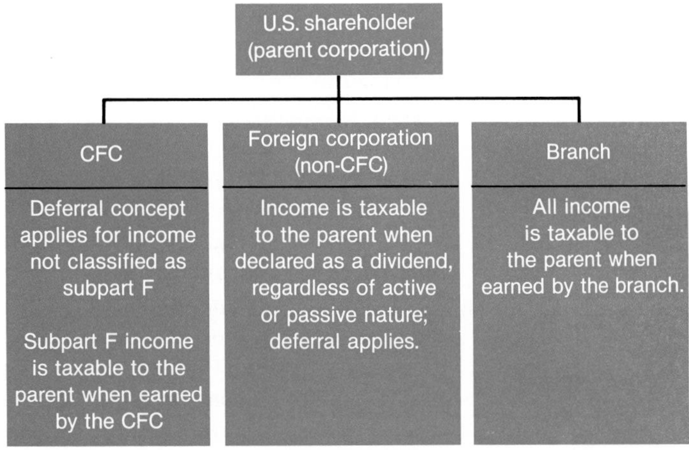

If a foreign corporation is not a CFC, income is not taxable until a dividend is received.

Subpart F income of a CFC is directly taxable to the parent.

The importance of distinguishing between a CFC and non-CFC and subpart F and active income is in the application of the deferral principle, which is summarized in Fig. 19.3. As long as a foreign corporation is not a controlled foreign corporation, its income is not taxable to the parent until a dividend is received by the parent. Thus the income is deferred from taxation in the U.S. If the foreign corporation is a controlled foreign corporation, the deferral principle applies to the active but not to the subpart F income, which is immediately taxable to the parent.

There is an exception, however. If foreign base company income is the lower of $1 million or 5 percent of gross income, none of it is treated as subpart F income. If foreign base company income is subject to a tax of at least 90 percent of the U.S. tax liability, the income also is not subject to U.S. tax.

Tax Credit

Every country has a sovereign right to levy taxes on all income generated within its borders. Problems arise when firms are owned by foreigners, such as foreign corporations, or are branches of foreign corporations. This problem has been important for U.S. firms because of the magnitude of foreign direct investment.

The IRS allows a tax credit for corporate tax paid to another country.

Credit is a dollar-for-dollar reduction of tax liability.

Credit must coincide with recognition of income.

As was mentioned earlier, the U.S. parent is able to defer recognition of active income until a dividend is declared to the parent. Then the parent gets credit for a portion of income taxes paid. For example, if 50 percent of the income of the foreign subsidiary is distributed as a dividend to the parent, the parent can claim no more than 50 percent of the tax as a creditable tax. Branches are not allowed the deferral privilege, so their income is taxed immediately to the parent, but all branch foreign income taxes are eligible for inclusion in the tax credit. Credit also is allowed for taxes paid by the parent to the foreign government on dividends paid by the foreign corporation to the parent. These taxes are called **withholding taxes.**

Credit is subject to the upper limit of what the tax would have been in the United States.

After the firm adds up its eligible credits, it finds that it is constrained by an upper limit imposed by the IRS. The upper limit is what the firm would have paid in taxes on that income in the United States. If the foreign source income is $1,000,000 and the applicable U.S. tax rate is 34 percent, the upper limit would be $340,000. If the tax credits added up from all over the world exceeded the $340,000, the firm could carry the excess credits back two years and re-compute their tax burden or carry them forward five years and try to use them. If the amount were less than the upper limit, the firm would be allowed the full amount.

In reality, the computation of the tax credit is significantly more complex than that. Foreign source income must be divided up into separate categories, or baskets: "overall" and "passive." The overall category would contain basically active income and probably generate excess credits. The passive category basically would contain subpart F income and probably use up all of its available credits with room to spare.

The Unitary Tax Debate

The unitary tax would impose a tax on a percentage of the corporation's total worldwide earnings.

The unitary tax debate has surfaced in recent years as a source of strong contention between the U.S. government and other governments around the world. This is especially true of governments of countries such as the United Kingdom and the Netherlands that have a number of firms investing in the United States. The basic concept of the **unitary tax** as developed in California is to tax a portion of a corporation's worldwide earnings. Taxable income is determined by applying to worldwide earnings a percentage based on the average proportion of the firm's in-state sales, property, and payroll to the firm's total sales, assets, and payroll. Thus the state income tax paid by a company may have no relationship to its profitability in that state. The states favor the unitary tax concept because it minimizes the possibility of a firm's using arbitrary transfer pricing techniques among its subsidiaries to manipulate profits and therefore taxes.

According to the water's edge concept, the unitary tax would apply to U.S. source income only.

A popular compromise to the worldwide concept of the unitary tax is the **water's edge concept.** According to this, taxable state income is determined on a base of income earned in the United States only, rather than of income earned worldwide. This method was adopted quickly by most states that had been using the worldwide unitary tax method.

Taxation of U.S. Citizens Abroad

Chapter 21 discusses some unique problems of compensating U.S. personnel working abroad. As noted in Chapter 21, a firm usually must offer an employee a significant salary to entice him/her to move abroad. The salary usually consists of the base salary plus additional compensation in the form of a housing allowance, a hardship allowance, an educational allowance for children, a cost-of-living differential, and so on. These additional allowances can escalate an employee's salary significantly and subject it to a higher income tax in the foreign country as well as in the United States.

U.S. employees working abroad can exclude $70,000 of their income and possibly a housing allowance from U.S. taxation.

The U.S. policy of taxing that foreign income has changed significantly throughout history. The more lenient the tax provisions, the easier it is for a firm to send employees abroad. The Tax Reform Act of 1986 changed the law considerably and has made it more costly for firms to send employees abroad. U.S. expatriates (that is, U.S. citizens working abroad) are allowed to exclude some of their foreign source income from U.S. taxation. That exclusion can take two forms. They generally are allowed to exclude $70,000 of their income from U.S. taxation. If their income abroad exceeds $70,000, they can treat their housing allowance separately. Housing in Hong Kong, for example, commonly costs $8,000 per month, which would result in a housing allowance of $96,000 a year. A portion of that allowance, as determined by a special formula, is excluded from taxation.

An expatriate might receive a significant amount of income that could be taxed by foreign and U.S. authorities. Income taxes paid to foreign governments can be treated as a credit or deduction, similar to the discussion on corporate taxes. However, the companies sending expatriates abroad generally must make up the difference between what the expatriate would have paid in taxes in the United States and what must be paid due to the foreign assignment. That tax-equalization practice can be quite expensive for the corporation.

NON-U.S. TAX PRACTICES

Problems with different countries' tax practices are related to:

- Lack of familiarity with laws
- Loose enforcement.

Differences in tax practices throughout the world often cause problems for U.S. firms operating overseas. Lack of familiarity with laws and customs can create confusion. In many countries, tax laws are loosely enforced, whereas in others taxes generally are negotiated between the tax collector and the taxpayer, if they are ever reported at all.

A variance among countries in GAAP can lead to differences in the determination of taxable income. This in turn could affect the cash flow required to settle tax obligations. For example, France allows companies to depreciate assets very quickly and allows additional depreciation for certain assets. In Sweden, companies can reduce the value of inventories, which tends to reduce taxable income.

In the separate entity approach, each unit is taxed when it earns income.

Taxation on corporate income is accomplished by one of two approaches in most countries: (1) the separate entity, or classical, approach and (2) the integrated system.[9] In the **separate entity approach,** which is used in the United States, each separate unit (firm or individual) is taxed when it earns income. For example, a corporation is taxed on its earnings, and shareholders are taxed on the distribution of earnings (dividends), which results in double taxation.

An integrated system tries to avoid double taxation of corporate income through split rates or tax credits.

Most other industrial countries use an **integrated system** to eliminate double taxation. In West Germany a split-rate system is used so that a lower corporate income tax rate is applied to distributed profits since the shareholders are taxed also. The rate on retained profits is 56 percent and on distributed profits only 36 percent. The other major way to eliminate double taxation is to give a dividend credit to shareholders, as is done in the United Kingdom. Resident shareholders in West Germany are allowed a tax credit in addition to the split-rate system.

Table 19.7 illustrates some of the differences in tax rates among countries. But it is difficult to make a simple comparison. Most of those rates are subject to conditions, such as tax treaties, that will be discussed next. Japan has different tax rates, depending on the amount of capitalization and whether the income is distributed or not. Switzerland has federal tax rates ranging from 3.63 percent to 9.8 percent. However, each canton, or local government, imposes its own income tax, which ranges from 5 percent to 35 percent.[10]

Different countries also have unique systems for taxing the earnings of the foreign subsidiaries of domestic corporations. Some countries, such as France, use a territorial approach and therefore tax only domestic-source income. Other countries, such as West Germany and the United Kingdom, use a global approach; that is, they tax the profits of foreign branches and the dividends received from foreign subsidiaries. The United States is the only country to tax unremitted earnings in the form of subpart F income.

Value-Added Tax

Under VAT, each firm is taxed only on the value added to the product.

The **value-added tax (VAT)** has been used since 1967 by most of the countries of Western Europe. The VAT is computed by applying a percentage rate on total sales less any purchases from other business entities. As the name

TABLE 19.7

TAX RATES OF SELECTED COUNTRIES, 1987 (Rate as Percent)

	Domestic Corporation	Branch of Foreign Corporation	Withholding Tax on Dividends
Brazil	35	35	25
Canada	46	46	25
France	45	45	25
West Germany	56	50	25
Hong Kong	18.5	18.5	0
Mexico	42	42	55
Singapore	33	33	0
United Kingdom	35	35	0
United States	40	40	30

Source: Ernst & Whinney, *1987 Foreign and U.S. Corporate Income and Withholding Tax Rates* (New York: Ernst & Whinney, 1987).

implies, VAT means that each independent company is taxed only on the value added at each stage in the production process. If one company was fully integrated vertically, the tax rate would apply to its net sales because it owned everything from raw materials to finished product.

Many countries rebate the VAT to an exporter.

The country rates in Europe vary significantly despite efforts toward a harmonization of different rates by the EC. The VAT does not apply to exports, since the tax is rebated to the exporter and thus is not passed on to the consumer, which results in an effective stimulus for exports. The VAT also is used as a basis for determining a border tax. A border tax in Europe is levied on imports at a rate approximately equal to the amount of internal excise and other indirect taxes paid by domestic producers of competing products. Border taxes are meant to put local goods and imports on the same competitive basis. Therefore, U.S. goods entering many European countries have to bear a VAT (often above 10 percent) in addition to the import duty, which may be much lower.

Tax Treaties: The Elimination of Double Taxation

The purpose of tax treaties is to prevent double taxation.

The primary purpose of most tax treaties is to prevent international double taxation or to provide remedies when they occur. The United States has active income tax treaties with approximately thirty-eight nations. The general pattern for withholding tax between two treaty countries is to grant reciprocal reductions on dividend withholding and to exempt royalties and sometimes interest payments from any withholding tax.

The United States has a withholding tax of 30 percent for owners of U.S. securities (individuals and corporations) who are from countries with which no tax treaties are in effect. Where a tax treaty is in effect, the U.S. rate on dividends generally is reduced to 15 percent, and the tax on interest and royalties either is eliminated or reduced to a very low level.

A good example of a tax treaty is one between the United States and Canada. Canadian dividends, interest, and royalties remitted to U.S. citizens and corporations normally are subject to a 25 percent withholding tax rate by the Canadian government, but for U.S. firms they are subject to only 15 percent as a result of the tax treaty between the two countries.

Planning the Tax Function

Firms should:

- Set up a branch in early years to recognize losses
- Set up subsidiaries in later years to shield profits.

Since taxes affect both profits and cash flow, they must be considered in the investment as well as the operational decision process. When a U.S. parent decides to set up operations in a foreign country, it can do so through a branch or a foreign subsidiary. If the parent expects the foreign operations to operate at a loss for the initial years of operation, it should operate through a branch, since it can deduct branch losses against the current year's income at the parent's level. As the operations become profitable, the firm should switch to a foreign manufacturing subsidiary. If the deferral principle applies to the subsidiary income, then the income of the subsidiary would not be taxed until a dividend is declared.

Debt versus equity financing has tax ramifications.

Tied in with the initial investment decision as well as with continuing operations is the financing decision. Both debt and equity financing affect taxation. If parent loans are used to finance foreign operations, the repayment of principal is not taxable, but the receipt of interest income is taxable to the parent. Also, the interest expense paid by the subsidiary is generally a business expense, which reduces taxable income in the foreign country. Dividends, which are a return to equity capital, are taxable to the parent and are not a deductible business expense to the subsidiary. As was pointed out in Chapter 10, international finance subsidiaries are set up outside the United States to escape withholding tax requirements.

Corporations should take advantage of tax-haven countries.

A multinational corporation aiming to maximize its cash flow worldwide should concentrate profits in tax haven or at least low-tax countries. This can be accomplished by carefully selecting a low-tax country for the initial investment; setting up tax-haven corporations to receive dividends; and carrying out judicious transfer pricing.

With proper planning and timing of dividend remittances, the parent firm can take advantage of the minimum distribution provision. Whenever possible, the parent also should utilize the 5 percent rule. If the parent has a profitable operating subsidiary in a relatively low-tax country, it can accumulate subpart F income there without worrying about U.S. taxes as long as that income does not reach 5 percent of total subsidiary income. For example, because of its low-tax status and membership in the EC, Ireland can be used both as a manufacturing center to supply the EC with goods and as a tax-haven corporation. The subpart F income provisions have complicated tax planning, but opportunities still exist.

Firms should utilize tax treaties to minimize taxes.

A judicious use of tax treaties also can be very helpful for corporations. For example, the treaty between the United States and the United Kingdom provides for a 15 percent withholding tax on dividends, whereas the treaties between the United States and the Netherlands and between the Netherlands and the United Kingdom provide for 5 percent withholding taxes. In addition, the Netherlands does not tax dividends from foreign sources. This policy would allow a U.S. firm to set up a holding company in the Netherlands that would receive dividends from a U.K. subsidiary and remit them to the U.S. parent at a combined withholding tax of only 10 percent rather than 15 percent.[11]

Tax law is very complicated, and a firm needs the counsel of an experienced lawyer. The following is a checklist that can assist a tax manager in proper tax planning:

1. Ask the respective controllers for tax projections that enumerate the items that are non–tax-exempt. Likewise, timing differences due to accelerated depreciation, and so on, should be shown.

2. Work out a minimum dividend distribution plan so that at year's end the group of companies can exploit any U.S. tax concessions.
3. Find avenues for bona fide reduction of the taxable profit (accelerated depreciation, inventory write-offs, etc.).
4. Check the local company's tax declarations.
5. Examine the local tax assessments and advise management of the non-deductibility of certain items so that corrective measures can be taken.
6. Verify that unjustified tax assessments are contested.
7. Verify that all relevant papers (tax returns, etc.) and tax receipts (photocopies) are forwarded to the parent company in order to obtain foreign tax credits.
8. Ensure that U.S. management is aware of major changes in local tax legislation so that corporate policy for such matters as future investments, cash flow, dividend remittances, and minimum dividend distribution can be formed accordingly.[12]

SUMMARY

- The MNE must cope with differing rates of inflation, changes in exchange rates, currency controls, customs, levels of sophistication, and local reporting requirements in performing its finance and accounting functions.
- Some of the major factors that influence the development of accounting objectives, standards, and practices are the nature of the enterprise, the enterprise's users of information, governmental users and regulators, other external users (such as creditors), local environmental characteristics, international influences, academic influences, and the accounting profession.
- There are important differences in worldwide accounting standards and practices. However, groups such as the EC and the International Accounting Standards Committee (IASC) are attempting to harmonize accounting practices and upgrade the accounting profession.
- In translating transactions denominated in foreign currency, all accounts are recorded initially at the exchange rate in effect at the time of the transaction. At each subsequent balance sheet date, recorded dollar balances representing cash and amounts owed by or to the enterprise that are denominated in a foreign currency are adjusted to reflect the current rate.
- The translation of financial statements involves measuring and expressing in dollars and in conformity with U.S. GAAP the assets, liabilities, revenues, and expenses that are measured or denominated in foreign currency.

- According to FASB Statement No. 52, the financial statements of most foreign firms are translated into dollars by using the current rate translation method. According to that method, all balance sheet accounts except stockholders' equity are translated into dollars at the current exchange rate in effect on the balance sheet date. All income statement accounts are translated at the average exchange rate in effect during the period.
- Foreign exchange gains and losses arising from foreign currency transactions are taken to the income statement during the period in which they occur. Gains and losses arising from translating financial statements by the current rate method are taken to a separate component of stockholders' equity. Those arising from translating according to the temporal method are taken directly to the income statement.
- International tax planning has a strong impact on the choice of location in the initial investment decision, the legal form of the new enterprise, the method of financing, and the method of setting transfer prices.
- The Foreign Sales Corporation (FSC) is a company incorporated in a foreign country or U.S. possession (except Puerto Rico). If it engages in substantial export services for its parent company, some of its income will be considered exempt from U.S. corporate income tax.
- Deferral means that income earned by a subsidiary incorporated outside of the home country is taxed only when it is remitted to the parent as a dividend, not when it is earned.
- A controlled foreign corporation must declare its subpart F income as taxable to the parent in the year it is earned, whether or not it is remitted as a dividend.
- The tax credit allows a parent corporation to reduce its tax liability by the direct amount paid to foreign governments on dividends declared by its subsidiary to the parent as well as by the amount of the corporate income tax paid by the subsidiary to the foreign government.
- The unitary tax debate was initiated by states wishing to tax a portion of a firm's worldwide income, rather than only income earned in those states, because they feared that MNEs were evading state taxes by reporting their income elsewhere.
- Policies in other countries vary as to what is taxable income, how honest taxpayers are in filing returns, and how taxes are assessed. The United States taxes each separate unit (the classical approach), whereas most other industrial countries use an integrated system in which double taxation of dividends is minimized or eliminated.
- The purpose of most tax treaties is to prevent international double taxation or to provide remedies when it occurs.

CASE:
THE COCA-COLA COMPANY[13]

From 1886, when Atlanta pharmacist J. S. Pemberton mixed up his first batch of Coca-Cola, to 1987, when Cuban Roberto C. Goizueta presided over the company as chairman and chief executive officer, Coca-Cola's worldwide revenues increased from $50 to $7.7 billion. Coke's rapid worldwide expansion has resulted in over sixty-five beverage trademarks worldwide and sales in 155 countries. From Figure 19.4 we can see that Coke's international revenues in 1987 were 55 percent of total revenues.

Coca-Cola's international presence has resulted in a number of interesting challenges and opportunities. In 1986 its operations were divided into three different product categories: soft drinks with 69 percent of total revenues; entertainment with 15.8 percent of total revenues; and foods with 15.2 percent of total revenues. Its soft drink business is particularly strong internationally, capturing over 40 percent of the soft drink market in the 155 countries where it is operating and a significantly higher percentage of the market in its major markets. Coca-Cola management feels that international markets are virtually untapped and are clearly the growth area of the future. Its entertainment is responsible for such productions as the television programs "Wheel of Fortune" and "Days of Our Lives" and the films "Stand by Me," "Karate Kid II," and "The Last Emperor." The food division produces products such as Minute Maid, Hi-C, and Bacardi fruit mixers.

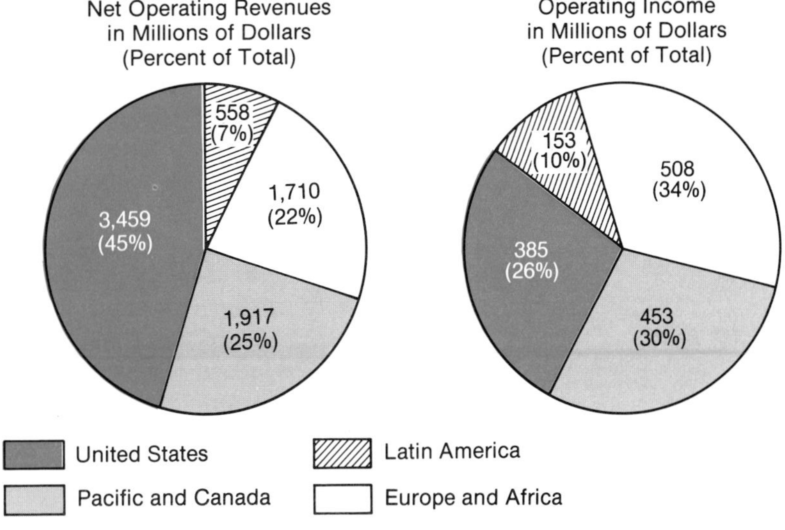

Figure 19.4
The Coca-Cola Company Geographic Segment Results

Source: 1987 Coca-Cola *Annual Report*

In 1984 and 1985, approximately 62 percent of Coke's soft drink sales volume was generated outside of the United States. In its 1985 *Annual Report,* Coke management noted that selected key hard currencies declined by an average of 9 percent against the U.S. dollar, which had an adverse effect on soft drink revenues. Although the actual impact on earnings was not discussed extensively in the *Annual Report,* Coca-Cola's chief financial officer disclosed in a newspaper interview that earnings per share of $1.84 were penalized by 22½ cents in 1985 due to the strong dollar.

Specific information was provided in the annual report on changes in the value of the West German mark, the Japanese yen, the South African rand, the British pound, and the Australian dollar. In 1984, other income (a category in the income statement) was reduced by $18 million due to transactions and translation losses, and in 1985, other income was increased by $27 million by transactions and translation gains.

In 1986, international sales volume grew by 12 percent over 1985, and a weak dollar helped push international operating income up so much that it exceeded the operating income of Coca-Cola only four years earlier. Management estimated that the exchange rates of key hard currencies increased against the dollar by 27 percent in 1986. Its worldwide market share in soft drinks increased to 43 percent in 1986 over 42 percent in 1985.

This growth continued in 1987, although sales volume increased by only 9 percent over 1986, compared with the 12 percent growth achieved the previous year. However, operating income increased 25 percent in 1987, aided partly by a 16 percent increase in key foreign currencies against the U.S. dollar.

Coca-Cola's other two product groups are not quite as international as the beverage category, but they are increasingly moving into international markets. In the entertainment division, primarily Columbia Pictures and Tri-Star Pictures, Coke hopes to begin producing more films that appeal to the tastes and preferences of international consumers. Its food division also is increasing its international sales, especially in Canada.

In 1987, Coca-Cola changed the way it accounted for its business groups, which resulted in only two divisions: soft drinks and foods. The entertainment division was not included as a separate business group.

As noted earlier, Coca-Cola operates in 155 different countries; it uses forty different functional currencies to translate its financial statements from foreign currencies into U.S. dollars. The dollar is the functional currency of operations in hyperinflationary economies, such as Brazil and Mexico. Exchange effects on foreign currency transactions and translation of balance sheet accounts in hyperinflationary countries are included in "other income" in the consolidated income statement.

In one place in its *Annual Report,* Coca-Cola's management noted that it had $249 million worth of debt in Japanese yen, over half of which is designated as a hedge against its net investment in Japan. The 1986 *Annual*

Report classified this as a Euroyen debt (Eurocurrency debt denominated in Japanese yen). In another place in the same report, it states that in general the company does not hedge its net investments in foreign operations. However, it sometimes enters into hedges to protect cash flows in foreign currencies.

An Accounting Procedures Manual. In the mid-1980s, Coke management saw that its intenational operations were increasing significantly and that the nature of its business had changed since its last accounting manual had been written. It needed a comprehensive, easy-to-reference accounting manual to help maintain strong financial controls over operations. Management felt that a better accounting manual would help the firm acquire reliable information about units all over the world in order to help local subsidiaries operate at peak efficiency and generate corporate-wide reports consistently.

A team consisting of a project manager and three senior accountants worked for eight months to develop an entirely new accounting manual. A universal chart of accounts was set up so that each account in the balance sheet and income statement would be consistent around the world. Based on the chart of accounts, definitions of each account were written and policies and procedures governing the use of each account and the flow of information into the financial statements was developed. A separate section was written about how to translate financial statements from local currencies into U.S. dollars. Drafts of the report were given to audit, legal, and tax managers for their comments, and other field accounting managers were asked for their input before a final draft was completed.

QUESTIONS

1. Explain how the changing value of the dollar affected sales and earnings of Coca-Cola in the period from 1984–1987.
2. Describe how Coca-Cola translates its financial statements into U.S. dollars. How do you think transactions and translation gains and losses are recognized in the financial statements?
3. What are some of the major problems that Coca-Cola management might have confronted in trying to write a uniform accounting policy manual?
4. What would you recommend that management do to resolve some of these problems?

NOTES

1. The data for the case are found in the Colgate-Palmolive *1986 Annual Report.*

2. Financial Accounting Standards Board, *Statement of Financial Accounting Concepts No. 1—Objectives of Financial Reporting by Business Enterprises* (Stamford, Conn.: FASB, 1979), paragraphs 34–54.

3. William P. Hauworth, "Problems in the Development of Worldwide Accounting Standards," *International Journal of Accounting,* Fall 1973, p. 24.

4. Financial Accounting Standards Board, *Statement of Financial Accounting Standards No. 52: Foreign Currency Translation* (Stamford, Conn.: FASB, December 1981), pp. 6–7.

5. Jeffrey S. Arpan and Lee H. Radebaugh, *International Accounting and Multinational Enterprises,* 2nd ed. (New York: John Wiley & Sons, Inc., 1985).

6. Albert J. Radler, "Taxation Policy in Multinational Companies," in *The Multinational Enterprise in Transition,* A. Kapoor and Philip D. Grub, eds. (Princeton: The Darwin Press, 1972), p. 30.

7. David Wessel, "Narrower Trade Deficit of $12.2 Billion in December Suggests Worst May Be Past," *Wall Street Journal,* February 16, 1988, p. 2.

8. Prentice-Hall, *A Complete Guide to the Tax Reform Act of 1984* (Englewood Cliffs, N.J.: Prentice-Hall, 1984), pp. 1791–1805. For more detailed information, *see* Jeffrey S. Arpan and Lee H. Radebaugh, *International Accounting and Multinational Enterprises,* 2nd ed. (New York: John Wiley & Sons, 1985), Chapter 7 ("Taxation and Transfer Pricing").

9. *See* M. A. Akhtar, *The Federal Reserve Board of New York Quarterly Review,* Summer 1977, pp. 27–32, for a more thorough discussion of this subject and for much of the information in this section.

10. Ernst & Whinney, *1987 Foreign and U.S. Corporate Income and Withholding Tax Rates* (New York: Ernst & Whinney, 1987).

11. George C. Watt, Richard M. Hammer, and Marianne Burge, *Accounting for the Multinational Corporation* (New York: Financial Executives Research Foundation, 1977), p. 410.

12. Ernst K. Briner, "International Tax Management," *Management Accounting,* February 1973, p. 50. Reprinted by permission.

13. Sources for the case were the 1985 and 1986 *Annual Reports* of the Coca-Cola Company; Timothy K. Smith and Laura Landro, "Profoundly Changed, Coca-Cola Co. Strives to Keep on Bubbling," *The Wall Street Journal,* April 24, 1986, p. 1; and Andrew L. Nodar, "Coca-Cola Writes an Accounting Procedures Manual," *Management Accounting,* October 1986, pp. 52–53.

20

CHAPTER

THE MULTINATIONAL FINANCE FUNCTION

To have money is a good thing; to have a say over the money is even better.
—Yiddish proverb

- To describe the multiple facets of the finance function and show how this function fits in the organizational structure of the MNE.
- To discuss the major internal sources of funds available to the MNE and show how these funds are managed globally.
- To explain the functions of bills of exchange and letters of credit.
- To explore the major financial risks of inflation and exchange rate movements.
- To compare operating strategies and forward contracts as protections against exchange rate risks.
- To highlight some of the financial aspects of the investment decision.

CASE:
DOLLAR VOLATILITY[1]

A major problem faced by U.S. corporate treasurers during the 1980s was the volatility of the U.S. dollar. The early 1980s was a period of intense strength for the dollar, but in 1985 the dollar began to fall. Volatility seemed to be the major issue, since treasurers had no idea how to plan the use of their firms' financial assets. As noted below,

> *In one recent three-week period, the dollar fell 2.2% against the mark and 2.8% against the British pound, only to then reverse course and climb 4.9% against the German currency and 4.5% against the British currency.*

In its 1986 *Annual Report,* for example, Coca-Cola estimated that the value of the dollar against major currencies rose an average of 9 percent in both 1984 and 1985 but fell against those same currencies by 27 percent in 1986. The trend continued in 1987, but the dollar became very erratic during that year.

Because of the dollar's strength and volatility in the early 1980s, firms used different approaches to protect liquid assets. Four companies that used four different approaches during the early part of 1984 were Westinghouse Electric Corp., Mack Truck Inc., Borg-Warner Corp., and General Electric Co. (GE).

Westinghouse is a high-technology company that produces products worldwide in such diverse and general product categories as defense, energy, industry and construction, and broadcasting and cable. In addition, it has specialized product areas in beverage bottling, transport, refrigeration, and financing services. Over a quarter of Westinghouse's business is international, including exports as well as foreign manufacturing.

Mack Truck Inc. is a Pennsylvania-based company that manufactures and exports trucks worldwide. In addition, it has some assembly operations outside of the United States.

Borg-Warner is an international manufacturing and services company with operations on six continents. Its major product lines are transportation equipment, chemicals and plastics, protective services, air conditioning, industrial products, and financial services. Borg-Warner exports a sizable amount of products each year, and sales of its foreign manufacturing operations represent 20 to 25 percent of corporate sales.

Finally, GE is a large manufacturing company that derives only about 15 percent of its sales from foreign manufacturing operations. However, it is also one of the largest exporters in the United States, with nearly 15 percent of its U.S. revenues coming from exports. It specializes in power systems, technical systems, aircraft engines, and a general category called services and materials.

Although the four firms product lines were very different, they shared one thing in early 1984: a strong but volatile dollar that made the management of liquid assets from exports and foreign operations extremely complex. The companies devised different solutions for their problems.

Westinghouse made use of the forward market to hedge some of its financial obligations worldwide. Regardless of the future spot rate, the forward rate guarantees an exchange rate at which currencies can be traded. Because of substantial receivables and royalties that it was to receive in the French franc, which was weaker than the dollar during 1983–1984, the Westinghouse treasurer decided to enter into forward contracts to secure the dollar equivalent of its receipts. As a result, the treasurer saved the company several million dollars.

Mack Truck was faced with a serious competitive situation in Western Europe that was causing pricing problems for its European distributors. To help solve that problem, Mack Truck decided to bill its European distributors in their own currencies so that the distributors needed to worry only about their competitive situation. However, that meant that Mack was faced with the task of managing its exposure since it would have substantial foreign currency receivables as a result of its export sales. Mack management felt that it was easier to centralize the exposure and deal with it at corporate headquarters and allow the local operations to deal with business strategy locally.

Borg-Warner also decided to centralize its foreign exchange exposure but for different reasons. Borg-Warner management thought that its large-scale international operations allowed it to net its exposure worldwide before going into the forward market or money markets to hedge its investments. It can balance off a sterling receivable position in one country, for example, with a sterling payable position in another.

GE uses the technique of "leads and lags" to manage its financial assets. For example, GE officials in early 1984 predicted a strengthening of the Japanese yen in 1984, so the company decided to take its yen dividends from Japanese operations and deposit them in yen certificates of deposit to earn interest. When the yen strengthened as anticipated, GE could convert its proceeds into dollars and remit them to the parent company at (management hoped) a greater profit than would have been the case if the dividends had been remitted earlier and invested in the United States or elsewhere.

As the dollar began to weaken in 1985, firms were faced with increased volatility on the downside. Once again, they had to respond. Many firms, such as Hewlett-Packard and Bio-Rad Laboratories, decided to enter into short-term forward contracts to protect exposed positions. As the VP-finance for Bio-Rad Laboratories pointed out, "If I lock in an exchange rate, I've lost flexibility. That's my main advantage as a small company. We had a lot of encouragement to lock in the yen for two years at ¥ 200: $1. If we had done that, we would be in horrible competitive shape right now."

INTRODUCTION

It is November 19, 1987, and you awaken from a good night's sleep to face a bright, sunny day. After a brisk 5000 meter run, you take a shower and think about your upcoming trip to Acapulco, where you will meet with the treasurer of your Mexican subsidiary. Made Latin American regional treasurer of your firm a month ago, you are eager to learn more about the Mexican operations, which constitute 20 percent of your region's sales and earnings.

As you sit down to breakfast you turn on the news, and hear the announcement, "Last night, the Banco de Mexico pulled out of the free peso market, prompting a free fall in the peso from P1720: $1 at the close of trading on November 16 to P2500: $1 at the opening of the market this morning."[2] What is your reaction? Do you spill orange juice on your new suit, or do you relax through breakfast, confident that your operations had been covered adequately?

The treasury function of an MNE can be exciting and challenging, but it also can be filled with surprises and headaches. As the treasurer of Volkswagen pointed out, "The function of a corporate treasurer is to integrate the various options of maintaining company liquidity. He has to integrate the entire system of cash flow, and he must be in a position to know about future liquidity needs."[3]

ORGANIZATION OF THE FINANCE FUNCTION

Types of parent-subsidiary relationships include:

- Complete decentralization at subsidiary level
- Complete centralization at parent level
- Varying degrees of centralization.

To optimize the flow of funds worldwide, the MNE must determine the proper parent-subsidiary relationship with respect to the finance function. There are three distinct patterns of parent-subsidiary relationships: (1) complete decentralization at the subsidiary level, (2) complete centralization at the parent level, and (3) varying degrees of centralization. These are referred to as ignoring the system potential, exploiting the system potential, and compromising with complexity.[4]

In complete decentralization, the subsidiary is independent of the parent.

In a decentralized situation the subsidiary is independent of the parent. The parent receives reports but generally issues only minor guidelines, especially when foreign sales comprise a small part of total sales and when the parent staff is relatively unfamiliar with the foreign environment.

In complete centralization, the parent dominates decision making.

In a centralized situation the parent staff dominates planning and decision making, whereas the subsidiary merely carries out orders. The idea behind this approach is that the more sophisticated parent staff understands the intricacies of moving funds across many national boundaries in order to serve the needs of the whole system at the greatest profit.

In compromise with complexity, guidelines are passed from the parent to regional or local operations.

The third approach, varying degrees, attempts to use the best aspects of centralization and decentralization by achieving high levels of financial sophistication on both parent and subsidiary levels. Because of this expertise, the subsidiary staff is better able to act within specified guidelines. The parent staff coordinates system activities and monitors results. To maintain close proximity to foreign financial information sources, many firms have organized regional financial decision making centers.[5] The parent staff continues to issue guidelines for decision making and coordinates the entire system, but the financial organization and management functions are turned over to the regional organizations.

As MNE management debates the relative advantages and disadvantages of different degrees of centralization of the finance function, it is forced to deal with several key issues in finance. Among the most important are the optimal utilization of funds internal to the firm, different means of financing imports and exports, the management of risk due to inflation and exchange rate changes, and financial aspects of the investment decision.

INTERNAL SOURCES OF FUNDS

Funds are the working capital or current assets minus current liabilities.

If a firm wants to expand operations or needs additional working capital, it can look to outside sources or to sources within the firm. In the case of the MNE the complexity of internal sources is magnified because of the number of related affiliates and the diversity of environments in which they operate. "Funds" can have many different definitions, and the term usually means cash. However, the term *funds* is used in a much broader sense in business and generally refers to working capital, that is, the difference between current assets and current liabilities.

Sources of internal funds include:

- Loans,
- Dividends,
- Intercompany receivables and payables.

Figure 20.1 illustrates a situation involving a parent firm with two foreign subsidiaries. The parent, as well as the two subsidiaries, may be increasing funds through normal operations. These funds must be used on a firm-wide basis. One possible way is through loans: The parent can loan funds directly to the French subsidiary or guarantee an outside loan to the Brazilian subsidiary. Another source of funds for the subsidiary is the receipt of more equity capital from the parent. Funds also can go from subsidiary to parent. The subsidiary could declare a dividend to the parent as a return on capital or could directly loan cash to the parent.

Figure 20.1
Internal Sources of Working Capital

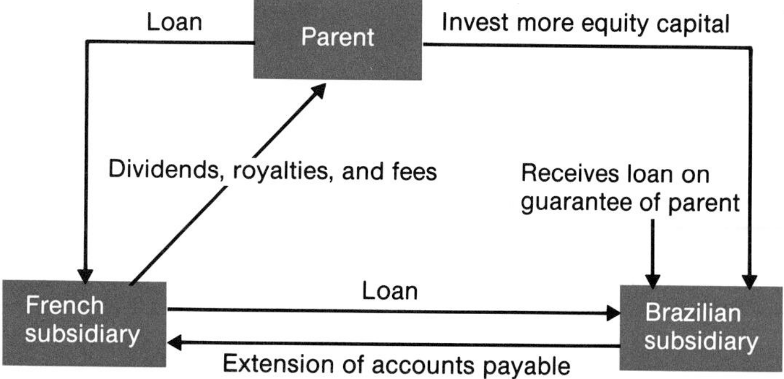

Intersubsidiary financial links become extremely important as the MNE increases in size and complexity. Goods as well as loans can travel between subsidiaries, thereby giving rise to receivables and payables. Although intercompany accounts can be used as sources of funds, some firms are surprisingly against this practice. The following illustrates what could happen:

> *To prevent intercompany accounts from being used as a financing tool, this particular company charges an interest rate on any account outstanding over thirty days. Since this charge is deducted from the annual bonuses of the executives responsible for the debt, it is a pretty effective deterrent.*
>
> *Nevertheless, the European treasurer of this company has tried to circumvent the rule. A few years ago the company's German subsidiary was short of funds and was reluctant to borrow from German banks at the then-going rate of 8 percent. The European treasurer tried to get the company's French affiliate, which routinely sells about $2 million worth of goods each year to the German affiliate, to forego payment on its German receivables for nine months, covering itself by borrowing francs locally at 4 percent. The French affiliate agreed, provided the Germans paid a 5 percent interest charge. Since this charge would come out of his bonus, the German treasurer balked and instead borrowed the $2 million from a Belgian bank at 5.5 percent. The German executive saved his bonus, but the company's rigid adherence to the rulebook cost $22,500—the difference between the Belgian and French cost of borrowing $2 million for nine months.*[6]

GLOBAL CASH MANAGEMENT

The problems of managing cash globally are complex. Cash management is complicated on an international level because of governmental restrictions on the flow of funds, differing rates of inflation, and changes in exchange rates.

General Principles

We can discuss some general principles of cash management without reference to the risks of inflation and exchange-rate changes. These principles are in addition to those in a domestic setting. Effective cash management is one of the chief concerns of the MNE, and three questions must be raised to ensure effective cash management:

1. What are the local and cooperate system needs for cash?
2. How can the cash be withdrawn from the subsidiary and centralized?
3. Once the cash has been centralized, what should be done with it?

The general cash flow cycle that a firm must deal with is illustrated in Fig. 20.2. The MNE must collect and pay cash in its normal operational cycle, and then it must deal with financial institutions, such as commercial and investment banks, in generating and investing cash.

Budgets and forecasts are essential in assessing a firm's cash needs.

Before any cash is remitted to a control center, whether on a regional or parent level, local cash needs must be properly assessed through cash

Figure 20.2
Cash Flow Cycle

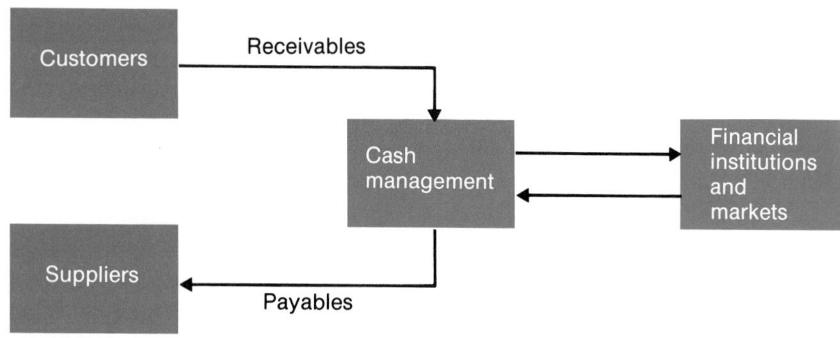

budgets and forecasts. Since the cash forecast will project the excess cash available, the manager also will know how much cash can be invested for short-term profits.

Four problems in getting good quality information:

- Language
- Local resistance
- Technical problems
- Governmental regulations.

An important aspect of global determination of cash needs is a good reporting system. However, there are four major reasons why foreign affiliates are often reluctant to provide good quality information to the parent: (1) language difficulties, (2) local resistance, (3) technical problems, and (4) governmental regulations.

Language problems are obvious. Local resistance is often cultural in that foreign affiliates sometimes tend to feel more independent than the parent company would prefer. Requests for information often are seen as a threat to the subsidiary's independence rather than a legitimate need.

Technical problems arise in cross-border data flows. In developing countries, there may be a lack of a good communications infrastructure. In other cases, the problem may be a compatibility of corporate and affiliate computer systems. MNEs use a variety of different communications links to cope with different environments. Governmental regulations range from rules about simply transferring information to rules about actually transferring funds. Governmental requirements that certain communications links be used and that data be put in a specific format often can create delays in the transfer of information.[7]

Local managers can distribute cash to the parent via dividends.

Once local needs have been adequately provided for, the cash manager must decide whether to allow the local manager to invest the excess cash or have it remitted to a central cash pool. If the cash is centralized, the manager must find a way of making the transfer. A cash dividend is the easiest way to distribute cash, but governmental restrictions may reduce the effectiveness of this tool. Exchange controls may prevent the firm's remitting as large a dividend as it would like. In some countries, the size of the dividend may be tied to the capital invested in the local operation. The parent must develop approaches, such as revaluation of fixed assets, to increase its subsidiary's investment base. In Brazil, for example, dividend remittances in excess of an annual average of 12 percent of the foreign registered capital over a three-year period are subject to a supplementary tax, which ranges from 40 to 60 percent of the amount remitted.[8] Cash also can be remitted through management fees, royalties, and repayment of principal and interest on loans.

Many of the developing countries with large foreign debt, such as Brazil, have created difficulties for firms attempting to transfer money abroad. This has been because they have tried to curtail the outflow of foreign exchange. One U.S. company with large operations in Brazil used dividends, loan repayments, and sales commissions to transfer funds out of Brazil. The Brazilian operation was treated as a manufacturing facility, and all export sales were made by a sales subsidiary of the parent firm in the United States. When the manufacturing facility was established in Brazil, it was financed primarily by debt rather than equity. The parent company could get more cash out of Brazil by paying off principal and interest than it could by paying a dividend, which was subject to such large taxes. When foreign sales were made, the Brazilian manufacturer was permitted to pay a commission to the sales company in the United States, which allowed it to transmit more funds abroad. The Brazilian government constantly tried to lower the amount of the commission, whereas the parent company tried to increase the amount of the commission.

Transfer Pricing

A transfer price is the price on inventory sold between related parties.

Transfer pricing is another way to move cash. A **transfer price** is the price on inventory sold between related entities. If the parent sells inventory to the subsidiary, a high transfer price would help concentrate cash in the central cash pool. The same effect would hold if the subsidiary were to sell inventory to the parent at a low transfer price.

In a survey on transfer pricing policies of U.S. firms, the most important influences on transfer pricing decisions found were: (1) market conditions in the foreign country; (2) competition in the foreign country; (3) reasonable profit for the foreign affiliate; (4) U.S. federal income taxes; (5) economic conditions in the foreign country; (6) import restrictions; (7) customs duties; (8) price controls; (9) taxation in the foreign country; and (10) exchange controls.[9] Management of cash flows itself was not considered important. However, when factors were grouped together according to common characteristics, influences on cash flows was rated the second most important factor grouping after the local environment.

One problem with making a transfer pricing decision is that multiple objectives could conflict with each other. For example, a high transfer price from parent to subsidiary would concentrate cash in the parent and also increase income because of the higher value placed on sales. However, if the corporate tax rate to the subsidiary is considerably lower than to the parent, it might be better to concentrate profits in the subsidiary to take advantage of the tax situation. This would require an opposite transfer-pricing approach from that just described. Obviously, the overall impact of a transfer-pricing scheme must be analyzed before a firm policy is selected.

An advantage of transfer pricing is that the cash is not subject to withholding taxes and restrictions.

The advantage of using transfer pricing to move cash is that the cash is not subject to the withholding taxes and restrictions that dividends and royalties are. This is especially true in countries with which the United States does not have a tax treaty and where withholding taxes are relatively high. Arbitrary transfer pricing can create problems in performance evaluation. Subsidiary managers find it very difficult to be motivated in a profit center context when they cannot control or influence pricing decisions.

Arbitrary transfer pricing can create difficulties in performance evaluation and with governments.

The choice of currency for transfer prices is also important. A U.S. company that determines all transfer prices in dollars is essentially shifting the burden for exposure management to the affiliates. As illustrated by the Mack Truck example in the case at the beginning of the chapter, if the transfer prices are set in local currencies, the burden is shifted to the parent company. Many firms began to shift to local currency transfer prices in the mid-1980s due to the high degree of volatility in currencies and the desire of the parent company to react to that volatility on a global basis.[10]

The firm should use surplus cash to retire debt, finance new investment, or acquire securities.

Once cash has been remitted to the central pool, the cash manager must decide what to do with it. Obviously the cash manager ensures that all system needs for cash are met. Then any leftover cash can be used to retire debt in the system, to finance new ventures, or simply to earn a return through the acquisition of marketable securities worldwide.

One successful example of that strategy involves the German pharmaceutical company, Bayer. In the late 1970s and early 1980s, Bayer invested billions of dollars in expansion (largely in the United States) when most other pharmaceuticals were being more cautious. That strategy seems to have paid off since Bayer is using its healthy cash flow worldwide to retire much of its investment-related liabilities. The company also used a lot of that liquidity to acquire inventory denominated in dollars as a hedge against rising prices and the rising dollar.[11]

The purchase of foreign securities is meant to diversify risk.

By purchasing securities in countries other than that of corporate headquarters a firm might be able to diversify its risk/return on investments. As world economies diverge in their growth cycles, the return on investments in strong countries could offset relatively weak returns in stagnant countries. However, as one pension fund manager pointed out, "You're dealing with the stability of foreign governments and with expropriations, [factors] we don't feel we have the ability to cope with."[12]

FINANCING INTERNATIONAL TRADE

A major aspect of global cash management is planning the outflow of money for imports or the inflow of money for exports. The flow of money across national boundaries is complex and requires the use of special documents. In addition, foreign trade usually is done by credit; exporters rarely get paid right away, due to collection and foreign-exchange problems.

Two major instruments of foreign exchange are:
- Commercial bills of exchange
- Commercial letters of credit.

Two major instruments of foreign exchange by which an exporter could receive payment from an importer are commercial bills of exchange and commercial letters of credit. In addition to these arrangements an exporter may wish to deal with the importer on an open account basis, especially where there is a parent-subsidiary or related-subsidiary basis between the exporter and importer. In especially risky situations, the exporter may wish to operate on a cash-in-advance basis.

Commercial Bills of Exchange

In a bill of exchange, the exporter instructs the importer to transfer the face amount of the bill of exchange at a specific time.

In a sight draft, payment must be made immediately.

In a time draft, payment can be made at a later period.

If payment were to be made by a **commercial bill of exchange,** the drawer (exporter) instructs the drawee (importer) to transfer the face amount on the bill of exchange at a given time. The transfer would be made to a designated payee, possibly to the exporter's bank where the drawer has an account, or directly to the exporter. The exporter could have requested that payment be made immediately, in which case the exchange instrument is known as a **sight draft.** Or, if the terms of agreement call for payment to be made in dollars at a later period (e.g., 30, 60, or 90 days after delivery), the instrument would be known as a commercial **time draft.**

Letters of Credit

A letter of credit obligates the importer's bank to accept a bill of exchange.

In the case of a bill of exchange, there is always the possibility that the importer will not be able to make payment to the exporter at the time agreed on by both parties. A **letter of credit,** however, obligates the buyer's bank in the importing country to accept a draft (a bill of exchange) presented to it, provided that the bill of exchange is accompanied by the prescribed documents.

The exporter who receives this guarantee from the importer's bank can rely on the credit of the bank in addition to the as-yet-unverified credit of the importer. The advantage of such an arrangement is that the seller can draw a bill of exchange on the importer's bank rather than on the importer and should therefore have no difficulty in selling or discounting the draft. Figure 20.3 explains the relationships among the three parties to the letter of credit.

An irrevocable letter of credit is a letter of credit that cannot be changed or cancelled without permission of all parties to the letter of credit.

Both exporter and importer may prefer an **irrevocable letter of credit,** which is a letter that cannot be cancelled or changed in any way without the consent of all parties to the transaction. By having the letter of credit denominated in the exporter's currency there is no risk of loss to the exporter as a result of possible exchange rate fluctuations. Figure 20.4 (on p. 646) shows an example of an irrevocable letter of credit. Notice that the importer's bank is obligated to pay and the bank will be willing to accept any drafts (bills of exchange) at sight, meaning that these drafts will be paid as soon as the correct documents are presented to the importer's bank.

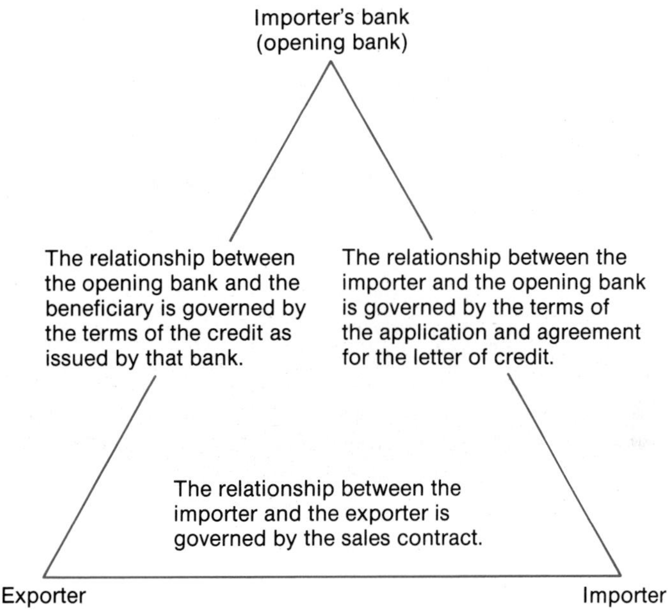
Importer's bank
(opening bank)
The relationship between the opening bank and the beneficiary is governed by the terms of the credit as issued by that bank.
The relationship between the importer and the opening bank is governed by the terms of the application and agreement for the letter of credit.
The relationship between the importer and the exporter is governed by the sales contract.
Exporter
Importer

Figure 20.3
Three-part Letter of Credit Relationships
Source: Adapted from *Export and Import Financing Procedures.* The First National Bank of Chicago, p. 22.

A confirmed letter of credit means that the exporter's bank is also obligated to pay the bill of exchange.

The letter of credit transactions may involve a confirming bank in addition to the parties mentioned above. A **confirmed letter of credit** means that in addition to having the guarantee of the bank in the importer's country, the exporter can have the guarantee of a bank in the exporting country. The greatest amount of protection to a shipper is provided by a confirmed, irrevocable letter of credit.

Open Account

In an open account, the exporter extends credit to the importer.

The exporter occasionally may sell on **open account.** This means the necessary shipping documents would be mailed to the importer before any payment or definite obligation on the part of the buyer. Releasing goods in this manner is somewhat unusual, since the exporter runs the risk of default by the buyer. An exporter ordinarily would sell under such conditions only if business with the importer had been conducted successfully for an extended period of time. This is generally the arrangement used when the importer and exporter are related entities.

Compensatory Trade

Compensatory trade is used when firms have difficulty collecting cash.

The previous discussion assumes that payment is a foregone conclusion. However, many developing nations and countries in Eastern Europe have relatively small holdings of convertible foreign currencies. So serious prob-

Figure 20.4
Export Letter of Credit

EXPORT LETTER OF CREDIT

Philadelphia National Bank
INTERNATIONAL DIVISION
P.O. Box 13866, Phila., PA 19101
CABLE ADDRESS: PHILABANK TELEX: 845-355

☐ To be collected at negotiation.
☐ We have debited your Account/ H. O. Account

L/C Advising Comm.	ACCOUNT NUMBER
$	
Confirmation commission	AMOUNT
$	$

IRREVOCABLE DOCUMENTARY CREDIT

ORIGINAL

OUR CREDIT NO.	CR NO-CORRESPONDENT	DATE	EXPIRY DATE	LETTER OF CREDIT AMOUNT
098765	010101	OCT.1,19XX	DEC.30,19XX	US$5,000.00

MAIL TO

BENEFICIARY
X Y Z COMPANY
C STREET
YOUR CITY, U.S.A.

CORRESPONDENT
A B C BANK
P.O. BOX 001
THEIR CITY, CEYLON

Gentlemen:

We are instructed by the above correspondent to advise you that they have opened their irrevocable credit in your favor for account of (NAME OF BUYER) available by your drafts on us AT SIGHT accompanied by the following documents:

1. SIGNED COMMERCIAL INVOICE IN TRIPLICATE
2. PACKING LIST
3. FULL SET OF CLEAN ON BOARD OCEAN BILL OF LADING PLUS TWO NON-NEGOTIABLE COPIES, CONSIGNED TO (BUYER'S NAME or CONSIGNEE) NOTIFY (BUYER'S NAME or CONSIGNEE) INDICATING THE AMOUNT OF FREIGHT CHARGES MARKED: "FREIGHT PREPAID" AND DATED NOT LATER THAN ____________

COVERING: ________ DESCRIPTION OF MERCHANDISE ________
TERMS: ____________

CORRESPONDENT BANK STATES:

SPECIAL INSTRUCTIONS:

SHIPMENT FROM: YOUR CITY TO: THEIR CITY

PARTIAL SHIPMENTS: NOT PERMITTED TRANSHIPMENTS: PERMITTED

THE ABOVE CORRESPONDENT ENGAGES WITH YOU THAT ALL DRAFTS DRAWN UNDER AND IN COMPLIANCE WITH THE TERMS OF THIS CREDIT WILL BE HONORED ON DELIVERY OF DOCUMENTS AS SPECIFIED IF PRESENTED AT THIS OFFICE ON OR BEFORE THE EXPIRATION DATE SHOWN ABOVE.

DOCUMENTS MUST CONFORM STRICTLY WITH THE TERMS OF THIS CREDIT, IF YOU ARE UNABLE TO COMPLY WITH ITS TERMS, PLEASE COMMUNICATE WITH YOUR CUSTOMER TO COMPLY WITH ITS TERMS, PLEASE COMMUNICATE WITH YOUR CUSTOMER PROMPTLY WITH A VIEW TO HAVING THE CONDITIONS CHANGED. THIS WILL ELIMINATE DIFFICULTIES AND DELAY WHEN YOUR DOCUMENTS ARE PRESENTED FOR NEGOTIATION.

THIS CREDIT IS BEING FORWARDED TO YOU AT THE REQUEST OF OUR CORRESPONDENT, AND CONVEYS NO ENGAGEMENT BY US.

ALL DRAFTS AND DOCUMENTS MUST INDICATE THE REFERENCE NUMBER OF THE CORRESPONDENT BANK AND THE REFERENCE NUMBER OF THE PHILADELPHIA NATIONAL BANK.

____
AUTHORIZED SIGNATURE

EXCEPT SO FAR AS OTHERWISE EXPRESSLY STATED, THIS DOCUMENTARY CREDIT IS SUBJECT TO THE "UNIFORM CUSTOMS AND PRACTICE FOR DOCUMENTARY CREDITS" (1983 REVISION), INTERNATIONAL CHAMBER OF COMMERCE, PUBLICATION NO. 400.

A CoreStates Bank

lems arise when they want to purchase much-needed industrial goods from Western countries. As a result, firms are often forced to resort to creative ways of settling payment, many of which involved trading goods for goods as part of the transaction. The term **compensatory trade** refers to any one of a number of different arrangements in which goods and services are traded for each other, either on a bilateral or multilateral basis. More specifically, it is defined as "any contractual commitment imposed as a condition of purchase, by the importer on the exporter, with the intention of creating quid pro quo benefits for the former."[13] Although it is nearly impossible to determine the extent of compensatory trade arrangements, an estimated 20 to 30 percent of international trade is tied in some form of compensatory trade.[14]

Barter is the trade of goods for goods.

Barter. The oldest form of compensatory trade, **barter,** occurs when goods are traded for goods of equal value without any flow of cash. Although there are many problems in negotiating a barter agreement, there are examples of it: Pepsico agreed to swap Pepsi syrup and bottling equipment for Russian vodka, and Occidental Petroleum arranged sales of fertilizer plants and pipelines to the Soviet Union in exchange for ammonia. In the past, Argentina has shipped wheat and frozen meat to Peru and received iron ore pellets in exchange. Indonesia bartered some of its oil for a sorely needed steelmaking complex from West Germany.[15] Figure 20.5 illustrates how a barter transaction might be structured.

A barter variation is when goods are traded for goods which are sold for cash rather than consumed.

A slight variation of barter trade includes goods and money. One example is when Mitsui, one of the largest Japanese trading companies, bought tanning material in the Soviet Union and shipped it to Argentina in exchange for plastic products. Mitsui marketed these products in the United States for cash.

In offset or countertrade, goods and services are sold for cash with the condition that the seller help the buyer earn foreign exchange through different means.

Countertrade. Another type of compensatory trade, called **offset trade** or **countertrade,** is becoming increasingly important. Countertrade exists "when reciprocal and contingent exchanges of goods and services are specified by contract and each flow of deliveries is valued and settled in monetary units."[16] A good example of how a firm might have to deal with offset involves McDonnell Douglas and the sale of F-18A fighter aircraft to the government of Canada. The sale of aircraft to Canada in 1980 was to net McDonnell Douglas

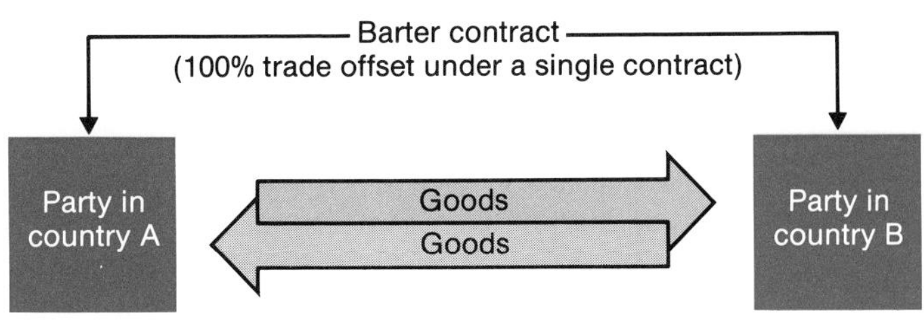

Figure 20.5
Model of a Barter Transaction
Source: Pompiliu Verzariu, *Countertrade, Barter, Offsets* (New York: McGraw-Hill Publishing Co., 1985), p. 26.

nearly $3 billion, a significant amount of money for one sale. Over the eight-year period involved in the delivery dates, this would result in average imports for Canada of several hundred million dollars per year. Given the weakness of the Canadian dollar relative to the U.S. dollar at the time of the sale, this was bound to concern the Canadian government. As a result, the negotiations for the sale of the aircraft involved not only the technical capabilities of the F-18A and the attendant costs, but also the industrial benefits that McDonnell Douglas could promise the Canadian government.

F-18A offset involves manufacturing, technology transfer, export promotion, and tourism promotion.

The Canadian offset program covers a period of fifteen years with a three-year grace period. The total program commitment of $2.9 billion must be covered from the following three areas: aerospace and electronics (minimum 60 percent), advanced technology (minimum 6 percent), and diversified activities (maximum 40 percent). The aerospace and electronics area is the most important of the three, and it involves designated production, co-production, technology transfer, and joint R&D. The diversified activities portion of the offset commitment involves investment/technology development, export development, and tourism development.

Evidence Account Transaction

Figure 20.6 shows how a complex transaction such as the F-18A sale to Canada might be structured. This type of transaction is sometimes known as an **evidence account transaction** because it requires that certain contractual obligations be adhered to. As noted, it involves the primary exporter, the importing government, and various other secondary exporters and importers.

Whether firms become involved in the complexities of offset trade depends mainly on the strength of demand for their products, alternative sources of supply, and foreign exchange problems in the buying country.

RISK MANAGEMENT

Currency risks are:

- Inflation
- Exchange rate changes.

Commercial risks are:

- Extending and receiving credit
- Collecting and paying accounts in different currencies.

The discussions of global cash management and the instruments involved in financing foreign trade have focused on the flow of money for specific operating objectives. In addition, an important objective of the financial strategy of an MNE is to protect against the risks of investing abroad. The strategies that a firm adopts to protect against risk may involve the internal movement of funds as well as the use of one or more of the foreign exchange instruments described above.

In examining the risk encountered in international business, it is important that firms consider: the nature of the risk; the circumstances under which it can occur; implications for the firm; and the best defense against it. Risks related to currency, commercial, and political factors are the major

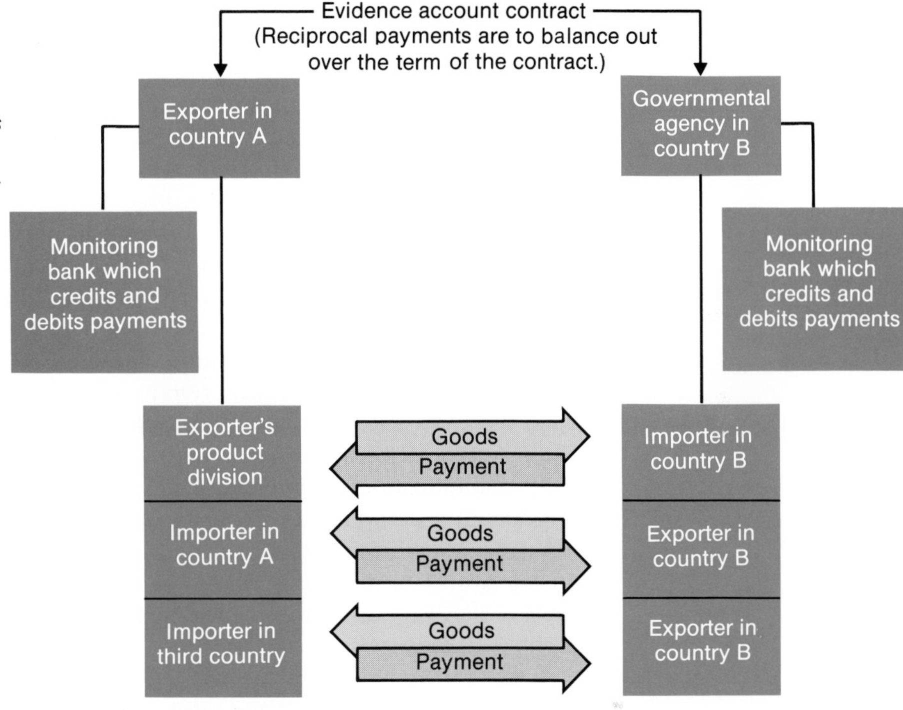

Figure 20.6
Model of an Evidence Account Transaction
Source: Pompiliu Verzariu, *Countertrade, Barter, Offsets* (New York: McGraw-Hill Publishing Co., 1985), p. 32.

Political risks are:
- Trade relations
- Expropriations.

ones. Currency risks include both inflation and exchange rate changes. Commercial risks involve the problems of extending or receiving credit and the difficulties of collection or payment of accounts in different currencies. Political risks (as was noted in Chapters 11 and 12) are extensive and cover trade relations, expropriations, and items that could be included as currency risks.

Inflation

Inflation occurs in varying degrees in nearly every country in which MNEs operate. Inflation tends to erode the value of financial assets and make financial liabilities more attractive. The attractiveness of liabilities is softened somewhat by the high interest rates that often accompany loans in countries with high inflation.

High inflation and a weak currency go hand in hand.

High rates of inflation often bring a variety of problems that influence the way an MNE operates. The most important ones are: (1) accelerated depreciation or devaluation of the local currency or a maxidevaluation; (2) tighter capital controls and import restrictions; (3) scarcer credit and higher borrowing costs; (4) a buildup of accounts receivable and lengthening of collection periods; (5) price controls to help bring inflation under control; (6) economic and political chaos and labor unrest; (7) capital flight, (8) and greater difficulty in evaluating the performance of foreign subsidiaries.[17]

In the Mexican example given in the introduction to this chapter, inflation was a major cause of the currency devaluation in 1987. Inflation in 1987 rose by 145 percent, compared with an increase of 106 percent in 1986, and it was expected to hit 180 percent in 1988.[18]

Price controls can be circumvented by:

- Modifying product line
- Reintroducing products with new name
- Changing containers.

Many companies faced with price controls need to get around controls through imaginative product development and pricing strategies. This may involve slight product modifications and brand-name changing in order to effect price rises. Quite frequently, MNEs are so brand-conscious that they refuse to exploit this strategy. A study conducted in Chile found that Chilean firms could modify a product line, reintroduce the product with a new brand name, and avoid price controls more efficiently than their U.S. counterparts.[19] Where brand image is important, however, this strategy may be impossible.

One multinational firm operating in Brazil got around price controls by introducing a brand name product in a smaller container but listing the product at a significantly higher price. However, it would sell the product for considerably less than list price in order to attract sales. Then it could increase the price according to inflationary trends up to the upper price limit established by price control authorities.

One of the major problems which the firm faced was trying to estimate inflation correctly. If it predicted inflation at 200 percent and priced accordingly, it would be in serious trouble if inflation was actually 500 percent. It would have underpriced its products and sold them for less than the replacement cost of raw materials. On the other hand, if inflation came in at less than 200 percent, the firm ran the risk of pricing itself out of the market.

Firms need to manage receivables and payables carefully in inflationary countries.

It is evident that a firm operating in an inflationary environment needs to manage receivables and payables carefully. Receivables must be collected on a timely basis through a well-trained credit and collection department and a sophisticated and reliable reporting system.[20] Once it is collected, idle cash should be kept at a minimum. Funds should be remitted to the parent cash pool, as noted in the previous section, or invested in income-producing assets that provide a return in excess of inflation.

Exchange-Rate Changes

If all exchange rates were fixed in relation to one another, there would be no foreign exchange risks. However, rates are not fixed, and currency values change frequently, as discussed in Chapters 8 and 9. Instead of infrequent one-way changes, currencies can fluctuate either up or down; this has especially been the case with the dollar since the mid-1980s.

A change in the exchange rate can result in three different exposures for a firm: translation exposure, transaction exposure, and economic exposure.

In translation exposure, as the rate changes, the value of the exposed accounts changes also.

Translation exposure. As explained in Chapter 19, foreign currency financial statements are translated into the reporting currency of the parent company (assumed to be U.S. dollars for U.S. companies) for a number of reasons, such as consolidation, performance evaluation, creditors, and taxation. The mechanics of translation were described in Chapter 19 also. Exposed accounts—those translated at the balance sheet or current exchange rate—either gain or lose command over dollars. For example, assume that a subsidiary operates in Mexico. The Mexican peso, weakened by inflation, depreciates in relation to the dollar from P1720: $1 to P2500: $1. The subsidiary's bank account of P172,000,000 would be worth only $68,800 after the depreciation instead of the $100,000 original value.

Translation gain or loss due to exchange rate change is not a cash flow gain or loss.

The combined effect of the exchange rate change on all exposed assets and liabilities is a gain or loss. If the foreign currency financial statements are translated according to the temporal method, the gains or losses are taken directly to the income statement. If the statements are translated according to the current rate method, the gains and losses are taken to a separate component of stockholders' equity. No matter which method is used for translation purposes, this gain or loss is not a cash flow effect. The cash in the bank in Mexico is only translated, not converted into dollars.

In transaction exposure the amount of receivables and payables changes when the exchange rate changes.

Transaction exposure. The accounting measurement of transactions in foreign currencies was discussed in Chapter 19. The treasury difficulty arises because the company has accounts receivable or payable in foreign currency that must be settled eventually. For example, assume that a U.S. exporter delivers merchandise to a British importer. If the exporter receives payment in dollars, there is no immediate impact to the exporter if the dollar/sterling exchange rate changes. If payment were to be received in sterling, however, the exporter could be exposed to an exchange gain or loss.

Key economic issues:

- Pricing of products
- Source of inputs
- Location of production.

Economic exposure. Economic impact includes such issues as the pricing of products, the source and cost of inputs, and the location of investments.

Economic exposure is the overall change in the value of the firm in relation to the change in exchange rate.

The economic impact on the firm is difficult to measure, but it is crucial to the operations of the firm in the long run. Aside from the immediate impact described earlier, there is a long-term impact that involves pricing strategies. The inventory sold to the British importer just discussed probably was sold to final users before the exchange rate fluctuated, but future sales would be affected. The following example illustrates what could happen. Assume that the exchange rate before the change was $1.80:£ and after the change was $1.85:£.

	Price in Britain	Revenue to exporter
Before change	£1,000	$1,800
After change		
Invoice in £	£1,000	$1,850
Invoice in $	£ 973	$1,800

If the merchandise had been invoiced in sterling, the strengthening of the sterling would have resulted in a gain of revenue to the exporter of $50. If the merchandise had been invoiced in dollars, the cost of the product to the importer in Britain would have decreased to £973. In the first case, the exporter must decide whether to reduce the price in pounds to maintain the same level of dollar revenues and (hopefully) increase market share. In the second case, the importer must decide whether to pass on the savings to consumers by reducing prices or keep the price the same and increase profit margins.

Several firms noticed the economic effects of exchange rate changes in 1985. For example, Ford Motor Company planned to close down production of tractors in Michigan and start producing the tractors in plants in England and Belgium primarily because of the strong dollar. Du Pont expanded production in Britain, France, the Netherlands, West Germany, and Luxembourg rather than in the United States for the same reason.[21]

In 1987, however, firms began reversing their strategies as the dollar kept weakening. Liz Claiborne Inc. pushed much of its clothing manufacturing operation to Asia in the early 1980s, partly in response to the strong dollar. But the weakening dollar contributed to the firm's closing down some of its Asian operations and renovating two factories in New York's Chinatown.[22]

KEY ISSUES IN FOREIGN EXCHANGE RISK MANAGEMENT

Key issues are:
- Define and measure exposure
- Establish reporting system
- Adopt hedging policy
- Adopt hedging strategy.

To protect assets adequately against risks from exchange rate fluctuations, it is important for management to: (1) define and measure exposure, (2) organize and implement a reporting system that monitors exposure and exchange rate movements, (3) adopt a policy on assigning responsibility for hedging exposure, and (4) formulate a strategy for hedging exposure.

Measurement

Most MNEs will be subject to all three types of exposure described above. In order to develop a viable hedging strategy, the firm must be able to forecast the degree of exposure in each major currency in which it operates. Because the three types of exposure are very different from each other, the actual exposure by currency must be kept separate. For example, the translation exposure in Brazilian cruzados should be kept separate from the transaction exposure. The reason is that the transaction exposure will result in an actual cash flow, whereas the translation exposure may not. Thus the firm may adopt different hedging strategies for the different types of exposure.

Forecasting Exchange Rates

Another key aspect of measurement involves forecasting exchange rates that are applicable to the identified exposure. Estimating future exchange rates is similar to using a crystal ball: Approaches range from gut feeling to sophisticated economic models. The factors used in estimating future exchange rates were discussed in detail in Chapter 9. As noted in Chapter 9, firms should group currencies together in like categories. For example, countries in the European Monetary System are expected to behave fairly closely, whereas the Brazilian cruzado or Mexican peso might behave very differently. Whatever a firm decides to do, its management should estimate ranges within which it expects a currency to vary over the relevant decision period.

Reporting System

Foreign input is important in assessing information.

Once the firm has decided to define and measure exposure and estimate future exchange rates, it must design, organize, and implement a reporting system that will assist in protection against risk. Because of the nature of the problem, substantial participation from foreign operations must be combined with effective central control. Foreign input is important in order to ensure the quality of information being used in forecasting techniques. Since exchange rates move frequently, firms must obtain input from someone who is attuned to the pulse of the country. In addition, the maximum effectiveness of hedging techniques will depend on the cooperation of personnel in the foreign operations.

Exposure of several entities may offset each other.

A central control of exposure is needed to protect resources more efficiently. Each organizational unit in the firm may be able to define its exposure, but the corporation itself also has an overall exposure. To set hedging policies on a separate-entity basis might not take into account the fact that exposures of several entities (i.e., branches, affiliates, subsidiaries, and so on) could offset one another.

Management should devise a uniform reporting system to be used by all units reporting to the MNE. The report should identify the exposed accounts the firm wants to monitor, the exposed position by currency of each account, and the different time periods to be covered. Exposure should be separated into translation and transaction components, with the transaction exposure identified by cash inflows and outflows over time.

Exposure should be considered for the long term as well as the short term.

The time periods to be covered depend upon the firm. One possibility is to look at long- as well as short-run flows. For example, staggered periods (thirty, sixty, and ninety days; six months, nine months, and twelve months;

and two, three, and four years) could be considered. The reason for the longer time frame is that operating commitments, such as plant construction and production runs, are fairly long-run decisions.[23]

Once each basic reporting unit has identified its exposure, this should be sent to the next organizational level for a preliminary consolidation. That level may be a regional headquarters (such as Latin America or Europe) or a product division. The organizational structure of the firm will determine what that level is. The preliminary consolidation allows the region or division to determine exposure by account and by currency for each time period. These reports should be routine, periodic, and standardized to ensure comparability and timeliness in formulating strategies. Final reporting should be at the corporate level. There, corporate exposure can be determined and strategies identified to reflect the best interests of the corporation as a whole.

Hedging Policy

Hedging policies should be established at the corporate level.

It is important for management to decide at what level hedging strategies will be determined and implemented. To achieve maximum effectiveness in hedging, policies should be established at the corporate level. With a larger overview of corporate exposure and the cost and feasibility of different strategies at different levels in the firm, the corporate treasury should be able to design and implement a cost-effective program for exposure management. As a firm increases in size and complexity, it may have to decentralize some decisions in order to increase flexibility and speed of reaction to a more rapidly changing international monetary environment. However, such decentralization should stay within a well-defined policy established at the corporate level.

Firms have very different points of view as to the degree of decentralization that will be allowed in the treasury function. For example, Northern Telecom, the Canadian telecommunications MNE, evaluates each subsidiary on a functional-currency budget, typically the Canadian or U.S. dollar, but also occasionally the currency of the country where the subsidiary is located. The corporate treasury devises a hedging strategy that the subsidiary must carry out. The foreign exchange center is treated as a cost center, which means that it has an operational budget and is not expected to generate a profit. In contrast, Mattel, the California toy maker, operates its foreign exchange department as a profit center. It uses two outside firms to manage its exposures and evaluates the firms on the basis of the profitability of the hedging techniques that they use.[24]

Hedging Strategies

Principal exposure devices are:

- Balance sheet management

Once a firm has identified its level of exposure, it can hedge, or protect, its position from exchange rate changes. A firm can adopt numerous strategies, each with cost/benefit implications as well as operational concerns. The

- Leads and lags
- Forward exchange contracts
- Currency options.

safest position for a firm to be in is a balanced position, in which exposed assets equal exposed liabilities. The principal methods that MNEs use to protect against exposure are balance sheet management, leads and lags, forward exchange contracts, and currency options.[25]

Balance sheet management. To reduce exposure through operational strategies management must determine the working capital needs of the subsidiary. Although it might be wise to collect receivables as fast as possible in an inflationary country where the local currency is expected to depreciate, the firm must consider the competitive implications of not extending credit.

A weak-currency situation suggests that firms:

- Quickly collect receivables
- Invest cash
- Pay liabilities at latest date.

In reality, working capital management under exchange risk assumes that currency values move in one direction. A weak-currency country generally (although not always) suffers from inflation. The approach to protecting assets in the face of currency depreciation also applies to protection against inflation. Inflation erodes the purchasing power of local currency, whereas depreciation erodes the foreign currency equivalent.

In the weak-currency situation, subsidiaries' cash should be remitted to the parent as fast as possible or invested locally in something that appreciates in value, such as fixed assets. Accounts receivable should be collected as quickly as possible when they are denominated in the local currency and stretched out when denominated in a stronger currency. Liabilities should be treated in the opposite manner.

A policy for inventory is difficult to determine. If inventory is considered to be exposed, it should be kept at as low a working level as possible. However, since its value usually increases through price rises, it can be a successful hedge against inflation and exchange rate moves. If the inventory is imported, it should be stocked before a depreciation since it will cost more local currency after the change to purchase the same amount in foreign currency. Where price controls are in effect or where there is strong competition, the subsidiary may not be able to increase the price of inventory. In this situation, inventory can be treated in the same way as cash and receivables. These principles can be reversed when an appreciation is predicted—that is, keep cash and receivables high, and liquidate debt as rapidly as possible. The safest approach is to keep the net exposed position as low as possible.

Borrowing locally provides a trade-off between the loss from exchange rate variations and the cost of borrowing.

The use of debt to balance exposure is an interesting phenomenon. Many firms have adopted a "borrow locally" strategy, especially in weak-currency countries. One problem is that interest rates in weak-currency countries tend to be quite high, so there must be a trade-off between the cost of borrowing and the potential loss from exchange rate variations. Protecting against loss from transaction exposure becomes very complex. In dealing with foreign customers it is always safest for the firm to denominate the transaction in its own currency. Alternatively it could denominate purchases in a weaker currency and sales in a stronger currency. If forced to make purchases in a strong currency and sales in a weak currency, the firm could resort to contractual measures or try to balance its inflows and outflows through more astute sales and purchasing strategies.

A lead strategy is to collect or pay early.

A lag strategy is to collect or pay late.

Leads and lags. Another strategy, known as "leads and lags," is often used to protect cash flows among related entities, such as a parent and its subsidiaries. The **lead strategy** involves collecting foreign currency receivables before they are due when the foreign currency is expected to weaken and paying foreign currency payables before they are due when the foreign currency is expected to strengthen. A **lag strategy** means that a firm will delay receiving foreign currency receivables if that currency is expected to strengthen and delay payables when the currency is expected to weaken. Another way to state this is to say that a company usually leads into and lags out of a hard currency and leads out of and lags into a weak currency. For example, the beginning case in this chapter pointed out that General Electric used a lag strategy in 1984 when the Japanese yen was relatively weak against the U.S. dollar. Because GE predicted a strengthening of the yen, it delayed remitting a yen dividend to the parent company until the yen began to strengthen.

Leads and lags are much easier to use among related entities in which a central corporate financial officer can spot the potential gains and implement a policy. There are two problems with the lead/lag strategy. First it may not involve the movement of large blocks of funds. If there are infrequent decisions involving small amounts of money, it is easy to manage the system, but as the number and frequency of transactions increases, it becomes difficult to manage. Second, leads and lags are often subject to governmental control since movements impact the balance of payments of a country. In Chile, for example, export lags and export leads are limited to 90 days, import lags are limited to 120 days, and import leads are not permitted at all.[26]

A forward contract is used to lock in exchange rates for future transactions.

Forward exchange contracts. In addition to the operational strategies just mentioned, a firm may resort to contractual arrangements. The major approach is the **forward contract,** a contract between a firm and a bank to deliver foreign currency at a specific exchange rate at a set date in the future.

A firm would use a forward contract for many reasons. Basically, the contract takes the risk out of future foreign currency transactions.

As noted in the opening case, Westinghouse was expecting to receive large amounts of French francs during a time when the franc was expected to weaken against the dollar. In order to protect the dollar value of those francs, management entered into forward contracts to deliver francs for dollars at an exchange rate they felt was more favorable than they could receive if they were to wait until the francs were remitted.

An option is the right, but not the obligation, to buy or sell foreign currency in the future at a set rate.

Currency options. As noted in Chapter 8, the foreign currency option is a relatively recent foreign exchange instrument. It is more flexible than the forward contract because it gives the purchaser of the option the right, but not the obligation, to buy or sell a certain amount of foreign currency at a set exchange rate within a specified amount of time.

Firms prefer to use forward contracts when the amount and timing of the future cash flow is certain. The flexibility of options makes them useful for firms when there is high uncertainty in the amount and timing of the cash flows. Although the option can appear to be more expensive than the forward contract, especially when exchange markets are highly volatile, its flexibility can make it very useful in some cases.

When the dollar began to weaken in 1985, firms were required to alter their hedging strategies. First many of them adjusted their time horizons; the volatility of the dollar caused many of them to focus on the short run rather than try to speculate on the long run. Second they began to look for techniques other than forward contracts, such as options. Third, they decided not to focus on translation exposures, but to allow the weak dollar to work in their favor. Assets denominated in a strong currency, such as the Japanese yen, gain value over time as the yen strengthens against the dollar. Finally, many firms began to send home dividends more quickly since dividends declared in a strong currency such as the British pound or West German mark yielded high dollar results.[27]

Many firms also began to alter some of their operating strategies. In particular, they diversified their sourcing and production bases in order to be able to take advantage of significant shifts in currency values. As the vice-president of finance of Bio-Rad pointed out, "In this environment, you need to be able to change strategies quickly."[28] Many firms also shifted to using local currencies to establish budgets and monitor performance. In 1982, a Business International survey found that only 9 percent of the firms sampled set budgets in local currency; by 1987, a new survey showed that this had increased to nearly 75 percent. Most firms stated that volatility in the foreign exchange markets was a key factor for this shift.[29]

FINANCIAL ASPECTS OF THE INVESTMENT DECISION

The foreign investment decision was discussed extensively in Chapter 16, but a few additional financial issues should be mentioned here. An MNE considering foreign investment has many financing options available, as explained in Chapter 10. The parent company must consider the mix of debt and equity that it will use. There are at least two basic reasons why the debt-equity ratio for a foreign subsidiary may differ from that of the parent. First, the attitude toward the debt-equity ratio in the host country may differ from that in the parent country. Firms in Japan and West Germany, for example, tend to be more highly leveraged than their U.S. counterparts, which means that they rely much more on debt than on equity capital.

Second, different tax rates, dividend remission policies, and exchange controls may cause a firm to rely more on debt in some situations and on equity in others. The debt-equity ratio of the MNE will be a weighted average of the debt-equity ratios of all entities in the corporate structure.

Discounted cash flows often are used to compare and evaluate investment projects. Several aspects of capital budgeting unique to foreign project assessment follow:

1. There is a need to distinguish between total cash flows of the project and cash flows remitted to the parent company.
2. Because of differing tax systems, restrictions on financial flows, local norms, and differences in financial markets and institutions, the financing and remittance of funds to the parent firm must be recognized.
3. Different rates of national inflation can be important in changing competitive positions (and thereby cash flows) over time.
4. Foreign exchange rate changes may alter the competitive position of a foreign affiliate.
5. Foreign exchange rate changes unmatched by different national inflation rates may alter the value of cash flows from affiliate to parent, and vice versa.
6. Political factors can reduce drastically the value of a foreign investment.
7. The final sale value is difficult to estimate because of possible divergent market values of a project to potential purchasers from the host, parent, or third countries.[30]

The parent firm must compare the net present value or internal rate of return of a project with that of other parent projects. At the same time, it should compare the project with others available in the host country.

Management must view cash flows from two perspectives: (1) the total flows available to the local operations and (2) the cash available to the parent. The outflows to the parent are important to consider in light of the original investment made, especially if the investment was with parent funds. Finally, the firm must analyze foreign political and exchange risks. The best approach is for the firm to adjust forecasted cash outflows to various plots representing different levels of risk.

SUMMARY

- The finance, or treasury, function deals primarily with: (1) the generation of funds for operating needs and expansion; (2) the management of working capital; and (3) the financial aspects of the foreign investment decision process.

- Three distinct patterns of parent-subsidiary relationships have surfaced with respect to the finance function: (1) complete decentralization at the subsidiary level; (2) complete centralization at the parent level; and (3) varying degrees of centralization.
- The major sources of internal funds for an MNE are: intersubsidiary loans; loans from parent to subsidiaries; dividends; royalties; management fees; the purchase and sale of inventory; and equity flows from the parent to subsidiaries.
- Cash management involves determining local and system needs for cash, methods of centralizing cash, and uses for cash.
- Global cash management is complicated by governmental restrictions on the flow of funds, differing rates of inflation, and changes in exchange rates. A sound global cash management system requires timely reports from affiliates worldwide.
- The transfer of money from country to country to settle transactions involves the use of specialized financial documents, such as bills of exchange and letters of credit.
- Many developing countries and Eastern European countries have severe foreign exchange problems, so firms that sell to those countries are often forced to enter into different types of compensatory trade in order to earn foreign exchange for their transactions.
- Management must protect corporate assets from loss due to inflation and exchange rate changes. Exchange rates can influence the dollar equivalent of foreign currency financial statements, the amount of cash that can be earned from foreign currency transactions, and production and marketing decisions of a firm.
- Foreign exchange risk management involves defining and measuring exposure, setting up a good monitoring and reporting system, adopting a policy to assign responsibility for exposure management, and formulating a strategy for hedging exposure.
- Forward contracts can lock the firm into a specific exchange rate for future obligations, which could result in gains or losses, depending on what happens to the future spot rate. However, the forward contract eliminates the uncertainty for the firm.
- Foreign currency options give the purchaser the option of buying or selling foreign currency in a certain amount, at a fixed exchange rate, during a period of time in the future. It is more expensive than a forward contract but has more flexibility.
- When deciding to invest abroad, a firm must consider its optimal debt-equity ratio, evaluate local currency and investor currency rates of return, identify cash flows unique to foreign investment, calculate a multinational cost of capital, and offset foreign political and exchange risks.

CASE:
OLIVETTI'S EXPOSURE[31]

In 1978, Carlo De Benedetti took over as CEO of Olivetti, known primarily as a typewriter company, and turned it into the leading European-based office-automation company and one of the largest manufacturers of IBM-compatible computers. De Benedetti's aggressive strategy thrust Olivetti into the international marketplace and forced management to reexamine its exposure to foreign exchange risk and determine whether or not the policies and procedures designed to protect against risk were adequate in light of its new international strategy.

The Company. When De Benedetti was offered the CEO spot at Olivetti in 1978, the company was losing $8 million a month, had a debt position in excess of liquid assets by more than $600 million, and also had a management team that was very discouraged. "We had only a few products and a local culture," recalls Elserino Piol, executive vice-president for corporate strategies. "We were sort of a country-boy company. As soon as De Benedetti came on board, he instituted massive layoffs, increased the research and development budget significantly, introduced new products, and replaced most of Olivetti's top management.

By 1986, sales were $4.9 billion, and earnings were $380 million. Of Olivetti's sales, approximately 49 percent are in Italy, 32 percent in other European countries, and 18 percent in non-European countries. Olivetti manufactures computers under the AT&T name and has struck strategic alliances with a number of MNEs, including AT&T, Matsushita Electrical Industrial Co., and Toshiba. As noted by De Benedetti, "The traditional multinational approach is *dépassé* [obsolete]. Corporations with international ambitions must turn to a new strategy of agreements, alliances, and mergers with other companies."

Olivetti has been so successful in its partnership with AT&T that AT&T brought in the head of Olivetti's North American Operations to run the Data Systems Division of AT&T. De Benedetti wants to move away from the narrow niche of being a hardware manufacturer to being a firm that solves business problems through hardware and software. Olivetti has entered into an arrangement with GM's Electronic Data Systems Corp. to provide computer services in Europe. Olivetti is the top computer maker in Italy, but it is struggling in Europe and the United States, in spite of its strategic alliance with AT&T. Given the size and strength of the U.S. market, especially in the hardware and software industry, De Benedetti is determined to improve Olivetti's position there.

The Olivetti Risk Management Strategy. Olivetti has production and distribution facilities scattered around the world. As a result, it has tried to establish good strategies for managing foreign exchange risk. Olivetti's strategy is developed by a committee made up of the group controller, the international treasurer, the chief economist, and a member of the operational planning department.

The first thing that the committee does is consider the relationship among three currencies: the local currency (the currency of the country where the operation is located); the currency of denomination (the currency in which a transaction actually is denominated); and the currency of determination (the currency used to determine the global price of products). The committee tries to see how fluctuations in the three currencies will affect Olivetti's competitiveness in the markets where it operates. Once a year, the committee simulates the effect of different exchange rate scenarios on the profitability of each unit and the company as a whole.

There is a strong interrelationship between the exchange rate and the economic environment. As noted by Angelo Fornasari, Olivetti's vice-president of finance: "To maintain market share and satisfactory profit levels, Olivetti must constantly consider the problems of sourcing product input, of funding in different currencies and markets, of reorienting marketing efforts, of seeking higher productivity levels, of shifting from one currency of invoicing (i.e., of denomination), to another, etc." Currently, Olivetti develops its economic exposure scenario three years into the future.

Although the major exposure for Olivetti is economic exposure, management also is concerned about translation and transaction exposure. The hedging strategy is centralized at the corporate level so that local managers can concentrate on operating decisions. Transaction exposure is centralized, and hedging activities are carried out for the balances of transactions actually booked, as well as for forecasts of what the balances are expected to be four months into the future.

A major event likely to have an impact on discussions at Olivetti was the currency scandal at Volkswagen in 1986. Burkhard Junger, the former chief currency trader of Volkswagen AG confessed to complicity with fugitive currency trader Joachim Schmidt, the owner of a small foreign-exchange brokerage in Frankfurt. Apparently, Junger and Schmidt entered into fraudulent forward contracts with the National Bank of Hungary to sell the bank U.S. dollars for German marks at a rate just under three marks per dollar. When the contracts turned up fraudulent, Volkswagen was left with dollars worth less than two marks each, and it lost $260 million, which was 80 percent of its net income in 1986. VW currency traders were allowed to trade contracts for a profit, a policy that many shareholders felt was inappropriate. They felt that foreign exchange conversion should only take place to support manufacturing operations, not to gain a profit. In addition, VW had adopted a policy not to hedge against foreign currency fluctuations, since it felt that those fluctuations would balance themselves out over the medium term.

QUESTIONS

1. Given the nature of Olivetti's products, markets, and strategic alliances, what different types of foreign exchange risks do you think it will encounter?
2. In terms of foreign exchange risk management, what difference does it make what the currency of determination is for Olivetti products?
3. Why do you think Olivetti does not look into the future more than three years to develop its economic exposure scenario?
4. What hedging activities would you expect Olivetti management to pursue? Do you think that Olivetti's hedging strategy is more realistic than VW's?
5. What is your opinion of Olivetti's policy of centralizing hedging strategies at the corporate level? What role should local management play in developing and implementing those strategies?

NOTES

1. Data for the case were taken from Michael R. Sesit, "Treasurers of Multinationals Plan Ways To Handle Currency Swings," *Wall Street Journal,* January 24, 1984, p. 35; the annual reports of the companies involved; and "Managing Currency Risk in Today's Unsettled Markets," *Business International Money Report,* December 7, 1987, p. 395.

2. "MNCs Ponder Peso's Future after Free Market Collapse," *Business International Money Report,* November 23, 1987, p. 377.

3. Nigel Bance, "The Man Who Manages the Finances of Europe's Largest Car Manufacturer," *Euromoney,* May 1976, p. 20.

4. Sidney M. Robbins and Robert B. Stobaugh, *Money in the Multinational Enterprise* (New York: Basic Books, 1973), pp. 37–48.

5. John T. Wooster and G. Richard Thoman, "New Financial Priorities for MNCs," *Harvard Business Review,* May–June 1974, pp. 58–68.

6. "How Multinationals Play the Money Game," *Fortune,* August 1973, p. 60.

7. "Successful Global Cash Management," *Financing Foreign Operations* (New York: Business International Corporation, March 1986), pp. 1–3.

8. Ernst & Whinney, *1987 Foreign Exchange Rates and Restrictions* (New York: Ernst & Whinney, 1987).

9. Jane O. Burns, "Transfer Pricing Decisions in U.S. Multinational Corporations," *Journal of International Business Studies,* Vol. 11, No. 2, Fall 1980, p. 25.

10. Brad Asher, "What New Currency Strategies Should Treasurers Adopt Now?" *Business International Money Report,* (New York: Business International Corporation, December 7, 1987,) p. 396.

11. "Bayer: Why the High Dollar Is No Headache," *Business Week,* October 29, 1984, p. 53.

12. Daniel Hertzberg, "Pension Managers Invest More Overseas, Aware of Risks but Hopeful about Profits," *Wall Street Journal,* July 2, 1981, p. 44.

13. *Ibid.,* pp. 23–24.

14. Pompiliu Verzariu, *Countertrade, Barter, Offsets* (New York: McGraw-Hill Book Company, 1985), flyleaf.

15. The illustrations in this section are from *Wall Street Journal,* May 18, 1977, p. 1.

16. Verzariu, *op. cit.,* p. 27.

17. "Financial Strategies in Risky Markets," *Financing Foreign Operations* (New York: Business International Corporation, January 1987), pp. 1–2.

18. "Business Outlook: Mexico," *Business International Money Report,* November 30, 1987, p. 382.

19. Richard W. Wright, "Organizational Ambiente: Management and Environment in Chile," *Academy of Management Journal,* March 1971, p. 72.

20. "Financial Strategies in Risky Markets," *op. cit.,* pp. 2–5.

21. Gary Putka, "Strong Dollar Has Led U.S. Firms to Transfer Production Overseas," *Wall Street Journal,* April 9, 1985, p. 1.

22. "Claiborne Comes Home," *Business Week,* January 11, 1988, p. 73.

23. Helmut Hagemann, "Anticipate Your Long-Term Foreign Exchange Risks," *Harvard Business Review,* March–April 1977, p. 82.

24. "New Directions in Exposure Management," *Financing Foreign Operations* (New York: Business International Corporation, November 1986), pp. 4–5.

25. For a more extensive treatment of these four devices, *see* "New Directions in Exposure Management," *Financing Foreign Operations* (New York: Business International Corporation, November 1986), pp. 5–14.

26. "New Directions in Exposure Management," *op. cit.,* p. 10.

27. Brad Asher, "What New Currency Strategies Should Treasurers Adopt Now?" *Business International Money Report* (New York: Business International, December 7, 1987), pp. 395–396.

28. *Ibid.,* p. 396.

29. *Ibid.,* p. 396.

30. David K. Eiteman and Arthur I. Stonehill, *Multinational Business Finance,* 4th ed. (Reading, Mass.: Addison-Wesley, 1986), pp. 330–331.

31. Sources for the case are as follows: Olivetti Annual and Extraordinary General Meeting, 1985; "How Olivetti Manages FX Risk To Protect Long-Term Profits," *Business International Money Report* (New York: Business International, November 2, 1987), pp. 349–351; William C. Symonds, Thane Peterson, John J. Keller, and Marc Frons, "Dealmaker De Benedetti," *Business Week,* August 24, 1987, pp. 42–47; Terence Roth, "Former Trader at VW Admits Role in Fraud," *Wall Street Journal,* September 14, 1987, p. 16.

21

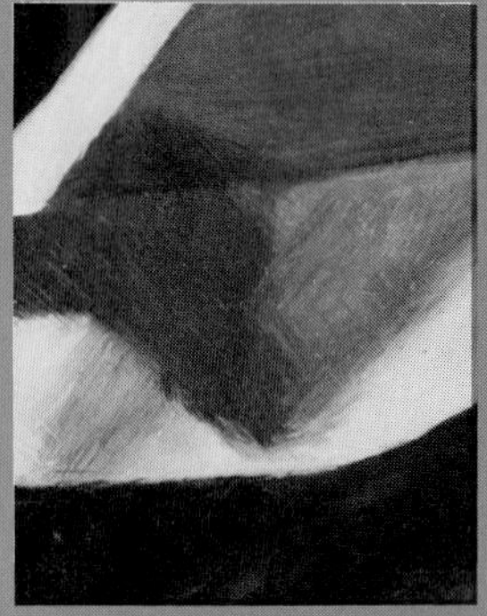

CHAPTER HUMAN RESOURCE MANAGEMENT

If the leader is good, the followers will be good.
—Philippine proverb

- To explain the unique qualifications of international managers.
- To evaluate the specific issues that occur when managers are transferred internationally.
- To examine the major alternatives for recruitment, selection, training, and compensation of international managers.
- To discuss how labor market differences among countries can affect optimum methods of production.
- To describe diversities in labor policies and practices on a country-to-country basis.
- To highlight some of the major international pressures on how MNEs can deal with labor worldwide.
- To examine the effect of transnational operations on collective bargaining.

CASE: DOW'S INTERNATIONAL MANAGEMENT DEVELOPMENT[1]

In 1987, Bulgarian-born Frank P. Popoff replaced Italian-born Paul Oreffice as chief operating officer of Dow Chemical, a U.S. company that is one of the world's largest chemical firms. Oreffice had replaced Hungarian-born Zoltan Merszei in 1979. On becoming chief at Dow, Mr. Popoff, who had once headed Dow's European division said, "I had a lot of international experience and I think, for a company that has over 50 percent of its sales outside the U.S., that's very important."

Some observers would argue that this placement of foreign-born and/or internationally experienced persons at the helm of the firm suggested the process of multinationalization. For example, Peter Drucker, a leading management authority, stated that a truly multinational firm "demands of its management people that they think and act as international businessmen in a world in which national passions are as strong as ever." A firm whose top management includes people from various countries and with varied country experiences presumably is less likely to place the interests of one country above those of others and supposedly will have a more worldwide outlook.

Whether nationality or birthplace of a firm's officers indicates a worldwide outlook is, of course, debatable. However, the experience of working abroad under some very different environmental conditions is very useful for grasping some of the problems that are not as prevalent in a purely domestic context. Paul Oreffice described his foreign experience at Dow as follows:

> *I would never have risen as far as I have in Dow if it hadn't been for my foreign experience. What I learned in Brazil in the 1960s influenced and advanced my career. Even though my training was technical, my job was about 70 percent a financial job, because that's what management in a high-inflation country is. The only way we could get dollars to import goods from the U.S. was to go to the exchange and bid on how many cruzieros we would pay per dollar for imported goods. It was so important to the job that every Tuesday morning I personally went to the exchange in Sao Paulo and stood there with my broker. I learned the maintenance of margins or replacement cost pricing which is the only way you can make sufficient profit to buy and build more.*

That Dow's chief executives have had considerable foreign experience indicates that international operations were an integral part of Dow's total commitment. Dow's dependence on foreign activities had increased very rapidly, and, to effect that growth, it had to gain a commitment to international business from a broad spectrum of managers. Until 1954, Dow's only foreign subsidiary was in Canada. The attitude in the late 1950s was expressed by a company historian as follows:

> *As for the overseas operations, a majority of the veterans regarded them as a sideline. The foreign market was all right as a place for getting rid of surplus products, but the only truly promising market was in the United States. They questioned the idea of the company becoming too deeply involved in countries whose politics, language, culture, monetary controls and ways of doing business were strange to them.*

Some of Dow's younger managers did not share this domestic attitude, but dramatic steps were needed to gain the commitment of the majority of managers to an international outlook. One method employed by the company's president in 1958 was to give international responsibilities to people who were widely perceived to be destined for top-level positions in the firm. C. B. Branch, who was managing Dow's fastest growing department, was appointed head of foreign operations. Herbert "Ted" Dow Doan, who at thirty-one was already a member of the board of directors, went to Europe on a fact-finding mission. (Ted Doan's father and grandfather both had been Dow presidents.) Both Branch and Doan went on quickly to become presidents of Dow. Thus the importance of international operations was readily apparent to any manager in the company.

By 1964, Dow's foreign sales still accounted for only about 20 percent of its total. Today, over half of the sales and profits are from foreign countries. Dow has a large portion of middle- and upper-level managers with foreign work experience. Although most of these managers are Americans who have had assignments in Europe, increasing numbers have experience in more remote areas. The firm estimated, for example, that about fifty senior executives had been moved into Saudi Arabia and Kuwait.

Although the discussion so far emphasizes the importance of international exposure for top-level managers in firms with global commitments, this experience is not the only international management consideration. Firms also must attract and retain high-quality personnel within each country where they operate. These are largely local personnel, and the needs change as corporate strategies evolve. For instance, Dow had to hire many more non-U.S. scientists and technicians in the early 1980s when the company was strengthening R&D in Europe and Asia. Firms also must transfer people to foreign locations when qualified local managers are not readily available. For example, Dow might have been much better off staffing with expatriate managers in a now-divested South Korean operation than depending on its governmental partner to supply personnel. The Korean government put retired army generals into top positions, which led Andrew Butler, an Englishman in charge of Dow in the Far East, to say that the government "brought no experience, clout, or technology to the joint venture."

When Dow sends managers to foreign operations, what type of qualifications should they have? Robert Lundeen, a former Dow chairman who had served twelve years as president of the Pacific division and three years as president of the Latin American division, gave some indication of his philosophy when he addressed the seventy-fifth anniversary meeting of the American Institute of Chemical Engineers. After speaking about the obvious technical needs, he said, "When I worked in Asia, I observed that many Americans seemed to delight in their insularity and that attitude hurts the ability of the U.S. to do business in foreign countries."

INTRODUCTION

The preceding case highlights one firm's experience in dealing with some international aspects of its personnel policies. Although companies have taken a variety of approaches, most agree on the importance of management internationalization if they are to achieve their foreign growth and operation objectives. For instance, the National Industrial Conference Board surveyed senior international executives from a broad range of U.S. industries to determine the most pressing and most enduring problems in international business. Of all the difficulties these executives reported, the finding, training, and holding of qualified managers drew the most comment. One executive summed up the personnel situation aptly when he stated,

> *Other executives might cite economic problems such as devaluations. I don't think it's wrong to say that virtually any type of international problem, in the final analysis, is either created by people or must be solved by people; hence, having the right people in the right place at the right time emerges as the key to a company's international growth. If we can solve that problem I am confident we can cope with all the others.*[2]

The need for highly qualified people to staff the organization cannot be overemphasized. Any company, whether international or purely domestic, must determine its labor needs, hire people to meet the needs, motivate them to perform well, and upgrade their skills so that they can move to more demanding tasks. The following summarizes the factors that make the management of international human resources different from the management of domestic resources.

1. *Different labor markets.* Each country has a different mix of available workers at different costs. This allows resource-seeking foreign operations to gain access to these human resource capabilities: For example, GM's Mexican upholstery operation employs low-cost production workers and IBM's Swiss R&D facility hires skilled physicists. Whether foreign operations are resource seeking or market seeking, the different labor markets may lend themselves to the production of the same product in different ways in different countries, such as substituting hand labor for machines.

2. *International mobility problems.* There are legal, economic, physical, and cultural barriers to the movement of workers to a foreign country. Yet it is often wise for an international firm to move people, especially when labor market differences result in shortages of needed skills. In such cases, companies often must develop special recruitment, training, compensation, and transfer practices.
3. *Management styles and practices.* As indicated in Chapter 3, attitudes toward different management styles vary significantly from country to country; norms among management practices and labor–management relations testify to this. These differences may strain relations between headquarters and subsidiary personnel or make a manager less effective when working abroad than at home. At the same time, the experience of working with different national practices offers some opportunities for transferring successful practices to other countries.
4. *National orientations.* Although an international company's goals may include attaining global efficiencies and competitiveness, its personnel (both labor and management) emphasize national rather than global interests. Certain personnel practices can help overcome the national orientations; and other operating adjustments may be necessary when the nationalistic orientations prevail.
5. *Control.* In Chapter 17 we showed that such factors as distance and diversity make the control of foreign operations more difficult than domestic ones. These factors affect the management of human resources in that personnel policies sometimes are used to gain more control over foreign operations. At the same time, these control factors inhibit the ability to conduct personnel policies as the international firm might prefer and cause practices to vary from one country to another.

This chapter emphasizes these points, differentiating between managerial and labor personnel.

MANAGEMENT QUALIFICATIONS AND CHARACTERISTICS

Headquarters–Subsidiary Relationship

Management must consider country and global needs.

Relations are affected by:
- Polycentrism versus ethnocentrism
- Benefits of independence.

International management staffing is two-tiered: First, the subsidiary level must employ persons who are equipped to manage the activities within the countries where they are located; second, people at corporate and/or regional headquarters must be equipped to coordinate and control the firms' various worldwide and regional operations. These two staffing dimensions are very much related, particularly since headquarters personnel usually choose and evaluate those who direct the subsidiaries abroad. These concerns also are related in that headquarters and subsidiary personnel must both be sufficiently aware of and acceptable of the trade-offs between the need to adapt to local environmental differences and the need to gain global efficiencies.

The balance of power in these trade-offs is complex, depending on such factors as the firm's philosophy (e.g., polycentric versus ethnocentric) and on how much operations in different countries may benefit from independence versus interdependence. When firms have a polycentric philosophy and their foreign subsidiaries are a federation of highly independent operations, there is much less effort to impose standard practices or a corporate culture abroad than when the philosophy is ethnocentric and foreign operations are interdependent with those in other countries.[3] Regardless of where the international firm lies between these extremes, it may face dilemmas because the technology, policy, and managerial style it has developed in one place may be only partially applicable elsewhere. International managers, at headquarters and subsidiaries, are responsible for introducing (or not introducing) practices new to a country.

Top-Level Duties Abroad

Top management in subsidiaries usually have broader duties than people with same size operation at home.

Subsidiary management. Although foreign subsidiaries usually are much smaller than their parents, their top-level managers often have to perform top-level management duties. This usually means being more of a generalist than specialist, more of a leader than a follower, having responsibility for all the wide variety of functions, spending more time on the job, and spending a larger portion of time on external relations with the community, government, and general public as well as outside business meetings. Managers with comparable profit or cost responsibility in the home country still may be performing middle-management tasks and lack the breadth of experience necessary for a top-management position in a foreign subsidiary.

Overseas managers must sell themselves, their companies, and the countries in which their firms are headquartered. Also, they must sell finished goods of dimensions and tolerances that may be new to the area.

Corporate staff abroad:

- Deal at top-level in many countries
- Have rigors of foreign travel
- Face difficulties if they have risen entirely through domestic divisions.

Headquarters travel. The corporate staff charged with responsibility for international business functions also must interact frequently with very high-level authorities in foreign countries. Such activities as negotiations for new or expanded plants, the sale of technology, and the assessment of monetary conditions require a high interaction by the corporate staff during their travels to foreign countries. In many ways their tasks are even more difficult than those of the subsidiary managers since they must be away from home for extended and indefinite periods while seeking the confidence and rapport of officials in many foreign countries rather than in just one. Even if they are not faced with the rigors of foreign travel, they may be ill at ease with the foreign aspects of their responsibilities if their rise to the corporate level has been entirely through work in domestic divisions.

Communications Problems of the Job

International communications are complex and more likely to be misunderstood than domestic ones.

Interpretation. International managers must communicate well to ensure that the intent of messages between the home and subsidiary operations is understood. This is no easy task for several reasons: The cost of overseas calls and cables; the problems of reaching people in different time zones by telephone, and the slowness of international postal service.

Communications between managers whose native languages are different are compounded further. Corporate communications, directives, and manuals of a U.S. firm, for example, probably will be sent worldwide in English. Even if all the content is understood perfectly abroad, the comprehension time will be likely longer than in a country for which English is the official language. Likewise, a manager working abroad, such as one from the United States at a U.S. subsidiary or one from France at the same firm's corporate headquarters, often must work harder to assure doing the same quality work that could be done at home.[4] These innate inefficiencies are often overlooked by the parent, yet international management is held responsible.

Recall from Chapter 3 that childhood socialization differences among countries cause differences in the intents and perceptions of what we transmit and receive in formal communications. Thus international managers may assume erroneously that foreigners will react the same way as their compatriots to such things as decision making and leadership styles. This is a particular problem when various nationalities are grouped, such as on a team project. Some of these differences may be lessened through the development of a common corporate culture, but even this may be of little use when managers must work internationally in the increasing number of cooperative ventures that include different nationalities and different firms, such as within joint ventures and licensing agreements.[5]

Use of English. English is today the international language of business because: (1) so much international business is conducted by firms from and in English-speaking countries and (2) English has become the major second language worldwide. Furthermore, managers cannot be expected to learn all the languages where their firms operate. Consequently, business between Mexico and Brazil or between Italy and Saudi Arabia may be conducted in the common second language of English. Even some multinationals from West Germany, Japan, Netherlands, Switzerland, and Sweden have adopted English as their official tongue.[6]

A working knowledge of the language spoken where a manager is operating can, nevertheless, help in adapting to the foreign country as well as gaining acceptance by people there. However, unless they are fully fluent in a common language, managers should consider employing good interpreters when they are attempting serious discussions.

Isolation

International managers are isolated and have less access to staff specialists.

The manager in a foreign subsidiary must be able to work independently because he or she may face a great deal of isolation in the job. Many staff functions are eliminated abroad because of the cost of duplication. At the home operation a manager can easily walk to the next office or make a few telephone calls to get advice from specialists. The manager abroad may not have these specialists close at hand; consequently, he or she ends up relying much more heavily on personal judgment.

Headquarters personnel traveling abroad on assignments may face the same isolation problems as do the managers in the foreign subsidiaries as well as isolation in their personal lives. Although many domestic positions require traveling, the domestic trips are apt to be of shorter duration because of the shorter time and lower expense of returning home for weekends.

FOREIGN MANAGERIAL TRANSFERS

Some Definitions

International firms commonly categorize managers as **locals** (citizens of the countries where they are working) or **expatriates** (noncitizens). The expatriate group is further categorized as **home country** and **third country nationals;** these are, respectively, citizens of the country where the company is headquartered and citizens neither of the country where they are working nor of the headquarters country of the firm. Locals or expatriates may be employed in the firm's home country or in the firm's foreign operations.

Expatriates: A Minority of Managers

Most managerial positions are filled by locals rather than expatriates in both headquarters or foreign subsidiary operations. The one exception is for project management in some developing countries, such as Saudi Arabia, where there is an acute shortage of qualified local candidates.

Problems in filling managerial slots:

- Many people don't want to move.
- Expatriates are more costly.
- There are legal impediments to using expatriates.

Mobility. Many people, regardless of nationality, simply do not want to work in a foreign country; this is particularly true if an assignment is perceived to be permanent or very long term. In many cases companies have had to set up special operating units to employ people who will not work where the company would prefer. For instance, this has been a motive for setting up R&D labs and regional staff offices abroad when the personnel refused to move to the global headquarters country.

The cost of using expatriates is another factor firms must face in filling managerial positions. Firms typically pay for moving expenses (including customs duties on household effects), settling-in expenses (such as the cost of adapting appliances to foreign electrical systems), and storage expenses for goods not shipped abroad, since employers may balk at moving pianos, antiques, boats, and hobby equipment. Generally it is more expensive for firms to maintain expatriates than local managers after the transfer. There are legal impediments as well, such as immigration restrictions that cause delays in filling positions. Since governmental regulations and their enforcement may change drastically and quickly, firms face considerable uncertainty.

Local competitive needs. The greater the need for local adaptations, the more advantageous it is for firms to use local management since they presumably understand local conditions better than someone from outside the country. These needs may arise because of unique environmental conditions, barriers to imports, or strong local competitors or customers.

Locals in management may help sales and morale.

The local image. Sometimes it is useful for the firm to create a local image for foreign operations, especially when there is animosity toward foreign-controlled operations. Local management may be perceived locally as "better citizens" because they presumably put local interests ahead of the companies' global objectives. This local image may play a role in employee morale as well, since many subsidiary employees prefer to work for someone from their own country.[7]

If top jobs are given only to expatriates, it may be hard to attract and keep good locals.

Incentives to local personnel. Proponents of employing local nationals sometimes argue that the possibility of advancement provides an incentive to employees to perform well; without this incentive, it is contended, they may seek employment with other firms. Opponents argue that practices restricting the best-qualified people, regardless of nationality, from positions are even more damaging to employee motivation. Anyone in the organization, they say, should have the opportunity to move up to any post, including positions in the corporate headquarters.

Expatriates may take shorter-term perspectives.

Long-term objectives. Since people transferred to subsidiaries usually expect to be there for only a few years, they are often more anxious than local nationals to choose short-term projects that will materialize during their tenure in the foreign location.[8] In producing highly visible and measurable results that help satisfy personal advancement needs when the foreign assignment is terminated, they may not be best serving the longer-range corporate goals. Local nationals who stay on for a longer duration therefore may take more heed of long-term objectives because of the probability of still working there when the instituted practices are completed.

Reasons for Using Expatriates

Despite expatriate managers being a minority within international firms, there are still several hundred thousand employed worldwide.

There are more shortages of technically trained personnel in LDCs.

Technical competence. When companies are asked why they use expatriate employees, especially in their foreign operations, the most frequent reply is that they cannot find a local candidate who has the technical qualifications for the job. The inability to find a locally qualified person is partly a function of the level of development of the country; thus expatriates constitute a much smaller portion of subsidiary managers in industrial than in developing countries. Also it is a function of how much it is necessary to infuse new home country developments abroad. When, for example, there is a transfer of new products or new production methods, usually there is a need for transfers of home country personnel to subsidiaries or of subsidiary personnel to the home country until the changes are running smoothly.

Multicountry experience gives upward-moving managers new perspectives.

Management development. MNEs transfer foreigners into their home country or regional operations and home country nationals abroad to train them about the overall corporate system.[9] In firms with specialized activities only in certain countries (extraction separated from manufacturing, for example, or basic R&D separate from applied), long-term foreign assignments may be the only means of developing a manager's integrative competence. These moves also enhance managers' ability to work in a variety of social systems and are therefore valuable training for ultimate corporate responsibility, including domestic and foreign operations.

People transferred from headquarters are more likely to know headquarters policies.

People transferred to headquarters learn the headquarters way.

Control. In Chapter 17 we showed that MNEs use both transfers and visits by headquarters staff to subsidiaries to control the foreign operations and coordinate organizational development. These goals are accomplished because the people who are transferred are used to doing things the headquarters way and because frequent transfers let them increase their knowledge of the company's global network.[10] Likewise, foreign nationals may spend time at worldwide or regional headquarters, thereby giving a foreign perspective to the firm's global direction. Through the greater interchange brought about by moves of both home and host country nationals, the new hybrid corporate culture can become a means of controlling the company's operations. Although a common international corporate culture would seem to emerge by bringing managers in closer contact, the evidence thus far indicates that national differences in approaches to managing are not overcome so easily.[11]

Where there is a need to adopt a more global strategy, there is a tendency to use more expatriates for control purposes. They are or become generally more familiar with the complexities of the business family system as a whole and tend not to see their own personal development so much in terms of what happens only in the country to which they are assigned.[12]

Home-Country versus Third-Country Nationals

Increasingly firms are considering the option of sending a national of a third country abroad rather than a home-country national. Certain factors help to explain the actual and ideal employment of one versus the other.

Decision makers are more prone to staff foreign operations with people they know.

Transfer decision process. The people who decide who will be transferred abroad are usually from the home country. Generally they seek someone they have observed personally because this is perceived to reduce the risk of making a wrong decision.[13] Since foreign operations generally are more independent of corporate headquarters than domestic facilities of comparable size, there is a greater chance that a home-country national rather than a foreign national will be considered seriously for a cross-national transfer. With recent improvements in travel and communications, the foreign national has been exposed more to corporate personnel and thus is increasingly employed as an expatriate.

Third-country nationals may be more knowledgeable of:

- Language
- Operating adjustments.

Qualifications. Most advances in technology, product, and operating procedures originate in the home country and are transferred into foreign operations later. Since the use of expatriates in foreign facilities is dictated in part by a desire to infuse new methods, the personnel with recent home-country experience (usually home-country citizens) are apt to have the desired qualifications.

In both technical and personal adaptive qualifications, third-country nationals might be expected in some instances to perform better than home-country expatriates. For example, a U.S. company used U.S. personnel to design and manage a plant in Peru until local managers could be trained. Several years later, the firm decided to begin manufacturing in Mexico. Management felt that the new plant in Mexico should resemble more closely the operations in Peru rather than those in the United States in terms of size, product qualities, and factor inputs. Therefore, Peruvian managers were used effectively in planning, start-up, and early operating phases in Mexico. The similar language and background facilitated the adaptiveness of the Peruvians and their families in Mexico.

Some Individual Considerations for Transfers

Job ability factors are usually the most important attribute.

Technical competence. Unless the foreign assignment is clearly intended for training the expatriate, local employees will resent someone coming in from a foreign country (usually at higher compensation) who, they feel, is no more qualified than they are. The opinions of senior international executives who make transfer decisions, expatriate managers themselves, and local managers with whom expatriates will work confirm that job ability factors are the most important determinants of success versus failure in overseas assignments.[14]

Not only must the expatriate know the technical necessities of the tasks as performed in the home country, he or she also must be able to adapt to variations in facilities and technologies due to different levels of economic and industrial development. Some of the most common of these are scaled-down plants and equipment, varying standards of productivity, lack of efficient internal distribution, nonavailability of credit, and restrictions on type of communications media selected.

Family adaptation is important.

Fixed-term versus open-end assignments are viewed differently.

Adaptiveness. About one-third of families transferred abroad return home prematurely, and some who complete their foreign assignments perform only marginally because of the employee's or family's adjustment problems.[15] An international move usually means a great disruption of the current way of living, especially since the greatest shortage of managers is in the LDCs. A move means new living and shopping habits, new school systems, and unfamiliar business practices. In addition, close friends and relatives—the personal support system—are left behind. Adaptation and performance in foreign assignments tend to be higher for people who have empathy with others' situations, who have traveled abroad before reaching adulthood, and who have foreign language abilities.[16] Since some individuals do enjoy and adapt easily to a foreign way of life, it is preferable to use them if possible when transfers are necessary. Some firms maintain a specific group of international employees who are the only ones assigned abroad.

A distinction needs to be made between a foreign assignment of fixed duration and one that is open-ended. Many more people can cope with a position abroad if they know that they will return home after a specific period of time than if the assignment may turn out to be permanent.

Expatriates may meet with local prejudice.

Local acceptance. Expatriates may encounter some acceptance problems regardless of who they are. For instance, it usually takes time for managers to gain recognition of their personal authority, and expatriates may not be there long enough to achieve this. Local employees may feel that the best jobs are given to overpaid foreigners. The expatriate may have to make unpopular decisions in order to meet global objectives. Or local management may have had experiences with expatriates who made short-term decisions and left before dealing with the longer-term implications.[17] If negative stereotypes are added to these attitudes, it may be very difficult for the expatriate to succeed. Therefore certain individuals are often excluded from consideration for transfer: A black manager in South Africa, a Jewish manager in Libya, a very young manager in Japan, or a female manager in Saudi Arabia, for example, might encounter insurmountable problems with employees, suppliers, and customers.

But do companies overreact to these acceptance problems? Take stereotypes of women, for example: They should not give orders to men, they are temperamental, their place is in the home, clients will not accept them, employees will not take them seriously, they don't have the stamina for harsh areas, they will not be given work permits. In response to these stereotypes, firms give very few expatriate positions to women. Yet women have succeeded as expatriates in such places as Japan, Thailand, and India.[18] Some suggestions have been made to improve the acceptability of women as expatriates that may be applied as well to improve the acceptability of other groups. These include the selection of very well-qualified older, midcareer women who could command more authority; the advance dissemination of information concerning the high qualifications; the placement of expatriate women in locations where there are already some local women in management positions; and the establishment of longer than normal assignments (e.g., seven or eight years) in order to develop role models of acceptance.[19]

Repatriation Problems

Coming home can be an adaptation in many areas:

- Financial
- Job
- Social.

Repatriation from foreign subsidiary assignments arise in three general areas: (1) personal finances, (2) adjustment to home country corporate structure, and (3) readjustment to life at home. Expatriates are given many financial benefits to encourage them to accept a foreign assignment; they are promised often that the assignment will enhance their careers. While abroad they may live in the best neighborhoods, send their children to the best private schools, socialize with the upper class, and still save more money than before. But this higher life-style is lost on return: An estimated 50-percent increase in salary would be necessary to maintain the same standard of living in the United States that U.S. executives enjoy overseas. The career advantages of the foreign assignment are extremely mixed, depending on how the foreign activities fit into the firms' strategies. Returning expatriates often find that many of their peers have been promoted above them in their absence, that they now have less autonomy in the job, and that they are now "little fish in a big pond." In addition to a drop in social status on return, many families who have successfully adjusted to a foreign life-style have problems in readjusting to schools and other aspects back in their home countries. Some suggestions for smoothing the reentry include early advice of return, maximum information on the new job, housing assistance, a reorientation program, bringing the expatriate manager frequently back to headquarters, and the use of a formal headquarters' mentor who will look after the manager's interests while he or she is an expatriate.[20]

Sometimes there is a specific problem for foreign nationals who are transferred to headquarters. If the assignment is a promotion from a manager's subsidiary post rather than part of a planned rotation, then the move to headquarters may be permanent. For example, the Brazilian head of the Brazilian subsidiary may have performed so well that the MNE wants to give that manager multicountry responsibility at the corporate offices in New York or Frankfurt. Since there would be no way to go back to Brazil without taking a demotion, the Brazilian manager might turn down the transfer; otherwise he or she would give up working in the home country permanently.

Expatriate Compensation

Firms must pay enough to entice people to move but not overpay.

If a U.S. company transfers its British finance manager, who is making $50,000 per year, to Italy where the going rate is $60,000 per year, what should the manager's salary be? Or if the Italian financial manager were to be transferred to the United Kingdom, what pay should be offered? Should the compensation be in dollars, pounds, or lire? Whose holidays should apply? Which set of fringe benefits should be used? These are but a few of the many questions that must be solved when firms move people abroad. On one hand, the firm must try to prevent excessive costs; on the other hand, the firm must maintain high employee morale.

The amount and type of compensation necessary to entice a person to move to another country vary widely by person and locale. For companies with very few expatriate employees a foreign compensation package may be worked out on an individual basis. As international activities grow, a company simply cannot work out each movement this way. Otherwise, questions of equity would be raised, since two people with quite diverse pay packages could end up in the same locale. As long as consistency is sought in transfer policy, some people inevitably will receive more than would be necessary to entice them to go abroad.

Living is more expensive abroad because:

- Habits change slowly
- People don't know how and where to buy.

Cost of living. Most people who move to another country find that their cost of living increases, primarily because they are used to living in a certain manner that is expensive to duplicate in a new environment. This does not imply that one living standard is necessarily better than another, but rather that habits are difficult to change. Knowledge of the local country is a second consideration. Food and housing may be obtained at higher than the local rate because expatriates may not know the language well, where to buy, or how to bargain for reductions.

Firms use various cost-of-living indexes and:

- Increase compensation when foreign cost is higher
- Do not decrease compensation when foreign cost is lower
- Remove salary differential when the manager is repatriated.

Most firms adjust salaries temporarily upward to account for higher costs of living in the area where a person is being transferred. Once the manager returns to the home country, the differential is removed, and the salary is adjusted downward again. When moves are made to foreign areas with a lower cost of living, firms are very reluctant to attempt to reduce the size of the employee's paycheck, since this would have a negative impact on morale; thus the expatriate may receive a windfall. A company therefore must resort to some type of average measurement to estimate a cost of living difference even though this measurement will not fit everyone's situation perfectly. Some commonly used sources are the U.S. State Department's cost-of-living index published yearly in *Labor Developments Abroad,* U.N.

indexes, and surveys by the *Financial Times, Business International,* and the International Monetary Fund *Staff Papers.* In using any of these indexes, firms must determine what items are included so as to adjust other expenditures separately. Some items commonly handled separately are housing, schooling, and taxes. The ultimate objective of cost-of-living adjustments is to ensure the expatriates' after-tax income will not suffer as a result of a foreign assignment. Since differences in inflation and exchange rates may quickly render surveys and indexes obsolete, it is necessary to update cost-of-living adjustments frequently.

Observers have suggested that cost-of-living differentials be reduced the longer the employees are in a given country. The rationale is that, as expatriates become better assimilated, they should be able to adjust more to local purchasing habits—for example, buying vegetables from a native market instead of using imported canned goods.

Transfer is more attractive if employees see it as an advancement.

Job status payment. Some employees may not accept a position abroad unless it is considered to be a promotion, and a promotion without a pay increase would naturally be considered inequitable by most people. Since individuals transferred abroad compare the equity of their compensation with other managers in both the country to which they are sent and the country of which they are citizens, companies additionally normally will raise the salary for individuals while they are working in a country where the going rate for the job is higher than in the home country.

Many companies make little or no provision for reincorporating the transferred employee into the home country operation after the foreign assignment. Because the overseas employees are removed from changes taking place in the home-country operations, they may fall behind in advancement, even to the extent that there is no place for the transferees in the organization upon their return. To alleviate some of the anxiety of the foreign assignment, some firms will pay additional money to the individuals who move abroad.

Employees may encounter living problems for which extra compensation is given.

Hardship allowances. There are bound to be things employees will have to do without when living abroad. Such sacrifices range from nuisance to hardship: For example, employees may miss a favorite brand of cigarettes or whiskey, certain foods, a holiday celebration, or television in the native language. Or children may have to attend school away from home, perhaps even in another country. There is also the adjustment to new cultures that may cause adverse psychological effects and social frustrations.

Few would deny that the living conditions in certain locations present particularly severe hardships such as harsh climatic or health conditions or political insurrection or unrest that places the employee and family in danger. For instance, in recent years, antigovernment groups kidnapped for ransom expatriate employees of such companies as Ford, Kodak, and Owens-Illinois.

In fact, the growing incidence of kidnapping and terrorism has caused firms not only to rethink their hardship allowances, but also to embark on training programs to advise personnel of dangers and how to deal with them. Corporations have been hit by legal suits from victims' families, which have alleged that companies mishandled ransom negotiations. Firms also have been hit by shareholder suits claiming that the company should not pay ransoms.[21]

Finally, a hardship may occur because of potential changes in total family income and status. In the home country, all members of the family may be able to work. Seldom will more than the transferred employee be given permission to work in a foreign country, so if an individual is moved abroad, his or her spouse may have to give up well-paying and satisfying employment.[22] Firms realize that changes in location present various types of hardship problems and attempt to compensate their employees accordingly.

At one time nearly all expatriates received a premium just for being in a foreign country. But there is a growing realization that not all foreign posts constitute a hardship and that it is easy to find people to accept jobs in the more desirable locations.

Salaries are usually a mixture of home and host currency.

Choice of currency. Expatriate employees' salaries are usually (but not always) paid partly in local currency and partly in the currency of the employee's home country. This allows employees to save in their home countries and often to forego host-country taxes on the home-country portion of income. Some other factors influencing the preference for payment in home versus host currencies include whether hard currency expenditures can be charged to the local operation, whether exchange control exists, and whether the expatriate can receive more local currency by exchanging the hard currency through a free market. The company must establish policies that somehow fulfill both its own objectives and those of the expatriate employees.

For their employees in remote areas, firms may have to give more fringe benefits.

Remote areas. Many recent large-scale international projects have been in areas of the world so remote that MNEs would get few people to transfer to these places if the companies did not attempt to create an environment more like the one at home or make other special arrangements. Lockheed Aircraft, for example, has set up its own color television broadcasting station in Saudi Arabia for its expatriates there. INCO has built schools, hospitals, churches, supermarkets, a golf course, yacht club, motel, and restaurant for its expatriates in Indonesia.[23]

Expatriate employees in these remote areas are often handled very differently from those in other locales. To attract the large number of people necessary for construction and start-up, MNEs usually will offer fixed-term contract assignments at high salary and hire most people from outside the firms. Some are attracted to these assignments and are willing to undergo different living conditions because they can save at a rate that would have been impossible at home.

MANAGEMENT RECRUITMENT AND SELECTION

College Recruitment

College recruitment is used at home and abroad, but the biggest need abroad is for higher-level managers.

International companies recruit through universities at home and abroad to find capable nationals of the countries where they have foreign facilities. This method has some drawbacks since the most acute personnel shortage in foreign facilities is for people who already have considerable experience. As one recruiter said, "I only hire people who have worked in multinational companies. I haven't got the time to teach someone what he should know already."[24] As the new hires gain experience, however, they may eventually move into higher-level management positions, thus decreasing the need for expatriates. These same firms also recruit home-country nationals, usually to work in their domestic operations until they have gained technical experience and know the corporate culture. After that, the nationals may be offered international responsibilities, either in a foreign location or at headquarters.

Management Inventories

Foreign personnel are not easily encompassed in inventories because

- Foreign operations may not be wholly owned
- There may be restrictions on cross-national data flows.

Many companies are moving toward a centralized maintenance and retrieval of personnel records, which includes home- and foreign-country nationals. Not only are the normal technical and demographic data maintained, but also such adaptive information as foreign language abilities, willingness to accept foreign assignments, and results of company-administered tests to indicate adaptiveness. There are some problems in bringing foreign managers into these systems because, if the firm owns less than 100 percent of the foreign facility, the other stockholders may complain.[25] Furthermore, restrictions on data flows among countries could inhibit future uses of centralized management inventories.

Adaptability Assessment

Test predictability for success in foreign assignments is not very high.

Since companies usually know more about their employees' technical rather than adaptive capabilities, they must focus on measuring adaptation abilities for foreign transfer purposes. People who have successfully adjusted to domestic transfers are more likely to adapt abroad. In addition, some companies use a variety of testing mechanisms to aid in the assessment. One is the Early Identification Program (E.I.P.), which assesses an individual's match with different environments. Many other tests assess personality traits that indicate a willingness to change basic attitudes: These include the Minnesota Multiphasic Personality Inventory, the Guilford-Zimmerman Temperament Survey, and the Allport-Vernon Study of Values.[26]

Some companies include spouses in tests and extensive interviews because a foreign assignment is usually more stressful for the spouse than for the transferred employee. The foreign assignment is generally an advancement for (in most cases) the husband; however, the wife must start to develop new social relations and learn how to carry out the day-to-day management of the home. The separation from friends and family often make the wife very lonely so that she turns to her husband for more companionship. But the husband may have less time because of his new working conditions. This may lead to marital stress which, in turn, affects work performance. Interviewers thus look not only at likely adaptiveness, but also at whether the marriage is strong enough to weather the stress and not impede employment duties.[27]

Although companies that follow a rigorous procedure of selecting and training people for foreign assignments experience a somewhat lower failure rate of expatriates, the difference is not very substantial relative to the cost of testing. Consequently, few companies administer tests to determine relational abilities.[28] Instruments have not yet been developed to predict adaptability with success.

The Help of Local Companies

Acquisitions and joint ventures secure staff but they may be:

- Inefficient
- Hard to control.

One way of attaining personnel for foreign operations is by buying an existing firm abroad and using the personnel already employed; however, firms should consider the possible efficiency problems of acquisitions as discussed in Chapter 15. Firms also may tie in closely with local companies in the expectation that these firms will contribute personnel to the operation as well as hire new personnel. In countries such as Japan, where the labor market is tight and people are reluctant to move to new firms, the use of a local partner may be extremely important. However, if a local partner handles staffing arrangements, the employees may see their primary allegiance to that partner rather than to the foreign investor.

Personnel Recruiters

Personnel recruiters are used extensively for finding technicians for remote areas.

For locations where there is a need for large numbers of expatriate specialists, companies must depend more heavily on outside recruiters to find personnel. One such area in recent years has been Saudi Arabia. Recruiters have used such methods as employment fairs and the direct mailing of brochures to as many as 10,000 engineers at a time to attract applications.[29]

MANAGEMENT TRAINING

Internationalizing the Organization

There is an increase in international studies in universities.

Preemployment training. As international business has grown and as transportation and communication have led to increased contact among people in different countries, it is probably safe to say that there is a lessened need worldwide to convince managers of the advantages of taking an international perspective on business. However, there is still a need to train managers in the differences in business operations brought about by the internationalization. Business schools are increasing their international offerings and requirements, but there is no consensus as to what students should learn to help prepare for international responsibilities. Two of the distinct approaches are (1) the conveying of knowledge specific to foreign environments as in area studies, and (2) training in interpersonal awareness and adaptability. For example, the former may tend to remove some of the fear and aggression that are aroused when dealing with the unknown. However, the understanding of a different culture does not necessarily imply a willingness to adapt to that culture.[30] Although either approach will help people adjust relative to those who lack the training, there appears to be no significant difference in the effectiveness of the two approaches.[31]

Postemployment training may:

- Include environment-specific information
- Include adaptiveness training
- Give on-the-job training within an unaffiliated firm abroad.

Postemployment training. Although more managers are gaining exposure to international business because of their firms' growth in the foreign area and more effort is being expended in formal business school training, many employees still may escape these internationalization processes. The result may be that they place domestic performance objectives above global ones or that they feel ill-equipped to handle worldwide responsibilities as they move in their organizations.

One approach to training has been to include international business components in external programs, such as at universities, where companies send managers regularly. Some companies have developed their own programs: For instance, General Mills and Celanese have year-long training programs in which foreign nationals spend time in all of the companies' domestic divisions. IBM has regional training centers in which managers from several countries are gathered for specific topics. Cummins Engine provides voluntary evening language courses that any employee may take and works toward overseas business trips for more than the "privileged management elite" so that large numbers of employees develop a foreign awareness.[32] Westinghouse developed cultural awareness workshops.[33]

Another approach has been to emphasize adaptability rather than knowledge of another environment. The Peace Corps, for example, uses sensitivity training, which is designed to develop attitudinal flexibility.[34] Another method is to expose a prospective candidate to subcultures within his or her own country. Still another has been for a firm in one country to train qualified engineers and managers from an unaffiliated firm in another country through on-the-job assignments lasting from one to two years.[35]

Easing the Expatriate Transition

The training activities described are geared toward employees, whether or not they might be sent abroad for transfers or short-term assignments. The purposes of those activities are to break down nationalistic barriers that may prevent an organization from achieving global efficiencies. These activities may be insufficient for employees who are assigned abroad.

For these people it may be difficult to know even what questions to ask, which is why the most common predeparture training takes the form of an informational briefing. Such factors as job design, compensation, housing, climate, education, health conditions, home sales, taxes, transport of goods, job upon repatriation, and salary distribution typically come to mind. But such issues as the foreign social structure, communications links, kidnapping precautions, and legal advice on the law of domicile are seldom considered before settlement abroad.[36]

Some firms go well beyond informational briefings by tapping people for foreign assignments at least a year in advance so that they can learn the culture, customs, language, and ways of doing business where they will be assigned.[37]

LABOR MARKET DIFFERENCES

External Reference Points

Firms should look to existing operations as reference for planning manpower needs in new operations abroad.

Typically, a company setting up a new operation in a foreign country is duplicating, perhaps on a small or slightly altered scale, a product, process, or function being performed at home. Past experience will have shown company officials that for the size of operation being built, what type and how many employees are needed. The company will probably have job descriptions for each category to be filled, and from past experience will know what types of people ideally fit into specific positions.

Appropriate Technology

Firms may shift labor or capital intensities if relative costs are different.

There is some danger in a firm's attempting to duplicate organizational structures and job descriptions abroad, particularly in LDCs. For one thing, labor-saving devices that are economically justifiable at home, where wage rates are high, may be more costly than labor-intensive types of production in a country with high unemployment rates and low wages. Labor-intensive methods also may ingratiate the firm with governmental officials, who must cope with unrest from the unemployed portion of the population. Because of differences in labor skills and attitudes, the firm also may find it advantageous to simplify tasks and use equipment that would be considered obsolete in a more advanced economy.

Critics have argued that MNEs have too often established capital-intensive rather than labor-intensive production methods, thus not contributing fully to the decrease needed in LDC unemployment. The term **appropriate technology** refers to that technology which best fits the factor endowment where it is used. The term usually is used to mean technology that is more labor-intensive than would be cost-efficient in an industrial country.

The evidence of whether MNEs do alter production possibilities to the extent that is cost-feasible is very mixed. On the one hand, there are undoubtedly engineering biases toward duplicating facilities with which the firm has recent experience; these are the plants built to save labor in industrialized countries. Management control systems also may place heavy emphasis on output per person, which is more relevant to production needs in industrialized countries. Likewise, many governmental authorities within the LDCs are anxious to have showcase plants to promote the message that the countries are modernizing rapidly. On the other hand, case studies point to substantial alterations by MNEs, such as replacing mechanized loading equipment with human efforts, because of local costs and availabilities.[38] As long as unemployment continues to be a major social and economic problem within LDCs, controversies will continue over the amount of labor that should be employed in the production process.

International Labor Mobility

There is pressure for labor to move from unemployed and low-wage areas to places of perceived opportunities.

Extent. At the same time that most developing countries have faced critical unemployment problems, many industrialized nations and the underpopulated oil-producing countries (e.g., Kuwait, Saudi Arabia) have been short of workers to run their factories and services. This has created a great deal of pressure for increased immigration, which in turn has been tempered by legal restrictions to minimize the economic and social problems for the countries absorbing large numbers of aliens.

Reliable figures on the amount of international migration are unavailable because of the large number of illegal aliens. However, the fragmentary evidence is rather startling. For example, remittances home from workers from such countries as Jordan, the Yeman Arab Republic, Pakistan, and Egypt exceed the value of exports from those countries.[39]

Companies are less certain of labor supply when they depend on foreign laborers because:

- Countries become restrictive
- Workers return home
- Turnover necessitates more training.

Work force stability problem. Migrant workers in many countries, such as New Zealand's workers from Fiji and Tonga, have permission to stay for only short periods of time, such as three to six months.[40] In many other cases, workers leave their families behind in the hope of returning home after saving sufficient money while working in the foreign country. In the mid-1970s, for example, France had a net loss in its work force as large numbers of Spanish workers returned home. Another uncertainty is the extent to which governmental authorities will restrict the number of foreign workers. Even if cutbacks are accomplished during a slack period in the economy, so that a firm may switch to using local versus foreign workers, a firm then may face the costly process of training workers who may leave as soon as the economy improves.

MNEs must build infrastructure in remote areas.

Employment adjustments. The ability of multinational firms to mobilize capital, technology, and management has fed the demand for migrant workers in remote parts of the globe. To construct facilities where minerals are located or in previously unoccupied areas of oil-producing countries, firms have had to bring in large numbers of skilled and unskilled workers from abroad. In doing this, MNEs have had to construct housing and infrastructure and to develop social services to serve the new population. Even in populated areas, housing shortages might prevent the influx of temporary workers if a company did not make provisions.

The influx and use of workers from different countries create additional problems in the workplace.[41] In the United States during the early twentieth century, large numbers of foreign laborers were secured to work in city industries, for railroads, and in construction. It was common for each nationality group to work under the auspices of its own interpreters and to do particular types of tasks. Barracks and kitchens, provided by employers, were separate, so ethnic separation was perpetuated. Similar practices exist in much of Western Europe today. Some of the results are: the relegation of certain nationality groups to less complex jobs owing to the language problem in training; the development of homogeneous ethnic work groups at cross-purposes with other groups in the organization; and the emergence of go-betweens who can communicate with management and labor.

LABOR COMPENSATION

Importance of Differences

MNEs may need to pay more than local firms to entice workers from existing jobs.

Compensation policies and practices directly affect a firm's competitive viability because they influence the competitive ingredient of attracting, maintaining, and motivating personnel. Labor cost differences among countries sometimes lead to competitive advantages and motivate many firms to establish foreign production facilities. The amount of compensation people receive depends on the estimated contributions made to the business, supply and demand ("going wage") for particular skills in the area, cost of living, governmental legislation, and collective bargaining ability. The methods of payment (salaries, wages, commissions, bonuses, and fringe benefits) depend on customs, feelings of security, taxes, and governmental requirements.

International firms usually pay slightly better than their local counterparts in the lower-wage countries, but far below the salary paid for similar jobs in the highest-wage countries. Some factors leading to higher wages by international companies relate to their management philosophy and structure: For example, techniques that lead to greater efficiencies allow for higher employee compensation. The international company's management philosophy, particularly in contrast to local, family-run companies, is often to attract high-level workers by offering higher relative wages. Furthermore, when a firm first comes into a country, experienced workers may demand higher compensation because they have doubts about whether the new operation will succeed.

Fringe Benefits

Fringe benefits vary substantially from country to country.

Fringe benefits differ radically from one country to another. Direct compensation figures therefore do not accurately reflect the amount a company must pay for a given job in a given country. The types of benefits that are either customary or have been required are also widely divergent. In Japan, for example, workers in large firms commonly receive such benefits as family allowances, housing loans and subsidies, lunches, children's education, and subsidized vacations meaning that fringe benefits make up a much higher portion of total compensation than is the case in the United States. Other types of benefits such as end-of-year bonuses of up to three months' pay, housing, payments based on the number of children, long vacations, and profit sharing are common in many countries.

In many countries it is impossible or expensive to lay off workers.

Job security benefits. Firing or laying off an employee may be either impossible or very expensive in many countries, resulting in unexpectedly higher costs for a company accustomed to the economies of manipulating its employment figures. In the United States, for instance, layoffs are not only permitted but have grown to be expected when demand falls seasonally or cyclically. In many countries a firm has no legal recourse except to fire workers—and then perhaps only if the firm is closing down its operations. In West Germany, for example, a fired worker may get up to eighteen months' salary as severance pay. To curtail operations there, a company must come to an agreement with its unions and the government on such issues as extended benefits and the retraining and relocation of workers.[42]

Workers or the company may be responsible for on-the-job injuries.

Liability for injuries. Company, worker, or third-party neglect may lead to various types of worker or company injury. Physical injury may result from negligent driving by transport workers, faulty maintenance of equipment, and lack of safety equipment. The firm may be injured monetarily from careless handling of cash, embezzlement of funds, and breakage of product and equipment. There is widespread variance in the extent to which companies or workers are held responsible for injuries.[43] The determination of responsibility should dictate how firms handle these contingencies. The amount and allocation of expenditures for insurance, training, and safety equipment thus vary substantially by country.

How to compare. Too often, compensation expenses are compared on a per-worker basis, which may bear little relationship to the total expense of the use of these individuals. People's abilities and motivations vary widely; consequently, it is the output associated with cost that is important. It has often been noted that seemingly cheap labor actually may raise the total compensation expenditure because of the need for more supervision, added training expenses, and adjustments in the method of production.

Labor–Cost Dynamics

Relative costs change, so firms must consider:

- Productivity change
- Labor rate change
- Conversion of labor rate to competitor's currency.

Differences among countries in amount and type of compensation are not static. Salaries and wages (as well as other expenditures) may rise more rapidly in one locale than another. Therefore the relative competitiveness of operations in different countries may shift. Since it is the output associated with cost that is most important in comparing labor competitiveness, an example will illustrate shifting capabilities. Assume U.S. productivity per worker in manufacturing increased by 2.8 percent, whereas hourly compensation rates went up by 10.2 percent. The result was a unit labor cost increase of 7.2 percent (1.102 ÷ 1.028). Meanwhile, productivity in the United Kingdom increased by 5.9 percent and hourly compensation in pounds sterling by 16.2 percent, amounting to a unit cost increase of 9.7 percent (1.162 ÷ 1.059) when measured in pounds sterling. This meant that labor costs were rising more rapidly in the United Kingdom than the United States in terms of local currencies. If sterling fell substantially in relation to the dollar, however, the unit labor cost measured in dollars could actually have become more favorable in the United Kingdom as compared to the United States.[44]

COMPARATIVE LABOR RELATIONS

In each country where an MNE operates, it must deal with a group of workers whose approach will be affected by the sociopolitical environment of the country and by the traditions and regulations of collective bargaining.

Sociopolitical Environment

Overall attitude in a country affects how labor and management view each other and how labor will try to improve its lot.

One of the striking international differences in labor–management relations is how each group views its relationship with the other. When there is very little mobility between the two groups, there may be little direct cooperation toward reaching an overall corporate objective. This type of separation may be enhanced if a marked class difference exists between management and labor. Certainly much labor strife may be traced to labor's and management's perceived involvement in a class struggle, even though labor may have been gaining a greater share of total income and wealth for some time.

In such countries as the United States, Brazil, and Switzerland, labor demands are largely met through an adversary process between the directly affected management and labor.[45] Unions have little influence on how members actually vote in political elections. In contrast, labor groups in many countries vote largely in blocs, resulting in a system in which demands are met primarily through national legislation rather than collective bargaining with management. Such mechanisms as strikes or slowdowns to effect changes may also be national in scope. This implies that a company's production or ability to distribute its product may be much more dependent on the way labor perceives conditions in the country as a whole. In 1984, for example, French truckers demanded lower taxes on diesel fuel and insurance and a subsidy to modernize French trucking. To make their demands known, they set up blockades, closed off major airports, and set fire to the Paris-Lyon railway line.[46] The entire economy was affected.

The use of mediation by an impartial party to try to bring opposing sides together varies as well. In Israel it is required by law; in the United States and the United Kingdom it is voluntary. Among countries which have mediation practices, attitudes toward it are diverse; for example, there is much less enthusiasm for it in India than in the United States.[47] Not all differences are settled through either changes in legislation or collective bargaining. Another means is the labor court or government-chosen arbitrator. For example, in Austria wages in many industries are arbitrated on a semiannual basis.[48] Settlements may be very one-sided if appointments to labor courts in a country have been made by political parties that are pro- or anti-labor.

Union Structure

Union structure can be:
- National versus local
- Industry versus company
- One versus several for the same company.

Companies in a given country may deal with one or several different unions. A union itself may represent workers in many different industries, in many different companies within the same industry, or merely in one company. If it represents only one company, the union may represent all plants or just one plant. Although there are diversities within countries, the most prevalent relationships vary from one country to another. For example, in the United States, unions tend to be national, representing certain types of workers (e.g., airline pilots, coal miners, truck drivers, or university professors) so that a company may deal with several different national unions. Each collective bargaining process is usually characterized by a single firm on one side, rather than an association of different firms, which deals with one of the unions representing a certain type of worker in all the company's plants. In Japan a union typically represents all the workers in a given company and has only very loose affiliations with unions in other companies. This allegedly explains why Japanese unions are less militant than those in most other industrialized countries: They seldom strike, and when they do, they may stop working for only a short period of time or continue working while wearing symbolic arm bands. Because of the closer company affiliation, Japanese union leaders are hesitant to risk hurting the company's ability to compete in the world markets.[49] In Sweden the bargaining tends to be highly centralized in that employers from numerous companies in different industries deal together with a federation of trade unions. In West Germany employers from associations of firms in the same industries bargain jointly with union federations.[50]

Protection from Closures and Redundancy

Worker takeover of plants has been done to publicize their plight.

In response to proposed layoffs, shifts in production location, and cessation of operations, workers in many countries increasingly have moved into plants to prevent the transfer of machinery, components, and finished goods.[51] They have even gone so far as to continue to produce until they ran out of raw materials and components and sold the output on the street in order to prolong their ability to occupy the plants. The results of these efforts have been mixed, sometimes preventing the plant's closing and other times not.

Notification of plant closings has been legislated in some countries.

The fact that workers will go so far to try to prevent a plant from closing indicates how important this issue is in some countries, particularly those in Western Europe where prenotification has been negotiated or legislated almost everywhere. The Western European situation is in contrast to that in Canada and the United States where fewer than one-fifth of contracts require employers to give more than a week's notice of closure.[52]

Lifetime employment in Japan:

- Is a dual system
- Helps institute certain efficiency measures.

The lifetime employment system within Japan offers some contrasts to labor practices in either North America or Western Europe. Within Japan some employees, usually skilled workers in large firms, enjoy lifetime employment. Other workers are considered temporaries; the number of temporaries is large, constituting about 40 percent of the work force even in a large firm such as Toyota. When business takes a downturn or when labor-saving techniques are introduced, companies keep the lifetime employees on the payroll by releasing the temporary workers, reducing the variable bonuses of lifetime employees, and transferring workers to other product divisions. Thus far this system has enabled Japanese firms to introduce robotics more effectively than firms elsewhere because there has been little concern about job security among unionized employees. It also has helped Japanese firms to spend heavily on training because the lifetime employees have a strong moral commitment to stay with their employers. The temporary workers have tolerated the system because of the labor shortage that has existed during recent decades in Japan.[53]

Codetermination

Some firms seek labor–management cooperation through sharing in leadership.

Another trend in labor relations, particularly in northern Europe, is the participation by labor in the management of firms. The most common means has been by having them represented on the board of directors, either with or without veto power. Management has at times proposed labor's participation, as at Chrysler's former U.K. facilities, in a belief that this would prevent frequent strikes and walkouts.[54]

Despite some voluntary moves toward codetermination, most existing examples have been mandated by legislation, such as in West Germany. These moves have been dictated not only by the philosophy of cooperative leadership but also by opinion that labor has risks and stakes in the organization as well as shareholders. Because of a belief that the interests of blue- and white-collar workers are different, recent efforts have been made to assure that each group is represented.[55] Although there were some early examples of effective blockage of investment outflows, acquisitions, and plant closures, codetermination apparently has had little or no effect on either the types of decisions reached by firms or the speed with which those decisions have been reached. One of the reasons given for the little or no effect is that workers are so divided in terms of what they want that it is hard for their representatives to take strong stances on issues. Where layoffs have been necessary, foreign workers have been given less protection than citizens.[56] The move to codetermination seems unlikely to temper the ability of MNEs to optimize on a global basis.

In West Germany, for example, workers elect representatives to serve on the Works' Council of the firm.[57] This council makes decisions on social matters (such as the conduct of employees, hours of work, and safety) so that when disputes arise between the Works' Council and the Labor Director of the firm, they are settled by arbitration. In economic and financial matters the Works' Council is provided information and consulted in decisions, but the Council does not have the same strength because, although the shareholders and employees have an equal number of representatives, the chairman (elected by shareholders) has the tie-breaking vote.

The Works' Council and the unions have different responsibilities. For instance, collective bargaining takes place between employer associations and the unions and covers all workers within a West German state or part of that state. Since the companies in the employer associations vary in size and ability to cover different possible wage rates, the negotiated annual wage rates are minimums and can be negotiated upward at the company level. But the unions are barred by law from negotiating at the company or plant level; this is the task of the Works' Council.

Quality Circles

To improve worker productivity, companies worldwide have experimented with a variety of means to commit workers to suggest ways to improve output.

Codetermination efforts have been motivated partially by this objective, and suggestion boxes are probably the most visible symbol of the movement. Because of rapid productivity increases in Japan recently, attention naturally has focused on Japanese approaches to worker involvement. One such activity is the **quality circle**, which involves about 8 million Japanese workers. The system involves small groups of workers meeting regularly to spot and solve problems in their areas. It is a participatory effort designed to get people to say things among their peers that as individuals they would be reluctant to communicate to managers.

Team Efforts

In some countries, particularly Japan and its investments abroad, there has been an emphasis on work teams in order: (1) to foster a group cohesiveness and (2) to get workers involved in multiple rather than a limited number of tasks. In terms of group cohesiveness, it is not uncommon for a portion of the compensation to be based on the group output so that peer pressure is created to reduce absenteeism and to increase efforts. In terms of worker involvement in multiple tasks, workers may rotate jobs within the group to reduce boredom and to develop replacement skills when someone is not present. Practices whereby workers' groups control their own quality and repair their own equipment also have been included.[58]

INTERNATIONAL PRESSURES ON NATIONAL PRACTICES

The ILO monitors labor conditions worldwide.

In 1919 the International Labor Organization (ILO) was set up on the premise that the failure of any nation to adopt humane conditions of labor is an obstacle in the way of other nations that desire to improve conditions in their own countries. Through ILO activities and the general enhancement of communications globally, people increasingly are aware of differences in labor conditions among countries. Among the newsworthy reports have been legal proscriptions against collective bargaining in Malaysia and wages below minimum standards in Indonesia. The ILO also brought attention to the prevalence of child labor in LDCs, many of whom are under 10 years old and receive practically no compensation.[59] Once these conditions have been noted, there have been varying efforts to pressure for changes through economic and political sanctions from abroad.

The most noteworthy example of efforts to effect internal changes in labor conditions has involved pressures on MNEs operating in South Africa. Through church groups, resolutions have been presented to stockholders proposing that firms cease, cut back, or report more fully on their South African operations. Reverend Leon Sullivan of the United States has set forth a list of principles on nondiscrimination and improvement of conditions for oppressed groups in the South African operations of MNEs. Progress has been slower than critics want, leading to concern among MNEs that in the future they may be caught in the middle, between pro- and anti-apartheid pressures. As a result, there was a large exodus of foreign direct investors from South Africa in the mid-1980s.

Another area influencing the labor practices of MNEs has been codes of conduct on industrial relations issued by the Organization for Economic Cooperation and Development (OECD) and the ILO. The EC and the United Nations also have been discussing their own codes. Although the OECD and ILO codes are voluntary, they may signal some transnational regulations of future MNE activities. Trade unions have been anxious to get interpretations of the guidelines and make them legally enforceable. The present complaint mechanism is slow; but it can strengthen national governments as they pressure MNEs.[60]

MULTINATIONAL OWNERSHIP AND COLLECTIVE BARGAINING[61]

MNE Advantages

There is disagreement on home-country employment effects of foreign direct investment but labor pushes to save home-country jobs.

Job security. It is often argued that, when the number of jobs is not growing, workers are concerned about employment stability rather than other work conditions. If MNEs have exported jobs from industrialized countries, then it should follow that labor demands in those countries have been tempered in the process. As we showed in Chapter 11, it is difficult to conclude whether MNEs have increased or decreased home-country employment by making direct investments abroad.

The composition of work forces in industrialized countries has moved more toward white-collar than blue-collar jobs. Although some of this internal realignment in work force composition may be inevitable with or without MNE activities, the result is nevertheless a shrinking of traditional bargaining units.[62] The white-collar workers, even when organized by unions, may not be as adverse to management as blue-collar workers are, since they may look forward to moving into the management positions themselves. MNEs may rationalize international activities by setting up production facilities in countries with low wages and high unemployment while simultaneously concentrating such functions as accounting, R&D, and staff support in industrialized countries. To the extent that they do this, they are contributing to work force composition changes that weaken the size of production bargaining units in industrialized countries.

Labor may be at disadvantage in MNE negotiations because:

- Country bargaining unit is only a small part of MNE activities
- MNE may continue serving customers with foreign production or resources.

Product and resource flows. If, during a strike situation in one country, an MNE can divert output from facilities in other countries to the consumers in the country where the strike occurs, there is less client pressure on the MNE to reach an agreement. Furthermore, since the operations in a given country usually comprise a small percentage of the MNE's total worldwide sales, profits, and cash flows, a strike in that country may have minimal effects on the MNE's global performance. The MNE's geographic diversification therefore is argued to be to its advantage when bargaining with labor in a given country. Some analysts contend that an MNE simply may hold out longer and be less affected in a strike situation.

MNE limitations come from capacity, legal restrictions, shared ownership, integrated production, and differentiated products.

Several factors moderate the MNE's ability to continue supplying customers in the country under strike. The MNE may divert output to other markets only if it has excess capacity and only if there is a homogeneous product produced in more than one market. If these two conditions are present, the MNE would still confront the cost and trade barriers that led to the initial establishment of multiple production façilities. If the operation under strike is only partially owned by the MNE, partners or even minority shareholders may be less willing and able to sustain a lengthy work stoppage. If the idle facilities normally produce components needed for integrated production elsewhere, then a strike may have much more far-reaching effects. This latter point is particularly important as firms have sought to decrease production costs through instituting just-in-time inventory systems. During the 1988 U.K. strike at Ford, Belgian facilities were shut down almost immediately because the firm needed British components; this may have speeded Ford to agree to a settlement.[63] It may therefore seem that the advantages of international diversification upon the collective bargaining process are present, but in only limited circumstances.

MNE may threaten workers with moving production abroad.

Even domestic firms face threats of foreign competition.

Production switching. There are documented examples of threats by MNEs to move production units to other countries if labor conditions and demands in one country result in changes in the least-cost location of production. A good case occurred when the chief executive of Hyster told employees in Scotland that the company was prepared to move two production lines from the Netherlands to Scotland and expand its Scottish operations if workers decided within 48 hours to take a 14 percent pay cut. The following morning, workers received letters saying that the company might go somewhere else unless its offer were accepted.[64]

Production shifts may occur because of changes in the least-cost location whether an MNE is involved or not; this is particularly true as economies have become more open to imports. During a rubber strike, for example, Firestone advertised that U.S. worker demands would lead to more imports of foreign-made tires. So the threat of international switches in production location is not purely the result of increased MNE activities.

Although there are circumstances in which shifts would seem more plausible when MNEs are involved, MNEs may be less likely to cause shifts in production than when national competitors are involved in various countries. The MNE must weigh the cost-saving advantages of moving its production location against the losses in terms of shutting down existing facilities, creating bad will, and becoming vulnerable through decreased diversification. A national company, such as a Korean firm producing in Korea, may not worry nearly so much about what happens to a Canadian-owned plant in Canada when it exports to the Canadian market.

Labor claims it has disadvantages in dealing with MNEs because:

- Decision making is far away
- It is hard to get full data on MNEs' global operations.

Structural problems. Observers often contend that it is difficult for labor unions to deal with MNEs because of the complexities in the location of decision making and the difficulties involved in interpreting financial data. If the real decision makers are far removed from the bargaining location, such as home-country headquarters, it is often assumed that this will lead to arbitrarily stringent management decisions. Conceivably, the opposite might take place, particularly if the demands abroad seem low in comparison with those being made at home. In reality, industrial relations tend to be very much delegated to the local subsidiary levels.

The question of interpreting financial data of MNEs is complex because of disparities among managerial, tax, and public disclosure requirements in home and host countries. Labor has been particularly leery of the possibility of artificial transfer pricing to give the appearance that a given subsidiary is unable to meet labor demands. These concerns seem to place an overreliance on a company's ability to pay, rather than the seemingly more important going wage rates in the industry and geographic area. Although MNEs may have more complex data, at least some set of financial statements must satisfy local authorities. This set should be no more difficult to interpret than that involving a purely local firm. In terms of transfer pricing, it is very doubtful that MNEs set artificial levels to aid in collective bargaining situations. To understate profits in one place would imply overstating elsewhere, which would negate the advantage, unless changes are made to reflect different contract periods. Tax authorities would not likely approve sudden price changes before contract negotiation. Furthermore, any artificial prices also would have to consider income taxes, tariffs, and opinions of minority shareholders.

Labor Responses and Initiatives

Labor might strengthen its position vis-à-vis MNEs through cross-national cooperation.

Information Sharing. The most common form of cooperation among unions in different countries is through an exchange of information. This helps them refute company claims as well as cite precedents from other countries when bargaining issues seem transferable. The exchange of information is carried out by international confederations of unions representing different types of workers and ideologies, by trade secretariats composed of unions in a single industry or in a complex of related industries, and by company councils that include representatives from an MNE's plants around the world.[65]

Assistance to foreign bargaining units. Labor groups in one country may support their counterparts in other countries in a number of ways. These include refusing to work overtime when that output would supply the market normally served by striking workers' production, sending financial aid to workers in other countries, and presenting demands to management through other countries. Although there are examples involving these types of assistance, for now they must be classified as potential rather than actual initiatives. There are more examples of refusals to cooperate in these matters than of successful collaboration.

Simultaneous actions. There have been a few examples of simultaneous negotiations and strikes.[66] Among the more notable have been meetings among the unions that negotiate with GE worldwide, a common strategy for unions from nine countries that represent St. Gobain, and simultaneous work stoppages in England and Italy against Dunlop-Pirelli. The concept of multinational collective bargaining seems less appealing to labor leaders now than it did in the 1970s. This is due to the relatively few successes and the national differences in terms of union structures and demands.[67] Furthermore, there has undoubtedly been a growing nationalism of workers as their fear of foreign competition has grown.

National approaches. Although there are numerous examples of cooperation among unions of different countries, their combat against MNEs has been primarily on a national basis. There is little enthusiasm on the part of workers in one country to incur costs in order to support workers in another country since they tend to view each other as competitors. Even between the United States and Canada, where there has long been a common union membership, there has been a move among Canadian workers to form unions independent of those in the United States. One Canadian organizer summed up much of the attitude by saying, "An American union is not going to fight to protect Canadian jobs at the expense of American jobs." The logic was that international unions will adopt policies favoring the bulk of their membership, which is bound to be American in any joint Canadian–U.S. relationship.[68]

Through national legislation, workers have managed in places to acquire representation on boards of directors, to regulate the entry of foreign workers, to limit imports, and to limit foreign investment outflows. Therefore it is probable that most regulations will be at the national rather than the international level.

SUMMARY

- Among the factors that differentiate between the tasks of international and purely domestic managers are that the internationals must know how to adapt home-country practices to foreign locales and usually must deal with high-level governmental officials.

- The top-level managers of foreign subsidiaries normally perform much broader duties than domestic managers with similar cost or profit responsibilities. They must cope with communications problems between the corporate headquarters and the subsidiaries, usually with less staff assistance.
- Reasons given for preferring local to expatriate managers are that: The locals understand regional operating conditions; demonstrate the opportunities for local citizens and the local interests of the operations; avoid the red tape of cross-national transfers; are usually cheaper; and may focus more on long-term operations and goals.
- Firms transfer people abroad in order to infuse home country business practices and technical competence to control foreign operations and to develop managers.
- When firms transfer personnel abroad, they should consider how well the people will be accepted, how to treat them when the foreign assignment is over, and how well they will adapt.
- When transferred abroad, an employee's compensation usually is changed because of differences in cost of living, job status, and hardship.
- Firms frequently acquire personnel abroad by buying existing companies. They also may go into business with local firms, which take on the major staffing responsibilities.
- Two of the major international training functions are: (1) to build a global awareness among managers in general and (2) to equip managers to handle the specific situations entailed in an expatriate assignment.
- When setting up a new operation in a foreign country, firms may use existing facilities as guides for determining labor needs. They should adjust, however, to compensate for different labor skills, costs, and availabilities.
- For some areas of the world a substantial portion of the labor supply is imported, which creates special stability, supervision, and training problems for the companies employing them.
- Owing to the enormous variance in fringe benefits, direct compensation figures do not accurately reflect the amount a company must pay for a given job. In addition, job security benefits (no layoffs, severance pay, etc.) add substantially to compensation costs.
- Although per-worker comparisons are useful indicators of cost differences, what is relevant for international competitiveness is the output associated with total costs. The costs may shift in time, thus changing relative international competitive positions.
- The sociopolitical environment will determine to a great extent the type of relationships between labor and management and affect the number, representation, and organization of unions among countries.

- Codetermination and quality circles are two types of labor participation in the management of firms. The purpose is usually intended to bring about a cooperative rather than an adversarial environment.
- In recent years there have been efforts to get firms to follow internationally accepted labor practices regardless of where they are operating or whether or not the practices are contrary to the norms and laws of the countries in which they are operating.
- MNEs are often blamed for weakening the position of labor in the collective bargaining process because of MNEs': (1) international diversification, (2) threats to export jobs, and (3) complex structures and reporting mechanisms.
- Cooperation between labor groups in different countries is small but has on occasion been used to combat multinational firms. Strategies include information exchanges, simultaneous negotiations or strikes, and refusals to work overtime if the intent is to compensate for a striking firm in another country.

CASE: THE OFFICE SYSTEMS COMPANY

In 1988, the Office Systems Company (OSC) had to replace its manager in San Salvador, El Salvador, because the then-managing director (a U.S. national) announced suddenly that he would leave within one month to start his own real estate business in South Florida. OSC manufactured a wide variety of small office equipment (such as copying machines, recording machines, mail scales, paper shredders) in eight different countries that was distributed and sold worldwide.

OSC had no manufacturing facilities in El Salvador (see Figure 21.1) but had been selling and servicing there since the early 1980s. OSC had first tried selling in El Salvador through independent importers but quickly became convinced that it needed to have its own staff there to make sufficient sales. Despite political turmoil, which had bordered on being a full-scale civil war over the last few years, OSC's operation in El Salvador (with about 100 employees) had enjoyed good and improving sales and profitability.

OSC was in the process of constructing a factory in El Salvador that should begin operations in early 1989. This factory would produce components for use in products to be assembled in the United States and employ approximately 150 people. El Salvador offered an abundant supply of cheap labor. Furthermore, by exporting the components, OSC expected to be able to ward off any import restrictions on the finished goods it sold within El Salvador. The construction of this plant was being supervised by a U.S.

Figure 21.1

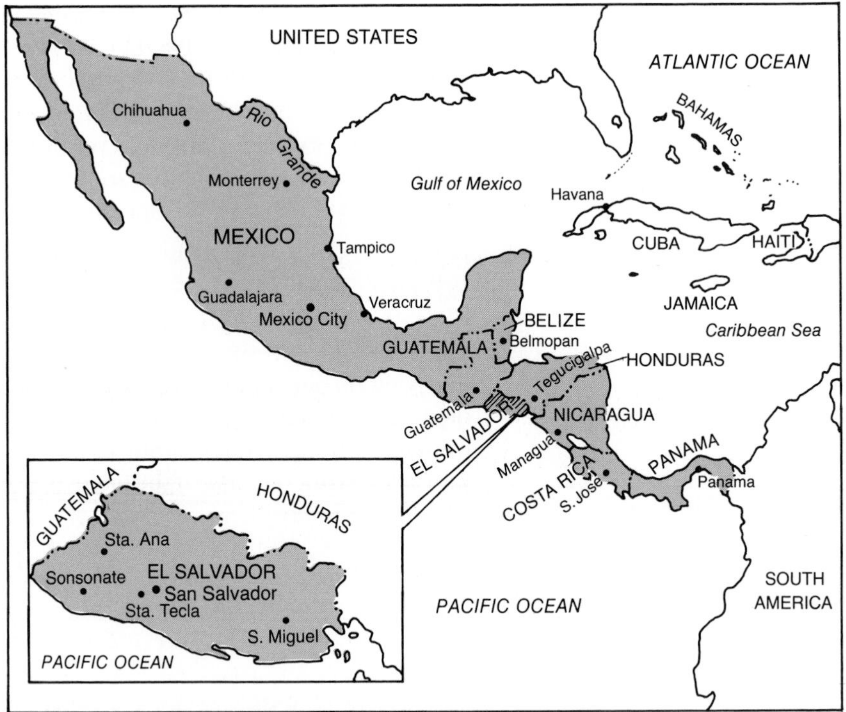

technical team; and a U.S. expatriate would be assigned to direct the production. This expatriate director would report directly to the United States on all production and quality control matters but would report to the managing director in El Salvador for all other matters, such as accounting, finance, and labor relations. There would be no marketing since all sales were captive ones, to the parent.

The option of filling the managing director position with someone from outside the firm was alien to OSC's policy. Otherwise, the options were fairly open. OSC used a combination of home country, host country, and third-country nationals in top positions in foreign countries. It was not uncommon for managers to rotate between foreign and U.S. domestic locations. In fact, it was increasingly evident that international experience was an important factor in deciding who would be appointed to top corporate positions. The sales and service facility in El Salvador reported through a Latin American regional office located in Coral Gables, Florida. A committee at the regional office quickly narrowed its choice to the following five candidates.

Tom Zimmerman. Zimmerman had joined the firm thirty years before and was well versed in all the technical and sales aspects required in the job. He had never worked abroad for OSC but had been on a sales team that visited South Africa a few years earlier. He was considered competent in the management of the duties he had performed during the years and would retire in about four and a half years. Neither he nor his wife spoke Spanish; their children were grown and living with their own children in the United States. Zimmerman was currently in charge of an operation about the size that the one in El Salvador would be after the factory begins operating. However, that operation was being merged with another, so his present office would become redundant.

Brett Harrison. At age forty, Harrison had spent fifteen years with OSC. He was considered highly competent and capable of moving into upper-level management within the next few years. He had never been based abroad but had worked for the last three years in the Latin American regional office, and he frequently travelled to Latin America. Both he and his wife spoke Spanish adequately. Their two children, ages fourteen and fifteen, were just beginning to study Spanish. His wife was a professional as well, holding a responsible marketing position with a pharmaceutical company.

Carolyn Moyer. Moyer had joined OSC after getting her MBA from a prestigious university twelve years earlier. At age 37 she had already moved between staff and line positions of growing responsibility. For two years she was second-in-command of a product group about the size of the expanded one in El Salvador. Her performance in that post was considered excellent. Currently she worked as a member of a planning staff team. When she joined OSC, she had indicated her eventual interest in international responsibilities because of her undergraduate major in international affairs. She had expressed a recent interest in international duties because of a belief that it would help her advancement. She spoke Spanish well and was not married.

Francisco Cabrera. Cabrera was currently one of the assistant managing directors in the larger Mexican operation, which produced and sold for the Mexican market. He was a Mexican citizen who had worked for OSC in Mexico for all his twelve years with the company. He held an MBA from a Mexican university and was considered to be one of the likely candidates to head the Mexican operation when the present managing director retired in seven years. He was 35, married with four children (ages two to seven). He spoke English adequately; his wife did not work outside the home and spoke no English.

Juan Moreno. At 27 he was assistant to the present managing director in El Salvador, a position he had assumed when he joined OSC after completing his undergraduate studies in the United States four years before and returned to his native country. He was considered competent, especially in employee relations, but lacking in experience. He had been quite successful in increasing OSC's sales, an advantage being that he was well connected with the local families who could afford to buy new office equipment for their businesses. He was not married.

QUESTIONS

1. Who should the committee choose for the assignment and why?
2. What problems might each individual encounter in the position?
3. How might OSC go about minimizing the problems that the chosen person would have in managing the El Salvador operations?

NOTES

1. The data for the case were taken from Edwin McDowell, "Making It in America: The Foreign-Born Executive," *New York Times,* June 1, 1980, Section 3, p. 1+; Don Whitehead, *The Dow Story* (New York: McGraw-Hill, 1968); *Annual Reports* of Dow Chemical Corporation for various years; Urban C. Lehner, "Pitfalls of Partnership," *Wall Street Journal,* January 5, 1983, p. 44; "Dow's Shifts in R&D Presage Overseas Work," *Chemical Week,* Vol. 128, No. 13, April 1, 1981, p. 17; "Lundeen Urges More Aid for Universities," *Chemical Marketing Reporter,* Vol. 224, No. 19, November 7, 1983, p. 3+; John Bussey, "Dow Chemical's Popoff Named President," *Wall Street Journal,* May 15, 1987, p. 49.

2. Michael G. Duerr and James Greene, The *Problems Facing International Management, Managing International Business,* No. 1 (New York: National Industrial Conference Board, 1969), pp. 1, 25.

3. Daniel Ondrack, "International Transfers of Managers in North American and European MNEs," *Journal of International Business Studies,* Vol. 16, No. 3, Fall 1985, pp. 1–19.

4. Bob Masterson and Bob Murphy, "Internal Cross-Cultural Management," *Training and Development Journal,* Vol. 40, No. 4, April 1986, pp. 56–60.

5. Peter Lorange, "Human Resource Management in Multinational Cooperative Ventures," *Human Resource Management,* Vol. 25, No. 1, Spring 1985, pp. 133–148.

6. Jean Ross-Skinner, "English Spoken Here," *Dun's Review,* March 1977, pp. 56–57; Urban C. Lehner, "When in Japan, Do as the Japanese Do, by Speaking English," *Wall Street Journal,* December 8, 1980, p. 1.

7. Dafna N. Izraeli, Moshe Banai, and Yoram Zeira, "Women Executives in MNC Subsidiaries," *California Management Review,* Vol. 23, No. 1, Fall 1980, pp. 53–63; Robert Shuter, "Assignment America: Foreign Managers Beware," *International Management,* Vol. 40, No. 9, pp. 93–96; Yves Doz and C. K. Prahalad, "Controlled Variety: A Challenge for Human Resource Management in the MNC," *Human Resource Management,* Vol. 25, No. 1, Spring 1986, pp. 55–71.

8. Yoram Zeira and Ehud Harari, "Structural Sources of Personnel Problems in Multinational Corporations: Third-Country Nationals," *Omega,* Vol. 5, No. 2, 1977, 167–168.

9. Anders Edström and Jay R. Galbraith, "Alternative Policies for International Transfers of Managers," *Management International Review,* No. 2, 1977, pp. 13–14; Asya Pazy and Yoram Zeira, "Training Parent-Country Professionals in Host-Country Organizations," *Academy of Management Review,* Vol. 8, No. 2, 1983, pp. 262–272.

10. Anders Edström and Jay R. Galbraith, "Transfer of Managers as a Coordination and Control Strategy in Multinational Organizations," *Administrative Science Quarterly,* June 1977, pp. 248–261; A. B. Sim, "Decentralized Management of Subsidiaries and Their Performance," *Management International Review,* No. 2, 1977, p. 48.

11. Alfred Jaeger, "Organization Development and National Culture: Where's the Fit?" *Academy of Management Review,* Vol. 11, No. 1, 1986, pp. 178–190.

12. Anders Edström and Peter Lorange, "Matching Strategy and Human Resources in Multinational Companies," *Journal of International Business Studies,* Fall 1984, pp. 125–137.

13. Edwin L. Miller, "The Selection Decision for an International Assignment: A Study of the Decision Maker's Behavior," *Journal of International Business Studies,* Fall 1972, p. 62.

14. Duerr and Greene, *The Problems Facing International Management,* p. 18; see also Richard D. Hays, "Behavioral Determinants of Success-Failure among U.S. Expatriate Managers," *Journal of International Business Studies,* Spring 1971, pp. 40–46.

15. Philip R. Harris and Robert L. Moran, *Managing Cultural Differences* (Houston: Gulf Publishing Company, 1979), p. 164 citing studies by the Center for Research and Education.

16. Richard J. Fleming, "Cultural Determinants for Selecting American Businessmen for Overseas Assignments," in *International Management in the Seventies: A Decisive Decade,* Richard J. Fleming, ed. (Norfolk, Va.: Old Dominion University, 1973), pp. 33–38.

17. Izraeli et al., *loc. cit.*

18. Mariann Jelinek and Nancy J. Adler, "Women: World Class Managers for Global Competition," *Academy of Management Executive,* Vol. II, No. 1, February 1988, pp. 11–19.

19. Izraeli, et. al., *loc. cit.* For some suggestions on how women may make themselves more acceptable, see Gladys L. Symons, "Coping with the Corporate Tribe: How Women in Different Cultures Experience the Managerial Role," *Journal of Management,* Vol. 12, No. 3, 1986, pp. 379–389; and Marlene L. Rossman, *The International Businesswoman* (New York: Praeger, 1986).

20. David M. Noer, "Integrating Foreign Service Employees to Home Organization: The Godfather Approach," *Personnel Journal,* January 1974, pp. 45–50; William F. Cagney, "Executive Reentry: The Problems of Repatriation," *Personnel Journal,* September 1975, pp. 487–488; J. Alex Murray, "Repatriated Executives: Culture Shock in Reverse," *Management Review,* November 1973, pp. 43–45; Philip R. Harris, "Employees Abroad: Maintain the Corporate Connection," *Personnel Journal,* Vol. 65, No. 8, August 1986, pp. 107–110.

21. Sam Passow, "Manager's Journal," *Wall Street Journal,* June 18, 1984, p. 18; Rod Willis, "Corporations Vs. Terrorists," *Management Review,* Vol. 75, No. 11, November 1986, pp. 16–27.

22. Joann S. Lublin, "More Spouses Receive Help in Job Searches When Executives Take Positions Overseas," *Wall Street Journal,* January 26, 1984, p. 35.

23. "Global Report," *Wall Street Journal,* July 11, 1977, p. 6; Barry Newman, "Mine over Matter," *Wall Street Journal,* August 25, 1977, p. 1.

24. Arnold Kransdorf, "The Hidden Benefits of 'Management Transfer,' " *International Management,* Vol. 41, No. 5, May 1986, p. 24 quoting Boyd Donawa, managing director of M&D Marketing Services in Milan.

25. A case of reduction of home office influence in subsidiary personnel staffing once the ownership became shared is described in Samir M. Youssaf, "The Integration of Local Nationals into the Managerial Hierarchy of American Overseas Subsidiaries: An Exploratory Study," *Academy of Management Journal,* March 1973, p. 29.

26. E. J. Karras, Roy F. McMillan, Jr., and Thomas R. Williamson, "Interviewing for Cultural Match," *Personnel Journal,* April 1971, pp. 276–279; Rosalie L. Tung, "Selection and Training of Personnel for Overseas Assignments," *Columbia Journal of World Business,* Vol. 16, No. 1, Spring 1981, p. 72; Canadian International Development Agency (CIDA), "Going Abroad with CIDA;" Bureau of Naval Personnel, *Overseas Diplomacy: Guidelines for United States Navy: Trainer* (Washington, D.C.: U.S. Government Printing Office, 1973); M. H. Tucker, D. Raik Rossiter, and M. Uhes, *Improving the Evaluation of Peace Corps Training Activities,* Vol. 3 (Denver: Center for Research and Education, June 4, 1973).

27. Michael G. Harvey, "The Executive Family: An Overlooked Variable in International Assignments," *Columbia Journal of World Business,* Spring 1985, pp. 84–92.

28. Tung, *ibid.,* pp. 75–77, showed a correlation of .63 between the rigor of the selection-training process and success in foreign assignments. Only about 5 percent of firms administer tests.

29. Erik Larson, "Saudi Rigors Toughen Task of Recruiters," *Wall Street Journal,* October 15, 1980, p. 31.

30. Tung, *op. cit.,* p. 71.

31. P. Christopher Early, "Intercultural Training for Managers: A Comparison of Documentary and Interpersonal Methods," *Academy of Management Journal,* Vol. 30, No. 4, December 1987, pp. 685–698.

32. Jeffrey L. Blue and Ulrich Haynes, Jr., "Preparation for the Overseas Assignment," *Business Horizons,* June 1977, pp. 61–67.

33. Philip R. Harris and Dorothy L. Harris, "Preventing Cross-Cultural Shock," *Management and Training,* May 1976, pp. 37–41.

34. R. Lynn Barnes, "Across Cultures: The Peace Corps Training Model," *Training and Development Journal,* Vol. 39, No. 10, October 1985, pp. 46–49.

35. Yoram Zeira and Asya Pazy, "Crossing National Borders to Get Trained," *Training and Development Journal,* Vol. 39, No. 10, October 1985, pp. 53–57.

36. Frank L. Acuff, "Awareness Levels of Employees Considering Overseas Relocation," *Personnel Journal,* November 1974, pp. 809–812; Kenneth Darrow and Bradley Palmquist, eds., *Trans-Cultural Study Guide* (N.P.: Volunteers in Asia, 1975, 2nd ed.) lists pertinent questions.

37. F. T. Murray and Alice Haller Murray, "SMR Forum: Global Managers for Global Businesses," *Sloan Management Review,* Vol. 27, No. 2, Winter 1986, pp. 75–80.

38. For a good survey of the various studies, see Peter Enderwick, *Multinational Business & Labor* (New York: St. Martin's Press, 1985), pp. 55–58.

39. R. Aggarwal and I. Khera, "Exporting Labor: The Impact of Expatriate Workers on the Home Country," *International Migration,* Vol. 25, No. 4, 1987, pp. 415–424.

40. R. J. Campbell and J. de Bres, "Temporary Labor Migration between Tonga and New Zealand," *International Labour Review,* December 1975, p. 445.

41. For a more complete discussion of business adjustments, see John D. Daniels, "International Mobility of People," *Essays in International Business,* No. 1, March 1980, pp. 3–7.

42. "Global Report," *Wall Street Journal,* August 29, 1977, p. 6.

43. Felice Morgenstern, "The Civil Liability of Workers for Injury or Damage Caused in Their Employment," *International Labour Review,* May-June 1976, pp. 317–328.

44. The cited example happened in 1981. For a good discussion on the calculation of the cost dynamics see Edwin Dean, Harry Boissevain, and James Thomas, "Productivity and Labor Costs Trends in Manufacturing, 12 Countries," *Monthly Labor Review,* Vol. 109, No. 3, March 1986, pp. 3–10.

45. Efrin Cordova, "A Comparative View of Collective Bargaining in Industrialised Countries," *International Labour Review,* July–August 1978, p. 423; and Eduardo B. Gentil, "Brazil's Labor Movement," *Wall Street Journal,* November 11, 1980, p. 34.

46. "The Europarking Lot," *Wall Street Journal,* February 24, 1984, p. 32.

47. Joseph Krislov, "Supplying Mediation Services in Five Countries: Some Current Problems," *Columbia Journal of World Business,* Vol. 18, No. 2, Summer 1983, pp. 55–63.

48. Frances Bairstow, "The Trend toward Centralized Bargaining—A Patchwork Quilt of International Diversity," *Columbia Journal of World Business,* Spring 1985, pp. 75–83.

49. Masayoshi Kanayabayasi, "Japan's Unions, Anxious to Avoid Fight, Again Likely to Accept a Modest Pay Raise," *Wall Street Journal,* February 9, 1984, p. 31.

50. Bairstow, *loc. cit.*

51. Donna Bridgeman, "Worker Take-Overs," ICCH Case 9-475-093, Harvard Business School, 1975; "Bulova Watch Plant Is Occupied to Protest Closing," *Wall Street Journal,* January 19, 1976; "ICL Workers Say They Took Over Plant to Prevent Closing," *Wall Street Journal,* November 11, 1980, p. 34; Barbara Ehrenreich and Annette Fuentes, "Life on the Global Assembly Line," *Ms.,* January 1981, pp. 53–71.

52. Bennett Harrison, "The International Movement for Prenotification of Plant Closures," *Industrial Relations,* Fall 1984, pp. 387–409; Walter S. Mossberg, "Plant-Closings Quarrel Distorts a Modest Idea," *Wall Street Journal,* April 25, 1988, p. 1.

53. P. Mourdoukoutas and S. N. Sohng, "The Japanese Industrial System: A Study in Adjustment to Automation," *Management International Review,* Vol. 27, No. 4, 1987, pp. 46–55.

54. Benjamin Prasad, "The Growth of Co-Determination," *Business Horizons,* April 1977, p. 27.

55. Peter F. Drucker, "The Battle Over Co-Determination," *Wall Street Journal,* August 10, 1977, p. 14; "Co-Determination Passes," *Business Europe,* March 26, 1976, pp. 99–100.

56. For early operational problems, see "Sweden: Worker Participation Becomes the Law," *Business Week,* June 21, 1976, pp. 42–46; G. McIsaac and H. Henzler, "Co-

Determination: A Hidden Noose for MNCs," *Columbia Journal of World Business,* Winter 1974, pp. 67–74; M. Warner and R. Peccei, "Worker Participation and Multinationals," *Management International Review,* No. 3 1977, pp. 93–98. For recent evidence on overall effects, see Wolfgang Scholl, Codetermination and the Ability of Firms to Act in the Federal Republic of Germany," *International Studies of Management & Organization,* Vol. XVII, No. 2, Summer 1987, pp. 27–37; and Giuseppe Benelli, Claudio Loderer, and Thomas Lys, "Labor Participation in Corporate Policy-making Decisions: West Germany's Experience with Codetermination," *Journal of Business,* Vol. 60, No. 4, October 1987, pp. 553–575.

57. Much of the information on codetermination in Germany is taken from Trevor Bain, "German Codetermination and Employment Adjustments in the Steel and Auto Industries," *Columbia Journal of World Business,* Vol. 18, No. 2, Summer 1983, pp. 40–47.

58. For two discussions of these efforts, see Duane Kujawa, "Technology Strategy and Industrial Relations: Case Studies of Japanese Multinationals in the United States," *Journal of International Business Studies,* Vol. 14, No. 3, Winter 1983, pp. 9–22; Wolf Reitsperger, "British Employees: Responding to Japanese Management Philosophies," *Journal of Management Studies,* Vol. 23, No. 5, September 1986, pp. 563–586.

59. "Child-Worker Abuses in Third World Draw Fire of Labor Group," *Wall Street Journal,* June 8, 1988, p. 26.

60. Richard L. Rowan and Duncan C. Campbell, "The Attempt to Regulate Industrial Relations through International Codes of Conduct," *Columbia Journal of World Business,* Vol. 18, No. 2, Summer 1983, pp. 64–72.

61. Unless otherwise noted, information in this section is taken largely from the following treatises: Gerald B. J. Bomers and Richard B. Peterson, "Multinational Corporations and the Industrial Relations: The Case of West Germany and the Netherlands," *British Journal of Industrial Relations,* March 1977, pp. 45–62; Duane A. Kujawa, "Collective Bargaining and Labor Relations in Multinational Enterprise: A U.S. Policy Perspective," paper presented at New York University Conference on Economic Issues of Multinational Firms, November 1976; Duane Kujawa, "U.S. Manufacturing Investment in the Developing Countries: American Labour's Concerns and the Enterprise Environment in the Decade Ahead," *British Journal of Industrial Relations,* Vol. 19, No. 1, March 1981, pp. 38–48; Roy B. Helfgott, "American Unions and Multinational Enterprises: A Case of Misplaced Emphasis," *Columbia Journal of World Business,* Vol. 18, No. 2, Summer 1983, pp. 81–86.

62. For some figures on the decreased unionized share of work forces, see Rick Melcher, John Templeman, John Rossant, Steve Dryden, and Bob Arnold, "Europe's Unions Are Losing Their Grip," *Business Week,* November 26, 1984, pp. 80–88.

63. Richard L. Hudson, "Strike at Ford Shows Problems of New Methods," *Wall Street Journal,* February 10, 1988, p. 14; Barbara Toman, "Ford, Unions Agree on Contract Offer in Breakthrough in 9-Day U.K. Strike," *Wall Street Journal,* February 17, 1988, p. 2.

64. Barry Newman, "Border Dispute," *Wall Street Journal,* November 30, 1983, pp. 1 +; see also "Ford Threatens to Move More Production Abroad," *Wall Street Journal,* April 22, 1981, p. 3.

65. Martin C. Seham, "Transnational Labor Relations: The First Steps Are Being Taken," *Law and Policy in International Business,* Vol. 6, 1974, pp. 347–354.

66. For a fairly comprehensive list for the 1965–1971 period, see I. A. Litvak and C. J. Maule, "The Union Response to International Corporations," *Industrial Relations,* February 1972, pp. 66–67.

67. Duane A. Kujawa, "International Labor Relations: Trade Union Initiatives and Management Responses," *Personnel Administrator,* February 1977, p. 50.

68. Douglas Martin, "A Canadian Split on Unions," *New York Times,* March 12, 1984, p. D12.

GLOSSARY

Absolute advantage: A theory first presented by Adam Smith, which holds that because different countries can produce different goods more efficiently than others, they should specialize and export those things which they can produce more efficiently in exchange for those things which they cannot.

Academic infrastructure: The term refers to the quality of accounting education offered as well as to the accessibility of this education.

Acquired advantage: Commonly referred to as technology.

Acquired group membership: Refers to affiliations not determined by birth, such as religion, political affiliation, and associations.

Active income: Income derived from the active conduct of trade or business.

Ad valorem duty: A duty (tariff) is assessed as a percentage of the value of the item.

Advance import deposits: A type of foreign exchange control in which importers must deposit some percentage of the value of a product with authorities for a specified period of time.

Anthropology: The study of human beings in relation to physical characteristics, environmental and social relations, and culture.

Appropriate technology: The term used to describe technology that best fits the factor endowment; often used to mean a more labor-intensive technology than that which would be cost efficient in an industrial country.

Arbitrage: To exchange foreign currency in more than one market and end up with more money at the end of the exchange than was had at the start of the exchange.

Arrangement Regarding International Trade in Textiles: Also known as the Multifibre Arrangement (MFA), this agreement among governments establishes rules on textile trade.

Ascribed group memberships: Refer to the affiliations determined by birth. These include differentiations based on sex, family, age, caste, and ethnic, racial, or national origin.

Association of South East Asian Nations (ASEAN): An economic integration agreement among a group of Asian countries.

Balance of payments: Statement which summarizes all economic transactions between a country and the rest of the world during a given period of time.

Balance of payments deficit: An imbalance for some

specific component within the balance of payments, such as on merchandise trade or the current account.

Balance of payments surplus: (See balance of payments deficit.)

Balance of trade deficit: The value of a country's imports is less than that of its exports.

Balance on goods and services: An exchange where a buyer in one country and a seller in another country exchange something of equal value.

Bank of International Settlements: A bank in Switzerland which facilitates transactions among central banks.

Barter: The exchange of goods for goods instead of for money.

Base currency: The currency whose value is one whenever a quote is made between two currencies. For example, if the cruzeiro was trading at 2962.5 cruzeiros per dollar, the dollar would be the base currency, and the cruzeiro would be the quoted currency.

Basic balance: The net current account plus long term capital within a country's balance of payments.

Bid: The amount a trader is willing to pay for foreign exchange.

Black market: The market for foreign exchange which lies outside of the official market.

Branch (foreign): A branch is a foreign operation which is not a separate entity from the parent.

Bretton Woods: An agreement among countries to promote exchange rate stability and facilitate the international flow of currencies.

Brokers: Specialists who facilitate transactions in the interbank market.

Buffer stock system: A commodity system that utilizes stocks of commodities to regulate prices.

Caribbean Community and Common Market (CARICOM): A customs union in Latin America.

Central American Common Market (CACM): A customs union in Central America.

Centralization: This implies a higher level of decision making, especially above the country level.

Centrally Planned Economy (CPE): (See Command Economy.)

Clearing House Interbank Payment System (CHIPS): An international electronic check transfer system that moves money between major U.S. banks, branches of foreign banks, and other institutions.

Command economy: An economy where resources are allocated and controlled by government decision.

Commercial Bill of Exchange: An instrument of payment in international business which instructs the importer to forward payment to the exporter.

Commercial paper: A form of IOU backed up by standby letters of credit.

Commission agent: A type of middleman who sells for commission without taking title on the goods.

Commodity agreements: Agreements among countries to influence prices of commodities by such means as restricting sales.

Common Agricultural Policy (CAP): An EC policy aimed at free trade, price supports, and modernization programs in agriculture.

Common market: A form of regional economic integration where countries abolish internal tariffs, use a common external tariff, and abolish restrictions on factor mobility. The term "Common Market" is also used to represent the European Community.

Communism: A form of totalitarianism initially theorized by Karl Marx.

Comparative advantage: The theory holds that there may still be gains from trade if a country specializes in those products that it can produce more efficiently than other products, whether or not the country has an absolute advantage or disadvantage vis-à-vis other countries.

Compensatory trade: Any one of several different arrangements in which goods and services are bartered.

Complete economic integration: A theoretical form of regional integration which presupposes the unification of monetary, fiscal, social, and counter-cyclical policies and requires the setting up of a supranational authority whose decisions are binding for the member states.

Compound duty: A tax placed on goods sent internationally, based on value plus units.

Concentration strategy: Going to one or a few countries and quickly building up operations before moving on to another.

Confirmed letter of credit: A letter of credit [see definition below] in which a bank in the exporter's country adds its guarantee of payment.

Consolidation: An accounting process whereby the financial statements of related entities (such as a parent and its subsidiaries) are added together to yield a unified set of financial statements. In the process, transactions among the related enterprises are eliminated so that the statements reflect transactions with outside parties.

Consortium: The joining together of several entities, such as firms or governments, in order to strengthen the possibility of achieving some objective.

Consortium bank: Several banks may pool resources to form another bank [the consortium bank] that engages in international transactions. The parent banks retain their separate operating identities, and the consortium bank becomes a new entity controlled by the parent banks.

Consumer sovereignty: The freedom of consumers to influence production through choice.

Controlled foreign corporation: A foreign corporation in which more than 50 percent of the voting stock is owned by "U.S. Shareholders" [taxable entities that own at least 10 percent of the voting stock of the foreign corporation].

Convertibility: When a currency can be exchanged into another currency without restrictions.

Coordinating Committee on Multilateral Export (Cocom): An agreement among Western industrial nations to limit militarily useful exports to Communist countries.

Corporate culture: The common values for employees in a corporation which form a control mechanism that is implicit and which help enforce other explicit control mechanisms.

Council for Mutual Economic Assistance (COMECON): A regional form of economic integration that is an association of communist countries. The members are essentially those considered to be within the Soviet bloc of influence.

Countertrade: A sale that involves obligations by the seller to generate foreign exchange for the buying country.

Country similarity theory: This holds that having developed a new product in response to observed market conditions in the home market, a producer will then turn to markets that are perceived to be the most similar to those at home.

Cross licensing: The exchange of technology by different firms.

Cross rate: An exchange rate between two currencies that is computed from the exchange rate of each of those two currencies in relation to the U.S. dollar.

Culture: The specific learned norms of a society, based on attitudes, values, and beliefs.

Culture shock: A generalized trauma one experiences in a new and different culture because of having to learn new cues when one's old ones will not work.

Current rate method: Translating foreign currency financial statements into the reporting currency. All assets and liabilities are translated by using the current exchange rate, also known as the exchange rate in effect on the balance sheet date. Income statement accounts are translated by the average exchange rate for the period.

Customs union: A form of regional economic integration which eliminates tariffs among member nations and establishes common external tariffs.

Debt service ratio: The ratio of interest payments plus principal amortization to exports.

Decentralized: This implies lower-level decision making in the organization; in international operations, decisions at the country-operating level rather than at headquarters.

Democracy: A political system which involves wide participation of citizens in the decision-making process.

Demography: The statistical study of populations and their subgroups.

Dependency: When one country is too dependent on the sale of one primary commodity and/or too dependent on one country as a customer and supplier.

Devaluation: The value of a currency is formally reduced in relation to another currency. The foreign currency equivalent of the devalued currency falls.

Direct foreign investment: An operation controlled by entities in a foreign country.

Direct investment: (See direct foreign investment.)

Direct quote: The number of units of the domestic currency given for one unit of the foreign currency.

Discount: A foreign currency sells at a discount in the forward market when the forward rate is less than the spot rate, assuming that the domestic currency is quoted on a direct basis.

Distribution: The course—physical path or legal title—that goods take between production and consumption.

Diversification strategy: Going to many countries quickly and then building up slowly in each.

Divestment: Reduction in the amount of investment.

Dualism: Progress that is confined to certain sectors of an economy while the rest of the sectors are left virtually untouched.

Dumping: The underpricing of exports (usually below cost or below the home country price).

Duty: A governmental tax (tariff) levied on goods shipped internationally.

Economic integration: The abolishment of economic discrimination between national economies.

Economic system: The system concerned with the allocation of scarce resources.

Economic union: A form of regional economic integration which combines the characteristics of a common market [see definition above] with some degree of harmonization of national economic policies.

Economies of scale: The lowering of costs with added output because of allocation of fixed costs over more units.

Edge Act Corporation: A banking corporation that allows banks to set up offices in money centers in the U.S. other than those where the bank is legally allowed to operate with the purpose of performing international banking activities.

Effective tariff: An argument used by developing countries which says that the real (effective) tariff on the manufactured portion of their exports is higher than indicated by the published rates because the ad valorem tariff is based on the total value of the product which includes raw materials which would have had duty-free entry.

Embargo: This is a specific type of quota that prohibits all trade.

Environmental climate: (See Investment Climate.)

Essential industry argument: A protectionist argument that a particular industry is needed for security purposes.

Ethnocentrism: The belief that one's own group is superior. Also used to describe the firm imbued with the belief that what worked at home should work abroad.

Eurobond: A bond that is sold in a currency other than that of the country of issue.

Eurocredit: A Eurodollar loan that has a medium term maturity of 3–5 years.

Eurocurrency: A currency that is banked outside of its country of origin.

Euroequity market: The market for shares sold outside of national boundaries of the issuing company.

European Community (EC): A form of regional economic integration in Europe. It most closely resembles the economic union form of regional integration. The EC is also known as the European Economic Community (EEC).

European Currency Unit: A basket of currencies comprised of the currencies of most of the members of the EC.

European Economic Community (EEC): (See definition of European Community.)

European Free Trade Association (EFTA): A form of regional economic integration involving a group of European countries that are not members of the EC. These countries have established a free trade area [see definition below].

European Monetary System (EMS): A cooperative foreign exchange arrangement involving most of the members of the EC that was designed to promote exchange stability within the EC.

European terms: When foreign exchange traders quote currencies on an indirect basis [see definition below].

Evidence account transaction: A requirement that certain contractual obligations be adhered to.

Exchange rate: The price of one currency in terms of another currency.

Expatriates: Noncitizens of the countries where they are working.

Experience curve: The measurement of percentage production cost reductions as output increases.

Export-Import Bank (Eximbank): A U.S. federal agency specializing in foreign lending to support exports.

Export-led development: An industrialization program emphasizing industries that will have export capabilities.

Export Management Company (EMC): A firm that buys merchandise from manufacturers for international distribution or that sometimes acts as an agent for manufacturers.

Export tariff: A tax on goods leaving a country.

Export trading company: A trading company sanctioned by law to become involved in international commerce. The law that established the ETC in the United States was designed to eliminate some of the antitrust barriers to cooperation.

Extraterritoriality: The term is used to describe the situation when governments extend the application of their laws to foreign operations of companies.

Factor proportions theory: Differences in countries' proportionate holdings of factors (land, labor, and capital) will explain differences in the costs of the factors so that the best export advantages are in production which uses the most abundant factors.

Favorable balance of trade: A country is exporting more than it is importing.

Fees: Payments for the performance of certain activities abroad.

Financial Accounting Standards Board (FASB): The private-sector organization in the United States that sets financial accounting standards.

First world countries: Nonsocialist industrial countries.

Fisher effect: The relationship between inflation and interest rates in two countries such that if the nominal interest rate in the home country is lower than that of the foreign country, one would expect the home country's inflation to be lower so that real interest rates would be equal.

Foreign bond: A bond sold outside the country of the borrower but in the currency of the country of issue.

Foreign Credit Insurance Association (FCIA): A U.S. federal agency that insures against non-payment on export sales.

Foreign currency swaps: Where one currency is traded for another currency with the agreement that the transaction would be reversed at some point in the future.

Foreign exchange: Currency from another country.

Foreign exchange control: A requirement to apply to governmental authorities for permission to buy foreign currency.

Foreign freight forwarder: A firm that facilitates the movement of goods from one country to another.

Foreign Sales Corporation (FSC): A special corporation established by U.S. tax law that can be used by a U.S. exporter to shelter some of its income from taxation.

Foreign Trade Organizations (FTO): Agencies, organized along product lines, which handle foreign sales and purchases in most centrally planned economies.

Foreign trade zones: Special physical sites where the government allows firms to delay or avoid paying tariffs on imports.

Forward contract: A contract between a firm or individual with a bank to deliver foreign currency at a specific exchange rate at a set date in the future.

Forward rate: A contractually-established exchange rate between a foreign exchange trader and the customer for delivery of foreign exchange at a specific date in the future.

Fractional reserve: An amount held by banks as a precaution which is generally much lower than the amount loaned and reloaned to users.

Franchising: A way of doing business in which one party (the franchisor) gives an independent party (the franchisee) (1) the use of a trademark that is an essential asset for the franchisee's business, and (2) continual assistance in the operation of the business.

Free trade area (FTA): A form of regional economic integration where internal tariffs are abolished but where countries set their own external tariffs.

Full convertibility: A situation in which both residents and nonresidents can purchase unlimited amounts of any currency.

Functional currency: In translating foreign currency financial statements, it refers to the currency of the primary economic environment in which the entity operates.

Gap analysis: A tool used to estimate why a market potential for a given produce is less than a company's sales in a country. The reasons may be due to a usage, competitive, product line, or distribution gap.

Generally Accepted Accounting Principles (GAAP): Those accounting standards accepted by users of statements in the area.

Glasnost: A Russian term referring to openness in political policies.

Global company: One that integrates operations from different countries.

Go-no-go decision: A basis of decision making, such as for foreign investments, which does not compare different alternative opportunities.

Grandchild: Also called second tier subsidiary; one that is under a tax-haven subsidiary.

Hard currency: A currency that is freely traded without many restrictions and for which there is usually strong external demand. Hard currencies are often called freely convertible currencies.

Hedge: A form of protection against an adverse movement of an exchange rate.

Hierarchy of needs: A well-known motivation theory stating that there is a hierarchy of needs and that people must fulfill the lower-order ones sufficiently before being motivated by the higher-order needs.

High-need achiever: One who will work very hard to achieve material or career success as opposed to a person who is more concerned with developing smooth social relationships or spiritual achievements.

Home country nationals: Citizens of the country where the company is headquartered.

Idealism versus pragmatism: In the former, people try to settle principles before they try to settle small issues; whereas, in the latter, people approach problem solving from the opposite direction.

Ideology: The systematic and integrated body of constructs, theories, and aims that constitute a society.

Imitation lag: One of the strategies to take advantage of temporary monopoly advantages by moving first to those countries most likely to develop competitors.

Import substitution: An industrialization policy whereby new industrial developments emphasize products that would otherwise be imported.

Import tariff: A tax placed on a good entering a country.

In-bond industry: An industry based on the processing of imported components which can enter the country free of duty, provided that they will be reexported.

Independence: A term referring to an extreme situation in which a country would not rely on other countries.

Indirect quote: A foreign exchange quote that is given in terms of the number of units of the foreign currency for one unit of the domestic currency. This is also known as European terms.

Indirect selling: This implies that the manufacturer deals through another domestic firm before entering the international marketplace.

Industrialization argument: A rationale for protectionism, stating that the development of industrial output should come about even though domestic prices may not become competitive on the world market.

Infant industry argument: The logic of the infant industry argument for protection is that initial output costs for an industry in a given country may be too high to be competitive in world markets, but that over a period of time, the costs will decrease sufficiently so that efficient production will be achieved.

Input-output: A tool that is widely used in national economic planning to show the resources consumed by different industries for a given output as well as the interdependence of economic sectors.

Integrated system: A tax system aimed at preventing double taxation of corporate income through split rates; for example, distributed profits versus retained earnings, or tax credits.

Inter-American Development Bank (IDB): An international organization aimed at improving economic conditions in Latin America, primarily by lending for public projects.

Interbank transactions: Foreign exchange transactions that take place between banks as opposed to those between banks and nonbank clients.

Interdependence: The development of mutually needed economic relations among countries.

Interest arbitrage: Investing in interest-bearing instruments in foreign exchange and earning a profit due to interest rate and exchange rate differentials.

Interest rate differential: An indicator of future changes in the spot exchange rate.

Internalization: The self handling of foreign operations, primarily because it is less expensive to deal within the same corporate family than to contract with an external organization.

International Accounting Standards Committee (IASC): The international private-sector organization established to set financial accounting standards that can be used worldwide.

International Bank for Reconstruction and Development (IBRD): A multi-government owned bank to promote development projects, primarily through low interest infrastructure loans.

International business: All business transactions involving two or more countries. The business relationships may be private or governmental.

International Development Association (IDA): A multi-government association through the World Bank in which developed countries subscribe funds to lend to LDCs on liberal terms.

International Finance Corporation (IFC): A member of the World Bank Group which fosters loans to private development in LDCs.

International Fisher effect: The relationship between interest rates and exchange rates that implies that the currency of the country with the lower interest rate will strengthen in the future.

International Monetary Fund: A multi-government organization organized to promote exchange rate stability and to facilitate the international flow of currencies.

International Sea-Bed Authority: A United Nations group aimed at determining coastal water rights and setting policy on the exploitation of resources on the sea bed.

International standard of fair dealing: A concept that prompt, adequate, and effective compensation will be received for investors in cases of expropriation.

International Trade Administration (ITA): A U.S. Department of Commerce agency that assists exporters.

Investment climate: It refers to those external conditions in host countries that could significantly affect the success or failure of a foreign enterprise.

Invisibles: (See Services.)

Irrevocable letter of credit: A letter of credit that cannot be changed without consent of all parties involved in the letter.

Joint venture: When two or more organizations share in the ownership of a direct investment.

Just-in-time (JIT): A manufacturing system that decreases inventories by having components and parts delivered as they need to be used in production.

Key industry: One that might affect a very large segment of the economy by virture of its size or influence on other sectors.

Lag strategy: A foreign exchange management strategy that results in delaying payments or delaying receipts in a foreign currency. This strategy usually occurs because one currency is expected to strengthen against another.

Latin American Integration Association (LAIA): A free trade area form of regional economic integration that involves most of the Latin American nations.

Lead strategy: The opposite of the lag strategy defined above. This strategy implies that firms would pay off foreign currency debts early and collect foreign currency receipts early. This is typically because the local currency is expected to weaken.

Learning curve concept: A concept used to support the infant industry argument for protection that costs will decrease as workers and managers gain more experience.

Leontief paradox: A surprising finding by Wassily Leontief that overall U.S. exports were less capital intensive and more labor intensive than U.S. imports.

Letter of credit: A precise document by which the importer's bank extends credit to the importer and agrees to pay the exporter.

Licensing agreements: Agreements whereby one firm gives rights to another for the use, usually for a fee, of such assets as trademarks, patents, copyrights, or other know-how.

Licensing arrangement (on trade): A procedure that requires potential importers or exporters to secure permission from governmental authorities before they conduct trade transactions.

Liquidity preference: A common concept to help explain capital budgeting, which when applied to international operations means that investors are willing to take less return in order to be able to shift the resources to alternative uses.

Locals: The citizens of the country where they are working.

London Interbank Offered Rate (LIBOR): The interest rate for large interbank transactions in the international banking market.

London International Financial Futures Exchange (LIFFE): An exchange dealing in futures contracts in several major currencies.

Management contract: An arrangement through which one firm assists another by providing management personnel to perform general or specialized management functions for a fee.

Maquiladora industry: Also known as in-bond industry. An industry concept developed by the Mexican government in which U.S.-source components are shipped to Mexico duty-free for assembly and are reexported to the United States.

Market economy: An economic philosophy where resources are allocated and controlled by consumers, who "vote" through buying goods.

Mercantilism: It is an economic philosophy, premised that a country's wealth is dependent on its holdings of treasure, usually in the form of gold. In order to increase wealth, countries attempt to export more than they import.

Merchandise exports: Goods sent out of a country.

Merchandise imports: Goods brought into a country.

Merchandise trade balance: The net of merchandise imports and exports within a country's balance of payments.

Mixed venture: A special type of joint venture, where a government is in a partnership with a private company.

Most favored nation: If a country, such as the U.S., gives a tariff reduction to another country, the U.S. must grant (with a few exceptions) the same concession to all other countries of the world.

Multidomestic company: A way of managing international operations whereby operations in each country are relatively independent of those in other countries.

Multifibre Arrangement (MFA): (See Arrangement Regarding International Trade in Textiles.)

Multinational corporation: (See Multinational Enterprise.)

Multinational enterprise (MNE): An integrated global philosophy encompassing both domestic and overseas operations. It is also sometimes used synonymously with Multinational Corporation and transnational corporation.

Multiple exchange rate system: A government sets different exchange rates for different transactions.

Natural advantage: A country may have a natural advantage in the production of a product because of climatic conditions or because of access to certain natural resources.

Neomercantilism: It is a term used to describe countries that apparently try to run favorable balances of trade, not to seek an influx of gold, but rather in an attempt to achieve some social or political objective.

Net buyer range: The price range in which the commodity buffer stock manager must buy more of the commodity in order to keep prices from falling too low.

Net seller range: The price range in which the buffer stock manager must sell more of the commodity in order to keep the price from rising too high.

Nonaccrual loan: A loan by a bank on which principal and/or interest have not been paid for 90 days.

Normal quote: Also known as a direct quote in foreign exchange [see definition of Direct Quote].

Offer: The amount for which a trader is willing to sell foreign exchange.

Official reserves: A country's holdings of monetary gold, Special Drawing Rights, and internationally acceptable currencies.

Offset trade: Also known as countertrade [defined above].

Offshore financial centers: Cities or countries that provide large amounts of funds in a currency other than their own.

Open Account: A situation in which the exporter extends credit directly to the importer.

Optimum Tariff: A situation in which a foreign exporter lowers its prices when an import tax is placed on its products.

Options: The right to buy or sell foreign exchange within a specific period or at a specific date.

Organization for Economic Cooperation and Development (OECD): A multilateral organization of industrial and semi-industrialized countries that helps them formulate social and economic policies.

Organization for European Economic Cooperation (OEEC): A sixteen-nation organization established in 1948 to facilitate the utilization of aid from the Marshall Plan. It evolved into the EEC and EFTA forms of regional economic integration.

Organization of African Unity (OAU): An organization of African nations, whose goals are primarily political.

Organization of Petroleum Exporting Countries (OPEC): A commodity agreement among major oil exporting countries.

Outsourcing: A situation in which a domestic company uses foreign suppliers for components or finished products.

Par value: The benchmark value of a currency, usually in terms of gold or the U.S. dollar.

Parallel market: A secondary currency market with currency rates different from those in the official market.

Passive income: Income, usually from operations in tax haven countries, resulting from investments and work of other affiliates.

Peg: To fix the value of a currency to some benchmark, such as another currency.

Planning: The meshing of objectives with internal and external constraints to set means to implement, monitor, and correct operations.

Pluralistic societies: Societies where different ideologies are held by numerous segments of society rather than one ideology adhered to by all.

Political science: A discipline that helps explain the patterns of governments and their actions.

Political system: The system designed to integrate the society into a viable, functioning unit.

Polycentrism: Characterizes an individual or organization that feels differences, real and imaginary, great and small, between its many operating environments.

Portfolio investment: Either debt or equity, but the critical factor is that control does not follow the investment.

Premium (in foreign exchange): The difference between the spot and forward exchange rate in the forward market. A foreign currency is selling at a premium when the forward rate exceeds the spot rate, and when the domestic currency is quoted on the direct basis.

Private enterprise: A system in which production is owned privately.

Private ownership: Individuals rather than the government own economic resources.

Product life cycle: The theory states that certain kinds of products go through a cycle consisting of four stages (introduction, growth, maturity, and decline), and that the location of production will shift internationally depending on the stage of the cycle.

Protestant ethic: A theory that says when work is viewed as a means of salvation and when people prefer to transform productivity gains into additional output rather than additional leisure, there is more economic growth.

Public ownership: The government rather than the individuals owns economic resources.

Pull: A promotion method which presells consumers before they reach the point of purchase, usually by relying on mass media.

Purchasing Power Parity (PPP): A theory to explain exchange rate changes based on keeping prices of goods in different countries fairly similar.

Push: A promotion method which involves direct selling techniques.

Quality circle: A production system in which small groups of workers meet regularly to spot and solve problems in their area.

Quantity controls: Government limitations on the amount of foreign currency that can be used in a specific transaction.

Quota: A limit on the quantitative amount of a product allowed to be imported into or exported out of a country.

Quota systems: A system in which producing and/or consuming countries divide total output and sales for a particular product.

Quoted currency: An exchange rate is usually quoted by relating one currency to the other. The currency whose numerical value is "one" is the base currency, and the other currency is the quoted currency. For example, if the exchange rate between the pound and dollar were to be quoted at $1.40 per pound, the pound would be the base currency, and the dollar would be the quoted currency.

Rationalized production: Companies increasingly produce different components or different portions of their product line in different parts of the world to take advantage of varying costs of labor, capital, and raw materials.

Reciprocal quote: The quote in foreign exchange that is also referred to as the indirect quote. This quote is the reciprocal of the direct quote. It is determined by dividing the direct quote into the number one.

Representative democracy: Individual citizens elect representatives to make decisions.

Revaluation: A formal change in an exchange rate where the foreign currency value of the reference currency rises. A revaluation results in a strengthening of the reference currency.

Royalties: The payment for use of assets abroad.

Second-tier subsidiaries: Ones that report to a tax-haven subsidiary.

Second world countries: Socialist countries (often referred to as centrally-planned economies or communist countries).

Secondary boycott: The boycotting of a firm doing business with a firm being boycotted.

Secular totalitarianism: A dictatorship not ruled by a religious party.

Separate entity approach: A tax system in which each unit is taxed when it receives income; for example, a firm is taxed on its profits and individuals are also taxed on the dividends paid from the firm's profits.

Services: International earnings other than for goods sent to another country. Services are also referred to as invisibles.

Sight draft: A bill of exchange that requires payment to be made as soon as it is presented to the party that is obligated to pay.

Silent language: Messages by a host of cues other than those of formal language.

Society: A broad grouping of people having common traditions, institutions, and collective activities and interests. The nation-state is often used as a workable term to denote society in international business.

Society of Worldwide Interbank Financial Telecommunication (SWIFT): A cooperative arrangement of banks worldwide to transfer funds instantaneously.

Sogo Soshas: Japanese trading companies that import and export merchandise.

Special Drawing Right (SDR): A unit of account issued to governments by the International Monetary Fund.

Specific duty: A duty tariff is assessed on the basis of a tax per unit.

Speculator: A person who takes positions in foreign exchange with the major objective of earning a profit.

Spillover effects: Situations whereby the marketing

program in one country results in awareness of the product in other countries.

Spot rate: The exchange rate quoted for immediate delivery (usually within two business days).

Spread (in the forward market): The difference between the spot and the forward rate.

Spread (in the spot market): The difference between the bid (buy) and offer (sell) rates quoted by the foreign exchange trader.

Tariff: A governmental tax usually on imports levied on goods shipped internationally. It is the most common type of trade control. (See also duty.)

Tax haven countries: Countries with low income taxes or no taxes on foreign source income.

Tax haven subsidiary: A subsidiary of a company that is established in a tax haven country for the purpose of minimizing income tax.

Temporal method: A method of translating foreign currency financial statements into the reporting currency of the parent company. It basically requires that monetary assets and liabilities be translated at the current balance sheet exchange rate, and other assets, liabilities, and owner's equity accounts be translated at historical exchange rates. Translation gains and losses are taken directly to the income statement.

Terms of trade: The quantity of imports that can be bought by a given quantity of a country's exports.

Theocratic totalitarianism: A dictatorship led by a religious group.

Theory of country size: Larger countries are generally more nearly self-sufficient than smaller countries.

Third-country nationals: Citizens neither of the country where they are working nor of the country where the firm is headquartered.

Third world countries: Developing countries, or those not considered socialist countries or nonsocialist industrial countries.

Time draft: An agreement calling for payment at a later period after delivery of sale.

Totalitarianism: A political system characterized by the absence of widespread participation in decision making, which is restricted to only a few individuals.

Transfer price: A price that is charged on goods sold between entities that are related to each other through stock ownership, such as a parent and its subsidiaries or subsidiaries owned by the same parent.

Transit tariff: A tax placed on goods passing through a country.

Translation: The restatement of financial statements from one currency to another.

Transnational corporation: A term with two different definitions. It is used to refer to a company owned and managed by nationals in different countries. It is synonomous with a multinational enterprise. This text uses the former definition.

Triangular arbitrage: The process of buying and selling foreign exchange at a profit due to price discrepancies where three different currencies are involved.

Turnkey operations: A contract for the construction of an operating facility that is transferred to the owner when the facility is ready to begin operations.

Underemployed: People who are working at less than their capacity.

Unfavorable balance of trade: Imports are more than exports.

Unit of account: A benchmark on which to base the value of payments.

Unitary tax: A method of taxing based on a percentage of a company's worldwide operations rather than on profits in the area where the taxing authorities are located.

U.S. shareholder: For U.S. tax purposes, a person or firm owning at least 10 percent of the voting stock of a foreign subsidiary.

U.S. terms: The quotation of exchange rates using the direct method [see definition above].

Value added tax: Each firm is taxed only on the value added to the product by that firm.

Vertical integration: Involves gaining control of different stages of a product moves from its earliest production to its final distribution.

Water's edge concept: A compromise between the unitary tax and the tax on state earnings in which a state taxes on a portion of national rather than global operations.

Withholding taxes: Taxes paid on dividends from the subsidiary to the parent.

Zero sum: One party's gain is another's loss.

COMPANY INDEX

NAME INDEX

SUBJECT INDEX